GW00648697
JOECROWFOOT

An Illustrated History of the EAST SUFFOLK RAILWAY

Ipswich

An Illustrated History of the

EAST SUFFOLK RAILWAY

John Brodribb

An imprint of
Ian Allan Publishing

Above:
On 4 September 1965 Type 2 No D5039 heads the 11.52 summer-Saturdays Yarmouth South Town to Liverpool Street into Oulton Broad South. Blue ex-Pullman camping coach No CC19 is berthed in the down siding. The signal behind the train is pulled off for a Lowestoft-bound working, with the smaller lower arm controlling access to South Side. *G. R. Mortimer*

First published 2003

ISBN 0 86093 572 8

Published by Oxford Publishing Co

an imprint of Ian Allan Publishing Ltd, Hersham, Surrey KT12 4RG.

Printed by Ian Allan Printing Ltd, Hersham, Surrey KT12 4RG.

Code: 0309/B1

Endpapers:
Steam over the Waveney. *An original painting by Joe Crowfoot*

Half title page:
A featherweight freight comes off the Framlingham branch in 1959 in the charge of 'J15' No 65389. *John Brodribb collection*

Title page:
A fine view of Ipswich station from over the top of the tunnel, looking north. Class 47 No 47580 is in charge of a Norwich–Liverpool Street train. Ipswich station signalbox is in the foreground, with Ipswich Goods Junction in the middle distance. The track layout remained substantially unchanged between 1912 and electrification in the 1980s. *L. A. Nixon*

Contents

Foreword 7

Introduction 8

1.	The Halesworth, Beccles & Haddiscoe Railway	11
2.	Building the East Suffolk	21
3.	Opening the East Suffolk	33
4.	East Suffolk Line Description — Ipswich to Melton	39
5.	East Suffolk Line Description — North of Melton	59
6.	East Suffolk Line Description — Halesworth and Beyond	83
7.	East Suffolk Journey's End — Beccles to Yarmouth South Town	107
8.	Framlingham Branch	135
9.	Snape Branch	145
10.	Aldeburgh Branch	149
11.	Lowestoft Branch	171
12.	Train Services on the East Suffolk	193
13.	What About the Workers?	218
14.	East Suffolk Survival and Renaissance	232

Index 254

Above:
170205 forms the very first scheduled through train of the Anglia Railways' era between Lowestoft and London Liverpool Street on Sunday 30 September 2001. *John Brodribb*

Below:
150235 rumbles over Oulton Broad Swing Bridge with a train for Ipswich on 8 May 2002. The equipment room can be seen on the right side of the structure. Only one of the two tracks remains in use. The photograph is taken from the signalbox. *John Brodribb*

Foreword

THE history of the railways is a fascinating one, with both the rise and fall of individual railways, and the industry as a whole, reflecting the social and economic development of the last 150 years.

The progress, in Victorian times, of railway development through East Anglia, with its flat or gently undulating landscape, must have been dramatic for the agrarian population with little experience of the effects of industrial revolution. I suspect even the most imaginative observer, looking up from his horse-drawn tilling, would not have dreamt of the changes which the railway would bring: standardisation of time, the telegraph, new goods, and importantly, new markets.

Helping to create this social change, with a largely untold story, were those 'working on the railway'. Working all hours of the day and night to operate this technically demanding and resource-hungry system, gazing stoically out of the old sepia photographs from platforms, footplates and signalboxes, they are part of the communities they served and in which they played such an important role. Industry and tourism grew with the railways, changing the way of life in East Anglia, as colourful railway posters for Lowestoft and other resorts remind us.

The establishment and development of the East Suffolk Railway was overshadowed in later years by the decline and traumatic closures of the late 1950s and then the Beeching cuts of the early 1960s. The railway link was a powerful economic symbol, even in decline. There was a human cost as work disappeared, not so obvious as the lost jobs in coal or steel, but equally important to the lives of those affected.

The East Suffolk line became a battleground for those communities wanting to save their railway. The efforts of groups such as the East Suffolk Travellers Association, quite simply, saved the line from closure in the 1960s. This enabled it to survive further changes in the 1980s, coinciding with the arrival of a new signalling system, preserving the route, albeit with a reduced service. The Radio Electronic Token Block (RETB) reduced the intermediate number of signalboxes to one: the signalling centre at Saxmundham. This, together with the arrival of automatic crossings, cut the staffing costs to the bare minimum.

It is only now, in the last few years, that we have again seen any real growth in services since the middle of the last century. The intervening years were ones of inexorable decline. It was, therefore, a proud moment for Anglia Railways in September 1999 when the first through train for 15 years ran from Lowestoft to London — something which many of us had not expected to see again.

The privatisation of the railways has ushered in a period of unprecedented change, but also of growth. For modern-day custodians, the challenge now is to respond to that growth and help to deliver a true renaissance for the East Suffolk line.

Tim Clarke
Managing Director
Anglia Railways

Introduction

THE East Suffolk has long been a railway that has inspired fierce loyalty and affection among those who use it, live in the area and who work on it. That any of it survives at all is a tribute to those people who have had to fight for it since the days of Dr Beeching, 40 years ago. Conceived as a system that would give Lowestoft and Yarmouth quicker connections to London, it achieved this aim admirably whilst bringing trade and prosperity to the string of towns that it served *en route* to Ipswich. However, its independence was confined to the period of its construction, and it never operated its own trains.

This book does not pretend or attempt to be a complete history of the East Suffolk. There is much material that has not been included, partly because the publisher has quite rightly resisted the temptation to go for a 10-volume boxed set, and also because there is much more to be discovered. History continues to be written, of course, and it is certainly one of my hopes that the East Suffolk has now passed its lowest point and is on its way back up. After scheduled through services to and from London were withdrawn at the start of the summer timetable in 1984 many feared that the line was entering a terminal decline, so that Anglia Railways' reintroduction of such services in 1999 using brand-new trains caused great pleasure and satisfaction locally. Work has been done at some stations to substantially upgrade the facilities, notably Woodbridge and Halesworth, although Beccles remains an eyesore at the time of writing despite heroic efforts to get things moving.

In this book, I have left spellings of place names and stations as they were at the time, whilst trying to say when they changed, so 'Aldborough' and 'Aldeburgh' both appear. Britain's railways were mostly built in Imperial units, and paid for in pounds, shillings and pence. Speeds were calculated in miles per hour, and the timetable was written with the 12-hour clock. Modern equivalents are not given in the text; if they were, a good half of it would be in brackets or appear as footnotes. For that reason, a summary of these systems is given here; readers above a certain age may skip this section!

Money: the United Kingdom went decimal in February 1971. Before that, the pound (£) was divided into 20 shillings (s), with each shilling containing 12 pennies, or pence (d). Note that three pence (3d) was *never* three dee, more like 'thrupp'nce', and similarly for other amounts. A penny could be divided into two halfpennies (hayp'nce, ½d) or four farthings (¼d). Silver coins before World War 1 were made of silver: there were the threepenny bit (later to become a 12-sided brass coin), sixpence (6d), shilling (1s), two shillings or florin, and half crown (2s 6d). Crowns (5s) had all but gone by the turn of the century. The sovereign (£1) and half sovereign (10s) were gold coins, but because of the demands of wartime, started to be replaced by notes from about 1914. The guinea was a nominal unit of coinage representing 21 shillings. Coins were much bigger than they are today: at decimalisation the shilling turned into 5p, and the florin into 10p. Both have since shrunk greatly in size and value. The sixpence, which remained briefly in circulation, was worth 2½p.

It matters more what these coins would buy. It probably is not much use to say that in 1900 one could get a gallon of 10-year-old Scotch whisky for 23s 6d (often written 23/6), or that W. Drake's 'Perfect Shirt' cost 4s 6d each, or six for 26s. A railway carriage washer in 1911 earned 21s for a seven-day week. After all his family's other expenses had been met, 8s 1d was left over for their food: there was the man and his wife and three children. Eleven loaves of bread cost 2s 7d. Half a pound of butter cost 6d, a pound of jam 3d, two pounds of sugar 4d, and tin of milk 4d. The family also spent 4d on cocoa, and 2d on suet. By the 1930s a very substantial new three-bedroomed semi-detached house in Beccles would cost about £400, just about within the reach of the better-paid railway grades, many of whom had housing provided by the company.

Wages and hours improved slowly. In 1891 a newly hired engine cleaner could expect to earn 5s per week, working five days of 12-hour shifts and a half day on Saturday. The top rate might be as much as 2s 6d a day, while a top-link engine driver would be getting something like 8s a day — and that was really good money. In the 1930s a job in a factory paid about 30s per week, while the railway offered 45s for permanent way men. It would take a full social history to go through all the changes in attitude and circumstances that have taken place, and it can be well worth pursuing this.

Weights and measures do not generally come into the picture quite as much. Weight on the old Imperial system was generally measured in ounces (oz) and pounds (lb), with 16oz equal to 1lb. The stone contained 14lb, and hundredweight (cwt) was 112lb. There were 20 hundredweight to the ton. In terms of metric equivalents, there are about 454 grams to the pound — a jar of jam — and a kilogram — a bag of sugar is about 2.2lb. The Imperial ton and metric tonne are actually very similar in size. Length on the Imperial system was complex, especially as the railways were originally surveyed and built long before many more modern simplifications. The mile is straightforward enough, and five miles are roughly equivalent to eight kilometres. The mile could be simply divided into halves and quarters, which is what the railways showed on their lineside posts, but could also be divided into 8 furlongs, or 80 chains (so 10 chains to the furlong), or 320 rods, or 1,760yd, or 5,280ft. In surveying, the other relevant measurement was that there were 100 links to the chain. In metric equivalent, a metre is just over a yard, or about 39in. In terms of area, the old and new units are the acre and hectare: the hectare is much larger, with 2.471 acres to the hectare, or 1 acre being 0.405 hectares.

A book such as this cannot be written without the help of a great many people. For this project the most important person has been Peter Punchard, widely regarded as Mr East Suffolk, and whose knowledge and understanding of the line are unrivalled. He has been willing throughout to make this available to me, to undertake research on many issues and has always been prepared to make constructive criticisms and suggestions as to how it should move forward. Alan Taylor, perhaps better known for his interest in the Southwold Railway, has also been of immense help.

Above:
Class B12/3 No 61535 leaves Beccles with the 4.44pm train to Yarmouth South Town in July 1956. On the left is Class F5 No 67201 with the 4.49pm to Lowestoft. *Dr Ian C. Allen*

There are many, many more, and in the list that follows (they are in no particular order) I hope that no one has been left out; I can only apologise if this is so. Some of those mentioned may have helped quite unwittingly: this has been going on for a long time, and some may sadly no longer be with us. The staff of the Public Record Office at Kew and the Norfolk and Suffolk Record Offices have been superb. Janet Huckle of the Halesworth & District Museum and Stephen Mael of the Long Shop Museum, Leiston, Wynn Baldry, Alan Chittock, John Sillett, John Thompson, Doug Baldry, Malcolm O'Neill, Richard Hardy, Sid Peace, George Lown, Monty Baskett, Albert Godfrey, Joe Crowfoot, Dave Francis and John Wilson of Network Rail, Tim Clarke and Peter Meades of Anglia Railways, John Blyth, Ray Beales, Ronnie Cockerill, Alfred Groves, Len Haylett, Chris Hines, Alan Richards, Rod Lock, Jim Skoulding, Ronnie Thompson, Ted and Miriam Vickery and Nick Sanderson have all been of assistance.

The East Suffolk is a working railway to this day, so do get out there and have a ride on it. Many of the stations are surprisingly intact and will repay a visit, and are gateways to other attractions if you have the family with you. Most of the lifted section of the Aldeburgh branch can be walked. There is little remaining of the trackbed of the Snape branch, but the station and Maltings are easily reached by bus or car. Between Beccles and Yarmouth the trackbed is largely intact as far as Beccles swing bridge, where the piers remain prominent. North of the river there are many crossing cottages, and Aldeby station is largely intact although in private ownership. There is no trace of Belton and Yarmouth South Town stations. The Framlingham branch stations are all intact but in private hands, but little of the trackbed is accessible. History is still being made: get out there, see it and be part of it!

I must, of course, thank my wife Wendy for her support and encouragement, and forbearance while the book was being written. Finally, I would be delighted to hear from anyone who has further information to add about the line, and can be contacted via the publisher.

John Brodribb
June 2003

Note on the Maps

The 25in Ordnance Survey maps reproduced in this book were published in three editions: the first edition maps were surveyed between 1882 and 1887; the second edition maps between 1902 and 1906 and the third edition between 1924 and 1929. Track layouts from the first edition should be treated with caution.

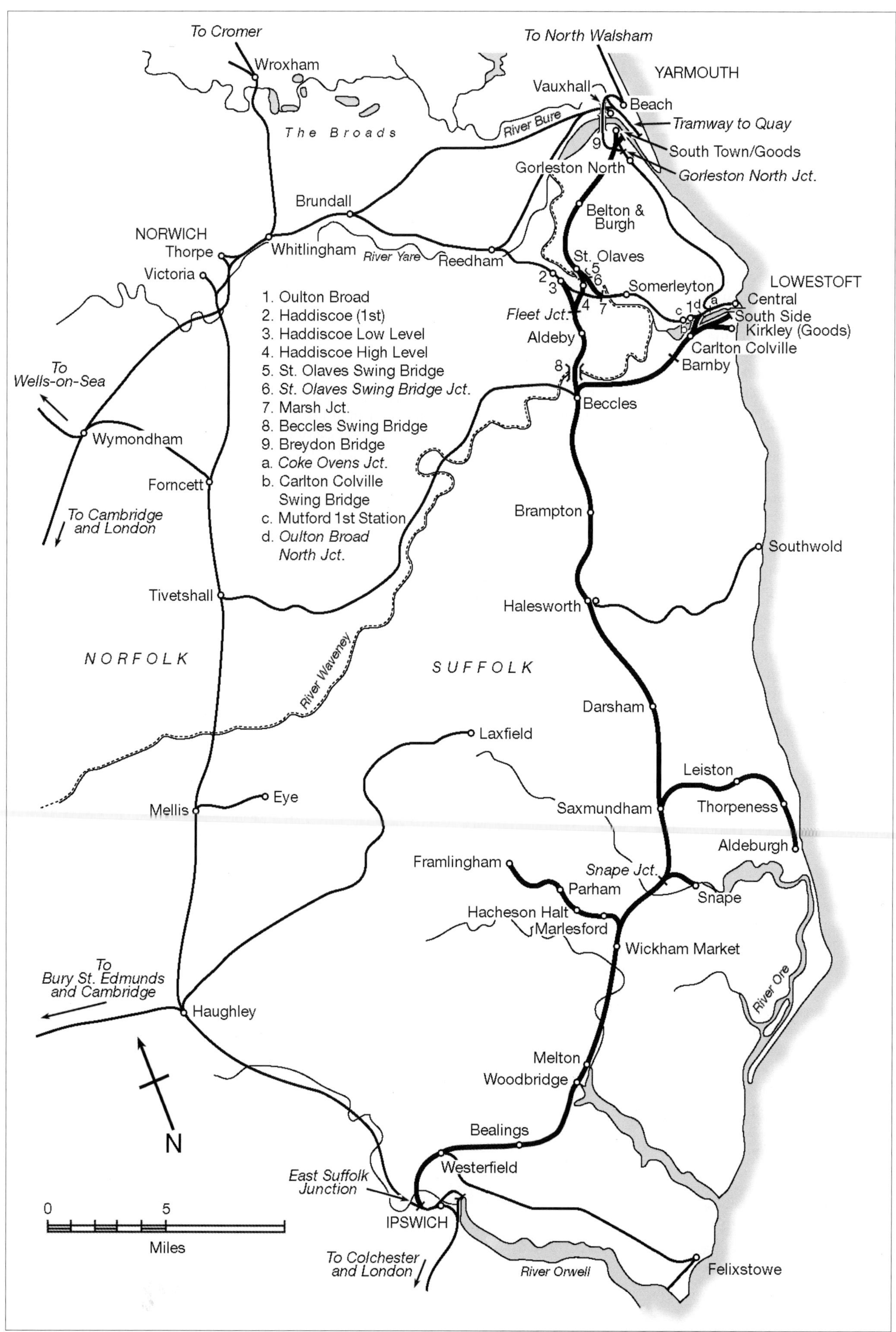
To Cromer
Wroxham
To North Walsham
YARMOUTH
Vauxhall
Beach
Tramway to Quay
River Bure
The Broads
South Town/Goods
Gorleston North
Gorleston North Jct.
Brundall
Belton & Burgh
NORWICH
Thorpe
Whitlingham
River Yare
Reedham
St. Olaves
Victoria
Somerleyton
LOWESTOFT
Central
South Side
Kirkley (Goods)
Fleet Jct.
Aldeby
Carlton Colville
Barnby
1. Oulton Broad
2. Haddiscoe (1st)
3. Haddiscoe Low Level
4. Haddiscoe High Level
5. St. Olaves Swing Bridge
6. St. Olaves Swing Bridge Jct.
7. Marsh Jct.
8. Beccles Swing Bridge
9. Breydon Bridge
a. Coke Ovens Jct.
b. Carlton Colville Swing Bridge
c. Mutford 1st Station
d. Oulton Broad North Jct.
To Wells-on-Sea
Wymondham
Beccles
Forncett
To Cambridge and London
Brampton
Southwold
Tivetshall
Halesworth
NORFOLK
SUFFOLK
River Waveney
Darsham
Laxfield
Leiston
Saxmundham
Thorpeness
Eye
Mellis
Aldeburgh
Framlingham
Snape Jct.
Parham
Snape
Hacheson Halt
Marlesford
Wickham Market
River Ore
To Bury St. Edmunds and Cambridge
Haughley
Melton
Woodbridge
N
Bealings
Westerfield
East Suffolk Junction
0
5
Miles
IPSWICH
To Colchester and London
River Orwell
Felixstowe

—1—

The Halesworth, Beccles & Haddiscoe Railway

RAILWAYS in East Anglia have a complex history. The Eastern Counties Railway (ECR) set out to construct a line from London to Chelmsford, Colchester, Ipswich, Norwich and Yarmouth, but after a protracted delay only the portion to Colchester was built. In any case, the published route north of Ipswich was quite different from that of today's line. At the same time the Northern & Eastern Railway was pursuing its railway from London to Cambridge, and this eventually reached Brandon, in Suffolk, which thus became the first town in the county to be joined to the iron road, although the station was actually across the county boundary in Norfolk.

The independent Yarmouth & Norwich Railway (Y&N) built its line from the east coast port to the county town via Reedham, and soon became the Norfolk Railway (NR), and linked with the Eastern Counties at Brandon, although construction of the swing bridge at Trowse caused some delay. It was not long again before Lowestoft was joined to the system, this time by Samuel Peto's Lowestoft Railway & Harbour Company, which was also involved in building the New Cut, which provided much more direct water navigation between Norwich and Lowestoft. Its new single-track railway, opened in 1847, joined the developing port to the Y&N at Reedham, and was the precursor of the present line. The junction between the two had originally been proposed to face the opposite direction from that built, and which exists today, so that trains could have run direct from Yarmouth to Lowestoft without reversal at Reedham, although the other alignment was shown as an alternative in the first plans. A branch to Loddon was also planned, the proposed junction being at Somerleyton. The Lowestoft Railway's station at Haddiscoe was on the single line on the Lowestoft side of the bridge where the Beccles to Yarmouth road crossed the New Cut.

The East Suffolk line can reasonably be said to have had its beginning with the Bill, lodged for the 1851 session of Parliament, for the Halesworth, Beccles & Haddiscoe Railway (HB&H), which proposed a line from the Lowestoft Railway, in Haddiscoe, to Beccles and Halesworth, with a branch in Haddiscoe. The branch referred to was a short length of track to allow through running between the HB&H and Lowestoft, since the main junction faced Norwich, although it appears that this line was never built. The authorised capital was £150,000, to be issued as 7,500 £20 shares, and the directors were Edward Leathes, Andrew Johnston, Frederick William Farr and Richard Till. The new line would cross the River Waveney near Beccles, the bridge needing the consent of the Lord High Admiral. There were 18 proposed level crossings, each of which had to have either a station or a lodge. Completion was to be within four years, and the Royal Assent was received on 5 June 1851.

The plans for the HB&H showed a line roughly the same as that later built and taken by the East Suffolk. Haddiscoe station was immediately on the east side of the level crossing where the turnpike road to Yarmouth crossed the line, which was shown as milepost 140¾. The proposed junction was about 12 chains east of MP141, and the new line curved gently away southward. At 4 furlongs' distance from the Lowestoft line, the branch diverged to form the other side of the triangle, rejoining the Lowestoft line at 141 miles 57 chains.

The proposed new line then ran straight and level for about a mile, crossing into the parish of Aldeby, and then climbed gently out of the valley bottom. From the site of the future station it then fell again towards the river, although a short rise was necessary to bridge the Waveney, which was to be crossed exactly 4 miles from Haddiscoe. A swing bridge was proposed, with a span of 25ft and a height above water of 10ft. After a short fall away from the bridge the line was then dead straight across Beccles Common, all of the land on this side of the river being owned by Beccles Corporation, until a pair of sharp reverse curves were reached at a distance of about 5 miles 2 furlongs.

The line was proposed to pass through Beccles much as at present, the central street plan then being almost exactly as now. However, the junction of Gosford Road and Grove Road was then a crossroads, and the small private road opposite the former was to be eliminated. St Anne's Road joined the present Fredericks Road near its junction with Ingate, and the new line cut through this, necessitating diversion of the former into a new junction with Ingate. Kemp's Lane was to be crossed to the west of the present line, and a bridge at a very oblique angle would have been needed: perhaps this accounts for the route as built.

From the level crossing at Grove Road (5 miles 6 furlongs) the line rose at about 1 in 100 to about 7 miles 4 furlongs, and then undulated through the parishes of Weston and Shaddingfield, largely following the present railway as far as Westhall Low Common. It then proceeded more or less in a straight line and just crept into the parish of Halesworth, the terminus being shown as about 1 furlong short of Quay Street, in an arable field with a pond, owned by John Crabtree and occupied by Isaac Mills. The total length of the line was to be 13 miles, 6 furlongs and 1 chain, and on its final approach it ran parallel to the Bungay road, but did not cross it. Level crossings were shown at about 2 and 5 furlongs from the terminus, with another about 1¼ miles from it.

Later, in 1852 a branch was proposed from the Lowestoft Railway, with a junction near Blundeston, going to Yarmouth. The Yarmouth & Lowestoft's line would have passed very close to the 'German Sea' at Gorleston and terminated at a site in Southtown, or Little Yarmouth, near to the later East Suffolk station. It was intended to be worked in connection with the Lowestoft Railway, and to give the port of Great Yarmouth links with the Waveney Valley, Beccles and Halesworth. All the parishes through which it passed (Oulton, Flixton, Blundeston, Lound, Hopton, Gorleston and Southtown) were then in Suffolk. Running powers over both the Lowestoft and Halesworth, Beccles & Haddiscoe lines were sought. This line was not realised, but those various railway concerns that were built in Norfolk soon amalgamated to

Left:
Map of the East Suffolk Railway.

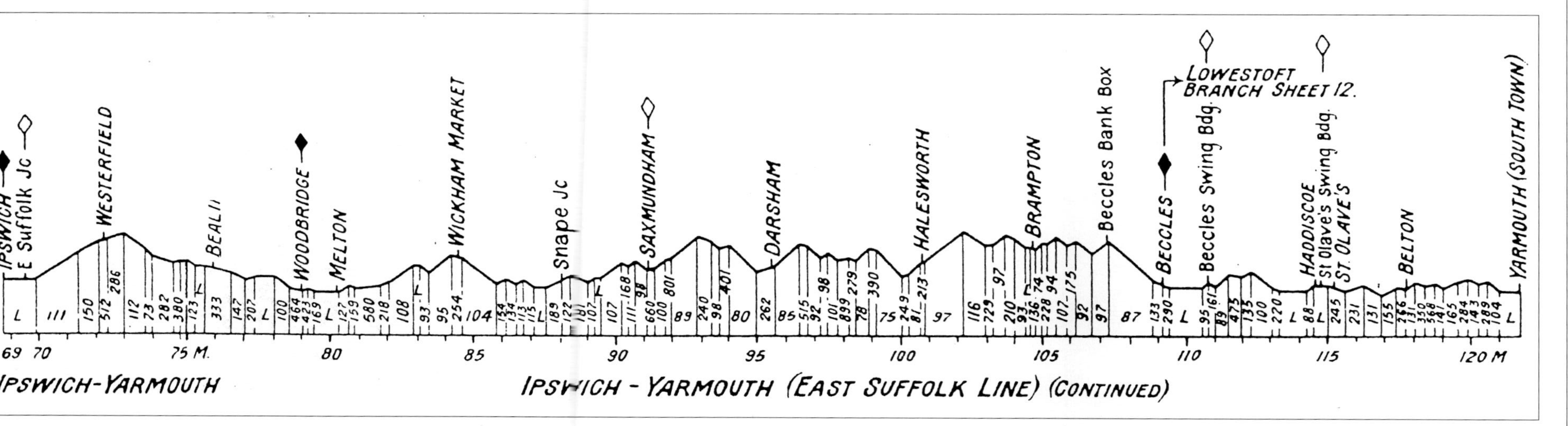

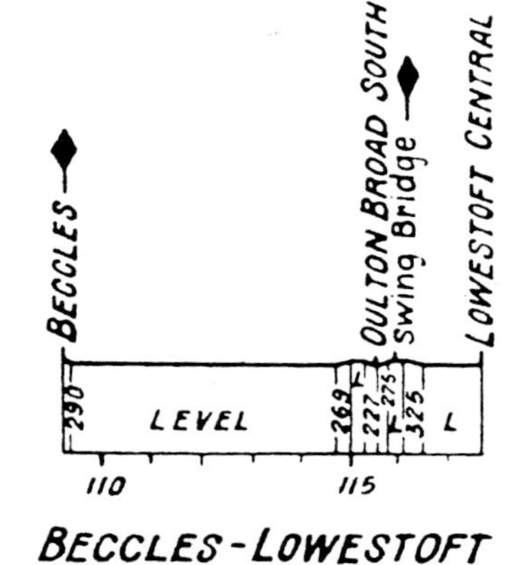

Gradient profiles on the East Suffolk:
Ipswich to Yarmouth and Beccles to Lowestoft.
Railway Magazine

Above:
The front of Ipswich station as it was in Edwardian days, with plenty of horse-drawn vehicles plus a Corporation tram. The station was originally built jointly by the Eastern Union Railway and the Ipswich & Bury St Edmunds Railway. *Alan Taylor collection*

form the Norfolk Railway, which in turn had a close relationship with the Eastern Counties, ultimately being worked and then taken over by it.

By 1852 the HB&H was considering changing its name to the 'East Suffolk Railway' and building a line onwards from Halesworth to Ipswich. The Earl of Stradbroke, Lord Lieutenant of Suffolk, gave his support to the proposal, and this considerably alarmed the Eastern Counties Railway. This company envisaged the whole area east of the Great Northern's main line as its own territory, and had already taken steps to control the lines other than its own already built or under construction. By October 1853 the HB&H had come to consider that it might be better to have a joint line involving the Eastern Union Railway (EUR), the Eastern Counties Railway and itself, and that a joint Bill should be promoted.

By 1854 the Haddiscoe, Beccles & Halesworth line was well advanced, construction being undertaken by Peto and Betts. Early in the year they donated 25 guineas to one of the navvies who had had both legs injured by a loaded truck. He had been taken to Beccles dispensary where they had been amputated, although he later recovered. Another accident on 27 May occurred at 10 o'clock to John West, described as a horse driver on the railway. One method of construction was to use wagons of spoil running on temporary track, which were run up to the end and tipped to form an embankment. West had been doing this, but the truck fell back onto him as he had been sitting on the frame. He was taken back to his lodgings at Westhall, and messages were sent to Halesworth and H. W. R. Davey, the railway's surgeon. He had serious internal injuries, and to his back, but was nevertheless expected to recover. A similar accident occurred on 31 July at Halesworth to Henry Emery, who slipped and had a loaded wagon run over both arms; he died two days later.

Although the railway was not yet open, communication with the outside world was still possible. A coach was advertised as leaving the White Hart Inn at Halesworth at 3.15am and ran via Framlingham to arrive in Ipswich in time to connect with the express, Parliamentary and excursion train to London. It returned when the 7.10am Parliamentary train arrived from London, calling also at the Crown & Anchor, Ipswich. At the same time the Eastern Union Railway was also advertising its own coach from Yoxford, Saxmundham, Wickham Market, Melton and Woodbridge.

The *Ipswich Journal* reported on 15 July that work was progressing very rapidly on the new railway. At Beccles the station house, engine house, water tank and goods sheds were erected. A great number of workmen were employed, and it was expected that a large proportion of the building work would be done here for various parts of the line. The permanent way was laid from Haddiscoe through Beccles and would shortly be completed to Halesworth, where excavation of the station area was very advanced. On the previous Saturday (8 July) one of the company's 'large and powerful ballast engines' had reached Beccles — the first to do so — and efforts were being made to finish the line for September. The station there was described as 'very picturesque' and of unique appearance, and its close proximity to the New Market through the intended new and handsome Station Road was felt to enhance the trade of the town. The opening was now expected in early September and advertisements from local livestock dealers reflected this, since they saw the benefits of being able to move stock quickly and cheaply to Norwich for the cattle fairs there.

Detailed negotiations were in progress during 1854 between the Eastern Counties Railway, the Norfolk Railway and the East Suffolk over the working of the new line. The local company's change of name was officially sanctioned in its 1854 Act which received the Royal Assent on 3 July of that year, and which also authorised the deviation from the original route between Westhall Low Common and Halesworth, on which no work had been done. At a meeting of the Joint Committee, which involved the Eastern Counties, Norfolk and Eastern Union Railways, on Tuesday 19 September an agreement about the new line was drawn up. Among the points were:

1. The EUR was bound to build the Ipswich–Woodbridge line, charging the 'United Companies' (ECR, EUR and NR) 1% of the cost
2. NR to work the HB&H; HB&H to have one-third of the revenue from traffic to Norwich, Yarmouth and Lowestoft, one-fifth of the traffic carried beyond its line by the NR
3. HB&H to have one-third of the harbour dues at Lowestoft *or* half the goods traffic
4. NR to provide the locomotives to work the line
5. HB&H may use its own engines to work to Norwich, Yarmouth and Lowestoft on Market Days
6. Through rates to be fixed by NR
7. No charge to be made for Halesworth traffic on the NR lines but such as are made on the branch
8. NR to work the branch if required
9. Present traffic at Haddiscoe to be as entrained and allowed to the NR
10. Accounts to be taken on 30 June and 31 December
11. Accounts to be open to inspection at all reasonable times
12. NR to have power to purchase branch
13. Differences to be settled by arbitration
14. Duration of the agreement to be 99 years

On the ground things did not go quite according to plan. Early September arrived, and the opening was not expected until October at the earliest. Part of the problem was that there had been a shortage of labour because of the harvest, although work was now progressing rapidly again. The line was now being called the 'East Suffolk Railway' (ESR) since its plans for expansion were already well under way. During the first week of September the approach road to Beccles station was almost complete, together with the working areas. The permanent way was complete as far as Westhall, and work at Halesworth was well advanced. A ballast engine had been over the line with heavy freights of ballast and iron, and this had bedded the track in well. In the meantime, the United Companies, in effect, the Eastern Counties Railway, took over the Norfolk Railway's commitments, and would thus work the line when it finally did open.

On 6 November 1854 the Joint Committee met at Woodbridge and inspected the quays where the proposed railway was to pass, and having stayed overnight at the Bull Inn a number of its members went over the line of country between Ipswich and Woodbridge, later going on to Saxmundham. Those in the party included David Waddington MP (Eastern Counties chairman), Samuel Anderson, Richard Till, John Chevallier Cobbold (Eastern Union chairman), James Packe, Henry Bruce and Lightly Simpson (chairman and deputy chairman respectively of the East Anglian Railway); also Mr Bidder (East Suffolk engineer) and the chief officers of the amalgamated companies (primarily the ECR, plus the EUR, NR, Newmarket Railway, East Anglian Railways and some smaller concerns — later constituents of the Great Eastern Railway) were present. At Saxmundham they met Peto, then chairman of the Norfolk Railway, Edward Leathes, ESR chairman, and Mr Long, a local landowner. The Earl of Stradbroke was waiting for them at Halesworth with other interested gentlemen, including directors of the ESR, and they were greeted by the ringing of church bells and a band. Having inspected the maltings they retired to the Angel Inn to enjoy a collation, with Edward Leathes presiding. After speeches from all concerned, David Waddington said that he would recommend Eastern Counties' shareholders to carry out the line as it had good prospects. The assemblage then went to the temporary station and took a special train to Haddiscoe; the line was expected to open for passengers on 1 December. It seems likely that the line was already open for goods traffic, since the *Ipswich Journal* for 11 November reported that Messrs Fenn & Crisp had held their first sale in a meadow adjacent to Beccles station, and that prices had been very good.

By 21 November the Special Joint Committee had received a letter from Edward Norton, secretary to the East Suffolk, saying that 'the entire management and working' of the new line between Haddiscoe and Halesworth would be undertaken by the United Companies from 1 December. However, Peto had written to the ECR objecting to the arrangements about traffic sharing, on the grounds that they were against the interests of the Norfolk Railway, and later he and Richard Till were appointed to negotiate for the NR. Work also remained to be done at Haddiscoe to carry forward the junction to the station. At the same time, the Joint Committee resolved that it was desirable to complete the Haddiscoe to Ipswich link as part of a united system, to seek cost estimates for the Ipswich to Woodbridge and Woodbridge to Halesworth lines from the Eastern Union and East Suffolk respectively, and to approach Robert Stephenson for his opinion of the value of the line from Halesworth to Haddiscoe.

In the meantime the HB&H line was inspected by Major Yolland on 14 September, although his report was dated 24 November and stated that opening for public conveyance of passengers must be postponed for one calendar month, and noted a number of important points. The line was single throughout, had sidings at Aldeby, Beccles and Halesworth, and was without works of any magnitude except for one swing bridge similar to others in the eastern counties. It appeared to be sufficiently strong and to work very satisfactorily: 'and I am informed (it) has been very severely tested'. There had been no deviation beyond the limits sanctioned. The permanent way was in good order but some fencing needed to be completed and some ballast was required. Some extra signals were required at Weston Cross level crossing because the sharp curve on the approach from the south allowed too little distance to stop for a train travelling at speed. There was no turntable so only tank engines could work the line, which was to be done by the Eastern Counties. Major Yolland forbade the opening until the stipulated works were carried out.

The line opened for public passenger traffic on Monday 4 December. The *Norwich Mercury* described it as running on the first two miles from Haddiscoe level with the marshes, and then entering the uplands, with cuttings and embankments in succession; Aldeby had a neat station, whilst that at Beccles was commodious, with a third station at Brampton. The *Mercury* thought that the works were heavier as the line neared Halesworth, but 'far from extensive'. The station at Halesworth was a very unpretending structure and understood to be temporary, and at a considerable distance from the town. Evidently the line was not yet completed, as there were wagons, temporary lines of rails and other debris to be seen, although the newspaper did not say whether this was only at the Halesworth end. It described the passage of trains as 'exceedingly easy', with the 13½-mile journey taking 40–50 minutes. The *Ipswich Journal* seems to have totally ignored the opening.

Above:
Beccles station is viewed from the top of one of the distant signals in 1911, with all platform faces clearly shown. Much of the background is maltings; cattle docks and animal pens are behind the water tank on the down platform. A line of wagons is standing across the station forecourt, probably being shunted to or from the maltings. *HMRS Hilton Collection*

By the middle of December 1854 the service seems to have become well established, the line being worked by the Eastern Counties Railway, which also worked the Norfolk Railway and hence the Reedham to Lowestoft line. Stations had been provided at Aldeby, Beccles, Brampton and Halesworth, trains using the Lowestoft Railway's station at Haddiscoe. Trains stopped at all stations and took 40 minutes each way for the journey, although unlike other local lines there was no service on the East Suffolk on Sundays. The Eastern Counties operated a Sunday service on its local lines on Christmas Day, but since the new line did not open on Sundays a special timetable was arranged, trains leaving Halesworth at 8.20am and 7.50pm, and returning from Haddiscoe at 9.50am and 9.5pm.

The scope for improvement was quickly recognised. By the end of the month Beccles had sent a memorial to the Postmaster-General, Viscount Canning, asking for mail to be sent to the town by train. It was currently travelling between London and Diss by rail, and thence by coach to Beccles, arriving at about 7pm. It could reach the town at 4.40pm by train, and the last collection for London of 5.30pm could be put back to 7.45pm. By early February the ECR had agreed to put on an extra train for the General Post Office. Another major advance for Beccles occurred on Thursday 8 February 1855 when the station was generally lit for the first time. John Thompson, a local man, had contracted with Peto & Betts for the lighting with gas of the station building, platform and goods shed, and on the 8th a special train ran for visitors from Halesworth who came to hear the 'English Glee and Madrigal Union' at the Assembly Rooms.

By March 1855 the timetable showed three trains from Haddiscoe on Mondays to Saturdays, with two from Halesworth, plus an extra on Saturdays. In April this had expanded to three each way, still with the Saturday extra from Halesworth, one in each direction being a mail train. In May another trip each way was added, with the additional bonus of two trains each way on Sundays, although these disappeared the following month.

On 11 May 1855 the Special Joint Committee met to consider a number of matters, one of which was a letter from Robert Stephenson. At its earlier request, he had inspected the Halesworth, Beccles & Haddiscoe line on 10 March and had sent in a detailed report, in which he described the line as substantially built, with stations convenient and sufficient for the anticipated traffic. He estimated the value of the line to the Norfolk Railway (under the 1852 agreement) as £6,000 per annum, or £150,000 outright, and called for the telegraph to be erected over the whole line. His comments on individual stations are most interesting:

- Aldeby: goods shed to get doors.
- Beccles: fence needed across the coal wharf, bottom to be chalked; small office to be provided; new siding to be put in connecting the present siding with the up road for the purposes of the up traffic; goods shed to be provided with doors. Water crane and coke platform to be erected at down end of platform. A siding to be put in to hold 30 wagons just beyond Beccles; he commented: 'Trains will have to be here rendering this siding necessary.'
- Brampton: goods shed, siding, coal and cattle accommodation to be provided.
- Halesworth: passenger platform to be covered, extra siding to be provided.

Above:
Brampton station building, also showing the entrance to the yard to the right. This was an original Halesworth, Beccles & Haddiscoe structure, so lacks the affinity with others on the line.
Peter Punchard collection

The entire costs of the Halesworth, Beccles & Haddiscoe from its opening until 30 June 1856 were £7,263 3s 11d, which included working expenses of £5,515 8s 8d. Repairs were also needed to Haddiscoe station. For the half-year ended 31 December 1856 receipts were £3,404 6s 8d, with working expenses £1,842 5s 10d. Later that year Mr R. Sinclair, based at Stratford, was able to report to the Eastern Counties board that the HB&H was in good condition, having surveyed it and the new lines under construction

During 1855 construction of the Waveney Valley line continued, its intended destination being Beccles. At its meeting on 1 November the ECR board heard that the 6½-mile section from Tivetshall to Harleston was completed and being operated on behalf of the local company, and that on the second section of 7 miles to Bungay, negotiations were in hand for acquisition of the land, whilst the third section to Beccles was in abeyance. Completion of the line, together with that of the East Suffolk, would give Beccles a third line of railway access, and the board felt it very questionable that the town's traffic justified this. They already had much of Harleston's traffic (population 1,509), and of Beccles (population 4,898), and the only remaining town of importance was Bungay (population 3,841), where the railway would be in competition with the coasting vessels using the Waveney Navigation. The ECR was reluctant to work a line that it felt to have a low traffic potential, but was persuaded to do so by a clause in the Waveney Valley Railway's Act giving it running powers over the rival Eastern Union!

By late 1855 serious problems were besetting the Eastern Counties Railway, which were to affect its dealings with its associated companies. On 7 December an adjourned General Meeting of the Proprietors received a very detailed report of the state of the company's lines and those of its associates, the preamble of which alleged mismanagement of the company with adverse effects upon the shareholders. Amongst other points it called for strenuous opposition to the Halesworth & Woodbridge railway, which was seen as competing with the ECR and thus reducing profit, and noted that the costly improvements that the company had recently been obliged to undertake at Lowestoft harbour had resulted in taking trade from Yarmouth, and finally — and perhaps most startling — that there was no provision at all for the maintenance of the company's permanent way! At least £150,000 was needed at once for the total of 548 miles.

Meanwhile the Eastern Counties board continued to receive regular reports on its new railway. At its meeting on 30 April 1857 the miles reported as run on the HB&H were 2,133 for the year ending 31 December 1854, when it had been open for only a few weeks, and 15,240 for the first full half-year ending 30 June 1855. Receipts for the half-year to June 1856 were £7,263 3s 11d, and expenses £5,515 8s 8d. For the remainder of that year, receipts were £3,404 6s 8d and expenses £1,842 5s 10d. The East Suffolk seems to have been making a tidy profit.

An event of considerable importance to the Halesworth, Beccles & Haddiscoe occurred in 1858, occasioned by the progress of work on the extensions. It had been previously agreed by all concerned that complete closure would take place on 31 May 1858 so that the work of doubling the track

could proceed, but Mr Birkley, the East Suffolk's engineer, asked for this to be brought forward. The ECR agreed, and accordingly an advertisement with the following wording was issued:

Eastern Counties Railway

> The East Suffolk Company, lately the Halesworth Beccles & Haddiscoe Railway Company having intimated to the Eastern Counties Railway Company that they are about to re-lay their line of Railway from Halesworth to Haddiscoe, the public is hereby informed that the line will be closed for traffic after Saturday 15th May next until further notice.
>
> Bishopsgate Terminus — J. B. Owen
> 29 April 1858 — Secretary

The East Suffolk Railway name had been adopted before the original Halesworth, Beccles & Haddiscoe was completed, and construction of the extended line was put in hand as soon as possible. The East Suffolk itself proposed to extend from Halesworth to Woodbridge, and construct branches to Framlingham, Leiston and Snape. Access to Ipswich was to be via the Eastern Union's line from Woodbridge, which had been mooted before, and which was later the cause of considerable difficulty. This was not the limit of the East Suffolk's ambitions, however, as it had its eye on the Yarmouth traffic, in which the port was a ready ally. There the Eastern Counties was regarded with considerable disfavour, since its route to London via Norwich and Cambridge was long, slow and expensive for goods traffic.

Above:
The station building at Aldeby in about 1940, seen from the top of the ramp down to the down platform. This was a Halesworth, Beccles & Haddiscoe building and so does not show the similarities to the standard East Suffolk style. The recently repaired steps lead to the up platform, and there is a large LNER enamel sign facing passengers entering from the road. The road bridge provided the only connection between the platforms for passengers.
HMRS Hilton Collection

The East Suffolk also looked to the rapidly developing port of Lowestoft as a source of traffic. Nominally separate companies were set up to promote the necessary connecting lines: the Yarmouth & Haddiscoe Railway and the Lowestoft & Beccles Railway (L&B). The former would run from a new station at Haddiscoe to Southtown in Yarmouth, with a swing bridge being needed at St Olaves. The L&B would diverge at Beccles, with a station at Carlton Colville, and terminate on the south side of Lake Lothing, with a branch to Kirkley. In due course another independent company, the Waveney Valley, completed its route across from Tivetshall Junction to Beccles, and much later still the Felixstowe Dock & Harbour Company built its line to Westerfield. At one stage fairly early in the life of the East Suffolk it was also associated with the proposed Colchester & Pitsea Railway,

Opening of the Halesworth, Beccles, and Haddiscoe Railway.

The Halesworth, Beccles, and Haddiscoe Railway was opened for general traffic on Monday, The line, which forms part of the East Suffolk scheme, and will be continued to Woodbridge and Ipswich, diverges from the Norfolk at Haddiscoe, and for the first two miles runs on a level with the marshes. It then enters the "uplands," and cuttings and embankments of a slight nature succeed each other. At Aldeby a neat station is erected, and the line soon after crosses the river Waveney by a swing bridge of a similar construction to those at Trowse, Reedham, and Somerleyton. At Beccles a commodious station has been built, and a third is placed at Brampton. As the line approaches Halesworth, the works become rather heavier, but are still far from extensive. The station at Halesworth, which is a very unpretending structure, is understood to be only a temporary one; and it is to be hoped this is the case, for it is placed at a considerable distance from the town. Waggons, temporary lines of rails, and other *debris*, show that the new line is not quite completed. Still the passage on the rails is exceedingly easy, and a journey of 13½ miles is speedily accomplished in from forty to fifty minutes. Three trains pass backwards and forwards daily, and it proposed to add two more on Mondays. On Sundays it is not proposed at present to work the line.

EASTERN COUNTIES AND HADDISCOE, BECCLES, AND HALESWORTH RAILWAYS.

FIRST, SECOND, and THIRD CLASS **MARKET TICKETS** will be ISSUED AS UNDER, at the PRICE OF A SINGLE FARE for the DOUBLE JOURNEY:—

Day.	To	From	At Morning.	Available for Return.
Tuesday	Halesworth	Norwich	9 30	By any available Train after 2 p.m.
		Brundall	9 45	
		Buckenham	9 55	
		Yarmouth	9 45	
		Reedham	10 5	
		Lowestoft	9 30	
		Mutford	9 35	
		Somerletton	9 45	
		Haddiscoe	10 18	
		Aldeby	10 25	
		Beccles	10 33	
		Brampton	10 44	
Friday	Beccles	Halesworth.........	11 5	By any available Train after 3 p.m.
		Brampton	11 15	
			A. M. P. M.	
		Norwich	9 30 or 1 5	
		Brundall	9 45 ,, 1 21	
		Buckenham	9 55 ,, 1 28	
		Yarmouth	9 45 ,, 11 45	
		Reedham	10 5 ,, 1 40	
		Lowestoft	9 30 ,, 11 30	
		Mutford	9 35 ,, 11 35	
		Somerleyton	9 45 ,, 11 47	
		Haddiscoe	10 18 ,, 1 55	
		Aldeby	10 25 ,, 2 3	
Saturday	[illegible]	Halesworth	7 15 ,, 9 0	By 4 15 p.m. Train.
		Brampton	7 25 ,, 9 10	
		Beccles	7 37 ,, 9 21	
		Aldeby	7 46 ,, 9 32	
			A. M. A. M.	
Wednesday ..	Yarmouth	Halesworth	9 0 ,, 11 5	By 4 40 p.m. Train.
		Brampton	9 10 ,, 11 15	
		Beccles	9 23 ,, 11 27	
		Aldeby	9 32 ,, 11 36	

THESE TICKETS ARE NOT TRANSFERABLE.

Coaching Superintendent's Office, Bishopsgate,
5th December, 1854.

BY ORDER.

(10,446

EASTERN COUNTIES RAILWAY.

ON CHRISTMAS-DAY,
TRAINS WILL RUN, AS UNDER, BETWEEN
Hadleigh and Bentley,
AND
HALESWORTH AND HADDISCOE.

From	Morn.	Even.	From	Morn.	Even.
Bentley	10 50	6 35	Hadleigh ...	8 20	5 5
Capel	10 58	6 43	Raydon	8 28	5 13
Raydon	11 10	6 55	Capel	8 38	5 23
Hadleigh ...	11 20	7 5	Bentley arr.	8 50	5 35
From	**Morn.**	**Even.**	**From**	**Morn.**	**Even.**
Haddiscoe ..	9 50	9 5	Halesworth	8 20	7 50
Aldeby	9 58	9 13	Brampton ...	8 30	8 0
Beccles.....	10 7	9 22	Beccles.....	8 42	8 12
Brampton ...	10 17	9 32	Aldeby......	8 51	8 21
Halesworth	10 30	9 45	Haddiscoe ..	9 0	8 30

Coaching Superintendent's Office, BY ORDER.
Bishopsgate Station, 7th Dec., 1854.

Top:
Norwich Mercury,
December 1854 report
of the HB&H opening

Above:
The first cheap fares
promotion for the HB&H.
Note the confusion about
the company's name.

Left:
Christmas Day 1854
train service

Right:
official notice of opening

EASTERN COUNTIES AND **Haddiscoe, Beccles, and Halesworth Railways.**

NOTICE.

THE LINE from HADDISCOE to HALESWORTH OPENED for General Traffic on MONDAY, the FOURTH of DECEMBER.

Trains will leave Halesworth at 9 and 11.5 a.m., and 4 p.m.; and Haddiscoe for Halesworth at 10.18 a.m., 1.55 and 5.10 p.m., every week-day.

An Extra Train on Mondays from Halesworth at 6.10 a.m.; Beccles, 6.33 a.m.; in conjunction with the Express due in London at 11 a.m.; returning in conjunction with the 5 p.m., Express from London, due in Halesworth at 9.55 p.m.

There will be no Trains on Sundays.

Market Tickets at reduced fares to London on Monday, Halesworth on Tuesday, Beccles on Friday, Norwich on Saturday, and Yarmouth on Wednesday.

For further particulars see time-bills and placards.

By order.

Coaching Superintendent's Office,
Bishopsgate, Nov. 30, 1854.

(10,401

promoted by Peto, whose principal purpose seems to have been to frighten the Eastern Counties by offering an alternative route, in combination with the ESR, all the way from Yarmouth to London.

The Halesworth, Beccles & Haddiscoe's line was not built exactly as planned. There were minor deviations between Haddiscoe and Westhall, although all were within the limits prescribed in the plans. Beyond Westhall Low Common, where a minor road passed under the line by a bridge, the East Suffolk's new line replaced the original, with the previously authorised terminus at Halesworth being relinquished. The new company was to have an authorised capital of £450,000 (which included that of the original HB&H), and the directors were recorded as Leathes, Johnston and Till, together with James Peto, Holland, Thomas Birkett and George Teed, to a total of not more than nine or less than four. The 1854 Act had authorised the East Suffolk's new main line from Westhall to Woodbridge, and so included the deviation from the HB&H's original plan. In addition, branches were to be built to Leiston, plus the Leiston extension (a tramway from Leiston station into Richard Garrett's engineering works), to Snape Bridge (a railway or tramway) and to Framlingham, with completion in five years. There were to be 14 level crossings between Haddiscoe and Westhall, 23 between Westhall and Woodbridge, six on the Leiston branch, two on the Snape branch and 11 on the Framlingham branch; the conditions for their provision remained the same as in the original Act. The East Suffolk Railway would afford facilities for all traffic to and from the Eastern Union. The Act received the Royal Assent on 3 July 1854.

Construction of the line was continuous with that of the original Halesworth, Beccles & Haddiscoe. The East Suffolk company had established its registered office at 43 Parliament Street, London, and in 1857 its secretary was William Day. The engineer at the time was Mr Berkley, who also acted for the other associated companies, although he was later replaced by Peter Bruff. Bruff had also worked for the Eastern Counties Railway in this capacity, but after putting in hand a great deal of remedial work to help pull the ECR from its parlous state he resigned in March 1857. He remained as engineer to the Eastern Union.

The passage of the East Suffolk's Act, and the subsequent construction of its lines met with considerable opposition from the Eastern Counties Railway. This company saw itself as having a monopoly of East Anglia, and viewed the possible development of the new lines with alarm, offering Lowestoft and Yarmouth their freedom. At first the Eastern Union and the Norfolk Railway associated companies were disposed to support the ECR's position, but this changed after a while. They set up a joint committee to pursue the matter, and for a time acted in concert.

In October 1853 the Eastern Counties and the Norfolk were united in wanting the Earl of Stradbroke to withdraw his support for an East Suffolk line between Halesworth and Ipswich in favour of one under the joint control of the associated companies. In their report to shareholders on 29 August 1854 the Eastern Counties directors noted that the East Suffolk's lines had received Parliamentary sanction, and that they were considering how to gain control of them. The general economic depression was causing problems. On 6 and 7 November members of the Joint Committee met at Woodbridge and went over the line of country to Halesworth, before then travelling over the line to Haddiscoe. On 21 November the Special Joint Committee again met and resolved that the United Companies would take over the entire management and working of the 'Halesworth branch' on and after 1 December. In fact the new line opened to passengers on 4 December 1854 and the following day the Joint Committee resolved that it was desirable to complete the line as far as Ipswich as part of a united system. The East Suffolk would be approached to get its costings for the Halesworth to Woodbridge line, whilst the Eastern Union was asked about the costs of the Ipswich to Woodbridge section, which it was obliged to build. Events continued to move ahead, with the Eastern Counties still trying to gain complete control. On 27 February 1855 the ECR directors reported to their shareholders that the Eastern Union was bound to build the Ipswich–Woodbridge section, and that only the intervening Woodbridge–Halesworth line, of 24 miles, with two branches of 10 miles, remained to be secured. This would 'complete the entire Railway System East of the Great Northern Railway, and which would be entirely under the management of this company'. The chairman asserted that the costs of the new line would be about £10,000 per mile, and that it should be very prosperous if the railways between Cambridge, Newmarket and Bury were a fair comparison. However, there was considerable opposition from the floor, especially to what were viewed as loss-making branches.

The Special Joint Committee met on Friday 11 May 1855 to consider a number of essential matters, and resolved, in line with a proposal from an East Suffolk deputation, that its lines should be handed over complete for working by the Eastern Counties at £10,000 per mile. The stations would be adequate to earn a dividend of 5% (allowing the same working expenses as the existing section) and Robert Stephenson would adjudicate on any disputes. A report from George Bidder, now engineer to the East Suffolk, was also received, and gave considerable detail of the costs of the proposed lines. The distance from the proposed Eastern Union station at Woodbridge to the temporary terminus at Halesworth was 22 miles 8 chains; the Framlingham branch 5 miles 58¼ chains; the Snape branch 1 mile 44½ chains; and the Leiston branch 3 miles 48½ chains. The costs of the main line came to £194,686 2s 6d (£8,812 per mile); the Framlingham branch £46,354 4s 2d (£8,064 per mile); Snape £10,601 12s 7d (£6,812 per mile); and Leiston £22,032 2s 8d (£6,109 per mile). Halesworth, Yoxford, Saxmundham and Framlingham would require the more important stations, while Bramfield, Campsey Ash, Melton, Leiston and Snape should also have stations appropriate to the traffic on offer. The quantities of land needed were 200 acres for the main line, and 36, 12 and 26 acres for the Framlingham, Snape and Leiston branches respectively.

At about this time the Eastern Counties board received a report from Messrs Moseley (the general manager), Capper (the outdoor manager) and Church (the coaching superintendent) about the desirability of taking over the East Suffolk, and concluding that it was essential if direct damage to the ECR were to be avoided. In a subsequent submission at the end of May 1855 they noted that the area served covered some 293,471 acres and had a population at the 1851 census of 104,760. It was a highly prosperous fertile agricultural district with many nobility and gentry, and with a number of watering places. Aldborough and Southwold were well situated and capable of much improvement, and there were also the ports of Aldborough (or Snape), Woodbridge and Southwold, as well as Yarmouth and Lowestoft. The only competing internal navigations were the River Waveney to Beccles, and the River Blyth to Halesworth. Comparison with the area served by the East Anglian Railway showed the new line to be a worthwhile venture.

Meantime the Eastern Union had set up a 'Woodbridge Committee' consisting of Sir Samuel Bignold MP, Mr Cayley MP and Messrs Hart, Josselyn and Wright, with J. C. Cobbold

MP in the chair. On 15 June 1855 they considered a letter from Peter Bruff saying that he could not get a reply from Mr Ogilvie on behalf of Peto and Brassey, concerning the execution of the work on the line. It had been surveyed and laid out, and work could start at once. He was currently working on plans for the bridges. In mid-July the committee authorised the secretary to raise a loan of £25,000 for land purchase.

Also by the middle of June the ECR board had resolved that it would be expedient to make an arrangement with the East Suffolk, and this was agreed by the shareholders the following month. The divisions within the board had already attracted a critical letter from Peto and Till of the Norfolk Railway, in which they took the Eastern Counties to task for holding up agreement to build the East Suffolk line, and accused them of showing conduct 'not likely to excite and keep the good feeling of the district'. Disagreement between the two companies heightened as the summer wore on.

At the end of July a letter from Peto to the ECR board pointed out that while an independent East Suffolk would be a disadvantage to the Eastern Counties, the latter's activities were leading to the Norfolk company being 'penned in' by the ECR, so that all NR traffic had to go via the ECR. The Norfolk Railway met the East Anglian Railway at Dereham, which line then ran to Wisbeach where it made connection with the Great Northern Railway (later to become part of the Midland & Great Northern Joint Railway). With the Eastern Union–East Suffolk line giving direct access to Lowestoft and Yarmouth, the Norfolk could not remain quiescent: an agreement between the Eastern Union, Norfolk and Eastern Counties would foster the traffic of the area. However, the East Suffolk's Bill, promoted by the Earl of Stradbroke, had forced the EUR to suspend its dividends until the Woodbridge–Ipswich line was built. The Norfolk company had promoted its own line between Halesworth and Woodbridge, in the interests of fostering its own traffic, and disliked the ECR's policy of buying out the East Suffolk on minimum terms, with no branches. Since the Norfolk was pledged to help build the line it had no option but to seek independent powers for unrestricted passage of the traffic of the district by extension and otherwise.

In the meantime the local landowners, led by the Earl of Stradbroke, were determined to make the Woodbridge–Halesworth link, and had forced the Eastern Union to stop its dividends until the Woodbridge branch was opened. All in all, Peto and Till wanted the East Suffolk to be incorporated with the United Companies, having obtained control on fair and equitable terms.

In August 1855 Peto again wrote to the Eastern Counties board calling for the East Suffolk to be single track only, but with proper provision for the handling of coal traffic. Later in the month the Eastern Union had heard from Alexander Ogilvie of Messrs Brassey & Co that they would construct the Ipswich–Woodbridge section as single track with double-track bridges for £120,000, or with double track throughout for £159,390 13s 0d. The EUR considered that although the works were heavy, the prices were too high. Meanwhile the *Railway Times* reported that the East Suffolk proper would cost £108,000 for a single line and £144,000 for double (which was what the EUR was prepared to offer), with the Eastern Union seeking the East Suffolk's opinion on the desirability (or not) of double track. At this time also George Bidder offered to resign as Eastern Counties' engineer, having been engaged to work for the East Suffolk, but the board declined.

By early September of 1855 the Eastern Union was ready to let contracts for its section of line, and Edmund Ayres (EUR secretary) wrote to his Eastern Counties counterpart, J. B. Owen, that his company was willing for the line to go into the East Suffolk system. By mid-October it was decided that the line was to be built double, with the agreement of the Norfolk Railway, at a cost of £144,000 (Ogilvie had reduced his price), since the extra cost compared with a single track was small. The Eastern Counties — seeing a potential part of its empire slipping out of its control — immediately looked for ways of cutting costs, but could not interfere with the Eastern Union's actions because of the provisions of the amalgamation agreement, although it did come round to agreeing that the line should be double. By 13 November Peto had arranged a loan of £10,000 for land purchase, and a further sum of £5,000 was agreed in December, secured against £8,000 of EUR 'Woodbridge' stock. On 11 January 1856 a letter from Ogilvie advised that he was loading a vessel with railway plant, including wagons, barrows, planks etc, for Ipswich, and that he was prepared to commence work on its arrival. Meantime, in October, Peto had resigned as chairman of the Norfolk Railway and had surrendered his Eastern Counties pass, although it at once returned it to him as he remained a director of a company worked by the ECR.

In the meantime, at the end of November Crowder Maynard, the Eastern Counties' solicitors, advised of the appearance of the notices for the Yarmouth & Haddiscoe and Lowestoft & Beccles railways. The board resolved to give the Bills the most vigorous opposition, and on 11 December it was agreed to pursue this via the Joint Committee. However, the Eastern Union was reluctant to give general support to this, although it did allocate £1,500 for the purpose. In March 1856 the Eastern Counties appointed Peter Bruff, its engineer, to conduct its opposition; within a week the Joint Committee had rescinded its earlier decision.

However, much trouble had been brewing within the Eastern Counties Railway, and although not bearing directly on the East Suffolk it had far-reaching effects. On 7 December 1855 an adjourned General Meeting of the company's proprietors received a long and very detailed report on the ECR and its joint companies. It alleged serious mismanagement with consequent adverse effects on shareholders, and (amongst others) called for strenuous opposition to the Halesworth & Woodbridge line and for immediate provision of £150,000 for permanent way maintenance, none having so far been made for the company's 548 miles! A motion of 'no confidence' in the chairman David Waddington MP was moved and carried, and an inventory of the company's assets was to be prepared. The 'Committee of Investigation' under Horatio Love was to be continued.

On 11 December the Special Board of the ECR met and Waddington stepped down, to be replaced by Henry Bruce. He then moved Waddington's resignation as a director. The parlous state of the company's assets was confirmed in a letter from Lt-Col Geo. Wynne RE, of the Board of Trade, considered by the Special Board on 7 January 1856. He commented on the state of bridges on the Eastern Counties, many of which were timber and in an advanced state of decay. Many sleepers had been replaced, but the track was still in bad condition and would probably need speed limits.

One interesting aside in all this wrangling — most meetings were taken up by it — was that a variety of insurances under £5,000 were proposed during February 1856, including some at Lowestoft: the passenger station, engine shed, carriage shed, goods warehouse, fixtures and fittings were covered for £1,500; the cattle sheds, fish markets and buildings on the harbour wharf, harbour office and telegraph office for another £1,500, and the ice house, buildings and sheds near the waterside for £500.

—2—
Building the East Suffolk

THE Bill for the construction of the Yarmouth & Haddiscoe Railway (Y&H) had been deposited for the 1856 parliamentary session, with Thomas Harrison and George Berkley as engineers. At Haddiscoe the new line would rise at 1 in 134 over the Lowestoft Railway, and would then cross the Waveney by a bridge 12ft high and with a span of 30ft, which was not at first planned to swing. A very large cutting was needed on the north side of the river, some 37ft 6in deep at its maximum. It would terminate in Southtown about a furlong from Yarmouth bridge, and a branch of just over 6 furlongs would curve southwards from a trailing junction near the terminus and go to the River Yare, by the gas works.

On Monday 5 May 1856 a meeting of the Eastern Counties Special Board resolved to ask the Norfolk Railway board to meet at once, to propose the doubling of the Reedham–Yarmouth section, with which the Norfolk company duly agreed. By this means the ECR hoped to convince the Board of Trade that Yarmouth's rail accommodation was satisfactory for the amount of traffic on offer, and hoped to have a clause inserted in the Yarmouth & Haddiscoe's Bill, under examination at the time, to delay construction for a year while the doubling was effected. Two days later the board's advisers told it that the case against the Y&H was so good that no further evidence was to be called. However, Peter Bruff still felt that the Bill was fraught with mischief for the ECR, and that the engineering and working features had not been scrutinised. The Eastern Counties' optimism was ill-founded. The bill for the Lowestoft & Beccles was passed unopposed, the ECR's case having been thrown out, and the preamble to the Yarmouth & Haddiscoe was proved. The ECR board now considered coming to an arrangement with the East Suffolk, but also resolved to continue its opposition in the House of Lords, and also to try to prevent building of the Yarmouth line by doubling its own route from Haddiscoe to Yarmouth Vauxhall. Later, J. C. Cobbold, Eastern Union chairman, wrote to the Eastern Counties expressing the view that its conduct had played into the hands of the promoters of the East Suffolk, and pointing out that the ESR was not promoting the Yarmouth and Lowestoft lines.

In September 1856 the East Suffolk company sent a circular letter to its shareholders prior to a general meeting to be held on the 23rd of that month at the Angel Inn, Halesworth. It contained four propositions, which were the propriety of laying double track on the new line; an offer by Peto to extend his proposed 14-year lease at 6% per annum to

Below:
Lowestoft station in 1911, viewed from the Yard signalbox. A fine selection of wagons, including two cattle trucks, is on view. The goods shed is on the left and the passenger platforms are in the distance. *HMRS Hilton Collection*

21 years; the propriety of amalgamation with the Yarmouth & Haddiscoe and Lowestoft & Beccles companies; and the powers to lease the whole line to Peto on the above terms. Before this meeting Moseley, the ECR manager, reported to his board that he had been at Halesworth on the 12th and seen large numbers of men and horses working on the new line to Woodbridge, and that the bridges were being made double. During October the Eastern Counties concluded that it had no power to influence whether the new line was double or single, and that it should come to an amicable arrangement with the East Suffolk, and also with Peto's Colchester & Pitsea Railway. The chairman, now Ralph Walters, and his deputy were to form a committee to carry out negotiations.

At the end of November 1856 Peto met with them, and reported that the new lines were being made. He proposed to alter the Lowestoft & Beccles line to terminate at Mutford and run into the Norfolk's station (later Lowestoft Central), and that the Eastern Counties should work Haddiscoe to Woodbridge and its branches, and Beccles to Lowestoft via Mutford on the same terms as it worked the Norfolk and Eastern Union lines, charging 50% for working expenses. All of the Woodbridge to Haddiscoe section would be double, with the branches single. However, the Eastern Counties board rejected Peto's proposition, wishing still to return to George Bidder's earlier idea of a line with no branches. The Norfolk did not wish to subscribe to the Eastern Counties' scheme until an amicable settlement had been reached.

Bidder then put forward complex proposals about the division of traffic when the East Suffolk was built, saying that all goods traffic between London and Yarmouth/Lowestoft should be divided between the Colchester and Cambridge routes, with that via Colchester being divided between the United Companies and the East Suffolk according to mileage. Traffic would be worked fairly between the ESR and the United Companies as regards speed and rates, and gross traffic to be guaranteed would be equal to that in 1856. There would be a minimum of five trains each way daily on the East Suffolk. The Colchester & Pitsea would be abandoned. This move, when it became public, was not welcomed by the people of Colchester, who wanted a much more central station and suggested extending the Sudbury line.

Meanwhile, the Ipswich to Woodbridge line continued to give problems. In December 1856 the Earl of Stradbroke wrote to J. C. Cobbold saying that as the Eastern Counties had no intention of completing the line by July, the East Suffolk would have no choice but to stop the Eastern Union's dividends from then, as provided for in its Act. Bruff also

Below:
An elevated view at Westerfield level crossing looking back towards Ipswich on 12 September 1911, with an up train due. Note the men working in the wagon. The tramway leading to the brick and tile works of Bolton & Laughlin can be seen branching off just before the siding joins the main line. *National Railway Museum*

wrote to Cobbold saying that the contractor was doing as well as could be expected, but that the clay embankments could not be forced on too fast, and that the same problems had delayed the Eastern Counties' line between London and Colchester. Cobbold wrote back to the Earl of Stradbroke pointing out that it was the Eastern Union making the Woodbridge line, not the ECR, and that there had been obstruction from landowners. He also wanted to resign from his East Suffolk directorship because of the opposition of the Eastern Union, Eastern Counties and Norfolk railways to the East Suffolk's extensions. He had delayed resigning in the hope of a reconciliation.

As with other railway schemes in the country the missionaries were also at work, and had set up an evening school at Halesworth, which was in operation in 1857. It offered a warm and comfortable room with a large number of books and periodicals of an amusing and instructive character. A scripture reader, who also ran the school, would teach any man to read and write.

On 22 January 1857 the Eastern Counties board received a letter from Edmund Ayres, the EUR's secretary, expressing his company's opposition to the Colchester & Pitsea, since the damaging effect of it would be considerable. The Eastern Union wanted an arrangement with the East Suffolk to prevent the building of the Colchester & Pitsea, and the ECR agreed to meet with the EUR and the Norfolk on the issue. At their meeting on 5 February the board received a memo about a meeting between Brassey (an Eastern Union director and proprietor, as well as being a major railway contractor), and Walters and Love of the ECR. In it, they agreed to account for the Yarmouth/Lowestoft to London traffic as if equally carried via the Cambridge and Ipswich routes, the East Suffolk taking the mileage proportion of the Ipswich half. Passenger fares and rates would be the same by both routes, while other traffic would be accounted as if carried by the shortest route. The ECR would give the East Suffolk a rebate of one-third of the ECR proportion of receipts for all traffic to and from all ESR stations other than Yarmouth and Lowestoft, and the Eastern Counties would not re-book traffic, under penalty. The rebates were on the net amounts after working expenses had been deducted.

As to the operation of the line, the Eastern Counties would work and maintain the East Suffolk, find the rolling stock and pay every charge, and would take these expenses from the gross receipts due to the East Suffolk, which would be charged at the same rate as the amalgamated companies. Not less than three passenger trains each way per day would run over the East Suffolk, and the line would be run as if an extension of the Ipswich–London line, with the same speeds. The agreement would terminate if any new lines were built between Colchester and London.

During January Brassey wrote to Richard Till opining that the East Suffolk would doubtless be built, and that they must push for an agreement with the East Suffolk. He also thought that not much additional stock would be needed to work the new line.

By early February 1857 the *Ipswich Journal* was able to report good progress, with formation of the line being faster than in the summer of 1856. Although it was a severe winter, embanking and excavating did not stop, even in heavy snow. With the better weather, bricklayers started altering the Holton Road bridge at Halesworth for double track, although there were vociferous complaints about its awkward appearance from local residents. The nearby bridge over the River Blyth was reported as largely complete since the large cast-iron girders had arrived. Work was also progressing on the pile bridge over the old river channel, and going ahead rapidly at Wenhaston, Bramfield, Yoxford, Kelsale and Saxmundham.

The Eastern Counties' problems continued through February. All of its proposed new railways were struck out, except for the Shenfield & Pitsea, and the company continued to petition against the East Suffolk's new lines. On 27 February Horatio Love took up the chair of the company, having previously headed the Committee of Investigation.

By the end of the month Peto had submitted plans for the Lowestoft & Beccles' terminus, which was to be at the rear of St John's Church in South Lowestoft, while in March the ECR appointed a Mr Edwards to look into the repairs needed at Mutford Lock. On 19 March the company inexplicably relieved Peter Bruff of his duties, whilst paying him until 20 June, and advertised for a new engineer. The half-yearly meeting of the East Suffolk company took place in March at its London headquarters, with S. M. Peto, James Peto, Leathes, Richard Garrett, Johnston, Messrs Burleigh and Norton and Lord Stradbroke recorded as being present. The chairman reported on the good winter, saying that 900 men were currently employed and that although the line could be finished by August there was no point, since there were delays on the Ipswich–Woodbridge section. There was also timidity on the part of the shareholders in advancing money! A provisional agreement had been reached with Peto for him to lease the line for 21 years at 6% on capital, with a security of £100,000 deposited.

Since the previous September 800 men had been employed all the time, and 350,000cu yd of earth and 45,000cu yd of ballast had been excavated. Ninety tons of iron girders had been fixed, and 17 of the 34 cuttings were complete, with the remainder advanced. Mr Berkley, the engineer, reported that the whole of the land had been purchased or arranged for on the main line, and that negotiations were also advanced for the Framlingham, Snape and Leiston branches. Several lines of rails had been laid for the transport of permanent way materials, and several timber and iron bridges were progressing. Much of the railway was already ballasted, and a great deal had been obtained from excavations adjacent to the line where the company had bought fields for the purpose. There were 32,000 sleepers at Lowestoft for both that line and the one to Yarmouth: 300 tons of rails and 1,000 chairs and fishplates for points were on order, while 1,000 tons of rails had already been delivered, enough for a single line throughout, together with all sidings and stations. Two million bricks were on hand. The working plans for the Lowestoft & Beccles and Yarmouth & Haddiscoe lines were complete, and negotiations for purchase of the land were in hand.

Mr Garrett then reported that he had walked over the line and was very pleased with the cuttings. The rails were of heavy double-headed iron, laid on kyanised Norway timber sleepers. The work was first-class, and half the line was finished and ready for rails. He praised Peto for his efforts. The company owed Peto a great deal in every sense of the word — it was already in debt to him to the tune of some £73,000 to £74,000 — and needed another £100,000 to complete the works. Peto agreed to advance this sum. John Cobbold, chairman of the Eastern Union company, then reported that the Woodbridge section would be completed by March 1858, with a view to opening in the first week of July. It was felt that the railway must open as a whole, and instructions were issued to have the lines to Lowestoft and Yarmouth complete by March. It was agreed to modify the Holton Road bridge to pacify Halesworth residents.

At the same time the Lowestoft & Beccles held its half-yearly meeting in the Royal Hotel, Lowestoft, with Edward

Above:
Woodbridge in festive mood, with huge crowds in the station yard and the flags flying. Note the two footbridges — the one for railway passengers is covered, while the other is open — and the proximity of the river to the station. *Alan Taylor collection*

Leathes taking the chair. The reports were exactly the same as for the East Suffolk, although there was much discussion of the Colchester & Pitsea line, for which the East Suffolk companies had petitioned in favour. The site of the fish market at Lowestoft was not yet known. The Yarmouth & Haddiscoe meeting, held at the Star Hotel, Hall Quay, Yarmouth, had the deputy chairman, Mr R. Hammond. in the chair, in the absence of the chairman, Sir E. H. K. Lacon. Work was progressing rapidly on the line.

In Beccles work on the Lowestoft line had commenced in earnest by mid-March of 1857, with the first sod being moved on the 10th. Many men were at work on the embankment. By May vessels were arriving at Woodbridge and Lowestoft with permanent rails and kyanised sleepers, and delivery was also taken of 15,000 logs which would be cut into twice that number of sleepers. A final call on shares required payment of £2 on every £10 share before 1 June. Agreement was reached between the East Suffolk and the Eastern Counties for the latter to work the new line.

Meanwhile, progress was considered to be satisfactory on the Woodbridge line. Work had got as far as Dale Hall Farm from Ipswich, through which area a cutting of great depth and length was needed. The soil was mixed and there was some danger, although there had been no serious accidents. The Norwich road had been bridged, as well as one other, and only the Westerfield and Henley roads remained to be crossed on the section to Martlesham. A fatal accident of an all-too-common type happened on Friday 29 May at 6am when William Waspe, a truck driver, stumbled and fell lengthways in front of his cart. He had been cautioned previously about running on the track, and left a widow and four children. Early in June some three million bricks from London were landed at Woodbridge.

The Eastern Counties Special Board met on Friday 8 May 1857 and considered a memo from Brassey about the working of the East Suffolk. This was essentially the same as that presented at the 5 February board meeting, although there was to be no rebate from the Eastern Counties for traffic originating from Woodbridge (inclusive) to Halesworth (exclusive) stations. The usual Railway Clearing House (RCH) terminals charges would apply. Other provisions in the memo concerned the possible routes into Yarmouth and Lowestoft. The East Suffolk would be allowed to divert its line into the Reedham–Lowestoft section at Mutford, and would then pay the ECR for the use of Lowestoft station. The Eastern Counties would also allow the East Suffolk to use its line between Haddiscoe and Yarmouth (Vauxhall) if the East Suffolk did not build its own line into Yarmouth, and the ESR would be allowed to double this at its own expense. In addition to the minimum three passenger trains each way there would be two on Sundays if desired, and they would all communicate with the Eastern Counties' trains from Woodbridge to London. A joint management committee with two members from each board would be set up to oversee matters concerning rates, accommodation and so on. All arrangements would be under the RCH agreements, and the agreement would replace that with the Halesworth & Haddiscoe. The board duly approved these points, whereupon Brassey was called in, and agreed to abandon the Pitsea, Maldon & Colchester line; the ECR also then agreed to withdraw its Shenfield–Pitsea branch Bill. The Norfolk and East Suffolk boards also gave their agreement at subsequent meetings.

By early July 1857 a 'very highly finished' locomotive had arrived at Halesworth from Birkenhead works, to be used for ballasting the Saxmundham–Woodbridge section. The *Ipswich Journal* said that 'it appears to be one of extraordinary power and size'. At its meeting on Thursday 9 July 1857 the Eastern Counties Board received a report from Mr R. Sinclair from Stratford. He had examined the planned stations at Wickham Market (or Campsey Ash), Saxmundham, Yoxford and Halesworth, and found them to be skilfully laid out and of sufficient extent for the probable traffic. At Wickham Market he would have preferred the goods shed to be parallel with the running line and at the same distance from it as the passenger station, so as to allow an extension of the platform if this proved necessary. All of the stations were conveniently sited except for Yoxford, which was too far from the village, but could not be got nearer.

Peto had earlier sent the block plans of the new stations to the ECR chairman, and had also gone from Ipswich to Lowestoft with Sinclair and Moseley. On the section between Ipswich and Woodbridge the excavation was very backward, and Peto expected that the line could not be completed for at least a year and a half. Only a small part of it was in a forward state, and parts were not yet begun. The Woodbridge station site was convenient for both the town and the river. From Campsey Heath, where the junction for the Framlingham branch was to be made, the party went on to the Framlingham, where the station was just outside the town and quite convenient. Having gone on to Saxmundham, Yoxford and Halesworth they concluded that the population of the area was undoubtedly scanty, but that it was a cultivated and wealthy district, the fields of which 'teem with corn of every kind'. The East Suffolk was in a much more forward state than the Ipswich–Woodbridge line. A meeting in August 1857 in Woodbridge Corn Exchange attracted almost one hundred people and heard of a plan to build a station at Melton, although the road crossing there to Wilford Bridge (half a mile on the Orford road) would need gates and probably a platform, bearing in mind the conditions imposed on level crossings. It was felt that Woodbridge station should be near Jessup's Wharf.

The August half-yearly meeting of the East Suffolk was held at the Angel Inn, Halesworth, with the Earl of Stradbroke in the chair. An agreement had been reached with the ECR for the carriage of traffic from Yarmouth and Lowestoft, although this did not prejudice the arrangement with Peto to make the line. Calls on shares had not raised enough money, so the company was still indebted to him. Much of the line was reported as complete, including most of the 18 miles of cuttings and 8 miles of permanent way which had an engine running daily over it. Purchase of the remaining small portion of the line to Woodbridge was in hand, and the branches were progressing satisfactorily. The engineer reported that the station plans were determined and that work had started on the most important of them. No bridges were yet built on the Snape or Leiston branches, although fencing was being erected. The Snape line was being laid to facilitate carriage of materials arriving at the quay on the River Alde. The Lowestoft and Yarmouth lines were also proceeding well, and the chairman expected the line to be open by March 1858, when a minimum service of three trains daily to London would be provided.

A letter to the *Ipswich Journal* of 19 September 1857 signed 'your obedient servant, AN IDLE MAN', makes interesting reading, describing a walk from Wissett (near Halesworth) along the new line. There was a steep incline down from the old line, with a heavy cutting of real gault, a type of heavy clay used for brick making. There was then an immense bridge over the navigable River Blyth flowing towards Southwold, followed by a high embankment across the marshes to Wenhaston where there was a magnificent five-arch brick bridge. The line continued onwards past Brook Hall, Bramfield, residence of the Rev Reginald Rabett who had fought against the railway, and then through woods belonging to Peto, and to Darsham level crossing. A deep ravine and bridges followed, bringing the 'idle man' to the Rookery at Yoxford, following which two massive iron bridges were needed to get to Saxmundham, together with another 'stupendous bridge over the turnpike' there. The line then passed the Buck Inn at Campsey Ash, whence it was a quarter mile to the station site, at the confluence of three roads, and which was marked by a huge heap of bricks. The railway was not advanced beyond this, and the line 'swarms with animals in shirts without sleeves — where the pickaxe, the barrow, and the tipping cart are in full requisition; where piles of timber and bricks and dingy sleepers forbode the assault and carry the delinquent place by storm . . .' The writer got to Ufford, where the line crossed the River Deben for the second time, and encountered unbroken ground at Loudham; otherwise the line was being made everywhere. The quality of the work was excellent.

At the September half-yearly meeting of the Yarmouth & Haddiscoe the chairman, Sir E. H. K. Lacon reported that more than the proceeds of the previous £2 call on shares had been spent, and another was ordered. The viaduct over the marshes at Haddiscoe was proving difficult, and the average length of the piles driven over a quarter-mile stretch was more than 80ft. However, all those for the swing bridge had been driven and this was going well. Much earth still had to be brought over the Waveney from the cuttings which had not yet been started. All of the materials necessary for a single line of track had been purchased and delivered. Peto reported that the value of work done by him to date was £23,000.

It had been decided to set up an operating committee of four for the new system, consisting of two representatives from the Eastern Counties and two from the combined East Suffolk companies, with an umpire. Three passenger trains per day would run in each direction, together with all necessary goods trains, and the same speed would apply throughout the system. Rates charged would be those applicable to the shortest route. Meanwhile it was reported to the Lowestoft & Beccles' half-yearly meeting that 6 of the 7 miles were in the company's possession, and that work was in hand to obtain the remainder. Work was proceeding rapidly and it was hoped to open throughout in March of the following year.

On 14 October 1857 a 'select party' inspected the works to date between Woodbridge and Saxmundham, and the *Ipswich Journal* carried an extensive report. The bridges were mostly of iron, from Richard Garrett's works at Leiston. The permanent way was described as being 'converted and prepared sleepers and rails' with ordinary chairs and keys, with fishplates at the joints, and fastened with prepared trenails, making 'a substantial road for fast trains'. The party travelled over the first part of the line in horse-drawn trucks and was loudly cheered by throngs of delighted spectators as it made its way along the level stretch to the site of Melton station. The party continued on its way through the slight cutting on Capt Brooke's land, then having the Deben on one side and Melton church and water mill on the other. A further mile brought them to an iron bridge on five brick piers over the Deben, with Bromeswell church on the north side and Ufford village on the other. On reaching Ufford bridge — a fine iron structure — they then had to walk for three miles as there was no track as yet! An extensive valley had yet to be filled as the line passed through the Loudham Hall estate, and in Pettistree parish work was progressing well on a heavy cutting.

Continuing onwards the party crossed over the Deben again before the site of Wickham Market station, and was able to board a train of open carriages and trucks, this time propelled by a locomotive, waiting at the crossing close to the proposed station. The works seem to have been largely complete for some way from here onwards. Beyond Blaxhall Hall the River Alde had been diverted to give the railway a better line with fewer bridges. The bridge at Beversham was described as being of iron and built on an entirely new principle using wrought-iron screw piles. These were of 9in diameter and were screwed through sand into solid gravel, and then braced with cross-ties. They were bolted together with wrought-iron collars and had wrought-iron caps or cross-girders which in turn carried the longitudinal cast-iron girders which were immediately under the bearings of the rails. It was a unique and expensive structure, but said to be strong and of extreme durability. The train passed over it several times as the party inspected it and no vibration was observed at all.

The line was apparently complete from here onwards. Another iron girder bridge with brick piles was crossed at Snape Junction, and later Rose Hill bridge, this time of brick, across the Aldborough turnpike. Another bridge then followed, taking the line under the London to Yarmouth turnpike, being made from six iron girders on brick piers, with counter-arches between the girders. The line then passed back onto the property of W. Long, in the parishes of Saxmundham and Benhall, whose mansion and park occupied land to the right of the line. A further brick bridge marked the end of the permanent way, and it was necessary to walk some 200yd into Saxmundham. The line crossed Rendham Road on the level, where there was to be a gatekeeper's lodge, shortly followed by another level crossing over Albion Street, where the station was to be on the north side of the crossing.

Another large bridge over the turnpike consisted of two brick abutments and four heavy cast-iron girders bolted by 1½in horizontal iron bolts. At this point Edward Leathes, vice-chairman of the East Suffolk Railway Company, joined the party, and they went by train to Snape Junction and Snape, the branch being some 1½ miles long. At the furthest extremity a timber bridge of seven openings, each of 20ft span, crossed the river, and the arrival of this first train was 'greeted by an immense concourse of the inhabitants . . .' There followed an inspection of the maltings of Newson Garrett, and a splendid cold collation had also been laid on for the party, which now exceeded 200 people, many of whom were ladies. In the course of many speeches, the construction of the East Suffolk line was compared with Peto's building of some 800 miles of railway in Canada. Ten days later the *Ipswich Journal* reported that several vessels flying the Norwegian flag had brought in 17,000 logs for sawing into 34,000 sleepers. In November the Bills for the amalgamation of the East Suffolk, Lowestoft & Beccles and Yarmouth & Haddiscoe companies were deposited, which also sought an increase in authorised capital and authorisation of the link with the Lowestoft & Reedham line via what later became Oulton Broad swing bridge.

Concern was expressed during February 1858 that the Holton Road bridge at Halesworth was obstructing the road. An accident had been caused when a wagon laden with whins higher than the bridge struck it and capsized, the horse nearly being strangled. The state of Ipswich station continued to exercise the East Suffolk company. In a letter to the *Ipswich Journal* of 27 February Cornelius Welton, an auditor to the company, complained bitterly about the likelihood of being shunted at Ipswich when the line opened, since the original station was still in use, necessitating a reversal at Halifax Junction. He condemned the 'present temporary and dilapidated building' and called for a new station. At the same time the matter was being brought before the town's council, which was also pressing for a new station. Reported in the same edition of the paper, the half-yearly meeting of the Eastern Union Company had been told that traffic was down for the first time since the union with the Eastern Counties, which appeared inexplicable. The EUR had raised objections to the ECR accounts, and it was noted that at the previous half-yearly meeting, the auditors had identified a number of irregularities, among them being shortages in the stated receipts, large charges which were not authorised by the amalgamation agreement and a number of large outstanding sums due to both the EUR and Norfolk Railway. The meeting also objected to remarks made by the Eastern Counties about Peter Bruff in its half-yearly report, and expressed strong support for its engineer. The Norfolk Railway's half-yearly meeting noted a similar drop in traffic.

In Norfolk and Suffolk in early March 1858 heavy snow caused difficulties in working local lines. On Tuesday 2 March the 4.45pm Norwich to Yarmouth left double-headed at about 6pm, to face a northeast wind and much drifting. It covered the first seven miles without trouble, but about a mile from Buckenham one engine left the rails and collided with some four or five trucks of a train passing on the other line. A permanent way inspector had his arm broken and driver Holroyd was badly scalded. Luckily no passengers were injured, and they were got back to Norwich. Both the Harleston and Halesworth branches were blocked by snow.

The half-yearly meeting of the East Suffolk had been held on the previous Saturday in Halesworth, with the Earl of Stradbroke in the chair. In spite of the tight state of the money market the works were well advanced, and he confidently expected the line southwards to Woodbridge to be finished on time, ready for opening in September. He was doubtful about the line to Ipswich, and called on the EUR to act on the inconvenience of Ipswich station. The matter of whether the line was to be single or double was also raised, and the answers were satisfactory. Unfortunately, it was not reported what they were! Presumably it was to be built as double track.

At the Yarmouth & Haddiscoe's half-yearly meeting Sir E. H. K. Lacon had reported expenditure of £11,279 for the six months to December, with £4,400 being due to Peto. By far the most difficult part of the works had been the construction of the swing bridge at Haddiscoe, which was complete, so that the heavy cutting at Herringfleet would now have the attention of the contractor. He also stressed the importance of a new station at Ipswich. The Lowestoft & Beccles' meeting had supported the amalgamation of the three companies, and received reports that expenditure on works had already reached £500,000. It was proposed to open the main line between Halesworth and Woodbridge in July, when the Leiston and Snape branches would also be ready. The Yarmouth to Haddiscoe, Beccles to Lowestoft and Framlingham branches would open in early September, when the EUR had assured them that the section to Ipswich would also be ready. It had been agreed to double the line, and application would be made to Parliament for the extra funds necessary, and also to lease the line to Peto at 6%. Legal authority was required for the working arrangements already made between the Eastern Union, Eastern Counties and Norfolk railways.

George Berkley, engineer to the Lowestoft & Beccles, presented a report showing that the works on the main line were nearly completed. Sixteen miles of single line had been made, as well as the greater part of the necessary sidings,

Above:
A very similar bridge to that at Beccles, the original St Olaves swing bridge was a single-track structure, although the lines had originally been gauntleted, later being converted to single track with points at each end. This fine view shows the old bridge on 26 July 1923. Trains to Yarmouth would travel to the left of the picture.
National Railway Museum

switches, crossings and so on. All the works had been constructed and the permanent way ballasted for double track. The station building at Halesworth had been roofed and would soon be finished, whilst others would be started in April. On the branches, rails were laid throughout the Snape line, with that to Leiston in a forward state, being ready for ballast and with rails provided. Earthworks and bridges were progressing well on the Framlingham line.

Strong support was expressed from the floor for the Mutford Lock line, and Peto gave his support to having a single station at Lowestoft. The Mutford route would be much better for sending fish to London, being shorter than the line via Haddiscoe, and the East Suffolk would handle goods at the Town Quay (on the south side of Lake Lothing). If there were any disagreement with the Eastern Counties there could still be independent access to London. He opined that there was no reason not to have the Mutford line open by September, and that one would be able to leave London at 4pm and be in Lowestoft by 8pm — '. . . which must have a visible effect on the passenger traffic to Lowestoft during the watering season'. In Mr Seppings' view there was 'no end to the fish that might be abstracted from the sea and the only two points necessary were to find persons to catch them, and to have the means of sending them away'.

In March 1858 the mayors of Norwich, Yarmouth, Bungay, Beccles, Eye and Southwold met members of the Eastern Counties board in Ipswich to press for a new station there, and were assured of their 'best attention'. On the same day, Thursday 13, an extraordinary meeting of East Suffolk shareholders at the Angel Inn, Halesworth, agreed to three Parliamentary bills: for the amalgamation of the various companies with the ESR, the building of the Mutford Railway, and alterations to the route of the Beccles–Bungay line. The existing line between Haddiscoe and Halesworth had just been closed for doubling of the track, and the Earl of Stradbroke was unable to say when it would reopen. John Cobbold, chairman of the Eastern Union, was also at the meeting, and was dubious about the proposed opening of the section onwards from Woodbridge in September, even though his engineer (Bruff) and the contractor (Ogilvie) had assured him that it would be ready. The works were proving to be very heavy. It also emerged that the line as built was single in parts and double in others, but would be doubled throughout as soon as possible at the East Suffolk's expense. Concerning the problems with Ipswich station, Cobbold opined that Horatio Love, Eastern Counties' chairman, was the cause of the trouble. However, by the end of May, Love and other ECR directors had inspected both the existing station and the proposed new site west of Stoke Tunnel and agreed that a new station was needed, and that steps were to be taken at once. In the meantime, the Eastern Counties had appointed a committee with Love in the chair to consider agreement with the East Suffolk. In spite of much discussion matters proceeded no further for some considerable time, but early June 1858 saw the first real signs of progress. The Eastern Counties board approved the spending of up to £5,000 by the Joint Committee on a new station, subject to it being put out to contract.

Trouble was brewing at Woodbridge. The proprietor of the roadway leading to Manby's Wharf and Hayward's Tide Mill had set a compensation value on it, and some time later had still not heard from the railway company. It was stated in the railway's Act to be a public highway, but had been purchased by the aforementioned proprietor, Mr R. K. Cobbold, who thus claimed it as private property. The East Suffolk and Eastern Union lines were to form an end-on junction at this point and were within 150 yards of each other, so Mr Cobbold proceeded to erect a long covered shed as a barrier between the two. The station itself, on Eastern Union territory, was proceeding well. Jessup's Dock was now connected with Hart's Quay by strong piling and ballast for the purpose of connecting it with the East Suffolk line, and parts of the foundations, sidings, cattle walls and permanent rails were laid.

By early July the problem of the 'private' roadway at Woodbridge was resolved. The land in question had given the appearance of being a public road, being gravelled and connecting a public road at one end with a public ferry at the other, and with no part of it fenced off. The Eastern Union had taken no steps for its compulsory purchase, believing it to be a public highway, but when the due time expired, Manby had sold it to R. K. Cobbold. He then filed a petition to the House of Lords against the railway company having the power to cross it. The matter came before a committee of the House, and it transpired that it had been the property of adjacent landowners, who were Manby and John Cobbold. Manby had sold his part to R. K. Cobbold, but it had not been conveyed, and the latter had then erected the shed. It appeared that he felt ill-treated by the railway company and one of its sub-contractors, and wanted a place to carry on his business of trading in coprolite; he already had much property on the other side of the river for this purpose. He had built the shed of second-hand materials bought from the railway as a delaying tactic, and a clause was inserted in the Bill for amalgamating the railways to resolve the matter.

The Bills for the construction by the East Suffolk of its branch between Carlton Colville and Mutford, and for the amalgamation of the East Suffolk, Yarmouth & Haddiscoe and Lowestoft & Beccles were under consideration by Parliament in May 1858. The former included provision for the ESR to use the Eastern Counties' Lowestoft station and to come to an agreement with the ECR over the working of the new branch. The Norfolk and Eastern Union companies opposed this, wanting also to be involved, and the ECR opposed the Bill.

By the end of the month extra borrowing powers for the East Suffolk had been approved by shareholders, extending the authorised amount to £120,000. All the necessary land had been bought, except for a few poles at Woodbridge. It was not possible to tell shareholders an opening date, although Ogilvie, the Eastern Union contractor, still maintained that its section would be ready in September, and a single line was finished from the north to Woodbridge. The Earl of Stradbroke insisted that the line would not open until the whole section between Yarmouth and Ipswich was ready. Landslips had retarded the work and there was the customary shortage of labour during the harvest months. However, it appeared that the whole line from Halesworth to Woodbridge, the Leiston and Snape branches, and the Framlingham branch except in Parham were complete by early August, although Cornelius Welton, now land agent for the East Suffolk, did not now expect the Ipswich to Woodbridge section to be ready before February or March 1859.

There was some slight movement at Ipswich towards the end of August, when the Joint Committee set up by the Eastern Counties and the associated companies (including the Eastern Union) sanctioned the general plans for a new station. Under the rules of the Joint Committee work was to be done by the company on whose land the site stood, with prior agreement of the committee. Also at the end of the month the first formal general meeting of the newly amalgamated East Suffolk company was held, with Edward Leathes in the chair. The Lowestoft–Beccles–Halesworth section was well advanced, but opening was said to depend on the bridge at Aldeby, which required widening for a double line. (It did not get it until well into LNER days!) Lack of labour was hindering progress on the southern section, and there were continuing engineering difficulties in the parishes of Playford and Rushmere. The development of modern communications was given a further boost in September, when it was reported that several vessels had arrived at Woodbridge laden with wire and other materials to connect the East Suffolk's wire with a submarine cable from Dunwich to The Hague. The anchors of vessels moored off Orfordness apparently often came in contact with the existing cable and the new one would resist any strain.

By the time of the next half-yearly meeting of the ESR at the end of September 1858 anxiety was being expressed about the delay in opening the line. A letter from Ogilvie to the directors told of sinking and slipping at Playford and Rushmere, and that consequent alterations had to be made to some brick bridges, converting them to timber viaducts. Opening was no longer possible before December. A letter had also been received from Bruff saying that he could have had the whole of the line ready including the branches, but that it was desirable that the embankments at Haddiscoe be given time to consolidate. Doubling had been completed over the greater portion of the line thence to Halesworth, said the chairman, but it was desirable not to open piecemeal. Mr Brooke, a shareholder, said that he had earlier been assured by the Eastern Union chairman, Cobbold, that Peto would open the Halesworth to Woodbridge section and provide screw steamers for the onward carriage of goods. Peto affirmed that the line was ready, but he was opposed to the partial opening, adding that there was no reason why the Halesworth–Haddiscoe section could not reopen. However, a train would run from Halesworth to Woodbridge after the meeting for shareholders. Agreement with the Eastern Counties for the working of the line had not yet been made, although drafts were being prepared for submission to both the Norfolk and Eastern Union railways for their prior approval.

On the evening of Tuesday 5 October Peto met Horatio Love, Eastern Counties' chairman, at the Crown Hotel in Woodbridge. The following day they set out in two first-class carriages with engineers and other gentlemen to examine the whole line, and it appears that they found all of it ready for passenger traffic. However, there was considerable dissatisfaction with the previous week's half-yearly meeting, and a deputation was waiting at Halesworth to meet Mr Love and press the case for an immediate opening to Woodbridge and reopening to Haddiscoe. In the words of the *Ipswich Journal* for 9 October 1858, Mr Love '. . . very politely received the delegation, uttered a good many words signifying nothing and rather brusquely bowed the gentlemen forming the delegation out again, very little wiser but a great deal more indignant'. The new station at Ipswich continued as a subject for argument rather than construction. At its meeting on 14 October 1858 the Eastern Counties board wanted Robert Sinclair to do all the design work, although the Joint Committee wanted Sinclair and Bruff.

On 16 October Horatio Love visited Woodbridge station with members of the Joint Committee, namely Messrs Bidder, Smyth, Bruce, Cobbold and Josselyn, and then went over the East Suffolk line. Generally they were very pleased with it, but the goods warehouse at Woodbridge station gave great cause for dissatisfaction in view of the likely amount of business to be done there. It abutted the passenger station, was extremely small and narrow, with no thoroughfare for trucks, all of which could have been avoided had the Eastern Union submitted plans to the Eastern Counties first. At

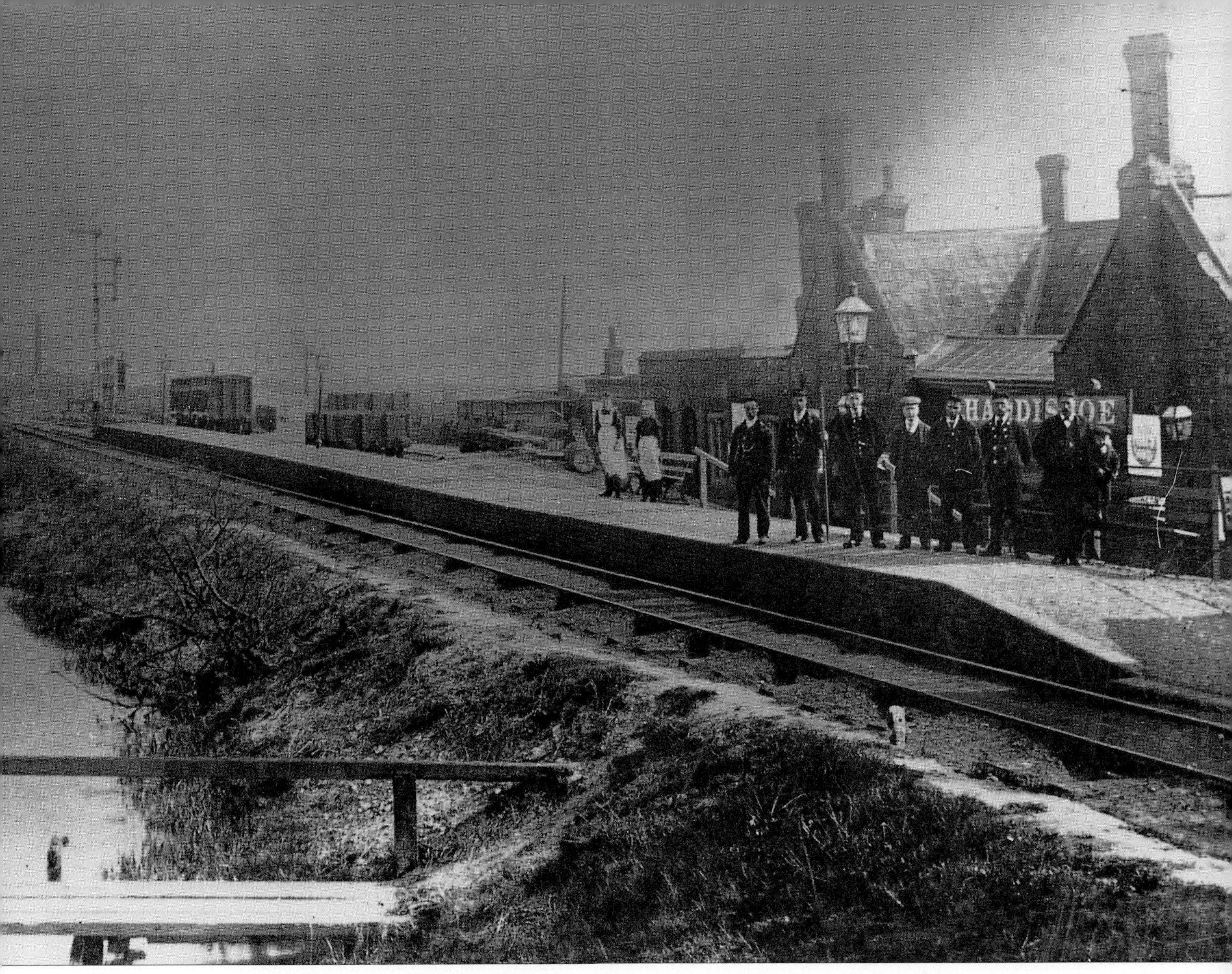

Above:
An extremely early view of the original Haddiscoe station and its staff. This is on the single-track line between Reedham and Lowestoft, and was the original terminus for the Halesworth, Beccles & Haddiscoe Railway. The station building has clear affinities with that at Cantley, only recently demolished. As the route was progressively doubled the line from Fleet Junction effectively terminated in the bay at the back of the platform, seen occupied by an open wagon. The original Yard box can just be made out. The station closed in 1904 when the new interchange was opened to the east — much less convenient for local people, as it was around half a mile further from the village. *Peter Punchard collection*

Halesworth John Crabtree put the case that the town was suffering the lack of a railway, 15 stands now being vacant in the Corn Hall because of it. Matters worsened on Saturday 13 November when the omnibus from Halesworth to Haddiscoe was withdrawn, leaving no means of getting to Lowestoft, Yarmouth and other local towns.

The Ipswich saga dragged on into November, with the ECR board complaining that the Joint Committee had not enabled them to commence building the station 'so necessary for the convenience of the public upon the opening of the East Suffolk lines'. However, on a brighter note the revised agreement for the working of the East Suffolk was accepted and signed, with copies being passed to the Norfolk and Eastern Union companies. Later in the month the Earl of Stradbroke wrote saying that it was essential to have the new station at Ipswich ready before the East Suffolk opened, and accordingly the ECR board resolved to erect it forthwith, advertise for tenders using Sinclair's plans, and have all works, such as buildings and junctions done by Sinclair under the board's direction. At the end of the month Peto wrote asking that the Mutford–Lowestoft line be doubled, a distance of only ¾ mile, 'this being the only portion of the East Suffolk route between London and Lowestoft which is not a double line'. This latter assertion was a little strange, since although the East Suffolk was certainly being built double, its branches, including the Lowestoft & Beccles, were not, and the work between Beccles and Carlton Colville was not done for many years afterwards. Nevertheless the Eastern Counties board approved the doubling of its portion, although this work was not done on any of the routes into Lowestoft until around the turn of the century.

By the end of the month things were starting to move again, with notice being given for the first time in the *Ipswich Journal* of 20 November that the East Suffolk was about to deposit a Bill for the extension to Aldborough, the standing orders for which duly passed the House of Lords in the following January. The following week the paper reported that '. . . Mr Walter Scott Jarvis, the indefatigable and much respected stationmaster of this town (Halesworth), has been temporarily moved to Cambridge to superintend the goods department at that place'. The editorial columns also noted that tenders had been let for the building of a new station at the north end of Stoke tunnel, Ipswich, and urged that no expense be spared. The new station seemed to be under way at long last, but disagreement soon surfaced between the

Eastern Union and Eastern Counties over the project, and it appears that the former had started the work out of exasperation at the delays from the ECR.

At the Eastern Counties Special Board meeting of 1 December it emerged that the Eastern Union was in process of erecting a new station, and the ECR gave notice that it must be carried out in accordance with the wishes of the Joint Committee. J. B. Owen, ECR secretary, wrote to his EUR counterpart Edmund Ayres presuming that the Eastern Union was compelled to do the work under terms imposed by the Corporation of Ipswich long before amalgamation with the Eastern Counties, and thus his company would not oppose the work, although traffic must not be interrupted. Ayres replied that the ECR had no power over EUR lines, and that the agreement of the Joint Committee was required only if the work were to be charged to that committee. It was not being undertaken under the Corporation of Ipswich agreement. The ECR had deducted a large proportion of the EUR's one seventh of the traffic receipts for 1857, so the ECR was not to be allowed to carry out any more new works. The Eastern Counties' reply characteristically disagreed with everything asserted by the Eastern Union.

At the end of January 1859 it was reported that the East Suffolk was considering opening to Woodbridge for goods traffic on 1 March, and although the station building was rapidly approaching completion at the time, there was no sign of the new approach road. On 5 February 1859 the *Ipswich Journal* reported that the junction had been made between the Eastern Union and East Suffolk at Woodbridge, allowing trains from the north access to the EUR station there, whereupon the Eastern Counties sent Sinclair to report if the junction was satisfactory. The newspaper also asserted that it had been positively informed that the line was to be opened in March, and that stationmasters and other officials had been appointed.

At the Eastern Counties' half-yearly meeting in February Horatio Love had given details of the East Suffolk line. It consisted of 45 miles of main line and branches, built at a cost of £450,000. The ECR had agreed to lease and work it for 21 years with quarterly payments of 40% of the gross to the ESR every three months, and to pay taxes, maintain the line, and provide rolling stock and staff. Traffic from Yarmouth and Lowestoft to London would be carried at the same fares whether routed via Cambridge or Woodbridge, and these receipts would be split in two halves, with one direct to the ECR and the other divided between the ESR and ECR, after expenses had been taken out. The Eastern Counties would set the rates. The new station at Ipswich, described as very commodious and convenient, ornamental and attractive, had made good progress by the end of February, with the brickwork appearing finished. Meantime work had begun in Woodbridge on the demolition and alteration of a house and other premises in Cumberland Street latterly belonging to Mr W. Page Wood in preparation for the new approach road.

On Friday 25 February at 10am a special train was run for East Suffolk shareholders from Woodbridge to Halesworth for their half-yearly meeting. It consisted of 12 first-class carriages and carried a number of gentlemen including Peto and Mr Wagstaff, the ESR's solicitor. It was conducted by Mr Lockey, a sub-agent to Messrs Peto, Brassey and Betts, and picked up passengers at almost all the intermediate stations. At Melton the large and handsome station was nearly completed, with considerable traffic being expected there, and it also had substantial cattle accommodation. The Station Hotel had been erected by Cobbold & Co. At Campsey Ash another considerable station had been erected, partly to serve Wickham Market, and since this was the first train to pass over this part of the line a great number of people were gathered to see it, and there was much excitement. The *Ipswich Journal's* reporter opined that this was some of the prettiest scenery in Suffolk, and considered that the line was exceedingly well constructed, with stations for both goods and passengers that were commodious and ample throughout the line.

The special train soon reached the junction at Campsey Ash and took the single line to Framlingham, reached at about 11am. At the station Mr Pearson and others were picked up, and again there were many local people to see the train. It was then reversed back to the main line and went on to Saxmundham, reached at about 11.40am, passing Snape Junction on the way. There were again crowds there, and the train continued to Darsham and Yoxford, where the fine station and hotel were approaching completion. Halesworth was reached around noon amidst the cheers of the inhabitants, the special trains from Lowestoft and Yarmouth having already arrived. The former had been conducted by Mr Stephenson, chief agent for Messrs Peto & Co, while the latter had been in the charge of Mr Watson, superintendent of the Norwich District of the Eastern Counties. The directors met upon the arrival of the trains, while shareholders convened at 1pm in the Market Hall, some 3-400 being present.

The secretary read the report. The railway was double from Woodbridge to Yarmouth, with single track branches to Framlingham, Leiston, Snape and Lowestoft, including the Mutford Junction line — a total of 64 miles. It was complete, and the Board of Trade had been requested to inspect it. The Eastern Union extension to Woodbridge was also complete, and required only the sanction of the Government inspector. The Aldborough extension of 4½ miles would cost about £40,000, and Morton Peto was willing to take it on the same terms as the rest of the line. The Amalgamation Act of 1858, authorising the merger of the East Suffolk with the Lowestoft & Beccles and Yarmouth & Haddiscoe Railways, had been passed, and a lease of the whole to Peto for 21 years agreed, as had working by the Norfolk, Eastern Union and Eastern Counties railways. A joint committee would fix the number of trains, fares, rates and accommodation to be given. At least three trains per day were to be run between Lowestoft, Yarmouth and London via Ipswich, with the traffic being worked as efficiently as if the line were part of the Eastern Counties itself. The directors felt that the public would be better served by a harmonious arrangement with the ECR than if the ESR worked its own line.

The amounts expended to 30 June 1858 were as follows:

on the East Suffolk	£556,439 5s 7d
Lowestoft & Beccles	£72,015 10s 5d
Yarmouth & Haddiscoe	£75,989 17s 6d
Total	£704,444 13s 6d

Additional sums to the end of December 1858 included land purchase at £20,918 12s 6d, engineers' fees £5,000, works £273,365, leaving a balance at the bank of £1,325 18s 0d. The grand total of expenditure was thus £1,006,054 4s 2d — which doesn't quite add up! It isn't recorded whether the matter was picked up at the time.

Much satisfaction was expressed at the meeting at the finishing of the line, and when the chairman said that the government inspector, Capt Tyler of the Board of Trade, would come over the line within a few days and give sanction to opening within a week, there was much cheering. It was dangerous to give promises, but he had every reason to expect a March opening. He asked for patience, and pointed out that the company had paid 6% on all investments to the day and hour. He expressed his regret at the death of George Game Day, the company's solicitor. A motion expressing thanks to

Above:
Darsham seen in Great Eastern days. Most traffic is evidently still horse-drawn, and the future A12 hardly looks busy. An up train waits to leave the station watched by a handful of cyclists and the inevitable small boy. *Alan Taylor collection*

Peto for the high standards of construction of the line was passed with much cheering. In replying, Peto commented that Ogilvie had been working night and day repairing the landslip and fallen embankment on the Ipswich–Woodbridge section, and he expected an opening on 13 March. He was also indebted to his agents, Watson and Currie, for overcoming the difficulties at Haddiscoe.

On 3 March the first engine to traverse the entire line from Ipswich to Woodbridge brought a quantity of materials for the electric telegraph. A large body of men was still employed at Rushmere and Playford where the engineering difficulties were extraordinary. The following day Capt Tyler went over the line from Woodbridge to Halesworth, and affirmed that the line from Ipswich should be open by the end of the month. At Yarmouth the railway was expected to open during the month, and a spacious and commodious station had been erected near the new bridge (Haven Bridge) in Southtown. A complete diversion of the Norfolk traffic to the new line was expected, with not less than 250,000 tons per annum of merchandise expected. However, full agreement had not yet been reached for the carriage of this traffic, for while the Norfolk and Eastern Union companies had assented to the arrangements made between the East Suffolk and Eastern Counties, the Norfolk felt that some clauses infringed its rights under the amalgamation agreement. The ECR accepted the Norfolk's modifications, and it received the company's seal on 11 May.

The Eastern Counties had been active at Lowestoft during April, and at the board meeting on Thursday the 14th heard that it had purchased cattle sheds for £3,000, and Thurneyssens Manure Factory for £1,000. Ayres wrote to the board informing it of the impending completion of the Woodbridge line, while at the same time Peto's submissions on timetables, rates and fares were approved. The Woodbridge to Ipswich section was almost ready for inspection, but the station at the former town still had much to be done, there being no sign of accommodation on the up side. In spite of the inspection of the line, no certificate had apparently yet been issued.

Nevertheless, on Monday 18 April the whole staff — stationmasters, clerks, signalmen and porters — had been employed and were taken down the line from Ipswich by Mr Dutton, superintendent of the district, and placed at their posts ready for active service. The Eastern Union refused to let them go via its line to Woodbridge and they were forced to travel via Norwich and Haddiscoe to get to the East Suffolk! The problem was due to the line still being in the possession of the contractors, and the passage of a train would thus have caused delay to the works. There also seems to have been argument about the connection at East Suffolk Junction. The Eastern Union claimed that the problem was due to the Eastern Counties' delays with installation. The ECR countered by saying that the EUR had made a single-line junction (the plans had allowed for either single or double), whereupon the EUR retorted that the work had also involved the underpinning of the London Road bridge. The ECR then claimed that although its engineer had offered to lay in the junction on 18 March, the Eastern Union had not replied until 1 April, and that the work had been done by 21 April. The earlier wrangling about the accounts also continued, the ECR still feeling that the cost of the Woodbridge–Ipswich line was excessive. However, the EUR said that although Ogilvie was connected with Messrs Brassey, he 'stood alone' on this contract, and that Bruff had advised that the price was fair. Ogilvie had constructed 75 out of 100 miles of the Eastern Union, and his work was 'most substantial'.

Capt Tyler of the Board of Trade duly inspected the final section on Monday 3 May 1859, the problems with the treacherous ground at Playford having been overcome. He also examined the alterations to the East Suffolk line proper that he had requested earlier, which had been carried out

Above:
This fine photograph shows the station building at Halesworth to good effect, although the bunting in the foreground is blurred. This was the largest of the line's station buildings, and is seen here decorated on the occasion of the Suffolk Show, held at nearby Chediston Park in 1905. The inscription over the entrance reads 'Success to Agriculture'. All of the upstairs was accommodation for the stationmaster and his family. From the right the upstairs windows were sitting room (2) and then four bedrooms. The front door was at the extreme right behind the fence.
Peter Punchard collection

immediately, although inspection had been delayed until he was again in the area. On 10 May William Day, ESR secretary, received the vital certificate for the line, although that for the Woodbridge–Ipswich section was still awaited, since Capt Galton, secretary to the Railway Department of the Board of Trade was away from London. This having been dated 26 May, the directors and officers inspected the line on 31 May and the system opened throughout for public traffic on Wednesday 1 June 1859. This involved the main line from the old Ipswich station south of the tunnel to Yarmouth South Town, and the branches to Framlingham, Snape, Leiston and Lowestoft. For most of these places it was the first time they had had a direct rail connection, and for Yarmouth and Lowestoft it substantially cut the distance to London. Halesworth, Brampton, Beccles and Aldeby regained their services now that the HB&H had been incorporated into the new line, and the whole was worked by the Eastern Counties. Snape never opened for passengers, despite promises, and the only significant extension to the system was the end-on junction at Leiston

Work had been going ahead on the line to Aldborough. In its 3 March 1860 edition the *Ipswich Journal* had 'pleasure in stating that the Aldeburgh [sic] branch line is now complete', describing the terminal station as covered over with a glass roof, and substantially built in white brick. Morton Peto and others had recently visited by rail, and indeed Peto's plant had been used to build the 2½-mile Aldeburgh [sic] Esplanade at the same time as the branch. Newspaper adverts gave the opening date of the branch as Monday 23 April, with a special excursion train running from Ipswich and all stations to Saxmundham, where it departed at 10.10am, calling at Leiston at 10.20 and reaching Aldborough at 10.30am. Connections and excursion fares were also available from the Framlingham branch, and the third class return fare from Ipswich was 2s 0d. However, the *Journal* had already reported that the line opened on Thursday 12 April, and advertised a service of four trains each way on Mondays to Saturdays, with two on Sundays. Perhaps there was an actual and official opening? The *Suffolk Chronicle* certainly reported the 12 April opening, commenting that Capt Tyler's inspection had been so favourable that authority to open had been granted immediately. As for the spelling, the Ordnance Survey used 'Aldborough' on its maps until the 1880 electrotype of the first edition 1in sheets, but it then appeared as 'Aldeburgh' on the 1884 and subsequent 25in maps. The local press tended to use 'Aldeburgh' when reporting on the building of the branch, although the railway called it 'Aldborough' until the name changed officially to 'Aldeburgh' on 1 June 1875.

—3—
Opening the East Suffolk

Above:
Saxmundham station building does not at first look similar to others on the line; in fact, it has the same basic structure with some extra bits added on, most of which are evident in this view from the road approach, which despite the LNER caption, probably dates from Great Eastern days. The level crossing is off the left side of the picture. *Alan Taylor collection*

THE East Suffolk line opened throughout between Ipswich and Yarmouth on Wednesday 1 June 1859, together with the Framlingham, Snape and Leiston branches. In its editorial of 4 June the *Ipswich Journal* waxed lyrical about the new line and its directors. The improvement of the district was due to the chairman, the Earl of Stradbroke, and the feelings of Suffolk should be testified to him as soon as possible. The East Suffolk had never been promoted simply for private advantage or pecuniary profit: it was a public utility serving a rich, cultivated district. Its construction had been well carried out by Peto, the Garretts and the shareholders. It marked the commencement of a new era in the agricultural and commercial annals of Suffolk, and would bring new impetus to the prosperity of Ipswich and East Suffolk. 'Right heartily do we congratulate our neighbours upon the prospects which are opening. Long have they invoked with the poet — "Come! bright improvement on the car of time".'

When it opened, the East Suffolk had stations on its main line at Westerfield, Bealings, Woodbridge, Melton, Wickham Market, Saxmundham, Darsham, Halesworth, Brampton, Beccles, Aldeby, St Olaves Junction, St Olaves, Belton and Yarmouth. It made Lowestoft 25 miles nearer to London, and Yarmouth 35, and gave the intermediate towns and villages the means to take advantage of new trade and commerce.

However, all was not as smooth as it might have been. At Woodbridge there were complaints that the Eastern Counties management had been up to its usual tricks: there were no time bills to be had and the day's mail did not arrive until Thursday. At Framlingham many people had had a trip during the day and sampled the novelty, although there had not been time to organise demonstrations by the local populace. Bells rang throughout the day and tea was provided for 40 gentry and inhabitants by Mr John Pipe of the Crown Inn. Songs were sung and a cricket match was played. Further celebrations were cut short by a serious accident at Framlingham station during the day. A concert had been advertised for 8.30pm in the Corn Exchange, the leader of the instrumental performers being one Edward Plantin, recently appointed as a light porter at the station. On the arrival of the 1.10pm Parliamentary train he was seriously injured, due 'to the desire on Mr Plantin's part to render himself as efficient as possible in the capacity that he fills'. The driver, who was not to blame, reversed his engine at once or Plantin would have been cut in two. Mr G. E. Jeaffreson, a surgeon, attended very promptly and Plantin had improved, although it was expected to be some time before he was fit to resume his duties.

Eastern Counties, Eastern Union, and East Suffolk Railways—Time Bill for May, 1860.

LONDON, COLCHESTER, IPSWICH, WOODBRIDGE, BECCLES, YARMOUTH, AND NORWICH, WITH BRANCHES TO MALDON, BRAINTREE, SUDBURY, HARWICH, HADLEIGH, FRAMLINGHAM ALDEBURGH, LOWESTOFT, BURY, AND HARLESTON.

DOWN TRAINS.—Week Days. — EAST SUFFOLK LINE.

FROM	1 2 3 class.	1 2 3 class.	B 1 2 3 class.	1 2 3 class.	Parl. 1 2 3 class.	Ml. 1 2 class.	1 2 3 class.	1 2 class.	1 2 3 class.	1 2 class.	Exp. 1 2 class.	1 2 3 class.	1 2 3 class.	1 2 3 class.	Ml. 1 2 class.	1 2 3 class.
IPSWICH arr.					11 10	11 37		2 20	—	6 17	6 35				11 25	
IPSWICH dep.		6 50			11 55			2 33			6 50					
Westerfield		7 0			12 5						7 1					
Bealings		7 11			12 16						7 11					
WOODBRIDGE		7 21			12 26			2 58			7 20					
Melton		7 26			12 31			3 3	1 2		7 25					
Wickham Market—Fr. J.		7 39			12 44			3 16	class.		7 38					
Fram. branch: Wickham Mar. dep		7 43			12 48			3 18	[illegible] 0		7 44					
Fram. branch: Marlesford		7 51			12 57			3 28	[illegible] 8		7 52					
Fram. branch: Parham		8 0			1 6			3 37	[illegible] 17		8 1					
Fram. branch: FRAMLINGHAM		8 10			1 15			3 45	[illegible] 23		8 10					
Snape Junction																
SAXMUNDHAM: Ald. J		8 0			1 5			3 32			7 57					
Aldb. brch: Saxmundham dep.		8 5			1 10			3 35	45		8 0					
Aldb. brch: Leiston		8 15			1 20			3 45	55		8 10					
Aldb. brch: ALDBOROUGH		8 30			1 35			4 0	10		8 25					
Darsham for Yoxford and		8 12			1 17			3 44			8 9					
Halesworth [Southwold		8 25			1 30			4 0			8 22					
Brampton		8 35			1 40			*			8 32					
Beccles—Lowestft. Br. Jn.		8 47			1 52			4 30			8 44					
Lowst. branch: Beccles dep.		8 50			1 55			4 33			8 48					
Lowst. branch: Carlton Colville		9 5			2 10			*			9 0					
Lowst. branch: LOWESTOFT		9 15			2 20			4 55			9 10					
Aldeby		9 0			2 5			*			8 56					
St. Olaves Junction		9 5						4 42								
E. C. Line to Norwich: Haddiscoe		9 30						5 4								
E. C. Line to Norwich: Reedham		9 40						5 13								
E. C. Line to Norwich: Buckenham		10 2						5 32								
E. C. Line to Norwich: Brundell		10 10						5 40								
E. C. Line to Norwich: NORWICH		10 25						5 55								
St. Olaves		9 13			2 18			*			9 9					
Belton		9 21			2 26						9 17					
YARMOUTH		9 35			2 40			5 5			9 30					
YARMOUTH dep.					5 30				10 20			3 15		5 45		
Belton					5 41				*			*		5 56		
St. Olaves					5 48							*		6 4		
E. C. Line fm. Nrwch: NORWICH									9 25			1 40		4 45		
E. C. Line fm. Nrwch: Brundell									9 40			1 56		5 0		
E. C. Line fm. Nrwch: Buckenham									9 48			2 5				
E. C. Line fm. Nrwch: Reedham									10 8			2 25		5 24		
E. C. Line fm. Nrwch: Haddiscoe									10 18			2 35		5 34		
St. Olaves Junction									10 43			3 38		6 12		
Aldeby					6 0							A		6 18		
Lowst. brnch.: LOWESTOFT dep.					5 40				10 32			3 30		6 0		
Lowst. brnch.: Carlton Colville					5 47							*		6 7		
Lowst. brnch.: Beccles Junct arr.					6 0				10 52			3 50		6 24		
Beccles dep.					6 10				11 0			3 55		6 31		
Brampton					6 22							*		6 43		
Halesworth [Southwold					6 31				11 20	1 2		4 18		6 53		
Darsham for Yoxford and					6 44				11 32	class.		4 30		7 6		
Aldb. brch: ALDBOROUGH dp					6 20				11 15	3 0		4 10		6 45		
Aldb. brch: Leiston					6 35				11 30	3 15		4 25		7 0		
Aldb. brch: Saxmundham J. ar					6 45				11 40	3 25		4 35		7 10		
SAXMUNDHAM dep.					6 55				11 45			4 42		7 18		
Snape Junction																
Fram. branch: FRAMLINGHAM					6 40				11 30	2 40		4 25		7 5		
Fram. branch: Parham					6 48				11 38	2 48		4 33		7 13		
Fram. branch: Marlesford					6 57				11 47	2 57		4 42		7 22		
Fram. branch: Wickham Mar J.a.					7 7				11 55	3 5		4 50		7 30		
Wickham Market dep.					7 14				12 2			4 57		7 38		
Melton					7 25				12 11			5 9		7 49		
WOODBRIDGE					7 30				12 20			5 15		7 54		
Bealings					7 40				*					8 4		
Westerfield					7 50									8 15		
IPSWICH arr.					8 5				12 50			5 45		8 30		

Sundays.

FROM	1 2 3 class.	1 2 3 class.	Parl. 1 2 3 class.	1 2 3 class.	1 2 3 class.	1 2 3 class.	E 8 1 2 3 class.	1 2 3 class.	Ml. 1 2 3 class.	1 2 3 class.
IPSWICH arr.			10 50				7 40		11 25	
IPSWICH dep.	8 0						7 47			
Westerfield	8 10						8 0			
Bealings	8 21						8 11			
WOODBRIDGE	8 31						8 21			
Melton	8 36						8 26			
Wickham Market—Fr. J.	8 49						8 38			
Fram. branch: Wickham Mar. dep	8 53						8 43			
Fram. branch: Marlesford	9 1						8 51			
Fram. branch: Parham	9 10						9 0			
Fram. branch: FRAMLINGHAM	9 20						9 10			
Snape Junction										
SAXMUNDHAM: Ald. J	9 10						8 58			
Aldb. brch: Saxmundham dep.	9 16						9 3			
Aldb. brch: Leiston	9 25						9 15			
Aldb. brch: ALDBOROUGH	9 40						9 30			
Darsham for Yoxford and	9 22						9 10			
Halesworth [Southwold	9 35						9 23			
Brampton	9 45						9 33			
Beccles—Lowestft. Br. Jn.	9 57						9 45			
Lowst. branch: Beccles dep.	10 0						9 50			
Lowst. branch: Carlton Colville	10 15						10 5			
Lowst. branch: LOWESTOFT	10 25						10 15			
Aldeby	10 10						9 57			
St. Olaves Junction										
E. C. Line to Norwich: Haddiscoe										
E. C. Line to Norwich: Reedham										
E. C. Line to Norwich: Buckenham										
E. C. Line to Norwich: Brundell										
E. C. Line to Norwich: NORWICH										
St. Olaves	10 23						10 10			
Belton	10 31						10 17			
YARMOUTH	10 45						10 30			
YARMOUTH dep.			6 0				6 0			
Belton			6 10				6 11			
St. Olaves			6 17				6 19			
E. C. Line fm. Nrwch: NORWICH										
E. C. Line fm. Nrwch: Brundell										
E. C. Line fm. Nrwch: Buckenham										
E. C. Line fm. Nrwch: Reedham										
E. C. Line fm. Nrwch: Haddiscoe										
St. Olaves Junction										
Aldeby			6 29				6 33			
Lowst. brnch.: LOWESTOFT dep.			6 15				6 20			
Lowst. brnch.: Carlton Colville			6 25				6 27			
Lowst. brnch.: Beccles Junct arr.			6 35				6 40			
Beccles dep.			6 42				6 46			
Brampton			6 53				6 58			
Halesworth [Southwold			7 2				7 8			
Darsham for Yoxford and			7 15				7 21			
Aldb. brch: ALDBOROUGH dp			6 55				7 0			
Aldb. brch: Leiston			7 10				7 15			
Aldb. brch: Saxmundham J. ar			7 20				7 25			
SAXMUNDHAM dep.			7 25				7 33			
Snape Junction										
Fram. branch: FRAMLINGHAM			7 15				7 20			
Fram. branch: Parham			7 23				7 28			
Fram. branch: Marlesford			7 32				7 37			
Fram. branch: Wickham Mar J.a.			7 40				7 46			
Wickham Market dep.			7 45				7 53			
Melton			7 56				8 4			
WOODBRIDGE			8 1				8 9			
Bealings			8 11				8 19			
Westerfield			8 21				8 30			
IPSWICH arr.			[illegible]				[illegible]			

East Suffolk Railway and Eastern Counties Railway timetables, *Ipswich Journal* 5 May 1860.

Above:
An up local to Wickham Market heads away from Framlingham. This card was sent in 1908. *Alan Taylor collection*

Lowestoft seems to have paid the opening relatively little attention, perhaps because it already had a railway and an important terminus. Peto, together with the East Suffolk and Eastern Counties directors, had arrived via the new line on Tuesday evening, and dined at the Royal Hotel. At 8am the following day they left by special train over the same route. There was no celebration in the town, apart from flag staffs at the Royal Hotel, fish market, telegraph office, various vice-consulates and the Suffolk Hotel, the last of which was also gaily dressed with flags. The branch now enjoyed four passenger and three goods trains per day.

At Woodbridge the tide was high in the Deben estuary as the noon train from Ipswich arrived on opening day, and some of the yachts in the river had their colours flying. Numerous groups of local people had collected to watch the passage of the trains, and others were gathered at succeeding stations to cheer their passage. At Saxmundham it was rather quiet, but Mr Richard Garrett alighted there and was thought to be the purchaser of the first ticket to Leiston from Ipswich station. At Darsham Mr Rouse, proprietor of the local coach, was waiting with his horses to take passengers on to Southwold, although his days of taking them all the way to Ipswich were finished. Halesworth station was decorated with a variety of flags.

The line thence to Beccles had been relaid with double track, and at the latter town the church bells pealed, and the station area was decorated with flags and evergreens. The lines onward to Yarmouth and Lowestoft were described by the *Suffolk Chronicle* as being little else but marshland, rivers and ditches. 'Indeed so different is the scenery, and so many of the arrangements on the line, such as the signal posts, the signal men's houses etc that one might be excused for thinking that he was not only in another county but another country.' South Town station was described as being very light, airy and pretty, with the train running in under cover, the platforms being enclosed with an open roof and skylights. The rolling stock is also mentioned in glowing terms, the first class described as 'luxurious', the second far more comfortable than usual (with cushioned seats!), and the carriages probably being confined to the line.

The train service in the first timetable was as follows. In the down direction (towards Yarmouth):

- The first left Ipswich at 6.50am and called at all stations to Yarmouth (arrive 9.35am), with connections for Lowestoft (9.15am), Framlingham (8am) and Leiston (8.15am).
- There was a 12 noon train from Ipswich to Yarmouth, which had no Norwich connection, but which was shown as connecting with the 7.25am Parliamentary from London, and also the 9.15am express from London.
- The 2.35pm from Ipswich omitted Westerfield, Bealings, Brampton, Carlton Colville, Aldeby, St Olaves and Belton, whilst
- The 6.45pm called at all stations (except St Olaves Junction, as there was no connection to Norwich).

On Sundays there were down trains at 8am and 7.47pm. Snape Junction was shown as a station but with no trains calling; Leiston was shown as 'for Aldborough', Darsham 'for Yoxford', and St Olaves Junction appeared after Aldeby, although only trains with a Norwich connection called since it was purely an exchange platform. In the up direction the pattern of service reflected that in the down, with trains leaving Yarmouth at 5.30am, 10.45am, 3.30pm and 5.45pm.

On the branches the passenger service was usually arranged to connect with the main line trains. In May 1860 Lowestoft received four trains on Mondays to Saturdays via the East Suffolk, with two on Sundays, when there were only the two main line trains. The Framlingham and Aldborough branches fared better, and each had an extra train, from

Saxmundham at 4.45pm and Wickham Market at 5pm. This extra train had been provided during the first year of operation, and indeed within the first month on the Aldborough branch. The last possible train from London was the 4.25pm express, which called only at Chelmsford, Witham, Mark's Tey, Colchester and Manningtree before arriving at Ipswich at 6.35pm, only 18 minutes behind the 3pm stopper. Both connected into the 6.45pm all stations to Yarmouth, reached at 9.30pm. This last East Suffolk train was quickly put back to 6.50pm, perhaps because the connection was too tight.

The East Suffolk company had nominated the Earl of Stradbroke and Edward Leathes as its representatives on the ESR/ECR Joint Committee, although the Eastern Counties had refused to give the ESR secretary and the other directors passes over its system. It did not grant Peto and the other ESR directors passes to travel over its own line until early November 1859.

Concern about Ipswich station continued, and in mid-May J. C. Cobbold wrote to Horatio Love expressing anxiety. By the end of September the ECR had informed the Eastern Union that it was suffering great loss because the new station was not ready, and that there was great danger because of the East Suffolk traffic coming into the old station. However, at the end of October 1859 the Eastern Counties board was advised by the EUR that it was expected to be ready in approximately a month, and that a large expenditure had already been made on the approaches. The new station at Ipswich finally opened on 1 July 1860.

One of the immediate changes that the railway brought was to the old coachmen. Mr Rouse at Darsham was '. . . . forced to greet the entrance of the train with a smile, although in great measure his "occupation's gone", for it is not in the power of horseflesh, even when handled by the civillest of Jehus, to compete with steam.' Richard Warner of Bungay advertised that on and after 2 June his coach would leave the King's Head there at 7.40am for Beccles railway station in time for the 8.50am train to Yarmouth, Lowestoft and Norwich. It would leave Beccles again at 11.16am, arriving at Bungay at 12.20pm, depart Bungay at 2.50pm to connect with the London train at 4pm and the London train at 4.12pm, returning to Bungay on the arrival of the 6.30pm from Lowestoft, Norwich and Yarmouth. Warner did not last long in this new role of feeder service to the railway, and he sank into melancholy and died in October 1865, by which time the Waveney Valley Railway had opened its line connecting Bungay and Beccles.

Excursion traffic started almost as soon as the line opened, the new opportunities for travel quickly and easily to the coast not being lost on either the railway or the public. On Whit Monday 13 June 1859 an excursion was run to London, leaving Yarmouth at 8am, and with connections from the Lowestoft, Leiston and Framlingham branches. It arrived in London at about 2pm, and the fares ranged from 21s first class, 16s second class and 11s third class from Yarmouth, Lowestoft and stations to Beccles, to 14s, 10s and 6s 9d respectively from Bealings. The special excursion tickets were available for return any weekday up to and including Saturday 18 June by any train except an express.

Another matter which was to affect the East Suffolk, if less directly, was beginning to gather momentum. The Amalgamation Committee, formed to consider the formal union of the so-called 'United Companies' reported that terms must be settled before a Bill was deposited, and accordingly recommended that it not be done that year, the time for all railway Bills being the end of November.

In early January the ECR Special Board met to consider the amalgamation, and discussed the Heads of Agreement already produced. The companies involved were as follows (the number of its directors on the board of the amalgamated company are shown in parentheses): the Northern & Eastern (2; it would remain a distinct company), Eastern Union (2), Norfolk (2), East Anglian (1) and Eastern Counties (8). The old ECR thus remained in the overall majority. The East Suffolk Railway was not directly involved.

At the start of June 1860 the Eastern Counties was able to find fault with the new, as yet unopened, Ipswich station. There was no water for the engines, and all those from both the East Suffolk and Norwich lines would have to run to the old station for this purpose, as well as for coking. The company complained that there would be no turntable for another month, and that two sets of waiting rooms had been provided when one would have been sufficient. Meanwhile the Traffic Committee was considering the absolute necessity of getting more rolling stock, since new lines such as the East Suffolk were placing a strain on resources. There was a need for 30 engines, 20 composite and 80 second-class carriages, six smoking saloons, 400 wagons and 100 timber trucks, although only 200 wagons were ordered. Sixty old second-class coaches were to be downgraded to thirds.

During July the Eastern Counties was advertising a through service between Yarmouth and Lowestoft via Beccles, taking 50 minutes in each direction. Trains left Yarmouth at 8.50am, 12 noon, 3.45pm and 8pm, with returns from Lowestoft at 10am, 1.10pm, 5.45pm and 9.10pm. Reduced fares were offered via both Beccles and Reedham, being respectively 1s 6d, 1s and 9d single, or 2s, 1s 6d and 1s day return. By October of the following year the Reedham and Beccles services were being advertised separately, although not billed as through trains, effectively giving eight local workings daily between the two seaside rivals. The Reedham trains used Yarmouth Vauxhall station. Also during the month the Eastern Counties considered Peto's proposal to dispose of surplus lands on the East Suffolk to traders for stores and warehouses. Sinclair had visited the stations and found that in almost every case they would be let to Mr Newson Garrett, which Sinclair felt would give him a monopoly and be prejudicial to the railway. The sites for the proposed buildings would (except at Brampton and Melton) occupy land most convenient for the loading and unloading of carts, and thus their erection would interfere with this traffic. At Beccles, Leiston, Framlingham, Yoxford and Wickham Market future extensions to the stations would be prevented. Sinclair thus wanted the land left in the company's hands, but was prepared to mark maps showing which parts could be disposed.

At the end of November 1860 the Eastern Counties Traffic Committee accepted a tender from Messrs Smith & Sons for the exhibition of advertisements and the sale of newspapers, periodicals and books at various stations on its lines. Thus started a partnership which lasts to this day, the firm of W. H. Smith being familiar to rail travellers throughout East Anglia.

At Beccles the need for changes at the station rapidly became apparent. In May 1863 the Engineers' Office of the Great Eastern Railway (GER) drew up plans for changes to the layout. At the time, the down platform was relatively short, and occupied the trackside immediately next to the station building, extending no further north than the later footbridges. The up platform was a little longer, and opposite the down. It had a water tank at the Ipswich end, and a waiting shelter opposite the station building. Passengers crossed between platforms at track level. The changes proposed involved the construction of a level crossing approximately on the site of the present-day footbridge, leading from the station forecourt on the down side to a 'new promenade', later to become The Avenue. This crossing would have bisected the up platform but passed at the northern end of the down. A footbridge would be sited immediately on the south side of the proposed crossing, which appears never to have progressed any further.

The citizens of the town were also becoming dissatisfied with their station. In a letter to the chairman and directors of the Great Eastern signed at a public meeting on 8 January 1863, the mayor complained that the station had been erected by the Halesworth, Beccles & Haddiscoe company, and was thus inferior to others in a similar situation. The line had since been doubled and extended, the Waveney Valley connection was about to be made, and Beccles was thus the junction for both the Waveney Valley and Lowestoft lines. There had been a great increase in passenger and general business, and greater accommodation was needed. There was especially a need for first- and second-class waiting rooms, and better protection from the weather; he demanded that both platforms be 'boarded' and covered over. There was a need to guard against delay and danger in crossing the line since it lacked a bridge of any sort.

In September 1864 plans were drawn up to acquire land (1 rood, 18 poles) for further sidings on the west side of the line, there already being some on the site. The matter of passenger facilities clearly was not settled, since the protests continued. The Great Eastern had evidently ignored the memorial presented in 1863, so on 22 June 1865 a well-attended public meeting in the Town Hall called again for improved accommodation at the station, noting that Halesworth station was 'plainer but more commodious', with waiting rooms. To add insult to injury, in the previous year Beccles Corporation had allowed the GER to take water from its land on condition that a bridge was provided within six months. It took the water but failed to build the bridge. It was rumoured that plans for a new station by Sinclair, the GER's engineer, was 'all that they desired', but that the board had rejected it.

However, on Monday 4 July the alterations finally started. A deputation from Beccles met James Goodson, GER chairman at the Victoria Hotel in Yarmouth, and told him that they were watching the alterations, and were disappointed at the lack of waiting rooms. The major change was the enlargement of the booking office which resulted in the narrowing of the platform, and there was as yet no bridge. However, by 19 August the engineer's office at Stratford had written to say that the matter was in hand, and that the bridge should arrive in the next week. The East Suffolk line had now been fully open for five years, and had become an integral part of the district that it served. Local communities and businesses along its length depended on its successful operation, and were quite prepared to press for the improvements they felt necessary; sometimes they succeeded, and sometimes not. Although much changed, a journey along the line now would still show many similarities and links with its early years. The next section explores the line and points out some of those features.

Below:
A fine photograph of uncertain date, illustrating goods traffic characteristic of the area. This wagon is being loaded at Beccles with osiers which have been cut locally on the marshes and were used for a wide variety of purposes. *Peter Punchard collection*

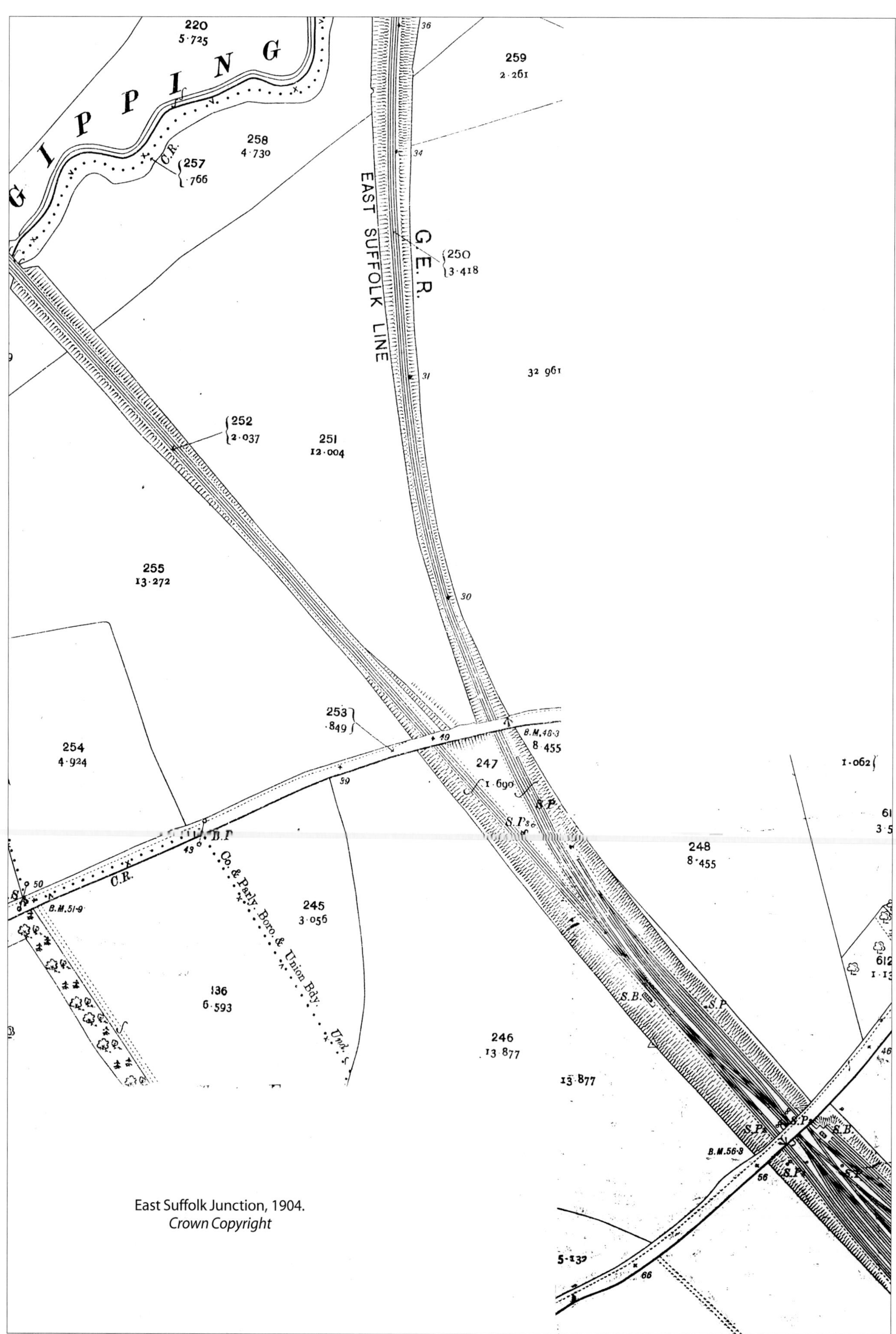

East Suffolk Junction, 1904.
Crown Copyright

—4—

East Suffolk Line Description Ipswich to Melton

Above:
Integrated transport Great Eastern style: a steady stream of travellers makes for Ipswich station, while a GER motor omnibus waits to leave. *Alan Taylor collection*

IPSWICH was a town almost completely surrounded by the Great Eastern Railway (formed in 1862 by the amalgamation, amongst others, of the Eastern Counties Railway and Eastern Union Railway). The EUR had first approached from the southeast from Colchester, changed direction a little and circled around the southern side before turning north again to Stowmarket and Bury, following which the East Suffolk covered the northeastern quarter, with encirclement almost completed by the Felixstowe line. The branches to the docks and quays on either side of the River Orwell made the embrace even closer. The building of the Ipswich & Bury St Edmunds Railway had necessitated the boring of Ipswich tunnel through Stoke Hill, and made the need for a new station inevitable. The East Suffolk line proper starts at East Suffolk Junction, which is about 69½ miles from Liverpool Street. Trains start or continue from Ipswich station, although for a brief period this was still the original on the south side of Ipswich tunnel, and they either had to reverse out of the station back to Halifax Junction, and then continue down the line to Yarmouth, or perform a similar manoeuvre in reverse when going towards London. The present station was originally one-sided, using what is now Platform 2 and the main station buildings, and acquired the island platform in 1883. The LNER also maintained a parcels and ticket booking office at 27 St Matthews Street, which facility was shared by, of all companies, the Great Western.

The first Ipswich station had stood on the site later occupied by the locomotive depot and its latter-day successor the electrification depot. This was not extended when the Ipswich & Bury Railway was being promoted — it had always been considered temporary, and so the new line bypassed it. The depot had an entrance in Croft Road, opposite which two pubs commemorated the origins of the railway, being respectively the 'Great Eastern' and the 'E.U.R', where the initials of the Eastern Union remain in the stonework. Around the corner in Wherstead Road, close by the bridge taking the Griffin Wharf branch over the road, was the new locomen's block, built in the 1950s, the depot being bounded by the main line and these streets.

The new station building was, and is, a very fine structure. It was designed by Sancton Wood in the Italianate style, and had originally been intended as a joint station between the Ipswich & Bury and Eastern Union Railways. It was executed in white brick, with reds used for quoins, plinths, lintels and so on. The arches were almost all circular. The central section was of two storeys with a hipped, slate roof,

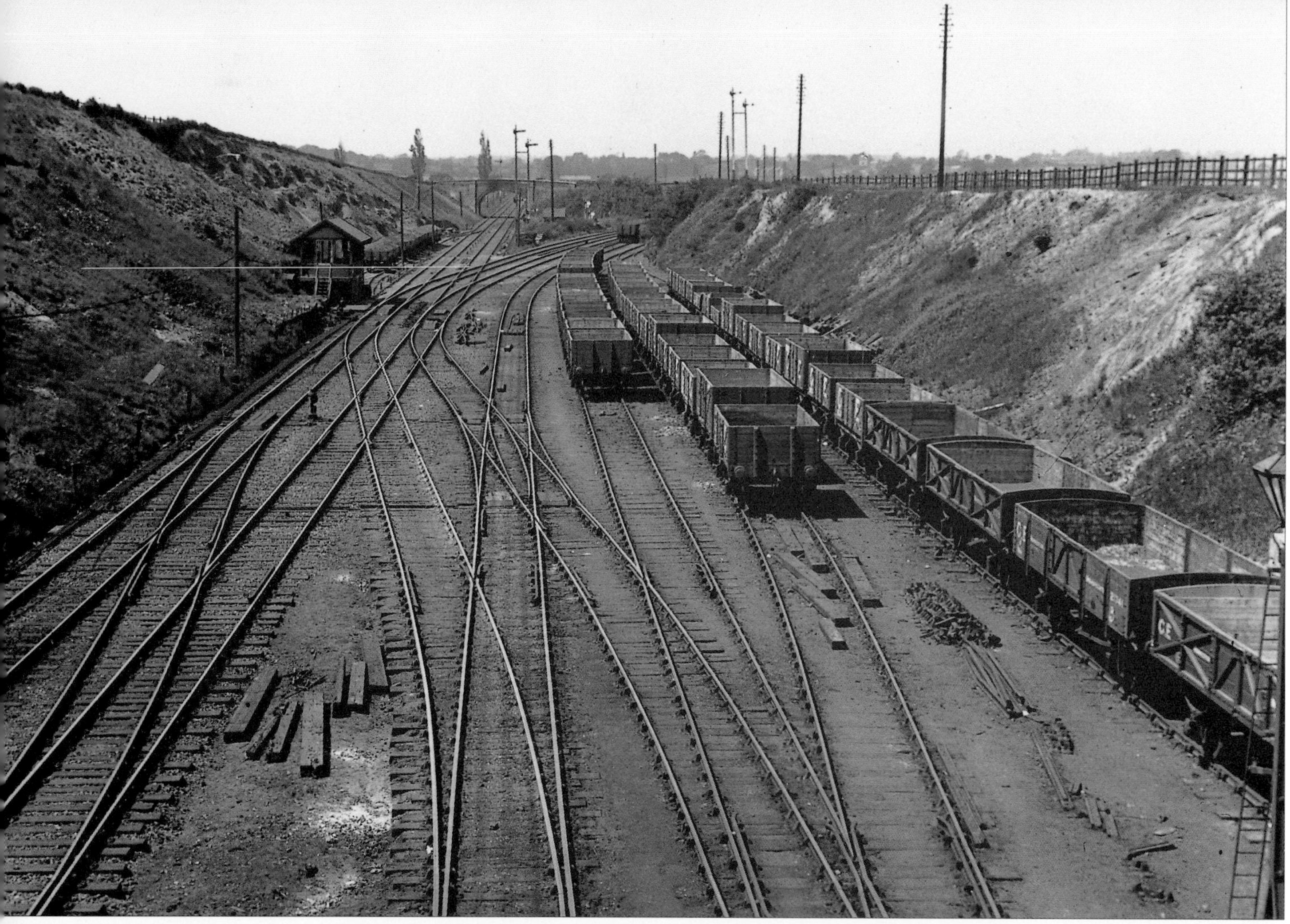

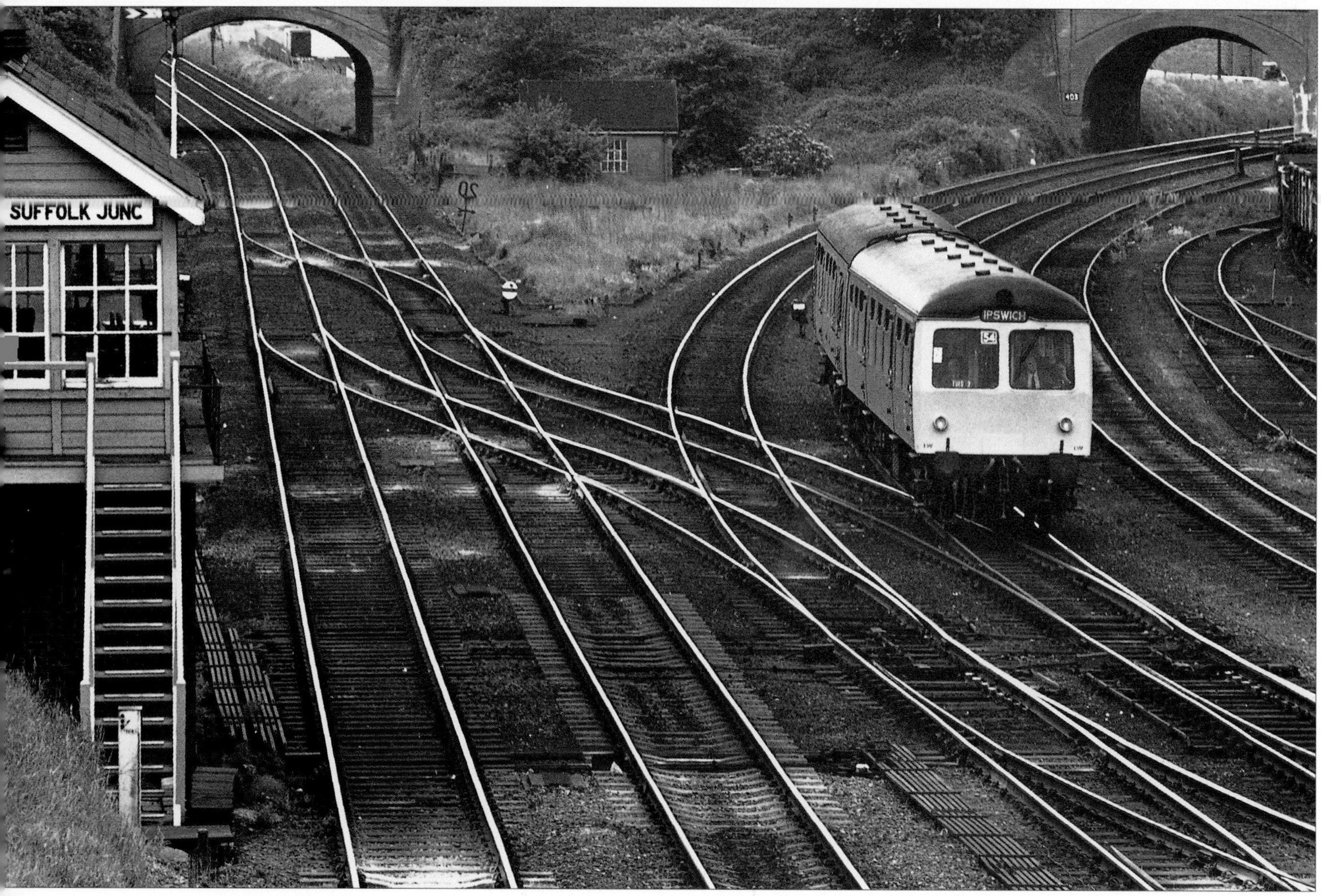
SUFFOLK JUNC
IPSWICH
54
403

and with prominent chimney stacks at each end and on both platform and road sides; the latter also had a small bell-tower. On the road approach side a large awning spanned the front of this block. The down main line served the north face of the island, No 3, whilst a sharp turnout, restricted to 15mph, gave access to the back platform, No 4. The up main did not serve a platform, with up Norwich trains calling at the through platform, No 2, having to be turned off the main line. No 1 was a Norwich-facing bay on the up side, today much truncated.

Ipswich station signalbox stood at the tunnel end of the island platform, and was provided as part of the 1883 station rebuilding. Two sharply curved short dock roads trailed into the up line close to the tunnel and were used for locomotive changing, the relieving engine waiting there for the up train to run in. The incoming engine, probably from Norwich or Yarmouth South Town depot, would come off and set back onto the middle road, whereupon the relief would emerge from the spur and couple up. After the train had gone the arriving crew would take their engine through the tunnel and into the depot, although much of the need to change engines was obviated when the 'Britannias' were introduced and through locomotive working between Liverpool Street and Norwich became the norm. After this there were fewer through trains between the East Suffolk and London, and as splitting of trains into Norwich and Yarmouth portions also involved engine changes, this practice also diminished. On the west side of the station were the carriage sidings, reached by trailing connections at the north end of the station. Today they are mostly used by Freightliner for locomotive stabling, though some electric and diesel multiple-units have short-term layovers there.

Top left:
East Suffolk Junction, looking north, before the new double track for the Norwich line was built between Ipswich station and the junction. The new track was on the left of the main line shown here, necessitating considerable earthworks and a new signalbox. *National Railway Museum*

Below left:
A two-car Cravens Class 105 nears Ipswich with the 14.50 from Lowestoft on 28 May 1981. Compare the layout shown here with that before quadrupling. *Brian Morrison*

Above:
East Suffolk Junction in its final form. The East Suffolk and the goods lines have both been singled and the junction simplified. East Suffolk Junction box has closed and control transferred to Colchester power box. The layout now has much less flexibility. The train is the 07.17 Lowestoft to Liverpool Street headed by Class 37 No 37049, and the date is 12 May 1984, the last day for this service, after which it was replaced by a DMU between Lowestoft and Ipswich. *G. R. Mortimer*

Movements here were controlled by Ipswich Goods Junction signalbox, which stood on the down side of the tracks, but with the down goods road passing behind it. Further to the north — 1,025yd to be exact — stood East Suffolk Junction signalbox, controlling trains to and from that line, and access into the upper goods yard from the north. Congestion here could be considerable, since a northbound goods train had to cross the up and down East Suffolk and the up main line to get onto the down main, the pair of East Suffolk running lines extending right into the station, rather than being single, as today. Between here and Ipswich Goods Junction there were

WESTERFIELD
JUNCTION FOR
FELIXSTOWE
DAILY MIRROR
2806

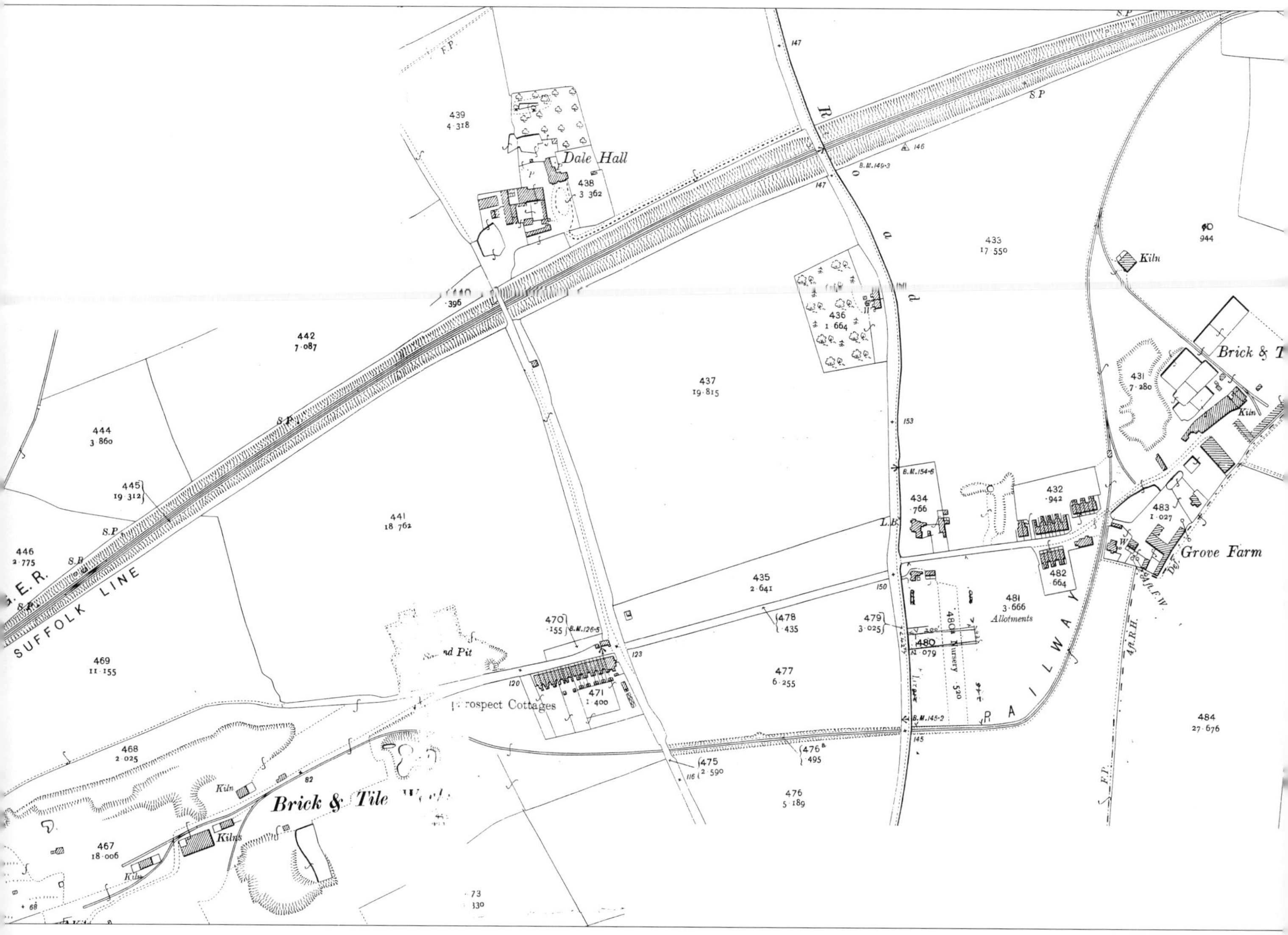
Dale Hall
Brick & Tile Works
Grove Farm
Prospect Cottages
SUFFOLK LINE
RAILWAY
Allotments
Nursery
Kiln
Kilns

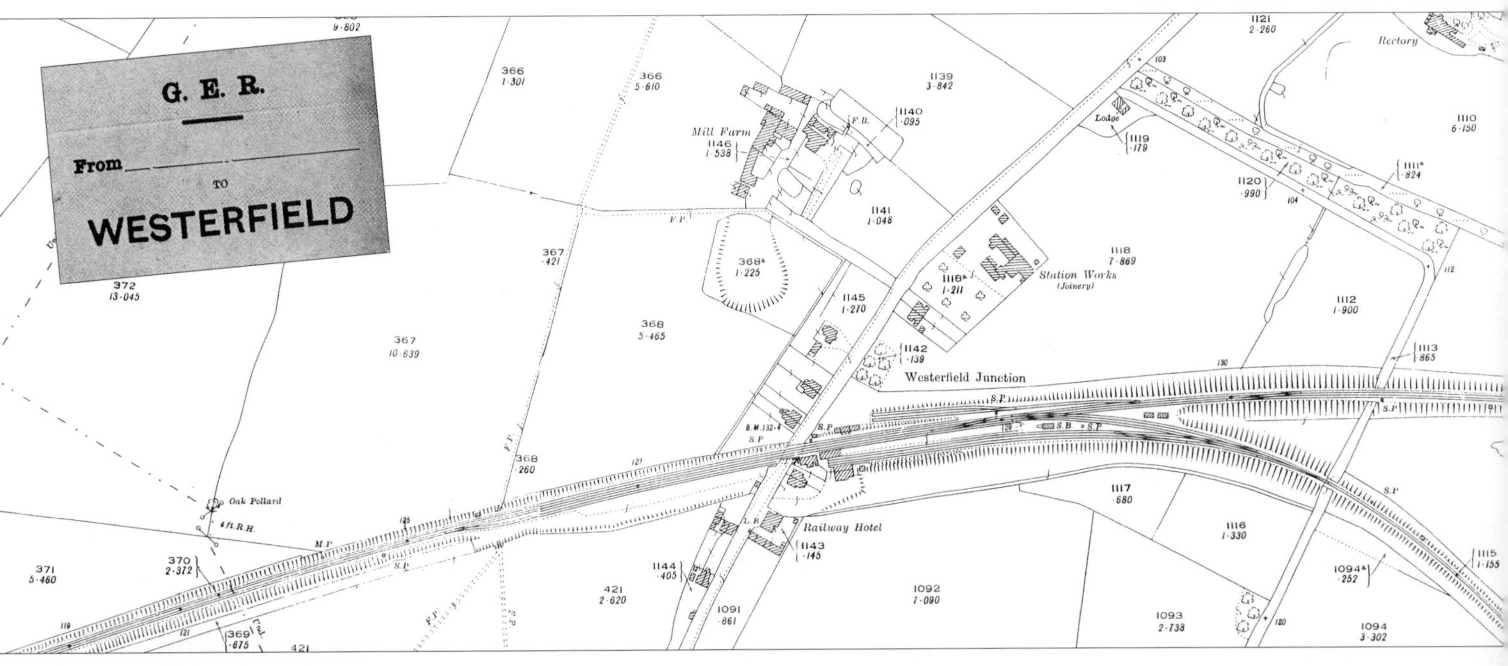

Top left:
Class B17 No 2806 *Audley End* heads a down express through Westerfield. *Alan Taylor collection*

Below left:
Westerfield brick works branch, 1904.
Crown Copyright

Above:
Westerfield station, 1924. *Crown Copyright*

Below:
On Sunday 21 August 1966 English Electric Type 3 No D6720 heads a troop train from Newquay to Lowestoft. Simplification of the track layout at Westerfield has meant the removal of sidings on the down side and all the track into the bay platforms. *G. R. Mortimer*

Above:
A two-car Metro-Cammell DMU heads away from Westerfield with a Felixstowe train. The bay platform is still partly in existence. This is the second signalbox, and survived until the Felixstowe branch was resignalled in 1999. *M. P. Jacob*

Below:
An elevated view of Westerfield from the Felixstowe branch, with the East Suffolk main line in the middle distance. Shunting is in progress, and two men are pushing a trolley on the down East Suffolk main line. This is the first Westerfield signalbox, which was replaced in 1913. *National Railway Museum*

Above:
Westerfield station in 1967, looking over the level crossing towards Ipswich. The station remains intact, with the Felixstowe Railway's wooden building still in use. *Stations UK*

six running lines: the main, East Suffolk and goods roads, the down East Suffolk leading straight into Platform 2. This represented the highest development of the layout here, and had been brought into use in August 1912, when a new pair of tracks was provided to the south of the existing running lines between Ipswich Goods and East Suffolk Junctions, the former lines becoming the East Suffolk and the new ones the Norwich road. Having formerly diverged at East Suffolk Junction, they now ran separately to that point. Both the up and down platforms were lengthened at this time at the Norwich end, and the Ancaster Road bridge was widened. At the same time the goods lines' junction was also reorganised at East Suffolk Junction. Ipswich was considered for rebuilding in 1956, when lengthening of the platforms, improvements to running facilities and revision of the signalling was proposed at a cost of some £500,000, in order to meet traffic requirements, although apart from the work in connection with the change to diesel traction, nothing was done until the advent of electrification in the 1980s when the layout was simplified and somewhat reduced.

Near Goods Junction box was one of the great railway features of Ipswich, the magnificent Great Eastern signal gantry which carried a total of 22 arms, and which was erected in 1912 when the two goods roads were added between Goods and East Suffolk Junctions. It spanned all six running lines, and apart from three down distants, all its arms were for up trains. The up Norwich home and up Yarmouth home were the highest at 45ft above rail level, and the gantry sported several GER 'drawahead' arms to the very end. The end came on the weekend of 27-28 July 1957 when it was replaced by just three four-aspect multi-lens colour-light signals with theatre-type route indicators. The one controlling the goods lines was at ground level for reasons of restricted clearance.

On the north side of the main line between the two boxes was the Upper goods yard, which handled considerable quantities of freight, and which is currently largely used for containers in transit to Felixstowe. It also gave access to the Dock branch, which wound down across Ranelagh Road, under Princes Street, through the lower yard and goods station, and then continued across Bridge Street to St Peter's Quay, where it divided. One branch went around the north side of the Wet Dock, serving a multitude of private sidings and wharves, including Albion Wharf, Common Quay, Neptune Quay and Orwell Quay and including firms such as Meux brewery and Ransomes, Sims & Jefferies. Much of the quay area on this side was not constructed until after World War 1, although authorised before. By 1937 Cliff Quay extended to 1,800ft and could accommodate ships of 28ft draught; electric cranes were also installed.

Trains for both Norwich and Yarmouth passed under the London Road bridge immediately before East Suffolk Junction, and Hadleigh Road bridge immediately after. East Suffolk trains then faced the start of Westerfield bank almost immediately, with the added disadvantage of the sharp curve to the right and the consequent speed limit. For much of its life the now-demolished bacon factory was a prominent feature of the area between the Norwich and Yarmouth lines. The East Suffolk, climbing steadily on a high embankment at 1 in 111, crossed the River Gipping immediately after MP70. About a quarter of a mile beyond Westerfield Bank box the gradient eased to 1 in 146, the box having been opened on the down side of the line in October 1898 to provide a break in the section; a crossover was installed at the same time. At about this point also the line went into a cutting, emerging only at Westerfield station. At 72 miles 20 chains this represented a brief respite in the climb for Yarmouth trains, with the gradient easing to 1 in 512 through the station but increasing to 1 in 286 until MP73, from where it fell steadily towards Woodbridge and Melton.

Westerfield became the junction for Felixstowe on 1 May 1877 when the Felixstowe Railway Company opened its line to the coastal town and port. What had been a wayside station with the usual two platforms and a level crossing acquired two bay platforms and new buildings to serve them. The Great Eastern would not, at first, let the newcomer use its tracks to gain access to Ipswich, so that intending passengers had to change at the junction; the situation did not change until 1885 when the company was vested in the Great Eastern.

The station was approached from the west over a level crossing of the Ipswich to Eye road, now the B1077. On the right a siding about 650ft long trailed from the up main line. This was built in 1888, together with a branch leading from it into the brick and tile works of Messrs Bolton & Laughlin. It curved away from the main line for a distance of about 110 chains (somewhat over 1¼ miles) to their works in Dales Lane (later Road), and also had a siding into Grove Farm and another adjacent brick and tile works. The junction of this siding was controlled by a four-lever dwarf frame with four working and four spare levers, and released from the Junction signalbox. This line was closed and lifted in the 1920s, but the brick and tile merchants Messrs Cubitt & Gotts continued to use the siding at Westerfield for many years for deliveries from the London Brick Company at Peterborough. The ubiquitous Thomas Moy, coal merchant, had an office at the station.

Both platforms were on the east side of the level crossing and, in contrast to the present layout, all Yarmouth and Felixstowe trains used the down platform. The bays were used for goods work, either loading and unloading or simply for stabling. There were also sidings on the down side running behind the platform. The first signalbox stood on the down side of the main line just beyond the junction, and was replaced in 1913 by a newer box off the eastern end of the up platform and about 3 chains closer to the station. This survived the introduction of Radio Electronic Token Block (RETB) signalling on 24 November 1985, but was finally abolished in March 1999 when the Felixstowe branch was resignalled.

Westerfield earned itself a place in railway history on Tuesday 25 September 1900 when the boiler of the engine hauling the late-running 7.20am goods from Ipswich exploded with great violence. The locomotive had been shunting the sidings on the up side of the level crossing, and was waiting to get into the station. The explosion tore the boiler from its frames and hurled it 40 yards forward, landing near the crossing and bouncing onto the porters' hut at the end of the down platform. It flew over the head of Porter Brand, who was opening the gates at the time. Meanwhile, the frames of the locomotive, and the tender, had embedded themselves in the track, whilst debris was strewn over a wide area. Police Constable Goodwin, who had been standing near the porters' hut, was trapped by a fallen telegraph or signal post, but it also saved him from being crushed. Rescuers spent several minutes freeing him as soon as they arrived on the scene. Driver John Barnard's body was found 150ft from the explosion in the coal yard, whilst the fireman, William MacDonald, was blown over the tender and into the third truck in the train. Both must have died instantly, and their bodies were charred and mutilated when they were found. The explosion was heard clearly in the Henley Road brickfields, over 1½ miles away. Two passenger trains had just left Westerfield, one for Ipswich and another for Felixstowe, and stationmaster William Henry Wilkes could offer no explanation for the explosion.

At the inquiry held at Ipswich Town Hall, attention naturally centred on whether there had been a fault on the engine. It appeared that there had been many leaks on the six-coupled goods locomotive, No 522. It was about a year old at the time, and entries in its log book referred to leaks of firebox stays and tubes, and that the top water gauge glass needed packing. Repairs had been repeatedly carried out, but it turned out that a bulge had been reported in the right side of the firebox about five weeks before. Remedial action was taken to drill out and tighten the stays around the area. The bulging was not thought to be unusual, but was not expected on a new engine. The Board of Trade had Mr E. A. Carlton examine the engine and firebox after the accident at Stratford works, and concluded that there had been no shortage of water in the firebox, but that a number of stays onthe left side were not properly attached, leading to a bulge. However, another expert witness, Thomas Knights of Manchester, said that the stays had overheated, indicating a shortage of water, and agreed with others that the bronze stays used were not as good as copper. James Holden, GER locomotive superintendent, also called as a witness, disagreed. Walter P. Sterricker was district locomotive super-

Right:
The aftermath of the boiler explosion on 25 September 1900, when No 522, only a year old, spread itself over a very wide area and killed its footplate crew. The usual crowd of onlookers has gathered at the level crossing.
Alan Taylor collection

Above:
All the major facilities except the signalbox were on the down side at Bealings. Here an Edwardian view towards Ipswich shows the layout of the main station building and goods shed, together with some of the staff and possibly members of their families.
Peter Punchard collection

intendent at Ipswich, and was also a witness. He said that the top row of small tubes in the boiler had sagged, indicating shortage of water. It also transpired that GER engines at the time were not fitted with a 'fusible tube' which would melt when the water level fell too low.

Driver Barnard and Fireman Macdonald were buried at Ipswich Cemetery on Saturday 30 September. Nearly 200 employees of the Great Eastern followed on foot from Stoke, where the men had lived, forming a procession ¼ mile long. The locomotive was repaired, being given a new boiler, and lasted until 1936.

Alfred Groves started work for the LNER in January 1928, and within three months had become an assistant clerk at Westerfield. Being a small station it had only two porters, but there were three regular signalmen. There was, of course, a stationmaster, although this post was later abolished and supervision undertaken from Derby Road. At the other end of his career in 1962 Alfred Groves was appointed to Derby Road and so once again took charge of Westerfield.

Westerfield very nearly became a three-way junction during the Edwardian era when the Mid-Suffolk Light Railway had ambitions to build a line thence to Kenton Junction on its Haughley to Halesworth line. A magnificent ceremony was held, at which the Duke of Cambridge cut the first sod, followed by the great and the good retiring to a large marquee for a commemorative repast. The duke and many other guests arrived at Westerfield via the Great Eastern, and duly left by the same means. The Mid-Suffolk's line did not progress, and although it appeared on a number of maps, construction did not proceed much further south than Debenham, and not at all from Westerfield.

The line onward from Westerfield falls steadily once past MP73, apart from a short rise of 1 in 207 just past MP77, and is relatively easily graded except for about half a mile of 1 in 100 where it drops down towards Woodbridge, into the Deben valley. It had been a difficult section to construct because of the nature of the land through which it passed. Having circumnavigated Ipswich the East Suffolk then follows the south side of the valley of the River Fynn (Finn until at least the 1930s) almost all the way to its confluence with the Deben just south of Woodbridge, running parallel to Martlesham Creek before swinging roughly northeast to follow the larger river. Most of this section is relatively straight, which necessitated successive cuttings and embankments to maintain its course a little way up the valley side.

The line runs in cutting for over a mile before picking up the Fynn valley, and it was the marshes and alder carr beyond this that had caused all the trouble when the line was being built. It continues through a succession of cuttings and embankments, passing Playford Hall and village, on the north side of the line at MP73, with the road from Playford to Kesgrave crossing on one of the characteristic red brick arched bridges. Curving slightly to the south to avoid Playford Mere it continues towards Little Bealings, intersecting the road from that village to Martlesham Heath at the level crossing immediately beyond Bealings station. This also served Great Bealings slightly to the north.

Bealings, at just under 76 miles from London, was a small station entirely on the west of the level crossing, and has the distinction of being the only closed passenger station on the existing operational East Suffolk line. The station buildings and goods accommodation were entirely on the down (north) side, with the signalbox at the Woodbridge end of the up platform. The red brick station building abutted the goods shed, which was served by a single siding, with another to the north used as a loading dock. This small goods yard could be reached from the down main line by a trailing connection and headshunt, or from the up main line by a trailing connection and crossing. This layout dated from October 1886, when the new connections between the sidings and the main line were put in, the down platform was extended towards Ipswich and

Top right:
Bealings in about 1928, looking towards Woodbridge. It may be summer, but there has been plenty of rain. The gardens look well tended. *Stations UK*

Below right:
Already into the British Railways era, this 1949 view is looking from the up platform across to the goods shed and main station building, with the signalbox just visible. The crossing gates retain the diamond pattern targets.
HMRS Hilton Collection

Below:
A collection of light engines heads towards Ipswich through Bealings. Although it has only another year before the passenger service is withdrawn, the station is still well looked after. There is not much sign of traffic in the goods shed, though.
Stations UK

Above:
A fine view of the signalbox at Bealings.
Robert Humm

Below:
Bealings station, 1926-8.
Crown Copyright

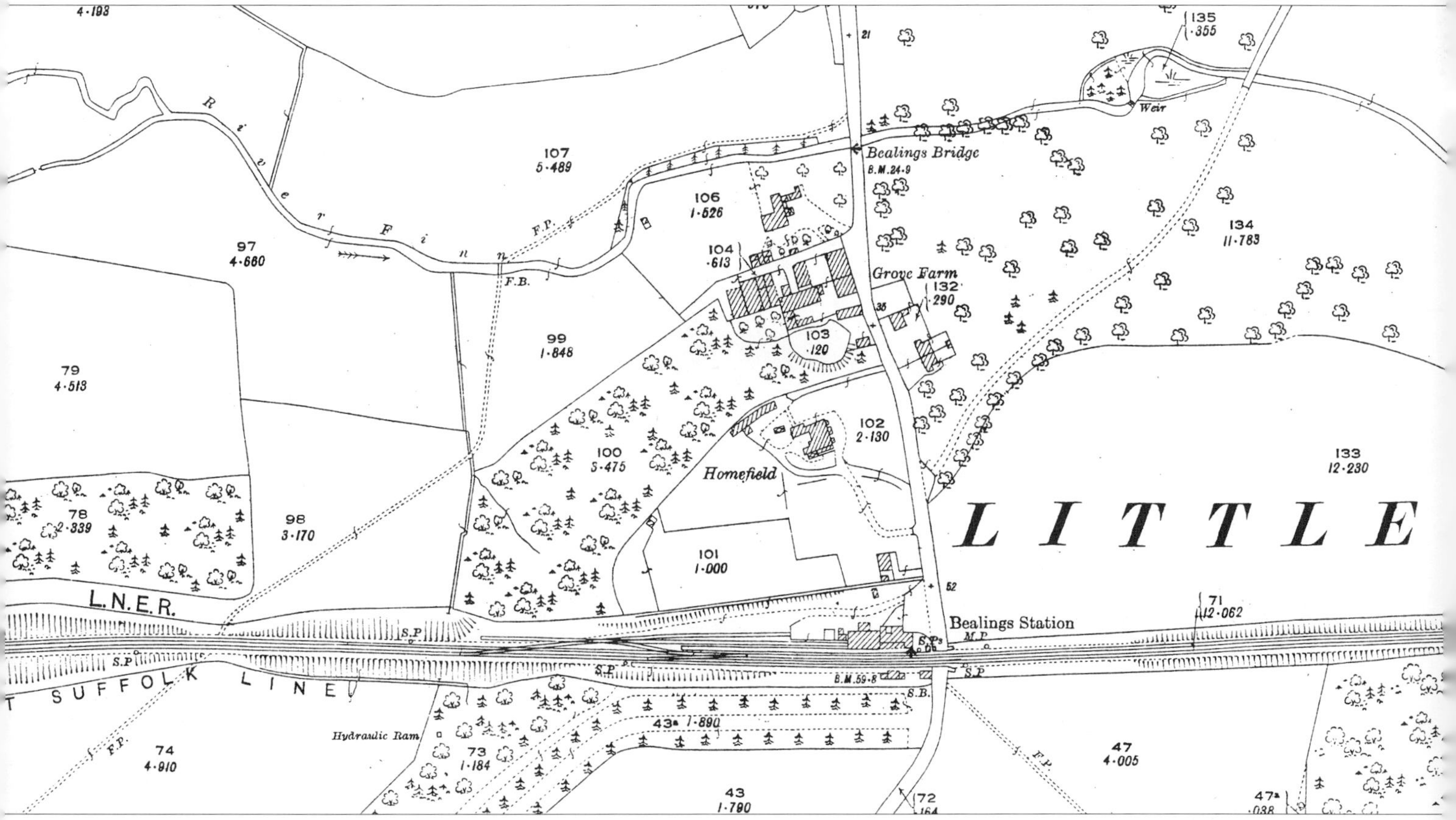

Above:
A down Ipswich to Yarmouth train passes the closed Bealings station on 19 June 1965. The signalbox continues to be a block post, the track layout appears intact and the grass banks are neatly trimmed. *G. R. Mortimer*

Below:
The 12.50 Saturdays-only from Yarmouth South Town to Liverpool Street nears Bealings on a fine 19 June 1965. *G. R. Mortimer*

the signalbox erected; this then lasted practically unchanged until closure to goods traffic. There was a small wooden shelter on the up platform. The signalbox survived much longer, albeit downgraded to a gate box, and was not demolished until just before the introduction of RETB, in April 1984, conversion to AOCL (Automatic Open Crossing Locally-monitored) operation taking place at the same time. Bealings was quite busy with goods, and received bricks and coal for a builders'/coal merchant. Traffic tended to be carried via the Snape bonus goods train, which shunted at Bealings on its way out. Most trains did not call at Bealings, which was an early closure to passengers on and from Monday 17 September 1956 (ie the final train service called on Sunday, 16 September). Goods traffic survived until April 1965. Unlike Melton, which had closed to passengers some 18 months earlier, it did not reopen.

Trains continue their descent towards Woodbridge, and because of the tight curve on the approach from Ipswich were limited to 20mph, and again on leaving the station as the line threaded its way along the Deben estuary. These limits were later raised to 25mph, but effectively lowered by conversion of four level crossings (from Woodbridge they are Ferry Lane, Haywards, Lime Kiln and Sun Wharf) to AOCL status in the 1980s, necessitating the imposition of a 15mph limit. As the line curves towards the northeast it runs through a deep cutting spanned by a tall brick arch bridge carrying a track towards Kingston, a small hamlet between the Fynn and Deben. Two level crossings immediately preceded Woodbridge station, one of which (Jetty Lane, now The Avenue) marked the furthest point to which the sidings reached. This crossing was locked from the signalbox.

Woodbridge was an important market town, the centre for a wide area around. It had a population of 4,480 in 1891 and continued to grow steadily. Being on the west bank of the Deben it had a number of ferries, although the tidal nature of the river made their operation more difficult. It had been a port in its own right for a time, but lost this status in the early 1880s. The platforms at Woodbridge were quite tightly curved, with Ferry Lane level crossing marking the Yarmouth end of the station. In later years a cinema backed onto the down platform, and film-goers felt the building tremble as trains went by. As with Bealings and Westerfield this was originally an Eastern Union station, so the style differed from those on the rest of the line. The main station building, on the down side, was of white brick, two storeys including the usual accommodation for the stationmaster, plus booking office and hall, and various other offices. It was surprisingly modest for a town of Woodbridge's importance. On the up platform the mostly wooden buildings included waiting rooms and toilets, and were provided with awnings at the Yarmouth end, as was the up platform. A typical Great Eastern lattice footbridge linked the platforms, with a second adjacent span allowing non-rail-users to get from the forecourt on the down side to the boatyards and river wall on the up.

Goods provision was at quite a high level. A substantial goods shed stood at an acute angle to the running lines on the down side, with a second siding outside it. There were cattle pens and loading docks, and another siding running parallel to the down line into another shed behind the down platform.

Below:
Woodbridge from the south, 1911. Jetty Lane level crossing is in the foreground, worked by a gateman from the station. The signalbox and goods sheds can be seen, with the sidings looking quite crowded. The line behind the up platform continues towards Melton as the tramway. *HMRS Hilton Collection*

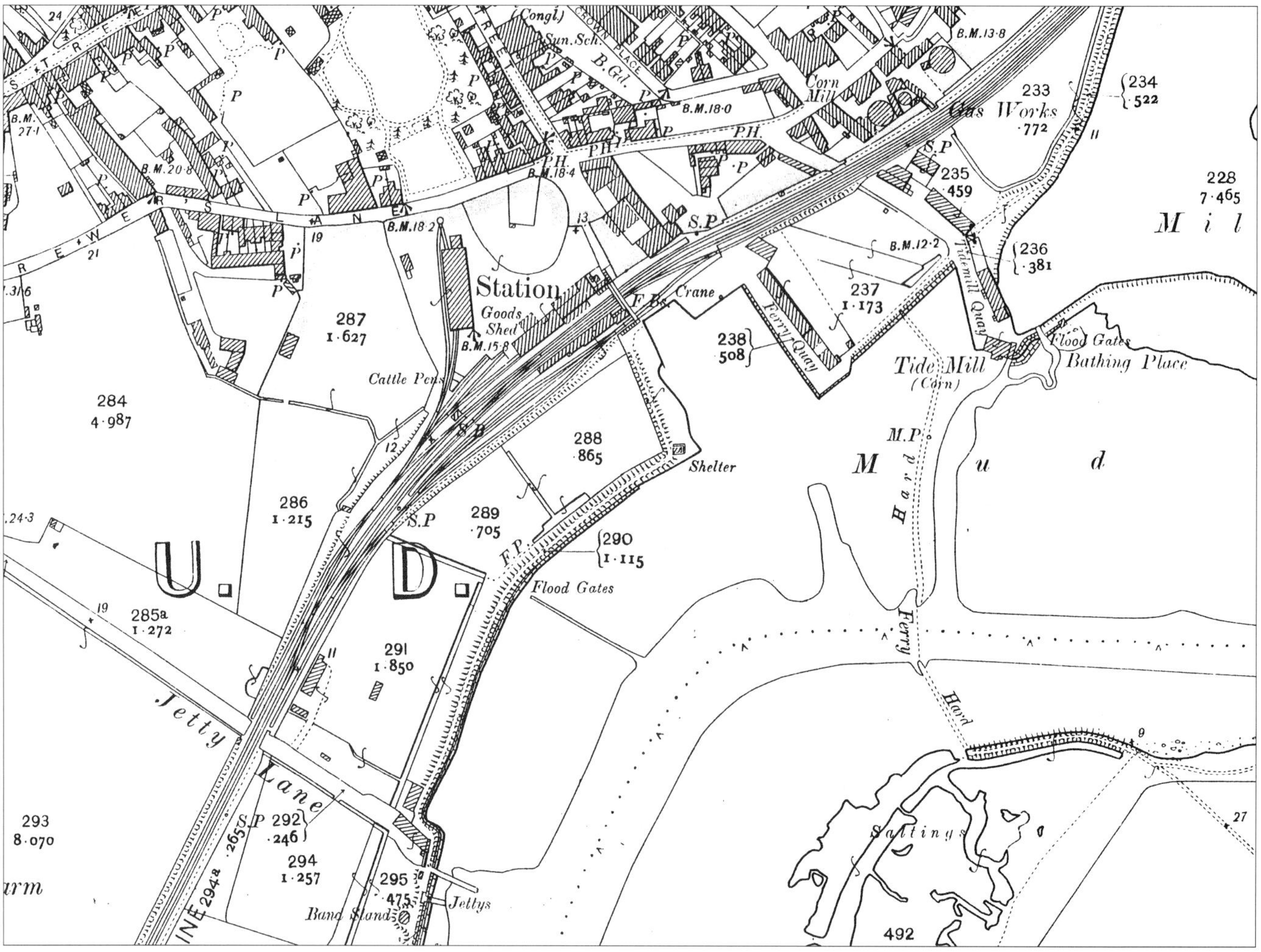

Above:
Woodbridge station, 1902-6.
Crown Copyright

Below:
Woodbridge from the south, 1911. The viewpoint is probably from the up starting signal. The signalbox and goods shed are prominent, and the covered footbridge is clear. The gas works is a source of traffic for the railway, and there are many wharfs and jetties along the River Deben, which is hidden by the buildings in the right background. *HMRS Hilton Collection*

Left:
The station building at Woodbridge is a modest structure on the down side, although by the time this picture was taken the goods shed which abutted the end at the right had been demolished, leaving only its end wall. This station was built by the Eastern Union Railway, not the East Suffolk.
Peter Punchard collection

Centre left:
Times change, and although the signalbox is still operational much of the track has gone in this 1967 photograph, certainly on the up side. What appears to be a Class 20 diesel stands in the down platform.
Stations UK

Below:
An elevated view of Woodbridge from a signal post. Haywards level crossing is nearest the camera, with Ferry Lane nearer to the station. The tramway is to the left of the East Suffolk main line.
HMRS Hilton Collection

Right:
Woodbridge, looking towards Yarmouth in 1967. The goods shed has been demolished around the crane, although no track remains. *Stations UK*

Right:
Woodbridge up side platform with its buildings intact and in use, and the signalbox open. *Lens of Sutton*

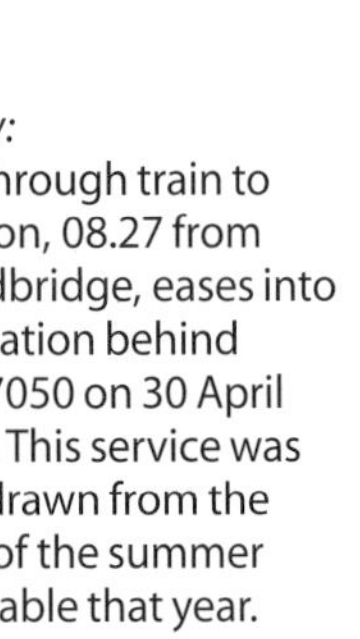

Below:
The through train to London, 08.27 from Woodbridge, eases into the station behind No 37050 on 30 April 1984. This service was withdrawn from the start of the summer timetable that year. *G.R.Mortimer*

Above:
No 37033 heads an up freight — probably coal empties from Melton — and is about to pass over Ferry Lane crossing at Woodbridge on 14 June 1976. *P.H. Wells*

Right:
Times have moved on at Woodbridge. A three-car Class 101 DMU works the 11.00 Lowestoft to Ipswich service on 4 March 1989, calling at Woodbridge. The aerial for RETB can be clearly seen on the front of the unit. At this time trains had to stop short of the station canopies because they would otherwise be too close to the level crossing and so activate it as they waited in the station. *Tim Edmonds*

Right:
Common sense at last prevailed with Ferry Lane crossing, which is now activated in the down direction by the driver pressing a plunger, so allowing trains to stop where there is shelter for their passengers. Ramped access has now been provided to the up platform. *John Brodribb*

Above:
Melton, looking north in LNER days, with shunting in progress as a 'J15' eases back into the siding. The building on the up platform is typical of many East Suffolk stations. *Stations UK*

A 1½-ton crane was provided. Several businesses were based at the station including a number of coal merchants such as R. B. Strickson & Sons and Chas Blake. George Chandler was a builder based at Lime Kiln Quay who also used Strickland's siding, as did Brooks & Son and the Deben Construction company, all in the 1930s. R. Coller & Sons and T. L. Lister & Sons also had their own sidings. There were some users of the station which seem a little surprising, though. The presence of W. H. Smith's bookstall and Finlays tobacconist kiosk are to be expected, but then there was Harry D. Cox, coal merchant and motor haulage contractor, and Jack Leonard Harrison, a cartage and motor haulage contractor who advertised 'estimates free, distance no object, lowest possible charges' and was still allowed to operate from the station house. In the mid-1950s there was still much goods traffic from Woodbridge, and there were several users of sidings. The Ipswich Malting Company had one, and T. L. Lister were still there. A. Hayward, Eastern Counties Farmers and A. V. Roberston had sidings, all officially between Woodbridge and Melton. The station continued to offer the full range of services and was still shunted by horses, one of the last to do so. In country areas many of the station staff seemed to have the same name — at Woodbridge it was Daines, and they were related, there being others at Melton. Signalmen, guards, and the horsemen at Woodbridge were included among their number.

Many other businesses were served from the station, Sun Wharf Ltd being coal merchants at Sun Wharf. There were a number of such locations along the estuary, such as Ferry Quay and Tidemill Quay, both close to the station on the Yarmouth side and served by their own level crossings. Lime Kiln and Sun Wharf were a little further on, and all were served by the tramway which ran from behind the up platform back towards Melton. Some sidings off it were reached by means of wagon turntables (Sun Wharf) whereas others (Lime Kiln) used a more conventional set of points. The tramway was worked by horse and ran over the several level crossings to the north of the station, but generally was not protected by the level crossing gates. The horses were also used to shunt the sidings on both sides of the line, and were notably sure-footed, knowing exactly where to tread to keep their footing. The sidings continued right round the back of the up platform and connected into the up main line, with the headshunt extending right up to Jetty Lane level crossing. For all its importance as a passenger station, Woodbridge did not generate the same volume of goods traffic as other stations on the East Suffolk — it was about the only one that did not load sugar beet, and Melton was generally more important.

The signalbox was just off the Ipswich end of the down platform and opened in July 1881, although there had been an earlier structure on the other platform. At this time various new works were brought into use by the Great Eastern, mostly being new connections and a new crossover, all at the Ipswich end of the layout. Jetty Lane crossing was locked from the signalbox, and both platforms were extended at the Ipswich end. At the end of 1882 further changes were made which involved the provision of a very short carriage dock at the Beccles end of the station, trailing from the up main. At this time Haywards level crossing was unusual in that its gates did protect the tramway, although trams had been forbidden to shunt across the level crossings when the changes above were introduced. In 1900 further work was undertaken. The trailing crossover which gave access to the down sidings from the up line had slips inserted so that it also became a crossover, there now being two in the layout. Some changes to the signalling were necessitated, and the signalbox now had all 24 levers in use. Alterations were also made to the connections between the up main line and the tramway and up-side sidings.

Beyond Woodbridge the main line was accompanied across the flat, marshy ground at the edge of the estuary by the tramway, which finished at about 79 miles 50 chains. Although the Deben narrows rapidly between Woodbridge and Melton, there were still some more quays beside the line, notably serving Melton Dock, where there were maltings and lime kilns. The railway served these from Melton station, with a long siding on the up side of the main line directly serving the malthouse that stood alongside, and giving access to the lime kilns and quay by means of another siding accessed by a wagon turntable.

Although Melton has now become more or less a suburb of Woodbridge it was not always so. Woodbridge had a population of 4,480 at the 1891 census, and Melton 1,510;

Right:
The platforms at Melton were staggered, and the down was very short indeed. In this view, looking towards Woodbridge, a train approaches the down platform, but may just be shunting. The signalbox is on the up platform.
Stations UK

Right:
Melton in 1967 has not had a passenger service for 12 years. It still looks smart, but lacks white lines on the platform edge and nameboards. Plenty of goods traffic is still in evidence in the yard.
Stations UK

Below:
Melton station, 1927.
Crown Copyright

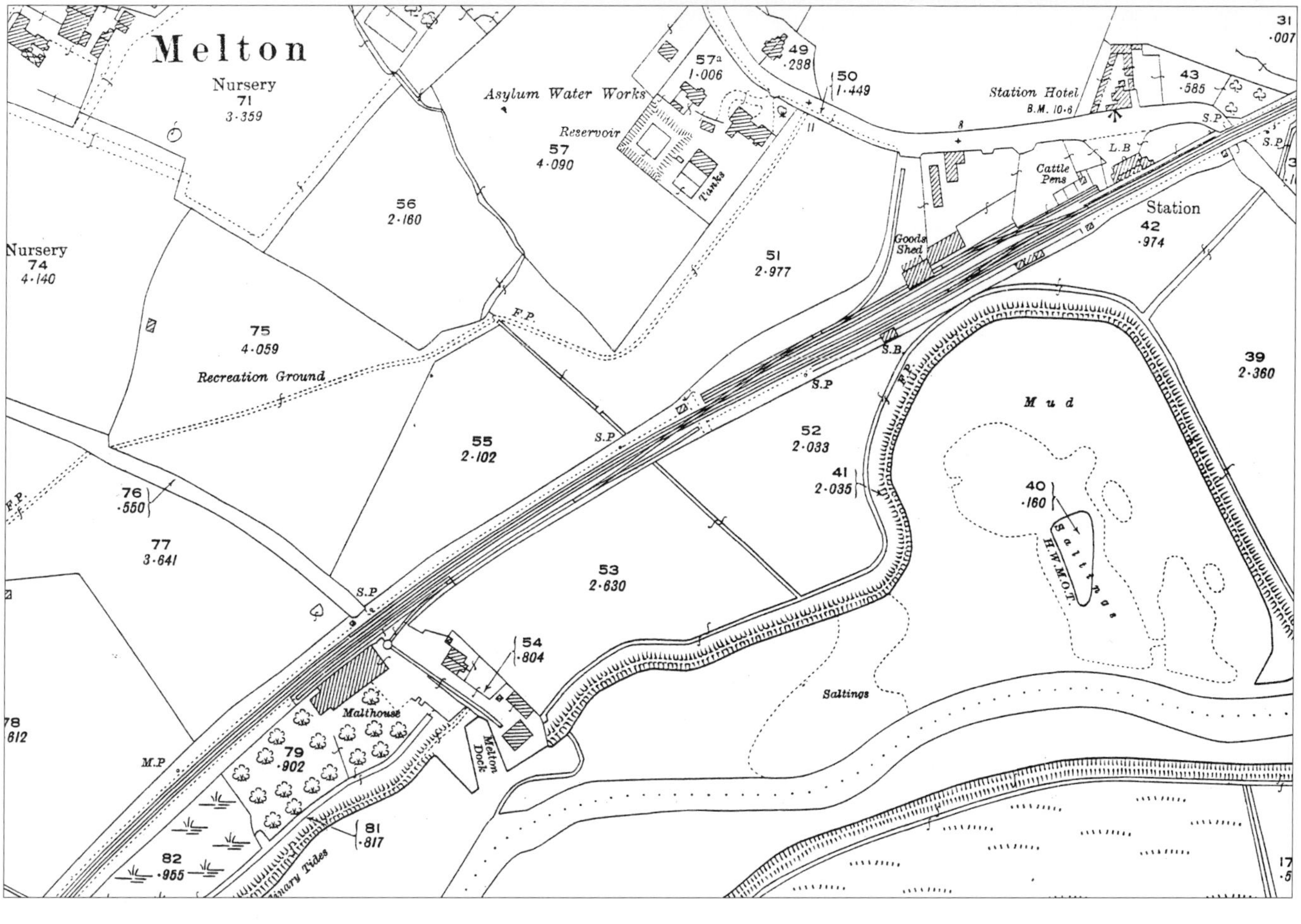

Right:
Into the late 1970s and things do not look nearly as good at Melton. The down platform is overgrown and the universal buddleia grows from the awning. *Lens of Sutton*

Below:
Looking back towards Woodbridge in the late 1970s the up platform has had its coping stones removed, although the signalbox remains open and the yard is intact. There is no rail traffic evident, although Melton continued to be used by local coal merchants. It reopened to passengers in May 1984.
Lens of Sutton

by 1931 they were respectively 4,734 and 2,197. Melton was an important settlement in its own right, and originally the main road ran through the middle of both. Its station was substantial, in what became the standard Great Eastern style, reflecting the fact that it was built by the East Suffolk company as opposed to the Eastern Union which had constructed the line as far as Woodbridge. The station buildings were largely on the down side, away from the river, together with the substantial goods shed and yard. The main building consisted of a sizeable two-storey structure in white brick with a characteristic awning forming an integral part of the platform side. At both ends a single-storey part of the structure extended beyond the main structure, and the awning stretched between these two. The passenger entrance to the station was through double doors on the road side, leading into the booking hall, and again through double doors onto the platform. The up platform had a wooden building with rooms at each end and an open roofed area between, similar in layout to that still in existence at Darsham, for passengers. It also hosted the signalbox, which was one of the longest survivors on the East Suffolk, not being abolished until the advent of radio signalling in the 1980s.

There were cattle pens at the back of the down platform, and two sidings also on the down side. Later another was added, curving away from the main line and reached via a facing connection from the goods shed road. The sidings could be accessed by rail from the up side, the connection trailing from the up main line at the Ipswich end of the layout, whilst at that end of the down platform there was a trailing connection into the down line. A 1½-ton crane was available. The station handled a substantial amount of livestock traffic — 322 tons in 1938, with a value of £553 to the railway. Fruit was also important, as well as the sugar beet usual for the area. The Melton Corn & Coal Company had one of the sidings.

—5—

East Suffolk Line Description North of Melton

BETWEEN Woodbridge and Melton the line is level all the way, although its sinuous nature severely limits speeds. Once over the level crossing at the latter there is a slight rise to get across the rapidly narrowing River Deben, and then very gentle gradients as it keeps to the side of the valley for another two miles. Ufford level crossing, at 81 miles 60 chains, has the usual cottage on the east side of the line where the minor road from Eyke to Ufford crossed the railway. The line again crosses the Deben just over ¼ mile beyond Ufford, and at about MP82 the line started another relatively short climb at 1 in 108, although for less than a mile. There is a brief respite at MP83, it falling briefly at 1 in 93 before continuing to climb towards Campsey Ash and Wickham Market station at 84 miles 43 chains. This section of the line has very gentle curves and less of the saw-tooth gradient profile than most parts of the East Suffolk, and required a number of shallow cuttings and embankments to help it along the edge of the valley. The remains of the lineside sandpit, on the east side at about MP 82½, give evidence of the nature of the countryside, and had been used to provide spoil during the construction of the railway. The nearby Sandpit Farm, about ¼ mile to the west of the line at this point also had a crag pit where the underlying clay was extracted. The spelling of 'Campsey Ash' has changed over the years, this version being in use when the line was built and until after World War 2, when it had changed to 'Campsea Ashe'; every combination seems to have been in use in the mid-1930s. At about 83½ miles the line crosses the River Deben for the last time, the river wandering away towards the northwest and Debenham, whilst the railway continues northeastwards. Here it passes the remains of Ash Abbey, and also a large decoy pond.

Almost all the way from Melton to Beccles and nearly to Yarmouth the East Suffolk traverses the Sandlings. This is an expanse of heathland, which is almost entirely a creation of human habitation over several millennia. The East Suffolk is never far from the North Sea coast — the German Ocean when the line was built — and the sea has a great influence on the landscape. The nature of the coastline has also ensured that the main line did not follow it, and necessitated branch lines to serve the string of fishing towns and villages.

Underlying the area is red and coralline crag. In East Anglia the term 'crag' implies estuarine or marine deposits, largely of shelly sand, but with pockets of clay interspersed. These components are rarely homogeneous, so that the quality and

Below:
The second of three up Whit Monday extra trains near Ufford, north of Melton, on 30 May 1966. This is the 16.10 Yarmouth South Town to Liverpool Street headed by No D6712. *G. R. Mortimer*

consistency are very variable. In many places the clay was extracted and used for making bricks and, if the quality was high enough, tiles. Differences in composition also led to different colour bricks, and in most cases production levels were not large enough for the brickworks to have had their own rail connection. Production declined sharply after World War 1, and had largely ceased by the end of the 1930s. In prehistoric times the first human settlers found the gently undulating land easy to clear of its tree cover, which provided them with fuel and land to till. Being sandy the nutrients soon leached out of it, reducing its use for growing crops, and so they had to move on and clear more of the forest. The old land was not abandoned, because it was then used for grazing, particularly by sheep, and in mediaeval times Suffolk supported huge numbers of the animals. They were particularly valued for the dung that they left on their night-time pastures, having grazed the open sheepwalks during the day. In this way even more nutrients were removed from the soil of the Sandlings, leading to an acid heathland vegetation characterised by heather and ling. Sheep farming had declined by the 17th century, but grazing by rabbits kept the heaths open and prevented trees from regrowing, and in many places artificial warrens were created for them. In East Suffolk there were prominent warrens at Snape, Wangford and Fritton.

The landscape of East Suffolk when the railway was built was thus quite open, much of it heathland and with relatively few trees. In 1783 approximately 16,000 hectares of the southern Sandlings were open heath, dropping to 13,000 hectares by 1880. The hostilities of World War 1 led to much tree planting, and in the Sandlings this mostly meant Scots pine: much of what can be seen today dates from after 1919. By 1931 the amount of open heathland had dropped to 9,000 hectares, and the decline has continued, with only 6,000 hectares left by 1965. Continued loss of sheep grazing was a major factor, and when the myxomatosis epidemic in the 1950s wiped out 95-99% of the rabbits there was almost nothing left to keep the heathland open. The landscape has therefore changed very greatly since the East Suffolk line was built, becoming progressively more wooded both because of forestry planting and colonisation by birch trees, and because of the encroachment of arable farming. In more recent years up to 6% of the loss has been due to golf courses! The railway has not benefited from the extraction of timber — the East Suffolk woodlands are not on the scale of Thetford forest — but the nature of the soil and the resurgence of rabbits is obvious in many places along the railway, where they can be a serious problem, destabilising the banks. On the other hand, there were many railwaymen, mostly on the branches, who regularly set snares and collected their dinner on the way back! There were quite a number of pheasants collected as well, although they may have been accidentally struck by the engine of a passing train. Some of the pine trees were planted so that they had to fly higher and give the guns a better shot at them, and today continue to give the line and its landscape their characteristic appearance.

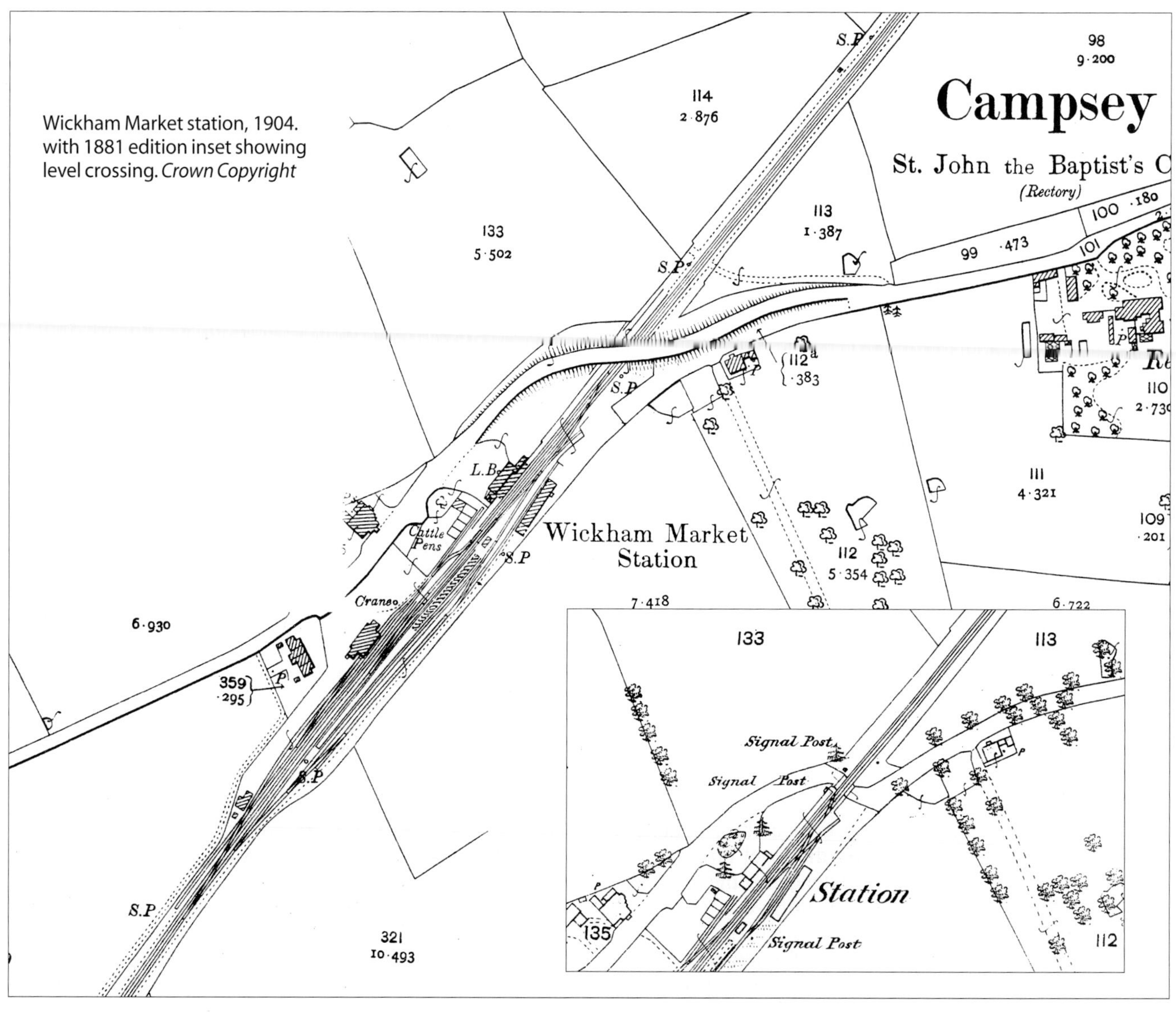

Wickham Market station, 1904. with 1881 edition inset showing level crossing. *Crown Copyright*

Left:
Wickham Market station, looking northwards in 1911. The road bridge replaced a level crossing in about 1903, and the opportunity was taken to extend the down platform. The photograph is taken from the end of the up platform which has the up main on one face, with Framlingham branch trains using the other. *HMRS Hilton Collection*

Below:
Wickham Market station, looking from the road bridge back towards Woodbridge in early spring 1950. The avoidance of facing connections is particularly clear in this picture. Both faces of the up platform remain in use. Steam and smoke obscure the goods shed, behind the station building, and will be unpopular with the stationmaster's wife, who has the washing hung out. *Stations UK*

Wickham Market station appeared in the timetables for much of its existence with a note to indicate that the station is at Campsey Ash, two miles distant. In the early days, however, it was simply shown as Wickham Market Junction for the Framlingham branch, although the physical junction was 71 chains to the north. When the line was built the road between Tunstall and Wickham Market crossed the railway on the level at the north end of the station. This was replaced by a bridge around 1903, leaving the approach from the east to serve the up side, while only slight modifications were needed on the west side to accommodate the new road embankment.

Despite its distance from the town it nominally served, Wickham Market station was a substantial affair. The main buildings were in the usual style, executed in white brick and with the customary awning. The platform on the down side hosted the main building, and had a dock at the Woodbridge end with cattle pens behind. After the level crossing was removed the platform was greatly extended at the north end, going under the new bridge. The up platform was to the south of the down, the two being connected by a barrow crossing, and had two faces. The outer was used by Framlingham branch trains and gave a convenient connection into the up main line services which used the other face. The station signalbox was at the Saxmundham end of this platform. It was a leisurely life for the staff: Wickham Market was a quiet station. Lady Graham and Viscount Ullswater were passengers, and staff had to mind their manners when they were about.

The large red brick goods shed was located on the down side, and was served by a siding running through the building. In 1881 this could be reached from either end: from the up main by a trailing connection across the down main, or from the down main by a trailing connection near the end of the platform. Another siding went between the goods shed and the main line. On the up side, alterations in 1881 saw a new connection installed at the Woodbridge end of the platform, effectively making it into a loop, together with new connections into the dock at the Saxmundham end. On the down side, new double slips were provided at each end of the goods shed, giving greater flexibility of access. The signalbox was erected at the same time, and interlocking of points and signals was concentrated there. Because of the falling gradient (1 in 101) towards Framlingham Junction, a set of runaway points was installed in the up line about 300yd from the station.

Above:
Wickham Market from the road approach side. There is a prominent bookstall run by W. H. Smith on the down platform. *Alan Taylor collection*

Below:
Some of the station staff pose on the down platform for the camera around 1950. The sign proclaims that Wickham Market (Campsey Ash) is the junction for Marlesford, Parham and Framlingham. Hacheston Halt never made it onto the nameboard.
HMRS Hilton Collection

Top:
The Framlingham branch train lurks in the yard on the down side, awaiting the opportunity to emerge into the down platform. Although a mixed working, there appears to be no goods traffic on offer, since there is only a brake van attached at the rear. *Ian Allan Library*

Above:
Wickham Market, looking north in about 1950. The up platform is intact with its buildings and awning, and retains the outer face for Framlingham branch trains. *HMRS Hilton Collection*

Right:
Wickham Market in late LNER or early BR days, looking north from the up platform. *Stations UK*

Above:
The 10.53 Ipswich to Yarmouth South Town pulls away from Wickham Market on 24 July 1965. Although everything looks intact, the signalbox (from where this picture is taken) is closed and has had its equipment removed, and the signal arms have gone.
G.R.Mortimer

Right:
Wickham Market Junction signalbox was close by Blackstock crossing and controlled the junction for the Framlingham branch. It retained green and cream livery to the end, in March 1971.
Robert Humm

Above:
By 1967 the up platform has only one face, and all but the main line itself has been lifted. The station building has lost its awning, the cattle pens have gone and the signalbox has gone. At least the main line is still open . . .
Stations UK

Left:
A closer view of the down platform, looking towards Saxmundham, after the signalbox was demolished. Only the blue enamel nameboard remains.
Lens of Sutton

Left:
Wickham Market up platform seen from the down side after the sidings had been lifted.
Lens of Sutton

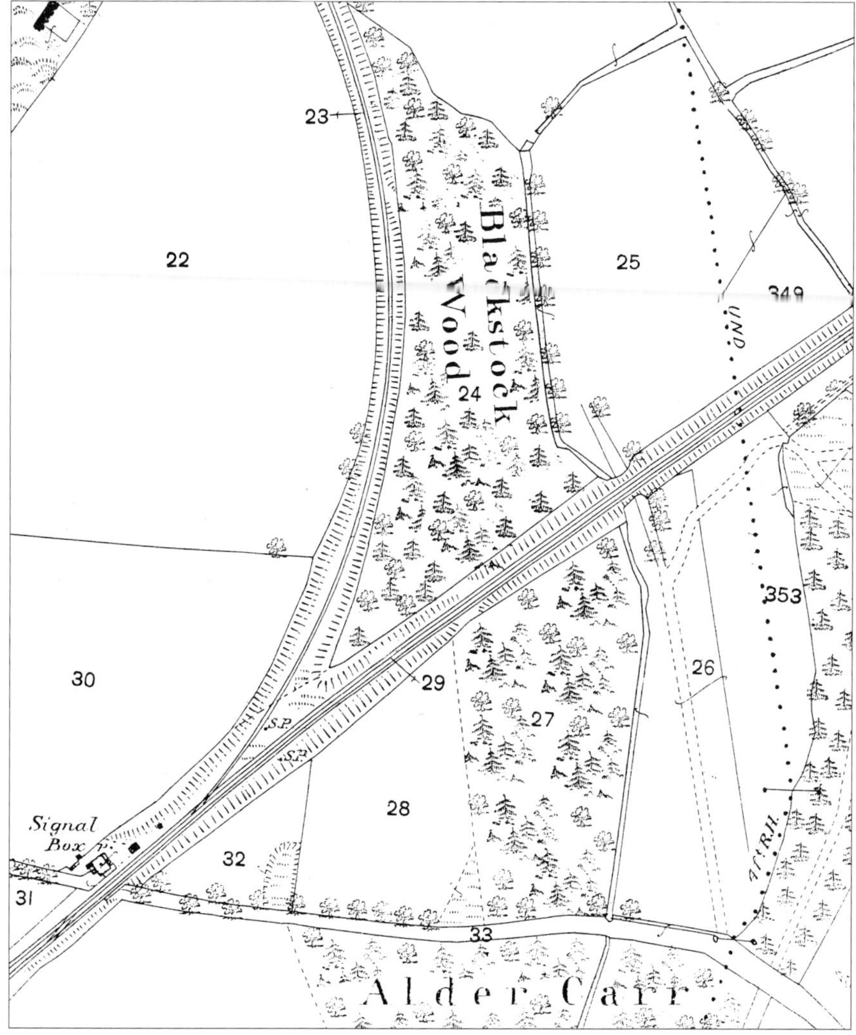

Above:
Class 40 No 40004 on a special working at Wickham Market, on Sunday 24 July 1983. Single line working is in force, as the train is working down the up main line.
Bryan Newman

Above right:
Snape Junction, 1902-6.
Crown Copyright

Left:
Wickham Market Junction, 1882-7.
Crown Copyright

In 1886 the up platform was lengthened by about 180ft, the siding running behind it was also extended and the connections at the Ipswich end changed. The signalbox now had 27 working and four spare levers. In April 1892 new connections between the up loop and the up main allowed it to be used for the departure of Framlingham trains. Some signalling alterations were needed, and a new siding at the Ipswich end was also installed. The down platform was extended as far as the level crossing. This was replaced by a bridge in about 1903, the old road becoming the access to the up side of the station. The down platform could then be extended under the bridge.

Wickham Market could handle all classes of traffic, and boasted a crane of 6 tons capacity. A livestock market was held on Mondays in the 1930s near the station, and in 1938 the traffic amounted to 508 tons, with a value to the railway of £776. The Cobbolds of Glemham Hall were also rail users, and sent cattle from the station. After shoots, pheasants would be sent up to London by train. Goods from Marlesford on the Framlingham branch were also accounted here. In the 1920s Boynton's had a siding at the station.

From Wickham Market the main line falls towards Wickham Market Junction. This was situated just beyond Blackstock crossing, which had the usual cottage for the keeper, where the minor road between Blaxhall and Wickham Market crossed the line. Here the main line passed through alder carr, while the branch curved away sharply northwards through a substantial cutting. The signalbox was just on the Saxmundham side of the crossing, and had only the connection to Framlingham, plus a crossover so that branch trains could gain the up main line. A brief rise beyond the junction marks the passage of the line out of the Deben valley, the River Ore joining it for a couple of miles or so on the inland side. It meanders under the line at Blaxhall Hall crossing (86 miles 33 chains) and very quickly back again. Beversham crossing (87 miles 15 chains), over the Blaxhall– Stratford road is at the start of a brief level section before the climb towards Snape Junction. The alignment here is very gently curved and high speeds were possible. At Screw Bridge, about a ¼ mile further, the railway swings round to head almost due east for a short distance, and then crosses the River Alde, into which the Ore flows a little to the north. For most of the distance from Blackstock crossing the line is carried on a low embankment so that it is a little above the marshy river valley. The line then turns back towards the north and maintains this general heading as far as St Olaves.

In sweeping around this long curve trains encountered Snape Junction at 88 miles 12 chains. The signalbox here was on the up side of the line at the exact point of divergence, with the branch curving away towards the east and dropping away rapidly from the main line. There was a level crossing about 300yd on the Saxmundham side of the junction, with the usual cottage for the crossing keeper, although the road itself was very minor indeed — little more than a rough track. There was a refuge on the down side, trailing back from the level crossing, and another on the up, trailing from the branch immediately before it joined the main line, both capable of holding 27 wagons. There was also a crossover near the crossing. Although it appears that the branch had been passed for passenger use when the system opened in 1859 this never happened, and in early 1908 a trap was provided in the branch, just short of the junction.

As the line climbs towards Saxmundham its character changes back to that of the open heathland of the Sandlings, after the encounter with the marshes of the Alde valley. The crossing at Snape Junction marked a minor summit, the line falling either side of it, although the respite for down trains was brief and they soon resumed their uphill progress at 1 in 107 to just beyond MP90, after which there were two small summits. The line curves slightly through a substantial cutting, and under the main Ipswich to Yarmouth road, once the turnpike, later the A12 and since bypassed. Soon after this there were two level crossings: Benhall at 90 miles 21 chains

Above:
'J15' No 65478 shunts at Snape Junction in the depths of winter.
Peter Punchard collection

and Brick Kiln at 90 miles 34 chains, both over very minor roads and both with cottages. The latter gained its name from the works a short distance west along Kiln Lane where the clay was both dug, shaped and fired, although there does not seem to have been any direct rail connection.

By now falling towards Saxmundham in a cutting, trains slowed for the station, one of the main traffic centres for the East Suffolk line. About 200yd from the station the line passed under a red brick arch bridge carrying a track between Park House and Howards Farm, the latter later becoming Park Farm cottages. The railway had been threaded through the old town, and so the station was very conveniently placed, although operationally difficult with its two closely spaced level crossings about 5 chains apart. The first of these was over Mill Lane (to the west of the line) and Chantry Row, later Road, and the second crossed Albion Street. In general the goods facilities were to the north of Albion Street, whilst the passenger station spread further. The up platform and main station building was also to the north of Albion Street, while the down was to the south.

In about 1874 or 1875 the Great Eastern built a new section of down platform to the south of Mill Lane, much to the consternation of the Board of Trade, which was understandably concerned that passengers alighting from trains were likely to find themselves stepping out into thin air. Maj-Gen Hutchinson inspected the station for the Board of Trade in May 1881 and refused to sanction use of the extension, although he was happy with the signalling alterations which had involved the provision of a new signal cabin. He also recommended provision of a bridge or subway between the platforms. This was later rectified when a new section of platform was built to link the old and new, and which was swung across the road when the level crossing needed to be opened for the passage of trains. It is thought that together with those at Halesworth, these swinging platforms were virtually unique in Great Britain. Access to this platform was from the Albion Road crossing, and a footbridge was provided some time after 1884 so that passengers could reach trains from the town even when the gates were closed across the road. This was initially covered, but the roof was removed in later days. Along the back of the platform was a substantial white brick wall, with the rear of the buildings forming the boundary for much of its length. The buildings were single-storey with an awning for almost all of their length, only the gentlemen's toilets at the south end not being so sheltered. Unlike the up side there were no stanchions supporting the awning, it being cantilevered out from the building and also supported by the usual spandrels. They had a flat roof, and accommodated, from the Ipswich end, the gentlemen's toilets, lock up store for station cleaning materials etc, the main waiting room, parcels lock-up, permanent way office and the ladies' waiting room and toilets. At the Beccles end of the platform was a water column, together with a water tank atop a brick base, with passenger access to the platform between the water column and station building.

On the Woodbridge side of the Chantry Road crossing a siding trailed from the up main line, initially provided with safety points close to the junction, and because the main line continued to fall towards the station the siding ended at a higher level. Immediately adjacent to this and parallel to the railway were two buildings, one of corrugated iron and the other a substantial malthouse, which received and sent out traffic by rail.

The up platform was served by the main building — booking office, stationmaster's accommodation and so on — in a fine two-storey white brick building of the same family as others on the East Suffolk-built sections, but with some significant variations. Wickham Market and Halesworth were almost entirely contained within an elongated rectangular plan, whilst most stations on the branches such as Marlesford, Parham or Carlton Colville were smaller versions. Saxmundham — perhaps because of restrictions of the site — had a relatively short frontage onto the platform, but then sported a substantial extension on the approach side, the centre of this being two storeys with a hipped roof, and single-floor

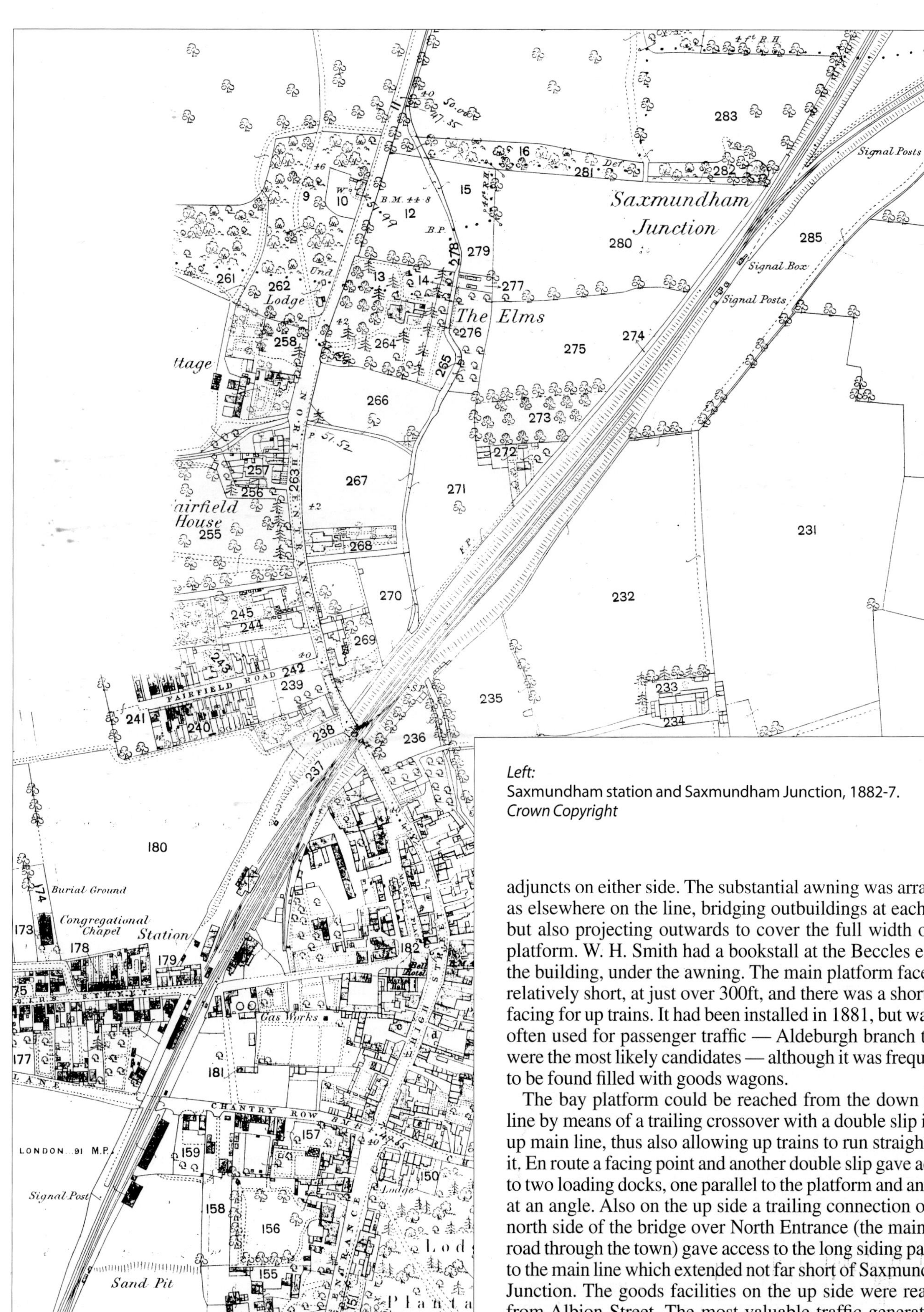

Left:
Saxmundham station and Saxmundham Junction, 1882-7.
Crown Copyright

adjuncts on either side. The substantial awning was arranged as elsewhere on the line, bridging outbuildings at each end, but also projecting outwards to cover the full width of the platform. W. H. Smith had a bookstall at the Beccles end of the building, under the awning. The main platform face was relatively short, at just over 300ft, and there was a short bay, facing for up trains. It had been installed in 1881, but was not often used for passenger traffic — Aldeburgh branch trains were the most likely candidates — although it was frequently to be found filled with goods wagons.

The bay platform could be reached from the down main line by means of a trailing crossover with a double slip in the up main line, thus also allowing up trains to run straight into it. En route a facing point and another double slip gave access to two loading docks, one parallel to the platform and another at an angle. Also on the up side a trailing connection on the north side of the bridge over North Entrance (the main A12 road through the town) gave access to the long siding parallel to the main line which extended not far short of Saxmundham Junction. The goods facilities on the up side were reached from Albion Street. The most valuable traffic generated at Saxmundham was livestock, which in 1938 amounted to 237 tons, worth £410 to the railway. It was mostly horses, pigs and cattle, with the pens being on the up side where the station car park is now situated. Timber was also important. Trees would be dragged into the station and then loaded onto rail using a hand crane, which stood in a siding. Silcock's had

Above:
The platforms at Saxmundham were staggered, with the down to the south of the Albion Street level crossing, ultimately straddling the Chantry Road crossing. This view is looking south, and part of the platform can be seen in the distance beyond the lorry going over the crossing. As at many stations on the line, the platform is very low. *Alan Taylor collection*

Right:
In some ways little changed after the platform was extended over the crossing. However, after an accident when a train ran into the movable platform section it was replaced by a gate and the far end was taken out of use. The awning has decayed somewhat in this 1970s view and the side gate has been taken off its hinges. The water crane has gone, and there is clearly much less parcels traffic — the barrows have gone. *Peter Punchard collection*

Left:
The down platform photographed around 1950. The movable platform is clearly visible, together with the gatekeeper and his hut. All the down-side buildings are visible, with the water tank seemingly on top of the awning. *HMRS Hilton Collection*

Above:
Times have changed at Saxmundham. The goods yard has been lifted and all that remains is the crossover. The station bookstall is closed, but the down platform remains on the other side of the level crossing. *Lens of Sutton*

Right:
Saxmundham down platform, looking north in 1967. The oil store which had stood on the right of the line just this side of the level crossing has been demolished, but otherwise things are largely unchanged since the end of steam. *Stations UK*

Right:
A general view, looking south about 1950, with the up platform and buildings and the signalbox visible. The level crossing gates are across the road, although no train is signalled. The same viewpoint today would be under the down platform! *HMRS Hilton Collection*

Left:
Shunting is in progress at Saxmundham; possibly this is an Aldeburgh train crossing over onto the down prior to setting back into the platform. There is plenty of traffic in the goods yard. The footbridge is covered. The warehouses on the right were largely demolished by the early 1920s. *Stations UK*

Below:
A two-car DMU for Yarmouth South Town pulls away from Saxmundham past the signalbox on 24 June 1961. The down platform can clearly be seen behind the train. Note the water column for up trains behind the up starter. *S. Creer*

a meal store, and feedstuffs would arrive by train and then be sent out to local farms by lorry. There were also malthouses adjoining the yard, and the town gas works between Albion Street and Chantry Road.

The main goods yard and shed was on the down side of the line. There was a trailing crossover through the Albion Street level crossing, and immediately on the north side a facing connection from the down main allowed trains into the goods yard. Space was tight, so a double slip acted as safety points for the yard, as well as giving access to the goods shed itself. Previously the layout had been simpler, and the change was made some time between 1884 and 1903, so giving more space. One through siding passed between the shed and the main line, and a further siding trailed from this back towards the goods shed from the North Entrance end. In effect there was a goods loop, it rejoining the down main a little way to the north of the main road bridge, which thus carried three tracks. Access to this yard was from Station Road, which itself did not appear until relatively late in the day, not having been built when the first edition of the 25in Ordnance Survey maps were being prepared around 1882, and was an extension of the goods yard access road.

Although the East Suffolk climbs fairly steadily since leaving the Deben valley a mile or so before reaching Snape Junction, Saxmundham station is in a dip, and trains climb out of it in both directions. To the north the line had been built on embankment, passing high over North Entrance and looking down on the houses either side of the line. The long siding on the up side seemed to fall away, but in reality stayed level as the main line rose. Saxmundham Junction signalbox was only 736yd from the station box, and much less from the far end of the up siding (not much more than 100yd). The two were in sight of each other: no tree growth was allowed to obstruct the view or scatter leaves on the line. At about MP92 the gradient steepens to 1 in 89 for a mile, the summit being just short of MP93, with East Green crossing just beyond.

Above:
The goods shed at Saxmundham stood on the down side of the line, to the north of the Albion Road level crossing. The present down platform stands where the siding runs in front of the building, which still stands.
Peter Punchard collection

Below:
The cramped nature of the yard on the up side is well illustrated here in this 1911 view looking back towards the up platform. A horse is shunting in the siding in the middle distance, and the bay platform is, as usual, occupied by goods wagons. There is a wealth of other detail including a re-railing ramp under the buffers in the foreground. *HMRS Hilton Collection*

Above:
Saxmundham signalbox changed little over the years until the introduction of RETB in the late 1980s. When this happened the box no longer needed levers to control signals and pointwork, and the frame was removed. A small panel is now used to control the barriers at both level crossings, and the box houses the RETB computer and its back-up. The entrance has been moved to the other end, and the upper part is now clad in UPVC instead of wood. Here, in the 1950s, the full frame is in operation and the layout is still intact. *Peter Punchard collection*

Below:
The 14.53 Ipswich to Lowestoft approaches Saxmundham on 25 June 1984. At this time the line had been singled between Saxmundham and Melton using the up line, and was using tablet working: the temporary catcher can just be seen by the cab. Because the crossover was beyond the platform only the up platform could be used by trains, so the 14.45 Lowestoft–Ipswich train was waiting on the up line behind the camera. At this stage the level crossing gates have not been replaced by lifting barriers, and the remains of the old down platform can be seen beyond the signalbox. The new down platform has subsequently been built on the site of one of the sidings. *S. C. South*

Right:
A classic view of the lineside at Saxmundham Junction in 1911, looking north, with the branch diverging to the right. Scarcely a blade of grass looks out of place! The Junction signalbox looks immaculate, and has not yet developed the pronounced lean of later years. The footpath on the left crosses the main line just past the junction, and still provides a good vantage point today. *HMRS Hilton Collection*

Below:
Fifty-five years later almost the same vantage point sees the 12.23 Aldeburgh to Ipswich coming off the branch and surrendering the tablet on 20 August 1966. The box certainly is now leaning backwards, but the lineside is just as beautifully trimmed. *G. R. Mortimer*

Right:
The leaning box of Saxmundham Junction is clearly seen from the footpath crossing, again looking back towards the station. *Adrian Vaughan collection*

Below:
The 10.05 Ipswich to Aldeburgh collects the tablet at Saxmundham Junction on 20 August 1966. The goods shed is clearly visible in the background. An idea of the gradient can be gained by looking at the up siding, which is about level. *G. R. Mortimer*

Above:
A fine view of Darsham station, looking north along the Yarmouth turnpike. The down siding is full of wagons, but there is still little traffic about. The Stradbroke Arms in the left foreground is evidently under new management.
Alan Taylor collection

Right:
The southern end of the station building at Darsham, as seen by an approaching passenger on 21 August 1959. This was one of the larger buildings, being L-shaped, the other side being along the down platform.
Peter Punchard collection

The countryside is open here, and the line is carried on a succession of minor cuttings and embankments. It now falls towards Darsham, with one stretch of a little under a mile at 1 in 80, Middleton crossing lying on this grade. Whilst East Green and North Green crossings are over minor roads, that between Yoxford and Leiston, now the B1122, is much more important, and so Middleton has always been much busier.

The line sweeps towards Darsham on a left-hand curve, rising gently at 1 in 262, although this steepens once through the platforms to 1 in 85. There was no rest for East Suffolk firemen! The station was built to serve the small town of Yoxford, and Darsham was the closest that the East Suffolk could reasonably reach. It remains well known for its level crossing over what is now the A12, at 95 miles 31 chains from Liverpool Street. Both platforms were on the north side of the crossing, with the main buildings on the down side. Again built in typical style in white brick, Darsham did not have the full-width awnings, but sheltered its passengers with only the narrower version joining the projecting out-buildings. The building was L-shaped, with the longer side along the platform and the shorter facing south, and passengers approaching from Yoxford. The awning continued around this end for the full width of the building. The goods shed stood at the Beccles end of the down platform, whilst the signalbox was on the up side of the line, south of the level crossing. There was a brick-built shelter on the up platform, with a covered waiting area open to the elements flanked by a waiting room at the north end and the lamp room at the other. The station bible was available for passengers using the up side waiting room.

Above:
Darsham, looking north along the railway in Great Eastern days, with an up express passing at speed. Almost the entire layout south of the crossing can be seen; note the lime-washed cattle pens on the extreme right and the coal yard on the left. The roof of the Stradbroke Arms is also visible on the left.
Alan Taylor collection

Right:
A 1911 view with an up train ready to leave, close to the signalbox, wagons, horse boxes and the immaculate cattle pens, all on the Ipswich side of the level crossing.
HMRS Hilton Collection

Below:
By the time this photograph was taken on 15 July 1976 the level crossing had been automated, the signalbox demolished and the railway reduced to just the two running lines. However the goods shed still stands.
Alan Taylor collection

The track layout at Darsham was complex. There was a very long siding on the down side, parallel to the main line and terminating just short of the level crossing at one end, and almost to the Westleton Road bridge at the other. It could be reached by a facing connection from the down main near the crossing, or a trailing one slightly further away and could also be reached from the up main. It had a loading dock near the crossing. On the up side, south of the crossing, were two more short sidings, one also with a short loading dock, and with the signalbox between it and the crossing. Both were accessed from the main road. North of the main road a long siding ran behind the down platform for most of its length, terminating by the station building. It then ran through the goods shed, which was just off the Halesworth end of the platform and very close to the main line, and continued for about another 130yd. Access to this siding was made more complex in 1886 when a trailing connection from the up main was installed, crossing over the down. There was also a trailing connection from the down main, the two connections themselves crossing over! The signalbox thereafter had 27 working and seven spare levers; the track layout was later simplified again. The down platform was lengthened by about 100ft at the same time. The goods shed had the usual lean-to office at the southern end of the building. Goods traffic was healthy: in 1938 Darsham loaded 2,458 tons of vegetables, mostly beet, and 1,165 tons of grain, together worth over £1,300 to the railway. The job of signalman at Darsham was the least enviable on the line, and got worse as traffic grew remorselessly on the A12. The gates had to be opened and closed continually, which meant that the signalman was always in and out of his box like a yo-yo. There was no gate wheel — the only one in the area was at Oulton Broad North, within sight of the East Suffolk but not on it.

Continuing northward, trains face a mile's climb at 1 in 85, with Darsham crossing (now Willow Marsh) just past MP96, followed by about 2½ miles of undulation, no particular gradient lasting more than a few hundred yards one way or the other. Curves are gentle and there are no earthworks of particular note. The minor road from Bramfield to Peasenhall goes over the line on a red brick arch bridge, with Hillhouse (now Bridge) Farm just to the west of the railway on that road, and Sillett's Wood just past Darsham crossing. Just beyond MP99 the downward gradient steepens abruptly to 1 in 75 for nearly a mile, with MP100 being the lowest point. The line then climbs again towards Halesworth, crossing the Blyth valley to reach this important town. The East Suffolk passes close to Bramfield village — about a quarter of a mile — and it is perhaps surprising that no station or any other rail facility was ever provided there. Presumably the distance from the adjacent stations of Darsham and Halesworth was considered too small: they are just over 5 miles apart, although Woodbridge and Melton are only about 1½ miles distant. Darsham station is much further from Yoxford.

At MP98, the nearest the line comes to the village, the road from Bramfield to Walpole crosses over the line, whilst a quarter of a mile to the north another minor road goes under. At around MP99 the line passes Railway Wood to the west, with the lane to Brookhall Farm going over on a skewed brick arch bridge. At 99 miles 19 chains Bramfield crossing, with its cottage on the up side, is where the main Ipswich to Halesworth road crosses the line, with Wenhaston crossing following soon after at 99 miles 52 chains. The main road, having crossed the line, curves sharply to run parallel with it

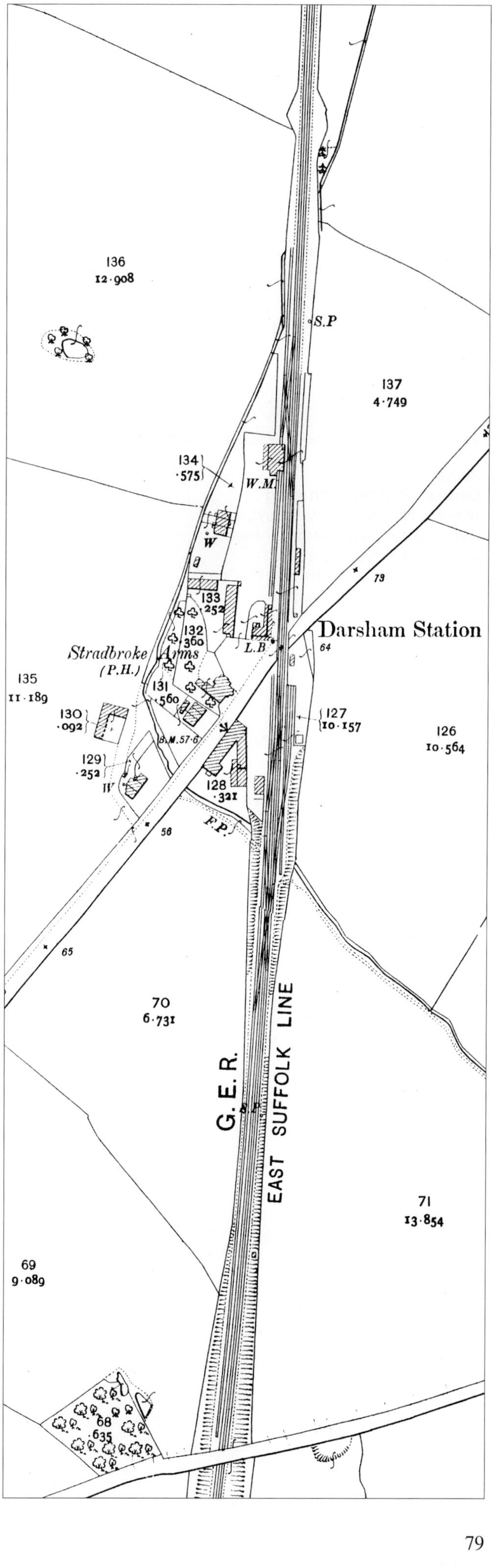

Right:
Darsham station, 1903. *Crown Copyright*

for a short distance, the road from Wenhaston and Mells joining it nearby. For many years the land enclosed by these roads and the railway was occupied by Mells Works making bricks and tiles, although this had certainly gone by 1937, and was probably defunct by 1920.

Having plunged down the side of the valley and passed its lowest point, the East Suffolk crosses the River Blyth by a viaduct. The river is complex and has a number of channels, this first passing to the south of the town and flowing from Walpole and Ubbeston in the west. About a quarter mile further on the railway crosses another channel by viaduct, this one flowing through Halesworth itself. Within 100yd the line crosses the New Reach by a brick arch bridge, this once-navigable waterway serving the quay to the south of Quay Street. Ironically, efforts to improve the river navigation near Blythburgh had had the opposite effect and stopped Halesworth's waterborne trade.

Above:
The up platform at Darsham, looking south towards Saxmundham in early summer in Great Eastern days, with the roses in full bloom. The shape of the station building is a little clearer in this view, but the shelter on this platform is almost hidden by the greenery. The crossover in the foreground gives access to the goods shed and yard on the down side. *Alan Taylor collection*

Having crossed the valley the line then starts to climb out of it at 1 in 81, soon reaching Halesworth station at 100 miles 49 chains. It was never a junction, although for 50 years it served as the interchange point with the celebrated narrow-gauge Southwold Railway. It might have been a junction had the various plans for the Mid-Suffolk Light Railway come to fruition, but they remained in the realms of 'might have been', and a favourite topic for modellers and enthusiasts.

Right:
The British Railways era has arrived at Darsham, although the station remains largely intact. The roses still bloom, there are wagons in the coal siding and the signalbox still stands.
Adrian Vaughan collection

Above:
A posed 1950 photograph on the down platform, with a particularly clear view of the level crossing. *HMRS Hilton Collection*

Below:
Later in the British Rail era the crossing has been modernised and the yard on the down side is beginning to look overgrown. The old electric lamps are still in place, though. *Stations UK*

Above:
The level crossing at Darsham on a rainy 11 September 1965, with the 14.30 Yarmouth South Town to Ipswich waiting at the up platform. *G. R. Mortimer*

Below:
Going south from Halesworth the East Suffolk crosses the New Reach and then the River Blyth by this six-arch bridge. On 8 April 1980 a Class 37 gathers speed as it heads the 07.22 Lowestoft to Liverpool Street just under a mile from the station. *G. R. Mortimer*

—6—

East Suffolk Line Description Halesworth and Beyond

HALESWORTH had been the original terminus of the Halesworth, Beccles & Haddiscoe Railway, but that line did not reach as far as the site of the permanent station, instead terminating to the north. Thus, although at first sight one of the oldest parts of the East Suffolk, the station shared the appearance of the newer sections.

Down trains approached the station on a fairly sharp curve, crossing the Holton Road bridge which had caused so much controversy during its construction. From 1875 the Southwold Railway curved in from the east about a quarter mile to the south, having its own bridge across Holton Road and its own station to the east of the Great Eastern. The railways reached the stations on substantial embankments, with much pointwork spreading out almost as soon as the road was crossed. The town lay largely to the south and west of the station, and most passengers arrived along Station Road, which became Bungay Road once past the level crossing. The Station Hotel offered sustenance to the traveller. It had been built in 1864 as the New Inn, becoming the Station Hotel in 1873 and later still was renamed the Railway Tavern before becoming the Labour Club. For as long as the Southwold Railway existed, certainly the larger proportion of the railway was on the east side of the East Suffolk, and even after this line closed most of it, mainly the transfer sidings, remained in use for dairy traffic. However, on the town side of the passenger platforms stood the substantial goods shed together with animal pens and loading docks, and also serving James Parry & Sons' maltings. They had other maltings in Quay Street, a very short distance away, and together with the other maltsters in the town (including Watney, Combe & Reid) generated a substantial traffic for the railway. At the Beccles end of the goods shed were the horse stables, with the goods office at the other. There was road access on the west side, and a mess room on its other side.

The main station building was on the down side, and was very substantial: it occupied most of the length of the platform. The upper floor provided the accommodation for the stationmaster, his family and domestic staff, whilst the lower contained the usual railway facilities including the booking office and hall, general waiting room and lock-up parcels room at the Ipswich end. The ladies' waiting room and toilets were on the Beccles side of the booking office, with the stationmaster's office and porters' room at the end of the building. The stationmaster had a living room on the ground floor at the end of the building, and this also had a door leading directly into the booking office. There was a W. H. Smith bookstall on the down platform, at the Beccles end under the awning, which ironically was run by a Mr Jarrold (namesake of well-known Norwich booksellers) in the 1930s. There was a single-storey red brick building on the up platform, housing ladies' toilets and waiting room, together with a general waiting room. The gents' toilets were in a separate structure nearer the gates. The signalbox, installed in 1881, was on the up side at the Ipswich end of the platform, and at a slight angle to the main lines because of the siding in front of it going into the milk docks. A footbridge spanned the main lines at this end, with staircases going to each GER platform, and another span going across to the Southwold station. This was blocked off when the latter closed, and was damaged by bombs during the war. The Southwold section was not taken down until 1962, and the rest about 1966.

Left:
Halesworth goods shed stood on the down side of the layout. This view shows the road side, and the lean-to offices at both ends. *Peter Punchard collection*

Right: Halesworth station, 1927. *Crown Copyright*

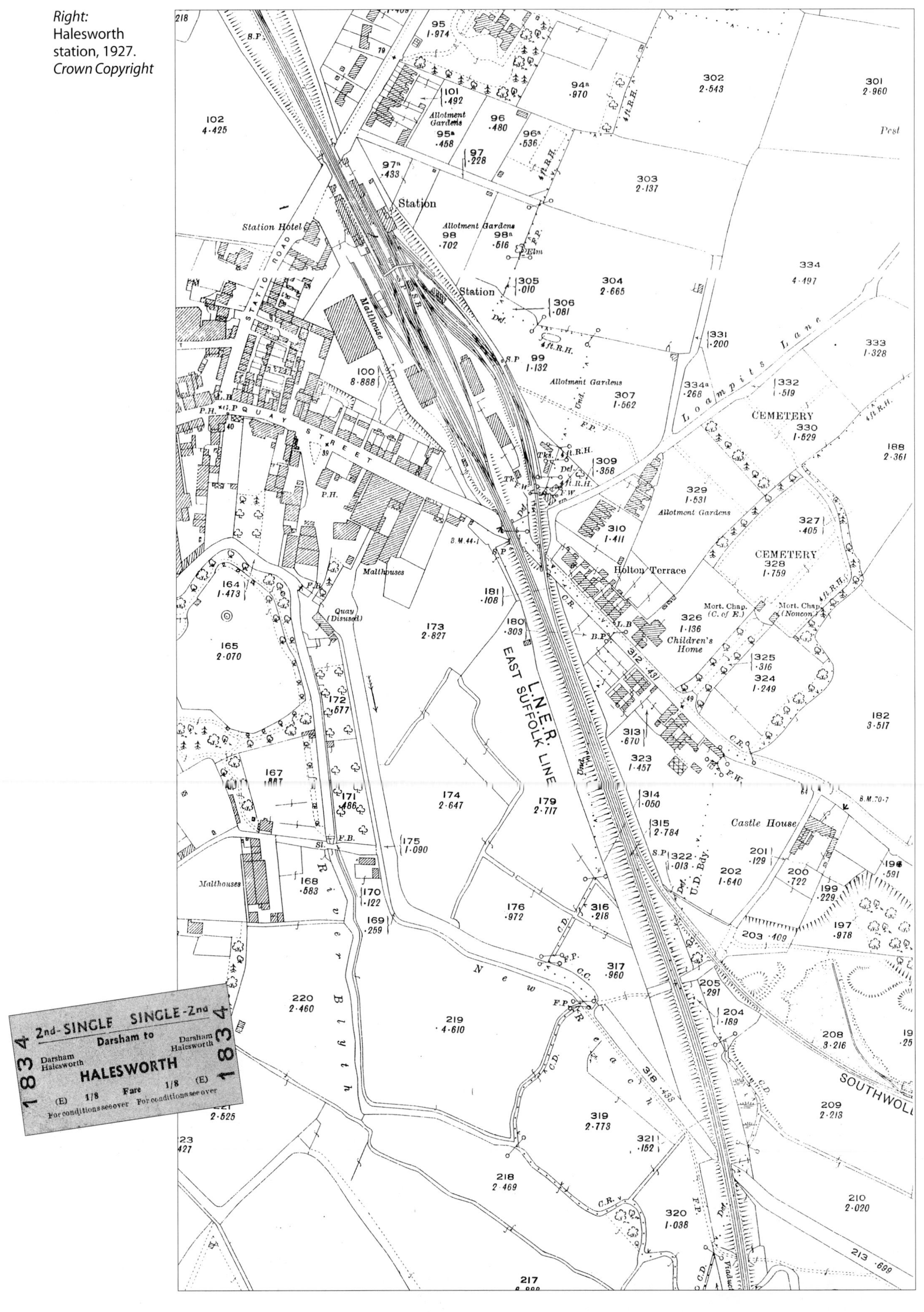

Above:
The down platform at Halesworth in 1962. The extent of the damage done in the war can readily be seen by comparing the size of the station building in this photograph with that on page 32. The wall supporting the awning was rebuilt, and it continued to cover much of the platform. Note the W. H. Smith bookstall and the collection of milk churns beyond the building. The platform is extremely low, only corrected in the late 1990s. *Peter Punchard collection*

Centre left:
Halesworth station from the up platform, looking south. The goods shed and a milk tank can be seen through the footbridge, which has had its connection to the former Southwold Railway station removed. The movable platforms are now fixed, and the roadway has been removed. *Stations UK*

Left:
A view from the footbridge, looking north, and showing the new road bridge in place. It is still 'Halesworth for Southwold', and the sidings behind the up platform are jammed with milk tanks. *Stations UK*

Above:
Class O1 No 63687 shunts the cattle dock on the down side at Halesworth. *Peter Punchard collection*

Quite apart from the Southwold interchange sidings, there was much goods activity on the up side because of the United Dairies depot there. This opened some time between 1924 and 1935, and provided heavy traffic for the railway. The highest figure was 15 tanks per day to Ilford in 1955-6. Some tanks held 3,000 gallons, with a few at 2,000. Milk in churns went to Clacton, Southend and Yarmouth, going to the latter destination mostly in the summer season when it could be up to 50-60 churns daily. They were all loaded in the guard's brake of passenger or stock trains, some going on the up stock train at around 11am and others on the 2pm up. The down train used was the stopper at 11.30–11.45am to Yarmouth. Tanks went on the afternoon stock train (about 2pm), or at about 3.45pm. They might also be attached to the 7pm up passenger working which had left Yarmouth just after 6pm. They were never sent by goods train.

Interchange traffic with the Southwold Railway required transhipment between wagons of each company because of the difference in gauge. There had been various schemes to convert the SR to standard gauge, but the only work done was to provide a new swing bridge at Southwold capable of taking the wider track and install a standard-gauge weighbridge on the harbour branch, to which a third rail was added. Arrival of the Mid-Suffolk at Halesworth would have given a little more impetus, but that line barely reached Cratfield, nearly six miles away, before the money ran out. Goods were manually transferred behind the up main line passenger platform, with two standard-gauge sidings separating it from the transfer platform. This was a substantial timber structure and had a narrow-gauge siding on its other side, which was actually a headshunt from the Southwold Railway passenger platform. The transfer shed was at the northern end of the platform and was also a timber structure, open on the main-line side but with more shelter for Southwold Railway wagons. The United Dairies depot had been built on the east side of the transfer sidings with access from Bungay Road, and after the Southwold Railway closed the transfer sidings were used instead for milk tanks. The siding adjacent to the transfer platform extended some way beyond it, so that loading could be done here. Another standard gauge siding extended south, next to the Southwold's run-round loop for passenger trains, and this allowed coal wagons to stand side by side so that the coal could be shovelled onto the narrow gauge. Milk was also carried in churns, the standard 10gal steel ones being used, which had to be loaded on the passenger platform. Because of their weight they would be spun along the platform using the rim of the base, two people being needed to load them up into the vans. A skilled porter could spin two empty churns — one with each hand — back towards the dairy. The siding finally closed on 30 April 1968, and the site has now been redeveloped for housing.

Apart from milk, Halesworth generated considerable goods traffic, as well as having much coming inward. The 1938 traffic returns show that the station forwarded 1,696 tons of vegetables, much of it sugar beet, and 313 tons of livestock, respectively worth £370 and £743 to the LNER. On sheep sale days, which were an annual event in Halesworth in the 1920s, over 3,000 head would be driven through the town to be loaded into wagons. Horse boxes were loaded using very heavily padded shuttering so that the horses were packed in tightly, to minimise the risk of injury. In the 1940s or earlier bullocks were loaded from the saleground, although this traffic had finished by the mid-1950s. Calves, only a few days old, came off the train with their legs folded up and tied in a sack. Station staff would ring the farmer as soon as they arrived and they were picked up very quickly. Day-old chicks would also arrive by train, sometimes 6-10 boxes at a time, and again the farmer would be rung to arrange immediate collection. As with many rural stations, homing pigeons arrived by train in baskets to be released. The staff would let them go, put the release time on the baskets, tip out the sawdust and send them back on the next train.

Livestock was only a small part of the picture, and there was much else carried. Five farms produced strawberries, which were loaded in fruit wagons, either parcels or ventilated vans, on the dock. Raspberries, blackcurrants and redcurrants were also handled. These vans were then attached to the 8pm stock train, with all the fruit in chip baskets which had to be manhandled in and out, four at a time. Loading was

Above:
A Yarmouth South Town to Ipswich train leaves Halesworth on 18 September 1965, formed from two two-car units because of the number of holidaymakers still about. *G. R. Mortimer*

Below:
A three-car unit for Ipswich waits at the up platform as the platform gates are closed behind it, and passengers run for the footbridge in the early 1960s. Work is in progress on building the new Norwich Road bridge which will replace the level crossing.
Peter Punchard collection

backbreaking work, even with the fruit farmers helping, and took so long that the stock train might stand an hour while it was being done. The shunter would either take the engine across to pick up the loaded vans, or the train would stand at the passenger platform for loading. Blackberries followed later in the season, and the fruit generally went to Chivers' factory at Histon. Chrysanthemums were sent away to Covent Garden from nearby Heveningham Hall. Other outward traffic included ordinary parcels and luggage in advance, especially from Southwold. Collections and deliveries were made by three lorries, one serving the town and two the surrounding country, with three drivers. They went out daily, but some villages were served only twice weekly. Southwold was served morning and afternoon, as was Halesworth itself.

Incoming traffic was very varied. Coal was a staple, the merchants at the station in the 1930s being James Parry & Son Ltd, who were also maltsters and dealt in animal feeds, lime and seeds, with William Sage nearby in the New Cut. The gas works, very close to the station in Wissett Road, was also supplied by rail. Wet fish, packed in boxes of ice, arrived daily from Lowestoft by the parcels trains and was sent to the fish fryers in the town and outlying villages such as Wangford, Laxfield and so on. Adnams Brewery at Southwold sent away beer and received spirits. Tobacco and cakes arrived, including Lyons and Sabona swiss rolls. Seed potatoes arrived in ventilated vans, and broken bags ensured that no railwayman ever had to buy them for the garden. James Parry owned fields on the east side of the station which were used as allotments, and many railwaymen and men working at the maltings had plots there. At Christmas poultry and game would be loaded, whilst the platforms would be full of mail and parcels bags inward and outward. There were special train workings to handle all this extra traffic. There were always postmen on the station, possibly three or four at Christmas. Post to and from Southwold was also handled at Halesworth.

One feature of Halesworth station that was almost unique, and shared only by the down platform at Saxmundham, was the level crossing bisecting the platforms. As with other stations the platforms were originally both low and short, and in this case stopped where the main road (Station Road to the south and Bungay Road to the north of the railway) crossed the line. The railway approached Halesworth from the south on an embankment across the Blyth valley, and was restricted by the Holton Road bridge and Southwold Railway, so that the platforms could not be extended in this direction. The only solution was to go north and construct the four swinging platforms, manually operated and interlocked with the signalling, which gave an extension of about 300ft on both up and down sides, this work being carried out in 1888. Other minor alterations, including the provision of a new trailing crossover on the Beccles side of the level crossing, followed in 1905. Four years previously a very long refuge had been provided on the up side north of the level crossing, and extending almost all the way to Wissett crossing, almost half a mile away. After all this work the 35-lever frame in the signalbox was left with only one spare. The platform gates

Above:
An early view of the level crossing at Halesworth, looking down Station Road towards the town and the Station Hotel.
Alan Taylor collection

Upper right:
The crossing gates are still partly over the line: an up train must be due, judging by the number of passengers on the platform.
Lens of Sutton

Lower right:
A very fine view of the crossing at Halesworth in British Railways days, but before the bridge was built, or any development had taken place on what was to be the Norwich Road. The gradient can be judged by the fact that the up refuge siding, seen beyond the end of the up platform, is roughly level. The down platform was subsequently cut short. The 'pull-in' gates are at the far end of the crossing from the photographer.
Eastern Counties Newspapers

Above left:
Halesworth signalbox late in its career. The siding in front of it has been lifted, and all the box controls is the block signals and a crossover. *David Pearce*

Above right:
Unlike almost all the other signalboxes on the East Suffolk, Halesworth survived the introduction of RETB, being bought by Peter Punchard and moved to the local middle school grounds where it is now a museum, together with some examples of local signalling. *Peter Punchard collection*

were renewed in 1922, the replacements being made by Boulton & Paul in Norwich, after which there were two short sections which slid in or out and performed the function of wicket gates, allowing pedestrians to cross when the main platforms were across the road.

Halesworth had been the scene of a serious accident on 20 August 1877, when the 5pm express from Yarmouth, running at normal speeds and not scheduled to call at the station, passed the home signal showing clear and ran into a goods train being shunted on the main line. Although the driver of the express applied his brakes hard, the engine smashed into the trucks and completely destroyed several. The express driver and fireman jumped clear, and although the latter survived uninjured, the driver badly damaged his leg. The express engine could not continue, and the train was taken forward by the goods locomotive, and was about three hours late leaving Ipswich. Single line working was put in place, and Ipswich immediately despatched a breakdown train. Astonishingly, there appear to have been no injuries among the passengers on the express train.

Halesworth station suffered serious damage during World War 2, when it was the target for a German bomber. On 18 January 1941 Gladys Rogers, a porter at the station, stood in the doorway of her house and watched the bomber pass overhead, straighten up and head for the railway. The station building took a direct hit, and the stationmaster Herbert Holland, his wife and their maid were killed, the only civilian casualties in the town during the war. Their daughter Miriam was at work at the nearby telephone exchange at the time and returned to a scene of utter devastation. Her brother Walter maintained the railway tradition and joined after the war, going on to become stationmaster at Norwich Thorpe.

In short, Halesworth was a busy station for both passengers and goods, and almost everything and everyone in the town passed through at some time. Down trains leaving the station faced a stiff climb of 1 in 97 for nearly 1½ miles before reaching the highest point on the line. The climb started with a sweeping curve to the right, initially with the long refuge on the up side, over Wissett level crossing (later Old Station Road), and from 1959 passing under the new Norwich Road bridge, built to replace the station level crossing, which was then closed and the gates fixed across the road. Much of this section of line is carried in a succession of shallow cuttings and embankments, passing under the ancient Roman road of Stone Street, now the A144 between Halesworth and Bungay, just short of MP102. Millpost crossing, with the usual keeper's cottage, was at 102 miles 20 chains and near the summit, the line here being at ground level, almost straight

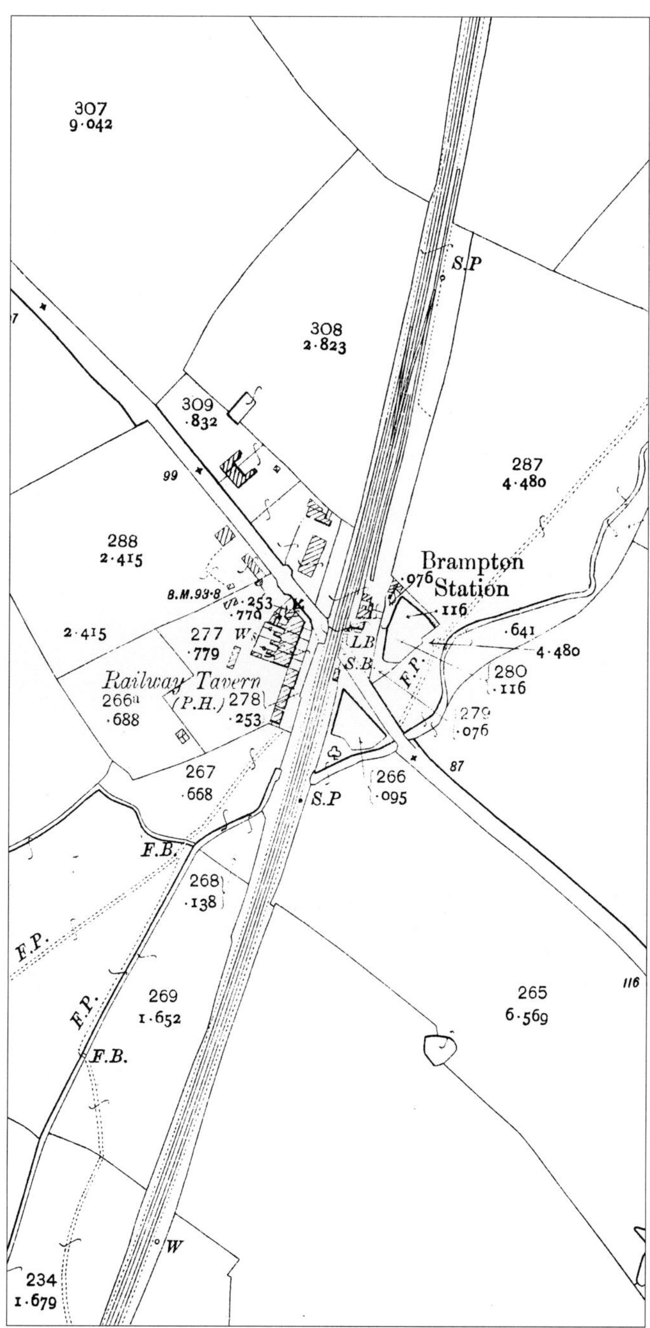

and with down trains now facing a saw-tooth profile as far as Beccles Bank signalbox at 107 miles 17 chains. The line curves briefly to the left as it approaches Westhall Low Common, where it crosses over the minor road between Westhall and Spexhall, here gaining the alignment originally planned by the Halesworth, Beccles & Haddiscoe Railway. From here it runs in an almost straight line to Brampton station at 104 miles 50 chains, passing Westhall level crossing at 103 miles 49 chains, and over the station level crossing at 104 miles 46 chains, with the signalbox on the Halesworth side of the crossing on the up side.

At Brampton the station did not resemble those to the south, being an original HB&H construction. Both passenger platforms were to the north of the crossing, with the buildings almost entirely on the up side. The track layout was simple, with a trailing crossover at the Beccles end of the platforms, and a long siding running behind the up platform, extending northwards past a loading bank, and joined to the up main line by a trailing connection just north of the crossover. The station was inspected by Maj-Gen Hutchinson for the Board of Trade on 29 October 1886, who observed that the up platform had been lengthened, the siding connection altered and that signalbox had 15 levers of which 10 were working. He also wrote that 'I was sorry to observe that there is no shelter on the down platform', which so galvanised the railway that one was moved from Great Ormesby soon after the Midland & Great Northern Joint closed in 1959!

The station building stood by the level crossing at the foot of the up platform ramp, the main part being two storeys and almost square, with a fully hipped roof. The entrance was on the platform side via an elaborate porch, with the booking office, waiting room and stationmaster's office all in one. There was always a fresh stationmaster at Brampton — it was a Class 5 station, in other words at the bottom of the pile, and so usually had a newly promoted clerk in the job. At the Beccles end of the building a single-storey extension housed the gents' toilets. Next to this, with double doors opening onto the platform, was the lock-up, which was three-quarters full of grain sacks — there were hundreds of them. A major activity at Brampton, as at many rural stations, was the loan of sacks to farmers. When they came back they had to be shaken out and then stowed 23 to a sack (total 24), which was a filthy job for the staff. There was a hand pump at the back of the station house, and it took 400 pumps from the pond nearest the house to fill the big tank on top of the

Above:
Brampton station, 1904. *Crown Copyright*

Right:
Brampton in Great Eastern days, before it was felt necessary to add the 'Suffolk' suffix to the nameboard. The yard is full: Brampton had a healthy goods traffic despite its apparent remoteness.
Stations UK

Right:
Looking north over the level crossing gate at Brampton in 1959. The lock-up is on the up platform, and there are wagons at the loading dock in the distance. *Stations UK*

Below:
Brampton station seen from the signalbox around 1970. The smart shelter on the down platform was installed after the M&GN closed in 1959, being moved from Great Ormesby, there having been nothing there since the line opened.
Peter Punchard collection

Above:
A four-car unit for Yarmouth South Town runs into Brampton in 1963. *Peter Punchard collection*

Lower left:
Looking in the up direction over the crossing, the starter is off for an up train. The down home, positioned for sighting round the curve, is preserved at Halesworth with the signalbox. *Lens of Sutton*

stationmaster's toilet, which also fed a tap in the house. This took half an hour. There was another pump on the cattle dock fed from another pond, and the big concrete drinking trough had to be filled if it was known that animals were being sent away, although this did not happen very often. There was another pond behind the signalbox.

Sugar beet was very important at Brampton, and in 1955 the station loaded 737 trucks for Cantley and Ipswich, beaten only by Barnby. When the special trains arrived in the morning, the empties had to be shunted in, which could take an hour or more. The lad porters had to label the loaded trucks, which mostly went to Cantley via Lowestoft, although if Cantley was full then the beet went to Ipswich. At Beccles the Waveney Valley beet would be attached, and Beccles itself could load up to 35 wagons a day. It was also possible for Brampton beet to go to Ipswich via Lowestoft; it would be attached to the up night goods which was not booked to call at Brampton. Most of the wagons attracted demurrage and so were turned round fast. Brampton was the only station on the East Suffolk where trucks could be legally towed by rope whilst shunting.

In the 1950s Mr Jones was a local coal merchant, and to save himself work always wanted his trucks left at the end of the siding, just inside the gate to the yard. On the subject of coal, an 'L1' 2-6-4T once failed at Brampton and was shunted into the siding onto the stops. It started with about three-quarters of a bunker of coal, but since it took nearly two months to take it away there wasn't much left when this finally happened!

On leaving the station trains continued their undulating progress towards Beccles Bank signalbox, passing Weston crossing, over the minor road between Redisham and Weston. The railway approached the crossing over a right-hand curve, but the shallow cutting and Eight Acre Covert on the east side of the line combined to make sighting poor for down trains, and one of the conditions imposed before the HB&H was allowed to open for passengers was the provision of an 'additional auxiliary signal'. Down trains today are limited to 45mph approaching the crossing for the same reason. The appearance of the line has changed here over the years, having originally been quite open, with Sparrow's Thicks covert on the west side extending northward along the lineside.

Once over the crossing the line is straight, passing the Bank box at the last of the 'saw-teeth' and then taking the precipitate plunge down Beccles bank for two miles, mostly at 1 in 87 including Cromwell's Lane (later Cromwell Road) and London Road crossings, easing slightly to 1 in 133 over Ingate Street and Ingate Road (later Grove Road) crossings into the station and then to 1 in 290 for the final short drop onto the flood plain of the River Waveney. Beccles Bank box had been opened in October 1885 as a block post, when a trailing crossover was installed. It had 10 levers including two spares, and runaway points were provided in the up line because of the steep gradient. The gradients seem mysteriously to have changed over the years, because they were given on the GER's official plan of 1885 as being 1 in 66 towards Cromwell's Lane, with 1 in 98 near the summit, and fell at 1 in 528 for 30yd towards Brampton, steepening to 1 in 88, instead of the 1947 figure of 1 in 97 in this direction. Beccles bank was the only location on the East Suffolk where banking was permitted, and then only for up freight and fish trains, the banker not being attached to the rear of the train. As soon as it reached the Bank box it dropped off the train, and was then crossed over to run back down to the station.

Both Cromwell's Lane and London Road had cottages for their crossing keepers, but Ingate Street and Ingate Road did not, being worked by Beccles station staff. By the beginning of the 20th century, however, all were worked by crossing keepers from Beccles (with the cottages being used as accommodation for railway staff), together with others in the immediate area such as Northgate Street, between Beccles station and the first river bridge on the Waveney Valley line. Perhaps because of the difficult approaches to the East Suffolk line crossings there was growing concern by the Board of Trade at the number of serious accidents involving the keepers, and it became obvious that remedial action had to be taken. Conditions for the gatemen were not good: they had to be out in all weathers, but had very little shelter apart from a small hut. They faced long periods of inactivity, but then had to operate the gates immediately a train approached. The Great Eastern had submitted an audit of traffic over the crossings for a 24hr period in both summer and winter. On a January 1910 weekday there were 10 trains each way between 7am and 7pm, and four each way between 7pm and 7am. On an August weekday the corresponding figures were 18 down and 17 up during the day, and five each way at night. All of these crossings, together with Jetty and Water Mill (Woodbridge) and Rendham Road (Saxmundham), had what was then a special dispensation which allowed the gates to be kept closed across the railway except when a train passed, the instructions stating that they '. . . must be closed across the Public Road in sufficient time to prevent delay to trains and engines'.

A report prepared for the Board of Trade in April 1910 detailed 10 accidents at the four Beccles level crossings on the East Suffolk, plus another at Northgate Street. (It may be useful to note that road names ending in '. . . gate' in places such as Beccles derive from Norse, and do not mean 'gate' as in modern English. They signify 'street' or 'road', and so the name 'Northgate Street' as used by the railway was a tautology, and it is actually called 'Northgate'.) On 24 June 1904 at Cromwell Road Gateman Drayton put the gate across the railway, went into his hut and forgot about it. It was hit by the 12.45am goods from Ipswich to Lowestoft. He was accused of falling asleep and denied it, but was suspended and sharply cautioned. He had failed to hear the ringing of the electric warning bell, which all these crossings had. Other accidents happened over the years, the worst being at Ingate Road on 19 January 1909, when Gateman William Drane failed to open the gates for the 8.50am Ipswich to Yarmouth passenger train until it was very close, and was fatally injured by the engine. The inquest returned a verdict of accidental death. A similar accident occurred on 12 February 1910 when Porter H. W. Fisk, who was relieving the regular gateman who was off sick, was struck and killed by the engine of the 8.15am goods from Lowestoft to London. The Board of Trade also complained about the excessive hours worked by enginemen at the time, the crew of the locomotive that killed Porter Fisk being booked on for 12¾ hours each. They had been on duty for 1½ hours when the accident occurred.

As a result, the crossing gates at Ingate Street and Ingate Road were modified, both going from having four to two gates, and special locks were provided on the wicket gates so that the gateman could prevent pedestrians using them when trains were nearby. Both crossings were busy with foot and vehicular traffic, and the gates being across the line provided an excuse for local schoolchildren to be late over very many years. Perhaps more importantly new distant signals were provided, for up trains 300yd on the Beccles side of Ingate Road, and for down trains 400yd on the Ipswich side of Ingate Street, the approach being down the steeply graded and sharply curved Beccles bank. Although the arms were of the fishtail pattern, they were red, and showed a red or green light, depending on their position. They were of a different pattern to the usual distant signal so that drivers knew they referred to the gates. New three-lever ground frames were provided at each crossing for working the signals and locking the gates, which were interlocked with Beccles station (Beccles South) signalbox. Col von Donop, who inspected the new arrangements for the Board of Trade, felt that sighting for the gates and lamps at Cromwell's Lane and London Road was so good that the provision of distant signals was unnecessary there.

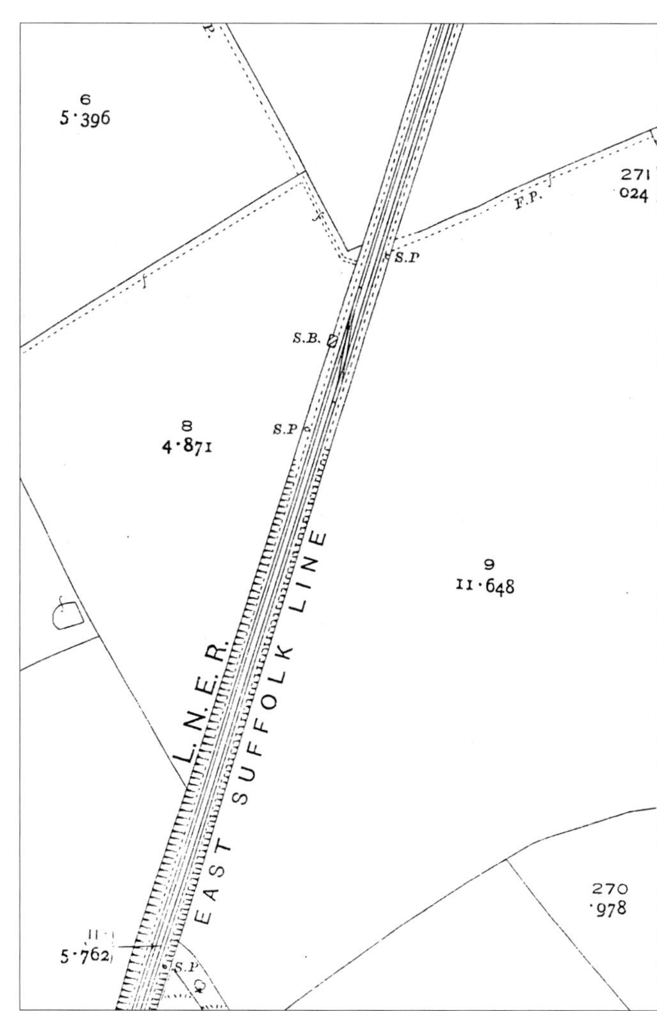

Above:
Beccles Bank signalbox, 1924-9. *Crown Copyright*

Beccles was easily the largest intermediate station on the East Suffolk, and at the end of the 19th century boasted a large and thriving variety of industries. There were several maltings including John Crisp's, at the station, Messrs J. K. & W. H. Garrod's tannery, Field's agricultural implement works, the Vulcan Iron Works of Messrs Elliott & Garrood, Laws & Son's nursery grounds, and many wind and steam corn mills. There was a corn market every Friday, and stock sales on alternate weeks by Messrs Henry & John Read in Blyburgate, and George Durrant & Sons adjacent to the railway station. Having rebuilt Wellington Street into Station Road in a style befitting the importance of the new railway, the Corporation then continued on the other side of the tracks in 1863 with The Avenue, a fine tree-lined drive from the station across to the Common.

Beccles was a major junction and traffic centre with a large and complex layout. The railway employed a very large number of people on and around the system in the town, and the fortunes of the two were inextricably bound for many years. In British Railways days it was the only station in the Norwich Division that could despatch four trains

Above:
An aerial view of Beccles in 1959. The town forms the main part of the picture, with the River Waveney to the right and the railway in the lower part of the picture. The Waveney Valley line curves away and can just be seen crossing the river, while Common Lane level crossing is visible at the bottom edge, with the four tracks of the Lowestoft and Yarmouth lines clear. The building with a light roof is the engine shed. The main part of the station is near the left edge of the picture. *Simmons Aerofilms*

Below:
No 70013 *Oliver Cromwell* heads an up express over Grove Road level crossing, soon after leaving Beccles. The speed limit leaving the station and the tight curves make the assault on Beccles bank the more difficult. *Alan Taylor collection*

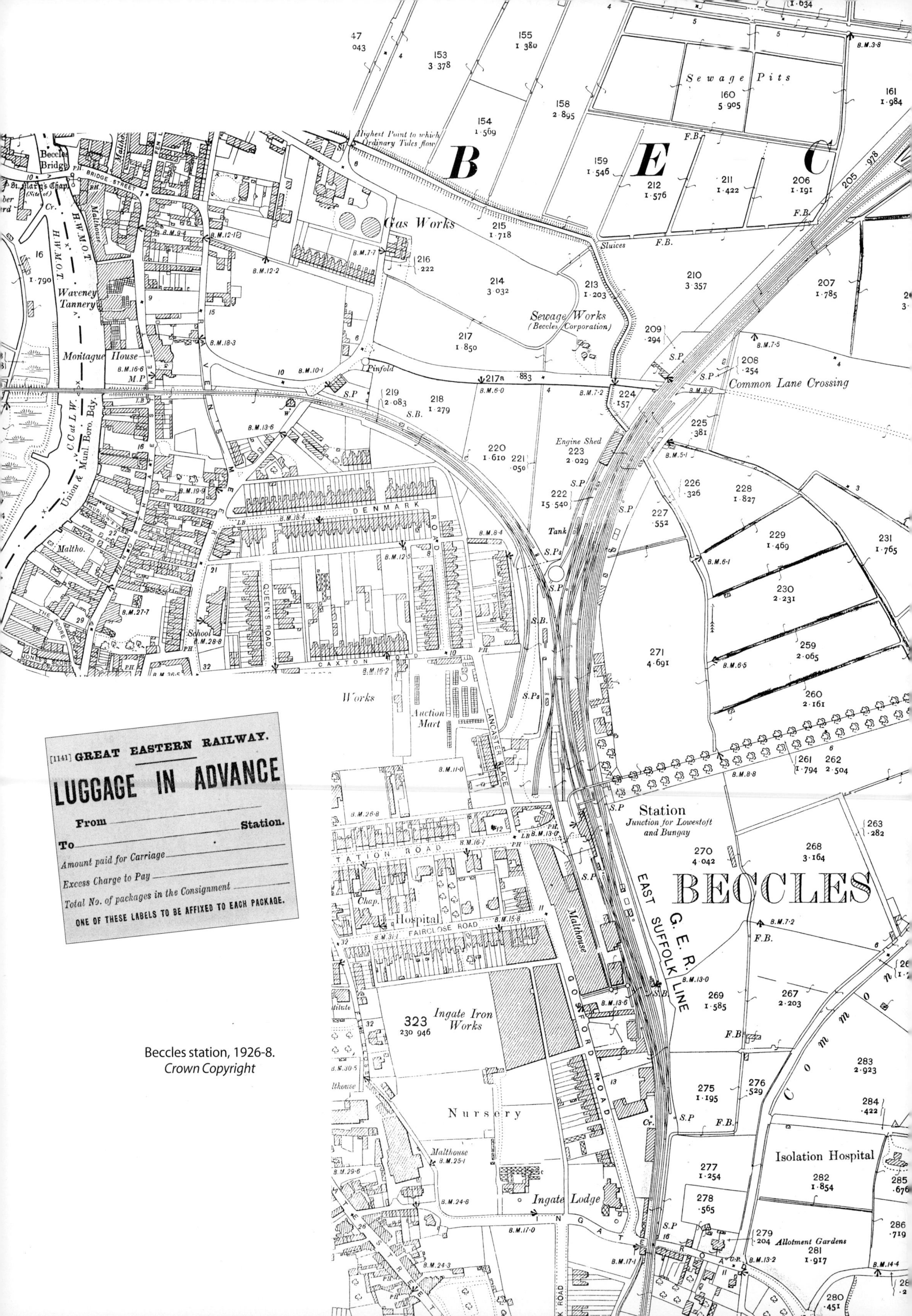

[1141] GREAT EASTERN RAILWAY.

LUGGAGE IN ADVANCE

From ______ Station.

To ______

Amount paid for Carriage ______

Excess Charge to Pay ______

Total No. of packages in the Consignment ______

ONE OF THESE LABELS TO BE AFFIXED TO EACH PACKAGE.

Beccles station, 1926-8.
Crown Copyright

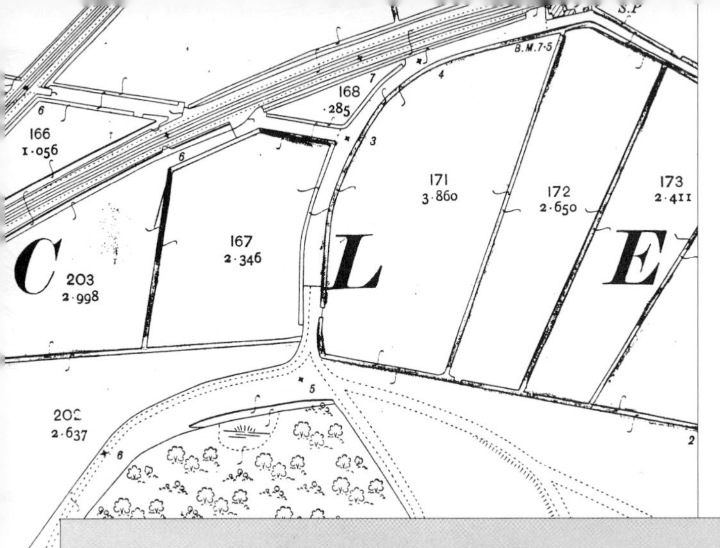

Below:
Looking south from Beccles South signalbox in 1911; Grove Road crossing is just out of sight round the curve. The track components are stacked neatly by the lineside. *HMRS Hilton Collection*

Bottom:
Beccles in 1911, this time looking north, with Beccles South box on the extreme right. The passenger station is visible in the distance. The water tank is just beyond the signalbox, and the goods shed on the left of the tracks. The other buildings form part of the extensive maltings, with a manure store housed in the wooden building in the left foreground. *HMRS Hilton Collection*

Right:
A closer view of the maltings on the down side at Beccles, 1911. They provided a major source of traffic for the railway.
HMRS Hilton Collection

simultaneously — even Thorpe couldn't manage this. It achieved this by sending one towards London, one to South Town, another to Lowestoft, and the fourth along the Waveney Valley line. The station had also developed greatly over the years, starting largely south of the point where the footbridges spanned the line, and extending northward so that most of the platforms and track layout were on this side. Beccles had its own engine shed and turntable, and six signalboxes for several years — Bank, South, North Junction, Lowestoft Junction, Swing Bridge South and Swing Bridge North. None now survives, although South lasted until the introduction of RETB in 1986.

The layout at Beccles had evolved greatly since the Corporation had been so agitated in 1865. The opening of the Waveney Valley line in March 1863 had necessitated the provision of the bay platform more or less where it remained throughout the life of the line, and started the move of the passenger platforms northwards. By 1880 the main down platform was only about 200ft long, but was now extended by a similar amount adjacent to the Waveney Valley bay. The up platform was opposite, also with a new section opposite the bay. There was not much change by 1888, although there were now three signalboxes controlling the station: South, North (Beccles Junction) and Lowestoft Junction, the last some 400ft beyond Common Lane crossing. Here the branch diverged from the main line by means of a double junction, the tracks quickly converging. At the passenger station a single footbridge landing close to the north end of the main building had replaced the original barrow crossing and allowed passengers to cross to the up platform, which was

Right:
Seen in a much later era, Beccles South signalbox was the last of many to survive, lasting until the introduction of RETB in 1986. All it has left in this 1980s view are the block signals for the double track, a crossover and a solitary siding.
Robert Humm

Above:
The south end of Beccles station, looking south, in the early 1960s. Note the fine collection of signal arms and the platform bridge. There are still a few wagons standing outside the goods shed, and the water tank and column still stand. The maltings have had a large square grain silo constructed behind them. *Peter Punchard collection*

Below:
The Beccles platform bridge in action in 1960. It was essential for getting milk churns onto the up platform for onward shipment. *Stations UK*

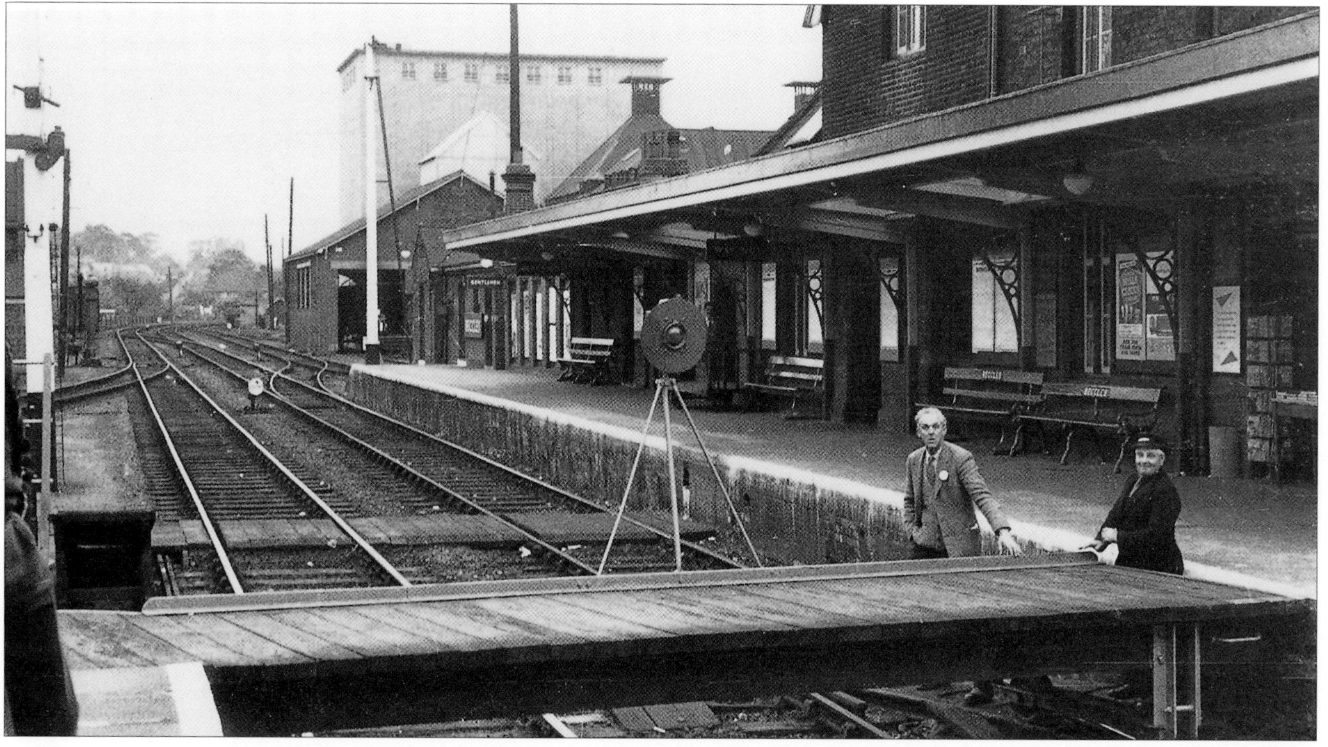

Left:
Class J20 No 64681 stands by the W. H. Smith bookstall on the down platform at Beccles station on 20 June 1959. The refreshment room was once here.
Peter Punchard collection

Below:
Viewed from the footbridge across to the Common, ex-Great Northern Class C12 No 67366 stands in the Waveney Valley bay, Platform 1, with the 12.33pm Beccles to Yarmouth South Town train on 28 May 1957. The cattle pens and market can be seen beyond the train.
Alan Taylor collection

opposite the down, single-sided and mostly to the south of the footbridge. It also took them across the tracks and onto the Common.

By March 1893 the footbridge had been replaced by the existing one across to the Common, and a separate one connecting the platforms. The down platform had been extended at the Yarmouth end, but the up was almost unchanged and retained its shelter opposite the booking office. The GER General Powers Act of 1898 included provision for doubling of the Lowestoft branch, which was then carried out in stages. At the Beccles end this involved utilising the former sidings that had run towards Common Lane, extending them over the crossing and converting them into the new line to Lowestoft. This meant widening the level crossing and providing new gates. At the same time the sidings on the up side at the station had to be rearranged, and the new up island platform provided. Lowestoft Junction signalbox became redundant, since the junction was effectively transferred to its later position and control transferred to an enlarged Beccles North Junction box. When Col G. W. Addison reported on his inspection of the works for the Board of Trade in October 1901 the junction arrangements at this end of the station were substantially as they remained until the Yarmouth line closed in 1959.

The station had thus reached its maximum extent soon after the turn of the 20th century. The main line approached from the south, with the down platform, No 2, on the town side having the main station buildings at its southern end. A bay, Platform 1, for Waveney Valley trains faced north. There was also a long island platform on the east side of the main line,

Above:
An Edwardian view of the frontage of Beccles station. Contrast this with the more modern views below, and the changes are obvious, including the repositioning of the main entrance, and the remodelling of the left-hand gable end. The track connecting the cattle docks and the maltings can be seen in the foreground.
Alan Taylor collection

Right:
The station frontage in LNER days, taken in 1946. Compare this with the Edwardian view: the changes are substantial, including the moving of the main entrance, the reconstruction of the left-hand gable end and the addition of a second single-storey part on the right. The lower part of the centre section was rebuilt completely.
HMRS Hilton Collection

Right:
Beccles station seen in the late 1960s soon after it had become unstaffed. The façade of the building underwent many changes over the years, and there used to be a siding running in front of it into the maltings.
Peter Punchard collection

Above:
An up train at Beccles on a Sunday afternoon. This looks like the Lowestoft portion being drawn forward from Platform 4 so that it can be set back onto the main Yarmouth train.
Alan Taylor collection

Below:
A Class D16/3 leaves Beccles with a local for South Town on 19 May 1951. This became the junction between the Lowestoft and Yarmouth lines, controlled by Beccles North Junction, when the Lowestoft branch was doubled. *Harold D. Bowtell*

Above:
'J15' No 65460 stands in the cattle dock at Beccles.
Alan Taylor collection

with its main face, No 3, used principally by up Yarmouth trains, and the most easterly face, No 4, by trains to and from Lowestoft. The island had a substantial wooden building containing toilets and waiting rooms, and was also protected by extensive awnings at each end of this building. A footbridge passed over the platforms and provided a public right of way for pedestrians between the station forecourt and The Avenue on Beccles Common, whilst another between this and the station building gave access for passengers between the platforms, and at one time had a roof where the other did not. There were sidings on the east side of the line. A siding and headshunt trailed from the Ipswich end of the down platform almost to Ingate Road level crossing, with another on its west side going through the goods shed. This in turn ran across the station forecourt in front of the ticket office and connected to a siding serving animal pens on the north side of the station. Access was gained via wagon turntables into the adjacent Crisp's Maltings and Elliott & Garrood's yard (they were general engineers and had iron and brass foundries). In 1938 1,660 tons of malt were sent out from Beccles, balanced by grain being brought in. Coal traffic was substantial, with the Co-op and Fowlers (later Craskes) having yards, and other merchants unloading in the Gresham Road yard.

Passengers arrived at the station through the booking office in the middle of the main building, having had to cross the tramway-type track passing in front of it. This was a red brick structure, originating from Halesworth, Beccles & Haddiscoe days, and had a slate roof. Perhaps not as grand as the standard pattern typified by Halesworth and other stations on the East Suffolk sections, it had been extended and modified over the years. From the London end it housed the foremen's office, shunters' room and public toilets. There was a weighbridge on the road side, and then the ladies' waiting room, general waiting room and the booking office. Beyond this had once been a dining room and the refreshment room, later replaced by W. H. Smith's bookstall.

Trains for Bungay, Harleston, Tivetshall Junction and Norwich (originally Victoria) left from the Waveney Valley bay, and could also go across onto the down main to Yarmouth, but not directly to Lowestoft. The Waveney Valley line had a long loop on its up side extending almost from the Pound Road level crossing, and a headshunt on the down side. Another siding from the latter swung towards Lancaster Place, later Gresham Road, Shell-Mex subsequently having a terminal here, where two or three tank wagons could usually be seen. Durrant's auction mart was on the opposite side of the road, and the rail yard and animal pens saw considerable use, 523 tons of livestock being forwarded in 1938. Durrant's held fortnightly stock sales, alternating with Read, Owles & Ashford in the town, and it was always the drovers who did the loading and unloading of livestock. Beccles North Junction signalbox was on the west side of the line where the Waveney Valley diverged, whilst in the vee was the turntable, with water tank beyond. Between the turntable and signalbox was the junction of the Yarmouth and Lowestoft lines, so that there were four running lines, plus the Waveney Valley, at this end of the station. Also on the west side of the line and a little further north was the engine shed, and just beyond this, Common Lane level crossing with a typical cottage for the keeper.

Saxmundham and Halesworth may have had whole sections of platform that swung across the line, but Beccles also had something similar, albeit on a smaller scale. As with

Above:
Beccles North Junction with the layout intact. This was the largest of the Beccles boxes, controlling many lines. The Waveney Valley curves away to the left, whilst the Lowestoft line curves away to the right beyond the engine shed, which is behind the '15' sign. The island platform is just in view. *Adrian Vaughan collection*

Below:
Times change at Beccles North Junction. The Yarmouth line has closed, and the layout is being simplified, taking out the junction and reducing the line from four to two tracks.
Peter Punchard collection

Above:
Beccles was a large station. This 1956 view is taken from the main down platform, with the Waveney Valley bay, No 1, on the right. The cattle pens and maltings can be seen in the background. The up platform had a wooden building with toilets and waiting rooms, and an extremely long awning over much of its length. A Lowestoft train waits in Platform 4.
Stations UK

Left:
In contrast, the same viewpoint only 11 years later. The awning has gone and only the building remains on the up platform. Shortly afterwards the station became unstaffed and it was all boarded up. *Stations UK*

many stations, considerable amounts of milk in churns was loaded — it went to United Creameries in Halesworth — as well as other heavy merchandise carried by passenger train. William Clowes, who had a very large printing works in nearby Newgate, often had urgent material in addition to the quantities of paper that arrived by train, and which was carted away from the station by the printers on an electric truck. Books were despatched. To make life easier for the porters the down and island platforms were connected by a movable 'bridge' which could be swung across from the Ipswich end of the island and then allowed barrows to be wheeled between the two. It was locked from the South box. Newspapers were another item that went over this bridge: they arrived via the overnight train from London. At Beccles bundles were unloaded for the 7am Waveney Valley departure, and also for Lowestoft at about the same time. Deliveries to W. H. Smith were easy as it had a bookstall at the station. At first this was on the down platform just north of the main building, but moved into the main building to replace the refreshment room when that closed in the late 1920s.

Above:
Class D16 No 62521 leaves Beccles with a train for Yarmouth on 6 September 1952. *R. E. Vincent*

Below:
'K3' No 61958 is pressed into passenger service on a special from Lowestoft to Ipswich, passing Beccles at about 11am on 24 February 1957. It carries Boy Scouts to a Baden-Powell centenary meeting. *Alan Taylor collection*

—7—

East Suffolk Journey's End Beccles to Yarmouth South Town

HAVING approached Beccles from the south, the railway curved steadily eastwards as it progressed further, with the Lowestoft line remaining level almost all the way to its termini. The main line to Yarmouth quickly swung back onto a more northeasterly course, and although not as flat, there was little more than gentle undulation on the rest of the journey to South Town. Passing Beccles Common as the Lowestoft branch curved away, the sewage works and sewage pits were on the other northwest side of the line, after which it set out across Beccles marshes in a straight line. With drainage dykes on either side, the line climbed briefly to get over Beccles swing bridge, before descending on the far bank of the River Waveney and passing through Stanley Carrs. For the first time the East Suffolk line had crossed into Norfolk, the river marking the county boundary. It crossed back into East Suffolk via St Olaves swing bridge, and remained in that county until only a mile or so from the terminus at Yarmouth South Town. In fact, until 1891 the terminus was still in Suffolk, Yarmouth until then encompassing parts of both Norfolk and Suffolk. The upheavals of the 1974 boundary changes came long after the closure of the main line north of Beccles.

The Waveney was, and is, a navigable river, having once had trading wherries sailing as far as Bungay, and presented a significant barrier to the railway. It describes a great loop as it flows eastwards through Beccles and on towards Lowestoft, then turns back to head northeast past St Olaves and thence to the River Yare, where both flow into Breydon Water. This creates almost a peninsula, often known simply as 'The Island', mostly bounded by the Waveney and smaller streams, and which has poor road access. The river had to be crossed north of Beccles and again at St Olaves, and swing bridges were dictated by reason of its status as a navigation.

Beccles swing bridge, structure No 476, at 110 miles 55 chains, was the older of the two, having been built for the Halesworth, Beccles & Haddiscoe Railway. It was a single-track structure, approached from both sides via wooden trestle viaducts, and with a turntable pier roughly in the middle of the river from which the bridge was cranked round manually. When the line was closed — for example, overnight at weekends — it had to be left open for boats, and so the bridge men had to row themselves back to the Beccles bank, there being a jetty for that purpose in both places. There was a signalbox at each end, and a pilotman conducted each train across. Initially the tracks across the bridge were gauntleted and were officially described as being double, but in 1894 this was altered to single track, with the installation of points at each end of the bridge. New signal cabins were erected at each end of the bridge at the same time. All trains had to be brought to a stand before crossing the bridge, and there was a severe speed restriction of 5mph for all trains. The whole operation was very labour-intensive.

As soon as World War 1 ended, concern arose about the condition of the bridges, as well as the operating restrictions that they necessitated. The Great Eastern had renewed four swing bridges in the area in the period 1904-7 at Trowse, Reedham, Somerleyton and Carlton Colville, and had intended to complete the programme by replacing those at Beccles and St Olaves. Although sanction was given by the 1912 General Powers Act, war had intervened, and they were extended until 1924. St Olaves was considered the more urgent despite being less old. During 1923 the Chief Civil Engineer's office prepared a series of reports on the bridges,

Below:
The first swing bridge was a single-track structure reached via wooden trestle approach spans. In this postcard view from the Great Eastern era the bridge is open to the river, with yachts passing either side. The bridge was cranked round by hand, and necessitated the men having a boat to get back to the shore. Note that the turntable pier is painted white for better visibility at night. *Alan Taylor collection*

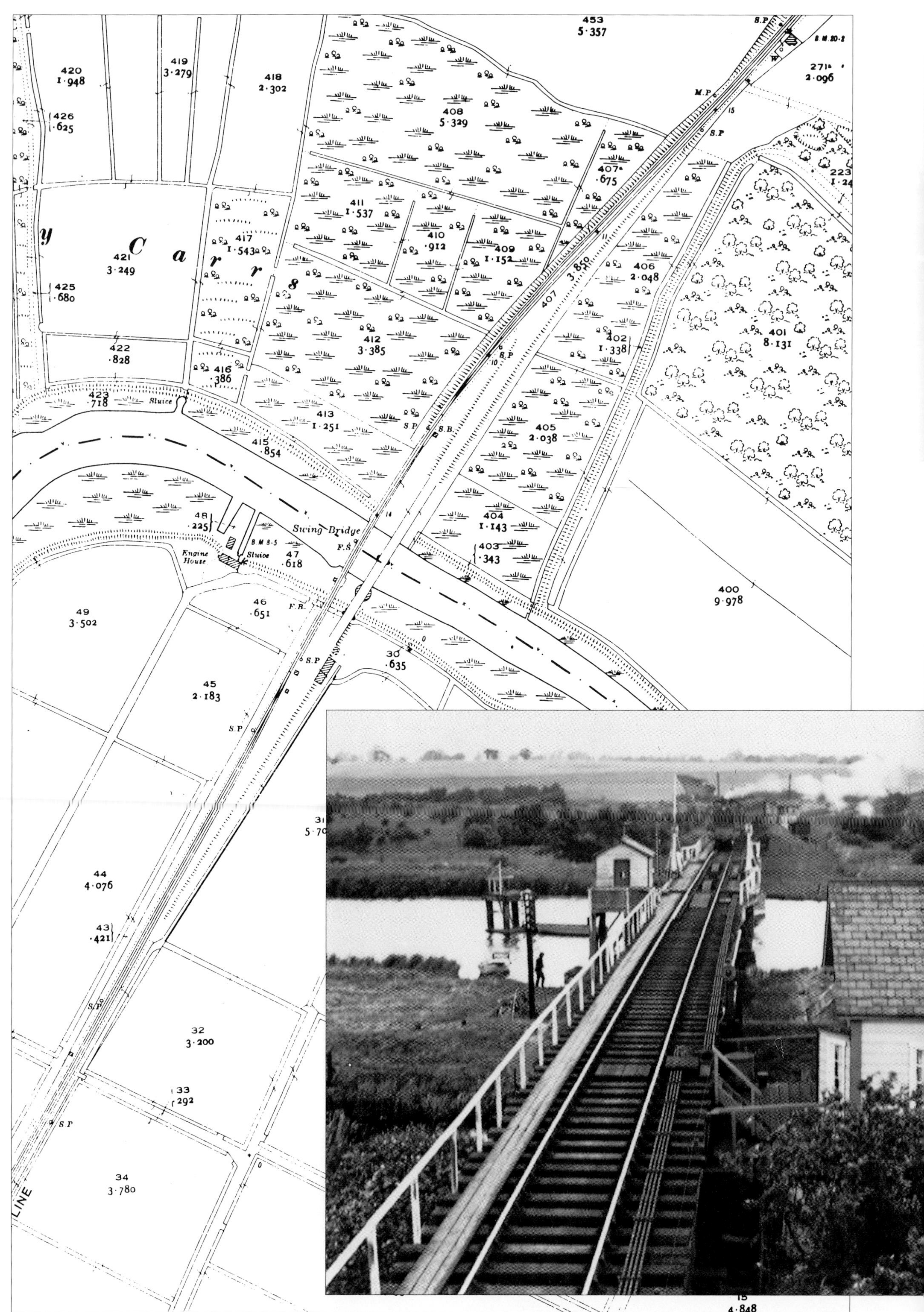

Swing Bridge
Engine House
Sluice
Sluice
y C a r r s
F.B.
F.S.
S.B.
S.P.
M.P.
B.M. 8.5
B.M. 20.2
LINE
453
5·357
420
1·948
419
3·279
418
2·302
426
·625
421
3·249
425
·680
422
·828
423
·718
417
1·543
416
·386
408
5·329
407a
·675
411
1·537
410
·912
409
1·152
412
3·385
413
1·251
415
·854
406
2·048
402
1·338
405
2·038
404
1·143
403
·343
401
8·131
400
9·978
271a
2·096
48
·225
47
·618
46
·651
49
3·502
30
·635
45
2·183
44
4·076
43
·421
32
3·200
33
·292
34
3·780
15
4·848

Left:
Beccles swing bridge, 3rd edition, 1927 . The new bridge had opened by the time the map appeared.
Crown Copyright

Below left:
Just into the LNER era the bridge was giving serious cause for concern. World War 1 had prevented its earlier replacement. This view is from the Beccles side looking towards Yarmouth, with a local train approaching. *Norfolk Record Office*

Above:
Another view of the old bridge on the same date, 26 July 1923. This time it is seen from the Beccles bank, so a train from left to right would be going from Beccles to Yarmouth. The winding mechanism can be seen to the right of the man on the swinging span.
Norfolk Record Office

Below:
The LNER had resolved to replace both the Beccles and St Olaves bridges together using identical designs, so saving on spares. In this view, taken on 11 February 1926, the turntable for the new bridge is being installed to the east of the old one. *National Railway Museum*

SOUTHERN AREA BET^{WN} BECCLES & ALDEBY.
BRIDGE Nº 476 AT 110M 55C. VIEW OF TURNTABLE.
11·2·26. Nº 1760

Above:
The new bridge is installed and open, and the old one has been demolished. It is 1927, but in this view looking north, the stub of the old main line has been left for the time being as sidings for recovery trains. *Norfolk Record Office*

Below:
The new bridge and its signalbox are seen on 19 October 1926 soon after opening. The new signalbox and generator house on the Beccles bank are in view. The river is on the right, and is much higher than the dyke shown here.
National Railway Museum

Above:
Class C12 No 67387 clears Beccles swing bridge on 6 September 1952 with a Yarmouth to Beccles local. *R. E. Vincent*

concluding that the cost would be around £80,000 for the bridge at St Olaves and £70,000 for Beccles, including the purchase of land and the diversion of track. Because the River Waveney was tidal at that point, approval was needed from both the Board of Trade and the River Authority.

At its December 1923 meeting the LNER's Works Committee gave permission to go ahead, the contracts being awarded to the Horsley Bridge & Engineering Co, which had tendered at £53,566 6s 4d. The new bridges would use Vickers electrical gear operable by just two push buttons. The bridges would be exact duplicates and one set of spares would cover both. They would be battery operated, although Beccles required smaller ones because lighting was not needed there. Each would have five approach spans of 45ft 6in and one half-through span of 65ft 0in, whilst the swinging span would be 55ft 0in and give a headroom of 14ft 6in above high water. Power houses 59ft x 17ft 6in would be provided, which would each contain a power room and battery room, the latter having access only from the outside so that battery acid fumes could not affect the machinery. Generating and motive power would be provided by a double-cylinder two-cycle vertical crude oil engine, with compressed air starting valve and receiver, and a compressor for the initial charging of the receiver operated either by hand or a bolt from the engine. The generator would be 330V dc and of 50kW capacity, capable of charging the batteries completely in one 8hr shift. There would be 120 accumulator cells in lead-lined wooden boxes, with a total capacity of 1,248 Amp-hours. They would be able to open and close the bridge 40 times a day for seven days and have a reserve of 5kW per day for seven days after a full 8hr charge. The 30bhp slewing motor would be series-wound and generate 550rpm, capable of opening or closing the bridge in one minute. A blocking motor (which withdrew or replaced the four blocks on which the bridge rested when across the river) of 15bhp and 220V dc was also to be provided. The switch gear would be built up from black enamelled slate slabs secured to an angle channel framework and stayed to the rear wall of the power house. The contractors boasted that this was 'the last word in Automatic Control' and 'so interlocked that it is impossible to do the wrong thing'. The centre pier was to be carried on a steel caisson 30ft 8in diameter, and all the piers would be sunk by air pressure. The bearings would be on Staffordshire blue bricks, and the steelwork to the LNER's specification.

By the time the Works Committee met on 19 February 1925 the material had been fabricated by Horsley to the value of £16,985, but as the foundations were not yet ready it could not go to site. Payment of two-thirds was authorised. Prices accepted by the LNER had been considerably higher than the initial estimate, being £56,012 for Beccles and £53,560 for St Olaves, on the grounds that the LNER's own work on making up the new formation, track and signalling needed to be accounted. Another span was to be added to the south end of the structure at St Olaves, and the Great Yarmouth Port & Haven Commissioners would require extra dredging. The Horsley company seems to have underestimated the figures by around £9,000 for Beccles and £5,000 for St Olaves, with design modifications further increasing costs by about the same again at Beccles, but a staggering £25,000 at St Olaves. The total costs were thus pushed up by nearly £37,000 over the authorised £150,000.

Land purchases did not account for much of this, and at St Olaves amounted to £60 paid to Lord Somerleyton and £200 to Mr Lee Barber. The work was carried out between 1924 and 1926, traffic being maintained over the old bridges, and by the time the October 1926 *Railway Magazine* appeared the new Beccles bridge was already in use and the old dismantled. Official photographs of St Olaves also show the

Above:
Aldeby station was a considerable distance from the village from which it took its name. The station was in a slight cutting, with the road bridge at the north end being used also for passengers to cross the platforms. The steps to both platforms can be seen in this view, as can the characteristic waiting shelters. The signalbox is behind the camera, and the yard at the south end of the up platform, further from the camera. *Stations UK*

Centre right:
In this 1959 view much has changed. The shelter on the up side has lost its awning, and the down one has been replaced completely. There are no steps to the down platform, and the path down the bank is hidden behind the shelter. The gardens remain well tended even though closure to passengers is imminent. *Stations UK*

Lower right:
From a little further back the layout is clearer, although the station building remains hidden behind the trees. Access to the yard is down the sloping road behind the fence. Staff have a board crossing between platforms. *Stations UK*

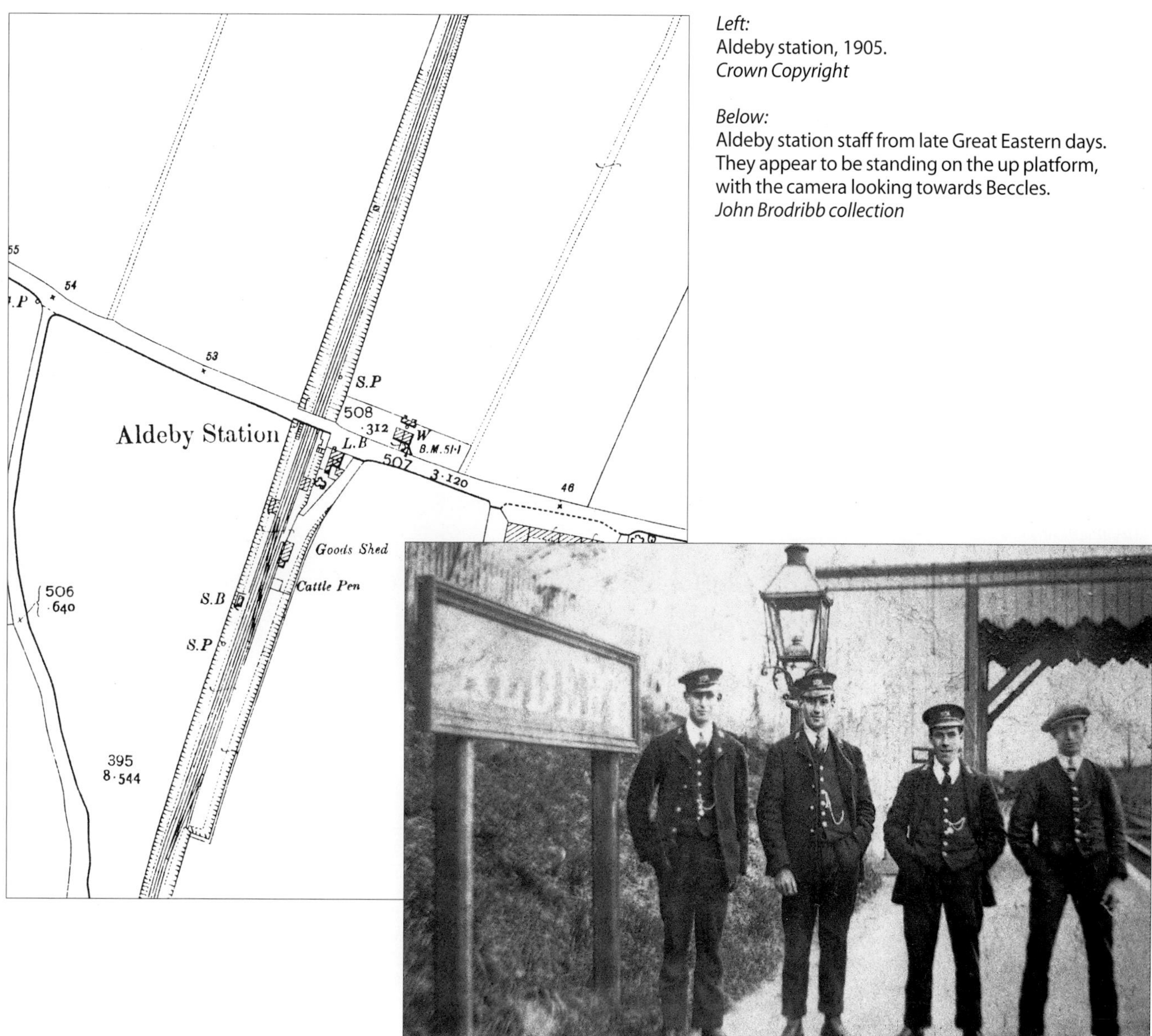

Left:
Aldeby station, 1905.
Crown Copyright

Below:
Aldeby station staff from late Great Eastern days. They appear to be standing on the up platform, with the camera looking towards Beccles.
John Brodribb collection

new bridge in use and the old dismantled by the end of October 1926. The old lines were retained briefly as sidings used by the recovery trains. The speed limit over the new bridges was 30mph, and the severe operational constraints of the two single-line sections were removed.

Having dropped down from the swing bridge the railway had to climb out of the valley towards Aldeby, although by comparison with the profile of the line thus far from Ipswich there was little to do. A brief stretch at 1 in 89 took the line onto the higher ground, and it then passed over three level crossings of minor roads, each with its crossing keeper's cottage, in quick succession before reaching Aldeby station at 112 miles 32 chains, running parallel to the lane between Aldeby and Haddiscoe for almost all the distance between Toft Monks crossing and the station. In fact, although the line passed within a short distance of the village, Aldeby station was not particularly close, and was nearer to Haddiscoe village than the station of that name.

The station was in a cutting, the line being spanned by the bridge carrying the road from Wheatacre and Burgh St Peter to Haddiscoe. The platforms were thus below the general land level and were slightly staggered, the up continuing under the bridge. The main station building was at road level and at right angles to the railway, whilst passengers had a waiting room on each platform. For London passengers this initially was provided in a wooden building with a deep awning, although later it was replaced by a brick structure with no awning. On the other side a small wooden shelter with awning sufficed for many years, later being replaced by a very basic shelter made from corrugated sheet. An old coach body resided on the up platform for many years. Near this was the access to the platform for barrows and carts etc, milk churns being loaded here or at the adjacent dock. A board crossing was provided for staff crossing the line. Passengers reached the platforms by means of steps, on the up side opposite the end of the station building, and on the down from the road bridge to the platform. These were later replaced by a sloping path. The platforms were oil lit up to the end, although electricity had been laid on to the waiting room in later years. Water had to be brought up from a well by means of a pump operated by a big wheel.

The track layout was simple, with a goods loop on the up side south of the Beccles end of the platform. There was a dock spur at the station end, and another spur at the other. A small goods shed on the dock completed the facilities. The signalbox was on the down side, just off the end of the platform, although its opening hours by the 1950s were restricted to the times needed for goods trains to call, or on summer Saturdays. The work here was done by a porter-signalman, who also issued tickets and looked after the usual

Right:
Two views of Fleet Junction soon after closure to passenger traffic. Here the main line has come across the marshes from Aldeby and can be seen rising to go over the Lowestoft line and the river at St Olaves swing bridge. The line branching to the left is the connection to Haddiscoe Yard and remained in use for sugar beet trains to reach Aldeby. The main line is severed and blocked by sleepers beyond the crossover. *Adrian Vaughan collection*

Right:
Looking back towards Aldeby at Fleet Junction. *Adrian Vaughan collection*

Far right:
Fleet Junction, 1902-6. *Crown Copyright*

platform work of despatching trains. The two men on this grade worked alternate earlies and lates, one week cleaning the lamps on earlies (there were only six running signals — distant, home and starter in each direction) and the next week on lates putting them out.

Access to the goods yard was by a trailing connection from the up line at the Beccles end, and by another trailing connection in the down main, crossing the up line by means of a single slip so that it could also function as a crossover. The station handled the usual goods traffic for an agricultural area, but beet was very heavy in season, over 3,000 tons being loaded in 1938. The passenger service was limited, which is not surprising given that the total population of its catchment area was only 487 in 1931.

Most passenger trains did not call at Aldeby, instead rushing through the station without check: soon after World War 2 the limit between Beccles and Yarmouth was 60mph. The line drops down towards Haddiscoe for almost a mile after the station, then levels out to cross the flood plain of the River Waveney once again before rising to pass over the Lowestoft to Norwich line. Originally, of course, the Halesworth, Beccles & Haddiscoe had stayed at river level and curved to the left to make its junction with the Lowestoft Railway, and this line remained as the single-line connection between Fleet Junction and Haddiscoe Junction. This was not used by regular passenger trains, and its normal function was to carry goods. There were no facilities at Haddiscoe High Level, so East Suffolk trains used the Low Level facilities, and there were other workings from the Norwich direction onto the East Suffolk. It certainly saw use as a diversionary route when the main line was closed, and in the days of steam traction relatively little time was lost travelling between Norwich and Ipswich by this route. It was also used by excursion traffic such as football specials, and there was a sharply curved face for use by such trains at the back of the up Lowestoft–Norwich platform. Goods traffic at Haddiscoe was quite heavy, and it handled much beet and other vegetables (4,731 tons in 1938) as well as livestock. The marshes here were much prized as summer grazing for fattening cattle.

The shunting required to get goods trains between Haddiscoe and South Town was complex. Trains were required to use Marsh Junction. Going towards Yarmouth they had to be propelled along the down Lowestoft line to Marsh Junction, crossed over to the up line, and then gain the Yarmouth line by the usual facing connection. Going the other way, they ran onto the down Lowestoft line from St Olaves Swing Bridge Junction, backed over the crossover

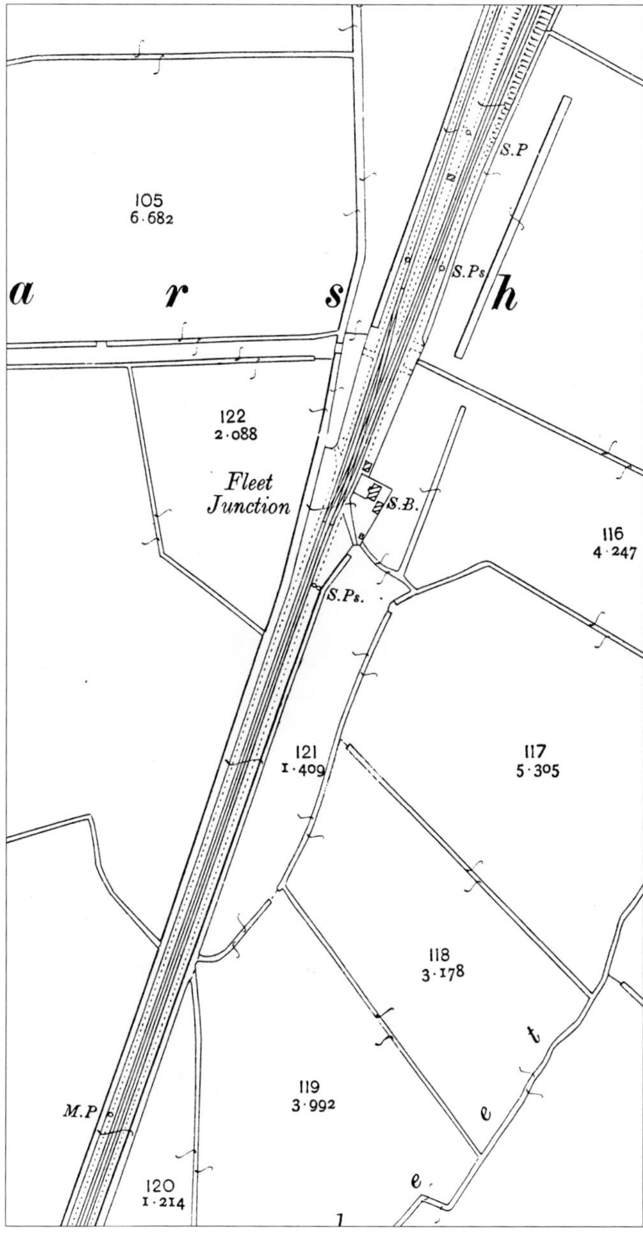

onto the up Lowestoft line and were then set back along this line to the yard.

In railway terms Haddiscoe was a complex place. It had started as the single-track Lowestoft Railway, itself an offshoot of the original line between Norwich and Yarmouth. Then the Halesworth, Beccles & Haddiscoe arrived, with its junction facing Norwich and the station remaining near the bridge where the main road, latterly the A143, crossed Peto's New Cut. Haddiscoe station was thus served by trains of two companies on two routes. Then the Yarmouth & Haddiscoe Railway arrived, extending onwards from the HB&H and becoming the East Suffolk main line, and climbing to cross the Lowestoft Railway about half a mile east of Haddiscoe bridge. The two lines remained connected between Fleet Junction and Haddiscoe Yard, and then also from April 1872 by a new single-track connection 31 chains long between Marsh Junction and St Olaves Swing Bridge Junction, allowing a Lowestoft to Yarmouth South Town service to operate. The staff for this line was square and yellow, contrasting with those for Marsh Junction to Somerleyton (triangular, red) and Marsh Junction to Haddiscoe (round and blue). Whilst the East Suffolk was double track when it opened, the Lowestoft line was progressively doubled and facilities increased over a long period.

The next major development came in 1879. The Board of Trade had been notified by the Great Eastern of extensive works in the area, the most important part of which was the building of a new two-level station, to be called 'St Olaves Exchange Station', although this had originally been proposed as 'St Olaves Bridge'. In practice it continued to appear in the timetables as 'St Olaves Junction'. Maj-Gen Hutchinson expressed grave concerns about its incompleteness at the time of his inspection in mid-May, although it had opened under provisional sanction on 1 May. There were no shelters at all at the High Level, and fencing was required at Low Level to stop passengers getting onto the lines. Lamps were needed on the platforms, and railings were needed along the outside of the viaduct to stop passengers stepping over the edge if an East Suffolk train stopped short. Maj-Gen Hutchinson also felt that a luggage lift was needed between High and Low Level, although the GER pointed out that most passengers went out and back the same day, and there was not much luggage. At the time there were long ramps between the two levels, and Maj-Gen Hutchinson wanted more direct stairs, and the risers on the existing steps to be closed in 'for decency's sake'. He did not recommend opening until all this work had been done and reinspected, but on the other hand felt that closure would cause great inconvenience.

Because it was still single there was only one Low Level platform on the river side of the Lowestoft line to the east of the East Suffolk bridge. The line from Fleet Junction curved round towards Norwich and ran parallel with the single line, but made no connection with it until reaching the old station, thus giving the appearance of double track for a short distance. In February 1886 Haddiscoe Junction signalbox was opened to control a revised layout involving additional passenger lines and sidings. The line from Fleet Junction now terminated in a bay platform on the south side of Haddiscoe's original station. A pair of crossovers to the east of the new box marked the point where the two single lines, from Lowestoft and Fleet Junction, became double, and another pair between the box and the passenger station connected the single line to Reedham and the bay platform. This marked the first genuine double track at this location. Work had taken place at Fleet Junction early in 1880, when the layout of a double junction from the main line going back to a single track on the Reedham line took more or less its final form, and the signalbox was provided. The section between Fleet Junction and Haddiscoe was controlled by a triangular red staff, with tickets also being used.

In 1904 a great deal of work was undertaken on the line between Reedham and Lowestoft which also had an important bearing on the East Suffolk. The section between Reedham station and Marsh Junction had been single track, with the line from Fleet Junction coming alongside at Haddiscoe Yard. The old layout was swept away and the route became double track, with a new Reedham swing bridge being built alongside the old single-track structure and brought into use in June 1904. Meantime a new Haddiscoe station was built 700yd on the Lowestoft side of the old, replacing the former St Olaves Junction or Herringfleet Low Level exchange platform, and allowing the original Haddiscoe station to close. The High Level exchange platforms on the East Suffolk were also renamed Haddiscoe, and the station opened for the public to start and finish their journeys on 9 May 1904. New signalboxes were provided at Haddiscoe Yard, Haddiscoe Junction, Reedham swing bridge and Reedham station, and the Sykes lock-and-block system introduced over the new double lines. A 25mph speed limit was enforced while the new lines were consolidated.

Right:
The other end of the line from Fleet Junction. There was a platform face at Haddiscoe Low Level, although it was never used by regular passenger trains. Haddiscoe Yard box is just visible in the distance. *Adrian Vaughan collection*

Far right:
Haddiscoe High Level and Low Level stations, St Olaves swing bridge and St Olaves station, 1905. Note Haddiscoe old station is intact and shown as disused. *Crown Copyright*

Right:
Looking towards Lowestoft at Haddiscoe Low Level, with the station straight ahead and the East Suffolk bridge visible in the background. The line to Fleet Junction branches away on the right. *Adrian Vaughan collection*

Below:
A year or so earlier, in 1959, a local East Suffolk train can be seen on the main line, while the signalling can also still be seen. *Stations UK*

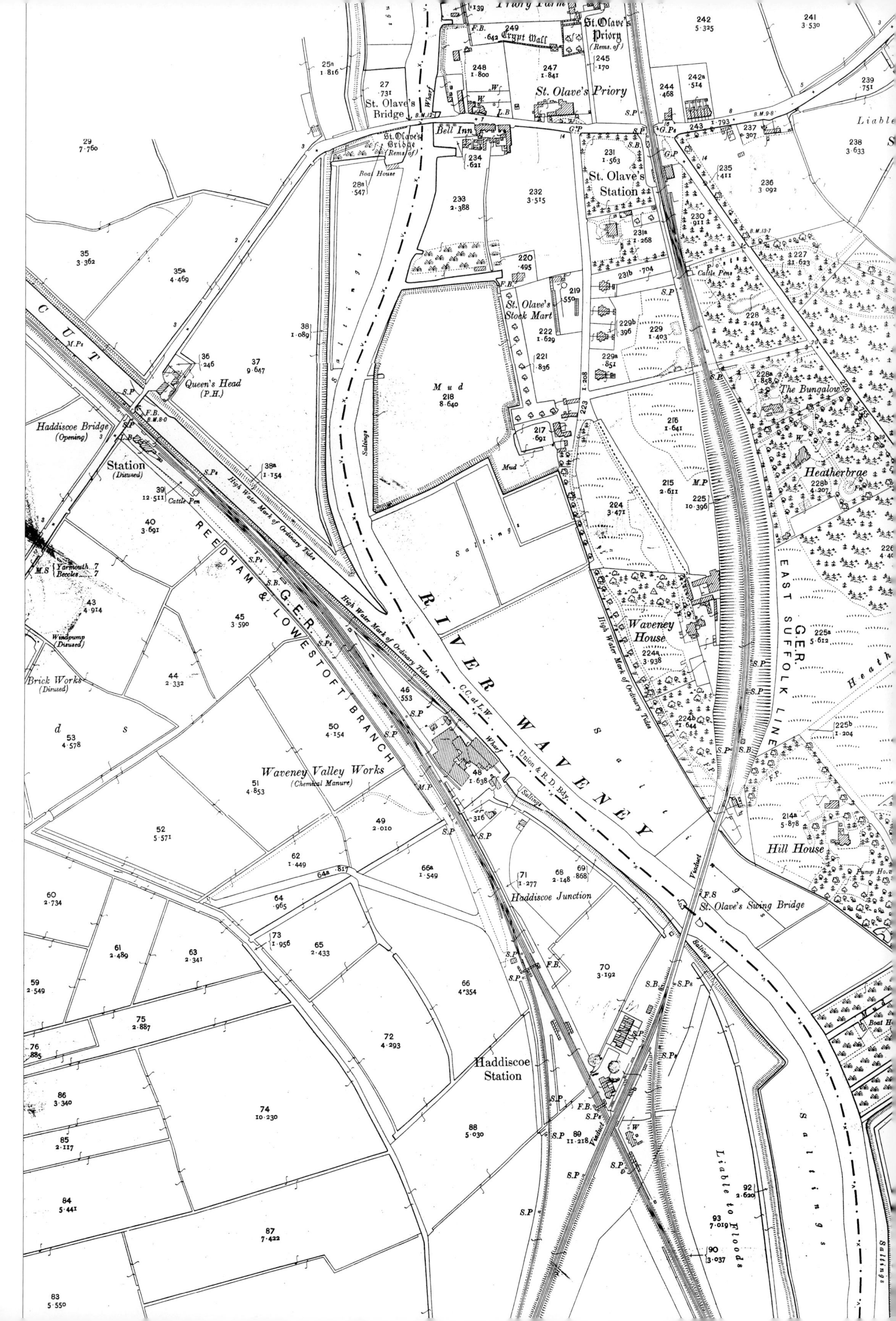
St. Olave's Priory
Crypt Wall
St. Olave's Bridge
Bell Inn
St. Olave's Bridge (Rems. of)
Boat House
St. Olave's Station
St. Olave's Stock Mart
Mud
Queen's Head (P.H.)
Haddiscoe Bridge (Opening)
Station (Disused)
CUT
REEDHAM & LOWESTOFT BRANCH
G.E.R.
High Water Mark of Ordinary Tides
RIVER WAVENEY
Saltings
Windpump (Disused)
Brick Works (Disused)
Waveney Valley Works (Chemical Manure)
Waveney House
The Bungalow
Heatherbrae
EAST SUFFOLK LINE
Hill House
Union & R.D. Bdy.
C.C. at L.W.
Wharf
Haddiscoe Junction
St. Olave's Swing Bridge
Viaduct
Haddiscoe Station
Liable to Floods
Cattle Pens
Cattle Pen

Above:
Haddiscoe Yard, with the signalbox just visible in the background. This 1911 view is looking towards Norwich, with the New Cut on the right, and the railway-owned toll bridge visible in the background. The original Halesworth, Beccles & Haddiscoe station was by this bridge, with the HB&H joining it via the curve from what later became Fleet Junction. *HMRS Hilton Collection*

Upper right:
The High Level platforms at Haddiscoe in 1959, looking towards St Olaves, with the swing bridge signalbox and other buildings evident. *Stations UK*

Lower right:
Only a few short years after closure the track has been lifted and the whole area is overgrown. Much of this still exists, but is in private hands and is not accessible. *Lens of Sutton*

Above:
The 12.10pm train from Yarmouth South Town to Liverpool Street, headed by Class B1 No 61253, crosses St Olaves swing bridge as it approaches Haddiscoe High Level on 21 April 1954. *R. E. Vincent*

The track over St Olaves swing bridge, No 481, was altered to become single instead of being gauntleted in June 1909, but instead of providing new signalboxes a new frame was installed in St Olaves Junction box, and St Olaves station box and signalling was modified. The small cabin on the north side of the river was retained, as at Beccles. As recounted earlier, the swing bridge was renewed at the same time as Beccles, and the new one opened by October 1926. At this point the railway crossed back into Suffolk, the county boundary not being changed until the local government reforms of 1974, long after the line had closed. The deviated line was to the east of the original, and the change necessitated some heavy earthworks in the deep cutting immediately to the north of the bridge. The line here swung round towards the northwest and the cutting avoided the need to climb to St Olaves station (115 miles 17 chains) about three-quarters of a mile from the High Level platforms at Haddiscoe. The station and bridge took their names from the ruined Augustinian priory nearby, and in fact were in the parish of Herringfleet, the name also given to the hills on the north side of the River Waveney here.

The East Suffolk crossed the main road to Yarmouth by means of a level crossing at the north end of the station, controlled by the station signalbox on the down side. As with all the boxes north of Fleet Junction, St Olaves station was open for all trains shown in the working timetable, plus others specially advised. The population of Herringfleet was very small — only 289 in 1931 — although the station had facilities to handle all classes of traffic. Its two platforms were immediately to the south of the main road, with the station building on the up side. The entrance for passengers and goods vehicles was just round the corner from the level crossing, on the road to Somerleyton. The building was of typical pattern with the main structure parallel to the tracks, a slate hipped-roof structure and with an awning on the platform and approach sides. A barrow crossing connected the two platforms by the signalbox, and the main nameboard on the up side proclaimed that the station was 'for Fritton'. A feature of the station was the large number of pine trees, themselves characteristic of the area to the north known as Fritton Warren. On the down platform there was an unusual brick-built shelter with its elliptical roof overhanging and providing an awning all round it, as if on an island platform.

There was a single siding on the up side, running back behind the passenger platform, and also having a loading dock near the station building. The siding extended southwards to a total length of just under 200yd, with hardstanding alongside for loading and unloading. There were cattle pens about half-way along. The only rail access to the siding was

Above:
On 15 October 1924 replacement work was in full swing. St Olaves Swing Bridge Junction box is just visible on the right. There is a feast for students of civil engineering here! *National Railway Museum*

Below:
Much progress has been made since the previous photograph. This was taken on 11 February 1926, and the new piers are complete, with the capping in place on the turntable. The extent of the earthworks needed to widen the cutting on the north bank can be appreciated in this view. *National Railway Museum*

Above:
By 9 June 1926 the new swinging span was being assembled on site, with temporary track to both sides of the new bridge.
National Railway Museum

Below:
When this photograph was taken on 27 October 1926 the new bridge was operational and the old had been removed, although the piers had yet to be demolished. The former main line remains as a siding and still runs onto the approach trestle on the north side.
National Railway Museum

Right:
St Olaves station was only a short distance to the north of Haddiscoe, and sported one of the standard buildings in the small size, standing on the up platform, seen in this 1951 view. The main road from Beccles to Yarmouth goes over the level crossing. *Stations UK*

Right:
A 1954 view looking from the level crossing back in the direction of the bridge, with the layout of the passenger station clearly visible. The nameboard reads 'St Olaves for Fritton'. *Stations UK*

Right:
A much earlier view, but again looking south from the level crossing. *Lens of Sutton*

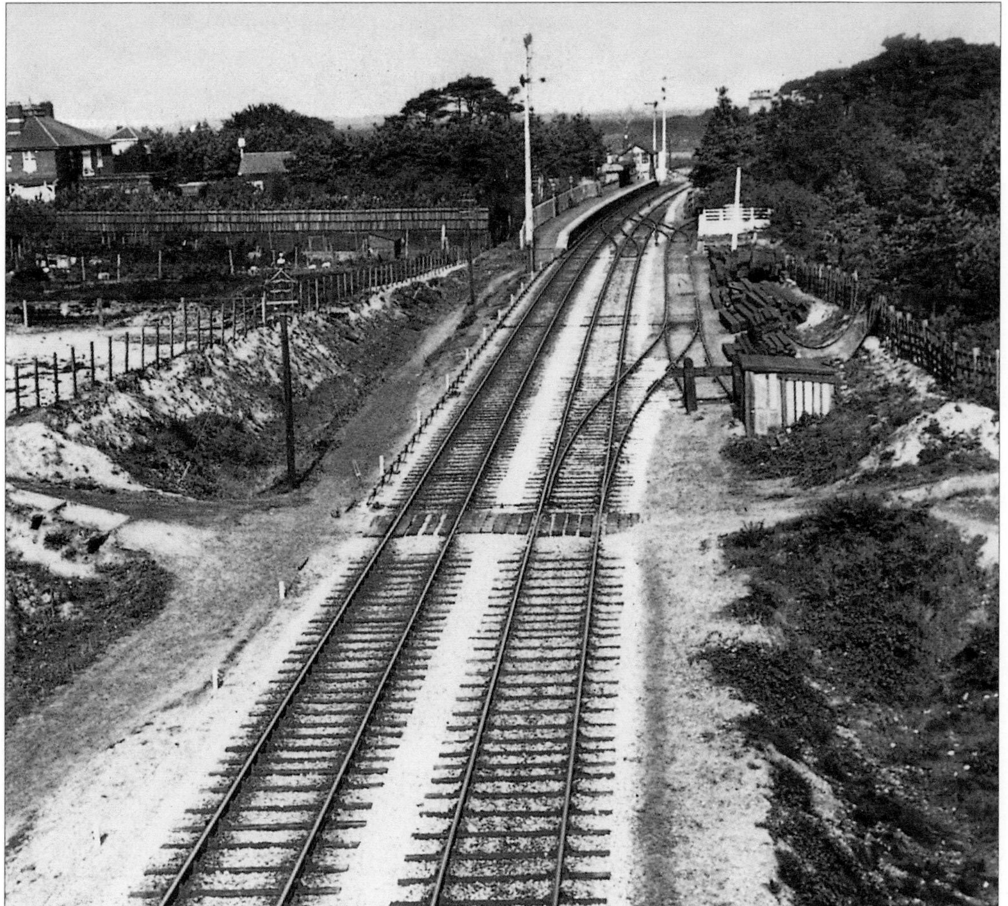

Above:
St Olaves already looks very sad in this photograph taken a few months after closure, early in 1960. The gates have gone, the lamps, signs and nameboards have been removed and the station will soon be no more than a memory.
Eastern Counties Newspapers

Left:
The track layout at St Olaves is neatly summed up in this photograph, looking north towards the station in 1911. The down platform and signalbox are in view, together with the cattle pens on the up side.
HMRS Hilton Collection

Above:
Two 1911 views of Belton.
This one peers through the crossing gate and looks towards Yarmouth, clearly showing the smaller pattern of station building and the small goods shed. *HMRS Hilton Collection*

Below:
This 1911 view is taken from the top of the up starting signal, again looking towards Yarmouth. The track layout is very clear, with carts working in the station yard and their horses waiting patiently. The extension to the down platform is visible, as is the down starter, which post also carries the up home signal. The land is intensively cultivated behind the down platform. *HMRS Hilton Collection*

Right:
Earlier days at Belton, looking towards Yarmouth, before the down platform was rebuilt. The station building is of the typical smaller type. The goods facilities are on the up side beyond the platform. *Stations UK*

by a trailing connection from the down line which crossed the up at the end of the up platform; there was also a trailing crossover in the main line a very short distance on the Haddiscoe side of this.

Travelling onwards from St Olaves trains continued their undulating but fairly undemanding course. The line swept round to head northeastwards again as it traversed Fritton Warren, an open heathland area running down to the River Waveney to the west. This has now changed greatly, having been forested since the railway closed. The line now headed almost straight for Yarmouth, over the level crossing of Staith Road in the middle of the Warren, passing Howard's Common to the north and Belton Common to the south before reaching Belton & Burgh station at 117 miles 58 chains. When the line was constructed this was still a fairly remote part of Suffolk. By 1891 the population of the area was only 752, and had risen to 833 40 years later. Being near the coast and the surrounding soil light and sandy, almost all of it was used for market gardening, and the station loaded a substantial tonnage of vegetables — 1,068 in 1938.

Belton & Burgh station was situated by a minor road which described a circuit of the village. It had been simply Belton until renamed by the LNER from 1 July 1923, the company providing a large enamelled nameboard on the end of the station building to demonstrate this. The platforms and other facilities were on the Yarmouth side of the level crossing, the station building being on the up side. As usual the awning here was on the platform side, although there was another sheltered area formed on the south side, where two rooms were built onto the end of the building. The main building had been extended in 1898 with a flat-roofed section at the north end to provide extra accommodation for the stationmaster, and there was a brick-built store and a wooden lock-up next to it further along the platform. This all gave the up platform a rather cluttered appearance, whilst the down side sported only a small brick shelter with a sloping roof. Goods facilities were provided by a single siding on the up side at the Yarmouth end, initially barely 60yd long, and trailing from the up main line. Later this was more than doubled in length, with a very short headshunt. The down platform had been greatly extended in 1898, but the up remained very short, since the siding prevented its lengthening.

North of Belton the line went into a shallow cutting after a short distance, passed under the Bell Lane bridge and then over two road bridges in quick succession, the first St John's Road by the King's Head pub. It continued through Bradwell on a succession of shallow cuttings or embankments. Passing close by Bradwell House to its right and Gapton Hall to its

Right:
In contrast, Belton & Burgh station in the summer of 1959. The up platform has been rebuilt, although it remains the same length as before. A large nameboard appeared on the end of the station building, although the passenger service was always fairly limited. Goods traffic appears still to be substantial even though complete closure is very near. *Stations UK*

Right:
Belton station, 1882-7.
Crown Copyright

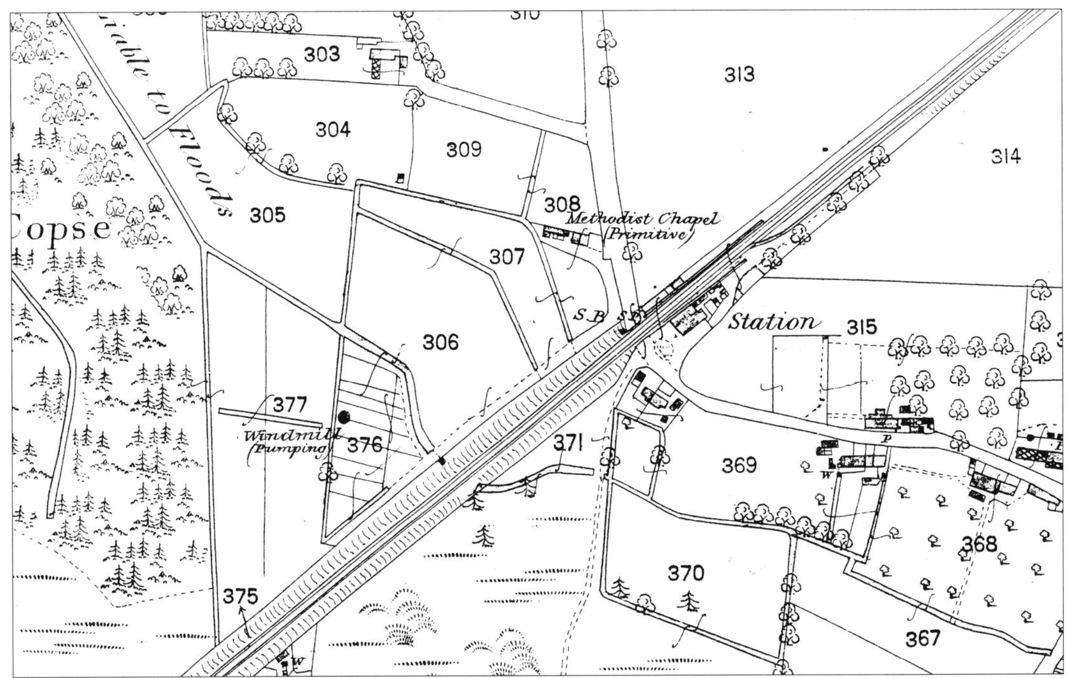

left, the line finally crossed back into Norfolk just short of MP121 and into the confines of the Great Yarmouth municipal boundary. The Norfolk & Suffolk Joint Committee's line to Lowestoft opened on Monday 13 July 1903, and the East Suffolk soon passed under the connecting Midland & Great Northern (M&GN) line across Breydon Water to Yarmouth Beach, with the former trailing in at Yarmouth South Town Junction on the east side a few chains further on. This marked the limits of the terminal station, and in later years the junction signalbox was abolished and control taken from the station box. It ceased to be a junction when the East Suffolk main line closed in 1959.

Below:
A very fine 1911 view looking towards London from a signal just to the south of the station box at Yarmouth South Town. The main lines are the two right-hand tracks, and the junction box is faintly visible to the right of the engine shed. *HMRS Hilton Collection*

Yarmouth South Town (121 miles 59 chains) was an imposing station which grew and developed much over the years. It was well placed to serve Yarmouth, being a very short distance from Southtown Bridge — later the Haven Bridge — connecting Cobholm and Southtown with the more easterly original area of town which had always been in Norfolk. Regarding spelling, this part of Yarmouth has always been referred to as Southtown, while the railway always called the station South Town. When the East Suffolk was first built even the terminus was still in Suffolk, since although the Borough of Yarmouth spanned the Yare and included Southtown, the river remained the county boundary. This was not altered until 1891, when Southtown and Gorleston were transferred to Norfolk.

The station started with two platforms, one for arrivals and one for departures, with a siding in between them. The brick station building stood across the end of the platforms and presented an impressive façade to the approaching passenger.

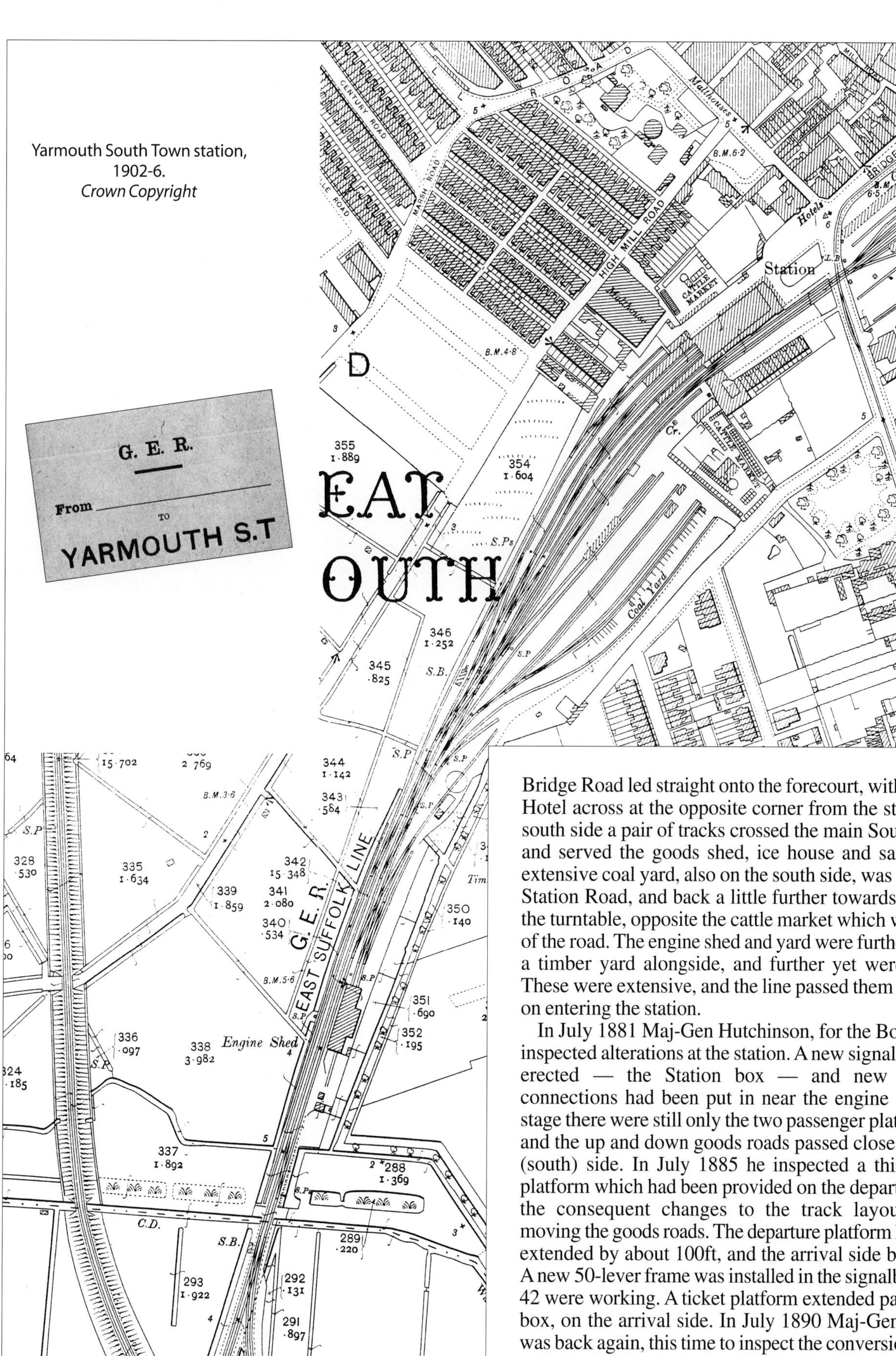

Yarmouth South Town station, 1902-6. *Crown Copyright*

Bridge Road led straight onto the forecourt, with the Railway Hotel across at the opposite corner from the station. On the south side a pair of tracks crossed the main Southtown Road and served the goods shed, ice house and saw mills. The extensive coal yard, also on the south side, was reached from Station Road, and back a little further towards Beccles was the turntable, opposite the cattle market which was at the end of the road. The engine shed and yard were further again, with a timber yard alongside, and further yet were allotments. These were extensive, and the line passed them on both sides on entering the station.

In July 1881 Maj-Gen Hutchinson, for the Board of Trade, inspected alterations at the station. A new signalbox had been erected — the Station box — and new sidings and connections had been put in near the engine shed. At this stage there were still only the two passenger platforms in use, and the up and down goods roads passed close by on the up (south) side. In July 1885 he inspected a third passenger platform which had been provided on the departure side, and the consequent changes to the track layout, including moving the goods roads. The departure platform had also been extended by about 100ft, and the arrival side by about 30ft. A new 50-lever frame was installed in the signalbox, of which 42 were working. A ticket platform extended past the signalbox, on the arrival side. In July 1890 Maj-Gen Hutchinson was back again, this time to inspect the conversion of a siding at the back of the arrival platform into a dock road to be used for the departure of trains. By now the main arrival platform was around 460ft in length and the departure one 520ft, with their outer faces somewhat shorter. The signalbox had been relocked and now had 48 working levers. The platforms were numbered from south to north, so that the departure side bay was No 1, the main departure platform No 2, main arrival No 3 and arrival side bay No 4. By the time of Maj Addison's

Above:
Class F6 No 67218 leaves Yarmouth South Town with the 2.15pm for Beccles on 19 May 1955, the station platforms just visible in the background. The original signalbox had been destroyed during World War 2 and was replaced by the modern brick structure shown here. *Peter Punchard collection*

Below:
An unusual view showing the lever frame in Yarmouth South Town signalbox. Almost every lever is in use; where the handle has been shortened it indicated that it operates something electrically and the usual force is not needed. Although it had had its own box when first opened, Yarmouth South Town Junction was also operated by the station signalbox. *National Railway Museum*

Above:
Dated 2 February 1933, this photograph is taken from Platform 3 and shows a wealth of detail. 'Claud' No 8880 leaves with an up local service, with more coaches on the centre road and in Platform 4. The construction of the canopies and train shed is very clear.
National Railway Museum

Below:
On the same date as the photograph above, the photographer also took this view inside the train shed, again from Platform 3, and again with a wealth of detail, especially of the coaches. There is a plethora of enamel advertising signs; note also the construction of the smoke vents overhead.
National Railway Museum

BOVRIL
BOVRIL
SUTTONS SEEDS
Worthington
NATIONAL
YARMOUTH, SOUTH TOWN STATION.
INTERIOR FROM ARRIVAL PLATFORM.
2·2·'33 — 4152.

Right:
Activity in the platforms at South Town, although whether shunting or a local departing is not quite clear. Where the photographer is standing (No 3) was the main arrival platform, with No 4 being added as an outer face later. The coaches stand in the main departure platform (No 2), the outer face again being added later. Modernisation of the signalling made the layout much more flexible. The goods lines went past the station on the right of this picture. *Stations UK*

Above:
A local train about to leave from Platform 3 in the charge of No 67199, probably to Beccles but possibly extended as far as Saxmundham, or alternatively to Lowestoft via Gorleston. The station has been rebuilt, as evidenced by the new lighting and the construction of the platform. *Ian Allan Library*

Right:
Taken from the very end of Platforms 1 and 2, a two-car Class 101 Metro-Cammell DMU leaves from Platform 3 on 11 September 1963. The view illustrates the new layout of the platforms. *S. Creer*

Above:
A closer view of the frontage of South Town station in British Railways days.
Eastern Counties Newspapers

Below:
Seen from outside the Railway Hotel, South Town station stands facing the town: a well-laid out, spacious forecourt and a simple and elegant building. The goods lines go past the building on the left. All of this has been swept away, and apart from some of the goods station there is now no trace of the East Suffolk in Yarmouth. *National Railway Museum*

Above:
Another view of the interior of South Town station, but this time after the 1953 rebuilding. The awnings have been completely rebuilt and there is no longer any cover over the tracks. The circulating area has been extended and remains covered, and there is much more glass, making everywhere much lighter. Sadly, the rebuilding did not ensure a long life for the station.
National Railway Museum

Right:
A train is about to leave from Platform 3, and the inspector checks passengers' tickets.
Eastern Counties Newspapers

Above:
Looking over the buffers from inside the station, an express waits to leave from Platform 2 in 1956. The refreshment room is through the door on the right, or passengers could buy their papers from the bookstall. They could also print out their name on an aluminium strip using the machine standing against the railings. *Stations UK*

Right:
From the side window this is the view looking towards the Haven Bridge and town centre from South Town station. Traffic on Beccles Road looks quite light. The goods station is visible behind the row of advertising hoardings, and the bus disappearing past the station building is crossing the tracks leading into it.
National Railway Museum

1895 inspection the signalbox needed more levers, now having 51 working and five spare, having been necessitated by further changes to the connections between the up line and goods sidings.

In 1903 the Norfolk & Suffolk Joint line from Lowestoft was opened, and brought a sudden increase in traffic to South Town station. A new junction was required about a quarter mile on the Beccles side of the station, and the platforms were lengthened again, the departure side by about 100ft and the arrival by 200ft. The station signalbox was replaced and a new box provided at the junction, with much new trackwork giving increased flexibility of operation. The new line and works had to be inspected, and H. G. Drury, the GER's superintendent of the line, suggested to Col von Donop of the Board of Trade that he take the 3.24pm express train to Yarmouth on Monday 20 July, arriving at 6.40pm, and stay at the Queens Hotel, then one of the finest. 'If,' he went on, 'you commence your inspection at Yarmouth at 6.15am on the Tuesday morning we could finish in time to return to the hotel for Breakfast and should you desire to go over the New Line to look at the few requirements named in your report (which have been carried out) I will arrange for a Special to leave Yarmouth South Town at 9.35am reaching Lowestoft about 10.30am.' Whether they finished within the hour that Drury expected, and so had their breakfast back at the hotel, is not recorded. The new line had opened for public traffic on 13 July, although trains had been running for the benefit of the contractors with a Great Eastern pilotman and guard for most of the year.

Yarmouth had three terminal stations, with Vauxhall serving the Great Eastern lines to Norwich, and Beach the

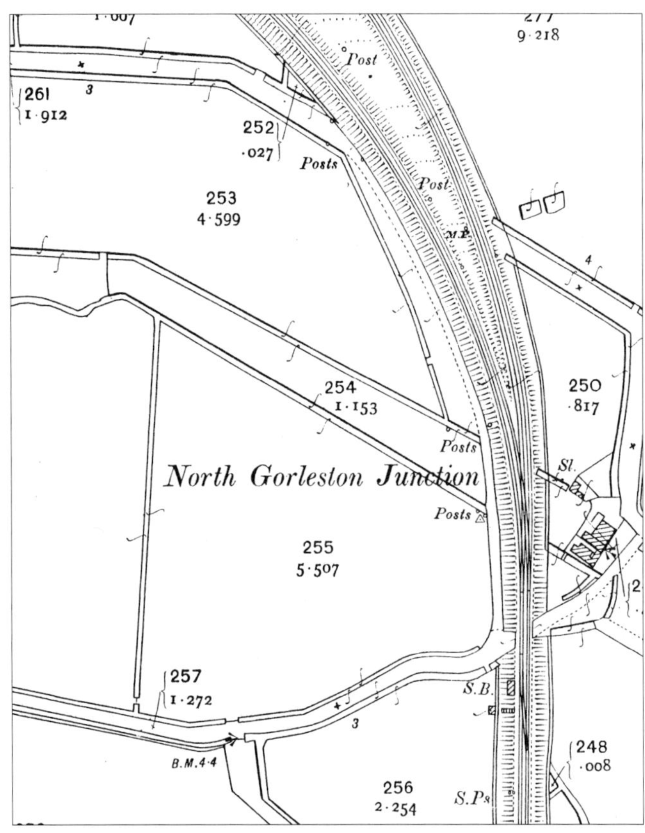

M&GN route to the Midlands via Melton Constable. The two Great Eastern stations worked together in many respects, so that railway staff were allocated to Yarmouth rather than one particular station. This was certainly true of footplate grades, and their duties saw them working over the East Suffolk, the Norfolk & Suffolk Joint to Lowestoft, the lines to Norwich and the tramways, not to be confused with the municipal undertakings. The docks had an extensive system and employed Sentinel geared locomotives, which could often be seen working their way through the streets. South Town did not have a direct connection with this system, although it was in theory possible to move by rail between any of the stations. In this case it would have necessitated going as far as North Gorleston Junction on the Joint line, and then via the M&GN over Breydon swing bridge into the Beach station. Because of this lack of a direct tramway connection fish traffic out of Yarmouth via the East Suffolk was taken by lorry from the quayside to the station for loading. Usually it would be packed into barrels, the top filled with salt, and the lid knocked on. Goods traffic was heavy, as befitted a major port, although the LNER did not break it down between stations in the annual returns. In 1938 the principal loadings were (in tons) ale and porter (2,721 — Lacon's was a major company), coal tar (2,389), timber (2,135), grain (1,242 — this included malt: Watney, Combe & Reid had its head office in Southtown High Road, and also W. D. & A. E. Walker and R. S. Watling & Son had maltings in the Borough), textiles and clothing (847) and livestock (375).

Above:
North Gorleston Junction, 1902-6. This is not on the East Suffolk Railway strictly speaking. The branch on the left hand side is the M&GN to Yarmouth Beach via Breydon bridge; the remainder is the Norfolk & Suffolk Joint (to Yarmouth South Town at top, Lowestoft at bottom.
Crown Copyright

Right:
An air of complete dereliction on the platform side at the same time, with the arrival platforms partly demolished. The station concourse had been walled in, as can be seen here, before the train service was withdrawn.
David Pearce

Right:
After final closure in 1970 the station was taken over for industrial use, although the clock and BR station name were left in place. This is how it looked on 4 May 1975.
David Pearce

—8—

Framlingham Branch

Left:
An Edwardian view of the platform at Marlesford, with a wealth of enamel advertisements, a weighing machine and an astonishing array of point rodding passing at the foot of the platform. A member of the station staff looks on.
Alan Taylor collection

THE line to Framlingham was the most southerly of the true East Suffolk branches in its junction with the main line. This was at Wickham Market Junction, the signalbox and physical connection being immediately to the north of Blackstock crossing. Branch trains almost always started from Wickham Market station, usually waiting in a siding on the down side, and sometimes in the goods shed itself, emerging into the down platform after the main-line train had gone. In the other direction branch passenger trains used the outer face of the island platform, so providing a convenient onward connection.

Having travelled the distance of just under a mile to the branch junction, trains diverged sharply from the main line, curving through more than 90° to take up a roughly north-westerly direction. Trains had to slow by the signalbox, a few yards before the junction, to collect the single-line staff, which was round and green, the branch being worked on the one-engine-in-steam principle since 25 January 1892, when the Great Eastern deposited a sealed certificate with the Board of Trade to this effect. ('Sealed' in this sense means that the document had the company's seal attached to it.) Tickets were not used for train working on the branch. It was also possible to use the branch as a refuge when trains needed to be passed by more important workings. If this happened, the signalman at the junction had to advise the stationmaster at Framlingham, who in turn had to advise the driver and guard of the branch train when they left to proceed cautiously when approaching the junction signals. It could even be done after the branch had closed for the night, although Framlingham had to be advised as soon as it opened if the train was still on the single line. The manoeuvre could not be performed during fog or falling snow unless fogmen were stationed at the branch distant and outer home signals.

The first half of the curve onto the branch was in a cutting, with Blackstock Wood on the right. The line then passed through another section of alder carr and quickly reached Marlesford station at 86 miles 23 chains, only about 1¾ miles from Wickham Market. There was a level crossing at the Framlingham end over what is now the A12. The village was small and part of it straggled along the main road, having a population of only 375 in 1891, which actually fell to 337 in 1931. Marlesford Bridge, over the River Ore, was a few yards to the north of the level crossing, and also had a ford to one side; the branch was very close to the river for its entire length. The single platform, which was never extended, was on the north side of the line, with the station building, at the level crossing end, of the standard design and executed in white brick. Its awnings provided shelter along the platform and the west end, and an old carriage body stood next to it at the other end. This is thought to have arrived around 1902 and was most likely to have been used as a lock-up store. The roof of the building was surmounted by a pair of chimney stacks, linked to form a housing for the station bell.

The small signalbox stood on the opposite side of the track and controlled the level crossing, although it was replaced in the early 1930s by a ground frame. In 1862 the original siding had been installed for a Mr Welton, who had not paid for it, but would do so if he could be confirmed as having possession. It was on the south side of the line opposite the passenger platform, and in its heyday had access from both ends. There was a crossover at the level crossing so that a very short headshunt was created running up to the main road, and another crossover at the other end, making a loop all of 180ft long. These 'headshunts' — more likely safety traps — appeared between the surveys for the 1882 and 1904 Ordnance Survey map editions. Towards the end of 1903 a

Right:
Marlesford level crossing and signalbox in 1912, looking north. This bustling main road is now the A12!
Alan Taylor collection

Above:
Marlesford, looking from the level crossing back towards Wickham Market. The station has reached its maximum development, with access to the siding from this end, the signalbox in operation and the siding into Gooderham & Heyward's mills beyond the far end of the platform. The stationmaster and two of his staff pose for the camera.
Alan Taylor collection

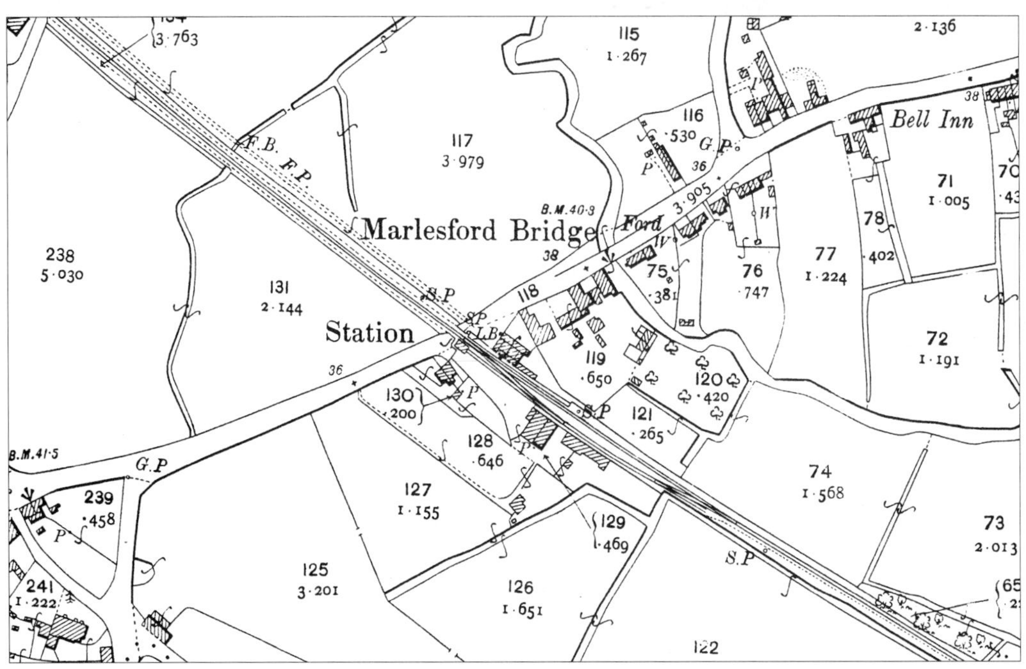

Right:
Marlesford station, 1902-6.
Crown Copyright

Above:
Passenger services had been withdrawn at the end of the 1954, although Marlesford still looks smart. The nameboard has gone, as have the platform lamps, barrows and trolleys. The ground frame which long ago replaced the signalbox can just be seen over the fence.
Stations UK

Left:
Marlesford station on 6 October 1952, looking towards the level crossing and Framlingham.
Rex Conway collection

new siding was built for Gooderham & Heyward, who had mills between the river and the station and whose head office was at the maltings at Snape. A set of points facing trains bound for Framlingham gave access via a gate to this siding running behind the station building. The connection and associated signals were worked from the existing signalbox, which now had 21 levers including one spare. The Ordnance Survey seems not to have noticed it, since the siding was not shown on either edition of the 25in OS map mentioned above, although it almost certainly survived to the final closure. An unusual operating provision, shown in the 1947 Sectional Appendix in connection with goods workings, was that up to six wagons could be propelled along the down main line from Wickham Market station to the junction and then along the branch to Marlesford. This tends to indicate that there was no other means of getting the wagons into the sidings in the absence of a loop, with towing not being permitted.

The station was hit during the war by a flying bomb which fell at 7.10pm nearby, shattering some of the windows in the station building. Marlesford had its moment of glory in 1956, after the end of the passenger service, when the Royal Train carrying the Duke of Edinburgh was stabled overnight there. Class B1 4-6-0 No 61252 was attached at the rear to provide steam heating, and also to haul the train back to the junction prior to continuation to Lowestoft. Unfortunately it made a rather sudden start, which caused the Duke to utter some decidedly colourful language and put his head out of the window, only to spy Dr Ian Allen photographing the train. The Duke having satisfied himself of the good doctor's motives, the train set out, being taken on down the main line by the train engine, No 61399.

Trains from Wickham Market had dropped down into Marlesford station, and having crossed the main road started to rise again towards the terminus. After a very short distance the line crossed the drive leading to Lime House and entered a short cutting. Shortly after this came Marlesford Street crossing, this time over the minor road leading to the main part of the village, which forded the River Ore on the north side.

Right:
An interesting viewpoint for Marlesford church, looking across the minor level crossing on the Framlingham side of the station. Marlesford Hall is in the distance. *Alan Taylor collection*

Above:
Class F6 No 67220 approaches Marlesford with an up goods train in 1952. The lineside allotment was a feature of most rural lines, now long gone with the staff and the lines themselves.
Rex Conway collection

Right:
No D5045 sets back into the siding at Marlesford on 12 April 1965, not long before withdrawal of goods services from the station. *H. N. James*

Left:
Hacheston Halt, around 1950. They don't come much more basic than this. *Stations UK*

Below:
Hacheston Halt, 1882-7. The halt did not appear until 1923.
Crown Copyright

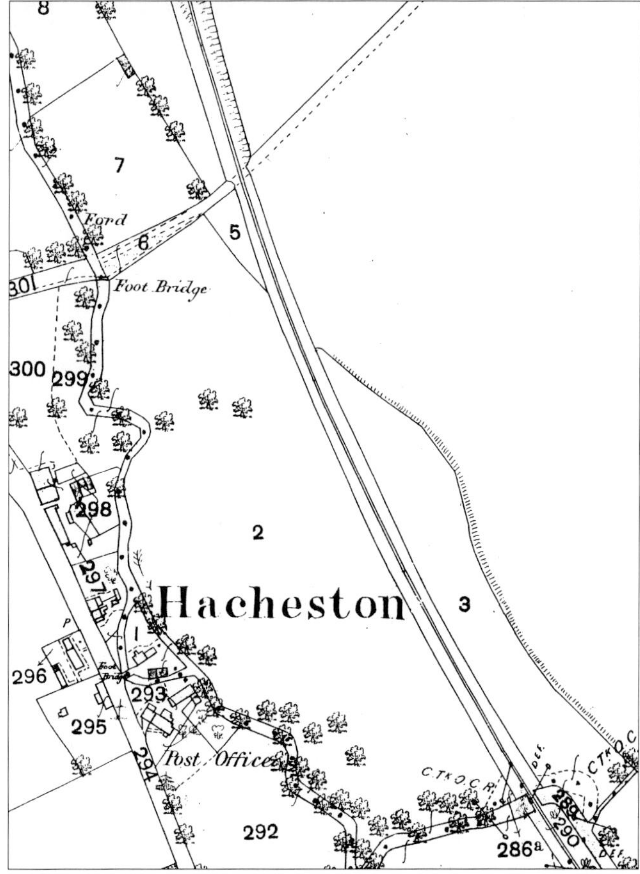

Another short cutting preceded a bridge over the river, all the while the branch heading in a northwesterly direction along the river valley towards Hacheston. The railway had put the river into a straight channel on the east side of the line, while the original meandered about on the west. The two came together again just before the halt was reached at 87 miles 58 chains. This opened very late in the day, in 1923, as part of a concerted programme started by the Great Eastern in 1922 and continued by the LNER in the early years of the Grouping. It was purely a ground level affair on the west side of the line, nearer the main road, with an ash surface retained by a sleeper edge, a nameboard and an oil lamp. When these halts were introduced the official GER line had been that passengers took shelter in inclement weather under the arch of a nearby overbridge — which was tricky, as there wasn't one on the branch! Passengers had to travel in the special coach provided, which had retractable steps, although when excursions were run the guard had to carry a ladder to allow them to board! It was not wholly unknown for the train to stop elsewhere for regular passengers, with the guard letting them off via the steps and the passengers then climbing over the fence!

By the time the branch had got much beyond Hacheston halt it was heading almost due north, still in the river valley and easily graded. This direction was not maintained for long, and it had not reached Parham station (88 miles 51 chains) before starting to swing round to the west again, closely following the River Ore all the while. Parham was reached over the level crossing of a minor road from the village which split in two almost at once, going both northward to North Green and Bruisyard, and eastward towards Little Glemham. The platform was on the east side of the line, together with the station building, of the standard East Suffolk type, with an awning along the platform face and at the level crossing end. A signalbox was provided at this end of the platform in 1892, having 20 levers including five spare, when the platform was also extended by some 90ft. Goods accommodation was provided by a siding of about 600ft on the same side as the platform, with access being possible from both directions. It had been extended by about 220ft in the 1892 alterations. In the down direction a home signal protected the crossing gates, a starter protected the siding and an advance starter was placed almost at the end of the siding. In the other direction a home signal protected the points into the siding from the Framlingham end, and a starter at the end of the platform controlled the crossing. There was a lamp hut and oil store opposite the signalbox; in later years a ground frame opposite the north end of the platform replaced the signalbox. Parham's goods traffic was accounted with Framlingham, and in 1938 the main loading was 134 tons of livestock, amounting to £253 for the railway.

Onwards from Parham — it was downgraded to a halt in later years — the line continued to turn westwards, and having done so then turned north again as the river meandered across the countryside. A short cutting around MP89 led into a straight stretch on a low embankment, and

Right:
A postcard view of Parham from the west, around the turn of the century. The River Ore is in the foreground. The height of the signal that can just be seen over the house is quite remarkable.
Alan Taylor collection

Above:
Parham, looking towards Framlingham from the level crossing on a winter's day. Something is clearly going on: there is bunting on the canopy, and this is not the only photograph being taken as a train for Wickham Market approaches. It may well be the last day of service, 1 November 1952, and given the reasonable amount of daylight is probably the 12.37pm from Framlingham, due away from Parham at 12.44pm.
Stations UK

Right:
Parham, looking towards Wickham Market, almost certainly on the same day. The ground frame which operated the siding points is in the foreground. *Stations UK*

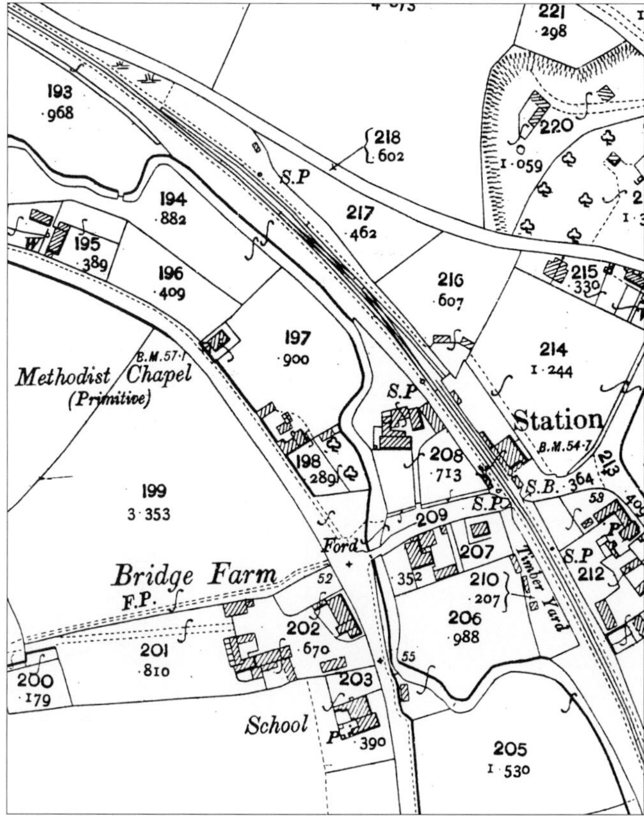

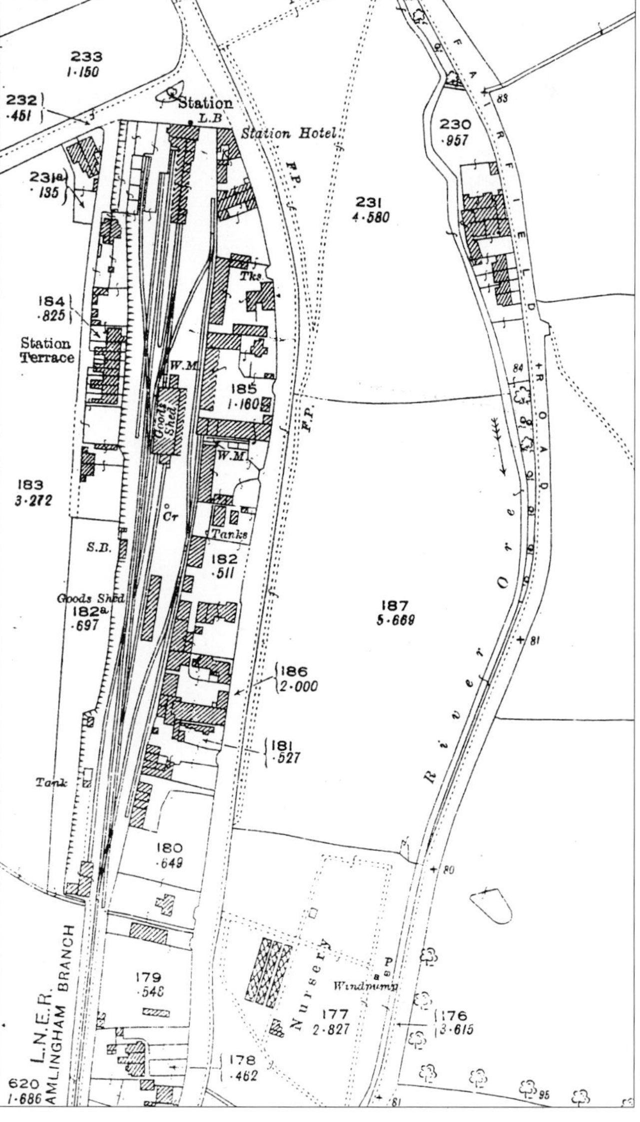

then to Bricklane crossing over the minor road to Framlingham via Cole's Green. The keeper's cottage here was on the north side of the line. Turning north again the line went over Broadwater crossing where the main road, now the B1116, had executed a sharp right-angle bend leaving the railway on its other side. Now crossing the river valley by the biggest engineering feature on the branch, it was first carried on a tall embankment and then over Broadwater Viaduct, almost at once plunging into the deep cutting through Hoggate (now Holgate) Hill. Just before reaching the viaduct there was a rifle range on the west side of the line. Almost at journey's end the branch went over the last crossing where the road from Brandeston and Kettleburgh joined Station Road, then past the backs of houses and into the terminus.

The railway had contributed greatly to the prosperity of Framlingham, although there had been a dispute early on when Newson Garrett (of Leiston) had been allowed to erect a building between the tracks at the station on East Suffolk land, and which other traders felt was unfair to them. Members of the Joint Committee of the East Suffolk and Eastern Counties agreed, and felt that it would hamper future development. The station was on the south side of the town, a short distance from the centre, and had attracted development along Station Road. Passenger trains ran into the single platform past a large grain store and then the goods shed on their right, coming to a stand exactly 91 miles from Liverpool Street, and just over 5½ miles from the junction. The main building stood across the end of the tracks, although it was L-shaped and so had a part which was parallel to the platform. Other single-storey facilities spread along the platform, which had a wide awning supported by the buildings and by columns and spandrels, whilst it too continued at right angles along the main building. A brick wall continued from the buildings towards the platform ramp, the back being finished off by iron railings. At the buffer end, opposite the passenger platform, was a loading dock, usable for end- or side-loading, and further over, served by another siding, were the cattle docks. It was not at all unusual for the loading dock to be occupied by the coaches which formed the branch train set. It seems never to have been possible for a locomotive to have run round a passenger train standing at the platform, and it was necessary for it to push back out before doing so. The goods facilities were completed by a long siding serving all the various buildings lining the east side of the station, which in the 1880s included a brickworks at the southern end, and in the 1930s a depot for the Anglo-American Oil Company, Eastern Counties Farmers, Framlingham & Eastern Counties Co-operative Egg & Poultry Society Ltd, Edwin G. Clarke & Son (corn, barley and coal merchants), Manby & Co (coal, corn and seed merchants), as well as the other coal merchants. The station generated much goods traffic, in contrast to its modest passenger usage, the main loadings in 1938 being livestock at 1,537 tons, and 3,779 tons of grain.

The latter was the mainstay of the freight traffic. Edwin G. Clarke had its own siding and was the largest customer, and in later years despatched malted grain in special covered bulk wagons, which was sent to brewers all over the country. Framlingham had also played an interesting role in developing the egg trade. The Framlingham & District Agricultural Co-operative Society had been active in developing it for some before World War 1, and was particularly

Top left:
Parham station, 1902-6. *Crown Copyright*

Lower left:
Framlingham station, 1927. *Crown Copyright*

exercised about the Great Eastern's increasing charges for carriage. However, towards the end of the war in 1917 the GER asked the Co-operative effectively to take control over the whole of the company's egg distribution business, involving over 150 million eggs per year. The operation proved to be highly successful, and the Co-operative established depots elsewhere in East Anglia. By the end of the 1920s, however, carryings by rail had almost died out as the traffic transferred to road.

The goods shed was served by a through road which then ran behind the platform and up to the station buildings, as well as connecting with the back siding. A 5-ton crane stood to the south of the shed. The engine shed stood right at the most southerly point on the layout, to the west of the running line, with a short spur reached via a wagon turntable just in front of it, although this did not survive until the 1927 OS survey. There was also a water tank here. In 1892 extensive alterations had been made to the signalling on the branch, with new cabins at Framlingham and Parham. At the terminus the platform had also been extended and the sidings and signals rearranged; the new cabin had 27 levers, of which seven were spare. It was located opposite the grain store, on the west side of the line.

BRITISH RAILWAYS
O. 6029 (G)
........................19..
From ....
POTATOES
To ....
.... Region ....
VIA ....
Owner and No. of Wagon 3
No. of bags ....
Whether carriage "Paid" or "To Pa[y]"
Consignee ....

BRITISH TRANSPORT COMMISSION
BRITISH RAILWAYS
USE BLOCK LETTERS
B.R. 21213
From........................19...
GRAIN
TO........................
Via........................Section
Letter Wagon | Number | 3 | of .... Sacks
Sender........................
Consignee........................
Lot/Contract No., Kiln or Code Letter........................

Top:
The station building was across the end of the station, but was built to the same design as others on the railway. The entrance to the yard is on the left between it and the Station Hotel, with warehouses visible between.
Station Road passes the left of the hotel.
Alan Taylor collection

Right:
Another view of the frontage of Framlingham station, taken in 1952, with the hotel in the background. *HMRS Hilton Collection*

Above:
Framlingham station basks in the autumn sunshine. The siding behind the platform contains wagons loaded with sugar beet. The siding on the left serves the cattle pens. *Rex Conway collection*

Below:
No 67230 eases the branch train to Wickham Market away from the platform at Framlingham in early BR days, although the totem era has not caught up with the lamp on the right. *Lens of Sutton*

Right:
A closer view of Framlingham's passenger platform, with a non-corridor coach left on the stops at the end. There are three cattle trucks in the siding. *Stations UK*

Below:
No 67230 again, this time waiting in the platform with a train for the junction, c1950. *Stations UK*

Left:
It is 1953 and passenger services have been withdrawn from the branch, although the terminal station continues to look smart and well cared for. The large goods shed beyond the platform is prominent, and the siding is full of vans. The station continued to see passenger trains until closure for the start and end of term at Framlingham College. *Stations UK*

—9—
Snape Branch

THE Snape branch diverged from the main line a little further north than that to Framlingham, at Snape Junction. The scenery here was probably more typical of the Sandlings than anywhere else on the East Suffolk, and in railway terms represented one of the racing stretches of the line as express trains stormed through the sweeping curve with the coast almost within sight in the distance. The branch was short, Snape station (89 miles 40 chains) being just under 1½ miles from the junction. It had originally been intended to operate a passenger service from there, and it was provided with much the same range and style of buildings as elsewhere. This did not happen at the outset, which caused the inhabitants to petition for one as early as August 1860, and which was rejected. In fact, Snape had a population rather larger than many others which did have a passenger station: in 1901 it was 529, compared with 354 for Marlesford and 375 for Parham.

Having collected the staff (square and green, no tickets used), trains diverged from the main line and dropped quickly away on a low embankment, earthworks being insignificant on the branch. The line curved away towards the southeast and headed for the marshy ground in the Alde valley, crossing two small streams and then the river by a wooden trestle bridge a short distance to the west of Snape Bridge. These bridges restricted the weight of locomotives that could be used on the branch, 'J15s' being the largest permitted. At Snape itself the road from Tunstall and Orford crossed the river, and the railway also crossed this road a little to the south. The station, known for most of its life as Snape Bridge, was between the road and river crossings, on the north side of the line. The main building was of the same pattern as elsewhere, built of white brick with a hipped slate roof, and with a short loading platform on the rail side. It may not have had passengers, but it certainly had very well-tended flower gardens and climbing roses. There does not appear to have been an awning attached, unlike the passenger stations, although there was a single-storey extension at the back. A loop was provided, the spacing between it and the running line being quite wide so that loading and unloading could be done easily. Almost opposite the main building was a goods shed with an awning on the rail side. It had a lean-to office at the road end, which survived after the main shed was demolished. Since both siding and running line crossed the road (now the B1069) tramway-style, access to the yard for carts and lorries was easy.

Much of the traffic at the station arose from the extensive maltings on the east side of the road where S. Swonnell & Son Ltd had one of its businesses, the other being at Oulton Broad. The buildings were imposing, rail access being gained through an archway in the three-storey office building, with a

Below:
The wooden trestle bridge over the River Alde was largely unchanged throughout its life, and provided a severe limitation on the axle loading of locomotives allowed to work the Snape branch. This official railway view shows it from the south on 11 June 1917, with the road bridge in the background. *National Railway Museum*

Left:
'J15' No 65389 prepares to leave with the bonus working back to Ipswich. This view is looking towards the maltings, with the station just out of sight on the left.
Adrian Vaughan collection

clock and bell tower over it. Wagons were shunted by horse over the road and into the maltings, although a Fordson tractor was substituted in later days. A flagman supervised the crossing. In front of the archway the loop and running line came together at a set of points, and there was then a wooden wagon turntable connecting the line continuing into the maltings with another at right angles in front of it. To the south it did not quite reach the end of the buildings, but on the other side extended to Snape Bridge, splitting into three and serving the wharf. There was a crane here which was used for the transfer of goods between barges and the railway. This connection, built at the very start of the line, had been important in bringing materials by boat for constructing the line. An extensive system of spurs and turntables served the maltings themselves once through the archway. Swonnell's had its own wagons for internal use, and in the late 1920s these were reported as being lettered 'S.S.&S. Ltd.' and fitted with dumb buffers, two-link chain couplings and no axleboxes. Grain and malt traffic was heavy, and 2,830 tons were loaded and taken away on the celebrated 'bonus' trains in 1938, of which more elsewhere. Operations on the branch had been simplified in 1892 when, at the same time as the Framlingham branch, one-engine-in-steam working had been adopted. The Snape Horse Fair, held every 11 August for many years, also provided a boost for traffic.

Below:
Snape station and maltings, and Snape bridge and wharf, 1902-6.
Crown Copyright

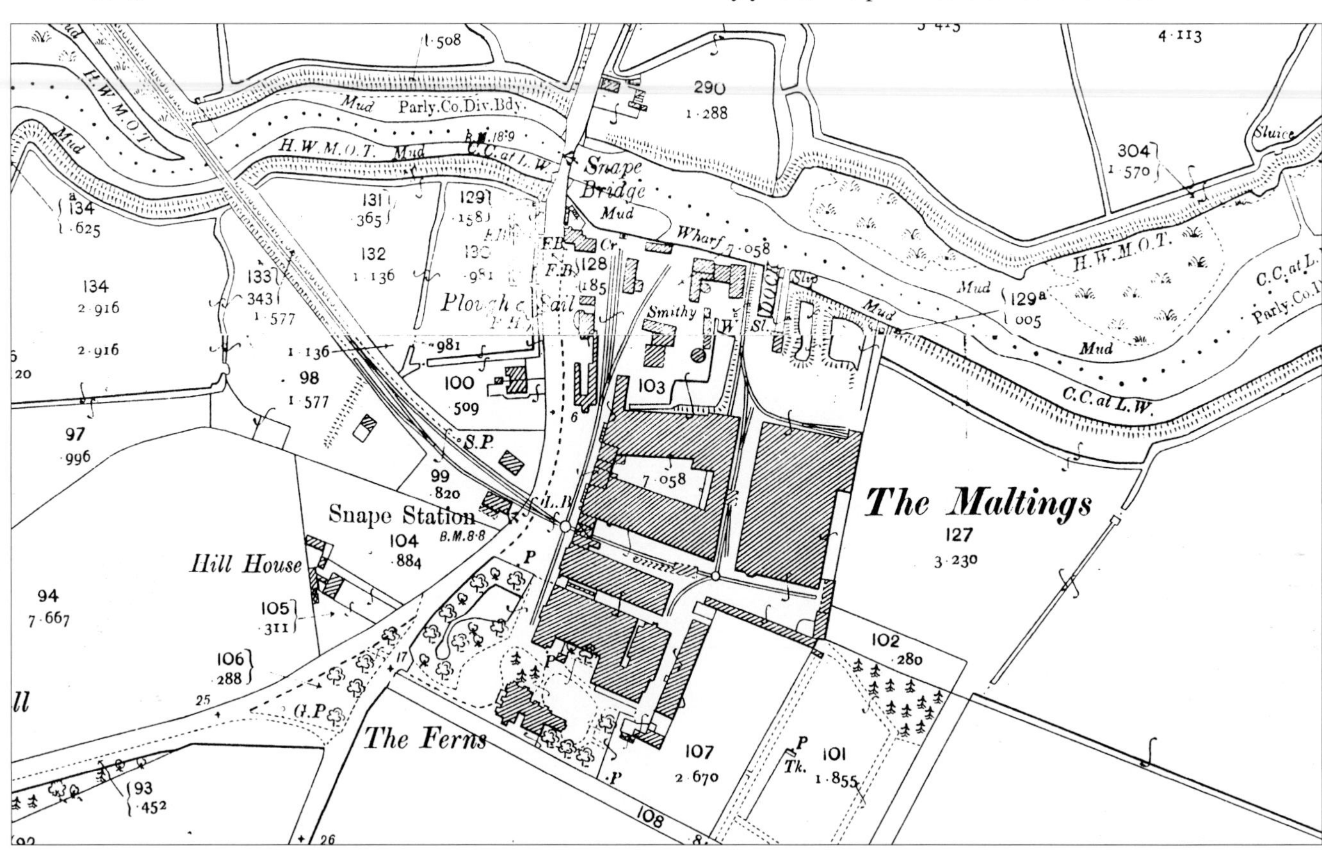

Above:
Snape station, looking back towards the bridge and junction. The station house is clearly similar to others on the East Suffolk, but without the awnings. The goods shed and its awning is clear on the left, with the lean-to goods office nearer the camera. The house and the office, but not the shed itself, still stand. *Stations UK*

Below:
Modernisation on the Snape branch on 16 April 1959, with a Fordson tractor being used for shunting wagons across the road to and from the maltings. The goods shed has been demolished, and the notice on the fence announces the withdrawal of goods services from Snape, Aldeburgh and Thorpeness. *John Brodribb collection*

— 10 —
Aldeburgh Branch

THE Aldeburgh branch was an important and busy line for both passengers and goods, serving the towns of Aldeburgh and Leiston, and later the new resort of Thorpeness. Garrett's works at Leiston had been the main reason for building the line in the first place, with the extension onwards being somewhat of an afterthought.

The branch used the split staff and ticket system and diverged from the main line at Saxmundham Junction, the signalbox being 34 chains from Saxmundham station box. The junction box, on the east side of the line, was perched precariously on the embankment and always on the lean, so much so that it was not possible even to fill a cup of tea. There was never electricity, only a Tilley lamp for lighting in later years, a coal fire and oven, and a bucket for a toilet. Coal was distributed to stations by truck, and the pilot locomotive would bring it out to signalboxes. Drinking water arrived at boxes via passenger trains in 3gal or 4gal cans. The branch was single track throughout, but although both Leiston and Aldeburgh had extensive track layouts they could not pass two passenger trains. There was a double junction with the main line, and branch trains had to collect the staff there, which occasionally caused problems. The climb away from the junction was a fierce 1 in 58 and tightly curved, and provided a stiff test for firemen. Initially on a low embankment, the climb lasted for about half a mile, by which time the branch was headed almost due east and the up distant signal had been reached. With almost no further earthworks, the branch went over Clayhills (now Knodishall) crossing at 92 miles 49 chains, then over the minor road from Knodishall Green to East Green, starting to curve southeastwards shortly before MP93. Westhouse crossing followed at 93 miles 32 chains, the lane here leading only to Westhouse Farm, and Saxmundham Road crossing, which had been a crossroads before the railway managed to thread its way through the middle. Having now almost regained its easterly heading, Buckleswood Road joined the railway on its north side and accompanied it for 200yd or so before coming into Leiston station, where MP95 was on the platform.

Leiston was a significant industrial centre in the 19th century, and had a population of 2,616 in 1891. Richard Garrett (the third of that name) established his engineering works in the town early in the 19th century, and oversaw a rapid expansion so that the works tripled in size between 1835 and 1855, before there was any real means of transporting goods over land. Much of the trade was carried out via Slaughden Quay, south of Aldeburgh, in which Garrett had a substantial interest. The building of the East Suffolk, of which Richard Garrett had become a director, provided a further spur to expansion, and allowed the development of new activities such as the boiler shop, opened around 1860, and a major expansion of the foundry around the same time.

Garrett's works was served by a private tramway from the station, which was itself at the northwest corner of the town where Buckleswood Road joined Theberton Road. Going south towards the town, part of the latter was renamed Station Road; north of the crossing it is now Abbey Road. The tramway curved off in a southeasterly direction opposite the passenger platform and crossed Station Road, threading its way between the backs of properties in that road and Foundry Lane (later Dinsdale Road). It then emerged to cross Saxmundham Road (Main Street) where the crossing was initially gated but later open, and entered the works, where there was an extensive system of sidings serving all parts. In the earlier days of operation, horses shunted wagons at the station as far as the start of the tramway, where they

Left:
Sirapite heads for Garrett's works along the tramway from the station. *Long Shop Museum*

Right:
A bird's-eye view from the new shaft at Garrett's works, looking north over the station. Station Road, the main station building, the signalbox and the goods shed can clearly be seen. In the distance the tramway into Carr's brickworks is visible beyond the road that curves away on the far side of the level crossing. The photograph is undated but was taken after the diversion of Carr's tramway into the branch, away from Garrett's tramway, but before the brickworks closed.
Frank Huxley collection

Brick Works
Pug Mill
Kilns
Yarmouth... 34
Aldeburgh.... 5
M.S.
TRAMWAY
New Haven
Police Station
Station
Brick Field
Kiln
Windmill
(Pumping)
Windmill
(Corn)
Burial Ground
Methodist Chapel
(Wesleyan)
Methodist Chapel
Vicarage
White Horse Hotel
Post Office
Smithy
Friends' Meeting House
School
Burial Ground
HIGH STREET
STATION ROAD
Gasometer
Congl. Chapel
Leiston Works
(Iron)
Crane
Hotel
Ivy Cottage
F.P.

Above:
'J15' No 65467 struggles up the bank towards Leiston with a special for Aldeburgh regatta in August 1955.
Dr Ian C. Allen

Right:
A 1922 postcard view of the tramway into Garrett's works at Leiston, crossing the main road, the works entrance being on the right with the railings. Note that there are no crossing gates and that trucks would hurtle across propelled by gravity.
Frank Huxley collection

Left:
Leiston station, Richard Garrett's works and tramway, 1884.
Crown Copyright

were allowed to run by gravity down towards the works, crossing the main street at some speed and eventually stopping because of the uphill gradient inside the works. A chain was then attached and the wagons wound up further by means of a winding drum powered by the boiler shop main drive. In the opposite direction the wagons were released at the top of the works yard and ran as far as possible before the horses took over. These Suffolk Punches were also used to pull the chain back out. This hair-raising procedure was altered in 1929 after a serious accident involving two wagons, following which an Aveling & Porter geared 0-4-0 tank locomotive named *Sirapite* was acquired from gypsum mines at Mountfield in Sussex. It was used for shunting, ostensibly being confined to Garrett's private tramway but in practice venturing into the sidings at Leiston station when necessary (and unobserved by Higher Authority). The locomotive's name had arisen from the obvious connection between gypsum and plaster of Paris, and had originally been intended as *Parisite*, until someone spotted the problem and reversed the first part of it. It worked at Leiston until the end of 1962 when it was replaced by a bright yellow battery-electric locomotive.

Above:
'J15' No 65447 heads an Aldeburgh train into Leiston on 9 September 1955, and passes *Sirapite*, the Aveling & Porter locomotive of Richard Garrett's works, in the sidings.
W. M. J. Jackson

Below:
A fine view of *Sirapite* in the sidings at Leiston. Garrett's new works are in the background.
John Brodribb collection

Garrett's carried out a very wide variety of activity. By the time of the Great Exhibition in 1851 the firm was making a range of agricultural machinery such as portable steam engines, reapers and threshers. At about this time building of the famous Long Shop began, and the foundry was enlarged. Boilers continued to be bought in for a while after the boiler shop was built, and the company developed its designs for fireboxes and smokeboxes to make its machines more efficient and easier to use by less skilled workers. The company had established its own gas works fronting Snape Road (later Haylings Road) in about 1850, and also supplied gas for public use. During the major wars the works was

Top:
The photograph is not quite as sharp as it might be, but the rarity of this view makes it worthy of inclusion. On 14 May 1956 *Sirapite* has climbed the steep incline into Garrett's works and has threaded its way further into the site. As ever, the locomotive is immaculate.
Long Shop Museum

Above:
Sirapite was not the only means of shunting at Leiston: here is a selection of alternative motive power. Horses were very widely used on the railway for over a century, for shunting and local deliveries. These two worked at Leiston around the turn of the century.
Alan Taylor collection

Above:
Sirapite was eventually retired and replaced by a yellow battery-electric locomotive, seen here about to cross Main Street into the works. Compare this with the 'Tea Time' postcard and the photograph of *Sirapite* threading its way along the tramway between the brick walls. *Long Shop Museum*

Below:
Taken from a postcard entitled 'Tea Time', this shows the entrance to the works in 1912. The tramway from the station approaches from the lower right and crosses Saxmundham Road (now Main Street). The Long Shop, now a fine museum, is just visible on the right. *Long Shop Museum*

Above:
Leiston played a fuller part than many in the World War 1 effort, because of its heavy industry. As with every town it sent away the best of its young men to fight in the trenches, and they wait on the platform for the troop train. The man in the right foreground is Frank Garrett senior (1845–1918) who had overseen so much of the works' development. *Long Shop Museum*

Right:
A rare World War 2 photograph of an armoured train and troops, probably somewhere on the Aldeburgh branch. Even the locomotive looks to be camouflaged. *Imperial War Museum*

Above:
The station building and staff from about the same time at the turn of the century, with a climbing plant (a clematis?) trained across the front of the awning, and roses around the building itself.
Lens of Sutton

Right:
Leiston around the same era as the previous photograph, but earlier in the year judging by the lack of growth on the roses and the heavy coats being worn.
Alan Taylor collection

Below:
Leiston a few years later.
A goods train shunts in the platform, and there are huge stacks of timber behind. The goods shed has acquired an awning over the platform.
Alan Taylor collection

Above:
A fine 1950s view of Leiston signalbox and the crane from the north side of the level crossing.
Peter Punchard collection

Below:
Leiston station from the signalbox window in 1952, looking back towards Saxmundham. Things are much quieter, with few wagons in evidence, although Garrett's still generated much traffic.
Rex Conway collection

Above:
Looking from the Saxmundham end of the platform towards the level crossing in 1955, the goods shed and office are prominent, whilst a BR locomotive shunts on the main line. *Sirapite* is also lurking on the loop in front of the signalbox. The lines to Garrett's works curve away on the right, the original having a wagon standing on it and that to the new part nearest the camera. There was a further connection some way beyond the Saxmundham end of the station. *Stations UK*

Right:
Evidence of Garrett's goods in this 1955 photograph which shows *Sirapite* shunting a conveyor loaded onto a wagon and about to be sent away to a customer by rail. *Stations UK*

converted for the production of munitions, and towards the end of its days made a name for itself with the development of automatic machinery for use in launderettes.

Unusually, Leiston did not load the usual agricultural traffic of other East Suffolk stations, and the 1938 returns mention only 1,228 tons of scrap iron. In fact, there were other private sidings at the station, such as that for the Leiston Gas Company, and also that into Carr's brickworks out on Theberton Road, to the north of the station. The works was in existence by 1880 and was served by a tramway which was a branch of Garrett's line, trailing into it soon after it had crossed Station Road, and then having a level crossing over the Aldeburgh line to the east of the level crossing. This was an awkward arrangement which had arisen because the brickworks tramway pre-dated the extension to Aldeburgh. In 1893 it was substantially altered, when a short siding was installed east of the crossing, facing for Aldeburgh-bound trains, into which the brickworks tramway trailed. A short spur was left running towards the branch, but the section crossing it and joining it to Garrett's tramway was removed entirely. The brickfields closed in March 1926.

Provision for other goods traffic was made by sidings on the north side of the line at the Saxmundham end of the station, where a siding ran along the back of the passenger platform, and was paralleled by another. Short spurs to the west completed the layout, which also had loading docks. The goods shed was close to the main passenger buildings — all being on the north side — and the siding ran through it. Major change came in March 1893 when Maj-Gen Hutchinson gave approval for the rearrangement and extension of the sidings, together with the lengthening by about 100ft of the passenger platform at the Saxmundham end. The siding

Above:
An October 1919 postcard view coincidentally taken at Leiston, and showing a group of strike-breaking volunteers on the footplate of GER No 569. *Long Shop Museum*

through the goods shed remained, and another on the far north side of the layout was installed. Two more trailed back towards the west, and it became much easier to reach the cattle pens. Two tracks went over the level crossing as before, the one opposite the platform continuing to form a loop, although not signalled as a running line. The signalling was remodelled and a new signalbox was installed, having a total of 35 levers including six spare. In 1912 Col von Donop approved a new connection on the down side, facing for trains to Aldeburgh, into the Leiston Gas Company's siding, its works being in Carr Road. This was about 400yd east of the station level crossing, and was worked by a six-lever ground frame. The company had started operations in the previous year and took over the supply of gas to the public from Garrett's. Overall Leiston had a huge goods traffic, with Garrett's works and the Gas Company's sidings, together with the general coal business. Leiston could handle all classes of traffic, and was provided with a crane of 30 tons capacity outside the western end of the goods shed. Passenger trains were not allowed to cross at Leiston, nor was the signalman allowed to accept trains from Aldeburgh and Saxmundham Junction at the same time. It was possible to accept a goods or ballast train from Saxmundham and refuge it in the down siding next to the running line, after which another train could be accepted from either direction.

Passenger provision was similar to other stations on the East Suffolk. The main building was of the usual design, although the goods shed adjoined it at the western end, and it was of red brick instead of the more usual white. In fact, the two buildings had originally been separate, with the siding emerging from the eastern end of the shed, via the usual wooden doors, for a very short distance. Later these were removed, and where there had been a low wall along the back of the platform with the siding behind, more single-storey stores were provided. The station building, reached by the public from Westward Ho, an extension of Bucklesham Road, was longer than many, and had the usual pattern of awning only along the platform side. It appears likely that it had once extended around the Station Road end as might be expected, but a further extension to the accommodation in GER days had removed it. Unusually, the goods shed also sported an awning for sheltering passengers, but there was a gap between the two. The signalbox was at the level crossing on the town side, opposite the passenger platform, with a loading dock immediately behind it. This was in the vee of the junction with Garrett's tramway, and could also be used for loading wagons from that line. It also had a very short spur between the loop and tramway which allowed end-loading of wagons. A set of points in the tramway immediately to the west of Station Road formed one end of what was effectively a loop, which joined the main-line loop beyond the end of the passenger platform.

Onward from Leiston, the branch continued in an easterly direction for about half a mile, before passing over a short embankment and Valley Road by a bridge. A shallow cutting followed as the line started to curve towards the south, then crossed the road to Sizewell at 95 miles 79 chains. The siding there was on the east side south of the crossing, with the connection facing for trains towards Aldeburgh. Much of the coal traffic for Leiston was handled here, and it was accounted with that station. The level crossing had its own keeper and cottage, and the siding was worked by a ground frame in a hut opposite the cottage. Until World War 1 a short headshunt trailed back towards the crossing. The siding was

Above:
A pair of Class 37s, probably No 37219 leading No 37216, head back to Saxmundham in 1988 as they approach Knodishall crossing with construction empties from Sizewell siding. *Peter Punchard collection*

Above:
Leiston in May 1988, from the site of the signalbox looking back towards Saxmundham. Some sidings still existed at the far end of the station, which was officially still open for goods traffic. A Class 37 shunts prior to heading back to Saxmundham. *Peter Punchard collection*

Below:
On 2 December 1993 Class 37 No 37379 stands in the platform at Leiston with the empty flasks for Sizewell siding. These trips usually operate on a Thursday. *David Pearce*

Above:
The branch continues in an easterly direction from Leiston station, and as it curves around the seaward edge of the town is carried on an embankment which takes it over Valley Road. On 2 March 1994 No 37023 heads a train of ballast wagons back towards Saxmundham.
David Pearce

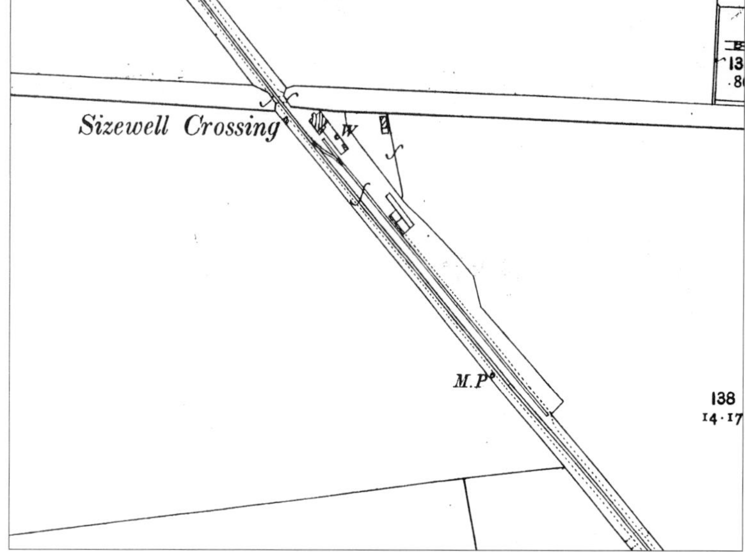

Right:
Sizewell siding and level crossing, 1902-6.
Crown Copyright

Below:
Sizewell level crossing from the Aldeburgh side, showing the keeper's cottage and the ground frame hut. The siding itself is on the right, with road access being behind the cottage. *Peter Punchard collection*

Above:
Radio-fitted No 37216, in green livery (disguised as No D6916 *Great Eastern*), shunts the flasks under the crane on 9 July 1992. The old siding had no run-round, so this had to be done at Leiston and the train propelled for the final part of its journey. Since it was extended to handle the construction traffic for Sizewell B power station a loop was provided, so running round can be done here, and the facility at Leiston has fallen into disuse. *David Pearce*

Right:
Ray Beales started at Halesworth as a lad porter soon after World War 2, and finished his railway career as a conductor on local trains in East Anglia. Here Ray (left) and his driver pose for the camera at Sizewell siding in 1987 in front of a construction train. *Peter Punchard collection*

Top:
Class J17 No 65560 ambles along between Leiston and Thorpeness on its way back to Ipswich with the Aldeburgh goods in September 1956. The countryside here is generally open heathland typical of the Sandlings. *Dr Ian C. Allen*

Above:
Thorpeness Halt opened on 29 July 1914 to serve the newly developed resort nearby. World War 1 put paid to any hope of much traffic, and in any case the mile distance between the station and the resort was too great. However, a substantial platform was built and facilities provided in a series of grounded coach bodies. The gardens are completely surrounded by rabbit-proof fencing. This view is looking towards Aldeburgh in 1955. The siding is facing for trains from Aldeburgh, and the buffers can be seen at the end of the garden. *Stations UK*

more than doubled in length before the end of the 19th century, but the headshunt was taken out later. In later years it came to be the terminus of the branch and handled freight traffic to and from Sizewell's nuclear power stations.

Passenger trains continued towards Aldeburgh, past MP96 and over Crown Lands crossing, soon ending up heading almost due south across The Walks and Aldringham Common. This part of Suffolk shows the Sandlings at their most pronounced, the terrain being open heathland kept in check for many years by huge populations of rabbits. The line threaded through this area on low banks or shallow cuttings, intersected by rough tracks every so often, and reaching Thorpe crossing over the road to the coast, now the B1353. When the railway was built, and until the early part of the 20th century, there was nothing more than the tiny hamlet of Thorpe sheltering behind the dunes. Just before World War 1 it was developed into the garden village of Thorpeness, which included the creation of The Meare, a shallow body of water on what had been marshy ground liable to flooding, and through which the Hundred River flowed. A country club, concert hall and theatre, dance hall, tennis courts and an 18-hole golf club were also provided, and so the Great Eastern built Thorpeness Halt on the south side of the crossing, opening it on 29 July 1914. This was a simple platform about 330ft long on the east side of the line, and with three old coach bodies providing the facilities. One stood at the foot of the ramp at the Leiston end and had almost all its windows boarded up. The other two stood at the back of the platform and provided the offices and waiting rooms, whilst there was also a wooden shelter about half-way along. Carefully tended gardens on the other side of the track were fenced against the rabbits. A short siding, facing for up trains, joined the running line a few yards beyond the Aldeburgh end of the platform, and terminated in a set of buffers about half-way along it. The access road for carts and lorries was on the west side of the line, completely separate from the passenger entrance. The halt could handle only passenger and general goods traffic, having only hardstanding — no loading dock, animal pens or crane.

Past Thorpeness the branch had to pass through The Fens on its west side, and The Meare on the east. Sheepwash crossing had a cottage and resident keeper, although over only a minor track. In the earliest days of the line a ballast branch had diverged towards the sea a few yards north of the crossing, heading east through what later became The Meare and terminating on the shore near Seaview Cottages, more or less where the B1353 first reaches the shingle bank today. This was disused and the junction removed by the time the Ordnance Survey carried out the work for its 1882 edition, and there was no trace by 1904, long before the area was flooded. The land to the south is very slightly higher, and so the aspect of the branch changed as it continued, with grazing marsh between it and the coast, and some slight cuttings. A little south of MP98 a brickworks and clay pit were passed on the inland side, becoming only the names of Brick Kiln cottage and Crag Pit Farm by the turn of the century. At long last the line entered the parish of Aldeburgh, and reached the station, about half a mile short of the hundred from Liverpool Street.

Aldeburgh was a substantial town, with a population of 2,150 in 1891, growing to 2,405 10 years later and 2,545 in

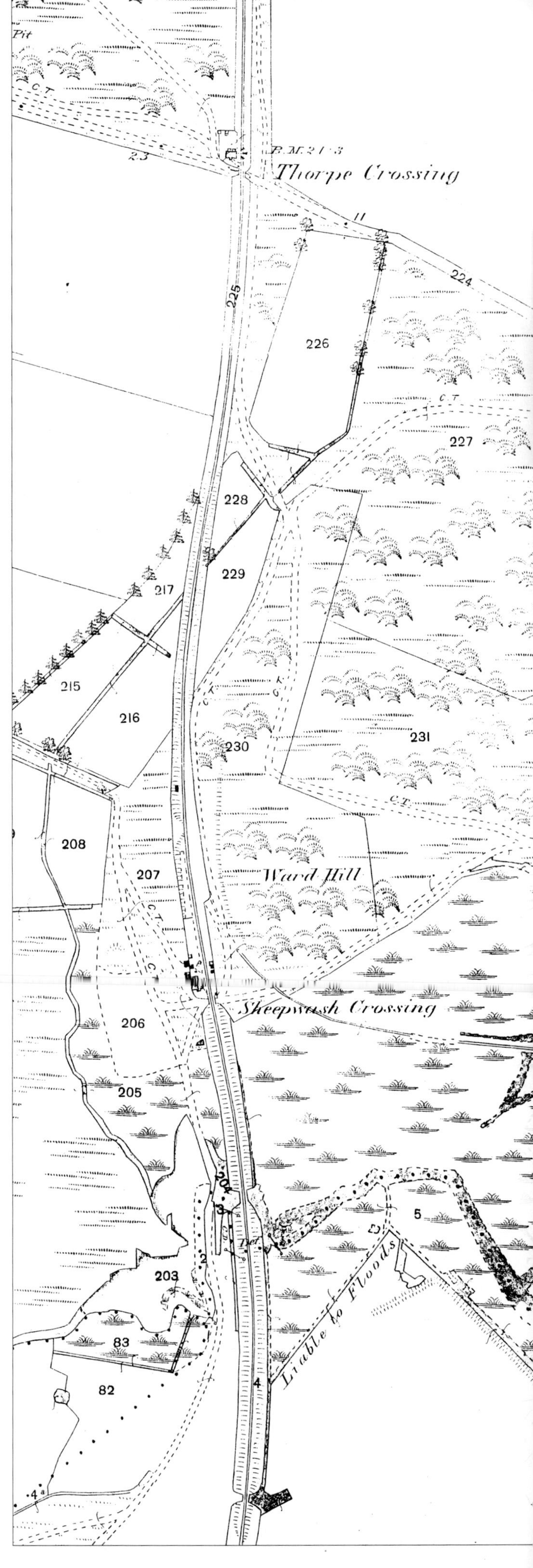

Right:
Thorpe crossing (later the site of Thorpeness Halt); also the ballast branch from Sheepwash crossing to Seaview Cottage, Thorpe, 1882. *Crown Copyright*

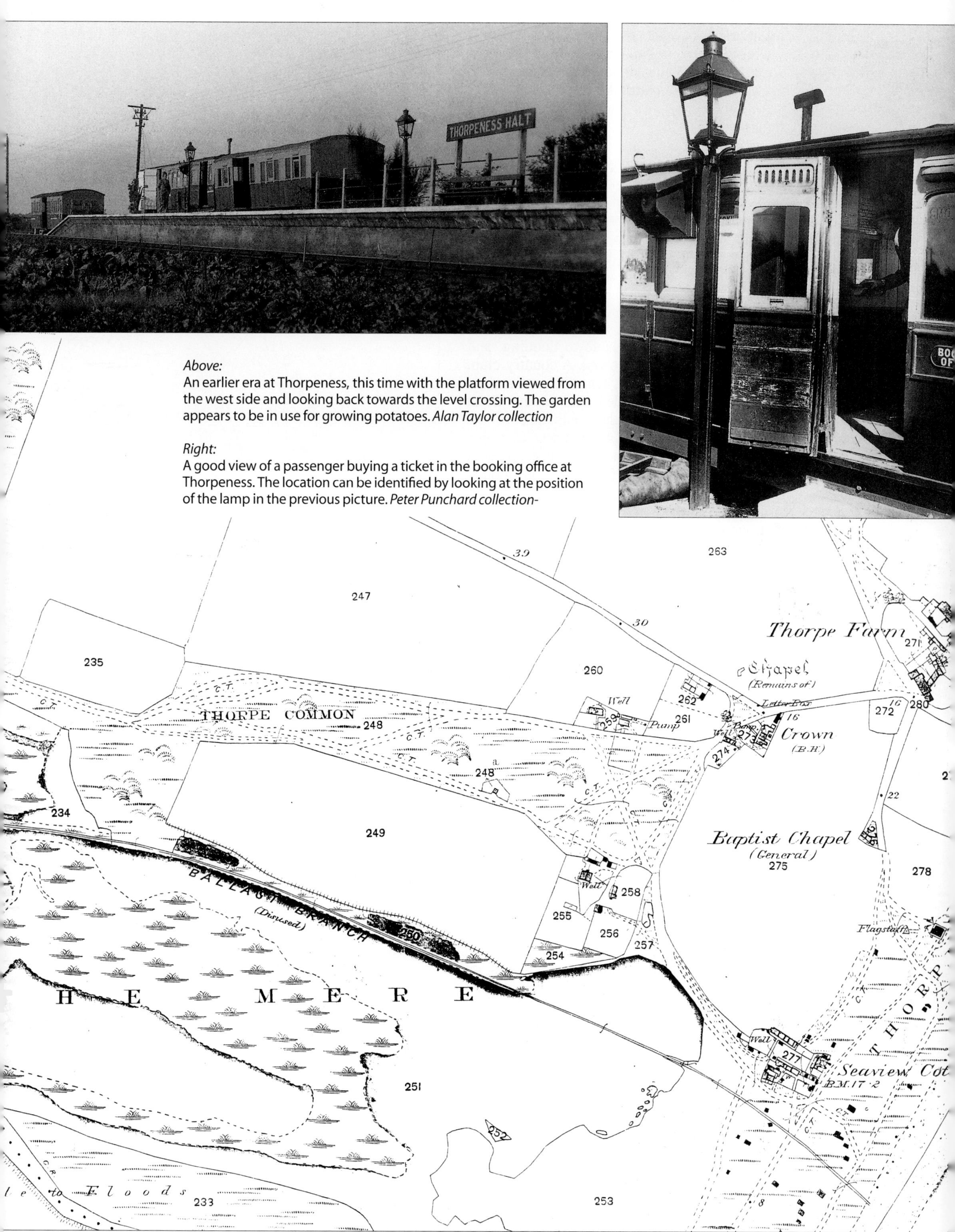

Above:
An earlier era at Thorpeness, this time with the platform viewed from the west side and looking back towards the level crossing. The garden appears to be in use for growing potatoes. *Alan Taylor collection*

Right:
A good view of a passenger buying a ticket in the booking office at Thorpeness. The location can be identified by looking at the position of the lamp in the previous picture. *Peter Punchard collection-*

1931. It was important for fishing and as a port in its earlier days, and continued to land substantial catches of sprats and other fish from its longshore boats throughout the 1930s. Over the years it became more and more popular after as a holiday resort, and offered many facilities for its well-to-do visitors including an 18-hole golf course, tennis courts, and the Aldeburgh Yacht Club. The town had its own lifeboat and station, and there was a lot of business traffic on the branch. The Great Eastern and LNER assiduously encouraged visitors with a range of tickets such as six-monthly tourist tickets, fortnightly, weekend and 'extra-journey' tickets that allowed members of holidaymaking families to make occasional trips back to London during the course of their stay. This sometimes backfired on the railway, since the rates for many of the coastal towns were lower than corresponding journeys terminating on the main line. In 1927 Mr J. O. P. Bland, who held a season ticket from Aldeburgh to London, wanted to get out at Saxmundham on his return journey, but the LNER refused to allow this on the grounds that the Aldeburgh ticket was cheaper than the rate to Saxmundham, despite the greater distance, and that if it were permitted, passengers from as far as Ipswich would book the cheaper Aldeburgh ticket, with consequent loss of revenue. Mr Bland wanted to travel by road for the final leg of his journey when there was no convenient train, and the LNER itself said that the local service 'is admittedly not very good'.

Aldeburgh station was originally intended to be south of the road from Snape and Saxmundham, but was built to the north. Arriving trains from Saxmundham passed the engine

Right:
An Edwardian postcard view of Aldeburgh station from the station entrance in Victoria Road. The typical nature of the main building can be made out, with the train shed added on to the platform side. The bookstall has not yet appeared.
Alan Taylor collection

Below:
A view probably taken at much the same time as the picture on the right, but this time showing several of the station staff. The ventilators in the roof of the train shed are clear, and the water tank to the right of the signalbox can also be seen. The painters were quite creative when they last attended to the awning over the entrance.
Alan Taylor collection

Above:
In 1952 Aldeburgh is a hive of activity as a passenger train prepares to leave, while there are wagons to be seen through the goods shed.
Rex Conway collection

Right:
In 1956 No 67239 stands lampless with a Saxmundham train. The bunting is out, probably for the regatta. The goods shed is on the right, while the rear coach stands under the train shed.
Peter Punchard collection

Right:
An LNER train of rather mixed origins stands under the roof, with a good collection of barrows lined against the fence. *Stations UK*

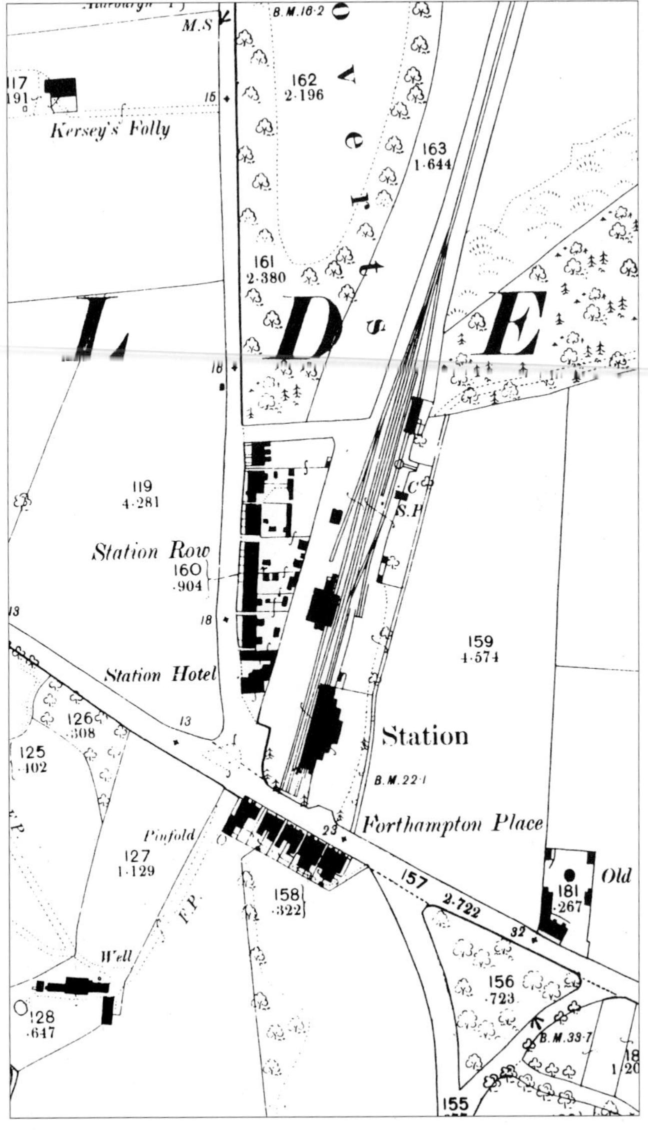

Above:
The end of the line is near. In the late 1950s Aldeburgh signalbox and engine shed are the centre of very little activity.
Peter Punchard collection

Left:
Aldeburgh station, 1882-7.
Crown Copyright

shed on their left and the goods shed on their right before running under the train shed which covered much of the single platform, with a rather commodious building on the east side. In fact, this was similar to others on the East Suffolk although not appearing so at first sight because of the overall roof. On the platform side a substantial wall had been added to the building, extending some way at each end, and with arches at intervals. Into these were cut the doors and windows, whilst on the other side of the track a similarly substantial wall, this time built up from ground level, supported the other end of the roof trusses. Because the points for the loop were back beyond the shed, an arrived train had to push back in order to run round, and then set back again to get under the roof. This was less of a problem when diesel railcars were introduced, although the roof was demolished not long afterwards. The usual offices and accommodation for the stationmaster were contained in the building, which stood almost adjacent to Victoria Road. W. H. Smith had its bookstall in a kiosk attached to the building at this end. Passengers could also take cover in a small waiting room about half-way along the platform.

The goods shed was another substantial structure, this time in red brick, with lean-to offices at both ends and a siding running through. It had a wide awning sheltering vehicles loading on the road side. There was another siding, an extension from the loop, between it and the running line. The signalbox stood at the foot of the ramp, with steps down onto the platform itself. It had been inspected by Maj-Gen

Left:
A 1959 view, looking back along the platform through the train shed, with the signalbox and goods shed in view. The bookstall, outside on the station approach, can also be seen behind the fence. *Stations UK*

Left:
The goods shed at Aldeburgh is seen from the road side, with a blood-and-custard-liveried delivery lorry backed up in the loading bay. The sign on the end wall reads 'Goods office at passenger station'. *Peter Punchard collection*

Hutchinson in February 1893 and built the previous year, when the signalling had been remodelled, and had 21 levers, including five spare. The platform was lengthened by about 170ft to 310ft, a new loading dock was provided behind the platform at the Leiston end, the loop was extended and the connections to the engine shed were altered. This was another substantial brick building with a single through road, and with a water tank and small coaling stage between it and the station, although in later days locomotives were often coaled direct from a truck by an Ipswich cleaner working nights. The branch had its own train crew, although it was often necessary for rest days and holidays to be covered from Ipswich. For many years the two drivers on the branch were Messrs Thurkettle and Moutel, replaced towards the end of steam by two men who were in complete contrast to each other. George Barnett had fired at March before World War 2, lived at Aldeburgh and enjoyed fishing and was very laid-back. On the other hand the driver-in-charge was Bill Runnacles, whose life centred around the Aldeburgh branch, and who was always ringing up for a fresh engine. He liked the fire to be made up as if he were going to the ends of the earth, with the engine blowing off. Driver Runnacles worried a great deal, but the branch was his life and he was extremely conscientious.

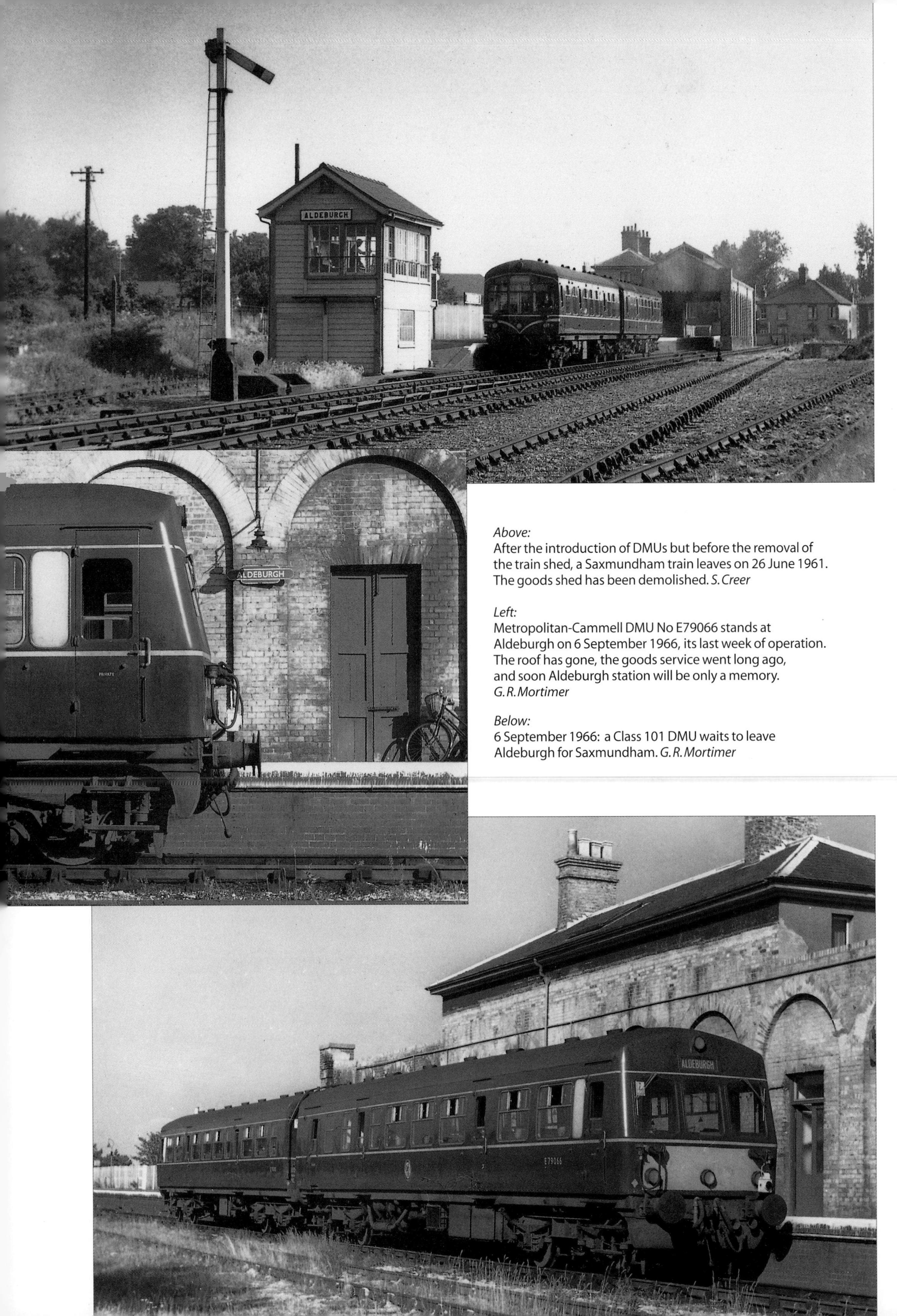

Above:
After the introduction of DMUs but before the removal of the train shed, a Saxmundham train leaves on 26 June 1961. The goods shed has been demolished. *S. Creer*

Left:
Metropolitan-Cammell DMU No E79066 stands at Aldeburgh on 6 September 1966, its last week of operation. The roof has gone, the goods service went long ago, and soon Aldeburgh station will be only a memory. *G. R. Mortimer*

Below:
6 September 1966: a Class 101 DMU waits to leave Aldeburgh for Saxmundham. *G. R. Mortimer*

—11—
Lowestoft Branch

Above:
A rare photograph of Barnby box, with the running lines on the right and the siding and yard on the left. *Peter Punchard collection*

Below:
Barnby siding, 1902-6. *Crown Copyright*

THE section of the East Suffolk between Beccles and Lowestoft was always considered as one of the branches, albeit an important one, and at first was not intended to go into what became Lowestoft Central. The East Suffolk's station would have been at South Lowestoft, with a branch to Kirtley (later Kirkley), which never saw a passenger service, although it did handle large amounts of goods traffic and outlived most stations on the line to Yarmouth, except the terminus itself. The main line was built as double track (although the original Halesworth, Beccles & Haddiscoe had been single) and the branch was single throughout. There was only one intermediate station, at Carlton Colville. The branch diverged from the main line about 400ft from Common Lane level crossing, and so about half a mile from Beccles station, and had a double junction with the two tracks rapidly converging into one. Lowestoft Junction signalbox was opened in April 1880 and controlled home and distant signals protecting the junction, and also locked the level crossing gates.

The line was almost completely level all the way. For most of its course between Beccles and Carlton Colville it was built over marsh, and whilst some parts needed much material to be tipped before a firm foundation was reached, most did not. Having swung round through 90° past Beccles, it then headed slightly south of east in a straight line to Barnby (originally Barnaby) at 113 miles 30 chains, passing through some fine grazing land and willow and alder carr, all the time roughly parallel with the River Waveney. There were a number of crossings, both public and occupation, notably Black Dam (109 miles 71 chains), Marsh Lane (110 miles 71 chains), North Cove (111 miles 69 chains) and Blindman's Gate (later Barnby Gate, 113 miles 22 chains). An early indication of operating practices was given by a report from a local newspaper of an accident at North Cove crossing gates. The exact date is unclear, but it happened on Monday 26th, probably sometime in 1865.

The inquest on the body of Maria Bayley was held at the Horseshoes Inn, North Cove, and the coroner, Gross, opened by commenting on the remarkable scarcity of accidents on the Great Eastern. John Nicklin was the driver of the train, the

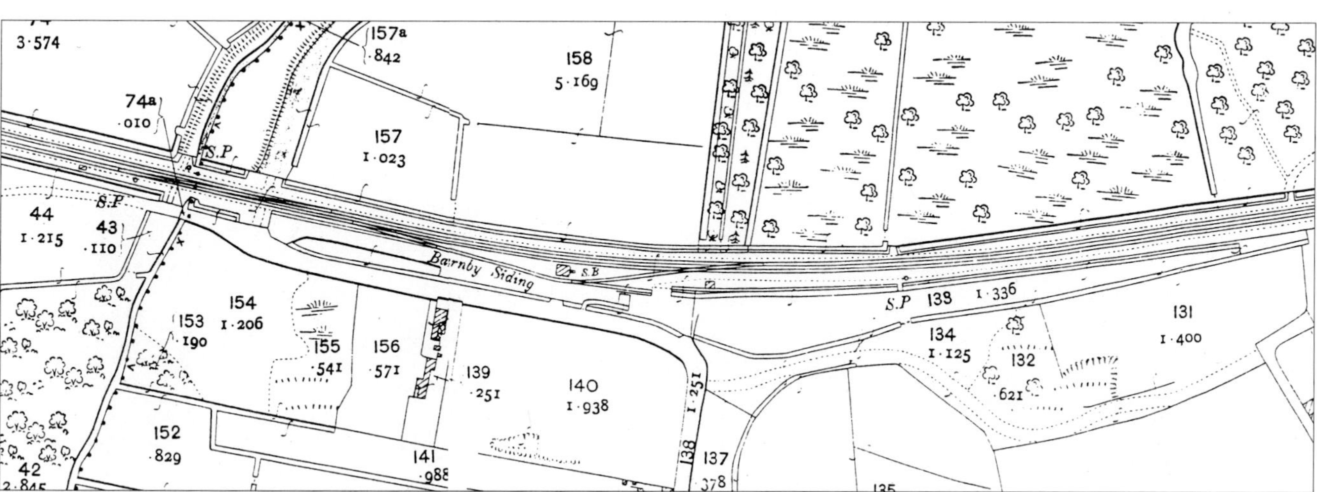

first up between Lowestoft and Beccles, and was due to pass the gates at North Cove at 6.5am. He said that it was a 'thick morning' and he had whistled 500yd from the gates. When the train was 400yd away the deceased closed one gate, and had the other held half open. He whistled for the break (sic), but the train was still travelling at 6mph when it hit and shattered the gate, the woman being struck down. The train stopped 27yd from the gate, whereupon Nicklin picked up the woman, who had one leg cut off and was fearfully cut, and 'she died in my arms'.

The district superintendent, Mr Thomas Stevenson, said that there was plenty of time to get the gates open. James Hall was the guard on the train, and heard the whistle when the train was 600yd away. He had looked out and applied the break, and the train had stopped 26-27yd beyond the gate. He had helped to get the woman back to the house, but she had died first. William Mudd was the gatekeeper at North Cove, and said that the deceased was his housekeeper, aged 29 years. She opened the gates when he was away, and he had been in Beccles at the time. He rarely received printed notices of train times from the Company (he estimated every five months) but said that she was well acquainted with the time of the morning train. Thomas Stevenson explained that he visited gatekeepers once or twice a year to explain their duties, and that no one was appointed to such a post unless a household member was available to do the gates in his absence.

Everett, foreman of the jury, opined that one or two gates needed attention, and that it was difficult to stop stock straying when crossing the line; he had had to get three or four persons to prevent it. He hoped that something could be done to prevent stock turning onto the line. In delivering the jury's verdict of accidental death, no blame was attributed to either the Great Eastern or its employees.

At Barnby the line curved gently back towards the north, passing Barnby Broad on the left, and continuing to follow the river about half a mile away. When first opened there were no facilities at all at this location, although they developed rapidly, serving the nearby villages of Barnby and North Cove.

In August 1885 Maj-Gen Hutchinson reinspected the site for the Board of Trade, most of the work having been done the previous year. A new passing place had been provided, with a new down line starting at Blindman's Gate crossing and continuing for about 800ft. A new signalbox was built about half-way along the loop on the south side, and worked up and down home and starting signals and distants, and also locked the gates. Only three years later the points at both ends of the loop were moved apart, lengthening it by around 150ft. Signalling alterations were also carried out, and the box now had 12 working and 10 spare levers. In October 1890 Maj-Gen Hutchinson approved the use of the new siding. This was on the south side of the line and passed behind the signalbox. A trailing connection was provided into the down loop at the Lowestoft end, with a crossing in the up loop; this was protected by a single-bladed trap in the siding. At the other end trailing points connected it to the up loop, with a headshunt stopping just short of the level crossing. A spur at the Lowestoft end served a loading dock with cattle pens. The relocked box now had 18 working levers and four spare.

Barnby siding was a surprisingly busy place. The procedure when calling was to stop the train from Lowestoft outside the box, uncouple, draw forward and then set back into the siding, pick up outward traffic, set back onto the train, pick up the inward traffic again and set it back into the siding, and then recouple onto the train and go forward to Beccles. In season there was always a supply of empty wagons for beet, which were filled by the farmers who had to fork them off their trailers onto an elevator for loading. Railway staff had to fill in the wagon cards with details of the farmer, destination and date, the cards then being clipped onto the wagon. Barnby loaded more sugar beet than almost anywhere else on the system: in 1955 Brampton loaded 737 trucks for Cantley and Ipswich, but Barnby beat it with 812 trucks. A wagon of coal arrived very occasionally, and a merchant's lorry would then appear, with his men sacking the coal. Farm machinery arrived for Wiggs, with tractors on a flat wagon, or balers, ploughs or other items. There was no loading dock, but plenty of hardstanding. There was once a wagonload of bricks, all of which came off by hand. Wagons were moved around by the use of pinch bars, with a long square handle. The single siding ended in buffers set into an earth bank.

At the end of its life, George Beckett was the only full-time signalman at Barnby, the box being switched in for the day shift only (in 1950, 10.5am to 5.25pm, Mondays to Saturdays). Milk was delivered to the box, and in summer was kept in a galvanised bucket of water outside the box.

Below:
Oulton Broad South (originally known as Carlton Colville), looking towards Beccles from the road bridge. Re-sleepering of the up road is in progress, and the gardens look very well tended. Today only the up platform is in use, although the building on the down platform still stands, minus its awning. A siding on the down side ran behind the platform, the connection being at the far end of the platform. *Stations UK*

There was a big black cast-iron range in the box, with the kettle always on, and the postman always came in for a cup of tea. The box was not open on Sundays.

Continuing on from Barnby the line was again almost completely straight, although more on the edge of the river valley and so with the marshes only on the north side. Hillings Road, Spratts Water and Dawdy's level crossings were within a mile of each other, the last being at 114 miles 76 chains, and Carlton Colville station at 115 miles 42 chains. The line to Lowestoft was single and this station was not a passing place. When first opened, the junction between the passenger line to what became Lowestoft Central and the goods line to South Side and Kirkley was at the west end of the station. There were two platforms, each serving one of the single lines, so that the southerly one with the main station building was not used by passengers. There was a siding on the north side which ran into a goods shed also on the north of the line, and which was at the west end of the passenger platform. When the branch was doubled between Beccles and Carlton Colville the station layout was substantially changed. The junction was moved to the other end of the station, so that the southern platform was brought into use for passengers. What had been the down line to Lowestoft (Central) was realigned at the west end, and continued through the station as a siding, with another crossover also being provided between it and the running line. The Board of Trade would not permit this to be used for passing trains. When the line was finally doubled through the station what now became the down platform was greatly extended and the goods shed demolished. The up platform remained in use when the branch was singled in the late 1980s with the introduction of RETB. The station building was on the south side platform

Above:
Oulton Broad South Junction signalbox stood in the junction between the main line and the goods branch. The main line curved very sharply past the box, turning through 90° to get to the swing bridge, and check-railed all the way round. *Robert Humm*

Right:
Oulton Broad South, looking towards Lowestoft in about 1950. The branch to Kirkley and South Side goes straight ahead, while the main line swings sharply to the left. The junction signalbox can just be seen through the bridge. The station building is one of the smaller type. *HMRS Hilton Collection*

Below:
Oulton Broad South seen from the Lowestoft end of the down platform in 1961, looking towards Beccles. Before the road bridge was built the main road had followed what is now the station approach and crossed the railway at an angle roughly where the nameboard and Morris Minor stand. *Stations UK*

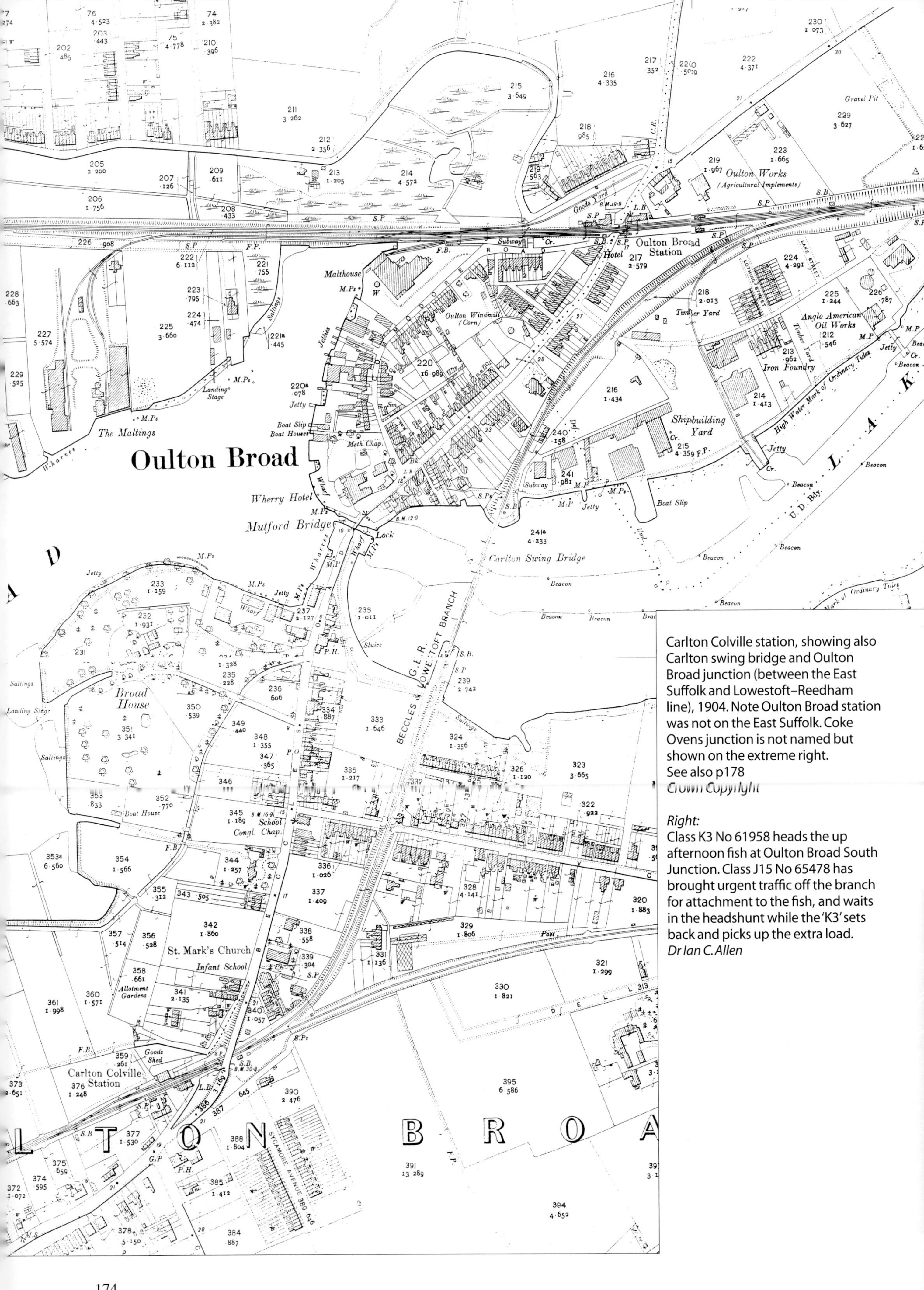

Carlton Colville station, showing also Carlton swing bridge and Oulton Broad junction (between the East Suffolk and Lowestoft–Reedham line), 1904. Note Oulton Broad station was not on the East Suffolk. Coke Ovens junction is not named but shown on the extreme right.

See also p178

Right:
Class K3 No 61958 heads the up afternoon fish at Oulton Broad South Junction. Class J15 No 65478 has brought urgent traffic off the branch for attachment to the fish, and waits in the headshunt while the 'K3' sets back and picks up the extra load.
Dr Ian C. Allen

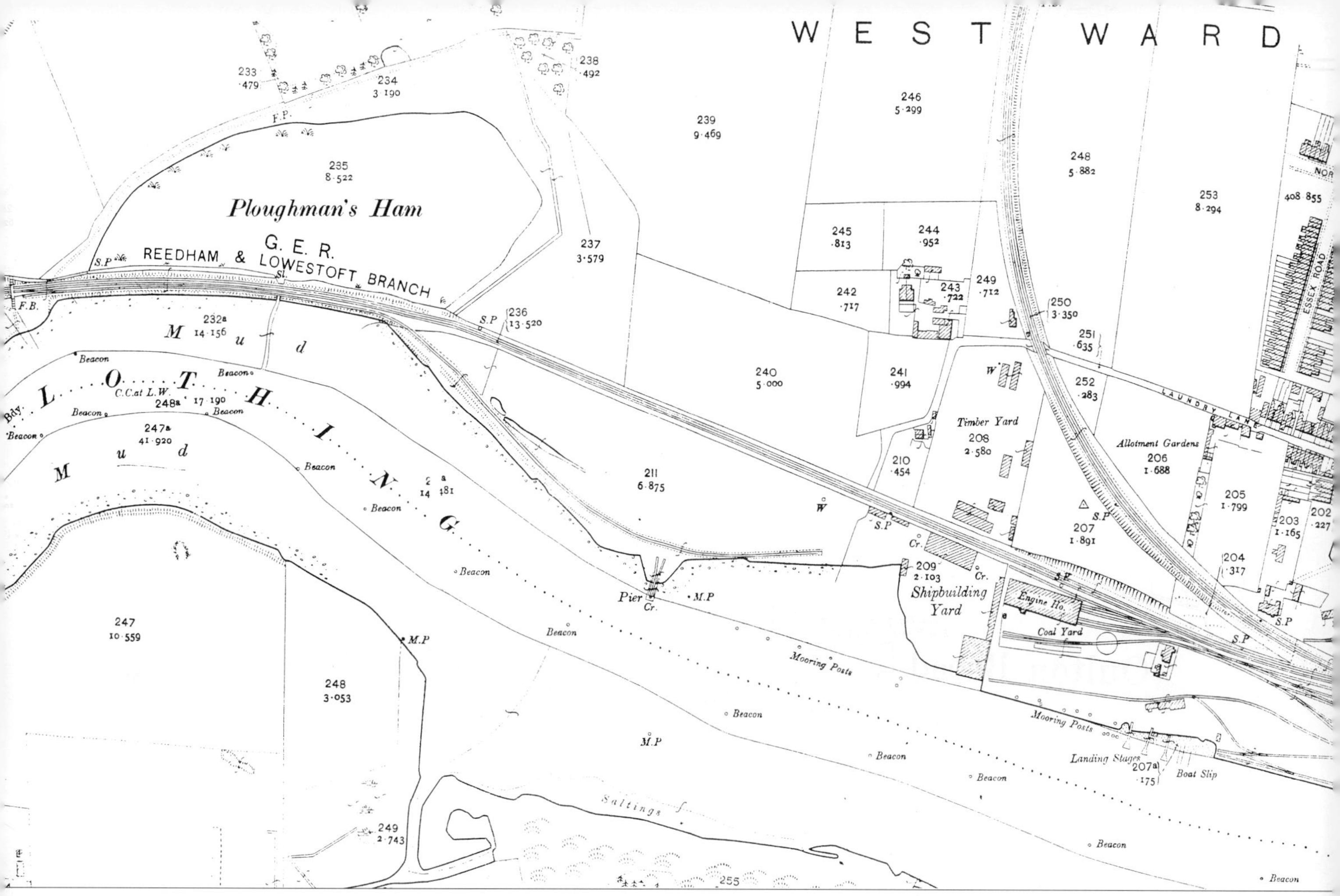
WEST WARD
Ploughman's Ham
G. E. R.
REEDHAM & LOWESTOFT BRANCH
LOTHING
Mud
Beacon
Timber Yard
Allotment Gardens
Shipbuilding Yard
Engine Ho.
Coal Yard
Pier
Mooring Posts
Landing Stages
Boat Slip
Saltings
ESSEX ROAD
LAUNDRY LANE
C.C.at L.W.
F.B.
S.P
M.P

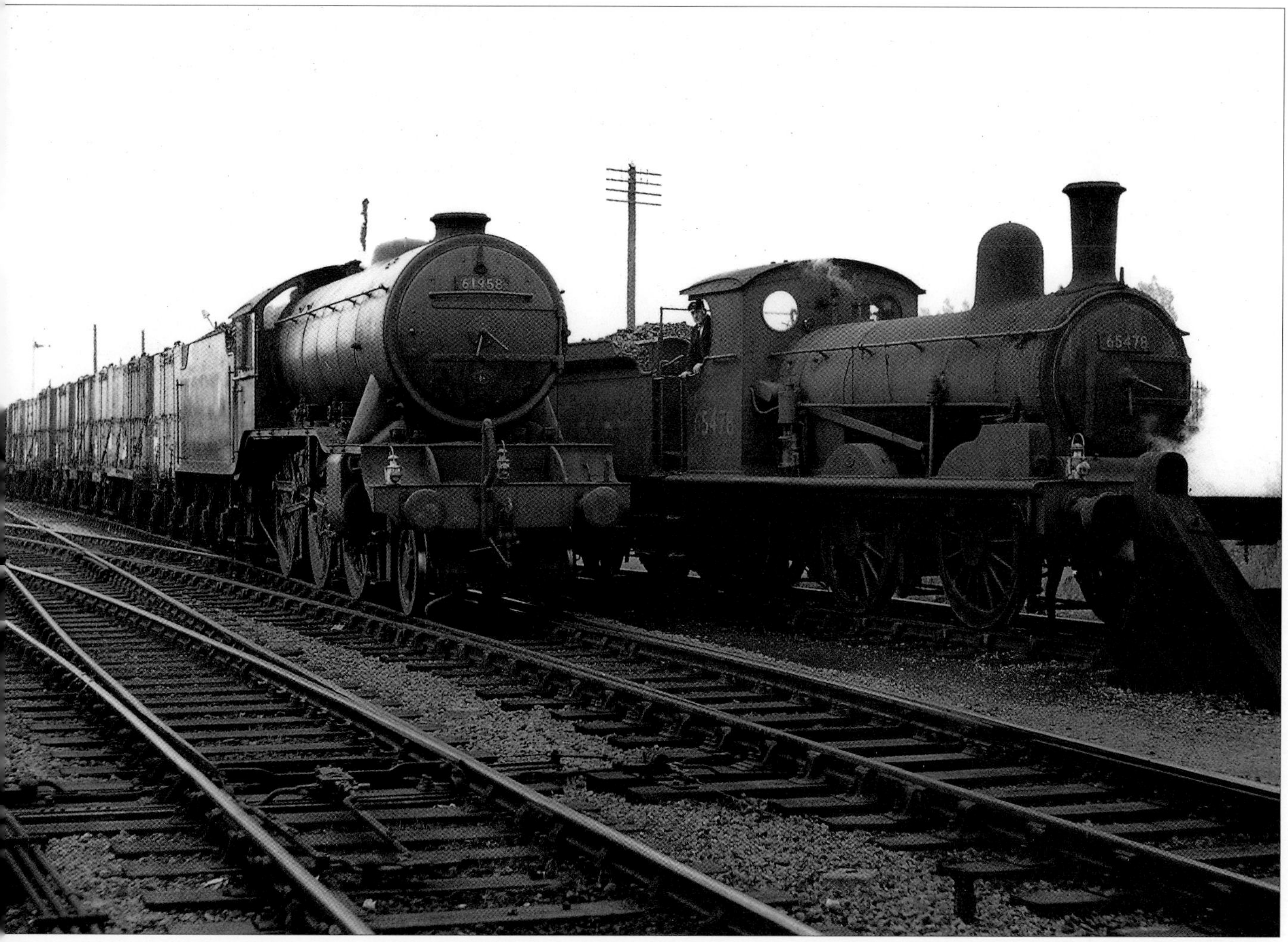
61958
65478

and of the usual pattern, but in the smaller size. The usual awning was on the platform side, continuing around the east end, and there was a small goods shed behind the passenger platform served by a short siding. Leaving Carlton Colville station, trains first passed over the level crossing at the east end of the station where Bridge Road crossed the railway, although this was replaced by a road overbridge before the 1884 Ordnance Survey of the area. The main line curved very sharply to the north — always heavily speed-limited — in order to reach the swing bridge over Lake Lothing at 115 miles 76 chains, going over Victoria Road level crossing (115 miles 62 chains) first. In later days Harbour Road (Gravel Pit) level crossing followed at 116 miles 12 chains, tightly curved as the line now swung back in an easterly direction to join the line from Reedham at Oulton Broad (North) Junction at 116 miles 27 chains. In the early days this was not strictly a junction, merely the point at which the East Suffolk and Reedham single lines converged, then running parallel as far as Coke Ovens (117 miles 13 chains). Eastwards from Oulton Broad the line had again been built over marshland, and had Lake Lothing and the inner harbour on the south side, together with the various rail-served works along the way, including Lowestoft motive power depot. Central station (so called after North opened on 13 July 1903) was reached at 117 miles 55 chains, and although not quite as imposing as South Town, was nevertheless a substantial and well-designed place after rebuilding in 1855 by Lucas Brothers.

The station had started with only two platforms, and after the reconstruction mentioned above boasted an L-shaped layout of its main buildings, with the booking, enquiry and parcels offices on the north side bordering Denmark Road, and the refreshment rooms at the east end opening onto Station Square. On the south side were toilets and the usual bookstall, whilst covering the concourse was a splendid overall roof extending some way over the tracks to provide a short train shed. In July 1885 Maj-Gen Hutchinson, for the Board of Trade, inspected alterations made by the Great Eastern which also involved rearrangements of track and

Below:
A fine aerial view of Lowestoft harbour and most of the railway, looking west. Central station can be seen on the right of the inner harbour, while there are numbers of trucks across the road in the trawl fish market, which is the smaller enclosed area on the right. There are also plenty of wagons on the North Pier Extension, the spit in the foreground, reached by lines which loop round the Waveney Dock behind this. Coke Ovens Junction can be seen further to the west, with the line to Yarmouth via Gorleston curving away to the right. A train appears to be coasting towards the junction, behind the Eastern Coach Works. Another train is on the line to Oulton Broad, just beyond Coke Ovens. On the other side of the harbour the line from Oulton Broad South can be seen curving round to reach Morton's factory and the South Side. *Simmons Aerofilms*

signalling between the station and Coke Ovens Junction. Whereas there had previously been two single lines from Oulton Broad, with a junction at Coke Ovens, the final section to the terminus was turned into double track, and an extra platform (the present No 4) added to bring the total to three; all were to be used for arrivals and departures. Two new signalboxes were provided — Coke Ovens on the south side of the line and Lowestoft Station on the north, having 28 working and six spare, and 36 working and eight spare levers respectively. Two dwarf frames were additionally installed. Maj-Gen Hutchinson required considerable extra interlocking and the removal of the smaller dwarf frame, which had been done when he reinspected in August. The line between Coke Ovens and Oulton Broad remained as two single tracks. Trains from Beccles arriving at Lowestoft were crossed over at Coke Ovens, as were those for Norwich. Further cross-overs close to the platform ends gave the flexibility needed for any platform to be used at the terminus.

Below:
A much lower-altitude view of Lowestoft at an earlier era. The tramlines are clear in the streets, and there are several horse-drawn vehicles about. Central station is very prominent, with its overall roof and main entrance in Denmark Road, on the right. The line to the trawl market in the left foreground is very clear. The yards are full of goods wagons, and the goods shed is in Denmark Road beyond the passenger station. *Simmons Aerofilms*

INNER HARBOUR
NORTH QUAY
SOUTH QUAY
COMMERCIAL ROAD
DENMARK ROAD
HERVEY STREET
MAIDSTONE ROAD
TONNING STREET
ALMA ROAD
ALMA STREET
ASHBY ROAD
STEVENS ST.
CLEMENCE STREET
SELBY STREET
NEPTUNE ST.
TRAFALGAR STREET
FLENSBURGH ST.
Coke Ovens Junction
Allotment Gardens
TRAMWAY
Goods Yard
Goods Shed
Hotel
Drill Hall
Oil Mill
BARBER'S WHARF
STERRY'S WHARF
Timber Yd.
DRY DOCK
Patent Slip
Lock
Iron Works
Ward Bdy.
Boatbuilding Yard
Crane
Kirkley Ham
Mud
Posts
Crown Works
(Boatbuilding, Engineering &c.)
Wharf
SOUTH WHARF
BELVEDERE ROAD
WAVENEY DRIVE
HORN HILL
Sluice
ST. JOHN'S ROAD
MILL ROAD
CLEVELAND ROAD
GROSVENOR ROAD
WINDSOR ROAD
LONDON ROAD SOUTH
PARADE ROAD SOUTH
FREEMANTLE RD.
SALISBURY ROAD
VICTORIA ROAD
WELLINGTON
MARINE PARADE
ESPLANADE
BEACH
Working Men's Institute
Mission Ch.
Mission Hall
Fire Sta.
Baths
Statue
Shelter
Low Water Mark of Ordinary Tides
Chap.
Sch.
SOUTH

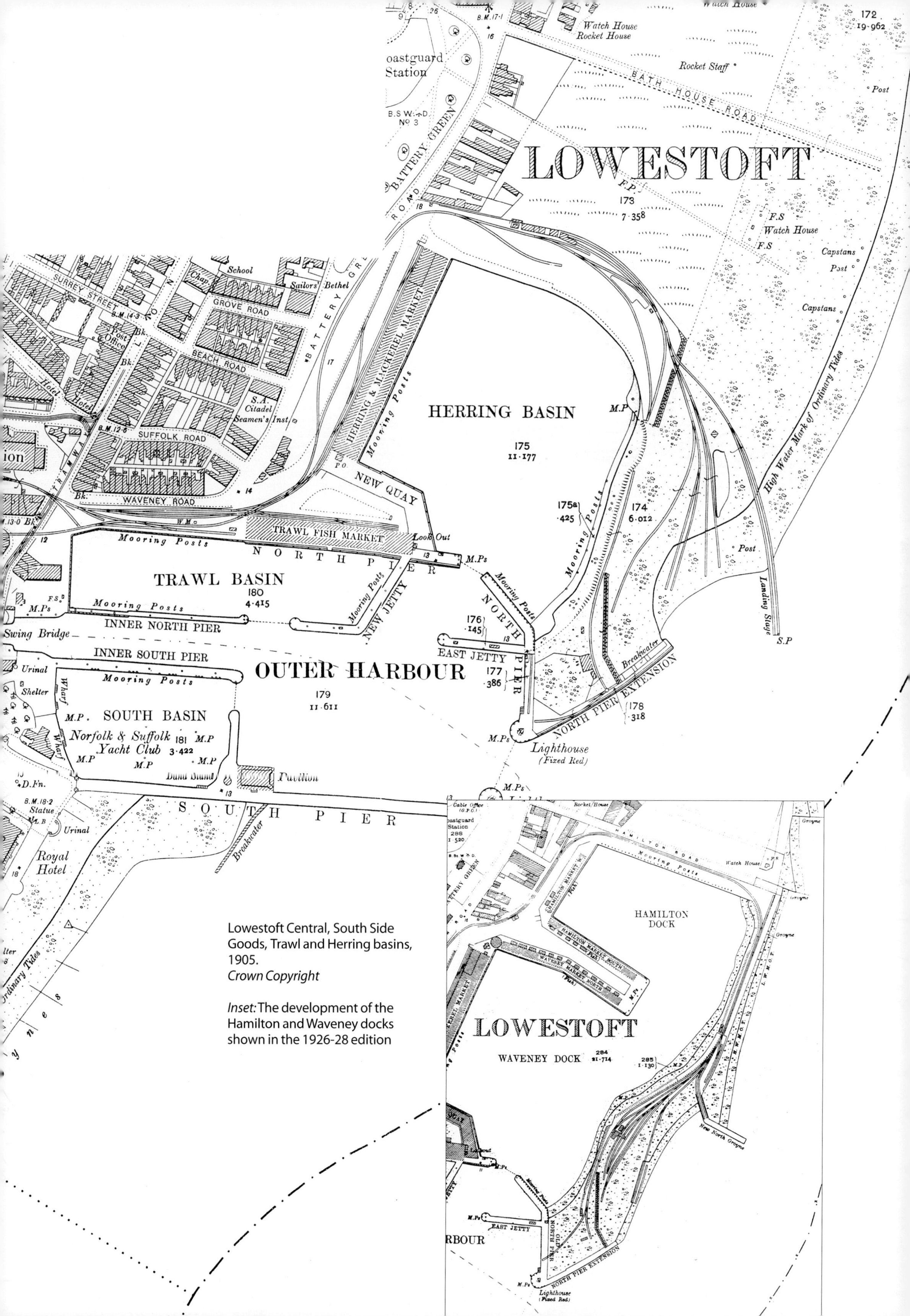

Lowestoft Central, South Side Goods, Trawl and Herring basins, 1905.
Crown Copyright

Inset: The development of the Hamilton and Waveney docks shown in the 1926-28 edition

Above:
A Great Eastern view of the south and east sides of the station from Station Square, with municipal tramlines prominent in the foreground. The GER tramlines to the trawl market cross these in the left foreground.
Lens of Sutton

Right:
The south side of the refreshment rooms, themselves at the east end of the station, seen in 1951.
HMRS Hilton Collection

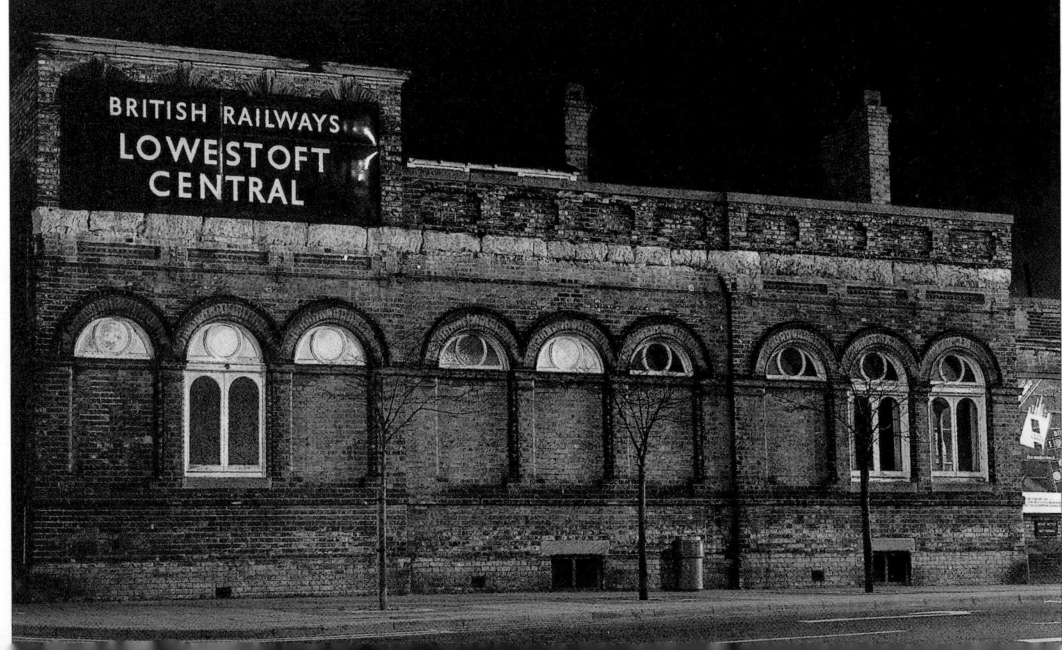

Right:
The east end of Lowestoft station on 12 November 1983. The blue enamel sign remains a feature of the station in 2003, but its future is threatened by redevelopment.
David Pearce

Above:
The interior of Lowestoft station, looking towards the buffers, with a train standing in Platform 4. There is an exit on the south side of the station just in front of the row of fire buckets in front of the bookstall. The roof has an air of solidity and permanence.
Stations UK

Below:
'Off to the Alps, May 19 1904' reads the caption on this postcard view. The party does not look unruly, although there are two policemen on hand. The platforms are wooden and the train waits in No 4, on the left. Since the Norfolk & Suffolk Joint line to Yarmouth opened in 1903 the station has been renamed 'Lowestoft Central', and the lamps are already so marked. *Alan Taylor collection*

Above:
Taken from a short distance along Platform 3, looking east towards the main station. The awnings have been largely removed but the overall roof is intact. Temporary lighting is being installed.
Lens of Sutton

Below:
A 1961 view, looking from the end of Platform 2 towards Oulton Broad. There are plenty of covered vans in the sidings, and the pilot, probably a Class 08, lurks in Platform 4.
Stations UK

Right:
A Yarmouth South Town to Liverpool Street train is ready to leave Lowestoft behind No D6717 on 27 June 1961. These workings entailed reversal at Lowestoft.
S. Creer

Below:
On 20 September 1977 the 12.26 to Norwich waits to leave, with a Cravens Class 105 DMU leading. Class 37 No 37056 is stabled in the yard. New lighting has been installed on the platforms.
Geoff Pinder

Above:
Despite the destination blind, this train is arriving as the 12.08 from Norwich, and will go out again as the 13.00 Lowestoft to Ipswich on 24 July 1982 after a 5 min turn-round. It is formed of two two-car Cravens Class 105 units. *R. S. Freeman*

Below:
A three-car Class 101 unit passes Lowestoft Yard box with an East Suffolk train from Ipswich on 29 April 1989. Note the radio aerial on the front of the unit, and the headlight fitted which aided sighting the many lineside reflective signal boards. *Michael J. Collins*

Above:
A most unusual visitor to Lowestoft on 3 September 1978 was 'Deltic' No 55015 which had arrived with an excursion from King's Cross via Cambridge, Ely and Norwich. It was about to return via the East Suffolk. The track in Platform 1 has been lifted. *David Pearce*

Below:
A typical sight at Lowestoft for many years was that of the yard pilot — in this case No 03370 — berthed alongside the station awaiting its next turn of duty. This view was taken on 1 July 1978.
David Pearce

Top:
The ultimate indignity to be heaped upon Lowestoft station was the removal of its overall roof. On 28 April 1992 the job has just been started. The 'Now Open' sign is very apt! *David Pearce*

Above:
Under the roof the station is a sorry sight. The former W. H. Smith bookstall looks forlorn as debris accumulates around it. The newly exposed concourse was subsequently refurbished. *David Pearce*

Above:
The end of an era: what most people thought was the final scheduled through train from London to Lowestoft via the East Suffolk ran on 12 May 1984, and here prepares to return to Norwich behind No 37115.
David Pearce

Below:
For many years Lowestoft was home to the Eastern Coach Works, which built bodies for buses. In the 1950s it turned its hand to building diesel railcars. Here are Nos Sc79959 and Sc79958 outside the works on 13 July 1958. The site is now occupied by a retail park.
Alan Taylor collection

The swing bridge at Carlton Colville had given cause for concern locally in the early 1890s when the local MP Mr J. C. Colman voiced complaints, and eventually the Great Eastern called in the Board of Trade to give it a thorough inspection. Maj-Gen Hutchinson duly arrived in February 1893, and gave a very full description of both the bridge and its approach viaducts in his report. The total length of the swing bridge was 85ft 6in, giving a clear opening of 32ft each side of the central support. The viaduct at the London end had 14 spans and that on the Lowestoft side seven, each with a length of about 17ft. The single line was laid with double-headed rails fixed in chairs secured to transverse sleepers 20ft long. The bridge itself was made of wrought iron and was cranked round by hand. Each pier was composed of four 13in x 13in vertical piles, with the two centre ones being directly under the rails and the outer about 5½ft from them. The piles were braced by 12in x 6in diagonals bolted to them, with caps and bolsters on the tops of the piles. Alternate bays were further braced by round iron diagonal ties. The height of the viaduct above high water was about 15ft, and the greatest depth of water at high water also about 15ft. Maj-Gen Hutchinson commented that he failed to discover any unsoundness about the bridge, and noted that although some of the upper timbers had been renewed from time to time, the piles themselves had never needed it, showing them to be of excellent quality. He found that the deflection of the longitudinals under the passage of an engine was between ⅜in and ½in, and felt that this was not excessive. In his opinion it was a lot more desirable to improve the arrangements at the junction of the fixed and swinging parts of the bridge, as was now being done at Beccles, than to tinker with the structure of the bridge itself.

The Great Eastern Railway General Powers Act of 1898 gave sanction for the widening of the line between Beccles and Lowestoft. The first part was undertaken between Beccles and Carlton Colville, a distance of about 6¼ miles, in 1899 and was inspected by Col G. W. Addison in October and incorporated a former siding on the up side at the Beccles end, although almost all the widening was on the down side. The five underbridges were reconstructed in wood to save delay in procuring girders, and a new brick arch bridge over the line was built at Carlton Colville. Common Lane crossing was rebuilt and received new gates, and the station yard at Beccles needed some slight alterations. The junction of the Lowestoft and Yarmouth lines was effectively moved back towards the station, with control of the points and signals taken over by Beccles North Junction box, now with 80 levers including four spare, making Lowestoft Junction redundant. At the other end, the doubling finished just short of Carlton Colville station, which was left with a single passenger platform and a signalbox with 19 working and four spare levers. Another ground frame had seven levers, all in use. Col Addison's report noted that the station had 'very indifferent accommodation' and was to be rebuilt. He decreed

Below:
A fine view of signalman Jack Howes in Oulton Broad Swing Bridge signalbox during its last week of operation before being downgraded to ground frame status. It is retained for working the bridge as required. The bridge indicator on the right of the block shelf shows that the bridge is in position for rail traffic, that the wedges are under it, and the bolts are in place; in other words, a train could pass over if signalled. *Eastern Counties Newspapers*

Above:
The modern swing bridge at Oulton Broad, seen from the west. It bridges Lake Lothing; boats reach Oulton Broad itself via Mutford Lock, out of the photograph on the left. The signalbox is also just out of shot on the left. *Alan Taylor collection*

that it must not be used as a passing place for passenger trains with its current layout. The signalbox at Barnby, until this scheme the only passing place on the branch, now became an intermediate block post with 17 working and five spare levers. Col Addison sanctioned the works being brought into use, subject to a 25mph speed limit until the track was fully consolidated.

Work at Coke Ovens in late 1900 involved extensive re-locking, although the tracks to the west remained as before: two single lines. Later in 1901 major works at Oulton Broad (now Oulton Broad North) brought about widening and other improvements. The station was completely rebuilt, the new one having two platforms on the Lowestoft side of the level crossing, a new station building incorporating booking office and hall, and a footbridge between the platforms which also allowed people over the line when the gates were across the road. There was also a small subway. The station signalbox, with 25 levers (five spare), and Oulton Broad New Junction box with 21 levers (four spare) were new. The railway thence to Coke Ovens was converted from two single lines to double track controlled by the signalboxes at each end. The East Suffolk remained single track, but with a double junction. Further work was needed at Coke Ovens in 1903 to accommodate the new Norfolk & Suffolk Joint line to Yarmouth, opened on 13 July.

Doubling between Carlton Colville and Oulton Broad Junction had to wait until 1907 before it was completed, despite having been authorised nearly 10 years earlier. At the latter place the junction itself was unchanged, although just about everything else was new. The new swing bridge was to be electrically locked at both ends from the signalbox, so that unless everything was in position for the passage of a train it could not be accepted or the signals lowered. Oulton Broad South Junction signalbox was new, in the vee of the junction, and the tracks were rearranged so that it made a double junction instead of the single track on the south side simply continuing on towards Kirkley. Carlton Colville station was almost entirely rebuilt. All of the down side was new — including the buildings, canopy and steps down from the road bridge, and the 500ft-long platform. On the up side a new shelter was provided half-way between the station building and the Beccles end of the platform, although otherwise this side was original. A new siding on the down side ran behind the platform. The main outgoing traffic was sugar beet.

Col von Donop inspected the remainder of the works in August 1908, they being officially completed on 8 July. The new double line between Carlton Colville and Oulton Broad had been deviated slightly towards the north, and laid with modern materials. The rail used was the standard 85lb/yd steel bullhead, with 95lb/yd used over bridges and viaducts. The swing bridge had been completely replaced and now had five spans, four being 44ft 9in and one 30ft 0in. They were of steel girders resting on brick abutments, with the two central spans forming the swinging portion. This bridge continues in use today, and was identical with the old bridge at Trowse, replaced when the main line to Norwich was electrified. There were two level crossings, one at Victoria Road and the other at what is now Harbour Road. Carlton Colville signalbox was new, with 28 levers including five spare. Oulton Broad South Junction retained its existing box but with all 29 levers in use, and the swing bridge box was also new, with 10 levers, including three spare. This last is one of the two remaining on the East Suffolk itself, the other being Saxmundham.

The goods line to Kirkley continued straight ahead at Carlton Colville (renamed Oulton Broad South by the LNER from 26 September 1927), which itself had limited facilities for this traffic. Curving gently to the south, it swung parallel to what became Victoria Road. This then turned sharply to the right a little under ¾ mile after the junction into what is now Kirkley Run, where there was a level crossing with cottage and keeper. By the turn of the century the main road had been diverted to the northeast just before this crossing, now reaching Lowestoft via Waveney Drive. Additional crossings also had to be built over Colville Road and Durban Road when they were constructed. About half a mile past Kirkley the line swung round towards the north, passing under the brick-arch Mill Road bridge and reaching Kirkley goods station after about a further half mile. Here the single line fanned out into two groups of sidings, one on each side of the yard, and both extending across Belvedere Road onto the South Quay, where wagon turntables were used to access the sidings there. Another siding, reached only by turntable, went

Above:
There is much of interest in this view of the railway, looking west at Oulton Broad North (or New) Junction. The station has been relocated to its modern position east of the level crossing, while the junction box controls the connection to the East Suffolk, which curves off to Carlton Colville on the left.
HMRS Hilton Collection

Below:
The complementary view, also taken in 1911, looking towards Lowestoft. Note that the signalbox is denoted 'Oulton Broad Junction'. The Norwich lines are on the left in the foreground, with the East Suffolk trailing in from the right. The siding on the right served boat builders and other businesses on Lake Lothing and in Harbour Road. *HMRS Hilton Collection*

parallel to the quay and into Morton's cannery in Belvedere Road. When the Co-op factory was built it, too, was given rail access, its siding diverging from the 'main line' just east of the Durban Road crossing, and curving round parallel to Waveney Drive then crossing it into the factory. Shunting into here required a flagman. The line was provided with a loop between Durban Road and Waveney Drive, and several sidings within the works, the main one running alongside Iceworks Road (later Riverside Road) and then turning westwards to serve the shipyards there.

Lowestoft South Side was worked on the 'one-engine-in-steam' principle, with the staff being blue. The far end of the staff section was the Durban Road crossing. Tickets were not used, but on rare occasions two trains might be worked down the branch by the simple expedient of the staff from the first being brought back by road. The most likely occasion for this was when Oulton Broad South needed to use the branch to refuge a train, which required the train to have the staff. It was often necessary for the trip from Central to South Side to be repeated if loads were heavy. The first would go down the branch loaded from Central, come back with empties, and then go back again with a second load. Often this involved coal, which arrived via Norwich into Central's yard, with steam coal for the trawlers being loaded from the North Side, and domestic coal tripped round to the South Side, where the yard was in Horn Hill. The Co-op received diesel oil and also

Above:
Oulton Broad North Junction as it is today. The signalbox is long gone, and Oulton Broad North station box, just visible under the bracket signal, controls the junction, swing bridge and South station. In this view taken on 29 April 1989 a private charter for VSOE from London to Lowestoft via Norwich is headed by No 47657. The East Suffolk has been singled and the crossover in the foreground is used to gain the down Lowestoft line. *Michael J. Collins*

empty wagons, and shunted its sidings in later days by tractor. Trains for the branch sometimes ran round in Oulton Broad South, and sometimes propelled down. They were always unpopular on Monday mornings when the washing was hung out! Two crews were required for a day's work, with the second coming on in the middle of the day and the first making its own way back to the depot.

Locomotives were not the only motive power used on the railway. There were some 30 horses at Lowestoft in the height of the season for various work, which included shunting coal for the fishing fleet on the North Quay; shunting fish vans in the trawl market, ice, and so on. A pair of horses would normally take one van loaded or two empty. On the South Side was another pair of horses shunting (for example) timber for Jewsons. Horses rarely went as far as the Co-op canning factory, since this was done by the shunting engine. There were normally eight pairs of shunting horses in all: three in

Left:
Class J15 No 65460 shunts into the Co-op factory, protected by flagmen across Waveney Drive and Durban Road. Evidently the driver got to and from the depot by bike.
Alan Taylor collection

the trawl dock, two on the south side and three on the north quay. Others were used on the vans. When making deliveries they could travel several miles — perhaps as far as Kessingland, Oulton Broad and other villages around Lowestoft. The stables were in Denmark Road next to the goods shed, before being established in Commercial Road.

Outward traffic included joinery work from Boulton & Paul's and cannery traffic. The Co-op generated 3-4 wagons per day, which would be tripped to Oulton Broad South and then attached to the front of the up fish, due out of Lowestoft at about 4.18pm. The fish traffic itself came entirely from the North Side. Overall, Lowestoft generated a large variety of freight, including, in 1938, 7,888 tons of confectionery and preserves (mostly from Mortons and the Co-op), 1,028 tons of manure and 2,962 tons of vegetables, mostly beet via Kirkley. Other substantial traffic included imports of Scandinavian timber used for permanent way items such as sleepers, and concrete. Lowestoft was a major centre for manufacture of railway materials, and its sleeper depot was always busy with manufacturing and pressure treating track materials. After Melton Constable works closed in 1936, Lowestoft took over as a centre for the manufacture of very many items such as fence posts, building parts and so on, and sent them all over the LNER and later British Railways Eastern Region. Products were largely despatched by rail, and there could be six or seven wagonloads daily. Latterly the staff included four carpenters in the mould shop, plus a wood machinist, six in the reinforcement shop making moulds, a mixer/driver and assistant, two auto-truck drivers and a loading gang of five or six men, the loading mostly being done manually, although with a steam crane at times. Others were employed in actually casting the concrete.

There was yet more to the railway. Lowestoft harbour was largely the responsibility of the railway, and had to be well maintained and kept in good order. In the late 1930s the quays were reconstructed from timber to concrete and steel, the South Pier having already been so treated by this time. Each of the pile frames used involved a steam boiler with attendant boilerman, winchman, between six and eight labourers and a chargehand. New concrete piles would be driven, and concrete poured behind them, possibly around a skeleton of beams. Steel piles were also used for many jobs. There were six or seven pile frames in use at any one time in the Harbour Works, always one on the South Pier head and one on the North Pier head extension. These had to have wooden piles for the safety of shipping, usually greenheart imported via the sleeper depot.

There was much more to Lowestoft goods traffic than South Side, of course. The fish market was reached by crossing the A12, and was worked with small tank engines or Sentinels. Fish that was unfit for human consumption was sprayed purple and spread on the fields, but all went away by rail. The traffic was lost to road partly because the price was raised too high, but perhaps what was not considered was the state of the fish at the end of its journey. It was packed in crates with ice, and on a rough road the fish rose to the top, out of the ice, whilst on rail the ride was much better and this did not happen. The fish market was worked daily. There might only be two trucks coming out, in which case a tractor would be used, with any more necessitating the use of a locomotive. A flagman was needed for crossing the road. The traffic was treated with great urgency and was passenger-rated, and was mostly sent to Spitalfields for Billingsgate; in the season most long-distance passenger trains from Lowestoft had three or four fish vans attached.

Right:
An unusual view taken in 1951, looking towards the terminus at Kirkley through the arch of the Mill Road bridge.
The trackbed here is now a cycle path.
HMRS Hilton Collection

— 12 —

Train Services on the East Suffolk

REFERENCE has already been made to the train services run on the line when it first opened, and in the immediate aftermath. It seems surprising today that, having spent so much time and capital on building the main line and its branches, a service of no more than four passenger trains each way daily was operated; the Snape branch initially had two goods trains. It says much about the relative size of staff wages that it was worth while for the railway companies, bearing in mind that the operation was much more labour intensive than now. On the other hand there were no signalboxes and the system of train control was primitive, so that fewer staff were needed for either operation or maintenance in this respect. The branches offered travel for all classes of passenger, including separate waiting rooms for first class passengers at many stations, while staff came to expect a Christmas box from the local squire — perhaps a brace of pheasants or the like. What follows here will try to give a picture of services once the line had become established, whilst also exploring developments that took place over the years and looking at what it might have been like to travel on the trains. The events leading up to the rundown and closure of lines are dealt with under a separate heading.

The *raison d'être* of the line was always to provide Yarmouth and Lowestoft with a fast route to London, whilst at the same time tapping into the rich agricultural hinterland of East Suffolk. Traffic developed steadily, and the range of passenger trains increased as the 19th century wore on. By July 1877 there were six trains between Ipswich and Yarmouth on Mondays to Saturdays, with one extra on Saturdays only, plus others which covered only part of the line. The 5.10am from Liverpool Street arrived at Ipswich at 7.5am, having made the journey in a very respectable 115min; it went on to terminate at Norwich Victoria at 9.18am, calling almost everywhere. The East Suffolk part of the journey was similarly a leisurely affair, with South Town not being reached until 9.35am. All the branches had a connection: Framlingham reached at 8.25am, Aldeburgh at 8.40am and Lowestoft at 9.35am, this last being a mixed working from Beccles. Carlton Colville had the dubious distinction of being the sole station where a stop was made only on request, which was true for all trains on the branch. Connections were also made at Beccles for the Waveney Valley line, and St Olaves Junction for Norwich, although the last involved a wait of 75min — ample for transferring between platforms. However, matters were better on Saturdays when there was a train from St Olaves Junction at 9.30am for Norwich market, returning to connect with the 6.38pm from there to Ipswich.

The next departure over the whole line was the 11.25am from Ipswich, all stations as before, except that it did not call at St Olaves Junction in the absence of a connection to Norwich. All branches again had connections. This train connected with both the 7.30am from Liverpool Street and the 9am, the former being the Parliamentary and the latter having pretensions to being an express service. The 12.3pm from Ipswich was the fastest train of the day by some margin, and was the through working of the 10am express from Liverpool Street, which had called only at Chelmsford, Colchester and Manningtree. On the East Suffolk its first call was at Saxmundham, where there was a connection for Aldeburgh (arrive 1.20pm), Beccles (for Lowestoft, arrive 1.35pm), and Yarmouth South Town, reached at 1.40pm. Framlingham did not have a connection from this train. The 2.20pm from Ipswich called at all stations except Belton, and had connections at all points, except that the branch train to Framlingham ran on Thursdays and Saturdays only. The 2.30pm express from Liverpool Street reached Ipswich at 4.31pm and reached Yarmouth at 6.30pm, calling en route at Woodbridge, Wickham Market, Saxmundham, Darsham (set down only), Halesworth and Beccles. Framlingham, Aldeburgh and Lowestoft had connections, but the Waveney Valley did not. The 6.52pm from Ipswich called at all stations and had connections onto all the East Suffolk branches, and was preceded on Saturdays only by the 6.49pm, calling only at Saxmundham for Aldeburgh, Beccles for Lowestoft, and Yarmouth. This was the last down train over the whole line, so the latest departure from London was at 4.20pm Mondays to Fridays, or 4.45pm on Saturdays.

There were additional trains from Beccles to Yarmouth at 10.15am Mondays to Fridays, and 11.10am Saturdays, plus the 5.40pm Mondays to Saturdays, calling at Aldeby, St Olaves and Belton, and the 9.55pm which called at the intermediate stations only on request. On the branches there were extra trains from Beccles to Lowestoft at 12.5pm, 2.15pm and 8.55pm, plus one from Saxmundham on the Aldeburgh branch at 9.30am Saturdays only, for the market. The solitary Sunday service left Ipswich at 6pm and called at all main line stations. Its only connection was at Beccles for Lowestoft.

In the up direction the first train was 5.40am from Yarmouth calling at all stations (St Olaves Junction on request); on reaching Ipswich at 8.12am passengers had a choice of the 8.20am express to Liverpool Street (arrive 10.22am), or the 8.33am Parliamentary, arrive 12.2pm. The 8.15am from Yarmouth was considerably faster, and called only at Beccles (connection from the Waveney Valley on Mondays and Thursdays, and Lowestoft Mondays to Saturdays), Halesworth, Darsham, Saxmundham (connection from Aldeburgh), Wickham Market (no Framlingham connection), Woodbridge and Bealings (for London passengers only), reaching Ipswich at 10.9am and pausing for only four minutes before leaving for London, calling at Manningtree, Colchester, Chelmsford and Stratford *en route*. Arrival in the capital was at 12.15pm. The 10.15am from Yarmouth called at all stations, had connections from everywhere and took 145min to reach Ipswich. The 11.40am had connections only from Lowestoft and Aldeburgh and reached Ipswich just 10min behind the 10.15am, having called only at Beccles and Saxmundham, and then gave an arrival of 3.37pm in Liverpool Street. The 3.25pm from Yarmouth called everywhere (Aldeby on Wednesdays and Saturdays only), and the 6.15pm was the last up train over the whole line, calling all stations except Westerfield and having

GREAT EASTERN RAILWAY—COLCHESTER LINE.

LONDON, COLCHESTER, IPSWICH, WOODBRIDGE, YARMOUTH, AND NORWICH, WITH BRANCHES TO MALDON, BRAINTREE, SUDBURY, HAVERHILL, BURY, HARWICH, HADLEIGH FRAMLINGHAM, ALDEBURGH, LOWESTOFT, AND BUNGAY.

DOWN TRAINS—Week Days.

EAST SUFFOLK DISTRICT.

FROM	Morn	Morn
IPSWICH arr.	7 5	11 15
IPSWICH dep.	7 10	11 25
Westerfield	7 20	11 36
Bealings	7 29	11 45
WOODBRIDGE	7 38	11 55
Melton	7 43	12 0
Wickham Market—Fr. J.	7 54	12 10
Fram. branch. Wickham Mar. dp.	8 0	12 40
Marlesford	8 8	12 47
Parham	8 16	12 57
FRAMLINGHAM	8 25	1 5
SAXMUNDHAM: Ald. J	8 9	12 45
Aldbr. branc. Saxmundham de.	8 15	12 55
Leiston	8 27	1 7
ALDBOROUGH	8 40	1 20
Darsham for Yoxford and	8 19	12 55
Halesworth (Southwold	8 32	1 7
Brampton	8 41	1 16
Beccles—Lowstt. Br. Jn.	8 55	1 30
Lowst. bra. Beccles dep.	9 5	1 35
Carlton Colville		
LOWESTOFT arr.	9 35	1 55
Waveney Val. bran. Beccles dep.	9 20	2 30
Bungay	9 41	2 54
Harleston	10 2	3 17
Tivetshall	10 20	3 35
Norwich, via W.V.	11 3	4 22
Aldeby	9 5	1 40
St. Olaves Junction	9 12	
Haddiscoe	10 29	
Reedham	10 37	
NORWICH arr.	11 12	1 48
St. Olaves	9 17	1 54
Belton	9 23	2 5
YARMOUTH (South Tar.)	9 3[illegible]	

FROM	Morn
YARMOUTH (Sth. T.) dep	5 40
Belton	5 50
St. Olaves	5 57
NORWICH dep.	
Reedham	
Haddiscoe	
St. Olaves Junction	6 5
Aldeby	
Tivetshall dep.	
Harleston	
Bungay	
Beccles	
LOWESTOFT dep.	5 50
Carlton Colville	
Beccles Junc. arr.	6 10
Beccles dep.	6 20
Brampton	6 32
Halesworth (Southwold	6 42
Darsham for Yoxford and	6 54
ALDBOROUGH dp	6 35
Leiston	6 47
Saxmundham J. ar	7 0
SAXMUNDHAM dep.	7 7
FRAMLINGHAM	6 50
Parham	6 57
Marlesford	7 5
Wickham Mar. J. a.	7 15
Wickham Market dep.	7 22
Melton	7 32
WOODBRIDGE	7 39
Bealings	7 49
Westerfield	7 59
IPSWICH arr.	8 12

A—Calls at Elmswell and Thurston for Passengers only. B—Horses and Private Carriages are not conveyed by these Trains between Ipswich and Norwich. C—1st and 2nd Class Passengers are conveyed to Chelmsford, Witham, Maldon, and Braintree, by Slip Carriage. Horses and Private Carriages not conveyed by this Train for these Stations or for Marks Tey, Stations on Sudbury and Bury Line, or Colchester. D—Will call at Bethnal Green Junction on Wednesdays. E—The 4.15 p.m. from Tivetshall to Beccles will start at 5.45 p.m. on Saturdays. F—Calls at Darsham to set down Passengers from London and Stations between London and Ipswich inclusive. G—Parliamentary to Stations between Ipswich and Yarmouth. H—Runs to Halstead and Haverhill on Mondays only. I—1st and 2nd Class Passengers conveyed to Marks Tey and the Sudbury Branch by Slip Carriage. J—Calls at Carlton Colville to set down Passengers only. K—This train will convey only Horses for Hunting to or from Brentwood, Ingatestone, Chelmsford, and Witham. Horses and Private Carriages are conveyed to or from Colchester and Stations beyond. L—IPSWICH MARKET.—The 3.48 p.m. Train from Ipswich calls at Ardleigh on Tuesdays. N—Will call at Aldeby on Wednesdays and Saturdays. O—Runs on Mondays and Thursdays only. Not Parly from Waveney Valley Line. P—Calls at Bealings when required to take up London Passengers only. S—Runs Thursdays and Saturdays only. T—Parly to Stations on the Bury Branch. U—Horses and Private Carriages not conveyed by this Train, except Hunting Horses, on Mondays only, locally between Beccles and Ipswich. V—Does not run from Haverhill and Halstead on Fridays. W—Calls at Bentley to set down Passengers only. Z—Starts from Bury at 5.20 p.m. on Wednesdays and runs from Haverhill and Halstead on Fridays only. NORWICH MARKET.—On Saturdays a Carriage is attached to a Goods Train leaving Ipswich for Norwich at 4.15 a.m., calling at Stowmarket, Haughley, Mellis, Diss and Tivetshall. A Market Train leaves St. Olaves Junction on Saturdays for Norwich at 9.30 a.m., in connection with the 7.10 a.m. train from Ipswich; returning from Norwich to St. Olaves Junction at 5.35 p.m., in connection with the 6.35 p.m. train ex St. Olaves Junction to Ipswich. * The Trains will stop at stations marked * when required to set down or take up Passengers: those who wish to alight must inform the Guard at the previous *stopping* Station to that at which they wish to be set down. †—Do not convey Horses and Private Carriages from Liverpool Street. ☞—Horses and Private Carriages will not be conveyed by these Trains. MIXED TRAINS.—These Trains being Goods Trains with Passenger Carriages attached for the general convenience of the Public the same punctuality cannot be observed as with ordinary Passenger Trains. RETURN TICKETS at Single Fares are issued every Sunday by all Trains to and from all Stations on the Eastern Union Division, that is, between Sudbury and Norwich, via Mark's Tey and Ipswich, Manningtree and Harwich, Haughley and Bury, available on the day of issue only.

Left: July 1877 timetable for the East Suffolk, with Sunday services, shown in the *Ipswich Journal*, 3 July 1877.

connections from all the branches. Additional trains over parts of the line included the 1.35pm, 5pm and 8.15pm from Yarmouth to Beccles, Lowestoft to Beccles at 12.40pm, 5.10pm and 9.30pm, and Framlingham to Wickham Market at 2.25pm on Thursdays and Saturdays. Aldeburgh had an additional train to Saxmundham at 2.40pm. On Sundays there were two up trains, at 7am and 5.30pm from Yarmouth, with connections only from Lowestoft and Aldeburgh.

Ten years later, the timetables for August 1887 showed further developments, but also that the pattern was fairly stable. The 5.10am from Liverpool Street ran much as before, with connections to all the branches; the Waveney Valley had them at both ends. Carlton Colville was now served by scheduled calls, Yarmouth was reached at 9.20am, and Halesworth now offered connections via the Southwold Railway. A fast train at 8am on Mondays only from Ipswich served Woodbridge, Wickham Market, Saxmundham, Darsham, Halesworth, Beccles and Yarmouth, with a connection to Lowestoft. The next service was the 10.20am all-stations to Yarmouth, with connections to all the branches, and then the 10.25am from Liverpool Street, which ran nonstop to Ipswich (arrive 12.10pm), then next stop Beccles, where the Lowestoft portion was detached, with South Town reached at 1.45pm. Connections were available via the 12.21pm semi-fast from Ipswich. The 12.30pm from Liverpool Street was another very fast service, but did call at Saxmundham for Aldeburgh; otherwise the 2.23pm from Ipswich provided the connections and covered the intermediate stops. Westerfield tended to be served by Felixstowe trains, and St Olaves Junction only when a connection to Norwich was possible. On Saturdays the 2pm express from Liverpool Street called first at Ipswich, although it slipped a carriage at Colchester, and then only at Beccles and Yarmouth, arriving at 5.15pm, with a connection for Lowestoft.

The 5.6pm from Ipswich was combined from the 2.36pm semi-fast from London and the 3.20pm express, and omitted some of the smaller East Suffolk main line stations but connected with all the branches. On the other hand, the 4pm from London split at Ipswich, with one part going fast to Beccles, Yarmouth and Lowestoft, and the other semi-fast, but not connecting for Framlingham or Aldeburgh. The 3.36pm stopper and 5pm express from Liverpool Street turned into the 6.50pm all-stations down the East Suffolk, although the 6.48pm departure from Ipswich ran nonstop to Beccles, beating it by nearly half an hour. The Lowestoft branch continued to have extra trains from Beccles, the latest now being 10pm, and there was also a 10.5pm Beccles to Yarmouth. The only extra to Framlingham was the 9.25am Tuesdays only. The Sunday service continued to be sparse, with trains only at 8.35am and 6.10pm down from Ipswich. Neither called at St Olaves Junction, and the former omitted Westerfield, Melton, Brampton and Aldeby as well. Both had connections to Aldeburgh and Lowestoft, but the Waveney Valley and Framlingham branches were closed on Sundays.

In the up direction the first train was now the 6.15am all-stations from South Town, reaching Ipswich at 8.35am, leaving again 10min later and reaching Liverpool Street at 10.30pm, with calls only at Bentley and Colchester. The 7.23am Mondays-only express from Yarmouth gave a very fast journey, calling only at Beccles, Halesworth and Ipswich on its way to London (arrive 10.45am), although it slipped a coach for Colchester. It gave a very tight connection out of the 7.30am from Southwold, passengers having a mere 2min to hurry between platforms. The 8am from Yarmouth was another fast train, and had a connection from Framlingham only on Tuesdays. The 11am and 12 noon from Yarmouth both called first at Beccles, but the first then called at all stations except Westerfield, while the second called only at stations with connections, which did not include Halesworth. The 2pm up from Yarmouth was easily the fastest train of the day, calling only at Ipswich *en route* to London, reached at 5.5pm. Intermediate stops were covered by the 3pm from Lowestoft, which unusually had no Yarmouth connection unless one counted the 1.10pm local to Beccles, necessitating a wait of just over 1¼hr.

The 4pm up from Yarmouth called only at Beccles before Halesworth, although it had a Lowestoft connection, but then served all stations except Melton as far as Colchester, finally reaching Liverpool Street at 8pm. The 5.45pm express from Yarmouth to London was followed up the East Suffolk by the 6.15pm Mondays-only to Ipswich (all stations from Beccles), and then the 6.5pm stopper to Beccles, which connected there with the 6.30pm, which then called at all stations to Ipswich and had connections from the branches. It was in turn followed by the 7.5pm express, with only a Lowestoft connection, and the two went forward at 8.50pm from Ipswich, reaching London at 11pm. The last up trains of the day were the 9.25pm from both Lowestoft and Yarmouth to Beccles. As before, most of the branches — notably Lowestoft — had extra services. Through tickets were available via Halesworth to stations on the Southwold Railway, although it was a separate company.

The benefits of the bracing air and coastal waters of East Anglia had prompted the Great Eastern to offer to supply small barrels of Lowestoft sea water to the masses in London. The burgeoning holiday trade on the coast prompted it to introduce summer-only nonstop expresses between Liverpool Street and Yarmouth and Lowestoft in the 1904 timetable. The trains were each scheduled to take 2½hr, and while the Yarmouth nonstops continued until the outbreak of war in 1914, resuming after hostilities ceased, the Lowestoft service was much less successful, and acquired a Felixstowe portion for 1905 which required unadvertised stops at Westerfield in both directions to attach or detach. From 1906 this ran as a separate working, so the Lowestoft train carried a portion for Aldeburgh instead. These trains also prompted the Great Eastern to introduce its first bus services, between Lowestoft, Oulton and Southwold, from July 1904.

By April 1910 there had been further developments, but there remained elements of the original pattern. The 5.5am from Liverpool Street continued to provide the first service to the East Suffolk, with connections along all the branches, and now to Gorleston via the Norfolk & Suffolk Joint line. Travel via both Yarmouth and Lowestoft was possible. The 8.33am from London was relatively fast on the main line, but called at all stations to Yarmouth on the East Suffolk. The 10am gave a faster journey, calling only at connecting stations, and while the 11.45am was named the 'East Anglian' and offered a luncheon car, it made its first call at Mark's Tey and thence all stations to South Town (arriving at 4.12pm) except Westerfield. The Norwich portion also called at all stations. The 1.30pm Saturdays-only express slipped coaches for Clacton, but was otherwise fast to Ipswich, and then Beccles, Lowestoft and Yarmouth only, with a connection to Gorleston via Lowestoft. Also continuing an earlier pattern, the 2.22pm semi-fast and 3.20pm express from London went forward as the 5pm from Ipswich, again calling only at Beccles, Lowestoft and Yarmouth. The last through train was the 5pm restaurant car service from Liverpool Street to Yarmouth, which carried a portion for Felixstowe and called only at connecting stations, not including Haddiscoe, on the East Suffolk. Local calls were made by the 6.56pm all-stations to South Town, reaching there at 9.5pm. Perhaps surprisingly, this was the last train down the East Suffolk in the evening, although strictly speaking this honour fell to the 7.55pm from Ipswich (5.30pm from Liverpool Street), which called at Westerfield on its way to Felixstowe.

There were other workings over parts of the line, such as the 9.53am and 6.7pm all-stations Beccles to Yarmouth, plus the usual extras between Beccles and Lowestoft, and more restricted services such as the 5.25pm Tuesdays-only Halesworth to Beccles. In addition, there was the through service between South Town and Lowestoft Central via Marsh Junction and St Olaves Swing Bridge Junction, which continued despite the opening of the direct route. There were five trains on weekdays from Yarmouth, and eight the other way, three of which were booked as 'via Haddiscoe'. This may simply have been a timetabling expedient, so that they were set back into the High Level station whilst another main-line service cleared the single line over the swing bridge. Lowestoft and Yarmouth had a further nine trains each way on Mondays to Saturdays via the Norfolk & Suffolk Joint line, running either to Beach or South Town, and taking about 33min for the slightly longer 12¼-mile route into the M&GN station. At 14½ miles the Great Eastern route took about 34min, although if running via Haddiscoe this could be prolonged to as much as 56min. There were, however, three trains each way on Sundays via St Olaves, and none on the new line.

In the up direction the pattern was similar to that earlier, with the 6.5am up from Yarmouth being an all-stations (except Haddiscoe) to Ipswich, with the choice of either fast or stopping trains to London. The 7.35am Mondays-only to Ipswich and London was very fast, taking only 3hr 10min overall. The 7.46am called at most stations to Ipswich and then nonstop to London, while the 8.20am restaurant car express called only at connecting stations. Most remaining trains ran through to London, with differing degrees of urgency, and the last weekday up working was the 6.27pm from Yarmouth to Ipswich, reached at 8.40pm. Sundays remained more or less unchanged, with trains at 7.15am and 5.40pm from Yarmouth, although in the other direction there was now an all-stations from Ipswich at 9am as well as the 6.7pm (4.15pm from Liverpool Street).

Little had changed in summer 1913, although the Framlingham branch sported a Sunday service of two trains each way, leaving Framlingham at 8.15am and 5.53pm, and returning from Wickham Market at 9.40am and 6.57pm. The Aldeburgh branch had three each way, at 8am, 5.36pm and 7.10pm, returning from Saxmundham at 9.55am, 6.12pm and 7.49pm. The Lowestoft branch enjoyed a Sunday service of six down and seven up trains, all calling at Carlton Colville except the 1.4pm express from Beccles (9.45am from Liverpool Street), and the 6.50pm up express to Liverpool Street, which would stop on request if there were passengers for Saxmundham, Ipswich or London. This train did not have a Yarmouth portion, and passengers had to use the 5.45pm connecting service via Somerleyton. There were four of these trains in this timetable, plus the 11.30am South Town to Beccles, and the 4.40pm South Town to Liverpool Street, calling all stations on the East Suffolk except Haddiscoe. The service was always slightly more generous in summer than winter.

There had been piecemeal alterations here and there to the timetable, but nothing of great importance for many years until Henry Thornton came on the scene, appointed as general manager of the Great Eastern Railway in May 1914. Bringing American management methods to bear on GER operations and timetables, he introduced radical alterations from October 1914, tightening running and operational times. Norwich and Cromer trains were now allowed only 3min to detach portions for the East Suffolk at Ipswich, and 4min to attach in the up direction. Cecil J. Allen reported one of the more interesting blunders in the new timetable, which was the requirement for the 6.28pm from Yarmouth to Liverpool Street to cover the 22 miles 29 chains between Saxmundham and Ipswich in 20min — a tall order, to say the least! However, the relentless demands of war soon made themselves felt, and standards of maintenance and the loss of men to the armed forces ensured that the brave new timetable withered and died.

In 1937 the timetable still showed recognisable similarities with earlier versions. The 5am from London continued to reach South Town at 9.20pm — no improvement since 1910. The 8.20am ran as far as Halesworth on Tuesdays only, while the next all-stations to Yarmouth was the 8.55am. The 8.15am from Liverpool Street left Ipswich at 10.38 and called at all stations, while the 11.32am all-stations to Saxmundham ran on Saturdays only. The 10.3am from London left Ipswich exactly two hours later and called only at Saxmundham, Halesworth, Beccles and Haddiscoe on its way to Lowestoft and Yarmouth. The 12.25pm Saturdays-only from London was faster, and left Ipswich at 2pm, and reached Yarmouth at 3.22pm. The 3.10pm express from Liverpool Street was another fast train, likewise the 4.55pm restaurant car service. The last train from Liverpool Street to serve the East Suffolk was the 5.18pm, although stations to Saxmundham could be reached off the 7.50pm on Wednesdays and Saturdays. On Sundays there were three trains each way, with two all-stations except Haddiscoe at 7.10am and 5.20pm up from Yarmouth, and 9.20am and 6.36pm from Ipswich, There were fast trains at 12.11pm from Ipswich and 6.55pm from Yarmouth, the last collecting a Lowestoft portion at Beccles and otherwise calling only at Saxmundham before Ipswich. Apart from Beccles to Lowestoft there were almost no other trains operating over parts of the line or the branches. The restaurant car express ran at 8.28am up from Yarmouth to London. As ever, there were some interesting quirks in the timetable, one of which was the Saturdays-only 9.30pm Yarmouth South Town to Harleston, calling all stations except Earsham, and arriving at 10.34pm.

It was not long before war again took its toll of the timetable, timings never really having got back to the standards envisaged by Thornton. The first train from Liverpool Street was brought forward to 4.40am but with timings largely unchanged, so that it reached South Town at 9.4am. The 8.40am all-stations from Ipswich still ran; through coaches off the 8.12am Norwich buffet car express departed Ipswich at 10.15am and provided a reasonably fast journey down the East Suffolk. The 10am restaurant car service from London also detached coaches for the East Suffolk at Ipswich, which then ambled along to Yarmouth calling everywhere. A buffet car express ran on Saturdays only to Yarmouth at 12.20pm from London, with the 1pm and 3.40pm expresses much as the 10am, without nearly as many stops between Ipswich and Yarmouth. The 4pm from London also had limited stops on the East Suffolk, and the next all-stations was not until 7.10pm from Ipswich, the 5.10pm from London. That was it for the day, although it is worth noting the one-class motor (auto-) trains between Beccles and Yarmouth, which left Beccles at 7.10am, 9.30am, 2.5pm (Mondays to Fridays, 3.25pm Saturdays) and 6.45pm. These trains sometimes performed triangular workings in either direction: out from Yarmouth to Beccles, then to Lowestoft and finally back to Yarmouth via Gorleston. All the Lowestoft to South Town trains were so worked during the war, there being only four return trains a day this way, and a further two in and out of Yarmouth Beach.

Table 8.

LONDON (LIVERPOOL STREET), COLCHESTER, CLACTON-ON-SEA, HARWICH, IPSWICH, NORWICH, BECCLES, LOWESTOFT AND YARMOUTH.

LONDON (Liverpool St.) to LOWESTOFT, YARMOUTH, NORWICH and CROMER

LONDON (Liverpool St.)
BURNHAM-on-CROUCH, SOUTHMINSTER, SOUTHEND-on-SEA — SHENFIELD (20¼)
CHELMSFORD (29¾)
MALDON — WITHAM (38¾) — BRAINTREE
(46½) MARK'S TEY — HALSTEAD, SUDBURY
BRIGHTLINGSEA, FRINTON-on-SEA, WALTON-on-NAZE, CLACTON-on-SEA — COLCHESTER (51¾)
PARKESTON QUAY, HOOK OF HOLLAND, FLUSHING, ANTWERP, ZEEBRUGGE, HARWICH TOWN — MANNINGTREE (59½)
IPSWICH (68¾)
WESTERFIELD (72¼) — FELIXSTOWE
STOWMARKET (80½)
FRAM-LING-HAM
WICKHAM MARKET (84¾)
LAX-FIELD
HAUGHLEY (83) — BURY ST. EDMUND'S, NEWMARKET, ELY, CAMBRIDGE
SAXMUNDHAM (91) — ALDEBURGH
DISS (95)
HALESWORTH (100¼)
TIVETSHALL (100½)
BUNGAY
(109¼) BECCLES
FORNCETT (104) — WYMONDHAM, WELLS-on-SEA
LOWESTOFT (Central) (117¼)
YAR-MOUTH (Vaux.)
NORWICH (Thorpe) (115)
YARMOUTH (South Town) (121¼)
WROXHAM (123½) — AYLSHAM
OVERSTRAND, MUNDESLEY-on-SEA — Nth WALSHAM (131) — SHERINGHAM
CROMER (139)

THE FIGURES INDICATE THE DISTANCES FROM LONDON (Liverpool Street)

For Local Service see Table	WEEKDAYS	a.m.	X a.m.	a.m.	a.m.	a.m.	a.m.	a.m.	TO a.m.
	LONDON (Liverpool St.) A dep.			5 0	5 30				
	Stratford A ,,			↓	↓				
	Ilford A ,,								
	Romford A ,,								
	Gidea Park and Squirrels Heath A ,,								
	Harold Wood A ,,			↓					
	Brentwood and Warley A ,,			5 29					
	Shenfield and Hutton A ,,			↓					
	Ingatestone A ,,								
	Chelmsford A ,,			5 50			6 1		
	Hatfield Peverel ,,			↓			6 10		
	Witham ,,						6 15		
	Kelvedon ,,			↓			To Braintree.		
	Mark's Tey ,,			6D13	↓				
	Colchester arr.			6 21	6 38				
32	Colchester dep.			6 34	7 5				
32	Walton-on-Naze arr.			7 39	8 54				
32	Clacton-on-Sea and Holland-on-Sea ,,			7 20	7 51				
	Colchester dep.			6 24	6 41	6 50	Stop	7 48	
	Ardleigh ,,			↓	↓	6 58		7 56	
	Manningtree arr.					7 4		8 2	
33	Manningtree dep.					7 6		8 27	
33	Harwich Parkeston Quay arr.					7E29		8 50	
33	Harwich Town ,,					7E38		8 58	
	Manningtree dep.			↓	↓			8 4	
	Bentley ,,							8 11	
	IPSWICH arr.			6 45	7 2			8 20	
	Ipswich dep.			6 55				8 25	
	Bramford ,,			↓				↓	
	Claydon ,,								
	Needham ,,			7 8			a.m.		
	Stowmarket ,,			7 18			8 5	8 40	
	Haughley ,,			7 25			8 10	↓	
	Finningham ,,			7 33			To Bury St. Edmund's	To Bury St. Edmund's	
	Mellis ,,			7 42					
	Diss ,,			7 49					
	Burston ,,			7 54					
	Tivetshall ,,			8 2					
	Forncett ,,			8 10					
	Flordon ,,			8 16					
	Swainsthorpe ,,			8 22					
	Trowse B ,,			8 32					
	NORWICH (Thorpe) B arr.			8 36					
66	Norwich (Thorpe) dep.			9 25					
66	Cromer arr.			10 21					
	Ipswich C dep.				7 7				8 38
	Westerfield C ,,				7 16				↓
	Bealings ,,				7 23				8 43
	Woodbridge ,,				7 31				8 49
	Melton ,,				7 35				8 53
	Wickham Market for Campsea Ash ,,				7 47				9 2
	Saxmundham ,,				8 0				9 16
	Darsham for Yoxford ,,				8 10				9 25
	Halesworth ,,				8 24				9 34
	Brampton (Suffolk) ,,				8 33				
	Beccles arr.				8 45				
	Beccles dep.	7 2			9 0				
	Oulton Broad South ,,	7 13			9 11				
	LOWESTOFT (Central) arr	7 19			9 17				
	Beccles dep.		7 50		8 50				
	Aldeby ,,		7 58		8 58				
	Haddiscoe arr.		8 1		9 1				
68	Haddiscoe dep.				9 12				
68	Reedham arr.				9 19				
68	Norwich (Thorpe) ,,				9 48				
	Haddiscoe dep.		8 2		9 2				
	St. Olaves ,,		8 5		9 5				
	Belton and Burgh ,,		8 11		9 11				
	YARMOUTH (South Town) arr.		8 18		9 18				
45	Yarmouth (South Town) dep.		8 32		9 34				
45	Gorleston-on-Sea arr.		8 39		9 43				

A Departure times or stations beyond Chelmsford. For complete service between Liverpool Street and Chelmsford see London Suburban Pocket Time Table No. 4.
B For other trains between Trowse and Norwich see Table 9.
C For other trains betweeen Ipswich and Westerfield see Table 40.
D Calls to set down passengers only.
E On Mondays, Fridays and Saturdays until **13th September** arrives 5 minutes later.
TO Tuesdays only.
X Third class only.

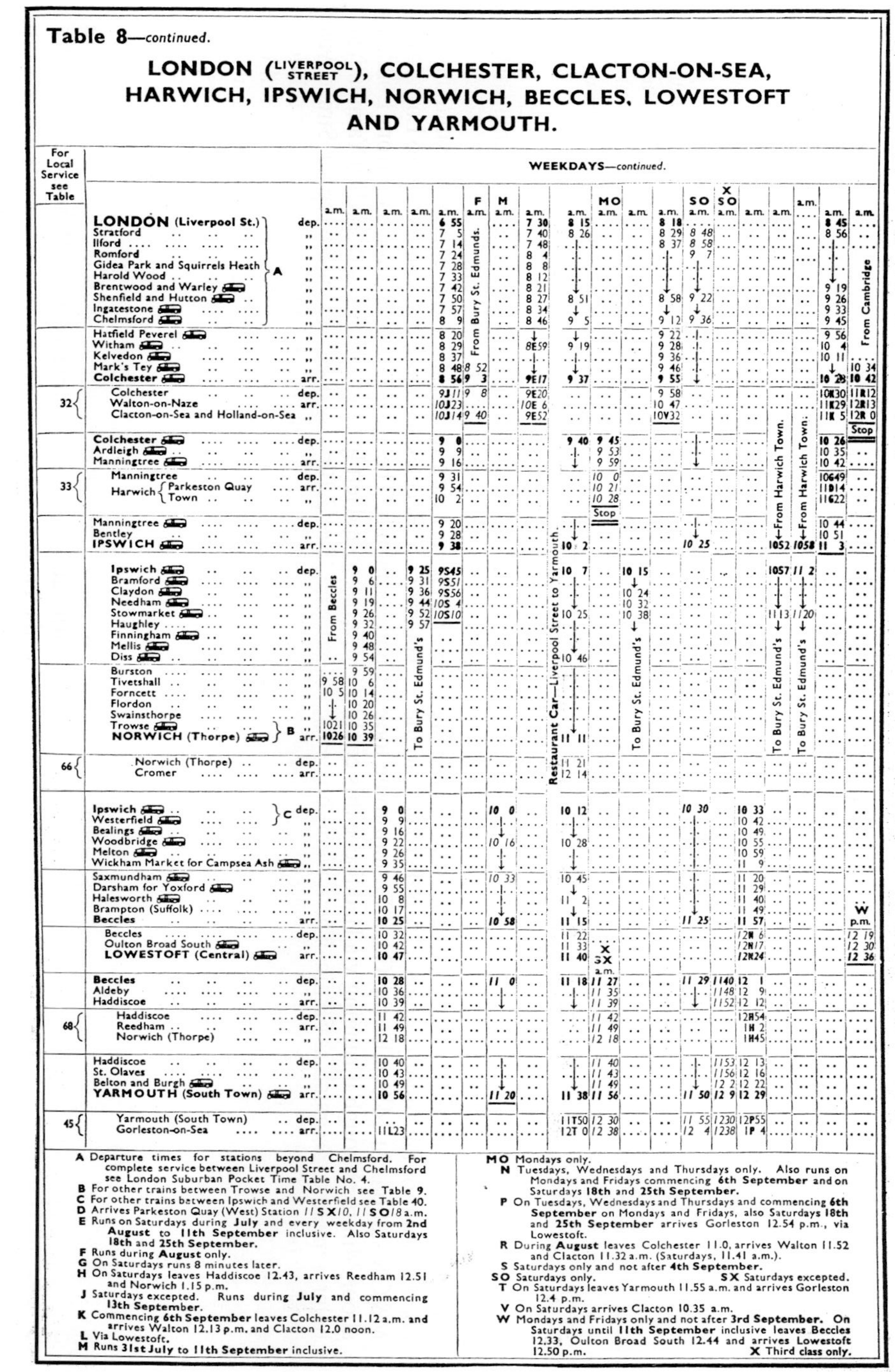

Table 8—*continued.*

LONDON (LIVERPOOL STREET), COLCHESTER, CLACTON-ON-SEA, HARWICH, IPSWICH, NORWICH, BECCLES, LOWESTOFT AND YARMOUTH.

For Local Service see Table	WEEKDAYS—*continued.*	a.m.	a.m.	a.m.	a.m.	a.m.	F a.m.	M a.m.	a.m.	a.m.	MO a.m.	a.m.	a.m.	SO a.m.	X SO a.m.	a.m.	a.m.	a.m.	a.m.	a.m.
	LONDON (Liverpool St.) A dep.					6 55	From Bury St. Edmunds.		7 30	8 15			8 18						8 45	
	Stratford A ,,					7 5			7 40	8 26			8 29	8 48					8 56	
	Ilford A ,,					7 14			7 48	↓			8 37	8 58					↓	
	Romford A ,,					7 24			8 4				↓	9 7						
	Gidea Park and Squirrels Heath A ,,					7 28			8 8					↓						
	Harold Wood A ,,					7 33			8 12											
	Brentwood and Warley A ,,					7 42			8 21										9 19	
	Shenfield and Hutton A ,,					7 50			8 27	8 51			8 58	9 22					9 26	
	Ingatestone A ,,					7 57			8 34	↓			↓	↓					9 33	
	Chelmsford A ,,					8 9			8 46	9 5			9 12	9 36					9 45	From Cambridge
	Hatfield Peverel ,,					8 20			↓	↓			9 22	↓					9 56	
	Witham ,,					8 29			8E59	9 19			9 28						10 4	
	Kelvedon ,,					8 37			↓	↓			9 36						10 11	
	Mark's Tey ,,					8 48	8 52		↓	↓			9 46						↓	10 34
	Colchester arr.					8 56	9 3		9E17	9 37			9 55	↓					10 28	10 42
32	Colchester dep.					9J11	9 8		9E20				9 58						10K30	11R12
32	Walton-on-Naze arr.					10J23			10E 6				10 47						11K29	12R13
32	Clacton-on-Sea and Holland-on-Sea ,,					10J14	9 40		9E52				10V32						11K 5	12R 0 Stop
	Colchester dep.					9 0				9 40	9 45			↓					10 26	
	Ardleigh ,,					9 9				↓	9 53								10 35	
	Manningtree arr.					9 16				↓	9 59			↓					10 42	
33	Manningtree dep.					9 31					10 0								10G49	
33	Harwich Parkeston Quay arr.					9 54					10 21								11D14	
33	Harwich Town ,,					10 2					10 28 Stop						From Harwich Town.	From Harwich Town.	11G22	
	Manningtree dep.					9 20				↓				↓					10 44	
	Bentley ,,					9 28													10 51	
	IPSWICH arr.					9 38				10 2				10 25			1052	1058	11 3	
	Ipswich dep.	From Beccles	9 0		9 25	9S45				10 7		10 15					1057	11 2		
	Bramford ,,		9 6		9 31	9S51				↓		↓					↓	↓		
	Claydon ,,		9 11		9 36	9S56						10 24								
	Needham ,,		9 19		9 44	10S 4						10 32								
	Stowmarket ,,		9 26		9 52	10S10				10 25		10 38					1113	1120		
	Haughley ,,		9 32		9 57					↓		↓					↓	↓		
	Finningham ,,		9 40		To Bury St. Edmund's							To Bury St. Edmund's					To Bury St. Edmund's	To Bury St. Edmund's		
	Mellis ,,		9 48																	
	Diss ,,		9 54							10 46										
	Burston ,,		9 59							↓										
	Tivetshall ,,	9 58	10 6																	
	Forncett ,,	10 5	10 14																	
	Flordon ,,	↓	10 20																	
	Swainsthorpe ,,		10 26																	
	Trowse B ,,	1021	10 35																	
	NORWICH (Thorpe) B arr.	1026	10 39							11 11										
66	Norwich (Thorpe) dep.									Restaurant Car—Liverpool Street to Yarmouth. 11 21										
66	Cromer arr.									12 14										
	Ipswich C dep.			9 0				10 0		10 12				10 30		10 33				
	Westerfield C ,,			9 9				↓		↓				↓		10 42				
	Bealings ,,			9 16												10 49				
	Woodbridge ,,			9 22				10 16		10 28						10 55				
	Melton ,,			9 26				↓		↓						10 59				
	Wickham Market for Campsea Ash ,,			9 35				↓		↓						11 9				
	Saxmundham ,,			9 46				10 33		10 45						11 20				
	Darsham for Yoxford ,,			9 55				↓		↓						11 29				
	Halesworth ,,			10 8						11 2						11 40				
	Brampton (Suffolk) ,,			10 17				↓		↓				↓		11 49				W
	Beccles arr.			10 25				10 58		11 15				11 25		11 57				p.m.
	Beccles dep.			10 32						11 22						12N 6				12 19
	Oulton Broad South ,,			10 42						11 33						12N17				12 30
	LOWESTOFT (Central) arr.			10 47						11 40	X SX a.m.					12N24				12 36
	Beccles dep.			10 28				11 0		11 18	11 27			11 29	1140	12 1				
	Aldeby ,,			10 36				↓		↓	11 35			↓	1148	12 9				
	Haddiscoe arr.			10 39							11 39				1152	12 12				
68	Haddiscoe dep.			11 42							11 42					12H54				
68	Reedham arr.			11 49							11 49					1H 2				
68	Norwich (Thorpe) ,,			12 18							12 18					1H45				
	Haddiscoe dep.			10 40				↓		↓	11 40			↓	1153	12 13				
	St. Olaves ,,			10 43							11 43				1156	12 16				
	Belton and Burgh ,,			10 49				↓		↓	11 49			↓	12 2	12 22				
	YARMOUTH (South Town) arr.			10 56				11 20		11 38	11 56			11 50	12 9	12 29				
45	Yarmouth (South Town) dep.									11T50	12 30			11 55	1230	12P55				
45	Gorleston-on-Sea arr.			11L23						12T 0	12 38			12 4	1238	1P 4				

A Departure times for stations beyond Chelmsford. For complete service between Liverpool Street and Chelmsford see London Suburban Pocket Time Table No. 4.
B For other trains between Trowse and Norwich see Table 9.
C For other trains between Ipswich and Westerfield see Table 40.
D Arrives Parkeston Quay (West) Station 11 **SX** 10, 11 **SO** 18 a.m.
E Runs on Saturdays during **July** and every weekday from **2nd August** to **11th September** inclusive. Also Saturdays **18th** and **25th September.**
F Runs during **August** only.
G On Saturdays runs 8 minutes later.
H On Saturdays leaves Haddiscoe 12.43, arrives Reedham 12.51 and Norwich 1.15 p.m.
J Saturdays excepted. Runs during **July** and commencing **13th September.**
K Commencing **6th September** leaves Colchester 11.12 a.m. and arrives Walton 12.13 p.m. and Clacton 12.0 noon.
L Via Lowestoft.
M Runs **31st July** to **11th September** inclusive.
MO Mondays only.
N Tuesdays, Wednesdays and Thursdays only. Also runs on Mondays and Fridays commencing **6th September** and on Saturdays **18th** and **25th September.**
P On Tuesdays, Wednesdays and Thursdays and commencing **6th September** on Mondays and Fridays, also Saturdays **18th** and **25th September** arrives Gorleston 12.54 p.m., via Lowestoft.
R During **August** leaves Colchester 11.0, arrives Walton 11.52 and Clacton 11.32 a.m. (Saturdays, 11.41 a.m.).
S Saturdays only and not after **4th September.**
SO Saturdays only. **SX** Saturdays excepted.
T On Saturdays leaves Yarmouth 11.55 a.m. and arrives Gorleston 12.4 p.m.
V On Saturdays arrives Clacton 10.35 a.m.
W Mondays and Fridays only and not after **3rd September.** On Saturdays until **11th September** inclusive leaves Beccles 12.33, Oulton Broad South 12.44 and arrives Lowestoft 12.50 p.m.
X Third class only.

Table 8—*continued.*

LONDON (LIVERPOOL STREET), COLCHESTER, CLACTON-ON-SEA, HARWICH, IPSWICH, NORWICH, BECCLES, LOWESTOFT AND YARMOUTH.

WEEKDAYS—*continued*

For Local Service see Table	Station		J a.m.	D a.m.	J a.m.	M a.m.	J a.m.	Q a.m.	E a.m.	SX a.m.	SO a.m.	J a.m.	G a.m.	R p.m.	SX a.m.	SO a.m.	Y p.m.	SX a.m.	SO a.m.	SO a.m.
	LONDON (Liverpool St.) A	dep.	9 36	9 48	9H48	9 52	9 52	10 0	....	10 3	10 3	10 5	10 12	....	10 20	10 20	....	10 23	10 23	10 26
	Stratford	,,	↓	↓	↓	↓	↓	↓		↓	↓		↓		↓	↓		10 35	10 35	↓
	Ilford	,,								10 19	10 20		10 31		10 37	10 37		10 44	10 44	
	Romford	,,																		
	Gidea Park and Squirrels Heath	,,																		
	Harold Wood	,,																		
	Brentwood and Warley	,,																		
	Shenfield and Hutton	,,																11 6	11 10	
	Ingatestone	,,																↓	↓	
	Chelmsford	,,											11 6		11 9	11 14		11 20	11 27	
	Hatfield Peverel	,,																↓	↓	
	Witham	,,																11 34	11 42	
	Kelvedon	,,																↓	↓	
	Mark's Tey	,,								11 11	11 19									
	Colchester	arr.	↓	↓	↓	↓	↓	↓		11 20	11 28		↓		11 38	11 43		11 52	12 1	↓
32	Colchester	dep.																11 55	12 3	↓
	Walton-on-Naze	arr.																12 41	12 59	
	Clacton-on-Sea and Holland-on-Sea	,,																12 32	12 49	12 23
	Colchester	dep.	↓	↓	↓	↓	↓	↓	11 23	11 22	11 31		↓		11 41	11 46				
	Ardleigh	,,							↓	↓	↓				11 50	11 [illegible]				
	Manningtree	arr.													11 57	12 2				
33	Manningtree	dep.						↓							12 10	12 10				
	Harwich { Parkeston Quay	arr.						11P38							12 34	12 34				
	Harwich { Town	,,						11 50							12 43	12 43				
	Manningtree	dep.	↓	↓	↓	↓	↓		↓	↓	↓		↓		11 59	12 5				
	Bentley	,,														↓				
	IPSWICH	arr.	↓	11 10	11 25	↓	↓		11 47	11 45	11 55		11K55		12 14	12 20				
	Ipswich	dep.		11 15	11 30				11 51					12 8			12 25			
	Bramford	,,		↓	↓				↓					12 14			↓			
	Claydon	,,												12 19						
	Needham	,,												12 27			12 38			
	Stowmarket	,,		11 34	11 49				12 7					12 35			12 46			
	Haughley	,,		↓	↓				↓					12 42			12 51			
	Finningham	,,												12 50						
	Mellis	,,												12 59						
	Diss	,,		11 57	12 13									1 6						
	Burston	,,		↓	↓									1 11						
	Tivetshall	,,												1 19						
	Forncett	,,		12 12	12 30									1 27						
	Flordon	,,		↓	↓									1 33						
	Swainsthorpe	,,												1 39						
	Trowse B	,,										↓		1 47						
	NORWICH (Thorpe) B	arr.		12 30	12H50									1 53						
66	Norwich (Thorpe)	dep.		12 42	12H58															
	Cromer	arr.		1 35	1H45															
	Ipswich C	dep.	↓			↓	↓			11 50	12 0				12 [illegible]6	12 26				
	Westerfield C	,,								↓	↓				↓	↓				
	Bealings	,,													12 [illegible]	12 40				
	Woodbridge	,,													12 [illegible]	12 47				
	Melton	,,													12 [illegible]	12 51				
	Wickham Market for Campsea Ash	,,													1 [illegible]	1 2				
	Saxmundham	,,								12 23	12 34				1 [illegible]	1 14				
	Darsham for Yoxford	,,								↓	↓				1 [illegible]	1 25				
	Halesworth	,,								12 40	12 51				1 [illegible]	1 37				
	Brampton (Suffolk)	,,	↓			↓	↓			↓	↓				1 [illegible]	1 46				
	Beccles	arr.	12 20			12 11	12 30			12 55	1 6				1 [illegible]	1 55				
	Beccles	dep.				12 19	12 33			1 3	1 14				1 [illegible]	2 5				
	Oulton Broad South	,,				12 30	12 44			1 14	1 24				2 [illegible]	2 16				
	LOWESTOFT (Central)	arr.				12 36	12 50			1 22	1 31				2 [illegible]	2 23				
	Beccles	dep.	12 24			12 15				12 59	1 10				1 5[illegible]	1 59				
	Aldeby	,,	↓			↓				↓	↓				2 [illegible]	2 7				
	Haddiscoe	arr.								1 8	1 19				2 [illegible]	2 10				
68	Haddiscoe	dep.								2 3	2 3					3 1				
	Reedham	arr.								2 11	2 11					3 8				
	Norwich (Thorpe)	,,								2 48	2 48					3 40				
	Haddiscoe	dep.	↓			↓				1 9	1 20				2 [illegible]	2 11				
	St. Olaves	,,								↓	↓				2 [illegible]	2 14				
	Belton and Burgh	,,													2 1[illegible]	2 20				
	YARMOUTH (South Town)	arr.	12 44			12 36				1 23	1 34	1Z25			2 2[illegible]	2 27				
45	Yarmouth (South Town)	dep.	12 55			12 55				1W40					2 2[illegible]					
	Gorleston-on-Sea	arr.	1 4			1 4	1L53			1W49	2T22				2 3[illegible]	3L 1				

Restaurant Car—Liverpool Street to Cromer. (D, J 9H48)

"FLUSHING CONTINENTAL" Restaurant and Pullman Cars (See page iv). Conveys passengers for Flushing. (Q)

From Clacton (dep. 10.45 a.m.) (E)

To Sheffield and Manchester. (E)

Via Cambridge. (J 10 5)

To Bury St. Edmund's (Y)

Restaurant Car (SO 10 26)

A Departure times for stations beyond Chelmsford. For complete service between Liverpool Street and Chelmsford see London Suburban Pocket Time Table No. 4.
B For other trains between Trowse and Norwich see Table 9.
C For other trains between Ipswich and Westerfield see Table 40.
D Until **11th September** inclusive does not run on Saturdays.
E Saturdays only and not after **18th September.**
G Mondays, Fridays and Saturdays only and not after **4th September.** Also runs Saturday **11th September.**
H Passengers for Norwich and Cromer leave Liverpool Street 9.45 a.m., arrive Norwich 12.33, depart 12.45 and arrive Cromer 1.35 p.m., with Restaurant Car (See Table 9).
J Saturdays only and not after **11th September.**
K On Saturdays arrives Ipswich 12.5 p.m.
L Via Lowestoft.
M Mondays and Fridays only and not after **3rd September.**
P Arrives Parkeston Quay (West) Station 11**SX**30, 11**SO**35 a.m. On Saturdays arrives Parkeston Quay 1[illegible].43 a.m.
Q On Saturdays during **July** and **August** conveys only passengers holding tickets to the Continent.
R On Saturdays runs 7 minutes later.
SO Saturdays only.
SX Saturdays excepted.
T Via Lowestoft. On **18th** and **25th September** leaves Yarmouth 1.40 and arrives Gorleston [illegible].49 p.m.
W On Mondays and Fridays until **3rd September** inclusive arrives Gorleston 1.53 p.m., via Lowestoft.
Y On Saturdays runs 4 minutes later.
Z Yarmouth (Vauxhall) station.

Table 8—*continued.*

LONDON (LIVERPOOL STREET), COLCHESTER, CLACTON-ON-SEA, HARWICH, IPSWICH, NORWICH, BECCLES, LOWESTOFT AND YARMOUTH.

WEEKDAYS—*continued.*

For Local Service see Table	Station		a.m.	a.m.	J a.m.	F p.m.	R p.m.	G p.m.	p.m.	p.m.	Y p.m.	p.m.	J p.m.	M p.m.	SO p.m.	SX p.m.	p.m.	SO p.m.	p.m.
	LONDON (Liverpool St.) A	dep	10 46	11H30	11 26	12 25	12 28	12 30	12 33	....	....	12 36	12 52	12 56	12 55	1 0	....	12 58	....
	Stratford	,,	10 58	↓	11 42														
	Ilford	,,	↓	11 45	11 52										↓				
	Romford	,,	11 12	↓	↓														
	Gidea Park and Squirrels Heath	,,	11 16																
	Harold Wood	,,	11 20												1 21				
	Brentwood and Warley	,,	11 29		12 11										1 29				
	Shenfield and Hutton	,,	11 35		12 17										1 36				
	Ingatestone	,,	11 42	↓	↓							↓			1 43				
	Chelmsford	,,	11 54	12 17	12 31							1Y24			1 55				
	Hatfield Peverel	,,	12 4	↓											2 5				
	Witham	,,	12 12	12 31											2 13				
	Kelvedon	,,	12 20	↓								↓							
	Mark's Tey	,,	12 32	12 44	↓				↓			1Y47							
	Colchester	arr.	12 40	12 53	1 0	↓	↓	↓	1Y42			1Y56	↓	↓		↓		↓	
32	Colchester	dep.		1K24	1 3							1Y59							
	Walton-on-Naze	arr.		2K24	1 49							2Y47							
	Clacton-on-Sea and Holland-on-Sea	,,		2K11	1 43							2Y36							
					Stop														
	Colchester	dep.	12 45	12 55		↓	↓	↓	1Y45	1Y50			↓	↓		↓		↓	
	Ardleigh	,,	↓	1 3					↓	↓									
	Manningtree	arr.	12 57	1 10						2Y 2									
33	Manningtree	dep.		1 38						2Y 3									
	Harwich { Parkeston Quay	arr.		2 1						2Y18									
	Harwich { Town	,,		2 10						2Y27									
										Stop									
	Manningtree	dep.	12 59	1 12		↓	↓	↓	↓				↓	↓		↓		↓	
	Bentley	,,	1 7	↓															
	IPSWICH	arr.	1 17	1 27		↓	↓	↓	2Y 8				↓	↓		2 30		2 39	
	Ipswich	dep.				↓	↓		2Y13		2 18						2 48		
	Bramford	,,							↓		2 24						↓		
	Claydon	,,									2 29								
	Needham	,,									2 37								
	Stowmarket	,,									2 45						3 5		3 12
	Haughley	,,									2 52						↓		3 17
	Finningham	,,									3 1								
	Mellis	,,									3 9								
	Diss	,,									3 16								
	Burston	,,									3 22								
	Tivetshall	,,									3 30								
	Forncett	,,									3 37								
	Flordon	,,									3 43								
	Swainsthorpe	,,									3 50								
	Trowse B	,,				↓	↓		↓		3 59								
	NORWICH (Thorpe) B	arr.							3Y 9		4 3								
66	Norwich (Thorpe)	dep.							3P15		4 30								Stop
	Cromer	arr.				3F22	3Q25		4P 7		5 25								
	Ipswich C	dep.						↓	2Y13				↓	↓		2 36		2 44	p.m. 2Z50
	Westerfield C	,,														↓		↓	2Z59
	Bealings	,,																	3Z 6
	Woodbridge	,,														2 54		3 2	3Z13
	Melton	,,														↓		↓	3Z17
	Wickham Market for Campsea Ash	,,																	3Z26
	Saxmundham	,,														3 16		3 24	3Z38
	Darsham for Yoxford	,,														↓		↓	3Z47
	Halesworth	,,														3 34		3 43	3Z58
	Brampton (Suffolk)	,,														↓		↓	4Z 7
	Beccles	arr.			p.m.			↓								3 49		3 58	4Z15
	Beccles	dep.			3 2								↓	↓		4 6		4 6	4 57
	Oulton Broad South	,,			3 13											4 17		4 17	5 8
	LOWESTOFT (Central)	arr.			3 19				3V52	X			3 41	3 36		4 23		4 23	5 14
	Beccles	dep.						↓		p.m. 2 55						3 53		4 2	4Z19
	Aldeby	,,								3 3						↓		↓	4Z27
	Haddiscoe	arr.						↓		3 7									4Z30
68	Haddiscoe	dep.								4 4									4N43
	Reedham	arr.								4 11									4N50
	Norwich (Thorpe)	,,								4 37									5N20
	Haddiscoe	dep.						↓		3 8						↓		↓	4Z31
	St. Olaves	,,								3 11									4Z34
	Belton and Burgh	,,						↓		3 17						↓		↓	4Z40
	YARMOUTH (South Town)	arr.						3 5		3 24						4 13		4 22	4Z47
45	Yarmouth (South Town)	dep.						3 17								4E20			
	Gorleston-on-Sea	arr.						3 27					4L28	4L28		4E30		5L48	5L48

Buffet Car—Liverpool Street to Ipswich (11H30)

Restaurant Car. (F)

Restaurant Car. (R)

To Sheringham (R)

Restaurant Car—Liverpool Street to Yarmouth. (G)

Restaurant Car—Liverpool Street to Cromer. (12 33)

Restaurant Car (J 12 52)

Restaurant Car (M 12 56)

To Maldon (East) and Heybridge (SO 12 55)

Restaurant Car (Mondays and Fridays only and not after 3rd September)—Liverpool Street to Ipswich. Restaurant Car (Tuesdays, Wednesdays and Thursdays. Also Mondays and Fridays commencing 6th September)—Liverpool Street to Yarmouth. (SX 1 0)

To Bury St. Edmund's (2 48)

Restaurant Car—Liverpool Street to Ipswich (to Yarmouth on 18th September). (SO 12 58)

To Bury St. Edmund's (3 12)

A Departure times for stations beyond Chelmsford. For complete service between Liverpool Street and Chelmsford see London Suburban Pocket Time Table No. 4.
B For other trains between Trowse and Norwich see Table 9.
C For other trains between Ipswich and Westerfield see Table 40.
E On Mondays and Fridays until **3rd September** inclusive arrives Gorleston 5.4 p.m., via Lowestoft.
F Mondays, Fridays and Saturdays only and not after **4th September.** On Saturdays arrives Cromer 3.15 p.m.
G Mondays, Fridays and Saturdays only and not after **4th September.** Also runs on Saturdays **11th** and **18th September.**
H On Saturdays until **11th September** inclusive will not convey Walton and Clacton branch passengers from Liverpool Street.
J Saturdays only and not after **11th September.**
K On Saturdays until **11th September** inclusive leaves Colchester 1.3, arrives Walton 1.49 and Clacton 1.43 p.m.
L Via Lowestoft.
M Mondays and Fridays only and not after **3rd September.**
N On Saturdays leaves Haddiscoe 5.37 and arrives Reedham 5.44 and Norwich 6.20 p.m.
P On Saturdays leaves Norwich 3.26 and arrives Cromer 4.22 p.m.
Q Runs Saturday **11th September** only, with **Restaurant Car.**
R Saturdays only and not after **11th September.** Until **4th September** inclusive runs to Sheringham only (arr. 3.45 p.m.). On Saturday **11th September** also runs to Cromer.
SO Saturdays only.
SX Saturdays excepted.
V Via Norwich. On Saturdays arrives Lowestoft 4.13 p.m.
X Third class only.
Y On Saturdays runs 4 minutes later.
Z On Saturdays runs 5 minutes later.

Table 41. WICKHAM MARKET AND FRAMLINGHAM.

For Local Service see Table			WEEKDAYS								
				TO	TX	TO	TSX	SO			
			a.m.	a.m.	a.m.	a.m.	a.m.	a.m.	a.m.	p.m.	p.m.
8	**LONDON** (Liverpool Street)	dep.	5 30	...	...	...	8 15	8 15	10 20	3 20	4 54
8	Colchester	,,	6 41	7 48	7 48	..	9 40	9 40	11B41	4 35	5 32
8	Ipswich	,,	7 7	8 30	9 0	9 0	10 33	10 33	12 26	5 3	6 24
8	Wickham Market	arr.	7 47	9 2	9 35	9 35	11 9	11 9	1 1	5 40	6 54
8	Yarmouth (South Town)	dep.	6 30	7 42	7 42	8 30	10 0	10 0	11 45	3 28	5 29
8	Lowestoft (Central)	,,	6 41	7 43	7 43	8 30	10 0	10 0	11 55	3 33	5 40
8	Wickham Market	arr.	7 55	9 2	9 2	10 15	11 32	11 32	1 10	4 54	7 3
	WICKHAM MARKET for Campsea Ash	dep.	7 56	9 6	9 40	10 20	11 40	11 50	1 14	5 44	7 4
	Marlesford	,,	8 2	9 11	9 46	10 26	11 45	11 55	1 19	5 49	7 9
	Hacheston (Halt)	,,	8 6	9 18	9 53	10 33	11 52	12 2	1 26	5 56	7 16
	Parham	,,	8 10	9 21	9 57	10 37	11 55	12 5	1 29	5 59	7 19
	FRAMLINGHAM	arr.	8 17	9 27	10 4	10 44	12 1	12 11	1 35	6 5	7 25

For Local Service see Table			WEEKDAYS							
			TO	TX		TO	TSX			
			a.m.	a.m.	a.m.	a.m.	a.m.	p.m.	p.m.	p.m.
	FRAMLINGHAM	dep.	7 14	7 18	8 36	9 45	10 40	12 36	4 23	6 30
	Parham	,,	7 21	7 24	8 42	9 51	10 46	12 42	4 30	6 36
	Hacheston (Halt)	,,	7 24	7 26	8 44	9 53	10 48	12 44	4 33	6 38
	Marlesford	,,	7 32	7 33	8 48	10 0	10 55	12 51	4 41	6 45
	WICKHAM MARKET for Campsea Ash	arr.	7 37	7 38	8 53	10 5	11 0	12 56	4 46	6 50
8	Wickham Market	dep.	7 47	7 47	9 35	11 9	11 9	1 1	5 40	6 54
8	Lowestoft (Central)	arr.	9 17	9 17	10 47	12 24	12C24	2A15	6 57	8 5
8	Yarmouth (South Town)	,,	9 18	9 18	10 56	12 29	12 29	2A22	6 57	8 2
8	Wickham Market	dep.	7 55	7 55	9 2	10 15	11 32	1 10	4 54	7 3
8	Ipswich	arr.	8 35	8 35	9 40	10 51	12 11	1 48	5 33	7 42
8	Colchester	,,	9 8	9 8	11 2	12 19	12 48	2 28	6 36	8 43
8	**LONDON** (Liverpool Street)	,,	10 23	10 23	11 15	1 13	2 3	3 42	7 52	9 24

A On Saturdays arrives Lowestoft 2.23 and Yarmouth 2.27 p.m.
B On Saturdays leaves Colchester 11.46 a.m.
C On Mondays and Fridays until **3rd September** inclusive arrives Lowestoft 12.36 p.m.

SO Saturdays only.
TO Tuesdays only.
TSX Tuesdays and Saturdays excepted.
TX Tuesdays excepted.

Tickets from Marlesford, Hacheston (Halt) and Parham are issued on the train.
Passengers to and from Hacheston (Halt) must join, or alight from, the special car provided.

Table 42. SAXMUNDHAM AND ALDEBURGH.

For Local Service see Table			WEEKDAYS																	SUNDAYS			
							D	SX	B	H	K	L		FO	FX	N	R	M	T				
			a.m.	a.m.	a.m.	a.m.	p.m.	p.m.	p.m.	p.m.	p.m.	p.m.	p.m.	p.m.	p.m.	p.m.	p.m.	p.m.	p.m.	a.m.	a.m.	p.m.	p.m.
8	**LONDON** (Liverpool Street)	dep.	5 30	...	8 15	[illegible] 20	...	1 0	12 58	12 58	...	...	3 20	4 5[illegible]	[illegible] 54	5 16	5 16	7 42	7 42	...	...	...	4 35
8	Colchester	,,	6 41	7 48	9 40	[illegible]E41	..	1 45	1 49	1 49	..	..	4 35	5 32	32	6 28	6 28	8 55	8 55	..	8 25	..	5 50
8	Ipswich	,,	7 7	9 0	10 33	[illegible]2 26	...	2 36	2 44	2 44	2J50	2 55	5 3	6 24	[illegible] 24	7 11	7 11	9 34	9 42	...	9 25	...	6 37
8	Saxmundham	arr.	8 0	9 46	11 20	1 14	..	3 16	3 24	3 24	3J38	3 43	5 52	7 7	7 7	7 57	7 57	10 20	10 28	..	10 11	..	7 24
8	Yarmouth (South Town)	dep.	6 30	8 30	10 0	2 23	...	...	...	2 35	3 28	3 28	...	5 29	6 35	6 59	7 30	6 55	7 30	7 45	...	5 15	7 28
8	Lowestoft (Central)	,,	6 41	8 30	10 0	2 22	..	..	..	2 33	3 33	3 33	..	5 40	6 38	7 7	7 33	7 3	7 33	7 4	..	5 25	7 10
8	Beccles	,,	7 3	8 56	10 35	2 48	...	...	...	3 3	4 2	4 2	...	6 6	7 2	7 31	7 57	7 27	7 57	8 9	...	5 49	7 50
8	Saxmundham	arr.	7 43	9 25	11 19	1 28	..	..	..	3 41	4 43	4 43	..	6 49	7 33	8 10	8 32	8 6	8 32	8 41	..	6 34	8 18
	SAXMUNDHAM	dep.	8 8	9 50	11 28	1 35	1 50	3 22	3 32	4 0	4 44	5 2	5 57	7 15	7 35	8 18	8 35	10 24	10 32	8 45	10 15	6 35	8 20
	Leiston	,,	8 21	10 0	11 38	1 45	2 0	3 32	3 42	4 10	4 55	5 12	6 7	7 25	7 45	8 28	8 45	10 34	10 42	8 56	10 26	6 46	8 31
	Thorpeness	,,	8 27	10 5	11 43	1 50	2 5	3 37	3 47	4 15	5 0	5 17	6 12	7 30	7 50	8 33	8 50	10 39	10 47	9 1	10 31	6 51	8 36
	ALDEBURGH	arr.	8 32	10 10	11 48	1 55	2 10	3 42	3 55	4 20	5 5	5 22	6 17	7 35	7 55	8 38	8 55	10 44	10 52	9 6	10 36	6 56	8 41

For Local Service see Table			WEEKDAYS																SUNDAYS			
							SX	SO	K	L	K	L	FO	FX	N	R	M	T				
			a.m.	a.m.	a.m.	p.m.	p.m.	p.m.	p.m.	p.m.	p.m.	p.m.	p.m.	p.m.	p.m.	p.m.	p.m.	p.m.	a.m.	a.m.	p.m.	p.m.
	ALDEBURGH	dep.	7 10	8 52	10 22	2 48	2 50	2 55	4 12	4 30	5 14	5 28	6 41	7 0	7 41	8 0	9 48	9 58	8 11	9 44	6 0	7 25
	Thorpeness	,,	7 15	8 57	10 27	2 53	2 55	3 0	4 17	4 36	5 19	5 33	6 46	7 5	7 46	8 5	9 53	10 3	8 16	9 49	6 5	7 30
	Leiston	,,	7 21	9 3	10 34	2 59	3 1	3 6	4 23	4 43	5 29	5 39	6 52	7 11	7 52	8 11	9 59	10 9	8 22	9 55	6 11	7 37
	SAXMUNDHAM	arr.	7 32	9 12	10 43	1 8	3 10	3 15	4 32	4 52	5 39	5 48	7 1	7 20	8 1	8 20	10 8	10 18	8 30	10 4	6 20	7 46
8	Saxmundham	dep.	8 0	9 46	10 45	1F12	3 16	3 24	...	...	5 52	5 52	7 7	7 57	...	...	10 20	10 28	...	10 11	7 24	9 23
8	Beccles	arr.	8 45	10 25	11 15	1F50	3 49	3 58	..	..	6 30	6 30	7 39	8 34	..	..	10 48	10 56	..	10 50	8 1	10 1
8	Lowestoft (Central)	,,	9 17	10 47	11 40	2F15	4 23	4 23	...	...	6 57	6 57	8 5	9 1	...	...	11 9	11 45	...	11 15	8 29	10 21
8	Yarmouth (South Town)	,,	9 18	10 56	11 38	2F22	4 13	4 22	..	..	6 57	6 57	8 2	9 6	..	..	11 10	11 18	..	11 20	8 32	10 30
8	Saxmundham	dep.	7 43	9 25	11 0	1 28	3 41	3 41	4 43	...	6 49	6 49	7V33	7 33	8 10	8 32	...	...	8 41	...	6 34	7 58
8	Ipswich	arr.	8 35	9 55	11 35	1 58	4 19	4 19	5 33	..	7 42	7 42	8V 5	8 5	9 2	9 4	..	..	9 17	..	7 25	8 28
8	Colchester	,,	9 8	11 2	12A19	2 28	5 19	5 19	6 36	...	...	...	8 43	8 43	9 53	9 53	...	...	10 3	...	7 57	9 5
8	**LONDON** (Liverpool Street)	,,	10 23	11 25	1A13	3 42	5 55	5 55	7 52	..	9 24	9 24	9 59	9 59	11 38	11 38	..	..	10 55	..	9 15	10 23

A On Saturdays arrives Colchester 12.48 and Liverpool Street 1.20 p.m.
B Saturdays only (Saturday **31st July** excepted).
D Runs Saturdays **31st July and 7th August** only.
E On Saturdays leaves Colchester 11.46 a.m.
F On Saturdays leaves Saxmundham 1.14 and arrives Beccles 1.55, Lowestoft 2.23 and Yarmouth 2.27 p.m.
FO Fridays only.

FX Fridays excepted.
H Runs Saturday **31st July** only.
J On Saturdays **10th, 17th, 24th July** also Saturdays commencing **4th September** runs 5 minutes later.
K Does not run on Saturdays **31st July** to **28th August** inclusive.
L Runs Saturdays **31st July** to **28th August** inclusive.
M Saturdays only. Commences **11th September.**

N Fridays only. Commences **10th September**
R Fridays only and not after **3rd September.**
SO Saturdays only.
SX Saturdays excepted.
T Saturdays only and not after **4th September.**
V From **6th August** to **10th September** inclusive leaves Saxmundham 7.17 and arrives Ipswich 7.58 p.m.

Pages 197-199:
LNER Summer timetables
5 July to 26 September 1937.

ALDEBURGH (Suffolk)
Miles 99½. Map Sq. 19.
Pop. 2,480. Clos. day Wed.
From Liverpool Street via Ipswich **and** Saxmundham.
1st cl.—Single **25/9**, Mth. Ret. **31/3.**
3rd cl.—Single **15/6**, Mth. Ret. **20/10.**

Liv. St.	Aldeb.	Aldeb.	Liv. St.
a.m.		a.m.	
4 40	8 21	7 15r	10 45
8 12r	11 23	8 37r	11 36
—	—	—	—
p.m.		p.m.	
1 0r	4 25	12 48	3 57
3 40r	6 29	6 38sr	10 10
5 10	8 26	6 38	10 10
—	—	—	—
—	—	—	—
—	—	—	—
—	—	—	—
—	—	—	—

No Sunday Trains.

e Not Sat. s Sat. only.
r Refresh. Car.
Bus facilities. From Saxmundham, Church St., 10 Weekday and **Sunday,** 30 min. journey.

FRAMLINGHAM (Suffolk)
Miles 91. Map Sq. 19.
Pop. 2,101. Clos. day Wed.
From Liverpool Street via Ipswich and Wickham Market.
1st cl.—Single **23/6,** Mth. Ret. **28/6.**
3rd cl.—Single **14/1,** Mth. Ret. **19/-.**

Liv. St.	Fram.	Fram.	Liv. St.
a.m.		a.m.	
4 40	9 56	8 42r	11 36
10 0r	1 31	—	—
—	—	p.m.	
p.m.		3 10	6 51
5 10	8 19	—	—

No Sunday Trains.

r Refresh. Car.
Bus facilities. From Ipswich, Old Cattle Market, 8 on Sunday 72 min. journey, and from Saxmundham, Church St., 2 on Sunday, 38 min. journey.

Crown Hotel. 'Phone : 22.
Comfortable Commercial and Family House, with good Standard in Cooking and Service.
For List of Trust Houses See Back of Map.

HADDISCOE (Norfolk)
Miles 114¾. Map Sq. 19.
Pop. 407. Clos. day Wed.
From Liverpool Street via Ipswich and Beccles.
1st cl.—Single **29/6**, Mth. Ret. **35/11.**
3rd cl.—Single **17/10**, Mth. Ret. **23/11.**
Served by most Weekday, all Sunday trains, to St. Olaves, 5 min. shorter journey.

HALESWORTH (Suffolk)
Miles 100¾. Map Sq. 19.
Pop. 2,024 Clos. day Thur.
From Liverpool Street via Ipswich.
1st cl.—Single **26/1,** Mth. Ret. **31/3.**
3rd cl.—Single **15/8,** Mth. Ret. **20/10.**

Liv. St.	Hales.	Hales.	Liv. St.
a.m.		a.m.	
4 40	8 6	7 36r	10 45
8 12r	11 9	8 50r	11 36
10 0r	1 33	9 58r	1 35
—	—	—	—
p.m.		p.m.	
12 20sr	2 51	1 12	3 57
1 0r	4 14	3 36	6 51
4 0	7 12	6 52	10 10
5 10	8 23	6 52sr	10 10
—	—	8 0	12 50
Sunday Trains.			
a.m.		a.m.	
10 0	1 44	10 1	1 40
—	—	—	—
p.m.		p.m.	
5 0	8 28	3 38	6 50
—	—	6 52	10 18
—	—	8 0	12 55

r Refresh. Car. s Sat. only.

SAXMUNDHAM (Suffolk)
Miles 91¼. Map Sq. 19.
Pop. 1,259. Clos. day Thur.
From Liverpool Street via Ipswich.
1st cl.—Single **23/6,** Mth. Ret. **28/6.**
3rd cl.—Single **14/1,** Mth. Ret. **19/-.**

Liv. St.	Saxmun.	Saxmun.	Liv. St.
a.m.		a.m.	
4 40	7 41	8 24r	10 45
8 12r	10 52	9 7r	11 36
10 0r	1 11	10 20r	1 35
p.m.		p.m.	
12 20sr	2 34	1 33	3 57
1 0r	3 52	3 58	6 51
3 40r	6 4	7 9	10 10
4 0	6 50	7 9sr	10 10
5 10	8 1	8 24	12 50
Sunday Trains.			
a.m.		a.m.	
10 0	1 19	10 23	1 40
—	—	—	—
p.m.		p.m.	
5 0	8 4	4 0	6 50
—	—	7 9	10 18
—	—	8 24	12 55

r Refresh. Car. s Sat. only.

Bell Hotel. 'Phone : 4. Comfortable Rooms. Hot and Cold Water in Bedrooms. Good Cooking.
For List of Trust Houses See Back of Map.

WOODBRIDGE (Suffolk)
Miles 79. Map Sq. 19.
Pop. 4,734. Clos. day Wed.
From Liverpool Street via Ipswich.
1st cl.—Single **20/5,** Mth. Ret. **24/9.**
3rd cl.—Single **12/3,** Mth. Ret. **16/6.**

Liv. St.	Wood.	Wood.	Liv. St.
a.m.		a.m.	
4 40	7 11	8 21r	10 45
8 12r	10 32	9 28r	11 36
10 0r	12 43	10 46r	1 35
—	—	—	—
p.m.		p.m.	
1 0r	3 29	1 54	3 57
3 40r	5 40	4 26	6 51
4 0	6 27	7 31	10 10
5 10	7 33	7 31sr	10 10
—	—	8 50	12 50
Sunday Trains.			
a.m.		a.m.	
10 0	12 48	10 51	1 40
—	—	—	—
p.m.		p.m.	
5 0	7 35	4 28	6 50
—	—	7 31	10 18
—	—	8 50	12 55

e Not Sat.
r Refresh. Car.
s Sat. only.
Bus facilities. From Ipswich, Old Cattle Market, frequent, 35 min. journey.

ABC Railway Guide
June 1941 timetable.

On the remaining branches, Aldeburgh was down to five trains each way, with no Sunday service, and Framlingham to two up and three down, compared to eight each way on the Aldeburgh branch (four each way Sundays) and six each way on the Framlingham branch in July 1938. Even the busy Felixstowe line, which used a section of the East Suffolk, was reduced to eight trains down and seven up, with the Pier station being closed and Beach only seeing three return trips. The Southwold Railway had long ago closed in 1929, owing to competition from buses, but the Waveney Valley still had five from Tivetshall to Beccles and six the other way.

In the postwar period the railways were nationalised from 1 January 1948, and the East Suffolk passed from LNER hands to British Railways. Little changed at first — even the style of the official lettering, the famous Gill Sans — remained the same, although gradually the LNER lozenge gave way to the BR double sausage. LNER green and cream liveries for stations and buildings certainly persisted for a very long time under the new owners, and can be seen today in some places. The postwar boom in incomes and leisure time helped some lines to see their highest levels of traffic ever during the 1950s, although others did not fare so well. The Framlingham branch lost its passenger services from 3 November 1952, the last trains running on Saturday 1 November; the rundown and closure of the system are dealt with elsewhere in this book. The Waveney Valley saw its last passenger trains on 3 January 1953.

Meanwhile, other changes were in the air. British Railways was building its new standard classes of steam locomotive, and Gerard Fiennes, then BR Eastern Region Assistant Superintendent at Liverpool Street, designed the new hourly interval service on the Great Eastern main line around them. Their power revolutionised the route, and they eventually appeared over much of East Anglia, including the East Suffolk. In the first place the new schedules on the main line affected the East Suffolk by reducing the number of services that dropped off coaches for Yarmouth South Town at Ipswich. For example, the 4.30am from Liverpool Street reached Ipswich at 6.17am, and then called at all stations to Norwich, while a connecting service left Ipswich at 6.41am for all stations to South Town and Lowestoft. The other effect was that it was often now quicker to reach Yarmouth Vauxhall via Norwich than to travel via the East Suffolk, with its undulations and sinuous curves. However, the best was still to come.

The 'Easterling' was introduced on 5 June 1950, departing Liverpool Street at 11.3am and running nonstop to Beccles, where it divided for Lowestoft, reached at 1.41pm, whilst the main train went forward to Yarmouth, arriving at 1.38pm. Intermediate stops were covered by through coaches detached from the 10.30am Norwich express at Ipswich, working forward at 12.31pm and reaching Yarmouth at 2.19pm. The train ran at 10.33am on Saturdays, with local stops this time covered by the 10.40am Liverpool Street to

Above:
Class B12 No 61564 has arrived at Ipswich with an up train from Yarmouth. 'Britannia' No 70012 *John of Gaunt* waits to take over for the journey to Liverpool Street. *John Brodribb collection*

Below:
'Britannia' No 70002 *Geoffrey Chaucer* heads an up express away from Halesworth whilst Class O1 No 63687 shunts the goods shed. *Peter Punchard collection*

Table 3 LONDON (Liverpool Street), COLCHESTER, CLACTON-ON-SEA, HARWICH, IPSWICH, NORWICH, BECCLES, LOWESTOFT, and YARMOUTH

Week Days

Miles		mrn	mrn	mrn	mrn	mrn	mrn	mrn	mrn	mrn	mrn		mrn	mrn	mrn	mrn	mrn	mrn	mrn	mrn	mrn	mrn
																B	U				B	
	LONDON (L'pool St) dep	..	..	..	4 40	..	To Braintree (Table 29a)	..	..	..	..	..	..	..	6 55	7 32	8 12	..	8 15	..	8 36	..
4	Stratford	..	..	..	..	..		..	..	..	..	..	..	..	7 5	7 43	..	..	8 26	..	8 47	..
7½	Ilford	..	..	..	..	..		..	..	..	..	..	..	..	7 14	7 50	..	..	8 35	..	8 59	..
12½	Romford	..	..	..	..	..		..	..	..	..	..	..	..	7 24	8 6	..	..	8 45	..	9 15	From Cambridge (Table 17)
13½	Gidea Pk & Squirrels	..	..	..	..	..		..	..	..	..	..	..	..	7 28	8 10	..	..	..	..	9 19	
15	Harold Wood [Heath]	..	..	..	..	..		..	..	..	..	..	..	..	7 33	8 14	..	..	..	..	9 23	
18¼	Brentwood & Warley	..	..	..	5 12	..		..	..	..	..	..	..	..	7 42	8 22	..	..	..	..	9 31	
20¼	Shenfield & Hutton	..	..	..	..	..		..	..	..	..	..	..	..	7 50	8 28	8 48	..	9 2	..	9 38	
23½	Ingatestone	..	..	..	5 23	..		..	..	..	..	..	..	..	7 57	8 35	..	..	9 9	..	..	
29¾	Chelmsford	..	..	..	5 34	..	5 50	..	..	..	..	..	..	..	8 9	8 47	9 3	..	9 21	..	9 53	
36	Hatfield Peverel	..	..	..	..	..	6 1	..	..	..	..	..	..	..	8 20	..	..	..	9 34	..	10 3	
38½	Witham	..	..	..	..	..	6G15	..	..	..	..	..	..	..	8R29	9 0	9 18	..	9 42	..	10 9	
42¼	Kelvedon	..	..	..	..	..	Stop	..	..	..	..	..	..	..	8 37	..	..	..	9 51	..	..	
46¾	Mark's Tey	..	..	..	6 0	..	..	..	..	..	..	..	..	..	8R49	..	..	..	10 1	..	..	1037
51¾	Colchester arr	..	..	..	6 9	..	..	..	..	..	..	..	..	..	8 59	..	9 36	..	1010	..	..	1047
70½	19 WALTON-ON-NAZE arr	..	..	..	8 3	..	..	..	..	..	..	..	..	..	..	..	..	..	1132	..	..	..
69¾	19 CLACTON-ON-SEA C	..	..	..	7 54	..	..	..	..	..	..	..	..	..	..	..	..	..	1123	..	..	..
—	Colchester dep	..	..	..	6 13	6 50	..	7 20	7 48	..	..	..	..	..	9 4	..	9 39	..	1015	..	..	..
56	Ardleigh	..	..	..	..	6 58	..	..	7 57	..	..	..	..	..	9 13	..	..	..	1025	..	..	..
59½	Manningtree arr	..	..	..	..	7 4	..	7 34	8 4	..	..	..	..	..	9 20	..	..	..	1032	..	..	..
69	21 HARWICH PARK. Q. arr	..	..	..	..	7 29	..	..	8 31	..	..	..	..	..	..	..	..	..	11 3	..	..	..
70¼	21 " TOWN "	..	..	..	..	7 40	..	..	8 40	..	..	..	..	..	..	..	..	..	1113	..	..	..
—	Manningtree dep	..	..	..	..	..	..	7 36	8 5	..	..	..	..	..	9 24	..	..	..	1035	..	..	..
63¼	Bentley	..	..	..	..	..	..	..	8 14	..	..	..	..	..	9 32	..	..	..	1044	..	..	..
68¾	Ipswich arr	..	..	..	6 37	..	mrn	7 53	8 24	..	..	..	..	..	9 42	..	10 4	..	1055	..	..	..
—	Ipswich dep	..	..	..	6 48	..	7 30	8 0	..	..	8 50	..	8 55	..	..	..	10 10	1025	..	1130	..	..
71½	Bramford	..	From Beccles (Table 23)	..	6 54	..	7 36	TC and Buffet Car to Bury St. Edmunds, Peterborough and York arr 1 30 aft. (Tables 32, 38, 61 & 1)	..	..	..	..	9 1	..	..	..	..	1031	..	1136	..	..
73½	Claydon	..		..	6 59	..	7 41		..	..	..	..	9 6	..	..	..	..	1036	..	1141	..	..
77	Needham	..		..	7 8	..	7 49		..	From Beccles (Table 23)	..	..	9 14	..	..	..	..	1044	..	1149	..	..
80½	Stowmarket	..		..	7 19	..	7 59		..		9 11	..	9 23	..	..	..	10 29	1053	..	1158	..	..
83	Haughley	..		..	7 27	..	8 5		..		9 19	..	9 31	..	..	..	..	11 0	..	12 4	..	..
86½	Finningham	..		..	7 36	..	b		..		b	..	9 40	..	..	..	..	b	..	..	..	..
91¼	Mellis	..		..	7 44	..	..		..		..	..	9 48	..	..	..	..	..	..	..	..	..
95	Diss	..		..	7 53	..	..		..		Stop	..	9 55	..	..	..	10 49	..	..	..	..	..
97½	Burston	..		..	7 59	..	..		..		..	..	10 1	..	..	..	..	..	..	..	..	..
100½	Tivetshall	..	6 30	..	8 8	..	..		..	9 53	..	..	10 9	..	..	..	11 0	..	..	..	..	..
104	Forncett	..	6 37	..	8 15	..	..		..	10 0	..	..	1016	..	..	..	..	..	..	..	..	..
106¾	Flordon	..	..	..	8 21	..	..		..	10 6	..	..	1022	..	..	..	..	..	..	..	..	..
109¾	Swainsthorpe	..	..	..	8 28	..	..		..	1013	..	..	1029	..	..	..	..	..	..	..	..	..
114	Trowse	..	..	..	..	..	..		..	..	..	..	..	..	..	..	..	..	..	..	..	..
115	Norwich (Thorpe) arr	..	7 0	..	8 38	..	..		..	1025	..	..	1039	..	..	..	11 20	..	..	..	..	..
139	45 CROMER arr	..	8 52	..	10 0	..	..		..	..	..	..	..	..	..	..	12 11	..	..	..	..	..
—	Ipswich dep	..	..	..	6 47	..	..		..	..	..	..	..	8 40	..	..	10 15	..	..	..	..	..
72¼	Westerfield	..	..	..	6 56	..	..		..	..	..	..	..	8 51	..	..	..	..	..	..	..	..
76	Bealings	..	..	..	7 3	..	..		..	..	..	..	..	8 59	..	..	..	..	..	..	..	..
79	Woodbridge	..	..	..	7 11	..	..		..	..	..	..	..	9 5	..	..	10 32	..	..	..	..	..
80¾	Melton	..	..	..	7 16	..	..		..	..	..	..	..	9 10	..	..	..	..	..	..	..	..
84½	Wickham Market D	..	..	..	7 28	..	..		..	..	..	..	..	9 21	..	..	..	..	..	..	..	..
91	Saxmundham	..	..	..	7 41	..	..		..	..	..	..	..	9 34	..	..	10 52	..	..	..	..	..
95½	Darsham, for Yoxford	..	..	..	7 52	..	..		..	..	..	..	..	9 45	..	..	..	..	..	..	..	..
100¾	Halesworth	..	..	..	8 6	..	..		..	..	..	..	..	9 57	..	..	11 9	..	..	..	..	..
104½	Brampton (Suffolk)	..	..	..	8 17	..	..		..	..	..	..	..	10 7	..	..	..	..	..	..	..	..
109½	Beccles arr	..	..	..	8 27	..	..		..	..	..	..	..	10 19	..	..	11 24	..	..	..	..	..
—	Beccles dep	..	..	7 18	8 35	..	..		..	..	..	..	..	10 30	..	..	11 32	..	..	..	..	..
115¾	Oulton Broad South	..	..	7 28	8 45	..	..		..	..	mrn	..	..	10 40	..	..	11 42	..	..	..	..	..
117¾	Lowestoft (Cen.) arr	X	..	7 33	8 50	..	..		..	..	X	..	..	10 45	..	..	11 47	..	..	..	..	..
—	Beccles dep	7 10	..	..	8 30	..	..		..	..	9 30	..	..	10 22	..	..	11 28	..	..	..	..	..
112¼	Aldeby	7 19	..	..	8 38	..	..		..	..	9 39	..	..	10 30	..	..	..	..	..	..	..	..
114¾	Haddiscoe arr	7 23	..	..	8 42	..	..		..	..	9 43	..	..	10 34	..	..	..	..	..	..	..	..
118¾	45 REEDHAM arr	8 2	..	..	8 54	..	..		..	..	..	..	..	11S54	..	..	..	..	..	..	..	..
131	45 NORWICH (Thorpe) "	8 34	..	..	9L35	..	..		..	..	..	..	..	12S34	..	..	..	..	..	..	..	..
—	Haddiscoe dep	7 24	..	..	8 46	..	..	..	..	..	9 44	..	..	10 35	..	..	..	..	..	..	..	..
115¼	St. Olaves	7 29	..	..	8 49	..	..	..	..	..	9 49	..	..	10 38	..	..	..	..	..	..	..	..
117¾	Belton and Burgh	7 35	..	..	8 56	..	..	..	..	..	9 55	..	..	10 44	..	..	..	..	..	..	..	..
121¾	Yarmouth (Sth. Town) arr	7 45	..	..	9 4	..	..	..	..	..	10 5	..	..	10 52	..	..	11 48	..	..	..	..	..
124¼	28 GORLESTON-ON-SEA arr	..	..	..	9X33	..	..	..	..	..	..	..	..	..	..	..	12 41	..	..	..	..	..

A For particulars of London Suburban Service see Suburban Time Table.
b To Bury St. Edmunds (Table 32)
C Clacton-on-Sea and Holland-on-Sea
G Arr 6 6 mrn
D Station for Campsea Ash
L Via Lowestoft
R Arr Witham 8 25 and Mark's Tey 8 45 mrn
S Saturdays only
TC Through Carriage
U Buffet Car Liverpool Street to Norwich (Thorpe)
X or X One class only
B Third class only

Table 3— *Continued* LONDON (Liverpool Street), COLCHESTER, CLACTON-ON-SEA, HARWICH, IPSWICH, NORWICH, BECCLES, LOWESTOFT, and YARMOUTH

Week Days—*Continued*

	aft	mrn	aft	aft	mrn	aft	aft	aft	aft	aft	aft	B		aft	B	aft	aft	aft	aft	aft	aft	aft	aft
		R				S			S	R		S		S	S				R		U		
LONDON (L'pool St) dep	..	10 0	..	..	1120	1220	..	..	1235	1 0	..	1251	..	1 30	1 36	..	..	2 15	3 40	..	3 46	..	3 30
Stratford	..	..	..	..	..	Buffet Car Liverpool St. to Yarmouth	..	..	..	..	..	..	..	..	..	..	..	2 26	..	..	..	..	3 40
Ilford	..	1016	..	..	1136		..	..	..	..	..	1 7	..	..	..	..	..	2 34	..	..	..	..	3 47
Romford	..	..	..	..	..		From Cambridge (Table 17)	..	..	..	..	..	..	..	1 58	From Cambridge (Table 17)	..	..	..	..	..	..	3 57
Gidea Pk & Squirrels	..	..	..	..	..			..	..	..	..	..	..	..	2 2		..	..	..	..	..	..	4 1
Harold Wood [Heath]	..	..	..	..	..			..	..	..	..	1 21	..	..	2 6		..	..	..	..	..	..	4 5
Brentwood & Warley	..	..	..	..	..			..	..	..	..	1 29	..	..	2 14		..	..	..	..	..	..	4 14
Shenfield & Hutton	..	1040	..	..	1158			..	..	1 35	..	1 38	..	..	2 20		..	2 55	..	..	..	..	4 23
Ingatestone	..	..	..	..	12 5			..	..	..	..	1 46	..	..	2 27		..	3 3	..	..	..	..	4 30
Chelmsford	..	1055	..	..	1219			..	1 23	1 50	..	1 58	..	2 21	2 38		..	3 16	..	..	4 34	..	4 39
Hatfield Peverel	..	..	..	..	1229			..	..	..	..	2 8	..	..	2 48		..	3 26	..	..	..	..	..
Witham	..	1110	..	..	1236			..	..	2 5	..	2 13	..	2 36	2 56		..	3 34	..	..	..	..	..
Kelvedon	..	..	..	..	1244			..	..	..	..	..	..	..	3 4		..	3 42	..	..	..	..	..
Mark's Tey	..	1124	..	..	1253		1 6	..	..	2 19	..	..	..	..	3 14	3 21	..	3 52	..	..	..	..	..
Colchester arr	..	1133	..	..	1 2		1 16	..	1 54	2 28	..	..	..	2 54	3 23	3 30	..	4 1	..	..	5 4	..	..
19 WALTON-ON-NAZE arr	..	1253	..	..	..		2E41	..	2 41	3F38	..	..	..	3 45	..	Stop	..	5 12	..	..	5 55	..	..
19 CLACTON-ON-SEA C "	..	1243	..	..	..		2E32	..	2 32	3F24	..	..	..	3 36	..	..	..	5 4	..	..	5 47	..	..
Colchester dep	..	1137	..	..	1 8		Stop	1 45	2 2	2 32	2 38	..	..	..	3 27	..	..	4 5	..	..	..	5 14	..
Ardleigh	..	..	..	..	1 17		..	..	..	..	2 49	..	..	..	3 37	..	..	4 14	..	..	..	5 23	..
Manningtree arr	..	1149	..	..	1 24		..	1 57	2 15	..	2 56	..	..	RC Liverpool St. to Clacton-on-Sea	3 44	..	..	4 21	..	..	..	5 30	..
21 HARWICH PARK. Q. arr	..	1218	..	..	..	..	..	..	..	..	3 21	..	..		..	..	..	4 53	..	..	..	..	..
21 " TOWN "	..	1228	..	..	..	..	..	..	..	..	3 31	..	..		..	..	..	5 3	..	..	..	..	..
Manningtree dep	..	1151	..	..	1 26	..	..	1 59	2 17	..	..	..	..		3 46	..	..	4 25	..	..	..	5 32	..
Bentley	..	..	..	..	1 34	..	..	2 7	..	..	..	..	..		3 54	..	..	4 33	..	..	..	5 40	..
Ipswich arr	..	12 6	..	..	1 45	1 56	..	2 17	2 33	2 57	..	..	..		4 5	..	..	4 45	5 13	..	..	5 50	..
Ipswich dep	..	1212	1220	..	..	2 7	..	2 26	Buffet Car, Liverpool St. to Ipswich.	3 3	..	..	..		..	..	..	..	5 19	5 35	..	Stop	..
Bramford	..	..	1226	..	..	..	..	TC to Bury St. Edmunds, Peterborough and Leeds (arr 8 46 aft) (Tables 32, 38, 1, and 89)		..	..	..	..		..	..	From Beccles (Table 23)	..	..	5 41	..	..	..
Claydon	..	..	1231	..	..	..	..			..	..	..	..		..	..		..	..	5 46	..	..	..
Needham	..	..	1239	..	..	..	..			..	..	..	..		..	aft		..	..	5 54	..	..	..
Stowmarket	..	1232	1251	..	..	..	..	2 46		3 22	..	..	..		..	3 35		..	..	6 3	..	..	..
Haughley	..	..	1259	..	..	..	..			..	..	..	..		..	3 42		..	..	6 9	..	..	..
Finningham	..	..	1 8	..	..	..	..			3 34	..	..	..		..	b		..	..	..	..	..	..
Mellis	..	..	1 16	..	..	..	..			..	..	..	..	..	..	..		..	..	..	..	..	..
Diss	..	1252	1 23	..	..	..	..			3 48	..	..	..	..	..	..		..	..	..	..	..	..
Burston	..	..	1 29	..	..	..	..			..	..	..	..	..	..	..		..	..	..	..	..	..
Tivetshall	..	..	1 37	..	..	..	..			4 0	..	..	..	..	..	..	4 22	..	..	..	..	..	..
Forncett	..	..	1 45	..	..	..	..			..	..	..	..	..	..	..	4 29	..	..	..	..	..	..
Flordon	..	..	1 51	..	..	..	..			..	..	..	..	..	..	..	4 35	..	..	..	..	..	..
Swainsthorpe	..	..	1 58	..	..	..	..			..	..	..	..	..	..	..	4 42	..	..	..	..	..	..
Trowse	..	..	..	..	..	..	..			..	..	..	..	..	..	..	..	..	..	..	..	..	..
Norwich (Thorpe) arr	..	1 20	2 16	..	..	3 6	..			4 22	..	..	..	..	..	..	4 52	..	6 1[illegible]	..	..	..	..
45 CROMER arr	..	..	3 27	..	..	..	..		..	5 29	..	..	..	..	..	..	6 4	..	..	..	..	..	..
Ipswich dep	1212	1220	..	..	..	2 2	..		..	3 8	..	..	..	..	..	..	..	..	5 24	..	..	..	..
Westerfield	..	1229	..	..	..	..	..		..	..	..	..	..	..	..	..	..	..	..	..	..	..	..
Bealings	..	1236	..	..	..	..	..		..	..	..	..	..	..	..	..	..	..	..	..	..	..	..
Woodbridge	..	1243	..	..	..	..	..		..	3 25	..	..	..	..	..	..	..	..	5 40	..	..	..	..
Melton	..	1248	..	..	..	..	..		..	..	..	..	..	..	..	..	..	..	..	..	..	..	..
Wickham Market D	..	1259	..	..	..	..	..		..	3 36	..	..	..	..	..	..	..	..	5 52	..	..	..	..
Saxmundham	..	1 11	..	..	..	2 34	..		..	3 48	..	..	..	..	..	..	..	..	6 4	..	..	..	..
Darsham, for Yoxford	..	1 21	..	..	..	..	..		..	3 58	..	..	..	..	..	..	..	..	..	..	..	..	..
Halesworth	..	1 33	..	..	..	2 51	..		..	4 10	..	..	..	..	..	..	..	..	..	..	..	..	..
Brampton (Suffolk)	..	1 42	..	..	..	..	..		..	..	..	..	..	..	..	..	..	..	..	..	..	..	..
Beccles arr	..	1 51	..	..	..	3 6	..		..	4 25	..	..	..	..	..	..	..	..	6 29	..	..	..	..
Beccles dep	..	2 0	..	..	..	3 20	aft		..	4 39	..	..	..	..	..	..	..	..	6 37	..	..	..	..
Oulton Broad South	..	2 10	..	E	..	3 30	S		..	4 49	..	..	..	..	..	..	..	..	6 47	..	..	aft	..
Lowestoft (Cen.) arr	..	2 15	..	X	..	3 35	X		..	4 54	..	..	..	..	..	..	..	..	6 52	..	..	X	..
Beccles dep	..	1 56	..	2 55	..	3 10	3 25		..	4 35	..	..	..	..	..	..	..	..	6 32	..	..	6 45	..
Aldeby	..	2 4	..	3 4	..	..	3 34	..	..	4 43	..	..	..	..	..	..	..	..	..	..	..	6 54	..
Haddiscoe	..	2 8	..	3 8	..	..	3 38	..	..	..	..	..	..	..	..	..	..	..	..	..	..	6 58	..
45 REEDHAM arr	..	..	..	4 9	..	..	4 9	..	..	..	..	..	..	..	..	..	..	..	..	..	..	..	..
45 NORWICH (Thorpe) "	..	..	..	4 50	..	..	4 50	..	..	..	..	..	..	..	..	..	..	..	..	..	..	..	..
Haddiscoe dep	..	2 9	..	3 9	..	..	3 39	..	..	..	..	..	..	..	..	..	..	..	..	..	..	6 59	..
St. Olaves	..	2 12	..	3 14	..	..	3 44	..	..	4 49	..	..	..	..	..	..	..	..	..	..	..	7 4	..
Belton and Burgh	..	2 18	..	3 20	..	..	3 50	..	..	4 55	..	..	..	..	..	..	..	..	..	..	..	7 10	..
Yarmouth (Sth. Town) arr	[illegible]Z12	2 26	..	3 30	..	3 28	4 0	..	..	5 3	..	..	..	..	..	..	..	..	6 52	..	..	7 20	..
28 GORLESTON-ON-SEA arr	..	3F34	..	..	..	..	..	..	..	5L49	..	..	..	..	..	..	..	..	7F54	..	..	..	..

A For particulars of London Suburban Service, see Suburban Time Table
b To Bury St. Edmunds (Table 32)
C Clacton-on-Sea and Holland-on-Sea
D Station for Campsea Ash.
E or E Except Saturdays.
F Via Lowestoft. One class only
L Via Lowestoft
R Restaurant Car Liverpool Street to Norwich (Thorpe)
RC Restaurant Car
S or S Saturdays only
TC Through Carriage
U Buffet Car Liverpool Street to Walton-on-Naze
X One class only
Z Yarmouth (Vauxhall) via Norwich
B Third class only

Table 3— *Continued* LONDON (Liverpool Street), COLCHESTER, CLACTON-ON-SEA, HARWICH, IPSWICH, NORWICH, BECCLES, LOWESTOFT, and YARMOUTH

Week Days—*Continued*

	aft	aft	aft	aft	aft		aft E	aft	3 E	aft S	aft	aft E	aft	aft	aft	aft	aft	aft	aft	aft	aft E	mrn	
LONDON (L'pool St) dep	4 0				4 18		4 54	5 10	5 16			6 0			6 20		7 30	8 45		9 5	1025		
Stratford "																				9 15			
Ilford "					4E34				5 33									9 2					
Romford "											From Haverhill (Table 17)			From Cambridge (Table 17)	6 43					9 31			
Gidea Pk & Squirrels "																				9 35			
Harold Wood (Heath "																				9 39			
Brentwood & Warley "					4 52													9 21		9 48			
Shenfield & Hutton "	4 35				4 59			5S45	5 54			6 36			7 1		8 6	9 28		9 57			
Ingatestone "					5 6				6 1						7 9		8 13			10 5			
Chelmsford "	4 50			4 56	5 17		5 43	6 1	6 13			6 50			7 20		8 25	9 43		1017	1114		
Hatfield Peverel				5 7	5 27				6 23						7 34		8 35			1028			
Witham	5 5			5 15	5 34		5 58		6 29			7 4			7 41		8 42	9 58		1035			
Kelvedon				5 23	5 42				6 36						7 50					1043			
Mark's Tey				5 35	5 51		6 12				6 58			7 27	7 59		8 55			1053			
Colchester arr	5 23			5 47	6 3		6 21	6 30			7 7	7 22		7 36	8 8		9 4	1018		11 2	1144		
19 WALTON-ON-NAZE arr							7 15	7S32				8 14			9 19		10 2						
19 CLACTON-ON-SEA C "							7 6	7S25				8 5			9 10		9 54						
Colchester dep	5 26		5 45					6 33				7 30			8 13		9 7	1023	1028	11 7	1151	Except Sunday mornings	
Ardleigh															8 22				1037	1116			
Manningtree arr	5 38						RC Liverpool St. to Clacton-on-Sea					7 42			8 29		9 19	1035	1044	1123			
21 HARWICH PARK.Q. arr	6 30											8 9			8 58			10N53					
21 " TOWN "	6 40											8 18			9 8			11N4					
Manningtree dep	5 41											7 44			8 32		9 21		1046	1125			
Bentley															8 40				1054	1133			
Ipswich arr	5 58		6 17					6 58				8 0			8 52		9 37		11 4	1145	1216		
Ipswich dep	6 4	6 14	6 30					7 5		7 20						9 0					1228		
Bramford		6 20								7 26						9 6							
Claydon		6 25								7 31						9 11							
Needham		6 33								7 39						9 19							
Stowmarket	6 25	6 42	6 53					7 26		7 48		Buffet Car Liverpool St. to Ipswich				9 28					1250		
Haughley		6 52								7 57						9 37					1 6	1 32	
Finningham		7 1								b						b							
Mellis		7 9																					
Diss	6 46	7 16						7 47					From Beccles (Table 23)									1 55	
Burston		7 22	TC to Bury St. Edmunds, Peterborough, York (arr. 12 50 ngt.) and Edinburgh, arr. 6 10 mrn (Tables 32, 38, 1, 103 and 157.)																				
Tivetshall		7 31											8 59										
Forncett		7 38											9 6										
Flordon		7 44											9 12										
Swainsthorpe		7 51											9 19										
Trowse																							
Norwich (Thorpe) arr	7 18	8 11						8 16					9 29									2 24	
43 CROMER arr	8E41							9 31															
Ipswich dep	6 10							7 10														1228	
Westerfield								7 19													To Bury St. Edmunds, Ely, and Peterborough (Table 32)		
Bealings								7 26															
Woodbridge	6 27							7 33														Except Sunday mornings	
Melton								7 38															
Wickham Market D	6 38							7 49															
Saxmundham	6 50							8 1															
Darsham for Yoxford	7 0							8 11															
Halesworth	7 12							8 26															
Brampton (Suffolk)								8 35															
Beccles arr	7 27							8 44															
Beccles dep	7 36							8 57															
Oulton Broad South	7 46							9 7															
Lowestoft (Cen.) arr	7 51							9 12														4K15	
Beccles dep	7 31							8 48															
Aldeby								8 56															
Haddiscoe arr								9 0															
45 REEDHAM arr																							
45 NORWICH (Thorpe) "																							
Haddiscoe dep								9 1															
St. Olaves								9 6															
Belton and Burgh								9 12															
Yarmouth (Sth. Town) arr	7 52							9 20														3Z36	
28 GORLESTON-ON-SEA arr																							

A For particulars of London Suburban Service, see Suburban Time Table
b To Bury St. Edmunds (Table 32)
C Clacton-on-Sea and Holland-on-Sea
D Station for Campsea Ash
E or E Except Saturdays
K Via Norwich
N Arr. 4 mins. later on Sats.
RC Restaurant Car
S or S Saturdays only
TC Through Carriage
Z Yarmouth (Vauxhall) via Norwich
3 Third class only

Table 3— *Continued* YARMOUTH, LOWESTOFT, BECCLES, NORWICH, IPSWICH, HARWICH, CLACTON-ON-SEA, COLCHESTER, and LONDON (Liverpool Street)

Week Days

Miles		mrn	mrn X	mrn	mrn		mrn	mrn	mrn	mrn	mrn		mrn	mrn	mrn	mrn	mrn R	mrn		mrn	mrn	mrn	mrn
	28 GORLESTON-ON-SEA dep																						
—	Yarmouth (Sth. Town) dp		5 55													6 44	7 30						
4	Belton and Burgh		6 4													6 52							
6½	St. Olaves		6 10													6 58							
7	Haddiscoe arr															7 0							
—	45 NORWICH (Thorpe) dep																						
—	45 REEDHAM "																						
—	Haddiscoe dep															7 1							
9¼	Aldeby															7 6							
12½	Beccles arr		6 22													7 13	7 49						
—	Mls Lowestoft (Cen.) dep															6 50	7 30						
—	2 Oulton Broad South															6 57	7 37						
—	8½ Beccles arr															7 7	7 47						
—	Beccles dep															7 15	7 56					TC from Edinburgh (dep 10 20 aft), York (dep 3 20 mrn) and Peterborough (Tables 157, 103, 1, 38, and 32)	
17¼	Brampton (Suffolk)															7 26							
21	Halesworth															7 36							
26¼	Darsham for Yoxford															7 47							
30¾	Saxmundham															7 57	8 24						
37¼	Wickham Market D															8 9							
41½	Melton															8 17							
42¾	Woodbridge															8 21							
45¾	Bealings															8 29							
49½	Westerfield															8 38							
53	Ipswich arr															8 45	8 54						
—	43 CROMER dep																6 30						
—	Mls Norwich (Thorpe) dp	From Peterborough, Ely and Bury St. Edmunds (Table 32)						7 0									7 46						7 56
—	1 Trowse																R						
—	5¼ Swainsthorpe							7 11															8 7
—	8¼ Flordon							7 18															8 14
—	11 Forncett						RC Clacton-on-Sea to Liverpool Street	7 24															8 20
—	14½ Tivetshall							7 34					Buffet Car, Ipswich to Liverpool Street.										8 27
—	17½ Burston																						8 34
—	20 Diss																8 15						8 42
—	23½ Mellis													Buffet Car, Walton-on-Naze to Liverpool Street									8 50
—	28½ Finningham							To Beccles (Table 23)													b		8 59
—	32 Haughley	1 26																			8 53		9 8
—	34¾ Stowmarket	1 35															8 36				8 59		9 15
—	3[illegible] Needham																						9 22
—	41½ Claydon																						9 29
—	43¾ Bramford																						9 34
—	46¼ Ipswich arr	1 53															8 52				9 16	9 25	9 41
—	Ipswich dep	2 3			6 32					7 29			7 50				9 3			9 12		9 33	
58½	Bentley									7 41										9 24			
62½	Manningtree arr				6 47					7 47										9 30			
—	21 HARWICH TOWN dep				6 11			Stop		7 0	7 25							8 50					
—	21 " PARK. Q. "				6 19					7 7	7 32							8 59					
—	Manningtree dep				6 48					7 48	7 57							9 22		9 32			
65¾	Ardleigh				6 57					7 57								9 31					
70	Colchester arr	2 29			7 4					8 4	8 10		8 17					9 38		9 45		10 0	
—	19 CLACTON-ON-SEA C dep						6 45						7 28	8 15									
—	19 WALTON-ON-NAZE "						6 40						7 22	8 10									
—	Colchester dep	2 35		6 28	7 6		7 32		7 42	8 6			8 23	8 51	8 56			9 40		9 47			
75	Mark's Tey			6 39	7 18				7 53					9 1	9 9					9 58			
79½	Kelvedon			6 48	7 27				8 2	8 21					9 18					10 7			
83½	Witham			6 56	7 36				8 11				8 42		9 26					1015			
85¾	Hatfield Peverel			7 5	7 44			mrn	8 20						9 34					1023			
92	Chelmsford arr	3 5		7 14	7 53		8 1	8d10	8 29	8 41			8 56		9 43			10 9		1032			
98½	Ingatestone "			7 28				8 21	8 42						9 55			1022					
101½	Shenfield & Hutton "			7 35			8 17		8 49									10D29		1048			
103½	Brentwood & Warley "	3 30						8 32															
106¾	Harold Wood (Heath "			7 46				8 38															
108¾	Gidea Pk & Squirrels "							8 42															
109¾	Romford "							8 46															
114½	Ilford "																						
117¾	Stratford "			8 3																			
121¾	LONDON (L'pool St) "	4 0		8 13			8 51	9 8	9 27				9 42	10 7	1036		1045	11 7		1121			

A For particulars of London Suburban Service, see Suburban Time Table.
b From Bury St, Edmunds (Table 32)
C Clacton-on-Sea and Holland-on-Sea
D Station for Campsea Ash
D Arr 2 mins later on Saturdays
d Departure time
R Restaurant Car Norwich (Thorpe) to Liverpool Street
RC Restaurant Car
TC Through Carriage
X or X One class only

Table 3—Continued YARMOUTH, LOWESTOFT, BECCLES, NORWICH, IPSWICH, HARWICH, CLACTON-ON-SEA, COLCHESTER, and LONDON (Liverpool Street)

Week Days—*Continued*

Station	mrn	mrn (RC Cromer to Liverpool Street)	mrn	mrn X	mrn	mrn		mrn	mrn		mrn R	mrn (To Beccles (Table 23))	aft	aft	mrn	aft	mrn X	mrn		aft		aft (Buffet Car Norwich to Liverpool St.)	aft
28 Gorleston-on-Sea dep	7F33					8X34											1041	11L40					
Yarmouth (Sth. Town) dp	8 5			8 15		8 55											12 5	12 30				1 Z5	
Belton and Burgh				8 24		9 3											1214						
St. Olaves				8 30		9 9											1220						
Haddiscoe arr				8 34		9 11											1224						
45 Norwich (Thorpe) dep				7 20													11V0						
45 Reedham "				7 57													11V36						
Haddiscoe dep				8 35		9 12											1225						
Aldeby				8 40		9 18											1230						
Beccles arr	8 24			8 50		9 24											1240	12 49					
Lowestoft (Cen.) dep	8 5					9 5									11 5			12 30				12K45	
Oulton Broad South	8 12					9 12									1112			12 37					
Beccles arr	8 22					9 22									1122			12 47					
Beccles dep	8 31					9 30									Stop			12 55					
Brampton (Suffolk)						9 41																	
Halesworth	8 48					9 56												1 12					
Darsham, for Yoxford						10 7												1 23					
Saxmundham	9 5					1018												1 33					
Wickham Market D	9 16					1031												1 44					
Melton						1039																	
Woodbridge	9 26					1044												1 54					
Bealings						1052																	
Westerfield						11 1																	
Ipswich arr	9 44					11 9												2 9				3 8	
43 Cromer dep		7 35				Stop					8 55											1240	
Norwich (Thorpe) dep		8 45							9 25		1020	11 5								1 10		2 10	
Trowse											R												
Swainsthorpe									9 36			1116								1 21			
Flordon									9 43			1123								1 28			
Forncett									9 49			1129								1 34			
Tivetshall									9 58			1140								1 43			
Burston									10 5											1 49			
Diss		9 14							10 13		1048									1 57			
Mellis									10 21											2 5			
Finningham									10 30					b						2 14			
Haughley								b	10 38					1241						2 23			
Stowmarket		9 35						1025	10 47		11 8			1248						2 31			
Needham									10 56					1256						2 40			
Claydon									11 3					1 3						2 47			
Bramford									11 8					1 8						2 52			
Ipswich arr		9 51						1042	11 14		1124			1 14						2 58		3 8	
Ipswich dep		9 59	10 7		1017			Stop	Stop		1130		1 0					2 10				3 15	
Bentley					1029								1 12										
Manningtree arr					1035						1146		1 18										
21 Harwich Town dep											11 0					1 19							
21 " Park. Q. "											11 9					1 26							
Manningtree dep					1036						1148		1 20			1 53							
Ardleigh					1045								1 29			2 2							
Colchester arr			1033		1053						12 1		1 37			2 10		2 41				3 41	
19 Clacton-on-Sea C dep			9 8								11 3		1242									2 13	
19 Walton-on-Naze "			9 3					mrn			1058		1234		aft							2 7	
Colchester dep			1037					11 2			12 5		1 42		2 0			2 42				3 44	3 50
Mark's Tey			1050			mrn		11N29 (To Cambridge (Table 17))	aft		1217		1 54		2U23 (To Cambridge (Table 17))								4P5 (To Cambridge (Table 17))
Kelvedon						(3)			(3)				2 3										
Witham			11 4			11 7			12 13		1231		2 14										
Hatfield Peverel						1115			12 21				2 22										
Chelmsford arr			1118			1124			12 30		1245		2 31										
Ingatestone "						1137			12 43				2 46										
Shenfield & Hutton "			1134			1144			12 50		1 1		2 53										
Brentwood & Warley "						1152																	
A Harold Wood [Heath "						1158																	
Gidea Pk & Squirrels "						12 2																	
Romford "						12 6							3 9										
Ilford "						1215							3 19										
Stratford "						1222							3 26										
LONDON (L'pool St) "		1136	12 7			1233					1 35		3 38					3 57				5 0	

A For particulars of London Suburban Service, see Suburban Time Table
b From Bury St. Edmunds (Table 32)
C Clacton-on-Sea and Holland-on-Sea
D Station for Campsea Ash
F Via Lowestoft. One class only
K Via Norwich
L Via Lowestoft
N Arr. 11 12 mrn.
P Arr 4 0 aft
R Restaurant Car. Norwich (Thorpe) to Liverpool Street
RC Restaurant Car
U Arr 2 10 aft
V Dep Norwich (Thorpe) 11 35 mrn and Reedham 12 11 aft on Sats
X or Y One class only
Z Yarmouth Vauxhall via Norwich
(3) Third class only

Table 3—Continued YARMOUTH, LOWESTOFT, BECCLES, NORWICH, IPSWICH, HARWICH, CLACTON-ON-SEA, COLCHESTER, and LONDON (Liverpool Street)

Week Days—*Continued*

Station	aft	aft S	aft	aft	aft	aft (TC from Leeds (dep. 10 30 mrn) Peterborough, and Bury St. Edmunds (Tables 89, 1, 38, and 32))	aft	aft R	aft	aft		aft (To Beccles (Table 23))	aft	aft	aft X	aft (Buffet Car (Sats only) Yarmouth to Liverpool Street)	aft	aft	aft (TC and Buffet Car from York (dep. 3 10 aft) Peterborough, and Bury St. Edmunds (Tables 1, 61, 38, and 32))	aft S	aft E	mrn (Except Sunday mornings; From Peterborough, Ely, and Bury St. Edmunds (Table 32))
28 Gorleston-on-Sea dep					2F9										3 34			6F38				
Yarmouth (Sth. Town) dp					2 40										5 30	6 10		7 0			10Z10	
Belton and Burgh					2 48										5 39			7 9				
St. Olaves					2 54										5 45			7 16				
Haddiscoe arr					2 56										5 48			7 19				
45 Norwich (Thorpe) dep					1 8										5 12			5 58				
45 Reedham "					1 33										5 36			6 30				
Haddiscoe dep					2 57										5 49			7 20				
Aldeby					3 2										5 54			7 25				
Beccles arr					3 9										6 3	6 29		7 33				
Lowestoft (Cen.) dep					2 48					4S7						6 10		7 10			8K40	
Oulton Broad South					2 55					4S14						6 17		7 17				
Beccles arr					3 5					4S24						6 27		7 27				
Beccles dep					3 15					Stop						6 35		7 40				
Brampton (Suffolk)					3 26													7 50				
Halesworth					3 36											6 52		8 0				
Darsham, for Yoxford					3 47													8 12				
Saxmundham					3 58											7 9		8 24				
Wickham Market D					4 11											7 20		8 37				
Melton					4 20													8 45				
Woodbridge					4 26											7 31		8 50				
Bealings					4 34													8 58				
Westerfield					4 43													9 7				
Ipswich arr					4 50											7 47		9 15			1a53	
45 Cromer dep							2 26					3 45				5 30		Stop			8 40	
Norwich (Thorpe) dep							3 35	4 20				4 55				6 45	7 20				11 35	
Trowse																						
Swainsthorpe							3 46	R				5 6					7 31					
Flordon							3 53					5 13					7 38					
Forncett							3 59					5 19					7 45					
Tivetshall							4 8	4 42				5 29					7 54					
Burston							4 14					Stop					8 0					
Diss							4 21	4 53								7 14	8 7				12a13	
Mellis							4 29			aft							8 14			S		
Finningham				b			4 38			b			b				8 22			b		
Haughley				4 16			4 47			5 50			6 35				8 30			1030	12‡30	1P26
Stowmarket				4 24		4 36	4 53	5 14		5 56			6 42			7 37	8 37		9 27	1036		1 35
Needham				4 30			5 0			6 3			6 50				8 43					
Claydon				4 36			5 7			6 9							8 49					
Bramford				4 41			5 12			6 14							8 54					
Ipswich arr				4 46		5 3	5 19	5 32		6 21		aft	7 4			7 55	9 0	aft	9 47	1053		1 53
Ipswich dep	3 28				5 0	5 13		5 37	5 44	Stop		6 35		7 15		8 8	Stop	9 35	9 55			2 3
Bentley	3 40											6 49		7 27				9 47				
Manningtree arr	3 46								5 59			6 55		7 33		8 24		9 53	1012			
21 Harwich Town dep	3 10								5 3			6 15				7 50						Except Sun. mrns
21 " Park. Q. "	3 17								5 11			6 22				7 57						
Manningtree dep	3 48								6 1			6 58		7 36		8 27		9 56	1015			
Ardleigh	3 57											7 7		7 45				10 5				
Colchester arr	4 5				5 28	5 42			6 14			7 15		7 53		8 40		1013	1035			2 29
19 Clacton-on-Sea C dep	3 18				4 33				5 25			6 10				7 45						
19 Walton-on-Naze "	3 10				4 27				5 20			6 4				7 39	aft					
Colchester dep	4 9		4 50		5 32				6 16	aft		7 20				8 47	8 55	1020				2 35
Mark's Tey	4 21	S	5 4						6 28	E		7 33					9 8 (To Sudbury (Table 17))	1033				
Kelvedon	4 30	(3)	5 14							(3)		7 43						1043				
Witham	4 39	5 0	5 25						6 43	7 8		7H55				9 8		1053				
Hatfield Peverel	4 47	5 10	5‡40							7 16		8 4						11 3				
Chelmsford arr	4 56	5 20	5 50		6 4				6 57	7 25		8 13				9 22		1113				3 5
Ingatestone "		5 35								7 38		8 29						1128				
Shenfield & Hutton "	5 12	5 42							7 13	7 45		8 36				9 41		1135				
Brentwood & Warley "		5 51								7 52		8 44						1145				3 30
A Harold Wood [Heath "		5 57								7 58								1151				
Gidea Pk & Squirrels "		6 1								8 2		8 52						1155				
Romford "		6 5								8 6		8 56						1158				
Ilford "		6 19								8 22		9 12						1223				
Stratford "	5 38	6 26								8 34		9 19						1233				
LONDON (L'pool St) "	5 49	6 36			6 51			7 18	7 47	8 45		9 30				1015		1250				4 0

A For particulars of London Suburban Service, see Suburban Time Table
a Mrn.
b From Bury St. Edmunds (Table 32)
C Clacton-on-Sea and Holland-on-Sea
D Station for Campsea Ash
E or E Except Saturdays
F Via Lowestoft. One class only
H Arr 7 50 aft
K Via Norwich
P Arr 1 14 mrn
R Restaurant Car. Norwich (Thorpe) to Liverpool Street
S or S Saturdays only
TC Through Carriage
U Arr 5 32 aft
X One class only
Z Yarmouth (Vauxhall) via Norwich
‡ Arrival time
(3) Third class only

Arr 7 25 mrn   S Saturdays only   For **OTHER TRAINS** between Ipswich and Westerfield, see Table 3

Table 26 — WICKHAM MARKET and FRAMLINGHAM

Miles		Week Days only									
		mrn			mrn			aft			
	3 London (L'pool St.).. dep	4 40	..	..	10 0	..	..	5 10	..	..	..
—	Wickham Market **A** .. dep	9 30	..	..	1 5	..	..	7 53	..	..	..
1¾	Marlesford	9 36	..	..	1 11	..	..	7 59	..	..	..
3¼	Hacheston Halt	9 43	..	..	1 18	..	..	8 6	..	..	..
[illegible]	Parham Halt	9 49	..	..	1 24	..	..	8 12	..	..	..
6½	Framlingham .... arr	9 56	..	..	1 31	..	..	8 19	..	..	..

Miles		Week Days only					
		mrn		aft			
	Framlingham .... dep	8 42	..	3 10	..	..	..
2¼	Parham Halt	8 49	..	3 17	..	..	..
3¼	Hacheston Halt	8 52	..	3 20	..	..	..
4½	Marlesford	9 0	..	3 28	..	..	..
6½	**Wickham Market A** .. arr	9 5	..	3 33	..	..	..
91	3 London (L'pool St.). arr	1136	..	6 51	..	..	..

Passengers to and from Hacheston Halt must join, or alight from the special car provided

NOTES

A Station for Campsea Ash

Tickets from Marlesford, Hacheston Halt and Parham Halt are issued on the train

Table 27 — SAXMUNDHAM and ALDEBURGH

Miles		Week Days								Sundays		
		mrn		mrn		aft		aft	aft			
	3 London (LiverpoolSt) dep	4 40	..	8 12	..	1 0	..	3 40	5 10	..	..	..
—	**Saxmundham** .... dep	8 0	..	11 3	..	4 5	..	6 9	8 6	..	..	..
4	Leiston	8 11	..	1113	..	4 15	..	6 19	8 16	..	..	..
6¼	Thorpeness	8 16	..	1118	..	4 20	..	6 24	8 21	..	..	..
8¼	Aldeburgh .... arr	8 21	..	1123	..	4 25	..	6 29	8 26	..	..	..

Miles		Week Days							Sundays			
		mrn	mrn		aft	aft		aft				
	Aldeburgh .... dep	7 15	8 35	..	1248	5 25	..	6 38	..	..	..	..
2	Thorpeness	7 20	8 40	..	1253	5 30	..	6 43	..	..	..	..
4¼	Leiston	7 26	8 46	..	1259	5 40	..	6 50	..	..	..	..
8¼	**Saxmundham** .... arr	7 35	8 55	..	1 8	5 50	..	6 59	..	..	..	..
99¼	3 **London**(LiverpoolSt.)arr	1045	1136	..	3 57	..	..	1015	..	..	..	..

Pages 202-204 and above:
LNER timetable book 4 May 1942, until further notice, showing the East Suffolk.

Yarmouth. In the up direction the train left Yarmouth at 7.17pm and reached London at 10pm, slightly later on Saturdays. By winter 1955-6 there were more trains travelling faster than ever before on the line, many at least being through carriages from London and others, such as the 3.33pm restaurant car services to South Town, even having a through portion for Felixstowe. Travel in the evenings became possible, and the last train from Liverpool Street with an East Suffolk connection became the 8.30pm semi-fast, which did not arrive at Ipswich until 10.25pm, but had a connection on Fridays and Saturdays at 10.43pm, and called at all stations except Westerfield, Bealings (Melton had closed to passengers), Brampton, Aldeby, Haddiscoe and Belton, reaching Yarmouth at 12.17am, and Lowestoft at 12.21am. The Sunday service was also better, although the first down train was not until 12.45pm from Ipswich (10.30am from London) and the next at 7.18pm.

In the up direction Yarmouth had at last acquired an early train to Ipswich at 5.43am, with a connection from Lowestoft leaving at 5.46am. Motor trains continued to work between Yarmouth, Beccles and Lowestoft, with more services than before, and also being used to provide late services such as the 10pm all-stations to Beccles on Saturdays only. The new diesel railcars were introduced on 5 January 1959 onto East Suffolk local services and quickly revolutionised them and passengers' perceptions. A service at roughly hourly intervals was provided between Ipswich, Lowestoft and Yarmouth via Gorleston, with local services continuing on the Yarmouth–Beccles–Lowestoft triangle. The Aldeburgh branch, which had had the new trains since June 1956, acquired some through workings to and from Ipswich as well as an increase in frequency, from about seven each way on weekdays to nine, plus a much better Sunday service, at least in summer. Conductor-guards had arrived on the line, and issued Aldeburgh and Thorpeness tickets on the train. This had happened previously on the East Suffolk on the Framlingham branch, where tickets from Marlesford, Hacheston halt and Parham — by then also officially classified as a halt — had been issued on the train as a wartime economy measure.

In 1959, with closure pending of the direct line between Beccles and South Town, the timetable format was altered so that trains were shown as reaching Yarmouth from Beccles via Lowestoft and Gorleston. Stations on the direct route were relegated to a separate table, although the service ran more or less as before, with the London trains to and from Yarmouth calling at Beccles to attach or detach the Lowestoft portion. From Mondays to Fridays the 8.35am carried a restaurant-buffet car, as did the 2.35pm and 6.2pm. On Saturdays the 8.20am, 11.50am, 2.20pm and 5.45pm all had these facilities, whilst the 10.55am, 12.55pm, 1.20pm, 1.55pm and 3.20pm all started from South Town, ran via Gorleston as Holiday Camps Expresses and were advertised as carrying light refreshments from Lowestoft to London. This system had operated for a number of years: traffic was very heavy on the Norfolk & Suffolk Joint on summer Saturdays, but not really at any other time.

After the axe fell on the main line, much the same pattern of services continued to operate except that trains reached South Town via Lowestoft, which necessitated reversal, and a journey of 18¾ miles instead of 12½ from Beccles. Beccles to Yarmouth direct and nonstop had taken 17min, all-stations 27min, whilst via Lowestoft timings varied but were about 45-50min with calls at Lowestoft and Gorleston, and were around the same for all-stations. Given that fares were still calculated on a mileage basis, passengers were less than ecstatic about the changes, although the direct line between Lowestoft and Yarmouth enjoyed its best service and had

Table 3 LONDON (Liverpool Street), COLCHESTER, CLACTON-ON-SEA, HARWICH, IPSWICH, NORWICH, BECCLES, LOWESTOFT, and YARMOUTH

Week Days

Miles	Station	mrn	mrn	mrn B	mrn	mrn	mrn	mrn	mrn	mrn	mrn	mrn	mrn	S mrn B	S mrn	mrn	mrn	mrn Z	mrn B	S mrn	S mrn	S mrn
	Notes			From Liverp'l St. dep 4 25 mrn.; To Braintree (Table 29a)	Through Buffet Car Train to Bury St. Edmunds, March, and York, arr. 1 16 aft, and Newcastle, arr. 3Y45 aft (Tables 32, 38, 61 and 1)	Does not run during School Holiday Periods			From Beccles (Table 23)		Runs 1st July to 7th September inclusive; Through Train Cambridge to Clacton-on-Sea (Table 17)	Runs 1st July to 7th September inclusive; Through Train Bury St. Edmunds to Walton-on-Naze and Clacton-on-Sea (Table 17)				RC (except on Saturdays) Liverpool Street to Norwich (Thorpe)					Runs 6th July to 7th September inclusive	Runs 1st June to 28th September inclusive
	LONDON (L'pool St) dep	..	4 25	..	..	..	..	..	..	..	..	..	6 50	8 0	8 8	8 1[illegible]	..	8 20	8 33	9 20	9 30	9 40
4	Stratford "	..	..	..	..	..	..	..	..	..	..	..	7 1	..	..	..	..	8 30	8 44	..	..	..
7¼	Ilford "	..	..	..	..	..	..	..	..	..	..	..	7 11	..	..	..	..	8 37	8 57	..	..	..
12¼	Romford "	..	..	..	..	..	..	..	..	..	..	..	7 21	..	..	..	..	8 46	9 13	..	..	..
13½	Gidea Pk & Squirrels Heath "	..	..	..	..	..	..	..	..	..	..	..	7 25	..	..	..	..	..	9 17	..	..	..
15	Harold Wood "	..	..	..	..	..	..	..	..	..	..	..	7 30	..	..	..	..	..	9 21	..	..	..
18¼	Brentwood & Warley "	..	4 57	..	..	..	..	..	..	..	..	..	7 40	..	..	..	..	..	9 29	..	..	..
20¼	Shenfield & Hutton "	..	..	..	..	..	..	..	..	..	..	..	7 48	..	..	8 4[illegible]	..	9 3	9 37	..	..	..
23¼	Ingatestone "	..	5 8	..	..	..	..	..	..	..	..	..	7 56	..	..	..	..	9 10	..	..	..	..
29¼	Chelmsford "	..	5 20	5 37	..	..	..	..	..	..	..	..	8 9	..	..	9 [illegible]	..	9 21	9 52	..	..	..
36	Hatfield Peverel	..	..	5 48	..	..	..	..	..	..	..	..	8 20	..	..	..	..	9 34	10 2	..	..	..
38½	Witham	..	..	6 C2	..	..	..	..	..	..	..	..	8R29	..	..	9 1[illegible]	..	9 41	10 8	..	..	..
42¼	Kelvedon	..	..	..	..	..	..	..	..	..	..	..	8 37	..	..	..	..	9 49	Stop	..	..	..
46¼	Mark's Tey	..	5 45	..	..	..	..	..	..	..	8 36	8 45	8R49	..	..	..	..	9 59	..	..	..	..
51¼	Colchester arr	..	5 54	..	..	..	..	..	..	..	8 46	8 55	8 59	..	..	9 3[illegible]	..	10 8	..	1033	..	..
70¼	19 WALTON-ON-NAZE arr	..	8 0	..	..	..	..	..	..	..	..	9 46	..	..	..	1044	..	11 2	..	1134	..	..
69¾	19 CLACTON-ON-SEA C "	..	7 50	..	..	..	..	..	..	..	9 28	9 38	..	9 50	..	1035	..	1050	..	11 5	..	..
—	Colchester dep	..	5 57	..	6 50	7 0	7 48	..	..	..	..	..	9 3	..	..	9 39	..	1020	..	..	..	..
56	Ardleigh	..	..	..	..	7 8	7 57	..	..	..	..	..	9 12	..	..	..	..	1028	..	..	..	..
59½	Manningtree arr	..	..	..	7 3	7 14	8 4	..	..	..	..	..	9 19	..	..	..	..	1035	..	..	..	..
69	21 HARWICH PARK. Q. arr	..	..	..	..	7 40	8 31	..	..	..	..	..	9 58	..	..	..	..	1110	..	..	..	..
70½	21 " TOWN "	..	..	..	..	7 56	8 41	..	..	..	..	..	10 8	..	..	..	..	1120	..	..	..	..
—	Manningtree dep	..	..	Stop	7 5	Stop	8 5	..	..	..	..	..	9 25	..	..	..	..	1037	..	..	..	..
63¾	Bentley	..	..	..	..	..	8 14	..	..	..	..	..	9 33	..	..	..	..	1045	..	..	..	..
68¾	Ipswich arr	..	6 21	mrn	7 21	mrn	8 24	..	..	..	..	..	9 43	..	9 54	10 [illegible]	..	1055	mrn	..	11 5	1116
—	Ipswich dep	..	6 33	7 5	7 33	7 40	Stop	8 50	..	9 0	..	..	..	..	..	1012	1025	Stop	1130	..	..	1124
71¼	Bramford	..	6 39	..	..	7 46	..	..	..	9 6	..	..	..	..	..	..	1031	..	1136	..	..	..
73½	Claydon	..	6 44	..	..	7 51	..	..	..	9 11	..	..	..	..	..	..	1036	..	1141	..	..	..
77	Needham	..	6 54	7 19	..	7 59	..	..	..	9 19	..	..	..	..	..	..	1044	..	1149	..	..	..
80¼	Stowmarket	..	7 6	7 28	..	8 8	..	9 10	..	9 28	..	..	..	..	..	103[illegible]	1052	..	1157	..	..	..
83	Haughley	..	7 15	7 35	..	8 15	..	9 18	..	9 36	..	..	..	..	..	..	11 2	..	12 3	..	..	..
86½	Finningham	..	7 25	b	..	b	..	b	..	9 45	..	..	..	..	..	..	b	..	..	..	..	..
91½	Mellis	..	7 35	Stop	..	..	..	Stop	..	9 53	..	..	..	..	..	..	..	..	..	..	..	..
95	Diss	..	7 45	..	..	..	..	..	..	10 1	..	..	..	..	..	105[illegible]	..	..	..	..	..	..
97½	Burston	..	7 51	..	..	..	..	..	..	10 7	..	..	..	..	..	..	..	..	..	..	..	..
100½	Tivetshall	..	8 0	..	..	..	..	..	9 53	1015	..	..	..	..	..	11 [illegible]	..	..	..	..	..	..
104	Forncett	..	8 7	..	..	..	..	..	..	1022	..	..	..	..	..	..	..	..	..	..	..	..
106¾	Flordon	..	8 13	..	..	..	..	..	..	1028	..	..	..	..	..	..	..	..	..	..	..	..
109¾	Swainsthorpe	..	8 20	..	..	..	..	..	..	1035	..	..	..	..	..	..	..	..	..	..	..	..
115	Norwich (Thorpe) arr	..	8 40	..	..	..	..	..	1013	1045	..	..	..	..	..	112[illegible]	..	..	..	..	..	1225
139	43 CROMER arr	..	1012	mrn	..	..	..	mrn	..	..	..	..	..	..	..	1230	..	..	..	..	..	1 28
—	Ipswich dep	..	Stop	6 41	..	..	..	8 40	..	..	..	..	..	..	10 0	101[illegible]	..	..	..	..	1113	1124
72¼	Westerfield	..	..	6 50	..	..	..	8 51	..	..	..	..	..	..	..	..	..	..	..	..	..	..
76	Bealings	..	..	6 58	..	..	..	8 59	..	..	..	..	..	..	..	..	..	..	..	..	..	..
79	Woodbridge	..	..	7 8	..	..	..	9 5	..	..	..	..	..	..	..	103[illegible]	..	..	..	..	..	..
80¼	Melton	..	..	7 13	..	..	..	9 10	..	..	..	..	..	..	..	..	..	..	..	..	..	..
84½	Wickham Market D	..	..	7 25	..	..	..	9 21	..	..	..	..	..	..	..	104[illegible]	..	..	..	..	..	..
91	Saxmundham	..	..	7 40	..	..	..	9 34	..	..	..	..	..	..	..	105[illegible]	..	..	..	..	..	..
95¼	Darsham, for Yoxford	..	..	7 52	..	..	..	9 45	..	..	..	..	..	..	..	..	..	..	..	..	..	..
100¾	Halesworth	..	..	8 6	..	..	..	9 57	..	..	..	..	..	..	..	111[illegible]	..	..	..	..	..	..
104¼	Brampton (Suffolk)	..	..	8 17	..	..	..	10 7	..	..	..	..	..	..	..	..	..	..	..	..	..	..
109¼	Beccles arr	..	mrn	8 27	..	..	..	10 19	..	..	..	..	..	..	10 54	113[illegible]	..	..	..	..	12 7	..
—	Beccles dep	..	7 18	8 38	..	..	..	10 30	..	..	..	..	..	..	11 5	114[illegible]	..	..	..	..	1220	..
115¾	Oulton Broad South	..	7 28	8 48	..	..	..	10 40	..	..	..	..	..	..	11 15	115[illegible]	..	aft	..	..	1230	..
117¾	Lowestoft (Cen.) arr	..	7 33	8 53	..	..	mrn	10 45	..	..	..	..	..	..	11 20	115[illegible]	..	X	..	..	1235	..
—	Beccles dep	7X10	..	8 33	..	..	9X30	10 22	..	..	..	..	..	..	11 0	113[illegible]	..	1240	..	..	1213	..
112¼	Aldeby	7X18	..	8 41	..	..	9X38	10 30	..	..	..	..	..	..	..	..	..	1248	..	..	..	..
114¾	Haddiscoe arr	7X22	..	8 45	..	..	9X42	10 34	..	..	..	..	..	..	..	..	..	1252	..	..	..	..
118¾	45 REEDHAM arr	7 58	..	8 59	..	..	1026	11S54	..	..	..	..	..	..	..	..	..	..	..	..	..	..
131	45 NORWICH (Thorpe) "	8 32	..	9 41	..	..	11 0	12S34	..	..	..	..	..	..	..	..	..	..	..	..	..	..
—	Haddiscoe dep	7X23	..	8 46	..	..	9X43	10 35	..	..	..	..	..	..	..	..	..	1253	..	..	..	..
115¼	St. Olaves	7X26	..	8 49	..	..	9X46	10 38	..	..	..	..	..	..	..	..	..	1256	..	..	..	..
117¾	Belton and Burgh	7X32	..	8 56	..	..	9X53	10 44	..	..	..	..	..	..	..	..	..	1 2	..	..	..	..
121¼	Yarmouth (Sth. Town) arr	7X40	..	9 4	..	..	10X0	10 52	..	..	..	..	..	..	11 20	115[illegible]	..	1 10	..	..	1233	1Z39
124¼	28 GORLESTON-ON-SEA arr	..	8X22	9X26	..	..	..	11L51	..	..	..	..	..	..	..	1 [illegible]	..	1 48	..	..	1X48	..

A For particulars of London Suburban Service, see Suburban Time Table.
b To Bury St. Edmunds (Table 32)
C Clacton-on-Sea and Holland-on-Sea
C Arrive 5 53 mrn
D Station for Campsea Ash
E or E Except Saturdays
L Via Lowestoft
R Arr. Witham 8 25 and Mark's Tey 8 45 mrn
RC Restaurant Car
S or S Saturdays only
TC Through Carriages
X or X One class only
Y Via West Hartlepool and Sunderland
Z Third class only on Sats, Liverpool Street to Clacton-on-Sea
Z Yarmouth (Vauxhall) via Norwich
B Third class only

Table 3—*continued* LONDON (Liverpool Street), COLCHESTER, CLACTON-ON-SEA, HARWICH, IPSWICH, NORWICH, BECCLES, LOWESTOFT, and YARMOUTH

Week Days—*continued*

Station	mrn	S mrn	mrn	S mrn	aft	mrn	S mrn	mrn	aft	S mrn	S aft B	S aft	E aft	S aft	S aft	aft	S aft	S aft B	S aft	aft R	aft	S aft B	S aft B
Notes	From Cambridge (Table 17)	To Felixstowe Beach (Table 25); Runs 6th July to 14th September inclusive.				To Felixstowe Beach (Table 25)			TC Harwich Town dep. 1 0 p.m. to Peterborough (North), arr. 5 0 p.m. (Table 32)	Runs 6th July to 14th September inclusive		Runs 6th July to 14th September inclusive			TC Liverpool Street to Sheringham (Table 43)	From Cambridge (Table 17)			To Felixstowe Beach (Table 25)			Arrive Witham at 2 20 aft; To Maldon (East) and Heybridge (Table 15)	
LONDON (L'pool St) dep	..	9 55	10 0	1020	..	1030	1034	1110	..	1135	12 4	1212	1230	1230	1233	..	1236	1239	1250	1 [illegible]	..	1253	1 30
Stratford "	..	..	..	..	..	..	1047	..	..	1146	..	..	..	..	..	..	..	..	..	..	..	..	..
Ilford "	..	..	1017	..	..	..	1055	1126	..	1154	..	..	..	..	..	..	..	..	..	..	..	1 9	..
Romford "	..	..	..	..	..	..	..	..	..	12 4	..	..	..	..	..	..	..	..	..	..	..	..	..
Gidea Pk & Squirrels Heath "	..	..	..	..	..	..	..	..	..	..	..	..	..	..	..	..	..	..	..	..	..	..	..
Harold Wood "	..	..	..	..	..	..	..	..	..	..	..	..	..	..	..	..	..	..	..	..	..	1 24	..
Brentwood & Warley "	..	..	..	..	..	..	..	..	..	..	..	..	..	..	..	..	..	..	..	..	..	1 32	..
Shenfield & Hutton "	..	..	1042	..	..	11 6	1119	1150	..	1223	..	..	..	..	..	..	..	..	..	1 36	..	1 45	..
Ingatestone "	..	..	..	..	..	..	..	1157	..	..	..	..	..	..	..	..	..	..	..	..	..	1 53	..
Chelmsford "	..	1043	1057	..	..	1121	1134	1210	..	1238	..	..	..	..	..	..	1 25	1 30	1 38	1 51	..	2 4	2 21
Hatfield Peverel	..	..	..	..	..	..	..	1220	..	..	..	..	..	..	..	..	..	..	..	..	..	2 15	..
Witham	..	..	..	..	..	1136	..	1228	..	..	..	..	..	..	..	..	..	..	1 53	2 6	..	2 30	2 36
Kelvedon	..	..	..	..	..	..	..	1236	..	..	..	..	..	..	..	..	..	..	..	..	..	..	..
Mark's Tey	1052	..	1122	..	..	..	..	1245	..	..	..	..	..	..	..	1 19	..	..	..	2 21	..	..	..
Colchester arr	11 2	1112	1131	..	..	1154	12 2	1254	..	1 6	..	..	..	..	..	1 29	1 53	2 0	2 12	2 30	..	..	2 54
19 WALTON-ON-NAZE arr	Stop	..	..	..	..	12E56	1258	..	..	1 57	..	..	..	..	..	2E41	2 36	3 2	..	3E40	..	..	3 37
19 CLACTON-ON-SEA C "	..	..	..	1215	..	12E43	1249	..	..	1 48	1 56	..	..	..	..	2E27	..	2 40	..	3E28	..	..	..
Colchester dep	..	1115	1134	..	..	1156	..	1259	..	..	..	..	..	..	..	Stop	Stop	..	2 15	2 34	2 46	..	..
Ardleigh	..	..	..	..	..	12 5	..	1 8	..	..	..	..	..	..	..	..	..	..	..	..	2 55	..	..
Manningtree arr	..	..	..	..	..	1212	..	1 15	..	..	..	..	..	..	..	..	..	..	2 28	..	3 2	..	..
21 HARWICH PARK. Q. arr	..	..	..	..	..	1243	..	1 56	..	..	..	..	..	..	..	..	..	..	..	..	3 29	..	..
21 " TOWN "	..	..	..	..	..	1255	..	2 6	..	..	..	..	..	..	..	..	..	..	..	..	3 38	..	..
Manningtree dep	..	..	..	..	..	1214	..	1 17	..	..	..	..	..	..	..	..	..	..	2 30	..	Stop	..	..
Bentley	..	..	..	..	..	1222	..	1 25	1 40	..	..	..	..	..	..	..	..	..	..	..	..	..	..
Ipswich arr	..	1139	1158	..	..	1232	..	1 35	1 50	..	..	..	2 0	2 7	2 14	aft	..	..	2 46	2 58	..	..	..
Ipswich dep	..	1147	12 8	..	1220	1240	..	..	1 57	..	..	1 58	2 10	..	2 20	2 30	..	..	2 55	3 7	..	..	..
Bramford	..	..	..	..	1226	..	..	..	..	..	..	..	..	..	..	..	..	..	..	..	..	..	..
Claydon	..	..	..	..	1232	..	..	..	..	..	..	..	..	..	..	..	..	..	..	..	..	..	..
Needham	..	..	..	..	1241	..	..	..	..	..	..	..	..	..	..	..	..	..	..	..	aft	..	..
Stowmarket	..	..	1227	..	12U54	..	..	..	2 17	..	..	..	..	..	..	2 50	..	..	..	3 27	3 36	..	..
Haughley	..	..	..	..	1 4	..	..	..	..	..	..	..	..	..	..	2 57	..	..	..	..	3 43	..	..
Finningham	..	..	..	..	1 14	..	..	..	..	..	..	..	..	..	..	b	..	..	..	3 42	b	..	..
Mellis	..	..	..	..	1 24	..	..	..	..	..	..	..	..	..	..	Stop	..	..	..	3 52	..	..	..
Diss	..	..	1248	..	1 32	..	..	..	..	..	..	..	..	..	..	..	..	..	..	4 2	..	..	..
Burston	..	..	..	..	1 38	..	..	..	..	..	..	..	..	..	..	..	..	..	..	..	..	..	..
Tivetshall	..	..	..	..	1 47	..	..	..	..	..	..	..	..	..	..	..	..	..	..	4 15	..	..	..
Forncett	..	..	..	..	1 55	..	..	..	..	..	..	..	..	..	..	..	..	..	..	..	..	..	..
Flordon	..	..	..	..	2 1	..	..	..	..	..	..	..	..	..	..	..	..	..	..	..	..	..	..
Swainsthorpe	..	..	..	..	2 8	..	..	..	..	..	..	..	..	..	..	..	..	..	..	..	..	..	..
Norwich (Thorpe) arr	..	..	1 14	..	2 31	..	..	..	..	..	..	..	3 6	..	3 16	..	..	..	..	4 40	..	..	..
43 CROMER arr	..	..	3 0	..	..	..	..	..	..	..	..	..	5 22	..	4 23	..	..	..	..	6 7	..	..	..
Ipswich dep	..	..	1216	..	..	..	..	..	..	..	..	2 2	2 10	2 14	..	..	..	..	..	3 15	..	..	..
Westerfield	..	..	1225	..	..	..	..	..	..	..	..	..	..	..	..	..	..	..	..	..	..	..	..
Bealings	..	..	1232	..	..	..	..	..	..	..	..	..	..	..	..	..	..	..	..	..	..	..	..
Woodbridge	..	..	1239	..	..	..	..	..	..	..	..	..	..	..	..	..	..	..	..	3 34	..	..	..
Melton	..	..	1244	..	..	..	..	..	..	..	..	..	..	..	..	..	..	..	..	..	..	..	..
Wickham Market D	..	..	1255	..	..	..	..	..	..	..	..	..	..	..	..	..	..	..	..	3 46	..	..	..
Saxmundham	..	..	1 8	..	..	..	..	..	..	..	..	2 37	..	2 50	..	..	..	..	..	3 59	..	..	..
Darsham, for Yoxford	..	..	1 18	..	..	..	..	..	..	..	..	..	..	..	..	..	..	..	..	4 9	..	..	..
Halesworth	..	..	1 30	..	..	..	..	..	..	..	..	..	..	3 7	..	..	..	..	..	4 22	..	..	..
Brampton (Suffolk)	..	..	1 39	..	..	..	..	..	..	..	..	..	..	..	..	..	..	..	..	..	..	..	..
Beccles arr	aft	..	1 48	..	..	..	..	..	..	..	..	3 2	..	3 20	..	..	..	..	..	4 37	..	..	..
Beccles dep	1242	..	2 0	..	..	..	..	..	..	..	..	3 10	..	3 30	..	aft	aft	..	..	4 50	..	..	..
Oulton Broad South	1252	..	2 10	..	..	..	..	..	..	..	..	..	..	3 40	..	S	E	..	..	5 0	..	..	..
Lowestoft (Cen.) arr	1257	..	2 15	..	..	..	..	..	..	..	..	3 25	..	3 45	..	X	X	..	..	5 5	..	..	..
Beccles dep	..	..	1 52	..	..	..	..	..	..	..	..	3 6	..	3 25	..	3 35	4 15	..	..	4 46	..	..	..
Aldeby	..	..	2 0	..	..	..	..	..	..	..	..	..	..	..	..	3 43	4 23	..	..	4 54	..	..	..
Haddiscoe arr	..	..	2 4	..	..	..	..	..	..	..	..	..	..	..	..	3 47	4 27	..	..	5 1	..	..	..
45 REEDHAM arr	..	..	..	..	..	..	..	..	..	..	..	..	..	..	..	3 59	..	..	..	5 39	..	..	..
45 NORWICH (Thorpe) "	..	..	..	..	..	..	..	..	..	..	..	..	..	..	..	4 35	..	..	..	6 3	..	..	..
Haddiscoe dep	..	..	2 5	..	..	..	..	..	..	..	..	..	..	..	..	3 48	4 28	..	..	5 2	..	..	..
St. Olaves	..	..	2 8	..	..	..	..	..	..	..	..	..	..	..	..	3 51	4 31	..	..	5 5	..	..	..
Belton and Burgh	..	..	2 14	..	..	..	..	..	..	..	..	..	..	..	..	3 57	4 37	..	..	5 11	..	..	..
Yarmouth (Sth. Town) arr	..	..	2 23	..	..	..	..	..	..	..	..	3 26	4Z5	3 45	..	4 5	4 45	..	..	5 19	..	..	..
28 GORLESTON-ON-SEA arr	..	..	3F17	..	..	..	..	..	..	..	..	..	..	4L37	..	..	..	..	..	5L52	..	..	..

A For particulars of London Suburban Service, see Suburban Time Table
b To Bury St. Edmunds (Table 32)
C Clacton-on-Sea and Holland-on-Sea
D Station for Campsea Ash
E or E Except Saturdays
F Via Lowestoft. One class only
L Via Lowestoft
R Restaurant Car Liverpool Street to Norwich
S or S Saturdays only
TC Through Carriages
U Arr. 7 minutes *earlier*
X One class only
Z Yarmouth (Vauxhall) via Norwich
B Third class only

Table 3— *continued* LONDON (Liverpool Street), COLCHESTER, CLACTON-ON-SEA, HARWICH, IPSWICH, NORWICH, BECCLES, LOWESTOFT, and YARMOUTH

Week Days—*continued*

Station	S aft	S aft 3	aft	E aft 3	S aft 3	aft	E aft	S aft 3	S aft	aft	aft	aft	aft	aft	aft	aft	aft	aft	S aft	E aft	E aft	E aft	S aft
Notes			From Cambridge (Table 17); From Beccles (Table 23)		To Sudbury (Table 17)				Runs 6th July to 14th September inclusive	RC except on Saturdays Liverpool St. to Cromer		TC to Bury St. Edmunds, Peterborough, York, arr 12 31 mrn., and Edinburgh, arr 5 27 mrn (Tables 32, 33, 1, 103, and 157)	Wednesdays and Saturdays; The Scandinavian							To Colchester, arr 7 32 aft	Buffet Car Liverpool St. to Walton-on-Naze		From Haverhill (Table 17)
LONDON (L'pool St) dep	1 34	1 42	..	2 10	2 10	2 30	..	3 15	3 20	3 40	3 48	..	3 55	4 0	4 18	4 54	5 6	..	..	5 16	5 30	..	
Stratford "	..	..	..	2 21	2 21	..	..	..			..	..		..	..	..	..	..	..	..		..	
Ilford "	..	..		2 29	2 29	..	..	..			..	..		..	4 34	..	..	..	..	..		..	
Romford "	..	2 4		..	..	..	..	..			..	..		..	..	..	..	..	..	5 42		..	
Gidea Pk & Squirrels "	..	2 8		..	..	..	..	..			..	..		..	..	..	..	..	..	5 46		..	
Harold Wood [Heath "	..	2 12		..	..	..	..	..			..	..		..	..	..	..	..	..	5 50		..	
Brentwood & Warley "	..	2 20		..	..	..	..	..			..	..		..	4 52	..	..	..	..	5 58		..	
Shenfield & Hutton "	..	2 26		2 52	2 52	..	..	..			..	..		4 38	4 59	..	5S43	..	..	6 9		..	
Ingatestone "	..	2 33		2 59	2 59	..	..	..			..	..		..	5 6	..	..	..	..	6 16		..	
Chelmsford "	2 27	2 44		3 11	3 11	3 23	..	..			4 34	..		4 53	5 17	5 43	5 58	..	..	6A25		..	
Hatfield Peverel	..	2 54		3 21	3 21	..	..	..			..	..		..	5 27	..	..	..	..			..	
Witham	2 42	3 1		3 26	3 28	3 39	..	..			..	..		5 9	5 34	5 58	..	..	..			..	
Kelvedon	..	3 9			..	3 47	..	..			..	..		..	5 42	..	..	..	..			..	S
Mark's Tey	..	3 19	3 28	Stop	3K48	3 58	..	..			..	..		..	5 52	6 12	..	..	..			..	7 8
Colchester arr	3 0	3 28	3 37	..		4 7	..	..			5 2	..		5 28	6 1	6 21	6 29	..	..		6 45	..	7 18
19 Walton-on-Naze arr	..	..		..		5 22	..	..			5 46	..	..	..		7E16	7S32	..			7 28		..
19 Clacton-on-Sea C "	3 42	..	Stop	..		5 14	..	4 58			5 38	..	..	6E22	Stop	7 E 7	7S25	..	S		7 20	E	..
Colchester dep	..	3 31	..	..		4 11	..	..	..	..	Stop	5 25	..	5 31	..	..	6 32	..	6 40		..	6 55	..
Ardleigh	..	3 40	..	..		4 20	..	..	..	..		..	..	5 41	..	..	..	..	6 49		..	7 4	..
Manningtree arr	..	3 47	..	..		4 27	..	..	..	..	..	5 37	..	5 48	..	..	..	..	6 56		..	7 11	..
21 Harwich Park. Q. arr	..	..	..	..		5 3	..	..	..	..	..	..	5 40	6 43	..	..	..	..	8 15	..	..	..	..
21 " Town .. "	..	..	..	..		5 13	..	..	..	..	..	..	..	6 53	..	..	..	..	8 24	..	..	..	..
Manningtree dep	..	3 49		..		4 31	..	..	..	..	..	5 39		5 51	..	..	..	..	6 58	..	..	7 13	..
Bentley	..	3 57		..		4 39	..	..	..	..	..	..		6 0	..	..	..	..	7 7	..	..	7 22	..
Ipswich arr	..	4 7		aft		4 50	..	..	5 2	5 10	aft	5 54		6 10	aft	..	6 56	..	7 20	..	..	7 35	..
Ipswich dep	..	..		4 45	..	Stop	..	..	..	5 20	5 31	6 5		6 19	6 33	..	7 4	7 15	..	..	..	..	..
Bramford	..	..		..	..	..	..	..	..	..	5 37	..		..	6 39	..	..	7 21	..	..	..	..	..
Claydon	..	..		..	..	..	..	..	..	..	5 42	..		..	6 44	..	..	7 26	..	..	..	..	..
Needham	..	..		..	..	..	..	..	..	..	5 50	..		..	6 53	..	..	7 34	..	..	..	..	..
Stowmarket	..	..		5 5	..	..	..	..	..	..	5 59	6 26		6 39	7 1	..	7 25	7 43	..	..	..	..	..
Haughley	..	..		b	..	..	..	..	..	..	6 7			..	7 11	..	..	7 50	..	..	..	..	..
Finningham	..	..		..	..	..	..	..	..	..	6 16			..	b	..	..	7 59	..	..	..	..	..
Mellis	..	..		..	..	..	..	..	..	..	6 24		..	..	..	..	..	8 8	..	..	..	..	..
Diss	..	..		..	..	..	..	..	..	..	6 32		..	7 1	..	..	7 48	8 16	..	..	..	..	..
Burston	..	..	aft	..	..	..	..	..	..	..	6 39		..	..	..	..	..	8 22	..	..	..	..	..
Tivetshall	..	..	4 26	..	..	..	..	..	..	..	6 46		..	..	..	..	8 2	8 30	..	..	..	..	..
Forncett	..	..	4 33	..	..	..	..	..	..	..	6 53		..	..	..	..	..	8 37	..	..	..	..	..
Flordon	..	..	4 39	..	..	..	..	..	..	..	6 59		..	..	..	..	..	8 43	..	..	..	..	..
Swainsthorpe	..	..	4 46	..	..	..	..	..	..	..	7 6		..	..	..	..	..	8 50	..	..	..	..	..
Norwich (Thorpe). arr	..	..	4 58	..	..	..	..	..	..	6 16	7 16		..	7 30	..	..	8 25	9 2	..	..	..	..	..
43 Cromer arr	..	..	6 7	..	..	..	..	..	..	7 15			..	8 43	..	..	9 41		..	..	..	..	..
Ipswich dep	..	..	..	..	..	..	..	..	5 9	5 30	Stop		..	6 29	..	..	7 12	Stop	..	..	..	..	..
Westerfield	..	..	..	..	..	..	..	..	..	..	..		..	..	..	..	7 21	..	..	..	..	..	..
Bealings	..	..	..	..	..	..	..	..	..	..	..		..	..	..	..	7 28	..	..	..	..	..	..
Woodbridge	..	..	..	..	..	aft	..	..	..	5 48	..		..	6 47	..	..	7 36	..	..	..	..	..	..
Melton	..	..	..	..	..	E	..	..	..	..	..		..	..	..	..	7 42	..	..	..	..	..	..
Wickham Market D	..	..	..	..	..	X	..	..	..	6 0	..		..	6 58	..	..	7 54	..	..	..	..	..	..
Saxmundham	..	..	..	..	..	5 10	..	..	..	6 12	..		..	7 12	..	..	8 7	..	..	..	..	..	..
Darsham, for Yoxford	..	..	..	..	..	..	..	..	..	..	..		..	7 22	..	..	8 18	..	..	..	..	..	..
Halesworth	..	..	..	..	..	5 32	..	..	..	..	..		..	7 35	..	..	8 31	..	..	..	..	..	..
Brampton (Suffolk)	..	..	..	..	..	..	..	..	..	..	..		..	..	..	..	8 40	..	..	..	..	..	..
Beccles arr	..	..	..	..	..	5 49	E	..	6 6	6 37	..		..	7 50	..	..	8 49	..	..	..	..	..	..
Beccles dep	..	..	..	..	..	..	6 10	..	6 17	6 48	..		..	8 0	..	..	9 0	..	..	..	..	..	..
Oulton Broad South	..	..	..	..	..	..	6 20	..	6 27	6 58	aft		..	8 10	..	..	9 10	aft	..	..	..	..	..
Lowestoft (Cen.) arr	..	..	..	..	..	..	6 27	..	6 32	7 6	X		..	8 15	..	..	9 15	X	..	..	..	..	..
Beccles dep	..	..	..	..	..	5 53	..	..	6 12	6 40	6 53		..	7 55	..	..	8 53	9 15	..	..	..	..	..
Aldeby	..	..	..	..	..	..	..	..	..	..	7 1		..	..	..	..	..	9 23	..	..	..	..	..
Haddiscoe arr	..	..	..	..	..	..	..	..	..	..	7 5		..	..	..	..	..	9 27	..	..	..	..	..
45 Reedham arr	..	..	..	..	..	..	..	..	..	..	..		..	..	..	..	..	..	..	..	..	..	..
45 Norwich (Thorpe) "	..	..	..	..	..	..	..	..	..	..	..		..	..	..	..	..	..	..	..	..	..	..
Haddiscoe dep	..	..	..	..	..	..	..	..	..	..	7 6		..	..	..	..	..	9 28	..	..	..	..	..
St. Olaves	..	..	..	..	..	..	..	..	..	..	7 9		..	..	..	..	..	9 33	..	..	..	..	..
Belton and Burgh	..	..	..	..	..	6 10	..	..	..	..	7 15		..	..	..	..	..	9 39	..	..	..	..	..
Yarmouth (Sth. Town) arr	..	..	..	..	..	6 20	..	..	6 32	7 0	7 23		..	8 15	..	..	9 13	9 47	..	..	..	..	..
28 Gorleston-on-Sea arr	..	..	..	..	..	6 38	..	..	..	7F58	..		..	..	..	..	9L55	..	..	..	..	..	..

A For particulars of London Suburban Service, see Suburban Time Table
A Arrival time
b To Bury St Edmunds (Table 32)
C Clacton-on-Sea and Holland-on-Sea
D Station for Campsea Ash
E or E Except Saturdays
F Via Lowestoft. One class only
K Arr 3 41 aft
L Via Lowestoft
RC Restaurant Car
S or S Saturdays only
TC Through Carriages
X One class only
3 Third class only

Table 3— *continued* LONDON (Liverpool Street), COLCHESTER, CLACTON-ON-SEA, HARWICH, IPSWICH, NORWICH, BECCLES, LOWESTOFT, and YARMOUTH

Week Days—*continued* / **Suns.**

Station	E aft		E aft	E aft	aft	aft	aft	S aft	E aft	aft	aft	aft	aft	aft	aft	aft	E aft	mrn	S aft	Suns. mrn	mrn	mrn	mrn 3
Notes			From Liverpool Street, dep 5 16 aft	To Ipswich (dep. Chelmsford 7 40 p.m.)	RC Liverpool Street to Norwich (Thorpe)	From Cambridge (Table 17)	From Beccles (Table 23)		From Liverpool St. dep. 6 8 p.m.; Wednesdays and Saturdays			Mondays, Wednesdays and Fridays; The Hook Continental RC Liverpool Street to Harwich (P.Q)					To Bury St. Edmunds, Ely, and Peterborough (Table 32)	Except Sunday mornings			From Southend-on-Sea (Table 14)		Runs 7th July to 15th September inclusive
LONDON (L'pool St) dep	5 42		..	6 8	6 40	..	6 44	6 30		7 20	..	8 0	8 5	8 45	..	9 5	1025	..	1025	..	..	..	7 7
Stratford "	..		..	6 18		..	..	..		..	..		..	..	..	9 15	..	..	..	..	..	..	7 20
Ilford "	..		..	..			..	..		..	..		..	..	..	..	..	..	..	..	..	..	7 32
Romford "	..		..	6 34			..	6 54		..	..		..	..	..	9 32	..	..	..	..	..	..	7 48
Gidea Pk & Squirrels "	..		..	6 38			..	..		..	..		..	..	..	9 36	..	..	..	..	..	..	7 52
Harold Wood [Heath "	..		..	..			..	..		..	..		..	..	..	9 40	..	..	..	..	..	..	7 56
Brentwood & Warley "	6 17		..	..			..	7 6		..	..		..	..	..	9 49	..	..	..	..	..	..	8 4
Shenfield & Hutton "	..		..	6 53			7 20	7B22		7 57	..		..	9 21	..	9 58	..	..	..	..	6 59	..	8 15
Ingatestone "	6 28		E	7 0			..	7 29		8 4	..		..	..	..	10 5	..	..	11 4	..	7 6	..	8 22
Chelmsford "	6 39		6 44	7A 9			7 34	7 40	7 40	8 16	..		8 53	9 35	..	1019	1114	..	1116	..	7 17	..	8 34
Hatfield Peverel	..		6 54				..	7 53	7 53	8 27	..		..	..	..	1029	..	..	..	..	7 27	..	8 48
Witham	6 54		7 0				7 49	8 0	8 0	8 34	..		..	9 50	..	1037	..	..	..	..	7 33	..	8 53
Kelvedon	..		7 8				..	8 8	8 8	..	..		..	..	..	1045	..	..	..	..	7 41	..	Stop
Mark's Tey	7 9		7 17			7 30	8 4	8 17	8 17	..	..		9 19	..	..	1055	..	..	..	..	7 49	..	
Colchester arr	7 18		7 32			7 52	8 13	8 26	8 26	8 52	..		9 28	10 8		11 5	1144	..	1144	..	7 58	..	..
19 Walton-on-Naze arr	..						9 12	..	..	..	..		1032	..		..	..		..	..	10C18		..
19 Clacton-on-Sea C "	..					Stop	9 3	..	..	..	..		1024	..		..	..		..	..	10C10		..
Colchester dep	7 21	7 26			..	..	Stop	8 30	8 30	8 55	..		9 32	10 12	1017	1110	1151		1149	7 0		..	..
Ardleigh	..	..			..	..		8 39	8 39	..	..		..	..	1026	1119	..		..	7 8		..	..
Manningtree arr	..	7 39			..	..		8 46	8 46	9 7	..		..	10 25	1033	1126	..		..	7 14		..	..
21 Harwich Park. Q. arr	..	7 55			..	..		9 18	9 18	..	..	9 40	..	10N44	..	..	..		..	7 39		..	..
21 " Town .. "	..	8 4			..	..		9 28	9 28	..	..	..	..	10N55	..	..	..		..	7 50		..	..
Manningtree dep	..	..			..	..		8 49	8 50	9 9	..		..	..	1034	1128	..		..	Stop		..	..
Bentley	..	..			..	aft		8 57	8 58	..	..		..	..	1042	1136	..		..			..	..
Ipswich arr	7 45	..			8 10	S		9 8	9 10	9 25	..		10 0	..	1052	1148	1216		1213	mrn		..	..
Ipswich dep	..	..		..	8 17	8 30		..	Stop	9 35	9 40		..	..	..	..	1228	..	..	6 40		9 0	..
Bramford	..	..		..	..	8 36		..		..	9 46		..	..	..	..	..	..	..	6 47		9 6	..
Claydon	..	..		..	..	8 41		..	..	..	9 51		..	..	..	..	..	..	..	6 53		9 11	..
Needham	..	..		..	..	8 49		..	..	..	9 59		..	..	..	..	..	..	..	7 1		9 19	..
Stowmarket	..	..	..	..	..	8 58		..	..	9 54	10 9		..	..	..	..	1250		..	7 10		9 27	..
Haughley	..	..	..	..	..	9 6		..	..	..	1017		..	..	..	..	1 R6	1 42	..	7 17	Stop	9 34	..
Finningham	..	..	..	..	..	b		..	..	..	b		..	..	..	..		..	..	b	..	9 43	..
Mellis	..	..	..	..	..	..		..	..	..	..		..	..	..	..		..	..	Stop	..	9 52	..
Diss	..	..	..	..	..	..		..		1015	..		..	..	..	..		2 7	..	..	..	10 0	..
Burston	..	..	..	..	..	..	aft	..		..	..		..	..	..	..		..	..	..	..	10 6	..
Tivetshall	..	..	..	..	..	..	9 4	..		1027	..		..	..	..	..		..	..	..	..	1014	..
Forncett	..	..	..	..	..	..	9 11	..		..	..		..	..	..	..		..	..	..	..	1021	..
Flordon	..	..	..	..	..	..	9 17	..		..	..		..	..	..	..		..	..	..	..	1027	..
Swainsthorpe	..	..	..	..	..	..	9 24	..		..	..		..	..	..	..		..	..	..	..	1034	..
Norwich (Thorpe). arr	..	..	..	..	9 13	..	9 34	..		1051	..		..	..	..	..		2 36	..	..	..	1048	..
43 Cromer arr	..	..	..	..	12P54	..	12P54			12P54			..	..	..	..		..	..	..	..	..	mrn
Ipswich dep	..	..	..	..	8 17	..	Stop	..		9 35	..		1012	..	..	..		1228	..	..	..	..	9 30
Westerfield	..	..	..	..	..	..	..	..		..	..		..	..	..	..		..	..	..	..	..	9 39
Bealings	..	..	..	..	..	..	..	..		..	..		..	..	..	..		..	..	..	..	..	9 46
Woodbridge	..	..	..	..	..	..	..	..		..	..	..	1031	..	..	..		..	..	..	..	..	9 52
Melton	..	..	..	..	..	..	..	..		..	..	..	..	..	..	..		..	..	..	..	..	9 57
Wickham Market D	..	..	..	..	..	..	..	..		..	..	..	1044	..	..	..		..	..	..	..	..	10 7
Saxmundham	..	..	..	..	..	..	..	..		..	..	..	1057	..	..	..		..	..	..	..	..	1019
Darsham, for Yoxford	..	..	..	..	..	..	..	..		..	..	..	11 9	..	..	..		..	..	..	..	..	1029
Halesworth	..	..	..	..	..	..	..	..		..	..	..	1122	..	..	..		..	..	..	..	..	1041
Brampton (Suffolk)	..	..	..	..	..	..	..	..	aft	..	..	..	..	..	..	..		..	..	..	..		1050
Beccles arr	..	..	..	..	..	..	aft	..	X	..	..	..	1137	..	..	..		..	..	..	mrn		1059
Beccles dep	..	..	..	..	..	..	9 30	..	1015	..	..	..	1147	..	..	..	..	..	..	..	9 37		11 8
Oulton Broad South	..	..	..	..	..	..	9 40	..	1023	..	..	..	1157	..	..	..	..	..	..	..	9 47		1118
Lowestoft (Cen.) arr	..	..	..	..	..	..	9 45	..	..	..	..	..	12 3	..	..	..	..	4K5	..	mrn	9 52		1123
Beccles dep	..	..	..	..	..	..	..	..	..	..	..	..	1142	..	..	..	..	..	..	9 0	..		11 3
Aldeby	..	..	..	..	..	..	..	..	..	..	..	..	..	..	..	..	..	..	..	9 9	..		1111
Haddiscoe arr	..	..	..	..	..	..	..	..	..	..	..	..	..	..	..	..	..	..	..	9 14	..		..
45 Reedham arr	..	..	..	..	..	..	..	..	..	..	..	..	..	..	..	..	..	..	..	9 26	..		..
45 Norwich (Thorpe) "	..	..	..	..	..	..	..	..	..	..	..	..	..	..	..	..	..	..	..	10 8	..		..
Haddiscoe dep	..	..	..	..	..	..	..	..	..	..	..	..	..	..	..	..	..	..	..	9 20	..		..
St. Olaves	..	..	..	..	..	..	..	..	1029	..	..	..	Hh	..	..	..	..	..	..	9 25	..		1118
Belton and Burgh	..	..	..	..	..	..	..	..	1035	..	..	..	..	..	..	..	..	..	..	9 31	..		1124
Yarmouth (Sth. Town) arr	..	..	..	..	10Z30	..	..	..	1043	11Z42		..	12 5	..	..	..	..	4Z36	..	9 40	..		1135
28 Gorleston-on-Sea arr	..	..	..	..	..	..	..	..	..	..	..	..	..	..	..	..	..	..	..	..	..	..	..

A For particulars of London Suburban Service, see Suburban Time Table.
A Arrival time
B Arr 7 11 aft
b To Bury St. Edmunds (Table 32)
C Clacton-on-Sea and Holland-on-Sea
C Runs 7th July to 8th September inclusive
D Station for Campsea Ash
E or E Except Saturdays
Hh Calls at 11 54 aft when required to set down
K Via Norwich
N Arr 6 mins later on Saturdays
P Saturdays only. Beach Station
R Arr 12 56 mrn
RC Restaurant Car
S or S Saturdays only
X One class only
Z Yarmouth (Vauxhall) via Norwich
3 Third class only

Table 26 WICKHAM MARKET and FRAMLINGHAM

Miles		Week Days only									
		mrn		mrn		aft		aft			
	3 London (L'pool St.)..dep	4 25	..	10 0	..	3 40	..	5 6	..	..	..
—	**Wickham Market A** .. dep	9 30	..	1 5	..	6 9	..	8 2	..	..	..
1¾	Marlesford	9 36	..	1 11	..	6 15	..	8 8	..	..	..
3¼	Hacheston Halt	9 43	..	1 18	..	6 22	..	8 15	..	..	..
4	Parham Halt	9 49	..	1 24	..	6 28	..	8 21	..	..	..
6½	**Framlingham** .... arr	9 56	..	1 31	..	6 35	..	8 28	..	..	..

Miles		Week Days only					
		mrn		aft		aft	
	Framlingham .... dep	8 38	..	3 15	..	6 57	..
2½	Parham Halt	8 45	..	3 22	..	7 4	..
3¼	Hacheston Halt	8 48	..	3 25	..	7 7	..
4¾	Marlesford	8 56	..	3 33	..	7 15	..
6½	**Wickham Market A** .. arr	9 1	..	3 38	..	7 20	..
91	3 London (L'pool St.). arr	11B30	..	6 51	..	1020	..

A Station for Campsea Ash
B 4 mins. later on Mondays

Tickets from Marlesford, Hacheston Halt, and Parham Halt are issued on the train.

Passengers to and from **Hacheston Halt must join, or alight from the special car provided.**

Table 27 SAXMUNDHAM and ALDEBURGH

Miles		Week Days only							
		mrn	mrn	E	C	G	aft	aft	aft
	3 London (L'pool St.). dep	4 25	8 12	10 0	10 0	1212	0	3 40	5 6
—	**Saxmundham** .... dep	7 58	1110	1 35	1 35	2 45	8	6 20	8 14
4	Leiston	8 9	1120	1 45	1 45	2 55	18	6 30	8 24
6¼	Thorpeness	8 14	1125	1 50	1 50	3 0	23	6 35	8 29
8¼	**Aldeburgh** .... arr	8 19	1130	1 55	1 55	3 5	28	6 40	8 34

Miles		Week Days only								
		mrn	mrn		aft	aft	aft		aft	
	Aldeburgh .... dep	7 15	8 30	..	1245	3 18	5 30	..	6 47	..
2	Thorpeness	7 20	8 35	..	1250	3 23	5 35	..	6 52	..
4¼	Leiston	7 26	8 41	..	1256	3 29	5 45	..	6 59	..
8¼	**Saxmundham** .... arr	7 35	8 50	..	1 5	3 38	5 55	..	7 8	..
99¼	3 London (L'pool St.). arr	1050	11B30	..	3 56	6 51	9C22	..	1020	..

B 4 mins. later on Mondays
C Sats. only. Runs until 29thJune incl. and from 21st Sept.
E Except Sats.

G or C Saturdays only. Runs 6th July to 14th September inclusive

Pages 206-207 and above:
LNER timetable book 6 May to 6 October 1946,
showing the Liverpool Street to Norwich and Yarmouth South Town services
and the Aldeburgh and Framlingham branches.

BEALINGS (Suffolk)
Miles 76. Map Sq. 19.
Pop. 567. Clos. day Wed.
From Liverpool Street via Ipswich.
1st cl.—Single 16/11, Return 33/10.
3rd cl.—Single 11/3, Return 22/6.
Served by most trains to Melton, 12 min. shorter journey

ABC Railway Guide
February 1954 timetable.

BECCLES (Suffolk)
Miles 109½. Map Sq. 19.
Pop. 6,869. Clos. day Wed.
From Liverpool Street via Ipswich.
1st cl.—Single 24/2, Return 48/4.
3rd cl.—Single 16/1, Return 32/2.

Liv. St.	Beccles	Beccles	Liv. St.
a.m.		a.m.	
4 30	8 27	6 16r	9 43
8 30r	11 37	6 59r	10 0
10 30sr	2 3	7 51r	10 31
10 30er	2 12	8 26r	11 23
p.m.		10 9e	1 34
12 33s	3 17	10 9s	1 40
1 30r	4 48	p.m.	
3 33r	6 11	12 37r	4 7
4 30	7 50	3 21	6 48
5 30r	8 44	5 53e	9 9
6 33r	9 24	6 36	9 56
8 30hr	12 2	7 58	12 9
Sunday Trains.			
a.m.		a.m.	
10 30	2 16	9 42	1 38
p.m.		p.m.	
5 0	7 59	3 16	6 40
5 30	9 14	6 36	9 29
7 45	11 3	7 46	12 17

e Not Saturday.
h Friday and Saturday only.
r Refreshment Car.
s Saturday only.

LOWESTOFT (Suffolk)
Miles 1 7¾. Map Sq. 19.
Pop. 42 337. Clos. day Thur.
CENTRAL STATION.
REFRESHMENT ROOMS.
From Liverpool Street via Beccles.
1st cl.—Single 25/11, Return 51/10.
3rd cl.—Single 17/3, Return 34/6.
Via Norwich.
1st cl.—Single 30/3, Return 60/6.
3rd cl.—Single 20/2, Return 40/4.

Liv. St.	Lowest.	Lowest.	Liv. St.
a.m.		a.m.	
4 30	8 59	5 55r	9 43
8 30r	12 3	6 36r	10 0
9 30sr	1† 5	7 25r	10 31
9 30er	2† 2	8 0r	11 23
10 30sr	2 29	9 43e	1 34
10 30er	2 38	9 43s	1 40
p.m.		10 0¶r	1a55
12 30er	5† 8	11†24s	3 30
12 33s	3 43	p.m.	
1 30r	5 14	12 10r	4 7
3 33r	6 37	12†26er	4 34
4 30	8 16	12†26sr	4 46
5 30r	9 11	2 55	6 48
6 33r	9 50	3†29r	7 45
7 30h	12† 9	4†15er	7 55
8 30hr	12 28	4†15sr	8 6
—	—	5†10s	9 9
—	—	5 25e	9 9
—	—	6 10	9 56
—	—	7 31	12 9
—	—	9†34e	3 56
Sunday Trains.			
a.m.		a.m.	
10 0	2†13	9 13	1 38
10 30	2 42	p.m.	
p.m.		1†11	5 20
5 0	8 25	2 50	6 40
5 30	9 40	6 10	9 29
7 45	11 28	7 20	12 17
—	—	9†10	3 56

a 2.6 p.m. on Fri. and Sat.
e Not Saturday.
† Via Norwich.
¶ Limited accommodation between Norwich and London. Advance reservation advisable.
h Friday and Saturday only.
r Refresh. Car. *s* Saturday only.

Suffolk Hotel. 'Phone 1015.
On the London Road. Close to Docks.
Open throughout year.
See page A173.
TRUST HOUSES LTD.
(For list see back of map.)

Royal Hotel. Premier position on Traffic-free promenade. Fully Licensed. Lift. Garage. A.A. R.A.C. 'Phone 1221. Apply Manager.
See page A173.

ST. OLAVE'S (Suffolk)
Miles 115½. Map. Sq. 19. Clos. day Thur.
From Liverpool Street via Ipswich.
1st cl.—Single 25/5, Return 50/10.
3rd cl.—Single 16/11, Return 33/10.

Liv. St.	St. Ol.	St. Ol.	Liv. St.
a.m.		a.m.	
4 30	8 51	6 2r	9 43
8 30er	12 50	6 46r	10 0
8 30sr	12 54	7 50r	11 23
10 30sr	2 24	9 46e	1 34
10 30er	2 33	9 46s	1 40
p.m.		11 49r	4 7
12 33s	3 51	p.m.	
1 30r	5 9	2 25	6 48
3 33r	6 38	5 30e	9 9
4 30§	8 7	5 45s	9 56
5 30r	9 6	6 13e	9 56
6 33§r	9 41	7 35	12 9
8 30h§r	12 19	—	—
Sunday Trains.			
a.m.		a.m.	
10 30	2 35	9 21	1 38
p.m.		p.m.	
5 30	9 33	2 55	6 40
7 45§	11 20	7 25	12 17

§ By request.
e Not Saturday.
h Friday and Saturday only.
r Refreshment Car.
s Saturday only.

YARMOUTH (GREAT)
(Norfolk)
Miles 121¾. Map Sq. 19.
Pop. 51,105. Clos. day Thur.
SOUTH TOWN STATION.
From Liverpool Street via Ipswich.
1st cl.—Single 26/9, Return 53/6.
3rd cl.—Single 17/10, Return 35/3.

Liv. St.	Yarm.	Yarm.	Liv. St.
a.m.		a.m.	
4 30	9 5	5 51r	9 43
8 30r	12 1	6 35r	10 0
10 30sr	2 38	7 25r	10 31
10 30er	2 47	8 0r	11 23
p.m.		9 31e	1 34
12 33s	3 41	9 31s	1 40
1 30r	5 23	p.m.	
3 33r	6 35	12 10r	4 7
4 30	8 14	2 55	6 48
5 30r	9 20	5 15e	9 9
6 33r	9 48	5 58e	9 56
8 30hr	12 26	6 10s	9 56
—	—	7 20	12 9
Sunday Trains.			
a.m.		a.m.	
10 30	2 50	9 10	1 38
p.m.		p.m.	
5 0	8 25	2 40	6 40
5 30	9 50	6 10	9 29
7 45	11 33	7 10	12 17

e Not Saturday.
h Friday and Saturday only.
r Refreshment Car.
s Saturday only.

Above:
An Aldeburgh train waits to leave from the down platform at Saxmundham in 1956, headed by Class F6 No 67239. *Peter Punchard collection*

Below:
Brush Class 31 No D5506 pulls away from Snape Junction with the 11.12am Holiday Camps Express from Liverpool Street to Gorleston on 30 August 1958. The signalbox is just visible at the back of the train. *John Brodribb collection*

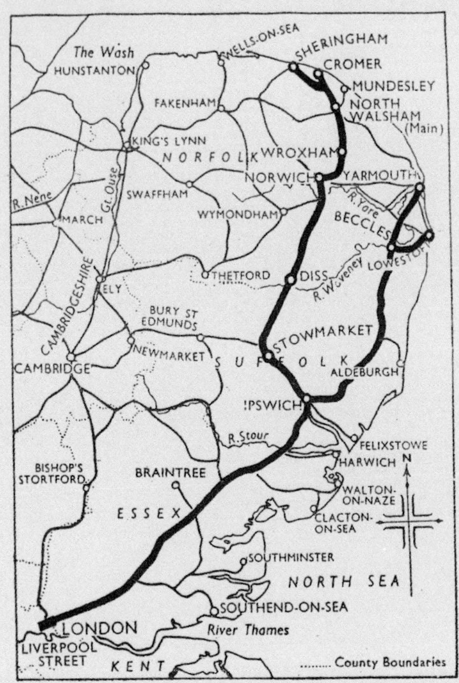

THE NORFOLKMAN

LONDON (LIVERPOOL STREET) IPSWICH NORWICH CROMER SHERINGHAM

THE EASTERLING

LONDON (LIVERPOOL STREET) LOWESTOFT YARMOUTH

THE BROADSMAN

LONDON (LIVERPOOL STREET) IPSWICH NORWICH CROMER SHERINGHAM

THE EAST ANGLIAN

LONDON (LIVERPOOL STREET) IPSWICH NORWICH

SUMMER 1955

Published by British Railways (Eastern Region) PP/316/61. Printed in Great Britain. Tinlings, Liverpool.

THE NORFOLKMAN

WEEKDAYS 13th JUNE TO 17th SEPTEMBER inclusive

	E	S
	a.m.	a.m.
London (Liverpool Street) ...dep.	9 30	9 30
Ipswich ... arr.	10 46	10 53
Ipswich ... dep.	10 49	10 56
Norwich (Thorpe)...arr.	11 40	11 51
	p.m.	p.m.
Wroxham ... ... ,,	12 10	12 20
North Walsham (Main) ,,	12 22	12 35
Gunton ... ... ,,	12 33	...
Cromer (Beach) ... ,,	12 47	1 4
West Runton ... ,,	1 2	1 17
Sheringham ... ,,	1 6	1 21

	E	S
	p.m.	p.m.
Sheringham ...dep.	4 26	4 26
West Runton ... ,,	4 30	4 30
Cromer (Beach) ... ,,	4 42	4 42
North Walsham (Main) ,,	5 5	5 5
Wroxham ... ... ,,	5 20	5 20
Norwich (Thorpe) ... ,,	5 45	5 45
Ipswich ... ... arr.	6 36	6 38
Ipswich ... ... dep.	6 38	6 41
London (Liverpool Street) ...arr.	7 55	8 6

E—Saturdays excepted **S**—Saturdays only

Seats can be reserved in advance at a fee of 1/- per seat at the seat reservation offices, Liverpool Street or any other London terminus, station booking offices Sheringham and Cromer, seat reservation office, Norwich (for journeys to Ipswich and London), or through the usual agencies.

THE EASTERLING

WEEKDAYS 27th JUNE TO 10th SEPTEMBER inclusive

	S	E
	a.m.	a.m.
London ... ...dep. (Liverpool Street)	10 33	11 3
	p.m.	p.m.
Beccles ... ...arr.	12 52	1 16
Lowestoft (Central) ... ,,	1 19	1 43
Yarmouth (South Town) ... ... ,,	1 14	1 38

	p.m.
Yarmouth (South Town) ... ...dep.	7 15
Lowestoft (Central) ... ,,	7 16
Beccles ... ... ,,	7 42
London ... (Liverpool Street) arr.	10 0

E—Saturdays excepted. **S**—Saturdays only

Seats can be reserved in advance at a fee of 1/- per seat at the seat reservation offices, Liverpool Street or any other London terminus, station booking offices Lowestoft (Central) and Yarmouth (South Town), or through the usual agencies.

THE BROADSMAN

WEEKDAYS 13th JUNE TO 17th SEPTEMBER inclusive

	a.m.
Sheringham ... ...dep.	6 23
West Runton ... ,,	6 27
Cromer (Beach) ... ,,	6 39
Gunton... ... ... ,,	6 54
North Walsham (Main) ... ,,	7 2
Worstead ... ... ,,	7 8
Wroxham ... ... ,,	7 16
Salhouse ... ... ,,	7 24
Norwich (Thorpe) ... ,,	7 45
Diss ... ... ,,	8 11
Stowmarket ... ... ,,	8 29
Ipswich ... ... arr.	8 42
Ipswich ... ... dep.	8 45
London (Liverpool Street) arr.	10 0

	E	S
	p.m.	p.m.
London (Liverpool Street)dep.	3 30	3 30
Ipswich ... ... arr.	4 43	4 53
Ipswich ... ... dep.	4 46	4 56
Norwich (Thorpe) ...arr.	5 30	5 51
Salhouse ... ... ,,	5 56	—
Wroxham ... ... ,,	6 3	6 16
Worstead ... ... ,,	6 12	—
North Walsham (Main) ... ,,	6 19	6 28
Gunton ... ... ,,	6 30	6 39
Cromer (Beach) ... ,,	6 44	6 53
West Runton ... ,,	6 58	7 6
Sheringham ... ... ,,	7 2	7 10

E—Saturdays excepted **S**—Saturdays only

Seats can be reserved in advance at a fee of 1/- per seat at the seat reservation offices, Liverpool Street or any other London terminus, station booking offices Sheringham and Cromer, seat reservation office, Norwich (for journeys to London and intermediate stations), or through the usual agencies.

THE EAST ANGLIAN

WEEKDAYS 13th JUNE TO 17th SEPTEMBER inclusive

	a.m.
Norwich (Thorpe) ...dep.	11 45
	p.m.
Ipswich ... ... arr.	12**D**36
Ipswich ... ... dep.	12**D**38
London (Liverpool Street) arr.	1**D**55

	p.m.
London (Liverpool Street)dep.	6 30
Ipswich ... ... arr.	7**C**45
Ipswich ... ... dep.	7**C**49
Norwich (Thorpe) ...arr.	8**C**40

C—On Fridays arrives Ipswich 7.53, departs 7.56 and arrives Norwich (Thorpe) 8.51 p.m.

D—On Fridays and Saturdays arrives Ipswich 12.38, departs 12.41 and arrives Liverpool Street 2.6 p.m.

Seats can be reserved in advance at a fee of 1/- per seat at the seat reservation offices, Liverpool Street or any other London terminus, station booking office Ipswich, seat reservation office, Norwich (Thorpe), or through the usual agencies.

REFRESHMENT CAR TRAINS

1955 timetable leaflet for the 'Easterling' and other named trains.
Peter Punchard

Left:
Just before World War 1 a goods train heads back to the junction over the River Alde, which is tidal at this point. It is headed by one of the ubiquitous Great Eastern Class Y14 0-6-0 locomotives which served the branch until it closed.
Alan Taylor collection

much work done on re-laying the track. The story of what happened, and the fight for the remaining railway in East Suffolk, is told in a later chapter.

Goods services were the mainstay of the line for many years, providing a large proportion of the revenue. Almost all stations had facilities to handle goods, with the Snape branch never doing anything else during its existence. The Framlingham line spent the last 12 years of its life as goods-only, although it did see occasional passenger trains at the start and end of school terms, and even Aldeby eked out a freight-only life for five years after losing its passenger trains. The pick-up goods — Class K — was responsible for much of this, ambling along calling at all stations and sidings to pick up and set down traffic, shunt the yards and carry out much unofficial internal business such as dropping off coal for gatekeepers and signalboxes, as well as official items such as churns of drinking water for remote spots. On the other hand there were the bonus trains, where the object was to get finished as soon as possible, since the size of the bonus depended on the earliness of the finish. With the importance of Lowestoft and Yarmouth as ports, the express fish trains ran to passenger timings and used the biggest available motive power. Halesworth's dairy necessitated similar urgency for its traffic and required to be served even on Christmas Day. Parcels and perishable traffic would go by passenger train, so that day-old chicks would arrive for immediate collection by local farmers, not to mention the livestock of many sorts. Whole farms moved by train, and when the Suffolk Show was held on the line, long and complex were the preparations and traffic arrangements. Market and sale days would see droves of livestock arriving at stations which would need feeding and watering *en route*. Railway staff had to be masters of a wide range of skills.

There was a very wide variety of goods services in 1913. The day started — it really went round the clock, of course — with the 12.55am Class A express goods from Ipswich, which called at Woodbridge for mail bags, Wickham Market, Saxmundham and Darsham when required to leave cattle, Halesworth and Beccles, which was reached at 3.5am. There it detached a portion for South Town, and continued to Lowestoft, arriving at 4am. The 11.18pm express goods from Bishopsgate and Spitalfields was about 1½hr behind it when leaving Ipswich, and was required to have a full load of trucks for the East Suffolk; it was limited to 40 wagons as far as Saxmundham. It called at Ipswich for mail bags only, and then called at Westerfield to remarshal trucks for Woodbridge, Wickham Market, Saxmundham and Halesworth, and also carried newspapers from Westerfield. This train did not run on Mondays; instead, there was a 9.25pm from Temple Mills, which was a little later reaching Ipswich but then did much the same. The 3am goods from Ipswich Lower Yard did not call at Westerfield, and did not run on Mondays, but then called at all stations to Beccles, arriving at 8.50am. It was shunted at Halesworth to let the 5.10am passenger train from Liverpool Street pass, due at 8.12am. The 3.30pm Tuesdays-only went as far as Darsham, reaching there at 5.25am and returning at 6.35am, and thus gave a means of clearing the cattle traffic from the Tuesdays-only Class B cattle train from Framlingham. The 11.45pm from March was sent forward when required from Ipswich at 3.50am or 3.55am depending on the day of the week, as far as Saxmundham. The 11.55am from Temple Mills left Ipswich at 5.40pm having spent 1¼ hours there, calling then at Wickham Market and all stations to Beccles, except Brampton, and going forward on Mondays to Lowestoft. The Aldeburgh goods left Ipswich at 6am and called at Woodbridge, Melton, Wickham Market and Saxmundham, leaving there at 9.55am and reaching Aldeburgh at 10.25am. It returned at noon, having a leisurely journey back to Ipswich, which was reached at 3.55pm.

The 1.10am from Goodmayes reached Ipswich at 4.50am and left again at 6.35am, calling first at Wickham Market and then all stations except Brampton to Beccles, and, except on Mondays, continuing to Lowestoft. It served Barnby siding and Carlton Colville when required, and reached the terminus at 10.28am. The 11.55pm from Temple Mills covered this on Mondays. The 12 midnight from Temple Mills arrived at Ipswich at 4.10am and left at 6.35am, calling at most stations to Yarmouth, and allowed time to attach at stations north of Beccles. Its progress was slower than most because it had to shunt at Woodbridge for the 5.10am down from Liverpool Street to pass, at Wickham Market for the 8.10am from Ipswich, and at Darsham for the 6.35am from Liverpool Street.

Table 3

LONDON (Liverpool Street), COLCHESTER, CLACTON-ON-SEA, HARWICH, IPSWICH, NORWICH, BECCLES, LOWESTOFT and YARMOUTH

MONDAYS TO FRIDAYS

Miles	Station	am D	am D	am	am D	am		am	am D	am D	am D	am	am D	am D	am D	am	am D	am D	am	am D	am D	am D
	LONDON (Liverpool St.) A dep			4 35															6 54			
20¼	Shenfield & Hutton A																		7 29			
29¾	Chelmsford A			5 37															7 42	7 50		
36	Hatfield Peverel			5 47				Through Train to Harwich Town												7 58		
38½	Witham			5c55															7 57	8 4	8 25	
42¼	Kelvedon																			8 10	8 31	
46¾	Mark's Tey			6 6																8 17	8 38	
51¾	Colchester arr			6 14															8 14	8 24	8 45	
70¼	24 Walton-on-Naze arr			7 45															1016	1016	1016	
69¾	24 Clacton-on-Sea F			7 40															9 1	9 1	10 0	
—	Colchester dep			6 16				6 45				7 17	7 48						8 16	8 25	8 46	
56	Ardleigh							6 55					7 55			From Harwich (Parkeston Quay) dep 8 0 am (Table 25)				8 33	8 53	
59½	Manningtree arr							7 2				7 32	8 1						8 29	8 38	8 58	
69	25 Harwich Park. Quay arr							7 45					8 33									
70¾	25 Harwich Town							7 57					8 39									
—	Manningtree dep											7 34	8 1						8 30	8 38	8 59	
63¼	Bentley												8 7							8 44	9 5	
68¾	Ipswich arr			6 36								7 51	8 15			8 28			8 45	8 52	9 13	
—	Ipswich dep			6 43					7 15	7 26		7 56	8 16		8 26	8 34				8 55		
73½	Claydon								7 22				8 23									
77	Needham			6 57					7 28				8 29									
80¾	Stowmarket			7d 7					7 34	7c44			8 35		8 42					9 12		
83	Haughley								7 38	7 48			8 39		8 47					9 16		
86½	Finningham			7 19					7 45													
91½	Mellis			7 27					7 51													
95	Diss			7d37					7 57						9 3							
97½	Burston								8 2	To Bury St. Edmunds (Table 30)		Through Train (RB) Colchester to Newcastle arr 3 29 pm via March and Spalding (Tables 30, 35, 44 and 1)	To Bury St. Edmunds (Table 30)							To Bury St. Edmunds and Cambridge (Table 30)		
100½	Tivetshall			7 47					8 7													
104	Forncett			7 54					8 13													
106¾	Flordon			8 0					8 17													
115	Norwich (Thorpe) arr			8 14					8 30						9 29							
141¾	42 Cromer (Beach) arr								9†26						10†32							
145½	42 Sheringham								9†38						10†50							
—	Ipswich C dep						6 53				7 40						8 40				9 15	
72¼	Westerfield C										7 46						8 46					
79	Woodbridge						7e13				7 57						8 57				9 30	
84½	Wickham Market						7 25				8 5						9 5					
91	Saxmundham						7e39				8 14					Through Train to Liverpool (Central) arr 3 10 pm (via March and Spalding) RC to Sheffield (Victoria) (Tables 30, 35, 44 and 63)	9 14			To Bury St. Edmunds (Table 30)	9 46	
95½	Darsham						7 49				8 22						9 22					
100¾	Halesworth B		6 47				8d 1				8 30						9 30				10 0	
104½	Brampton (Suffolk)						8 8				8 36						9 36					
109¼	Beccles arr		6 59				8 16				8 44						9 44				1013	
	Beccles dep		7 0			8 25	8 30				8 45						9 45				1013	
115¾	Oulton Broad South		7 9				8 40														1023	
117¾	Lowestoft (Central) arr		7 13				8 46														1027	
	Lowestoft (Central) dep	6 58	7 17		7 58									8 58				9 58			1030	10 58
120	Lowestoft (North)	7 2	7 21		8 2	Via Haddiscoe (Table 3a)								9 2				10 2				11 2
121¼	Corton	7 6	7 25		8 6						Via Haddiscoe (Table 3a)			9 6			Via Haddiscoe (Table 3a)	10 6				11 6
123½	Hopton-on-Sea	7 10	7 29		8 10									9 10				10 10				11 10
124½	Gorleston Links Halt	7 13	7 32		8 13									9 13				10 13				11 13
125½	Gorleston-on-Sea	7 16	7 35		8 16									9 16				10 16			1042	11 16
128	Yarmouth (South Tn.) arr	7 22	7 41		8 24	8 50					9 8			9 22			10 8	10 22			1048	11 22

D Diesel Train

† Second class only
‡ Arrival time
A Departure times for stations beyond Chelmsford. For complete service between Liverpool Street, intermediate stations and Chelmsford, see Table 13

B Station for Southwold
C For other trains between Ipswich and Westerfield, see Table 27
c Arr 3 minutes *earlier*
d Arr 4 minutes *earlier*
e Arr 5 minutes *earlier*

F Clacton-on-Sea and Holland-on-Sea
RB Buffet Car
RC Restaurant Car
TC Through Carriages

For COMPLETE SERVICE and intermediate stations between Beccles and Yarmouth (South Town) via Haddiscoe see Table 3a

Table 3—*continued*

LONDON (Liverpool Street), COLCHESTER, CLACTON-ON-SEA, HARWICH, IPSWICH, NORWICH, BECCLES, LOWESTOFT and YARMOUTH

MONDAYS TO FRIDAYS—*continued*

Station	am D	am		am	am	am D	am D	am	am	am D	am D	am	am	am D	am D	am	am		am D	pm D	am	am
LONDON (Liverpool St.) A dep				8 5	8 30			8 33	8 40				9 30			9 33		9 38			10 5	
Shenfield & Hutton A				8H26	8‡46			9 4				9 25				9G39		9G39				1015
Chelmsford A				8 54	9 11			9 18				9 39				1011		1016				1029
Hatfield Peverel																						
Witham				9 9	9 24			9 31	CONTINENTAL SERVICE	9 39								1028				
Kelvedon										9 45												
Mark's Tey	8 48									9 52												
Colchester arr	8 55			9 26	9 39			9 46		9 59		10 4	THE NORFOLKMAN	From Harwich Town dep 10 15 am (Table 25)		1034		1043				1054
24 Walton-on-Naze arr	1016			1016				1032		10L44		1044				1114		1142				1142
24 Clacton-on-Sea F	10 0			10 0				1022		10 57		1057				11 6		1133				1133
Colchester dep	9 0		9 10		9 41					10 0								1045				
Ardleigh	9 7		9 19							10 7												
Manningtree arr	9 12		9 25		9 52					10 13												
25 Harwich Park. Quay arr	9 38				10 27				10P15	11 25		Commences 20th July									11P36	
25 Harwich Town	9 44				10 33					11 31												
Manningtree dep	9 13		9 26		9 53					10 13												
Bentley	9 19		9 33							10 19				1045								
Ipswich arr	9 27		9 43		10 5					10 27			10 43	1053				11 5				
Ipswich dep	9 35				10 8								10 46	1055	11 0							
Claydon	9 42			Through Train Liverpool Street to Clacton-on-Sea																		
Needham	9 48																					
Stowmarket	9 53				10 23									1111	1116							
Haughley	9 58																					
Finningham	10 4												RB Liverpool Street to Norwich					RB Liverpool Street to Yarmouth				
Mellis	1011																					
Diss	1016				10 39			CLACTON INTERVAL SERVICE RB Liverpool Street to Clacton-on-Sea TC to Walton-on-Naze	Runs on Friday, 24th July and Mondays, 27th July, 3rd and 10th August			Through Train Romford dep 9 9 am to Walton-on-Naze			1135	CLACTON INTERVAL SERVICE RB Liverpool Street to Clacton-on-Sea					THE DAY CONTINENTAL Restaurant Car	TC Romford dep 9 57 am to Clacton-on-Sea and Walton-on-Naze
Burston	1021																					
Tivetshall	1026													To Bury St. Edmunds (Table 30)	1143							
Forncett	1032																					
Flordon	1036																					
Norwich (Thorpe) arr	1049				11 0								11 30		12 2							
42 Cromer (Beach) arr					12†3								12†25									
42 Sheringham					12†15								12†38									
Ipswich C dep			9 46			1015	1020											11 8	1115			
Westerfield C							1026												1121			
Woodbridge						1030	1037											1124	1132			
Wickham Market							1045												1140			
Saxmundham	Through Train from Bury St. Edmunds (Table 22)		1021		RC Liverpool Street to Norwich	1046	1054											1141	1149			
Darsham																			1157			
Halesworth B			1038			11 0												1154	12 5			
Brampton (Suffolk)																			1212			
Beccles arr			1051			1113												12 6	1219			
Beccles dep		1056	11 1			1113											1211	1216	1220	1225		
Oulton Broad South			1112			1123												1227		1234		
Lowestoft (Central) arr			1117			1127												1232		1239		
Lowestoft (Central) dep						1130	To Aldeburgh arr 11 13 am (Table 28)		Conveys only passengers holding tickets to the Continent		1158									1245	Conveys only passengers holding tickets to the Continent	
Lowestoft (North)											12 2											
Corton		Via Haddiscoe (Table 3a)									12 6						Via Haddiscoe (Table 3a)		Via Haddiscoe (Table 3a)			
Hopton-on-Sea											1210											
Gorleston Links Halt											1213											
Gorleston-on-Sea						1142					1216									1257		
Yarmouth (South Tn.) arr		1114				1148					1222		12Z36				1228		1243	1 3		

D Diesel Train

† Second class only
A Departure times for stations beyond Chelmsford. For complete service between Liverpool Street, intermediate stations and Chelmsford, see Table 13
B Station for Southwold

C For other trains between Ipswich and Westerfield, see Table 27
F Clacton-on-Sea and Holland-on-Sea
G Change at Chelmsford
H Change at Chelmsford. Second class only
L Until 17th July arr Walton-on-Naze 11 4 am

P Parkeston Quay West Station
RB Buffet Car
RC Restaurant Car
TC Through Carriages
Z Yarmouth (Vauxhall) via Norwich (Thorpe) (Table 43)

For COMPLETE SERVICE and intermediate stations between Beccles and Yarmouth (South Town) via Haddiscoe see Table 3a

Table 3—*continued*

LONDON (Liverpool Street), COLCHESTER, CLACTON-ON-SEA, HARWICH, IPSWICH, NORWICH, BECCLES, LOWESTOFT and YARMOUTH

MONDAYS TO FRIDAYS—*continued*

	am	am D	pm D	am	am	pm D	am D	pm	am	pm D	am	pm D	am	pm	pm D	pm	pm D	pm D	pm	pm	pm D
LONDON (Liverpool St.) dep				10 30	1033				11 3		11 30		1133			230			12 33	1238	
Shenfield & Hutton A „				10H44	11 2						11H44		12 2						12H44		
Chelmsford „				11 8	1116						12 8		1216		1221				1 11	1 16	
Hatfield Peverel															1229						
Witham				11 21	1129						12 21		1229		1235					1 28	
Kelvedon															1241						
Mark's Tey	1052						1148								1248						
Colchester arr	11 2			11 36	1144		1155				12 36		1244		1255				1 34	1 43	
24 Walton-on-Naze arr	12 7				1226		1 7						1 26		2 4				2 16	3 7	
24 Clacton-on-Sea F „	12 0				1217		1 0		1236				1 17		1 57				2 7	3 0	
Colchester dep	11 3			11 38			12 0				12 38				1 5					1 45	
Ardleigh	1111						12 7								1 12						
Manningtree arr	1119			11 49			1213				12 49				1 18						
25 Harwich Park. Quay arr				12 13							1 43				1 43						
25 „ Town „				12 19							1 49				1 49						
Manningtree dep	1119			11 51			1213				12 51				1 18						
Bentley	1127						1219								1 24		1 45				
Ipswich arr	1137			12 3			1227				1 3			1 25	1 32	1 43	1 53			2 5	
Ipswich dep		1155		12 7			1235	1255			1 7			1 31	Stop	1 46	1 55	2 0			
Claydon		12 2					1242														
Needham		12 8					1248														
Stowmarket		1214		12 22			1254	1c13			1 22			1 49			2 11	2 16			
Haughley		1218					1258														
Finningham							1 5														
Mellis							1 11														
Diss				12 38			1 17				1 38							2 34			
Burston							1 22														
Tivetshall							1 27											2 43			
Forncett							1 33														
Flordon							1 37														
Norwich (Thorpe) arr				1 0			1 50				2 0					2 30		3 2			
42 Cromer (Beach) arr				2† 3							3† 3					3†33					
42 Sheringham „				2†15							3†15					3†42					
Ipswich C dep						1215						1 15								2 8	2 15
Westerfield																					2 21
Woodbridge						1230						1 30								2 24	2 32
Wickham Market																					2 40
Saxmundham						1246						1 46								2 41	2 49
Darsham																					2 57
Halesworth B						1 0						2 0								2 54	3 5
Brampton (Suffolk)																					3 12
Beccles arr						1 13						2 13								3 6	3 19
Beccles dep						1 13						2 13								3 11 / 3 16	3 20
Oulton Broad South						1 23						2 23								3 27	
Lowestoft (Central) arr						1 27						2 27								3 32	
Lowestoft (Central) dep			1258			1 30				1 58		2 30			pm D 2 58						
Lowestoft (North)			1 2							2 2					3 2						
Corton			1 6							2 6					3 6						
Hopton-on-Sea			1 10							2 10					3 10						
Gorleston Links Halt			1 13							2 13					3 13						
Gorleston-on-Sea			1 16			1 42				2 16		2 42			3 16						
Yarmouth (South Tn.) arr			1 22			1 48				2 22		2 48			3 22					3 28	3 43
Notes		To Bury St. Edmunds and Cambridge (Table 30)		RC Liverpool Street to Norwich	CLACTON INTERVAL SERVICE RB Liverpool Street to Clacton-on-Sea TC to Walton-on-Naze		Through Train from Haverhill (Table 22)	To Bury St. Edmunds and Cambridge (Table 30)	Through Train Liverpool Street to Clacton-on-Sea		RB Liverpool Street to Norwich		CLACTON INTERVAL SERVICE RB Liverpool Street to Clacton-on-Sea TC to Walton-on-Naze	From Harwich Town dep 12 41 pm (Table 25); To Bury St. Edmunds, Ely, March and Peterborough (East) arr 4 3 pm (Tables 30 and 35)		RC Liverpool Street to Norwich	From Harwich Town dep 1 15 pm (Table 25); To Bury St. Edmunds (Table 30)		CLACTON INTERVAL SERVICE RB Liverpool Street to Clacton-on-Sea TC to Walton-on-Naze	RB Liverpool Street to Yarmouth; 3 11 Via Haddiscoe (Table 3a)	Via Haddiscoe (Table 3a)

D Diesel Train

£2 or † Second class only

A Departure times for stations beyond Chelmsford. For complete service between Liverpool Street, intermediate stations and Chelmsford, see Table 13

B Station for Southwold

C For other trains between Ipswich and Westerfield, see Table 27

c Arr 3 minutes *earlier*

F Clacton-on-Sea and Holland-on-Sea

H Change at Chelmsford. Second class only

RB Buffet Car

RC Restaurant Car

TC Through Carriages

For COMPLETE SERVICE and intermediate stations between Beccles and Yarmouth (South Town) via Haddiscoe see Table 3a

Table 3—*continued*

LONDON (Liverpool Street), COLCHESTER, CLACTON-ON-SEA, HARWICH, IPSWICH, NORWICH, BECCLES, LOWESTOFT and YARMOUTH

MONDAYS TO FRIDAYS—*continued*

	pm D	pm D	pm D	pm	pm D	pm D	pm	pm D	pm D	pm	pm D	pm D	pm	pm D	pm	pm	pm D	pm	pm	pm D	pm	pm D
LONDON (Liverpool St.) dep				1 30			1 33			2 30			2 33		3 5	3 30		3 33	3 38			
Shenfield & Hutton A „				1H44			2 2			2H44			3 2					3H44				
Chelmsford „				2 8			2 16			3 8			3 16	3 21				4 11	4 16			
Hatfield Peverel														3 29								
Witham				2 21			2 29			3 21			3 29	3 35					4 28			
Kelvedon														3 41								
Mark's Tey								2 50						3 48								
Colchester arr				2 36			2 44	2 57		3 36			3 44	3 55				4 34	4 43			
24 Walton-on-Naze arr							3 26	4 6					4 27	4 57				5 16	6 0			
24 Clacton-on-Sea F „							3 17	4 0					4 17	4 44				5 7	5 51			
Colchester dep				2 38				3 0		3 38				3 56					4 45			
Ardleigh								3 7						4 3								
Manningtree arr				2 49				3 13		3 49				4 9								
25 Harwich Park. Quay arr				3 12						4 43				4 43	4 34							
25 „ Town „				3 18						4 49				4 49								
Manningtree dep				2 51				3 13		3 51				4 9								
Bentley								3 19						4 15							5 6	
Ipswich arr				3 3				3 27		4 3				4 23		4 43			5 5		5 14	
Ipswich dep	2 55			3 7				3 35	3 55	4 7						4 46	4 55				5 30	
Claydon								3 42									5 3				5 37	
Needham	3 6							3 48													5 43	
Stowmarket	3 12			3 22				3 54	4 11	4 22							5 14				5 49	
Haughley	3 17							3 58	4 15								5 18				5 53	
Finningham								4 5													6 1	
Mellis								4 11													6 8	
Diss				3 38				4 17		4 38											6 14	
Burston								4 22													6 18	
Tivetshall								4 27													6 24	
Forncett								4 33													6 29	
Flordon								4 37													6 34	
Norwich (Thorpe) arr				4 0				4 50		5 0						5 30					6 46	
42 Cromer (Beach) arr				5† 3				6† 1		6† 1						6 44					8†18	
42 Sheringham „				5†15				6†16		6†16						7 5					8†50	
Ipswich C dep					3 15						4 15								5 8			5 29
Westerfield																						
Woodbridge					3 30						4 30								5 24			5 44
Wickham Market																						5 53
Saxmundham					3 46						4 46								5 41			6 2
Darsham																						6 9
Halesworth B					4 0						5 0								5 54			6 17
Brampton (Suffolk)																						
Beccles arr					4 13						5 13								6 6			6 31
Beccles dep		3 25			4 13						5 13								6 11 / 6 15	6 30		6 32
Oulton Broad South		3 34			4 23						5 23								6 27	6 39		
Lowestoft (Central) arr		3 39			4 27						5 27								6 32	6 44		
Lowestoft (Central) dep		3 45	3 58		4 31	4 58					5 30	5 58								6 46		
Lowestoft (North)			4 2		4 34	5 2						6 2										
Corton			4 6		4 38	5 6						6 6										
Hopton-on-Sea			4 10		4 42	5 10						6 10										
Gorleston Links Halt			4 13		4 45	5 13						6 13										
Gorleston-on-Sea		3 57	4 16		4 48	5 16					5 42	6 16								6 59		
Yarmouth (South Tn.) arr		4 3	4 22		4 54	5 24					5 48	6 22				6Z24			6 28	7 5		6 55
Notes	To Bury St. Edmunds and Cambridge (Table 30)			RC Liverpool Street to Norwich			CLACTON INTERVAL SERVICE RB Liverpool Street to Clacton-on-Sea TC to Walton-on-Naze	Through Train from Cambridge (Table 22)	To Bury St. Edmunds and Cambridge (Table 30)	RC Liverpool Street to Norwich			CLACTON INTERVAL SERVICE RB Liverpool Street to Clacton-on-Sea TC to Walton-on-Naze		Except Mondays; THE SCANDINAVIAN Buffet Car; Conveys only passengers holding tickets to the Continent	THE BROADSMAN TC Liverpool Street to Sheringham; RC Liverpool Street to Cromer	To Bury St. Edmunds (Table 30)	CLACTON INTERVAL SERVICE RB Liverpool Street to Clacton-on-Sea TC to Walton-on-Naze	RB Liverpool Street to Yarmouth; 6 11 Via Haddiscoe (Table 3a)		From Harwich Town dep 4 36 pm (Table 25)	Via Haddiscoe (Table 3a)

D Diesel Train

† Second class only

A Departure times for stations beyond Chelmsford. For complete service between Liverpool Street, intermediate stations and Chelmsford, see Table 13

B Station for Southwold

C For other trains between Ipswich and Westerfield, see Table 27

F Clacton-on-Sea and Holland-on-Sea

H Change at Chelmsford. Second class only

RB Buffet Car

RC Restaurant Car

TC Through Carriages

Z Yarmouth (Vauxhall) via Norwich (Thorpe) (Table 43)

For COMPLETE SERVICE and intermediate stations between Beccles and Yarmouth (South Town) via Haddiscoe see Table 3a

Table 3—*continued*

LONDON (Liverpool Street), COLCHESTER, CLACTON-ON-SEA, HARWICH, IPSWICH, NORWICH, BECCLES, LOWESTOFT and YARMOUTH

MONDAYS TO FRIDAYS—*continued*

	pm D	pm	pm D	pm	pm D	pm	pm	pm D	pm	pm D	pm	pm	pm D	pm D	pm D	pm	pm D	pm	pm	pm D	pm D
	From Cambridge dep 3 1 pm (Table 22)	Through Train Colchester to Peterborough (North) arr 9 7 pm, York arr 12 9 am, Edinburgh (W.) arr 4 43 am and Glasgow (Queen St.) arr 5 56 am (Tables 30, 35 and 1)		RB Liverpool Street to Norwich		CLACTON INTERVAL SERVICE RB Liverpool Street to Clacton-on-Sea TC to Walton-on-Naze	RB Liverpool Street to Clacton-on-Sea TC to Walton-on-Naze		THE ESSEX COAST EXPRESS RB Liverpool Street to Clacton-on-Sea		RC Liverpool Street to Norwich	To Bury St. Edmunds and Cambridge (Table 30)				CLACTON INTERVAL SERVICE RB Liverpool Street to Clacton-on-Sea TC to Walton-on-Naze		Through Train Liverpool Street to Harwich Town	THE EAST ANGLIAN RC Liverpool Street to Norwich	From Harwich Town dep 7 15 pm (Table 25) To Bury St. Edmunds and Cambridge (Table 30)	
LONDON (Liverpool St.) dep				4 30		4 36	4 58		5 27		5 30					5 40		5 45	6 30		
Shenfield & Hutton A „				4G44		5 4					5G42							6 18			
Chelmsford „				5 8		5 18	5 36	5 41			6 8					6 18	6 25	6 36			
Hatfield Peverel								5 49									6 33				
Witham				5 21			5 49	5 55								6 30	6 39	6 50			
Kelvedon								6 1									6 45				
Mark's Tey	4 52						6 1										6 52	7 3			
Colchester arr	4 59			5 36		5 41	6 9	6 14	6 23							6 45	6 59	7 12			
24 Walton-on-Naze arr	6 0					6 27	6 52		7 0							7 27	7 45				
24 Clacton-on-Sea F „	5 51					6 17	6 42		6 53							7 17	7 38				
Colchester dep		5 15		5 38				6 15									7 0	7 14			
Ardleigh		5 24						6 22									7 7				
Manningtree arr		5 31		5 49				6 28									7 13	7 27			
25 Harwich Park. Quay arr		6 0		6 22				6 49									7 44	7 44			
25 „ Town „		6 6		6 28				6 56									7 59	7 59			
Manningtree dep		5 33		5 51				6 28									7 13				
Bentley																	7 19			7 45	
Ipswich arr		5 49		6 3				6 41			6 48						7 27		7 43	7 53	
Ipswich dep		6 0		6 8							6 51	6 55	7 0						7 46	7 55	8 0
Claydon													7 7								
Needham												7 6	7 13								
Stowmarket		6d22		6 28							7 6	7 12	7 19							8 11	8 16
Haughley												7 17	7 23								
Finningham													7 30								
Mellis													7 36								
Diss				6 45							7 23		7 42								8 34
Burston													7 47								
Tivetshall													7 52								8 43
Forncett													7 58								
Flordon													8 2								
Norwich (Thorpe) arr				7 7							7 46		8 15						8 30		9 2
42 Cromer (Beach) arr				8†18							8†38										10†10
42 Sheringham „											8†50										10†22
Ipswich C dep					6 15									7 15							
Westerfield																					
Woodbridge					6 30									7 30							
Wickham Market					6 39																
Saxmundham					6 48									7 46							
Darsham					6 55																
Halesworth B					7 3									8 0							
Brampton (Suffolk)																					
Beccles arr					7 16									8 13							
Beccles dep					7 16									8 13							
Oulton Broad South					7 26									8 23							
Lowestoft (Central) arr					7 30									8 27							
Lowestoft (Central) dep			6 58		7 33					7 58				8 30	8 58						
Lowestoft (North)			7 2							8 2					9 2						
Corton			7 6							8 6					9 6						
Hopton-on-Sea			7 10							8 10					9 10						
Gorleston Links Halt			7 13							8 13					9 13						
Gorleston-on-Sea			7 16		7 45					8 16				8 42	9 16						
Yarmouth (South Tn.) arr			7 22		7 51					8 22	8Z37			8 48	9 22						

D Diesel Train

† Second class only
‡ Arrival time
A Departure times for stations beyond Chelmsford. For complete service between Liverpool Street, intermediate stations and Chelmsford, see Table 13

B Station for Southwold
C For other trains between Ipswich and Westerfield, see Table 27
d Arr 4 minutes *earlier*
F Clacton-on-Sea and Holland-on-Sea
G Change at Chelmsford

RB Buffet Car
RC Restaurant Car
TC Through Carriages
Z Yarmouth (Vauxhall) via Norwich (Thorpe) (Table 43)

For COMPLETE SERVICE and intermediate stations between Beccles and Yarmouth (South Town) via Haddiscoe see Table 3a

Table 3—*continued*

LONDON (Liverpool Street), COLCHESTER, CLACTON-ON-SEA, HARWICH, IPSWICH, NORWICH, BECCLES, LOWESTOFT and YARMOUTH

MONDAYS TO FRIDAYS—*continued*

	pm	pm	pm D	pm D	pm D	pm	pm	pm	pm D	pm D	pm	pm	pm	pm D	pm	pm	pm	pm D	pm	am	pm
	CLACTON INTERVAL SERVICE RB Liverpool Street to Clacton-on-Sea TC to Walton-on-Naze	RB Liverpool Street to Yarmouth; 9 11 from Beccles Via Haddiscoe (Table 3a)	Via Haddiscoe (Table 3a)	To Bury St. Edmunds (Table 30)		From Sudbury (Table 22)		RC Liverpool Street to Norwich			CLACTON INTERVAL SERVICE RB Liverpool Street to Clacton-on-Sea TC to Walton-on-Naze	THE HOOK CONTINENTAL Restaurant Car; Conveys only passengers holding tickets to the Continent	RC Liverpool Street to Norwich	Through Train from Cambridge dep 7 38 pm (Table 22)	To Bury St. Edmunds (Table 30)	Fridays only; also runs on Wednesdays 15th July to 26th August inclusive. CONTINENTAL SERVICE Restaurant Car; Conveys only passengers holding tickets to the Continent	CLACTON INTERVAL SERVICE TC Liverpool Street to Walton-on-Naze		To Bury St. Edmunds, Ely, March and Peterborough (Tables 30 and 35)		
LONDON (Liverpool St.) dep	6 33	6 38					6 45	7 30			7 33	8 0	8 30			8 45	9 33		10 40		1150
Shenfield & Hutton A „	6H37							7H44			8 2		8G47				10 2		10G44		11H42
Chelmsford „	7 11	7 16					7 35	8 8			8 16		9 8				1016		11 22		1233
Hatfield Peverel							7 45										1026				
Witham		7 28					7 52	8 21			8 29		9 21				1033				1248
Kelvedon							8 0										1041				
Mark's Tey						7 41	8 8							9 35			1049				
Colchester arr	7 34	7 43				7 54	8 17	8 36			8 44		9 36	9 42			1058		11 45		1 5
24 Walton-on-Naze arr	8 16	9 4				9 4					9 26		10 26	11 4			1146				
24 Clacton-on-Sea F „	8 7	8 59				8 59					9 17		10 21	1059			1137				
Colchester dep		7 45					8 19	8 38					9 38					11 5	11 52		1 7
Ardleigh							8 28											1112			
Manningtree arr							8 35	8 49					9 49					1118			
25 Harwich Park. Quay arr								9 13				9 25	10 11			1015					
25 „ Town „								9 19					10 17								
Manningtree dep							8 36	8 51					9 51					1118			
Bentley							8 44											1124			
Ipswich arr		8 5					8 54	9 3					10 3					1132	12 13		1 30
Ipswich dep				8 45				9 7					10 7		1012				12 23		
Claydon				8 52																	
Needham				8 58											1024						
Stowmarket				9 4				9 22					10 22		1030				12 45		
Haughley				9 8											1034				1L 1	1 32	
Finningham								9 33													
Mellis																					
Diss								9 47					10 38							1 54	
Burston																					
Tivetshall								9 57													
Forncett																					
Flordon																					
Norwich (Thorpe) arr								1014					11 0							2 20	
42 Cromer (Beach) arr																				7†21	
42 Sheringham „																				7†56	
Ipswich C dep		8 8	8 15							9 15											
Westerfield			8 21																		
Woodbridge		8 24	8 32							9 30											
Wickham Market			8 40							9 39											
Saxmundham		8 41	8 49							9 48											
Darsham			8 57							9 55											
Halesworth B		8 54	9 5							10 3											
Brampton (Suffolk)			9 12							1010											
Beccles arr		9 6	9 19							1017											
Beccles dep		9 11 / 9 16	9 20		9 30					1018											
Oulton Broad South		9 27			9 39					1027											
Lowestoft (Central) arr		9 32			9 44					1032			11K49							6K43	
Lowestoft (Central) dep					9 46				1015	1035											
Lowestoft (North)					9 51				1019												
Corton					9 54				1023												
Hopton-on-Sea					9 59				1027												
Gorleston Links Halt					10 2				1030												
Gorleston-on-Sea					10 5				1033	1047											
Yarmouth (South Tn.) arr		9 28	9 43		1011				1039	1053										4Z 7	

D Diesel Train

† Second class only
A Departure times for stations beyond Chelmsford. For complete service between Liverpool Street, intermediate stations and Chelmsford, see Table 13

B Station for Southwold
C For other trains between Ipswich and Westerfield, see Table 27
F Clacton-on-Sea and Holland-on-Sea
G Change at Chelmsford

H Change at Chelmsford. Second class only
K Via Norwich (Thorpe)
L Arr Haughley 12 51 am
RB Buffet Car
RC Restaurant Car
TC Through Carriages
Z Yarmouth (Vauxhall) via Norwich (Thorpe) (Table 43)

For COMPLETE SERVICE and intermediate stations between Beccles and Yarmouth (South Town) via Haddiscoe see Table 3a

Table 3a

BECCLES, HADDISCOE and YARMOUTH (South Town)

MONDAYS TO FRIDAYS

Miles		am	am	am B	am B	am B	am G	am A	am B	am	pm A	pm B	pm	pm A	pm B	pm	pm A	pm B
—	3 Liverpool Street dep	..	..	4 35	..	..	6 54	9 38	9 38	1030	1238	1238	1 30	3 38	3 38	4 30	6 38	..
—	3 Ipswich "	....	....	6 53	7 40	8 40	9 46	11 8	1115	1215	2 8	2 15	3 15	5 8	5 29	6 15	8 8	8 15
		D	D		D	D			D	D		D	D		D	D		D
—	**Beccles** dep	6 55	8 14	8 25	8 45	9 45	1056	1211	1220	1 50	3 11	3 20	4 50	6 11	6 32	7 50	9 11	9 20
3¼	Aldeby	7 1	8 20	8 31	8 51	9 51	....	....	1226	1 56	....	3 26	4 56	....	6 38	7 56	....	....
5½	**Haddiscoe** arr	7 5	8 24	8 36	8 55	9 55	..	..	1230	2 0	..	3 30	5 0	..	6 42	8 0	..	..
21¾	43 Norwich (Thorpe) arr	7 53	....	....	9 45	11 4	....	....	1 45	2 36	....	4 36	5 56	....	7 43	8 34	....	....
—	**Haddiscoe** dep	7 5	8 24	8 36	8 55	9 55	..	..	1230	2 0	..	3 30	5 0	..	6 42	8 0	..	..
6	St. Olaves	7 7	8 26	8 38	8 57	9 57	....	....	1232	2 2	....	3 32	5 2	....	6 44	8 2	....	....
8½	Belton and Burgh	7 12	8 31	8 43	9 2	10 2	..	..	1237	2 7	..	3 37	5 7	..	6 49	8 7	..	..
12½	**Yarmouth** (South Tn.) arr	7 18	8 37	8 50	9 8	10 8	1114	1228	1243	2 13	3 28	3 43	5 13	6 28	6 55	8 13	9 28	9 43
15	3 Gorleston-on-Sea arr	7 36	..	9 6	9 36	1036	1136	..	1 6	2 36	..	4 6	5 36	..	7 7	8 36	..	..

SATURDAYS ONLY

	am	am B	am B	am B	am B	am B	am B	pm B	pm B	pm B	pm B	pm B	pm B
3 Liverpool Street dep	..	4 35	..	..	7 50	9 58	10K38	1N30	3 38	4 39	5 30	6 38	7 30
3 Ipswich "	....	6 53	7 38	8 38	9 38	11 38	12 34	3 38	5 38	6 15	7 15	8 15	9 15
Beccles dep	7 5	8 25	8 52	9 48	10 52	12 48	1 51	4 52	6 52	7 29	8 18	9 32	1026
Aldeby	7 11	8 31	8 58	9 54	10 58	12 54	1 57	4 58	6 58	7 35	8 24	9 38	....
Haddiscoe arr	7 16	8 36	9 3	9 59	11 3	12 59	2 2	5 3	7 3	7 40	8 29	9 43	..
43 Norwich (Thorpe) arr	7 53	....	9 50	11 5	11 42	1 50	2 45	5 56	7 43	8 34	9 46	1036	....
Haddiscoe dep	7 16	8 36	9 3	9 59	11 3	12 59	2 2	5 3	7 3	7 40	8 29	9 43	..
St. Olaves	7 18	8 38	9 5	10 1	11 5	1 1	2 4	5 5	7 5	7 42	8 31	9 45	....
Belton and Burgh	7 23	8 43	9 10	10 6	11 10	1 6	2 9	5 10	7 10	7 47	8 36	9 50	..
Yarmouth (South Tn.) arr	7 30	8 50	9 17	10 13	11 17	1 13	2 16	5 17	7 17	7 54	8 43	9 57	1043
3 Gorleston-on-Sea arr	8 26	..	9 27	10 27	11 26	1 27	2 26	5 51	7 36	8 36	9 36	1052	..

SUNDAYS

	am B (Commences 28th June)	am A (Runs 28th June to 6th Sept.)	am A	pm A (Runs 28th June to 6th Sept.)	pm A	pm B	pm B
3 Liverpool Street dep	6‡15	10 3	1033	12 8	5 35	..	7 0
3 Ipswich "	9 25	1152	1238	1 50	7 18	7 50	9 7
Beccles dep	1045	1257	2 1	2 46	8 23	9 10	1018
Aldeby	1052		2 8		....	9 17	....
Haddiscoe arr	..		..		..	..	..
43 Norwich (Thorpe) arr	....		....		....	....	....
Haddiscoe dep	..		..		..	..	..
St. Olaves	1057		2 14		....	9 23	....
Belton and Burgh	11 3		2 19		..	9 28	..
Yarmouth (South Tn.) arr	1110	1 17	2 26	3 6	8 40	9 35	1039
3 Gorleston-on-Sea arr	..	..	2 36	3 36	..	9 47	..

MONDAYS TO FRIDAYS

Miles		am	am C	am	am C	am H	am C	am H	pm	pm C	pm H	pm	pm	pm H	pm H	pm J	pm	pm C
—	3 Gorleston-on-Sea dep	..	..	7 16	7 35	8 16	1042	..	1257	1 42	..	3 57	5 16	5 42	6 16	..	6 59	7 45
		D	D	D	D		D		D	D		D	D				D	D
—	**Yarmouth** (South Tn.) dep	6 25	6 50	7 25	8 20	8 35	1120	1135	1 20	2 20	2 35	4 20	5 45	6 2	6 39	6 55	7 20	8 20
4	Belton and Burgh	6 31	..	7 31	8 26	..	1126	..	1 26	2 26	..	4 26	5 51	..	..	..	7 26	8 26
6½	St. Olaves	6 36	6 59	7 36	8 31	....	1131	....	1 31	2 31	....	4 31	5 56	....	....	....	7 31	8 31
7	**Haddiscoe** arr	6 38	..	7 39	8 33	..	1133	..	1 33	2 33	..	4 33	5 58	..	..	..	7 33	8 33
—	43 Norwich (Thorpe) dep	6 0	....	7 15	....	....	1015	....	1215	1 15	....	3 15	5 15	....	....	....	6 15	7 15
—	**Haddiscoe** dep	6 38	..	7 42	8 33	..	1133	..	1 33	2 33	..	4 33	5 58	..	..	..	7 33	8 33
9¼	Aldeby	6 42	....	....	8 37	....	1137	....	1 37	2 37	....	4 37	6 2	....	....	....	7 37	8 37
12½	**Beccles** arr	6 49	7 9	7 49	8 44	8 52	1144	1152	1 44	2 44	2 52	4 44	6 9	6 19	6 57	7 13	7 44	8 44
53	3 Ipswich arr	....	8 17	8 56	9 50	9 57	1250	1257	....	3 50	3 57	6 43	7 22	7 22	8 16	8 29	....	9 50
121¾	3 Liverpool Street "	..	9 59	1029	1128	1128	2 28	2 28	..	5 31	5 31	..	8 53	8 53	1016	..	..	12a1

SATURDAYS ONLY

	am	am C	am C	am C	pm C	pm C	pm C	pm C	pm C	pm C	pm C
3 Gorleston-on-Sea dep	..	..	7 35	9 16	1216	2 54	3 42	4 16	6 15	7 16	8 16
		D	D								
Yarmouth (South Tn.) dep	6 25	6 50	8 15	9 45	1245	3 3	3 58	4 58	6 50	8 3	9 5
Belton and Burgh	6 32	..	8 21	9 52	1252	3 10	4 5	5 5	6 57	8 10	9 12
St. Olaves	6 36	6 59	8 26	9 56	1256	3 14	4 9	5 9	7 1	8 14	9 16
Haddiscoe arr	6 37	..	8 28	9 59	1259	3 17	4 12	5 12	7 4	8 17	9 19
43 Norwich (Thorpe) dep	6 0	....	7 15	9 15	1215	2 5	3 8	4 25	6 15	7 15	8 15
Haddiscoe dep	6 39	..	8 28	9 59	1259	3 17	4 12	5 12	7 4	8 17	9 19
Aldeby	6 43	....	8 32	10 3	1 3	3 21	4 16	5 16	7 8	8 21	9 23
Beccles arr	6 50	7 9	8 39	1010	1 10	3 28	4 23	5 23	7 15	8 28	9 30
3 Ipswich arr	....	8 17	9 45	1119	2 19	4 45	5 42	6 40	8 34	9 43	1040
3 Liverpool Street "	..	9 59	1129	1F 6	3 58	6 28	7 24	8 45	..	12 1	..

SUNDAYS

	am H (Commences 2nd August)	am H (Not after 26th July)	pm H (Commences 28th June)	pm H	pm H (Runs 28th June to 6th Sept.)	pm C	pm H	pm C	pm C	pm C (Runs 28th June to 6th Sept.)
3 Gorleston-on-Sea dep	..	..	..	2 16	..	5 16	6 16	..	7 16	..
Yarmouth (South Tn.) dep	9 21	10 7	2 22	3 15	5 0	5 34	6 26	6 40	7 26	9 22
Belton and Burgh	..	..		3 25		5 42	..	..	7 34	
St. Olaves	9 32	1018		3 30		5 47	....	....	7 39	
Haddiscoe arr	..	..		..		..	..	..	..	
43 Norwich (Thorpe) dep	....	....		....		....	....	....	....	
Haddiscoe dep	..	..		..		..	..	..	..	
Aldeby	9 37	1023		3 3[illegible]		5 52	....	....	7 45	
Beccles arr	9 43	1029	2 40	3 4[illegible]	5 18	5 58	6 46	6 58	7 52	9 40
3 Ipswich arr	11 8	1150	3 55	5 [illegible]	6 16	7 18	8 0	8 8	9 18	1054
3 Liverpool Street "	1 4	1 57	5 37	6 47	7 53	9 11	9 36	1025	1157	..

D Diesel Train

‡ Second class only between Liverpool Street and Shenfield

A Through Train Liverpool Street to Yarmouth (South Town)

a am

B Through Train Ipswich to Yarmouth (South Town)

C Through Train Yarmouth (South Town) to Ipswich

F On 20th June, 5th and 12th September arr Liverpool Street 1 20 pm

G Through Train from Colchester dep 9 10 am

H Through Train Yarmouth (South Town) to Liverpool Street

J Through Train to Colchester arr 9 6 pm

K Until 29th August dep Liverpool Street 11 0 am

N Until 5th September dep Liverpool Street 1 38 pm

Table 28

SAXMUNDHAM and ALDEBURGH

(Diesel Trains)

Week Days

Miles		am	am C	am E	am S	pm S	pm E	pm E	pm S	pm E	pm S	pm E	pm E	pm S	pm E	pm S
—	3 London (L'pool St) dep	4 35	8 30	9 38	9 38	12 38	12 38	1 30	1T38	3 38	3 38	4 30	5 30	5 30	6 38	6 38
—	**Saxmundham** dep	7 48	10 54	11 54	1157	2 49	2 54	4 6	4 20	5 50	6 20	6 56	7 54	8 0	8 54	9 13
4	Leiston	7 57	11 3	12 3	12 6	2 58	3 3	4 15	4 29	5 59	6 29	7 5	8 3	8 9	9 3	9 22
6¼	Thorpeness	8 1	11 8	12 8	1210	3 3	3 8	4 19	4 34	6 3	6 33	....	8 8	8 13	9 8	9 26
8¼	**Aldeburgh** arr	8 7	11 13	12 13	1216	3 8	3 13	4 25	4 39	6 9	6 39	7 13	8 13	8 19	9 13	9 32

Sundays

	am C	am	am	am	pm C	pm	pm
3 London (L'pool St) dep	6†15	..	10H 8	10 33	3 30	..	5 35
Saxmundham dep	9 22	10 30	12 32	1 30	6 18	7 40	8 48
Leiston	9 31	10 39	12 41	1 39	6 27	7 49	8 57
Thorpeness	9 35	10 43	12 45	1 43	6 31	7 53	9 1
Aldeburgh arr	9 41	10 49	12 51	1 49	6 37	7 59	9 7

Week Days

Miles		am	am C	am	pm C	pm E	pm S	pm E	pm S	pm	pm S	pm E	pm E	pm S	pm C E	pm C S
—	**Aldeburgh** dep	7 10	8 23	11 18	12 23	3 23	3 25	5 0	5 40	6 23	7 10	7 17	8 23	8 30	9 18	9 41
2	Thorpeness	7 14	8 27	11 22	12 27	3 27	3 29	5 4	5 44	6 27	7 14	....	8 27	8 34	9 22	9 46
4¼	Leiston	7 20	8 33	11 28	12 33	3 33	3 35	5 10	5 50	6 33	7 20	7 25	8 33	8 40	9 28	9 52
8¼	**Saxmundham** arr	7 29	8 42	11 37	12 42	3 42	3 44	5 19	5 59	6 42	7 29	7 34	8 42	8 49	9 37	10 0
99¼	3 London (L'pool St) arr	9 59	10 45	2 28	3B20	6 24	6 28	..	8 45	8 53	1015	1016	12 1	12 1	3 46	..

Sundays

	am	am	pm	pm C	pm	pm	pm C
Aldeburgh dep	9 57	11 56	12 56	2 22	6 58	8 6	9 12
Thorpeness	10 2	12 1	1 1	2 27	7 3	8 11	9 17
Leiston	10 8	12 7	1 7	2 33	7 9	8 17	9 23
Saxmundham arr	10 16	12 15	1 15	2 41	7 17	8 25	9 31
3 London (L'pool St) arr	12L48	..	..	5 20	9 36	11 57	3a56

Tickets from Aldeburgh and Thorpeness are issued on the train

† Second class only between Liverpool Street and Shenfield

a am

B On Saturdays arr Liverpool Street 3 4 pm

C Through Train from or to Ipswich (Table 3)

E or **E** Except Saturdays

H Runs 28th June to 6th September incl.

L Until 26th July arr 1 4 pm

S Saturdays only

T On 12th September dep Liverpool Street 1 30 pm

Pages 212-215:

Final BR Eastern Region 15 June to 13 September 1959 public timetable for Beccles–Yarmouth via Haddiscoe, plus complete times for the remainder of the line including the Aldeburgh branch. Note that the timetable continued in force until November because of a printers' strike.

After this the bulk of the service was passenger trains. The next goods working was the 10.55am from Ipswich, calling at Westerfield and Bealings as required, then all stations to Snape Junction and Snape. It left there at 2.50pm, and went on to Saxmundham, finally reached at 3.25pm. It returned at 4.40pm from there, and had to wait for an hour at Wickham Market while the 3.55pm and 4.3pm expresses from Yarmouth and Lowestoft respectively passed, and then the 4.3pm from Yarmouth which could convey loaded horse boxes, carriage trucks and 'foreign' trucks, loaded or empty, these being the days before common usage of wagons had been introduced. The 'Snape goods' finally reached Ipswich, after clearing Bealings and calling at Westerfield to attach perishable traffic, at 6.45pm.

At 12.40pm Beccles despatched a goods train to Lowestoft via Haddiscoe, although it went to Norwich instead on Saturdays. The 11.25am from Norwich called at Haddiscoe, and then went via Marsh Junction to South Town, calling at St Olaves and Belton if required. On Beccles market day, Friday, an express cattle special left for Haddiscoe at 6.20pm, arriving via Fleet Junction at 6.40pm. They had to return with a special goods via Marsh Junction and Swing Bridge Junction. With the exception of the 12.55am Class A from Ipswich, noted above, there were no down goods trains on Sundays.

Down goods workings took place largely at night, and by far the majority had already reached their destinations by the time the passenger services started for the day. It was not as clear cut in the other direction. Yarmouth despatched a goods train for Beccles at 1am on weekdays except Mondays, which called at Belton and St Olaves if required. Apart from the Tuesdays-only express cattle from Framlingham and Darsham, the next working was the 9.30am up goods from Beccles to Ipswich, calling only at Halesworth, and Wickham Market on Saturdays for cattle, arriving at 11.55am. The Aldeburgh goods returned from Saxmundham at 12.57pm, and the 10.5am from Wensum Junction via Fleet Junction reached Beccles at 12.25pm. The 4.23pm from South Town was an important train for London traffic, being intended mainly for meat and perishables, and called at all stations except Westerfield to Ipswich. All trucks at Saxmundham had to be taken up in one shunt, and detaching was generally not allowed, unless cattle were involved. Coal empties could not be conveyed on this train, which reached Spitalfields at 1.40am. The 5.20pm from South Town reached Norwich via Marsh Junction, calling at Belton and St Olaves as required. The 4.35pm from Lowestoft called at Carlton Colville and Barnby, and called at all stations to Ipswich to attach important traffic. At 8.15pm the up fish left Lowestoft, calling only at Beccles and Halesworth — the latter to attach fish for London that had arrived via the Southwold Railway — and then ran fast to Ipswich, and on to Spitalfields via Goodmayes, arriving at 2.30am. It ran rather later on Saturdays, and as a Class B instead of the usual Class A. The Yarmouth fish followed, leaving there at 8.40pm, but transferring its fish to the Lowestoft train at Beccles if loadings permitted, and then calling at Halesworth, Saxmundham, Wickham Market and Woodbridge to load mail. On Saturdays it carried cattle from Norwich, which had arrived via Fleet Junction and Beccles, and set them down at stations along the East Suffolk, as required.

There was little goods on Sundays, the only important workings being the 9pm mail from Yarmouth, which was attached at Beccles to the 8.30pm from Lowestoft. This then attached any Southwold fish at Halesworth, as well as loading mail, and also called at Saxmundham, Wickham Market and Woodbridge on its way to Ipswich.

The demands of traffic changed over the years, and so goods train working had to adapt. Much was seasonal, obvious examples being the landings of fish or the harvesting of sugar beet. On weekdays in 1937 the pattern was still much the same as before. In the down direction the 8.50pm from Temple Mills to Lowestoft reached Ipswich at 1.3am and left at 1.40am. This train did not run from London on Mondays, but started from Ipswich at the same time, and then called at Saxmundham, Halesworth and Beccles. The 11.5pm from Spitalfields carried brake goods, also ran to Lowestoft, and was allowed 20-25min for delay at Witham if it had to be shunted for excursion trains to pass. This train also did not run on Mondays, when it was replaced by the 10.55pm from Temple Mills.

The Aldeburgh goods now left Ipswich at 4.45am and called everywhere except Bealings, reaching Saxmundham at 7.32am. It shunted there, not leaving until 9.10am, and reached Leiston at 9.22am, also spending much time there shunting: there was much exchange traffic with Garrett's works. It finally left at 10.56am, reaching Aldeburgh at 11.15am and calling at Thorpeness if required. The trip was booked for working by a dual-braked engine on Saturdays. It left the terminus at 12.15pm, following the 12.2pm passenger, again spending time shunting at Leiston while the 12.38pm passenger from Saxmundham called at 12.47pm. Saxmundham was reached at 1.35pm; more time was spent shunting there, with departure at 2.40pm. Calls were made as required at Snape Junction, Melton and Bealings, and certainly at Wickham Market and Woodbridge, before Ipswich was reached at 4.50pm (5.15pm on Saturdays). The branch had another goods working, this time conditional, at 8.10pm from Aldeburgh, calling at all stations, returning from Saxmundham at 9pm. The 5.14pm passenger from Aldeburgh reached Leiston at 5.24pm and became mixed, reaching Saxmundham at 5.39pm.

Back on the main line the 6.10am from Ipswich connected with the 11.50pm from Temple Mills and made its first call at Saxmundham, then Darsham and Beccles before running to Haddiscoe via Fleet Junction. It then continued to South Town, calling at St Olaves and Belton & Burgh as required. A light engine left Lowestoft at 8.5am and ran to Darsham, due at 9am. It shunted there and picked up any traffic, and went back to Halesworth, where it shunted the yard, including milk tanks for the dairy. This lasted nearly three hours, after which it left for Brampton at 1pm and shunted as needed, leaving at 1.50pm for Beccles and Lowestoft, calling at Barnby and Oulton Broad South if required. On Saturdays in summer (from 6 June) the 10.28am parcels train from Ipswich called at all stations except Westerfield for Yarmouth South Town, a journey of 130min. The 8.20am from Wensum Junction — rather later than in previous years — reached Beccles via Fleet Junction at 11.35am, having already called at Haddiscoe and Aldeby. It retraced its steps at 12.35pm, calling again at Aldeby, where it had to be shunted to let the 12 noon express from Ipswich pass, which had left Beccles at 1.4pm. Having spent another hour at Haddiscoe it was propelled back to Fleet Junction and set off for Yarmouth, due 3pm, calling at St Olaves and Belton as required. On Fridays — market day — Beccles despatched a goods train to Norwich Thorpe at 5.20pm, and that was about it for down workings.

In the up direction some of the trains have already been mentioned. As before, there was little goods activity, although the 'Snape goods' ran much as before, due off the junction at 2.35pm and back from Snape at 3.5pm. It had to wait until 4.10pm to leave Snape Junction again, and shunted everywhere except Westerfield on its way back to Ipswich. A parcels train left Yarmouth at 3.40pm, calling at most stations

Left:
No D5045 pulls off the Framlingham branch on 12 April 1965. The lineside remains in pristine condition even though final closure is only a week away. Note that the signal arms are at right angles to each other because of the sharp curvature of the branch. *H. N. James*

BRITISH TRANSPORT COMMISSION
BRITISH RAILWAYS
USE BLOCK LETTERS
B.R. 21223
From..19....

SPECIAL VEHICLE URGENTLY REQUIRED

TO..
....
....
Via...Section
....

THIS WAGON MUST NOT BE DELAYED

Wagon	Letter	Number

Consignee..

except St Olaves, Haddiscoe and Westerfield, and running to Liverpool Street. This traffic was passenger rated. The 3.50pm Lowestoft to Goodmayes (Spitalfields on Saturdays) called at all stations including Barnby to Melton, reaching Ipswich at 8.48pm. Yarmouth despatched a goods train to Norwich via Fleet Junction at 7.5pm (7.15pm Fridays only). The 8.20pm Lowestoft to Spitalfields called only at Beccles and Halesworth on its way to Ipswich, which it passed at 10.25pm (11.5pm Saturdays). The 8.20pm from South Town to Spitalfields, which terminated at Ipswich on Saturdays, also called at Saxmundham.

On the Framlingham branch much of the goods traffic was carried on mixed trains. The 7.56am and 9.40am (9.6am Tuesdays-only) from Wickham Market, and the 7.18am (7.14am Tuesday-only) and 4.23pm from Framlingham were so designated, although there was also a goods working from the terminus at 1.55pm, reaching Wickham Market at 2.32pm after calling at Parham and Marlesford as required, and returning at 2.45pm, being booked to call at Marlesford on its way back. Beccles was at one end of the Waveney Valley line, although in the 1937 timetable there were no booked goods workings through onto the East Suffolk. Later it became the practice for them to go to and from Lowestoft. Between Beccles and Lowestoft there were many through trains, but also the workings to and from South Side, plus the Anglo-American Oil Company's siding to be served which was officially at Oulton Broad North, at the junction with the East Suffolk. The 10.7am from Darsham was booked to do this last. The 9.30am from Central was due at South Side at 9.55am, having shunted at Oulton Broad South, but ran earlier on Saturdays. It returned from South Side at 3pm on Saturdays, or 4.35pm Mondays to Fridays, and conveyed important traffic from the Co-op factory for despatch via the 5.25pm from Lowestoft to Norwich. Passengers from Beccles travelling home by the 5.2pm on Fridays might well be accompanied by cattle from the market: this train was allowed to attached fitted wagons for this purpose, as was the 7.47pm on Wednesdays.

By the mid-1950s goods traffic was looking altogether thinner, although the pattern of services remained much the same. In summer 1956 the 11.25pm from Goodmayes stopped at Ipswich at 1.31am to change crews and take water, and then ran nonstop to Beccles and Lowestoft. The 12.25am from Goodmayes called at Ipswich Goods yard before running nonstop to Halesworth (where it spent nearly 50min), Beccles and South Town. The 1.45am from Goodmayes ran only from 26 June to 17 August, called at Ipswich for crew change, then Darsham and overtook the 12.25am at Halesworth, going on to call at Beccles and Yarmouth. None of these trains ran on Mondays, and the last not Saturdays either.

The 9.10am Class K goods from South Side reached Lowestoft Central at 9.41am. The 5am Class H goods from Ipswich called at Saxmundham and all stations to South Town, except St Olaves and Belton & Burgh. It took rather longer to reach its final destination on Saturdays since it frequently had to be shunted to let passenger trains pass. The Aldeburgh goods had become a bonus turn and left Ipswich at 7.10am, shunting everywhere as required, except Westerfield. The Snape bonus was a law unto itself, and ran without the benefit of booked timings. A light engine was despatched from Ipswich MPD at about 8am to run to Wickham Market, where it worked the 9.30am goods to Framlingham, arriving at 10.15am. A conditional path was provided at 10.50am for a train as far as Parham and back, which begs the questions of why it was needed and how often it was used in practice. The goods returned at 11.50am (11.55am Saturdays), after which the locomotive returned light to Ipswich. Traffic could be picked up either by the Snape or Aldeburgh bonus trips, both of which had 'as required' calls at Wickham Market.

By summer 1956 closure of parts of the East Suffolk was not far away, although the dramatic falls in railway goods traffic were not yet fully apparent: road improvements and the relentless rise of road haulage had not yet got into its stride. All parts of the East Suffolk were still open for traffic, even if there was very little in some cases. The next decade was to prove traumatic.

— 13 —
What About the Workers?

IT is all very well to look at the train services, the track layouts and the station buildings, but there would have been no railway without the men and women who worked on it. There were the glamorous jobs such as driving the engines, although there were many who pointed out that the public did not see the unsocial hours and the grime of the steam locomotive depot. Other front-line staff worked in the booking offices, booked parcels and luggage in advance, delivered the same, worked as guards and conductors, or — with a certain aura of mystery — retreated into their signalboxes and did strange things with bells and crashing levers. Occasionally they emerged to open the level crossing gates! Many, many more unsung workers maintained the track, signalling and the telegraph. Unseen armies of fitters kept the locomotive fleet in working order, or did the preparation work or washed out boilers. The general public often complained about the service and then flocked to it when weather conditions closed the roads, expecting the railways to carry on as normal, which they usually did.

There were important motive power depots at Ipswich, Yarmouth and Lowestoft, with sub-sheds on the branches at Aldeburgh and Framlingham. Beccles had its own shed and allocation of locomotives before World War 2. Ipswich was easily the largest and most important shed, and covered a very large amount of work on the Norwich and Yarmouth main lines, as well as the various branches, and had responsibility for covering absences, rest days and so on at its sub-sheds. Lowestoft crews worked over the East Suffolk and Norwich lines, and ranged far afield with goods work in particular. On the Great Eastern section Yarmouth shed was not differentiated between Vauxhall and South Town, and crews there worked the lines served by both stations. Most of what follows here concerns the situation after World War 2, when the East Suffolk was intact, enjoying the postwar passenger boom at least on the main lines, and still largely steam operated.

In the early 1950s there was occasionally some confusion about who was in charge in the locality. The shedmaster at Yarmouth was W. A. (Bill) Hardy and at Norwich D. W. (Bill) Harvey, so with Richard (Dick) Hardy at Ipswich the confusion was greatly compounded! The shedmaster at Lowestoft was George Leverick.

Anyone joining the railway needed a reference. Aspiring footplatemen then had to see the shedmaster and fill in the application form and then took a medical and eyesight test, probably in Norwich. Newly recruited cleaners at Yarmouth straight after World War 2 started on a weekly wage of £2 10s 0d. It was very, very cold in January 1946, and at South Town shed there was a gas-lit run-down carriage used as a mess hut, which also contained a square cast-iron stove which could be used for keeping bottles of tea warm, and which gave out heat for the hut. The lid of the tea bottle had to be loosened, otherwise the extra heat would burst it. The railway was always full of practical jokers, and sometimes a smart alec would screw the caps hard down, so if anyone saw a bottle of tea going a funny colour they knew it would explode and got out of the way very quickly. New cleaners signed on at 8am, and the foreman allocated engines by number. There was usually only one cleaning gang with six or seven members, and within the gang there were two on the boiler, two tender and two wheels. The youngest recruit (and seventh member) got the motion to clean. If the weather was frosty he was given a square tin split in two, one half with paraffin (for cleaning) and the other engine oil (to stop rusting). A scraper was supplied for the removal of thick grease. If it was very cold the oil would not flow, so a half-gallon can was put over a fire to make it run.

Juniors were given the donkey (the steam-driven air compressor which worked the Westinghouse brake and other equipment) to clean, which was very oily and needed scraping. If an engine was being cleaned for a special job the senior boy would be given a lump of wax which was then used to make a pattern on the tender. This could not be seen straight on, but had to be viewed at an angle. All staff were issued with a new clean cloth every day on an exchange system. The new cloths were used to wash hands and face when about to go home, and the old ones were then paraffin-washed, returned to the depot and used to wipe the engines dry. It was possible for a gang to clean six engines in one day, although if there was a motive power shortage they had very little time on shed and had to be cleaned very quickly.

An essential job, mostly unremarked, was that of call-boy, which paid an extra 10s or £1 for working nights — well worth having on top of a cleaner's basic wage. At South Town he signed on at 10pm, and took half an hour later in his shift as a meal break. One of the jobs was to go on all the engines and get gauge lamps and oil bottles, often by looking through tool boxes, take them to the stores and make sure they were filled with paraffin, engine oil, gauge lamp oil etc, ready for the next shift. The donkey required 3 pints of black oil; ½gal of engine oil and ¼ pint of paraffin were also needed. Gauge lamps did not use paraffin because they would have caught fire, so rape oil was used instead. The call-boy also checked that there was an in-date, sealed tin of detonators on each engine, which were vital for train protection, especially in foggy weather.

Another job was to do a set of tubes — 100-150 per locomotive. These had to be rodded through so that they were clear, as did the superheater tubes at the top of the smokebox, of which there were usually about 30. Rodding tubes was a very dirty job which got the call-boy covered in soot and dust. This would take him up to about midnight — meal time — and then he would be off to see the foreman to find out which drivers needed calling, usually eight or 10 of them. Each man had to be called an hour before he was due on, and they might be all over town — one out at the Pleasure Beach, the next at Newtown and so on. The first might have to be called 10min early and the next 10min late, and although the railway had an official bike for the call-boy, it was not worth using. One driver had a garden that was 20ft long, and all that was needed was to shine the torch at his window and waggle it about, and he woke up. For others it was necessary to knock gently at first, and then harder and harder. Sometimes the call-boy would be stopped by police after midnight but he would simply holler 'railway' and keep going. In wartime each railwayman had an oval badge with 'LNER' plus an engine

Left:
Inside the goods office at Halesworth, where the clerk, Stanley Goodard is at work. There is a wealth of detail here from a time when all records were on paper, before the dawn of the computer era.
Peter Punchard collection

on the front, and his own check number on the back. This was his identification if stopped by the police, but he also carried a national identity card.

Passed cleaners at Yarmouth started their day at 6am by lighting the shedmaster's fire. He had a guard's brake stove, and the office was a sweatbox by 8am if he was on duty. If soft coal was used it lit easily, gave out lots of heat and cracked the asbestos stove pipe! If a coal man was sick then the boys had to help coal locomotives from trucks. Two more loaded ashes from the pit, thus keeping it clear.

Ipswich, as with large sheds everywhere, used a 'link' structure for its footplate staff, so that someone joining the railway started as a cleaner, and gradually gained knowledge and experience, first becoming a passed cleaner and being allowed to fire engines, working up to become a fireman. As they gained experience and route knowledge, firemen moved up through various links, each succeeding level requiring greater skill and bearing greater responsibility, until eventually the big day came to pass out as a driver. A passed fireman could drive when the need arose, but would probably continue firing until he had accumulated enough driving turns, when he started in the lowest of the driving links. The Great Eastern and its successors had been unusual in that drivers with the greatest experience and in the most senior link were not doing express passenger work. Instead they finished in the 'Old Man's Gang', a singular GER practice, which included the Snape bonus. This link paired very young firemen with the most experienced drivers and gave them a great chance to learn railway work. They did not just fire — they participated unofficially in all the train working. After the shed closed at Framlingham it also became a bonus trip in the Old Man's Gang. Other links tended to be associated with particular types of work, and therefore with the locomotives used. The progression for drivers at Ipswich was, with the most junior first: Shed Relief, Shunting, Goods, Spare, 'Bl2', 'B1', No 2 Passenger, No 2 Goods; while for fireman it was: No 2 Goods, No 2 Passenger, No 1 Goods, Spare, 'B12', 'B1' until passed for driving.

The goods link covered the 5.25am to Yarmouth, which was very, very slow, and was worked by the worst passenger engine at Ipswich. In the early 1950s this was Class B17 No 61647, recently transferred from Woodford Halse. This was a large link with 30 or so men who worked everywhere, and covered all the main line working to Lowestoft and Yarmouth, plus the Aldeburgh bonus. The Lowestoft fish came through Ipswich at about 5.40pm, with Lowestoft men working through to Spitalfields, and had once been a lodging turn at Stratford. Driver Freeman, often known as 'Bluebeard', had a reputation as a mad devil and drove Class K3 No 61959, whilst Driver Johnson had No 61958. Various fast goods ran at night, usually with Class J39s or remanned London engines. The Aldeburgh goods bonus working ran with a Class J17, either No 65560 or No 65510. The Snape bonus ran thus: 11.40am on duty, 12.40pm ex-yard. It then called at Woodbridge and Wickham Market before running to Saxmundham for water, where it also ran round. It went back to Snape Junction, propelled down the branch, hauled back up to the junction and back along the main line to Woodbridge, where it made up a full train and went hell-for-leather back to Ipswich. The Snape bonus gave quite a short day of five hours or so, and was better paid if the crew returned early.

At Yarmouth the tramways on the quay were worked by the Old Man's Gang, which also covered pilot and ballast work. There were two chain-driven Sentinels for this work, and timekeeping on the quay was not really important. The lines went right down as far as the fish wharf, but were gradually cut back over the years. Much coal was taken in for the fishing fleet, and the tramway went right into Vauxhall. In summer there were lots of coal trucks on the quay, and holidaymakers would duck underneath them whilst crossing the road, so shunters were always on the lookout for them, and moved the trains gently, although occasionally a car would argue with the wagons and get dented. The Yarmouth trams were generally out from 6am to 10pm, although this might be all night in the fishing season. Much fish went into wagons ready for the 1am train, and some fish was taken by lorry to South Town and loaded onto wagons in the goods yard there. The fish was packed in barrels, salt was put into the top and the lid knocked on.

The most testing jobs were on the loose-coupled goods, either Class 3 unbraked or Class 2 partly fitted. The section of

Above:
An interesting set of photographs showing the interior of the station at Halesworth, all taken on 11 March 1962 for railway records. The first shows the booking hall looking rather tatty and in need of a coat of paint. It is still gas lit, and the booking window is closed. There is still a willingness to seek out traffic, since the blackboard advertises a return fare to Ipswich of 6s 3d on 9 March to see Ipswich Town play Sheffield Wednesday, using either the 4.49pm or 5.55pm trains from Halesworth and returning by the 9.23pm, which has been specially retimed to 9.38pm.
Peter Punchard collection

Top right:
This time it is the parcels counter inside the booking office, again with a wealth of detail including the scales, telegraph instruments, the LNER clock and the immaculate stove.
Peter Punchard collection

Lower right:
The interior of the booking office, this time showing the ticket window, ticket racks and much more. *Peter Punchard collection*

line from Melton to Wickham Market was downhill at 1 in 104, followed by the saw-tooth profile past Snape Junction. Drivers had to keep steam on through the dips, with the guard, who needed to know the road well, braking at the back so that the couplings were kept taut. The train then had to roar up the grade with the brake being taken off at just the right moment and reapplied just before the summit. It was often said that 'if you can work a freight train over the East Suffolk you can do it anywhere'.

Not all Ipswich links had work over the East Suffolk. 'B12' men covered an early train to Yarmouth, with the crew coming on duty at Ipswich at about 4.30am and returning from South Town at about 8-9am, reaching Ipswich at about 11am. The locomotive then went to the shed, this particular train not being worked by Ipswich men to Liverpool Street. The locomotive off the 7.32am to Yarmouth came back with the 11.55am from South Town to Beccles and principal stations to Liverpool Street. Generally these 'B12' turns were remanned at Liverpool Street by the opposite crew, each locomotive being allocated to two sets of men. The following week the two crews reversed.

After the arrival of the 'Britannias' Ipswich lost its Norwich work, but gained the Mondays to Fridays 'Easterling'. The crew worked up on the 7.17am semi-fast from Ipswich to Liverpool Street and then back to South Town with the 'Easterling' at 11.3am, arriving at 1.38pm. They then returned to Ipswich 'on the cushions'. In the other direction they travelled down passenger to South Town, worked the 'Easterling' up to London, and then worked back to Ipswich. The train was particularly busy when race meetings were on, and would leave Liverpool Street full. It loaded 10 coaches, of which three dropped off at Beccles for Lowestoft. 'B1s' did not do well on this train, and ran hot when they were tried. '2800s', usually Nos 2849 *Sheffield United* and 2869 *Barnsley*, were preferred. There were also two of them at South Town, Nos 2864 *Liverpool* and 2865 *Leicester City*. *Liverpool* was a rough rider, and the shedmaster had had two iron bars fitted in the cab for the crew to hold on to! On Saturdays the 'Easterling' was a Stratford job.

THE SUNDAY TIMES
1962 MARCH 1962
BRISTOL
SUMMER COMPETITIONS 1962 
EASTERN REGION
CENTRAL STORES,
E.R. PETERBOROUGH.

Most through workings to Liverpool Street were covered by Yarmouth men working right through to London. One such was the train which left Ipswich at around 9am and formed the 1.33pm down from Liverpool Street. Another express left Liverpool Street for South Town at 3.33pm, calling at Ipswich at 5.5pm. Another South Town slow left Yarmouth at 9am behind a 'Claud', but this one turned round in Ipswich station. Men off the 2.15pm from Ipswich (about 12.10pm from South Town) reached Liverpool Street at about 4.6pm and came back with the 6.33pm buffet car express to Yarmouth. The former streamliners Nos 61670 *City of London* and 61659 *East Anglian* both worked Lowestoft and Yarmouth expresses.

Whilst they were open for passengers and remained steam operated, the branches had their own sheds and footplate staff. Framlingham had a standard set-up similar to that at Aldeburgh; both were small single road sheds with a pit and coal stage for hand coaling, often done direct from a truck by an Ipswich cleaner on nights. The Framlingham branch locomotive was an 'F6', but if there was a shortage of power a 'J15' or even a 'Claud' would be sent from Ipswich. The branch train had two bogie coaches and a number of freight wagons, plus a guard's brake in the rear. Sunday excursions off the branch were re-engined at Ipswich and could be taken onwards by almost anything from a 'J15' to a 'B12'. The wooden trestle bridge at Snape limited that branch to a 'J15', an English Electric 350hp diesel shunter (which was far too slow), or the Paxman 800hp diesels which could not handle a full load up Bealings bank. This is why a 'J15' stayed on until the branch was closed, so making No 65389 the last steam engine in service shedded at Ipswich. As well as the speed induced by the promise of bonus payments, the Snape turn involved several other practices which were not in the rule book. In Snape yard any maltings box wagon or truck would be given a good hit so that when uncoupled by the shunter it would go sailing across the road and through the arch into the maltings. If the crew did not fly shunt the truck there was a horse that pulled the trucks with chains into the various tracks inside the maltings. As the aim of the crew was to be as quick as possible they did not dispose of the locomotive on arrival at Ipswich, irrespective of the hours worked. In order to maintain steam on the return trip the fireman usually cleaned the fire whilst shunting backwards and forwards over the wooden bridge that spanned the river immediately before Snape yard. This involved removing clinker by way of the pricker and long slice, and was very much against the rules as the hot clinker could get caught in the baulks of timber forming the superstructure of the bridge. It was always a relief to see and hear the hiss and cloud of steam as the clinker hit the water. In the summer there were several swimmers in the water and the crew used to shout to them to get out of the way of the hot cinders. What would the Health & Safety Executive think of this today?!

At Aldeburgh the branch started with a 1 in 58 gradient from Saxmundham Junction, but was otherwise almost level. The branch engine was an 'F6', popularly known as 'Gobblers', of which there were three at Ipswich. Nos 67220 and 67239 were good and 67230 was truly dreadful. These three rotated on the Aldeburgh branch, which used a set of three coaches, later reduced to two. Ipswich crews often had to cover turns on the line. One of these involved leaving Ipswich on a train at about 6pm or 6.30pm and travelling passenger to Saxmundham and catching the last train to Aldeburgh, sleeping there overnight. The Ipswich men were supposed to find lodgings, but used to sleep in an old hut that was used for a canteen, which was all right during the summer but was very cold and draughty in the winter. What then happened was that the engine would be coupled to the train ready for the morning and the fire brought to the back of the firebox so that it would stand overnight. It would then be spread out in the morning ready for the first train. During cold weather the steam heating would be connected to the carriages and the crew slept in the train. They would then work the Aldeburgh branch all day and get the bus back to Ipswich at night, although they were supposed to stay overnight at Aldeburgh again and then get the first train back the following day. Crews used to get a lodging allowance, which was not much, and as they were in uniform the bus conductor seldom charged the fare back into Ipswich.

Lowestoft locomotive shed was a busy depot with a variety of work. There were almost 100 staff in all, many of them passed cleaners. Daily routine started with signing on, picking up tools and oil bottles and taking them to the engine. The driver would set the engine so that the rods were

Right:
Lowestoft and Yarmouth shared the distinction of hosting a small fleet of Sentinel locomotives, used for shunting work. At Lowestoft they were often to be seen in the sleeper depot, where No 41 was photographed on 20 October 1962. *Alan Taylor collection*

Above:
Local engine Class B17 No 61670 *City of London* stands outside the shed at South Town in 1958. Still being very well cared for, this locomotive was one of two that had been streamlined before the war to work the 'East Anglian' between Norwich and Liverpool Street. *Rex Conway collection*

in the right place for oiling, which involved many parts including the big ends and all the oiling underneath. Locomotives were coaled from the tower, which was filled by two coalmen using trolleys, and if a driver did not position his locomotive exactly right under the tower, coal went everywhere! Once on the engine the coal often had to be broken up to make it a usable size.

Lowestoft men generally worked passenger trains along the East Suffolk main line only as far as Beccles, where trains were taken on by Yarmouth crews, but they did work through over the Waveney Valley line. The Lowestoft train would work into Platform 4, where the shunter would cut off the Lowestoft engine. It ran round and awaited the next down Yarmouth, and then took the Lowestoft portion, the rear three coaches, down the branch; sometimes a locomotive would work light to Beccles for this purpose. Train working was particularly difficult in fog — between Oulton Broad South and Beccles crews counted the culverts and listened for the detonators at distant signals so that they knew where they were. Through workings onto the Waveney Valley from Lowestoft arrived in the bay at Beccles (Platform 1), and then set back towards Pound Lane level crossing where the engine ran round and set its train back into the bay, and would then go and turn. The same procedure applied to both goods and passenger trains.

Goods working was another matter, and allowed Lowestoft crews to travel more widely. They worked the Goodmayes as far as Ipswich, leaving Lowestoft at around 7pm. There they would have a meal break and then pick up the return at about 2am. The down train was so long that when it pulled up in the platform to change footplate crews the brake van was still in the tunnel, and they had to pull up again to let the guards change over. Much coal was brought into Lowestoft for the fishing fleet, as well as for locomotives, but this arrived via Norwich. The only coal carried on the East Suffolk was for domestic use.

The fish trains were lodging turns. Crews worked up one day to Spitalfields, leaving Lowestoft at about 10am, lodged, then came back the next day. These trains usually ran with a 'K3' as motive power. They were assembled in Lowestoft yard with stock brought over from the fish market, and were very heavy, sometimes needing banking up from Beccles. Bird's Eye traffic from Yarmouth went out via Beccles. Milk in churns was collected at Beccles and other stations and taken to Halesworth, where it was put in tanks and sent forward in bulk. This happened even on Christmas and Boxing Days, when sugar beet was also worked from places like Haddiscoe where it had been stockpiled in readiness. The road lorries did not work over the holiday, so it had to be taken into Cantley by rail, since the factory worked continuously.

Many other staff were involved in the operation of the trains. In steam days on the Aldeburgh branch the engine had to run round at each end, so a shunter was needed at Saxmundham. Push-pulls arrived there from Yarmouth on Saturday afternoons, and when he knew that such a train was coming the shunter could go home early, although he had to stay if an 'ordinary' engine arrived. Saxmundham had a water crane to be used by branch and freight trains, the latter including the Aldeburgh, Framlingham and Snape turns. At this and other local stations such as Melton, the old staff who

Above:
LNER 2-6-0 No 4667 turns at Lowestoft locomotive depot in 1939.
Rex Conway collection

Below:
A 1911 view of Lowestoft turntable and engine shed, with coal stacks in the background. *HMRS Hilton Collection*

Above:
A photograph of just a few of the railway staff at Halesworth in 1917. There is a mixture of GER cap badge styles, and it is worth noting that there are also Southwold Railway staff in the picture.
Peter Punchard collection

helped with the shunting and station work never got any extra for it unless the guard dropped them a half crown.

Saxmundham had a porter, shunter and gate boy (on the bottom — Chantry Road — gates) on each of the three shifts. There was a foreman and two other men in the goods shed, and three lorries that delivered to the villages and Framlingham after the branch closed. One of the traffics was meal, and there were stores everywhere. The filthiest traffic of all was fish, which was carried on the stock trains, together with milk churns to Halesworth. Then there were the permanent way men. Each main station had its gang: the ganger at Saxmundham in the 1950s was a hard man with a good gang, including a lot of youngsters. They really earned their money in fog and falling snow when they would be called out by the signalman to stand by signals and place detonators on the track to give an audible warning to train crews. Their only protection then was a small 'sentry box'. Many lived in gate houses where the wife worked the gates, although her husband would be passed out to work them so that she could have an occasional day off. They were 'chained' to the crossings, but it provided a regular wage for women when this was far from usual. Most gates were normally closed to the road, although some locations with much road traffic were exceptional, including Bramfield, although this was staffed at night by another man, and also had block repeaters.

Halesworth was an important and busy station, the more so on summer Saturdays when the gatemen could not even get into their hut for a cup of tea — they sat drinking it on the platform instead! The Halesworth pilot left Lowestoft at about 4am and returned at about 3pm, and needed two or even three sets of men, always from Lowestoft, and was used for shunting the dairy traffic, although on Saturdays it would be pressed into service as a banker as far as Wissett (Old Station Road) crossing, and would then come back wrong-line, quite unofficially! This was a strictly local initiative between the driver, guard and signalman, the latter being the kingpin of the operations. The stationmaster was involved in train working only when something major happened such as a derailment, or single-line operation. There was no water crane at Halesworth, so the shunting engine had to be filled from a hose and tap in the cattle pens, which allowed the crew (this turn was in the Old Men's link) to take an hour's nap. The milk traffic had to be ready when the stock train from Yarmouth arrived: the empties came off the down train from Ipswich. Halesworth would generate 20-30 churns a day of 'special milk' such as Jersey, which probably went to Yarmouth in the holiday season. There was always milk at Halesworth for making the tea! The loss of the steam engine had a major unforeseen consequence: there was no coal anywhere. There had always been (unofficially) a barrowload for each signalbox, crossing, waiting room and so on, and suddenly it had to be bought in.

On the LNER in 1947 at Halesworth the lad porter — a new recruit — had many duties, including helping with the level crossing gates. The first job of the day — always a lousy one — was cleaning out the toilets, including the ladies'. Other duties included meeting trains from Ipswich and London, and unloading the many parcels from each onto a four-wheeled barrow which was taken up to the brake van for this purpose. The porter would shut the train doors and help passengers with luggage, looking all the time for a 'weasel', or tip. In the late 1940s and early 1950s the Southwold bus left from the station, and there were also the taxis, with holidaymakers possibly good for two bob! Another job which had to be done was sweeping out the stationmaster's office at night. This gave a chance to read his correspondence, which he left out on his desk, and also allowed station staff to work out when they could take holidays to best suit themselves. He and all senior staff were called 'Mister', at least to their face, and the staff were always most polite when presenting him with a fait accompli about their leave!

Livestock provided an interesting diversion, as well as some very hard work and not infrequently some overtime which might or might not be welcome. Saxmundham and Halesworth handled racing pigeons which were sent there for release. Station staff entered the time on the crates and they were then despatched back to the starting station such as Beccles or Lowestoft. Cattle could cause some very bad jobs, especially if they got down, when it was difficult to get them up again. One way of doing this was to twist their tails. An occurrence like this could make up to five hours' extra work. If a full truck reached a station with, say, 10 beasts in it and one down, staff could only get at the stricken animal if the others were unloaded, usually at the cattle dock. These had water troughs, and naturally the animals would drink. After finishing the task of getting the fallen animal up, the others had to be got back in the truck; however, drinking made them expand, so where 10 came out only eight would fit back in! This extra time could be a nuisance during the day, but the overtime might be welcomed at night when a finish at 6am was little different from one at 3am.

Floods and Other Catastrophes

Much of East Anglia is low lying and has been affected by flooding at one time or another, often with devastating effects on local people and the train services. One of the worst episodes occurred at the end of August 1912, although Yarmouth seems to have escaped relatively lightly on this occasion. Even so, trains were stopped for a while. Torrential rain occurred on Bank Holiday Monday, 26 August, and the month had already been noticeably wet. The line from Yarmouth to Norwich was closed for four days west of Brundall, and the East Suffolk main line between Melton and Wickham Market was closed briefly by a collapsed culvert. On this occasion trains were worked to either side of the break and passengers and luggage transferred between them! The East Suffolk was also closed between Beccles and South Town, with Beccles Corporation marshes being entirely flooded. The area between Beccles and Oulton Broad was described as a big lake, and the coastal route between Lowestoft and Yarmouth was closed. The Lowestoft branch of the East Suffolk was reopened by 30 August, although the track was still flooded to a depth of 2ft in places and trains were proceeding at caution. The main line to South Town was still closed and all traffic to Yarmouth was still being sent this way. Norwich to Brundall had at last reopened, and it was hoped that the 5.42pm from Beccles would be the first train to reach South Town. The East Suffolk was described as 'running to time' by the *East Anglian Daily Times*, although it also noted that no trains were more than 40min late and praised the Great Eastern for its efforts. Beccles was very badly flooded and the local harvest was devastated, with orchards and fruit gardens particularly hit.

In 1938 an exceptionally high tide on 12 February wreaked serious damage at Lowestoft harbour and many other places along the east coast. About two miles of the East Suffolk were submerged by the River Deben between Woodbridge and Ufford, and the line was blocked for about an hour. The flood subsided after the tide turned, and trains were then let through under caution.

Much more serious were the 1953 floods, when a deep depression combined with strong onshore winds breached sea defences right along the coast, over 300 people being drowned in the subsequent inundation. On the night of 31 January floodwater breached the banks of Oulton Broad, flooding Lowestoft station and other parts of the railway to a depth of 3ft. A few minutes later the south wall of Breydon Water burst, inundating Yarmouth South Town station, where the water rose a foot above platform height, and the locomotive depot. An hour later the north wall burst and it was Vauxhall station's turn to be flooded. Inland water surging up the tidal rivers burst through and flooded the East Suffolk at Belton and Aldeby, and the Lowestoft–Norwich line at Haddiscoe. Before the full extent of the flooding

Right:
The floods of August Bank Holiday 1912 devastated much of East Anglia, not least the East Suffolk line. The water is relatively shallow in this postcard view of the gate house at North Cove.
Alan Taylor collection

Left:
The floods of August 1912 caused a culvert to collapse at Ufford, north of Melton, so that trains had to be worked to either side of it and passengers and luggage transferred across the gap. In this photograph repairs are in progress.
Alan Taylor collection

became apparent at least one train between Beccles and Yarmouth managed to make its way into Beach station via Breydon bridge. Further south the Snape branch was flooded, and the Deben once again breached the railway between Woodbridge and Melton. Great havoc was caused elsewhere. Although some of the damage was relatively slight, much was not, and it took months for the railway to be fully restored. Ironically at the time the water struck, South Town station was in the middle of extensive renovation. The concourse had been rather a gloomy place, being at one end of the train shed. This had a high roof with smoke vents along the ridge, and continued over the tracks far enough to shelter about two coach lengths. Its wooden façade had become grimy over the years. The platforms themselves had awnings supported on sturdy posts and wholly made of timber. The rebuilding replaced the train shed with a modern concrete and steel structure much truncated in length, with glass replacing the timber front, so that much more light was let in. The platform awnings were also replaced with concrete and glass structures, also giving much better light, and the platforms themselves were rebuilt in modern materials. The main building, however, was substantially unaltered.

Rain was not the only weather hazard to hit the railway. Extreme cold and snow caused their own problems, and one notable occasion came in 1929. On Tuesday 12 February there were bitingly cold easterly winds of 25-30mph, and slight snow. Linen was frozen before it could be pegged out, and milk froze in churns. The following night was the coldest in Yarmouth for 45 years, and on the Thursday in Ipswich the maximum temperature was 26°F (-3°C), with a minimum of 18°F (-8°C). Barges were iced in at Woodbridge, and temperatures of 20°F (-7°C) allowed skating on Oulton Broad. The northwest corner of Lowestoft's Hamilton Dock iced over, which was very rare. By the following Monday (18 February) there were four inches of ice on Oulton Broad, and games of football were played on it. By the following Saturday it was all over, with temperatures now 21°F (12°C) higher than a week ago. One consequence for the railway was that the Leclanché cells, which used a strong salt solution as an electrolyte and were used to power the telegraph circuits, froze — the only time it was known to have happened.

Intense frosts began on Thursday 23 January 1947 and continued almost unbroken through February and March. East Anglia was the first area of the country to be affected by heavy snow during 25 and 26 January, and the branch lines were kept open only by ploughing, with yards unworkable. Further heavy snow fell on 2 and 3 February, with more on 9 February. Strong winds caused it to drift onto lines that had been cleared, and some branches were badly affected. Passenger train services were reduced, the Cabinet having given absolute priority to coal traffic from 14/15 January. Despite the cuts passenger loads were low, so there was no overcrowding. The railways were still suffering from the general lack of maintenance because of the war, shortages of wagons through arrears of repairs and the poor quality of coal which was affecting the steaming of locomotives.

There had, of course, been other man-made problems with which the East Suffolk and other railways had to cope. One was the various episodes of industrial action that took place, the best known being the General Strike of 1926. There was increasing unrest in the early years of the 20th century, leading to the first national strike on the railways in 1911. This was a result of low wages and rising inflation, whereupon the Government declared martial law. The 1912 Railways Act permitted the companies to raise rates to pay for wage increases, although many, such as the Great Eastern, felt it unwise to do so, and found cost savings through greater co-operation between the companies and better use of resources. Railwaymen had still not achieved an 8hr day when war broke out in 1914.

Unrest continued after the war, since inflation had roared ahead and wages had not. Action early in 1924 gave a foretaste of things to come, and the Eastern Counties Farmers' Co-operative Association advertised that its feedstuffs, manure and so on were not dearer because of the recent rail strike. Road haulage, it said, was as cheap as rail, and that by making arrangements before the strikes they had large supplies available at trade prices. Industrial unrest continued, and by the very end of March 1926 coal miners were coming out on strike, every colliery in the country being idle by Monday 3 May. The TUC directed all its members to strike from the following Tuesday in support of the miners, and the National Union of Railwaymen told the LNER that its members would leave work after their shifts on Monday. The strike started on Tuesday 4 May. At Lowestoft 5,000 tons of coal were in stock, and although the 8pm fish to London had been expected to run on Monday evening the traffic was sent by sea if possible, or road. Newspapers were unable to publish because of the strike, and the next issue of the *East Anglian Daily Times* appeared a week later on Tuesday 11 May. Train services were extremely sparse despite the use of volunteers, and almost the only service on the East Suffolk appeared to be the 11.10am Yarmouth to Ipswich. On Wednesday 12 May the *East Anglian Daily Times* reported that 'the one need throughout the railway system of the country is signalmen, and these are being trained as quickly as possible and despatched to those parts of the country where their services are specially needed. The railway companies are absolutely inundated with offers of help and the thousands of volunteers are found work as quickly as circumstances permit.' The paper did not report whether there had been any volunteers to help mine coal. The Southwold Railway and the Aldeburgh branch had reopened, as had Derby Road and Westerfield stations where the stationmasters had been on strike. They had been replaced.

By Thursday 13 May another 1,000 LNER strikers had gone back to work and emergency timetables continued in operation. There had been no track inspection since the action started, but many railwaymen were still on strike. The Framlingham branch still had no service. On Saturday 15 May it was announced that the railway dispute had been settled, although only a strike service was possible on that day. Normal service was resumed as far as possible on the following Monday, with about 30% fewer trains on the main line and a 50% cut on the branches. A limited number of excursions were to be run for the Whitsun holiday on the following weekend, and inter-company ticket availability was kept in force for the time being. One such train was the 8.30am from Ipswich to South Town, offering return fares of 6s 8d from Ipswich down to 2s 8d from Halesworth, and returning at 7.15pm. The railways refused to take many of their men back because the miners were still on strike and there was less traffic. Coal rationing was in force, with households being allowed a maximum of 1cwt per fortnight and factories and offices half their normal amount.

World War 2 was another cataclysmic event for the railways, although the East Suffolk escaped relatively unscathed, except for Halesworth, which was bombed on 18 June 1941. Several buildings were damaged at Lowestoft on 13 June in the same year, with Belton also hit by incendiary bombs which burned out the lamp room. Lowestoft had been badly hit earlier in the year, on 7 February, when bombs damaged many buildings in the harbour area including the district engineer's harbour works office, joiners' shop and blacksmiths' shop. Eight railwaymen and one customs officer were killed, and 34 injured. South Town station was closed on 8 July by bomb damage, which included the signalbox being wrecked. On 19 February 1942 Lowestoft Yard signalbox was damaged in an explosion, and the instruments affected. The signalman was treated in hospital for shock. On 7 May 1943 there was much enemy action in Great Yarmouth, and South Town station and six coaches were slightly damaged by a blast bomb. Lowestoft was hit five days later, and machine gun fire damaged telephone wires. On 13 May the trawl market roof and office were badly damaged. Four unexploded anti-personnel bombs were found on the line between Leiston and Aldeburgh at about 9.30am on 4 October, causing the service to be replaced by buses until it reopened at 4pm. On 3 November Westerfield was hit by high-explosive bombs causing four large craters to block both lines for two days. The following day several unexploded incendiary bombs were found on the line between there and East Suffolk Junction, but traffic was not disrupted. Much of the damage on the line was to the overhead wires of the signal and telegraph, and this occurred in many places.

The Punchard Family

There were hundreds of railway people involved with the East Suffolk at any one time, and some of the obvious jobs have been mentioned already. There are far too many to mention individually, even if their names were all known. Many had fleeting connections: they may not have worked for long on the railway, or they may not have had many firing turns over the line, or never even have visited it, yet helped to build or repair rolling stock. All of them played an important part, often unseen and almost always unsung. Just as importantly, the people who worked on the railway were an integral part of their local communities. When first built, the railway had lifted the wages of those in previously agricultural areas, and gave ordinary men and women the opportunity to travel for the first time. They could enjoy undreamt-of luxuries for the first time, and the prices of basic commodities such as coal fell. The railway was a big employer, and the work was relatively steady even when the economy was in the grip of recession. There were certain people in any town or village who were viewed as pillars of the community: the vicar, the headmaster at the local school, and the stationmaster. Among this band of railwaymen and women were some families whose roots were deeply grown into the East Suffolk, and who were part of it for generations. One such were the Punchards of Halesworth.

The railway history of the Punchard family started with William, born at Halesworth in 1837. In 1872 he changed jobs from agricultural labourer to platelayer on the Great Eastern, living in the gate house at North Green, Kelsale, with his wife Sarah who was the gatekeeper. She died of hypertrophy of the heart on 25 May 1895, age 56, having borne many children. William Punchard's obituary in the GER magazine noted that he 'died in September last (1922) having retired on the pension fund in 1906 after 34 years service'. He was widely known and respected in the Darsham area.

The eighth child of William and Sarah, who had 11 children in total, was Isaac Robert Punchard, born on 13 February 1874 at North Green crossing. The family continued to live at North Green, as did all the children at some time in their lives. Isaac later moved to Halesworth, and entered railway service on 29 June 1891 aged 17 years four months, having been recommended by Rev C. R. Rayner of Middleton. His first job was gate lad at Rendham Road, Saxmundham, at a weekly wage of 8s, increased to 10s on 18 July 1892. On 25 June 1894 he was promoted to probationary gateman and night shunter at Saxmundham at a wage of 12s, being further promoted to gateman and shunter on 23 July 1894 at a wage of 14s, moving up to being a porter (still a shunter as well) on 21 December 1896 (wage 15s). He then transferred to Ipswich on 12 March 1900 as a probationary pointsman and signalman (17s), finally being appointed as signalman at Ipswich No 2 Goods Yard box on 25 March 1901 at 19s. He stayed there until 1907, when he transferred to Halesworth signalbox on 21 April at a wage of 21s. He stayed there for the rest of his working life, his highest weekly wage rate (71s 6d) being during January, February and March 1921. It then fell steadily, being 58s 6d from 1 January 1922 when it became a Class 5 job, reaching a low of 52s from July of that year. The wages shown here cannot be directly compared with present-day levels, and the hours were much longer. It was generally a steady job,

Above:
William and Sarah Punchard outside their home at North Green crossing, Kelsale. She died in 1895, and they had 11 children in all. He was a platelayer on the Great Eastern, and she was the crossing keeper. *Peter Punchard collection*

Left:
Isaac Punchard was one of William and Sarah's sons, and served on the railway all his working life. He was a keen gardener and is seen here in his garden at home in Halesworth.
Peter Punchard collection

although staff had to be prepared to move wherever the railway sent them, often at short notice. When the economy of the country went down, so did wages and conditions.

Isaac Punchard was a staunch Methodist, a superintendent and teacher at Sunday school, and often composed sermons whilst on duty during his 40-year service in signalboxes. As with so many railwaymen he was also a keen gardener. He married Emma Annie Podd at Saxmundham on 31 August 1896, and retired in 1939 having completed 48 years of service, of which 40 were as a signalman. The Halesworth stationmaster, Mr H. W. Holland, presented him with an easy chair which had been subscribed for by all the staff at the station, and commended his 'faithful and long service to the railway company'. He had a keen interest in the railway and was held in great esteem by his fellow workers. Testimonies were also given by Mr Jas Kidby (signalman), Mr Coleman (chief goods clerk) and Mr J. Hembling JP (motor driver), and a letter of appreciation from the superintendent of the line was read out. Isaac Punchard died aged 77 on 21 February 1951, and in his obituary it was noted that when there was a danger 31 years ago of the church being closed, he kept the cause going. His recent illness had been borne with fortitude and faith, and he was a 'fine Christian gentleman'.

Above:
Jack Punchard was one of Isaac Punchard's sons, and carried on the railway tradition.
Here he is on the steps of the family home.
Peter Punchard collection

Isaac was one of a large family, and several of his brothers also had railway connections. James William was born on 6 June 1868, and entered railway service on 8 October 1883, aged 15, on the recommendation of Rev Daines of Kelsale Rectory. He started as a gate lad at Saxmundham in October 1883 on weekly wage of 10s, progressing three years later to the post of porter at Norwich Thorpe, earning an extra 12s per week. In 1886 he went to Thorpe-le-Soken as a porter, where he met his future wife, Mary Anne Rowland, and they were married on 7 November 1889 in the parish church there. Mary wore a green dress and was then aged 22, while he was described as a 'railway servant age 21'. In March 1913 he went on to become foreman-porter at Ipswich, and was at Manningtree for three years and Harwich for 13 before moving back to Ipswich. He died aged 49 on 11 April 1917. The *Ipswich Evening Star* for Monday 14 April 1917 reported that upwards of 50 members of the GER Ipswich District uniformed staff formed a cortège from his residence in Ranelagh Road to the cemetery, which was followed by a glass carriage and four mourning coaches.

Another of Isaac's elder brothers was Henry Thomas, born on 4 December 1869, who entered railway service on 7 February 1887 as gate lad at Middleton Crossing, which then came under nearby Darsham. Two years later he moved to Saxmundham, where he lost his right foot in an accident. In 1891, aged 21, he was recorded as being a points signalman at Wenhaston GER. He moved to Welnetham, between Long Melford and Bury St Edmunds, in 1895 as a probationary signalman. Another brother, Herbert Punchard, eventually emigrated to South Africa to work on the Transvaal & Orange River Colony Railway, while younger brother Arthur did not start railway service until September 1894.

Jack Eric Punchard was born at Halesworth on 20 June 1906, and was Isaac's only son. His railway career started on 18 July 1921 at Halesworth, although he had to serve a probationary period until 16 November 1923 before being appointed to a permanent job. Throughout his working life he kept a small notebook in which he carefully recorded the money he made each year, although not all of the entries now make sense. In 1924, when he was a horse lad at Halesworth station, his wages amounted to £72 8s 6d, supplemented by tips of £11 6s 5d. Being older, his wages rose considerably the next year and his income then totalled £105 5s 9d. In July 1926 he transferred to Felixstowe Beach as a porter, followed by Lowestoft North and Ipswich. Wages were again higher, although it is worth noting that a small element of this — £2 11s 6d — came from strike pay.

In 1927 he moved on to carriage cleaning at Ipswich, also working there as a parcels porter, and he noted an income of £2 11s 4d from 'cups', the meaning of which remains unclear, but which appears in several subsequent years. Perhaps they were tips left by restaurant car customers? In this year Jack had time off through illness, and duly recorded sickness benefit of £2 11s 6d, presumably from the GER Benevolent Fund.

In 1929 he moved back to Halesworth and in both this and the following year benefited from tips for loading sugar beet, and received a Christmas box. Once one of his jobs was to take two shunting horses out along the Southwold Railway's track to pull a failed train into Halesworth. In 1931 the Depression struck at millions of working people, and Jack Punchard was fortunate to retain a job on the railway. For the next five years he worked at Leicester, Wembley, Northolt Park, Harrow and finally Culworth before moving back to East Anglia. On 11 November 1936 he started work at Pulham St Mary on the Waveney Valley line, as a porter-signalman. At long last, in 1949, he returned to Halesworth, starting on 1 March as a signalman at an annual wage of £357 11s 7d. This gradually crept upwards so that he cleared £505 in 1954, although this attracted income tax of £28 14s 0d. During this time an 8hr shift as signalman would often be supplemented by a further four hours on the platform on lower grade duties such as portering, giving welcome extra income and the chance of earning tips.

Jack Punchard was a pillar of his local community, being a Methodist church trustee, society steward, leader of the junior church and lay preacher. Many sermons were composed during the quieter moments in Halesworth signalbox. He died in Ipswich hospital at the tragically early age of 49 on 19 October 1955 after nine months' illness, and his funeral was attended by railway colleagues from along the East Suffolk line. They included the Halesworth stationmaster Mr A. H. Flunder and station staff R. Banham, C. Balls, H. Baker, F. G. Masters, H. Grant, L. Taylor, A. E. Duncan, J. E. Kiddy, C. Coleman and J. Evans. A. D. Pratt came from Brampton, H. Havers from Saxmundham and J. Baugham from Darsham.

Jack's son Peter Punchard joined British Railways as a lad porter at Brampton in 1954, so becoming the fourth generation of the family to work on the East Suffolk. There was a Christmas box for station staff from the farmers, usually 5s or a brace of pheasants, for letting them use the dock for loading beet, which saved them having to throw it up into the trucks. Another job for the lad porter on Saturday afternoon was to scrub the booking office floor on his hands and knees. At Brampton the booking office, waiting room and stationmaster's office were all in one.

Russell Garrod was a Lowestoft goods guard for many years, and later went on the Paytrains as a conductor-guard. At Brampton he taught Peter Punchard how to use a shunting pole, and, more importantly, how to use his head: stand and think where the full and empty trucks were going, and plan out the moves before starting shunting. The lad porters duties included labelling the trucks, most of which contained beet and went to Cantley via Lowestoft.

Before very long Peter Punchard moved to Halesworth, still as lad porter. His duties included the crossing gates, which were always difficult. If there was a 30–45min gap in the service all four gates would be swung across the track, and a pre-warning allowed two to be swung early in readiness for a train. If an express was due the wicket gates were not pulled in, but a porter would stand in each gap to block the way. A train from Darsham had 3min before arrival time at the gates, and the porters' hut was warned by a big bell, rung from the signalbox by the signalman. A fast from Brampton gave one minute's warning. In summer the lad porter (Peter Punchard because he was the smallest) crawled into the gates on Fridays and oiled them, so that they were easier to push on Saturday.

Peter Punchard moved to Saxmundham Junction as signalman in 1961. Normally a new recruit to this grade had to go to signalling school at Ilford, but his father had been on the railway and Peter was keen. He had about a fortnight with the existing signalman, and then the district S&T inspector, Bob Spencer from Ipswich, came down and saw him work the box for several hours. He also asked questions about the rules and procedures. The next day Peter had to go to his office in Ipswich and spend the day on rules and regulations, and was duly passed out. His wage at this time was about £7 5s 0d per week, as it was a Class 4 box.

In due course Peter Punchard moved back to Halesworth, where he was still living, to take up the duties of signalman there, following in the footsteps of his father and grandfather. There he remained until 1986, watching the goods traffic disappear and the passenger service diminish, until the line was modernised and rationalised. He worked in the box until it closed at 08.00 on 16 February 1986, and in due course bought and moved it, on 11 May the same year, the short distance up the road to the local middle school, where it is now a museum. He continued working on the East Suffolk, now based at Saxmundham, as part of a mobile team (the other half was Monty Baskett) looking after the stations on the line. Even then their work could be very varied. A new yard was being laid down at Sizewell siding for the nuclear construction traffic in connection with Sizewell B power station. Trains were taken down in the morning, and could load up to a thousand tons of cement, fly ash and later steel. Peter Punchard and Monty Baskett conducted the construction trains along the branch, sometimes two per day. Nuclear flasks continued to travel on Thursdays, with as many as three at any one time. Both men were qualified to drive the crane at Sizewell siding, and both worked on the branch on flask days. Peter Punchard later joined Railtrack, and is now retired, bringing to an end the family's remarkable connection with the East Suffolk, spanning almost its entire existence.

Above:
Peter Punchard is the fourth generation of the family to follow in the railway tradition, and is seen here in 1954, at the start of his railway career, in the garden of the family home in Halesworth. *Peter Punchard collection*

Below:
The lad porter — a youthful Peter Punchard — pulls in the gate on the up side. This was done last so that pedestrians could cross until the last moment before a train arrived. Sometimes the staff simply stood in the way rather than pull them in.
Peter Punchard collection

— 14 —
East Suffolk
Survival and Renaissance

At its greatest extent the East Suffolk comprised a main line of just over 52 miles between East Suffolk Junction and Yarmouth South Town, plus the branches to Framlingham (6¾ miles), Snape (just under 1½ miles), Aldeburgh (8 miles) and Lowestoft (about 7 miles to Oulton Broad North Junction), plus the South Side branches, amounting to around 80 miles or so. The main line was double track, as was the Lowestoft line. In the immediate postwar period the LNER had proposed improvements at Lowestoft, involving the provision of a new goods shed and offices, and an altered layout for the yard at a cost of £31,500. At Ipswich there was a £90,000 scheme to lengthen the platforms, together with another to reconstruct the goods shed and provide an extension for the goods offices. The total cost of this was estimated at £258,000, of which £120,000 was for remodelling the goods shed at the Lower Yard, provision of a double-track bridge over the river and new sidings. Naturally the LNER expected the Government to fund much of this via compensation for the damage caused by the war but in the event little of these plans was actually implemented. Apart from the work at Lowestoft no first-priority schemes were planned for the East Suffolk, and today the line is partly singled and open only as a branch between Ipswich and Lowestoft, with the section as far as Sizewell siding surviving for the occasional flask traffic for the nuclear power station.

The first casualties on the line were Melton and Bealings stations. Melton closed to passenger traffic on and from Monday 2 May 1955, meaning that the last train called on Sunday 1 May. Bramford, on the main line between Ipswich and Stowmarket, closed at the same time, and the *East Anglian Daily Times* compared their demise. It noted that Bramford Parish Council was actively seeking to reopen its station and was contesting the British Transport Commission's revenue figures. It said that 'railway stations at Bramford and Melton stations closed yesterday, Bramford under strong local protest, Melton without any voice being heard'. The irony is that Melton did reopen in 1984, whilst there is no trace of Bramford station. Melton remained open for general goods traffic until 1 June 1972, and even then the yard continued to handle coal traffic and occasional loads of stone. The coal survived until 1984, and the yard was lifted at the same time the line was finally singled and Radio Electronic Token Block (RETB) introduced in February 1986.

Most trains did not call at Bealings, which was another early closure to passengers, on and from Monday 17 September 1956, although goods traffic survived until April 1965. Unlike Melton it did not reopen, although the buildings remain largely intact and in good condition. The signalbox survived to control the level crossing, and was not abolished until it was converted to the locally-monitored open type (AOCL — Automatic Open Crossing Locally-monitored) on 31 March 1984, being demolished the following month.

The Framlingham branch was the next casualty. Its passenger service was infrequent and inconvenient: there were only four trains each way Mondays to Saturdays in the final timetable, and although connections at Wickham Market were generally quite good, it was a long way round for local people getting to Saxmundham or Ipswich. The buses were cheaper and certainly more frequent. The Eastern Region of British Railways had a policy of cutting out loss making branch lines, and Framlingham was one of a number, including the Waveney Valley line and Mid-Suffolk, to lose their services at this time. The axe fell on

Right:
The new era dawns at Bealings as the signalbox is dismantled on 7 April 1984. The new AOCL crossing is in operation. It was later replaced by an ABCL type with half-barriers. *Russell Whipps*

IPSWICH TO FELIXSTOWE, ALDEBURGH, LOWESTOFT AND YARMOUTH

DOWN

M. C.	M. C.	M. C.	Station		No.	A	C	C	B	B	B	B	B	B	B	B	B
Mileage						News	ECS	Diesel ECS		Rail Motor	Rail Motor		Rail Motor	Rail Motor			Diesel
											SX	SO					
						am	am	am	am	am	am	am	am	am	am	am	am
0 0	0 0		**IPSWICH**	arr	1												
				dep	2	4 30		6†10							6 53		
3 42	3 42		Westerfield	arr	3												
				dep	4	4 36		6 15							6 59		
	6 7		Derby Road	arr	5												
				dep	6												
	9 23		Orwell	arr	7												
				dep	8												
	14 15		Trimley	arr	9												
				dep	10												
	15 56		**FELIXSTOWE TN.**	arr	11												
				dep	12		6†28										
	17 6		**FELIXSTOWE BCH.**	arr	13		6†31										
10 18			Woodbridge	arr	14									On FO to call at Beccles Swing Bridge when required for S. & T. Staff.	7 8		
				dep	15	4 44		6 24							7 13		
15 64			Wickham Market	arr	16										7 23		
				dep	17	4 52		6 32							7 25		
22 27		0 0	**SAXMUNDHAM**	arr	18	5 0		6 40							7 34		
				dep	19	5 2	To work 6.54 am to Ipswich	6 42							7 39		7 51
22 61		0 34	Saxmundham Jn.		20			6 43									7 52
		3 75	Leiston		21			6c52									8 0
		6 22	Thorpeness Halt		22												8 5
		8 26	**ALDEBURGH**	arr	23			7† 0									8 10
26 58			Darsham		24										7e50		
31 73			Halesworth	arr	25										7 58		
				dep	26	5 15									8 2		
35 69			Brampton		27										8 9		
40 39	0 0		**BECCLES**	arr	28	5 26									8 17		
				dep	29	5 32			7 5	7 10				8 15	8 26	8 31	
	6 28		Oulton Broad South	arr	30				7 15							8 41	
				dep	31				7 16							8 42	
	8 40	0 0	**LOWESTOFT CEN.**	arr	32				7 24							8 47	
				dep	33			To work 7.10 am to Saxmundham			7 19	7 19	7 57				
		2 15	Lowestoft North		34						7 26	7 26	8 4				
		3 48	Corton		35						7 30	7 30	8 8				
		5 56	Hopton-on-Sea		36						7 35	7 35	8 13				
		6 57	Gorleston Links Halt		37						7 38	7 38	8 16				
		7 57	Gorleston-on-Sea	arr	38						7 40	7 40	8 18				
				dep	39			Runs as C Pcls. Saxmundham to Aldeburgh			7 42	7 42	8 20				
43 58			Aldeby		40					7 17				8 22	8 33		
45 40			Fleet Jn.		41												
45 72			Haddiscoe	arr	42					7 21				8 26	8 37		
				dep	43					7 22				8 27	8 38		
46 43			St. Olaves		44					7 25				8 30	8 41		
49 4			Belton and Burgh		45					7 30				8 35	8 46		
53 5		10 29	**YARMOUTH S.T.**	arr	46	5 49				7 37	7 48	7 48	8 26	8 42	8 53		

IPSWICH TO FELIXSTOWE, ALDEBURGH, LOWESTOFT AND YARMOUTH

No.			B	B	B	B	B	B	B		B	B		B§	A	B	B		
								Rail Motor							7.42 am from Liverpool St.		Rail Motor		
							SO								SO HC	SX			
			am	am	am	am	am	am	am		am	am		am	am	am	am		
1															9 13				
2			6 58	7 34		8 5					8 35			9† 0	9 20	9 20			
3			7 5	7 41							8 42					9 27			
4			7 6	7 42		8 12					8 44			9 7	9 26	9 28			
5			7 11			8X17								9†13	Not Advertised	9 33			
6			7 12			8 21								9X17		9 34			
7			7X18			8 27										9 40			
8			7 19			8 28								9 23		9 41			
9			7 26			8 35										9 48			
10			7 27			8 36								9 29½		9 49			
11			7 31			8 40								9 33		9 53			
12			7 40											9 42		10 0			
13			7 43											9 45		10X 3			
14				7 52							8 54								
15				7 53							8 55				9 34				
16				8 3							9 5								
17				8 4							9 6				9 42				
18				8 13							9 15								
19				8 14				From 24th June to 7th September inclusive			9 17			§ECS Ipswich to Derby Road	9 49				
20																			
21																			
22																			
23																			
24				8 23							9 26								
25				8 31							9 34								
26				8 32							9 37				10 1				
27											9 44								
28				8 44							9 52				10 12				
29				8 49	8 54				9 38		9 57	10 2			10 16				
30					9 4							10 12							
31					9 5							10 13							
32					9 10							10 18							
33							8 54	9 25							From 29th June to 24th August inclusive Limited Load 9 Bogies		10 11		
34							9 1	9 32									10 18		
35							9c 6	9 36									10 22		
36							9c12	9 41									10 27		
37							9 15	9 44									10 30		
38							9 17	9 46									10 32		
39							9 19	9 48									10 34		
40				8 56					9 45		10 4								
41																			
42				9 0					9 49		10 8								
43				9 1					9 50		10 9								
44				9 4					9 53		10 12								
45				9 9					9 58		10 17								
46				9 16			9 25	9 54	10 5		10 24				10 34		10 40		

L80 WEEKDAYS — IPSWICH TO FELIXSTOWE, ALDEBURGH, LOWESTOFT AND YARMOUTH

DOWN			B	A	B	A	C	C	B	B	B	B	B (unclear)	B	B	B	C
			Rail Motor	7.58 am from Liverpool St.		8.1 am from Liverpool St.	ECS	ECS			9.10 am from Colchester						ECS
				SO HC	SO	SO HC	SX	SO	SX	SO	SX	SX	SO	SO	SX	SO	SO
			am	am	am	am	am	am	am	am	am	am	am	am	am	am	am
			From 24th June to 7th September inclusive	Limited Load 9 Bogies		Until 7th September inclusive Limited Load 9 Bogies	To work 10.4 am to Felixstowe Beach; From 8th July to 30th August inclusive	To work 10.4 am to Felixstowe Beach; From 13th July to 31st August inclusive	From 8th July to 30th August inclusive	From 13th July to 31st August inclusive	From 24th June to 6th September inclusive	From 24th June to 6th September inclusive	From 29th June to 24th August inclusive	From 29th June to 24th August inclusive			After working 7.58 am from Liverpool St.
IPSWICH	arr	1		9 24		9 38					9 45						
	dep	2		9 29	9 34	9 45	9†45	9†48			9 55		10 [illegible]		10 6	10 7	
Westerfield	arr	3			9 41										10 13	10 14	
	dep	4		9 35	9 42	9 51	9 52	9 55			10 1		10 [illegible]		10 14	10 15	
Derby Road	arr	5			9 47		9†57	10† 0							10 19	10X20	
	dep	6			9 48				10 4	10X 4					10 20	10 21	
Orwell	arr	7			9X54				10 10	10X10					10X26	10 27	
	dep	8			9 55				10 11	10 14					10 29	10 28	
Trimley	arr	9			10X 2				10 18	10 21					10 36	10 35	
	dep	10			10 5				10X21	10 22					10 37	10 36	
FELIXSTOWE TN.	arr	11			10 9				10 25	10 26					10X41	10X40	
	dep	12			10 18				10 37	10 37					10 49	10 49	
FELIXSTOWE BCH.	arr	13			10 21				10 40	10 40					10 52	10 52	
Woodbridge	arr	14															
	dep	15		9 43		9 59					10 9		10 14				
Wickham Market	arr	16															
	dep	17		9 51		10 7					10 17		10 22				
SAXMUNDHAM	arr	18									10 25		10 30				
	dep	19		9 58		10 14					10 27		10 32				
Saxmundham Jn.		20															
Leiston		21															
Thorpeness Halt		22															
ALDEBURGH	arr	23															
Darsham		24															
Halesworth	arr	25									10 41		10 46				
	dep	26		10 11		10 26					10 43		10 48				
Brampton		27															
BECCLES	arr	28		10 23		10 37					10 55		11 0				
	dep	29		10 25		10 40					11 0	11 5	11 5	1 10			
Oulton Broad South	arr	30										11 15		1 20			
	dep	31										11 16		1 22			
LOWESTOFT CEN.	arr	32		10 40								11 21		1 27			
	dep	33	10 40	10 52													
Lowestoft North		34	10 47														
Corton		35	10 51	11c 2													
Hopton-on-Sea		36	10 56	11c 8													
Gorleston Links Halt		37	10 59														
Gorleston-on-Sea	arr	38	11 1	11 13													
	dep	39	11 4														11†20
Aldeby		40															
Fleet Jn.		41															
Haddiscoe	arr	42															
	dep	43															
St. Olaves		44															
Belton and Burgh		45															
YARMOUTH S.T.	arr	46	11 10			10 57					11 17		11 22				11†30

IPSWICH TO FELIXSTOWE, ALDEBURGH, LOWESTOFT AND YARMOUTH — WEEKDAYS L81

	B		A	B			B	B		B	A	B	B		B	A	B	B	B
	Diesel										9.43 am from Liverpool St.		Rail Motor		Rail Motor	9.53 am from Liverpool St.	Diesel	Diesel	
			HC								SO	SO	SX		SO	SO HC	SX	SO	
	am		am	am			am	am		am	am	PM	PM		PM	am	PM	PM	PM
			On MSO from 24th June to 7th September inclusive formed by 8.33 am from Liverpool St.					From 8th July to 31st August inclusive								From 29th June to 7th September inclusive			
1																11 35			
2	10 16		10 26				10 34	10 46		11 3	11 12					11 40			
3	10 21½						10 41	10 53		11 10						11 47			
4	10 22		10 32				10X42	10 54		11X11	11 17					11 48			
5							10 47	10†59		11 16						11X53			
6							10 48	11X 5		11 18						11 54			
7							10X54	11 11		11 24									
8							10 58	11 12		11 25						12 0			
9							11 5	11 19		11X32						12 7			
10							11 6	11 20		11 33						12 8			
11							11 10	11X24		11 37						12X12			
12							11 19	11 33		11 46						12 21			
13							11 22	11 36		11 49						12 24			
14	10 32		10 41																
15	10 33		10 43								11 25								
16	10 41		10 53																
17	10 42		10 54								11 33								
18	10 50		11 3																
19	10 51		11 5								11 40						12 3	12 8	
20	10 52																12 4	12 9	
21	11 0																12 12	12 17	
22	11 5																12 17	12 22	
23	11 10																12 22	12 27	
24																			
25			11 19																
26			11 21								11 52								
27																			
28			11 33								12 3								
29			11 38	11 43							12 8	12 13							12 30
30				11 53								12 23							
31				11 54								12 24							
32				11 59								12 29							
33													12 15		12 20				
34													12 22		12 27				
35													12 26		12 31				
36													12 31		12 36				
37													12 34		12 39				
38													12 36		12 41				
39													12 38		12 43				
40																			12 37
41																			
42																			12 41
43																			12 42
44																			12 45
45																			12 50
46			11 55								12 25		12 44		12 49				12 57

L82 WEEKDAYS — IPSWICH TO FELIXSTOWE, ALDEBURGH, LOWESTOFT AND YARMOUTH

DOWN		B	C	A	B	A	A	B	A	A	C	B	C	B	B
			Pcls.	10.15 am from Liverpool St.		10.33 am from Liverpool St.			11.3 am from Liverpool St.		ECS	Rail Motor	Pcls.		
		SO	SX	SO HC	SX	SO	SO		SX	SX	SO	SX	SX	SX	SX
		PM	am	am	PM	PM	PM	PM	PM	PM	PM	PM	PM	PM	PM
IPSWICH .. arr	1			11 44											
dep	2		11 49	11 50		12 1		12 14	12 25					12 31	
Westerfield .. arr	3							12 21						12 38	
dep	4		11 55	11 56		12 6		12 22	12 30					12 39	
Derby Road .. arr	5							12 27							
dep	6							12 28							
Orwell .. arr	7							12X34							
dep	8			Limited Load 9 Bogies		From 29th June to 7th September inclusive	From 29th June to 7th September inclusive	12 35	From 1st July to 6th September inclusive	From 1st July to 6th September inclusive					
Trimley .. arr	9							12 42							
dep	10							12 43							
FELIXSTOWE TN. arr	11							12 47							
dep	12							12 56							
FELIXSTOWE BCH. arr	13							12 59							
Woodbridge .. arr	14		12 6	12 4										12 49	
dep	15		12 8			12 14			12 38					12 51	
Wickham Market .. arr	16		12 20	12 12										1 1	
dep	17		12 23			12 22			12 46					1 3	
SAXMUNDHAM .. arr	18		12 32											1 12	
dep	19		12 36	12 19		12 29			12 53					1 14	
Saxmundham Jn.	20										After working 10.15 am from Liverpool St.				
Leiston	21														
Thorpeness Halt	22														
ALDEBURGH .. arr.	23														
Darsham	24		12c46										←	1 23	
Halesworth .. arr	25		12*54										12 54	1 31	
dep	26		1*12	12 31		12 41			1 5				1 12	1 33	
Brampton	27		→										1 20	1 40	
BECCLES .. arr	28			12 42		12 52			1 16				1 29	1 48	
dep	29	12 35		12 47	12 55	12 57	1 2		1 21	1 26			1 40	1 53	2 0
Oulton Broad South .. arr	30	12 45			1 5										2 10
dep	31	12 46			1 6										2 11
LOWESTOFT CEN. arr	32	12 51		1 4	1 11		1 17			1 41					2 16
dep	33			1 10								1 35			
Lowestoft North	34											1 42			
Corton	35			1e21								1 46			
Hopton-on-Sea	36			1e28								1 51			
Gorleston Links Halt	37											1 54			
Gorleston-on-Sea .. arr	38		••	1 33								1 56			
dep	39										1†48	1 58			
Aldeby	40												1 47	2 0	
Fleet Jn.	41														
Haddiscoe .. arr	42												1 51	2 4	
dep	43												1 52	2 5	
St. Olaves	44												1 55	2 8	
Belton and Burgh	45												2 0	2 13	
YARMOUTH S.T. .. arr	46					1 14			1 38		1†58	2 4	2 9	2 20	

IPSWICH TO FELIXSTOWE, ALDEBURGH, LOWESTOFT AND YARMOUTH — WEEKDAYS L83

		A	B	B	A	B	B	A		B		A	B	B	B	B	B	B	A
		10.40 am from Liverpool St.		Rail Motor	10.40 am from Liverpool St.			11.12 am from Liverpool St.				12.3 pm from Liverpool St.				Rail Motor	Rail Motor		10.52 am from Leicester London Road
																			M67
		SO HC	SO	SO	SO	SO	SX	SO HC		SO		SO HC	SO	SO	SX	SO		SX	SO
		PM	PM	PM	PM	PM	PM	PM		PM		PM	PM	PM	PM	PM	PM	PM	PM
1		12 30			12 30			12 44				1 26							
2		12 40			12 40		12 44	12 50		12 58		1 32		1 51	1 58				
3					12 47		12 51	12 57		1 5				1 58	2 5				
4		12 46			12 48		12X52	12 58		1 6		1 38		1 59	2 6				
5							12 57			1X11				2 4	2 11				
6							12 58			1 15				2 5	2 12				
7							1X 4			1 21				2X11	2X18				
8		Until 31st August inclusive	Until 31st August inclusive		Commences 7th September	Commences 7th September	1 8	Until 31st August inclusive		1 22		Until 31st August inclusive	Until 31st August inclusive	2 16	2 19				
9							1 15			1X29				2X23	2 26				
10							1 16			1 30				2 24	2 27				
11							1X20			1 34				2 28	2 31				
12							1 29			1 42				2 37	2 40				
13							1 32			1 45				2 40	2 43				
14		12 55			12 58														
15		12 57			1 0			1 10				1 46							
16		1 7			1 10														
17		1 9			1 12			1 21				1 54							
18		1 18			1 21			1 29				2 2							
19		1 20			1 23			1 31				2 4							
20																			Until 7th September inclusive
21		Limited Load 9 Bogies																	
22																			
23																			
24					1 32			1 40											
25		1 34			1 40			1 48											
26		1 36			1 42			1 49				2 17							
27					1 49			1 56											
28		1 48			1 57			2 4				2 28							
29		1 53	1 58		2 2	2 7		2 7				2 33	2 38					2 53	
30			2 8			2 17		2 17					2 48					3 3	
31			2 9			2 18		2 18					2 49					3 4	
32			2 14			2 23		2 23					2 54					3 9	3 14
33				1 56				2 31								2 47	2 51		3 16
34				2 3												2 54	2 58		
35				2 7	Limited Load 9 Bogies			2c41				Limited Load 9 Bogies				2 58	3 2		3 25
36				2 12				2g49								3 3	3 7		3 30
37				2 15												3 6	3 10		
38				2 17				2 54								3 8	3 12		3 35
39				2 19												3 11	3 14		
40		2 0			2 9														
41																			
42		2 4			2 13			Limited Load 9 Bogies											
43		2 5			2 14														
44		2 8			2 17														
45		2 13			2 22														
46		2 20		2 25	2 30							2 50				3 17	3 20		
47																			

L84 WEEKDAYS — IPSWICH TO FELIXSTOWE, ALDEBURGH, LOWESTOFT AND YARMOUTH

DOWN			A	B	B	B		B	C	C	B	B	E	B	B	B	
			12.33 pm from Liverpool St.			Diesel			ECS	Pcls.			12.50 pm from Liverpool St.		Rail Motor		
			SO HC PM	SO PM	SX PM	PM		SO PM	SO PM	SO PM	PM	SO PM	SO PM	SX PM	PM	SX PM	
IPSWICH	arr	1	2 2										3 5				
	dep	2	2 8 Limited Load 10 Bogies			2 20			Until 7th September inclusive	2 25	2 37	2 56	3 10			3 21	
Westerfield	arr	3									2 44	3 3				3 28	
	dep	4	2 14			2 25				2 32	2X45	3 4	3 17			3 29	
Derby Road	arr	5									2 50	3 9	3 22			3 34	
	dep	6									2 51	3 10	3 23			3 35	
Orwell	arr	7									2 57	3 16				3 41	
	dep	8									2 58	3 17	3 29			3 42	
Trimley	arr	9									3 5	3 24				3X49	
	dep	10									3 6	3 25	3 35			3 53	
FELIXSTOWE TN.	arr	11									3 10	3 29	3X40			3 57	
	dep	12									3 19	3 38	3 4[illegible]			4 6	
FELIXSTOWE BCH.	arr	13									3 22	3 41	3 5[illegible]			4 9	
Woodbridge	arr	14				2 34				2 46			Limited Load 9 Bogies		From 24th June to 7th September inclusive		
	dep	15	2 22			2 36				2 47							
Wickham Market	arr	16				2 44				3 1							
	dep	17	2 30			2 46				3 4							
SAXMUNDHAM	arr	18	2 38			2 54				3 14							
	dep	19	2 40			2 56				3 18							
Saxmundham Jn.		20				2 57											
Leiston		21				3 5											
Thorpeness Halt		22				3 10											
ALDEBURGH	arr	23				3 15											
Darsham		24							After working 10.52 am from Leices er	3c30							
Halesworth	arr	25	2 54							3 40							
	dep	26	2 56							3 45							
Brampton		27								3 56							
BECCLES	arr	28	3 8							4 8							
	dep	29	3 13	3 19	3 19			3 20		4 15				4 19			
Oulton Broad South	arr	30		3 29	3 29												
	dep	31		3 31	3 31												
LOWESTOFT CEN.	arr	32		3 36	3 36												
	dep	33													4 38		
Lowestoft North		34													4 45		
Corton		35													4 49		
Hopton-on-Sea		36													4 54		
Gorleston Links Halt		37													4 57		
Gorleston-on-Sea	arr	38													4 59		
	dep	39							3†47						5 0		
Aldeby		40						3 27		4 24				4 26			
Fleet Jn.		41															
Haddiscoe	arr	42						3 31		4 28				4 30			
	dep	43						3 32		4 29				4 31			
St. Olaves		44						3 35		4 32				4 34			
Belton and Burgh		45						3 40		4 38				4 39			
YARMOUTH S.T.	arr	46	3 30					3 47	3†57	4 46				4 46	5 6		

IPSWICH TO FELIXSTOWE, ALDEBURGH, LOWESTOFT AND YARMOUTH — WEEKDAYS L85

	B	B	B	B	B		B	B	A	G		A	B	B	B	B	G	B	C
					Diesel			Rail Motor	3.0 pm from Liverpool St.	LE		3.33 pm from Liverpool St.		Diesel	Rail Motor	Rail Motor	LE		ECS
	SO PM	SO PM	SX PM	SX PM	PM		SO PM	PM	SO PM	SO PM		HC PM	PM	PM	SO PM	SX PM	SO PM	PM	PM
1												5 1							
2	3 24 Until 7th September formed by 1.33 pm from Liverpool St eet		3 28 On MFO formed by 1.33 pm from Liverpool Street				4 6		4 25			5 8						5 15	
3																		5 22	
4			3 34				4X13		4 30 Until 7th September inclusive			5 14 Limited Load 9 Bogies						5 23	
5							4 18											5X28	
6							4 19											5 32	
7							4X25											5 38	
8							4 26											5 39	
9							4X33											5X46	
10							4 37											5 47	
11							4 41											5 51	
12							4 50			5‖15									6† 0
13							4 53			5‖18									6† 3
14	3 39		3 43				From 14th July to 31st August inclusive					5 23					Until 7th September inclusive		Until 6th July inclusive and commencing 2nd September
15	3 41		3 45						4 38			5 25							
16	3 51		3 55																
17	3 52		3 56						4 46			5 34							
18	4 1		4 5									5 42							
19	4 4		4 8		4 22				4 53	To work 7.22 pm to Ipswich		5 44		5 54					
20					4 23									5 55					
21					4 31									6 3					
22					4 36									6 8					
23					4 41									6 13					
24	4 13		4 17														After working 3.0 pm from Liverpool Street		
25	4 21		4 25									5 58							
26	4 24		4 28						5 5			6 0							
27	4 31		4 35																
28	4 39		4 43									6 12							
29	4 44	4 49	4 48	4 53					5 15			6 17	6 22			6 24			
30		4 59		5 3									6 32						
31		5 0		5 4									6 33						
32		5 5		5‡ 9					5 30				6 38						
33				‡5.10 pm				5 9	5 37						6 9		6‖20		After working 5.15 pm from Ipswich
34								5 16							6 16				
35								5 20	5e48						6 20				
36								5 25	5g56						6 25				
37								5 28							6 28				
38								5 30	6 1						6 30				
39								5 32	6 6						6 32				
40	4 51		4 55													6 31			
41																			
42	4 55		4 59													6 35			
43	4 56		5 0													6 36			
44	4 59		5 3													6 39			
45	5 4		5 8													6 44			
46	5 11		5 15					5 38	6 12			6 34			6 38	6 51	6‖51		

DOWN		B	B	B	B	B	B	B	B	G	B	B
						Rail Motor			Diesel	LE	Diesel	
		PM	PM	PM	PM	PM	PM	PM	PM	FO PM	PM	PM
IPSWICH arr	1											
dep	2	5 30		5 38	6 18		6 28		Until 22nd June and commencing 9th September	6‖50	From 24th June to 7th September inclusive	7 0
Westerfield arr	3											7 7
dep	4	5 36		5X45	6 25		6 34			6 57		7 8
Derby Road arr	5			5 50	6 30							7X13
dep	6			5 52	6 31							7 17
Orwell arr	7			5X58	6X37							7X23
dep	8			5 59	6 38							7 26
Trimley arr	9			6 6	6 45							7X33
dep	10			6 7	6 46							7 37
FELIXSTOWE TN. arr	11			6 11	6X50							7 41
dep	12			6 20	6 59							7 49
FELIXSTOWE BCH. arr	13			6 23	7 2							7 52
Woodbridge arr	14	5 45		From 8th July to 31st August inclusive			6 43					
dep	15	5 46					6 45			7 8		
Wickham Market arr	16	5 56					6 55					
dep	17	5 57					6 56			7 18		
SAXMUNDHAM arr	18	6 6					7 5					
dep	19	6 8					7 9		7 23	7 30	7 35	
Saxmundham Jn.	20								7 24		7 36	
Leiston	21								7 32		7 44	
Thorpeness Halt	22								7 37		7 49	
ALDEBURGH arr	23								7 42		7 54	
Darsham	24	6 17					7 18					
Halesworth arr	25	6 25					7 26					
dep	26	6 27					7 28			7 47		
Brampton	27											
BECCLES arr	28	6 39					7 40					
dep	29	6 44	6 51				7 45	7 53		8 3		
Oulton Broad South arr	30		7 1				St. Olaves arr. 7DR55 pm Yarmouth S.T. arr. 8.6 pm	8 3				
dep	31		7 2					8 4				
LOWESTOFT CEN. arr	32		7 7					8 9		8‖22		
dep	33					7 24				After working 3.53 pm from Lowestoft C.		
Lowestoft North	34					7 31						
Corton	35					7 35						
Hopton-on-Sea	36					7 40						
Gorleston Links Halt	37					7 43						
Gorleston-on-Sea arr	38					7 45						
dep	39					7 47						
Aldeby	40	6 51										
Fleet Jn.	41											
Haddiscoe arr	42	6 55										
dep	43	6 56										
St. Olaves	44	6 59										
Belton and Burgh	45	7 4										
YARMOUTH S.T. arr	46	7 11				7 53	8 2					

DOWN		B	B	B	B	A	B	B	B	B	B	B	B	B	B
				Rail Motor		6.33 pm from Liverpool St.		Diesel	Rail Motor						
		PM	PM	PM	PM	HC PM	PM	PM	PM	PM	PM	WSO PM	PM	PM	night
IPSWICH arr	1					8 1									
dep	2	7 5			7 58	8 10				8 27	9 12		10 34	10 42	
Westerfield arr	3	7 12			8 5					8 34			10 41		
dep	4	7 13			8X 6	8 16				8X35	9 19		10 42	10 48	
Derby Road arr	5				8 11	Limited Load 9 Bogies				8 40	9X24		10 47		
dep	6				8 12					8 41	9 31		10 48		
Orwell arr	7				8X18					8X47	9X37		10X54		
dep	8				8 22					8 51	9 38		10 55		
Trimley arr	9				8 29					8 58	9 45		11 2		
dep	10				8 30					8 59	9 46		11 3		
FELIXSTOWE TN. arr	11				8X34					9 3	9 50		11 7		
dep	12				8 43						9 59				
FELIXSTOWE BCH. arr	13				8 46						10 2				
Woodbridge arr	14	7 23				8 25			From 24th June to 7th September inclusive					10 57	
dep	15	7 25				8 27								10 59	
Wickham Market arr	16	7 35				8 37								11 9	
dep	17	7 36				8 39								11 11	
SAXMUNDHAM arr	18	7 45				8 48								11 20	
dep	19	7 47				8 50		8 57						11 22	
Saxmundham Jn.	20							8 58							
Leiston	21							9 6							
Thorpeness Halt	22							9 11							
ALDEBURGH arr	23							9 16							
Darsham	24	7c57												11c32	
Halesworth arr	25	8 5				9 4								11 40	
dep	26	8 7				9 6								11 42	
Brampton	27	8 14													
BECCLES arr	28	8 22				9 18								11 54	
dep	29	8 27	8 34			9 23	9 28					10 35		11 59	12 4
Oulton Broad South arr	30		8 44				9 38								12 14
dep	31		8 45				9 39								12 15
LOWESTOFT CEN. arr	32		8 50				9 44								12 20
dep	33			8 55		St. Olaves arr. 9DR33 pm Yarmouth S.T. arr. 9.44 pm			9 27					St. Olaves arr. 12DR9 Yarmouth S.T. arr. 12.20 night	
Lowestoft North	34			9 2					9 34						
Corton	35			9 6					9 38						
Hopton-on-Sea	36			9 11					9 43						
Gorleston Links Halt	37			9 14											
Gorleston-on-Sea arr	38			9 16					9 47						
dep	39			9 17					9 49						
Aldeby	40	8 34										10 42			
Fleet Jn.	41														
Haddiscoe arr	42	8 38										10 46			
dep	43	8 39										10 47			
St. Olaves	44	8 42										10 50			
Belton and Burgh	45	8 47										10 55			
YARMOUTH S.T. arr	46	8 54		9 23		9 40			9 55			11 2		12 16	

Pages 233-237:
BR ER passenger WTT 17 June to 15 September 1957.

Saturday 1 November 1952, when the final train, the 6.52pm from Framlingham, was strengthened by five extra coaches to cope with the 400 passengers making their final journey over the line. Ironically it was seen off from the booking office by Mr Edgar Gladwell, who had been transferred from Laxfield at the end of July when the 'Middy', as the Mid-Suffolk had been affectionately known, had closed. According to the *East Anglian Daily Times* there had been only five passengers a day prior to closure, and the final working, the 8pm from Wickham Market, was delayed by one passenger pulling the communication cord.

The passengers appear to have been in a good mood generally, perhaps because so few would have been inconvenienced by the loss of the service. At Wickham Market refreshments and gifts were given to the railway staff, and the right-away for the final departure was sounded by a hunting horn. Lord and Lady Alistair Graham and Sir Peter Greenwell were dressed in Edwardian clothes, Lord Graham placing a laurel wreath on the engine bearing the inscription 'RIP'. Fireworks were let off at the level crossings as the train passed, and Parham was decorated with fairy lights and streamers. Hacheston halt did not have any passengers for the final train, but the driver, Jack Turner, recalled the thousands of American servicemen who used it during the war when it was a short cut for them to get to Parham airfield. He had been one of the regular drivers on the branch, but the fireman on the last trip was Alan Chittock of Ipswich, as the local man 'Pony' Moore had a rest day. The engine and coaches were worked back to Ipswich the same evening by Ipswich driver Harold Double and fireman Chittock.

Above:
The two newest swing bridges were closed and demolished first. Beccles is here being dismantled soon after closure of the main line.
Peter Punchard collection

Traffic had picked up rapidly after the end of World War 2, and the LNER had proposed a great deal of new work. Morton's proposed big extensions to its factory at Lowestoft, most of the produce being moved by rail. There had been a scheme to rationalise the railways at Yarmouth and divert all lines into the Beach station, which was the most convenient of the three, but in the end, of course, it was Vauxhall that survived — the least convenient. An omen of things to occurred came as early as 1946 when Messrs Speight & Partners gained contracts to resurface the Ipswich to Shotley road and the Woodbridge bypass, and agreed with the LNER to install tar mixing plant at Westerfield and Melton stations, all to help the roads along. About 3,000 tons of granite were expected to arrive by rail. Despite initiatives such as the introduction of the 'Easterling' and the burgeoning Holiday Camps and their summer Saturday expresses, the rise of the motor car and lorry proved to be inexorable. Travel to Yarmouth became quicker for much of the time via Norwich, and the East Suffolk suffered.

Proposals to close the main line between Beccles and South Town emerged in 1959. Much has already been written about British Railways' 1955 Modernisation Plan, which had continued the policy of closing uneconomic lines. Acquisition of modern diesel and electric traction was proceeding apace — not always with complete success — and was seen as a means of speeding and increasing capacity on some lines and so allowing closure of parallel routes. The heavy maintenance costs of the East Suffolk north of Beccles militated against it, and there was a suspicion that St Olaves swing bridge had been damaged in the 1953 floods. Even though they were easily the newest bridges on the system, the costs of replacing this and Beccles swing bridge were cited as reasons why the line had to close. None of the intermediate stations was felt to be important, and it was thought that passengers would be happy to travel the extra distance between Beccles and Yarmouth, together with reversal at Lowestoft, as well as paying higher fares. The introduction of the winter timetable was delayed until 2 November by a printers' strike (the last day of the summer service should have been Sunday 13 September), and so the line kept running for a few more weeks, with the Yarmouth & Haddiscoe Railway just making it to its centenary.

Services were withdrawn on and from Monday 2 November 1959, with the last trains running on the Sunday. To add insult to injury on the day, single line working was in force at Wickham Market because of engineering works. A few of the Sunday trains were dated, and had finished on 6 September, and there was none booked to call at Haddiscoe High Level on Sundays, which thus saw its last services on Saturday 31 October. The last steam working left Beccles for Yarmouth at 9.15pm (7.50pm from Ipswich, due out of Beccles at 9.10pm) and provided St Olaves and Belton & Burgh with their very last passenger trains. The driver gave several blasts on the whistle, but there was no public interest, said the *Eastern Daily Press*. The very last train was formed of a well-filled two-car DMU and left Beccles dead on time at 10.18pm, 'just as unceremoniously as it had done on other Sunday nights'. The closure seems to have been unlamented and largely unreported by the local press, although when it had been proposed in February local politicians in both Yarmouth and Lowestoft had opposed it. The East Anglian Transport Users' Consultative Committee (TUCC) supported the closure. The *Yarmouth Mercury* made a note of the event, while the *Eastern Daily Press* and *Eastern Evening News* carried identical reports, mentioning the lone railway enthusiast who made a special journey to Beccles station to see the last train to Yarmouth via Haddiscoe. However, the local papers certainly did notice the opening of the M1 motorway at the same time, and reported that the Minister of Transport, Mr Ernest Marples, was appalled at the speed of traffic using it.

The withdrawal of services over the Snape branch cannot go unrecorded. It had seen its only passenger train on 30 September 1956 when the Railway Enthusiasts' Club 'Suffolk Venturer' visited the line, with Class E4 No 62797 hauling the train down the line. It then propelled back up to the junction and was held for the passage of the Halesworth milk. However, it was unable to restart on the 1 in 53 gradient and eventually Class J15 No 65447 was sent to assist. The wooden trestle bridge over the River Alde near the terminus had restricted the classes of locomotive that could be used, and towards the end a solitary 'J15' was kept at Ipswich for working the branch. The only nod that had been made to modernisation had been to substitute a Fordson tractor for the shunting horse, and with wagonload goods traffic falling fast, the decision to close came as no surprise. The service was withdrawn from Monday 7 March 1960 and the line closed completely.

Amidst the furore of the Beeching closures another East Suffolk outpost closed when goods services were withdrawn from Marlesford and Parham on 13 July 1964, and Framlingham on 19 April 1965. Between these dates Aldeby lost its remaining freight services from 28 December 1964. It had been retained for the sugar beet traffic and closed at the end of the season, having been served as a long siding using the former up main line from Fleet Junction, plus the siding on the up side.

The clouds were gathering over Britain's railways, the link with the motorways being Ernest Marples, Minister of Transport, whose connections with the country's biggest road-construction company were well known. He had appointed Dr Richard Beeching to be chairman of the newly constituted British Railways Board in late 1962, with a remit to bring its finances under control and to reshape the railway to suit modern conditions. This was to lead to the famous Beeching Report, properly *The Reshaping of British Railways*, which appeared early in 1963. Among the means by which it proposed to bring about change was to eliminate unprofitable parts of the system, although it did not pretend to say which parts could ultimately be made to pay their way; it merely sought the removal of parts which were obviously unsound. It proposed to eliminate duplication, so that places served by two or more routes would in future have only

Below:
The only passenger train on the Snape branch, REC 'Suffolk Venturer' in 1956, finally struggles back to the main line after being rescued by 'J15' No 65447. The train engine, 'E4' No 62797, had been unable to restart the train after being checked at the junction. *Stations UK*

DOWN

Mileage M C	Mileage M C	Mileage M C	Mileage M C	Station		No.	3-66	1-59	2-75	1-71	1C12	1-71
							19.38 Parcels Brentwood to Whitemoor	22.30 Sun. from Liverpool St. to Yarmouth Vauxhall		Postal	22.50 Postal from Liverpool St. to Peterboro' North	Postal
									DU			
							MX	MO ♠ HC	MO	MX	♠ HC	
0 0				LIVERPOOL ST. (Z)	dep	1						
68 59			0 0	IPSWICH	arr	2					0 24	
					dep	3				0 30	0 40	
77 8				Needham		4						
80 49				Stowmarket	arr	5		0 08½			0 53½	
					dep	6		0 10½	0 17		0 58½	
82 75	0 0			HAUGHLEY	arr	7			0 21		1 03	
					dep	8		0 14½	0 22	0 47	1 18	1 45
86 46				Finningham		9						
91 30				Mellis		10		[2½]				
94 79				Diss	arr	11		0 28				1 58½
					dep	12		0 30				2 03½
97 39				Burston		13						
100 44				TIVETSHALL	arr	14						
					dep	15		0 37		1 04		2 10½
104 7				Forncett		16						
106 54				Flordon		17		[3]				
113 77				Trowse		18						
114 77				NORWICH THORPE	arr	19		0 55		1 20		2 26
					dep	20		1 06				
				UP								
	3 46			Elmswell		21			0D28½	Detached off 22.50 from Liverpool Street		
	8 5			Thurston		22			0 34		1 30	
	12 12	0 0		BURY	arr	23			0 40		1 36	
					dep	24					1 42	
	15 29	3 17		Saxham and Risby		25					[4]	
	18 62	6 50		Higham		26						
	21 67	9 55		Kennett		27						
	24 52	12 40		Chippenham Jn.		28	0 02				2 03	
		13 29		Warren Hill Jn.		29						
		14 32		Newmarket Yd. Jn.		30						
		14 60		NEWMARKET	arr	31						
				DOWN								
					dep	32						
0 00				Newmarket (Down)		33						
0 28				Newmarket Yd. Jn.		34				Not advertised		
1 31				Warren Hill Jn.		35						
2 20	25 34			Snailwell Jn.		36	0 04				2 05	
	28 36			Fordham		37	[3]				2e14	
	31 37			Soham	arr	38						
					dep	39	0X15				2 19	
	33 56			Barway Siding		40	0 19				2 23	
	36 5			Ely Dock Jn.		41	0 23				2 27	
	36 41			ELY	arr	42					2 30	
					dep	43	0 24				2 37	
				UP								
		17 72		Dullingham		44						
		20 57		Six Mile Bottom		45						
		24 5		Fulbourne		46						
		29 21		CAMBRIDGE	arr	47						
			3 42	Westerfield		48						
			10 18	Woodbridge		49						
			15 64	Wickham Market		50						
			22 32	SAXMUNDHAM	arr	51						
					dep	52						
			26 58	Darsham		53						
			31 73	Halesworth	arr	54						
					dep	55						
			35 74	Brampton		56						
			40 39	BECCLES	arr	57						
					dep	58	Same as page 79	Same as pages 83 & 85				
			46 67	Oulton Broad South	arr	59						
					dep	60						
			48 79	LOWESTOFT CEN.	arr	61						
					dep	62						
			51 14	Lowestoft North		63						
			52 47	Corton		64						
			54 55	Hopton-on-Sea		65						
			55 56	Gorleston Links Halt		66						
			56 56	Gorleston-on-Sea	arr	67						
					dep	68						
			59 28	YARMOUTH S.T.	arr	69						

No.	1-59	1-13	2-75	3-73	1-72	3-01	3-72	2-72	2-72	2-28	2-00	2-71	2-72	2-51
	News to Yarmouth Vauxhall	News to Lowestoft	News	ECS	News	Parcels	ECS							
				DU		DU	DU			DU		DU	DU	
	♠ HC													HC
1	2 45													4 30
2	4 04													6 40
3	4 10		4 20	4†50	5 00	6 00								7 05
4														
5			4 37											7 20½
6			4 57											7 23½
7			5 03											7 27½
8	4 24½		5 04											7 28
9														7a35
10														7 42
11	4 35½													7 47
12	4 48											7 11½		7 50
13												7 16		7 54½
14												7 21		7 59½
15	4 55											7 21½		8 02½
16												7 27		8 08
17	[5]											7 31½		8 12½
18														
19	5 15											7 44		8 25
20	5 26	5 36												
21			5 12											
22			5c21											
23			5 28											
24										7 05				
25										7 11				
26										7 16½				
27										7 21½				
28										7 25½				
29										7 27				
30										7X29½				
31										7 31				
32										7 33				
33											7 45			
34											7 46½			
35											7 49			
36											7 50½			
37											7g58½			
38										[3] Fulbourne to Cambridge	8 03½			
39											8 04			
40											8 08½			
41											8 12½			
42											8 14½			
43									[1] Gorleston to Yarmouth S.T.					
44										7 39				
45										7 43½				
46										7 49				
47										8 01				
48				4 55½	5 07	6 05½								
49				5 05	5e20	6a16½								
50					5e33									
51				5 20	5 44	6 31								
52				5 36	5 54				(‡7.02)					
53					6c04									
54				5†54	6 13									
55							To work 6.18 to Ipswich		6 28½				[1] Gorleston to Yarmouth S.T.	
56									6 36½					
57									6 46					
58									6 50					
59									7 01½					
60									7‡04					
61									7 09½					
62				To work 6.11 to Ipswich	Not advertised	Forms 6.37 (Code 2-01) to Aldeburgh	5†48	6 16	7 15				7 55	
63								6 20½	7 19½				7 59½	
64								6 24	7 23				8 03	
65								6 28½	7 27½				8 07½	
66								6 31½	7 30½				8 10½	
67								6 33½	7 32½				8 12½	
68								6 34½	7 33½				8 13½	
69							6†08	6 40	7 40				8 20	

F72 WEEKDAYS — IPSWICH TO NORWICH, LOWESTOFT AND CAMBRIDGE‑YARMOUTH S.T.—IPSWICH TO ELY AND CAMBRIDGE

DOWN		2-72	2-25	1-85	0-73	2-72	2-73	2-65	1M72	1N48	2-71	3-00	2-72	1-52	2-52	
				To Liverpool St.	LE			7.20 from Colchester	7.30 Harwich to Manchester (Piccadilly)	7.50 Colchester to Newcastle		9†52 ECS from Reedham				
		DU	DU			DU		DU			DU	DU	DU			
				HC	SO				HC	HC				SX	SO	
LIVERPOOL ST.(Z) dep	1													7 00	7 00	
IPSWICH .. arr	2							7 47	8 13	8 19				8 45	8 45	
dep	3	7 10		7 24	7‖40			7 50	8 15	8 25	8 30 [1]		8 50	8 50	8 50	
Needham	4			7a35½				8 02								
Stowmarket arr	5			7 41½				8 07	8 28½		8 46					
dep	6			7 42½				8 08	8 29½		8 47					
HAUGHLEY arr	7			7 47				8 12			8 51					
dep	8			7 48				8 12½	8 34	8 41	8 51½		SX until 17th July and daily commencing 7th September	From 20th July to 4th September inclusive	Until 5th September inclusive	
Finningham	9										8 58					
Mellis	10															
Diss arr	11							[3] Thurston to Bury			9 08½					
dep	12										9 09½					
Burston	13															
TIVETSHALL arr	14															
dep	15										9 17					
Forncett	16															
Flordon	17										[2]					
Trowse	18															
NORWICH THORPE arr	19										9 38					
dep	20									[2]						
Elmswell	21			7a56	Until 5th September inclusive			8 19								
Thurston	22			8a04				8 25½	8 44	8 53						
BURY arr	23			8 11				8 34½	8 50	8 59						
dep	24		7 49	8 12					8 53	9 02						
Saxham and Risby	25															
Higham	26		7 59													
Kennett	27		8 04													
Chippenham Jn.	28		8 08	8 30		Until 5th September inclusive			9 10	9 19						
Warren Hill Jn.	29		8 09½	8X32												
Newmarket Yd. Jn.	30		8X12	8 34½												
NEWMARKET arr	31		8 13½	8 36												
dep	32		8 14½	8 37												
Newmarket (Down)	33	[1] Oulton Broad South to Lowestoft Cen. (‡ 8.30)														
Newmarket Yd. Jn.	34						Commences 7th September									
Warren Hill Jn.	35															
Snailwell Jn.	36								9 12	9 21			[1] Oulton Broad South to Lowestoft [1] Gorleston to Yarmouth S.T.	[1] Oulton Broad South to Lowestoft	[1] Oulton Broad South to Lowestoft [1] Gorleston to Yarmouth S.T.	
Fordham	37															
Soham arr	38															
dep	39								9X20	9 29						
Barway Siding	40								9 24	9 33						
Ely Dock Jn.	41								9 28	9 37						
ELY arr	42								9 30	9 39						
dep	43								9 33	9 41						
Dullingham	44		8 20½			[1] Gorleston to Yarmouth S.T.										
Six Mile Bottom	45		8 25													
Fulbourne	46		8 30½													
CAMBRIDGE arr	47		8 39½	8 57								To work 11.20 to Lowestoft Cen. Until 5th September inclusive				
Westerfield	48	7 15½			7 47								8 55½	8 57	8 57	
Woodbridge	49	7 26			7 56					Not after 5th September			9a06	9a08	9a08	
Wickham Market	50	7 34											9 14		9a19	
SAXMUNDHAM arr	51	7 42											9 22	9 26	9 30	
dep	52	7 43			8 14								9 23	9 27	9 31	
Darsham	53	7 50½		Cambridge dep. 9.00									9 30½		9a40	
Halesworth arr	54	7 58											9 38	9 42	9 49	
dep	55	7 59			8 29								9 39	9 43	9 50	
Brampton	56	8 06											9 46		9a58	
BECCLES arr	57	8 13½											9 53½	9 57	10 08	
dep	58	8 14½			8 46	8 58	8 58						9 55½	9 58	10 10	
Oulton Broad South arr	59	8 23½				9 09	9 09						10 04½	10 09	10 21	
dep	60	8 24				9 09½	9 09½			♠ beyond Ely			10 05	10 10	10 22	
LOWESTOFT CEN. arr	61	8‡29			8‖59	9 15	9 15					10 10	10 10	10 16	10 28	
dep	62	8 32				9 20						10 13	10 15	10 21	10 33	
Lowestoft North	63	8 36½				9 24½							10 19½		10a38	
Corton	64	8 40				9 28							10 23	10a30	10a42	
Hopton-on-Sea	65	8 44½				9 32½							10 27½	10a36	10a47	
Gorleston Links Halt	66	8 47½				9 35½							10 30½		10a50½	
Gorleston-on-Sea arr	67	8 49½				9 37½							10 32½	10 41	10 52½	
dep	68	8 50½				9 38½							10 33½	10 42	10 53½	
YARMOUTH S.T. arr	69	8 56				9 45						10†33	10 40	10 48	11 00	

IPSWICH TO NORWICH, LOWESTOFT AND YARMOUTH S.T.—IPSWICH TO ELY AND CAMBRIDGE — WEEKDAYS F73

	2-28	2-28	3-28	2-00	2-72	0-73	2-71		1-52	1-51	2-01	2-73	3-73		2-72	1-52	2-75	2-72	1-52
			ECS			LE					To Aldeburgh		Parcels						
	DU		DU	DU	DU		DU				DU	DU				DU	DU	DU	
		SO			SX	SO			SO HC	♠ HC			SX		SX	SO			SO HC
1									8 06	8 30						8 50			9 10
2									9 36	9 50						10 16			10 34
3	8 55	8 55			9 10	9‖25	9 30		9 39	9 55	9 58	9 58	10 06		10 10	10 19	10 25		10 37
4							9 42										10 37		
5	9 10½	9 10½					9 47			10 08½							10 42		
6	9 12	9 12					9 49			10 10½							10 43		
7	9 16	9 16					9 53										10 47		
8	9 16½	9 16½	Runs SO until 5th September Daily commencing 7th September				9 53½			10 14½							10 47½		
9							10a01			[2½]									
10							10 08												
11							10 13		Not after 5th September	10 28									
12							10 14½			10 30									
13							10 19										[2] Thurston to Bury		
14							10 24												
15							10 24½			10 37									
16				From 27th July to 5th September inclusive			10 30½												
17							10 34½			[3]									
18							[1]												
19							10 48			10 55									
20																			
21					[1] Oulton Broad South to Lowestoft [1] Gorleston to Yarmouth S.T.										[1] Oulton Broad South to Lowestoft Cen.	[2] Gorleston to Yarmouth S.T.	10 54		
22	9 28	9 28															11 00½		
23	9 34	9 34															11 09		
24	9 36	9 36	9†45																
25	9 42	9 42																	
26	9 47½	9 47½																	
27	9 52½	9 52½																	
28	9 56½	9 56½	10 08																
29	9 58	9 58	10 11																
30	10 00½	10 00½	10X13																Not after 12th September
31	10 02	10 02																	
32	10 03	10 03	10 14																
33				9 20															
34	[2] Fulbourne to Cambridge	[2] Fulbourne to Cambridge		9 21½															
35				9 24															
36				9 26	From 20th July to 4th September inclusive	Until 5th September inclusive					Until 5th September inclusive	Commences 7th September	Commences 7th September		Not after 4th September (‡11.30)	Not after 5th September			
37				9a31															
38				9 36½															
39				9 37½															
40				9 41½															
41				9 45½															
42				9 47															
43																			
44	10 09	10 09																	
45	10 13½	10 13½																	
46	10 19	10 19																	
47	10 30	10 30	10†41													[1]			
48			After working 7.20 from Colchester		9 15½	9 32			9 46		10 04½	10 04½	10 14		10 17	10 25½		[1] Gorleston to Yarmouth S.T.	10 44
49					9 26	9 41			9 55		10 15½	10 15½	10c28		10a28	10a36			10 53
50					9 34						10 23½	10 23½							
51					9 42						10 31½	10 31½	10 50		10 46				11 10
52	SX until 4th September inclusive Daily from 7th September				9 43	9 59			10 11		10 32½		10 54		10 47	10 50			11 11
53					9 50½														
54					9 58								11 10		11 02	11 03			
55					9 59	10 14			10 24				11 20		11 03	11 04			11 25
56					10 06														
57					10 13½								11 37		11 17				11 38
58					10 15½	10 27			10 36				11 41		11 18	11 16½			11 39½
59					10 24½										11 29	11 25			
60		Until 5th September inclusive			10 25				[8]						11‡33	11 25½			[5]
61					10 30	10‖40			10 58½				12 00		11 40	11 30			12 00
62					10 35				11 03½						11 45	11 35		11 55	12 05
63					10 39½													11 59½	
64					10 43				11a12½									12 03	[2]
65					10 47½				11b19									12 07½	
66					10 50½													12 10½	
67					10 52½				11 24						11 58	11 46½		12 12½	12 20
68					10 53½				11 26						11 59	11 47½		12 13½	12 22
69					11 00				11 32						12 05	11 55		12 20	12 28

F74 WEEKDAYS — IPSWICH TO NORWICH, LOWESTOFT AND YARMOUTH S.T.—IPSWICH TO ELY AND CAMBRIDGE

DOWN		No.	1-51	2-72	2-28	1-50	3-28	1-52	1-52	1-51	2-72	1-52	2-75	2-72
						To Sheringham	10†30 ECS from Felixstowe Beach							
				DU	DU		DU				DU		DU	DU
			♠ HC			SO HC	SX	SO HC	SO HC	♠ HC		SO HC		SO
Notes				[1] Oulton Broad South to Lowestoft; [1] Gorleston to Yarmouth S.T.	[2] Thurston to Bury; [3] Fulbourne to Cambridge	Not after 5th September	To work 13.38 to Haverhill; Until 4th September inclusive	Not after 12th September; [2] Gorleston to Yarmouth S.T.	Not after 5th September; [1] Gorleston-Yarmouth S.T.		Runs SX until 4th September Daily commencing 7th September; [1] Gorleston to Yarmouth S.T.	Not after 5th September; [2] Gorleston to Yarmouth S.T.		[1] Gorleston to Yarmouth S.T.; Until 5th September inclusive
LIVERPOOL ST. (Z)	dep	1	9 30			9 45		9 50	10 10	10 30		10 50		
IPSWICH	arr	2	10 42			11 08	11 14	11 20	11 38	11 50		12 16		
	dep	3	10 44	10 50	10 55	11 10	11 20	11 23	11 40	11 55		12 19	12 25	
Needham		4											12 37	
Stowmarket	arr	5			11 10½					12 08½			12 42	
	dep	6			11 11½					12 10½			12 43½	
HAUGHLEY	arr	7											12 47½	
	dep	8	10 58½		11 15	11 27	11 38			12 14½			12 48	
Finningham		9								[2½]				
Mellis		10												
Diss	arr	11								12 28				
	dep	12								12 30				
Burston		13												
TIVETSHALL	arr	14												
	dep	15	11 13			11 44				12 37				
Forncett		16												
Flordon		17	[2]							[3]				
Trowse		18												
NORWICH THORPE	arr	19	11 30			12 00				12 55				
	dep	20				12 06								
UP: Elmswell		21											12 54½	
Thurston		22			11 25		11 48						13 01	
BURY	arr	23			11 33								13 08	
	dep	24			11 35		11 54							
Saxham and Risby		25			11 41									
Higham		26			11 46½									
Kennett		27			11 51½									
Chippenham Jn.		28			11 55½		12 10							
Warren Hill Jn.		29			11 57½		12 12½							
Newmarket Yd. Jn.		30			11 59½		12 14							
NEWMARKET	arr	31			12 01									
DOWN:	dep	32			12 02		12 15							
Newmarket (Down)		33												
Newmarket Yd. Jn.		34												
Warren Hill Jn.		35												
Snailwell Jn.		36												
Fordham		37												
Soham	arr	38												
	dep	39												
Barway Siding		40												
Ely Dock Jn.		41												
ELY	arr	42												
	dep	43												
UP: Dullingham		44			12 08									
Six Mile Bottom		45			12 12½									
Fulbourne		46			12 18							[1]		
CAMBRIDGE	arr	47			12 30		12†45							
Westerfield		48		10 55½				11 30	11 47			12 27		
Woodbridge		49		11 06				11a41	11 56			12a38		
Wickham Market		50		11 14										
SAXMUNDHAM	arr	51		11 22					12 13					
	dep	52		11 23				11 58	12 14			12 55		
Darsham		53		11 30½										
Halesworth	arr	54		11 38				12 12				13 09		
	dep	55		11 39				12 13	12 28			13 10		
Brampton		56		11 46										
BECCLES	arr	57		11 53½					12 41					
	dep	58		11 55½				12 26	12 42½			13 23		
Oulton Broad South	arr	59		12 04½				12 36				13 35		
	dep	60		12 05				12 37	[2]			13‡36½		
LOWESTOFT CEN.	arr	61		12 10				12 43	13 00			13 42		
	dep	62		12 15				12 48	13 05		13 45	13 47		13 55
Lowestoft North		63		12 19½							13 49½			13 59½
Corton		64		12 23				12a57			13 53			14 03
Hopton-on-Sea		65		12 27½				13a03			13 57½			14 07½
Gorleston Links Halt		66		12 30½							14 00½			14 10½
Gorleston-on-Sea	arr	67		12 32½				13 08	13 18		14 02½	14 00		14 12½
	dep	68		12 33½				13 10	13 20		14 03½	14 02		14 13½
YARMOUTH S.T.	arr	69		12 40				13 18	13 27		14 10	14 10		14 20

IPSWICH TO NORWICH, LOWESTOFT AND YARMOUTH S.T.—IPSWICH TO ELY AND CAMBRIDGE — WEEKDAYS F75

No.	1-52	1-51	2-72	2-28	2-71	1-52	1M77	1-52	1-50	1-51	2-28	2-01	2-75	2-72
							12.40 Harwich to Rugby (Midland)		To Sheringham			To Aldeburgh		
			DU		DU						DU	DU	DU	DU
	SO HC	♠ HC				SO HC		SO HC	SO HC	♠ HC				
Notes	Not after 7th September; [1] Gorleston to Yarmouth S.T.		[1] Oulton Broad South to Lowestoft; [1] Gorleston to Yarmouth S.T.	[1] Thurston to Bury; [3] Fulbourne to Cambridge		Not after 5th September; [2] Gorleston to Yarmouth S.T.		Not after 5th September; [2] Gorleston to Yarmouth S.T.	Not after 5th September		[3] Fulbourne to Cambridge		[1] Thurston to Bury	Not after 5th September; [1] Gorleston to Yarmouth S.T.
1	11 10	11 30				11 50		12 10	12 20	12 30				
2	12 35	12 42				13 19	13 24	13 39	13 45	13 50				
3	12 37	12 44	12 50	12 55	13 00 [1]	13 21	13 30	13 41	13 47	13 55		13 54	14 00	
4					13 12								14 12	
5				13 10½	13 17		13 46			14 08½			14 17	
6				13 14	13 19		13 47			14 10½			14 18	
7					13 23								14 22	
8		12 58½		13 17½	13 23½		13 53		14 04	14 14½			14 22½	
9					13a31					[2½]				
10					13 38									
11					13 43					14 28				
12					13 44½					14 30				
13					13 49									
14					13 54									
15		13 13			13 54½				14 21	14 37				
16					14 00									
17		[2]			14 04½					[3]				
18					[1]									
19		13 30			14 19				14 37	14 55				
20									14 43					
21													14 29	
22				13 27½			14 03						14 35½	
23				13 34			14 09						14 44	
24				13 35			14 12				14 35			
25				13 41							14 41			
26				13 46½							14 46½			
27				13 51½							14 51½			
28				13 55½			14 29				14 55½			
29				13 57							14 57			
30				13 59½							14 59½			
31				14 01							15 01			
32				14 02							15 02			
33														
34														
35														
36							14 31							
37							14a38							
38							14 44							
39							14 46							
40							14 51							
41							14 56							
42							14 58							
43							15 01							
44				14 08							15 08			
45				14 12½							15 12½			
46				14 18							15 18			
47				14 30							15 30			
48	12 44		12 55½			13 28		13 48				14 00½		
49	12 53		13 06			13 37		13 57				14 11½		
50			13 14									14 19½		
51	13 10		13 22					14 14				14 27½		
52	13 11		13 23			13 53		14 15				14 28½		
53			13 30½											
54			13 38			14 07								
55	13 25		13 39			14 08		14 29						
56			13 46											
57	13 38		13 53½					14 42						
58	13 39½		13 55½			14 21		14 43½						
59			14 04½			14 31		[1]						
60	[5]		14 05			14 33								
61	14 00		14 10			14 39		15 00						
62	14 05		14 15			14 44		15 05						15 15
63			14 19½											15 19½
64	[2]		14 23			14a53								15 23
65			14 27½			14a59								15 27½
66			14 30½											15 30½
67	14 20		14 32½			15 04		15 18						15 32½
68	14 22		14 33½			15 06		15 20						15 33½
69	14 29		14 40			15 14		15 28						15 40

DOWN			1-52	1-51	2-72	2-28	3-71	2-00	2-72	1-51	2-71	2-25	1-52
							ECS	16.22 Railbus from Ely					
					DU	DU	DU		DU		DU	DU	
			SO HC	♠ HC						♠ HC			SO ♠ HC
LIVERPOOL ST.(Z)	dep	1	13 10	13 30						14 30			15 20
IPSWICH	arr	2	14 35	14 42						15 50			16 34
	dep	3	14 37	14 44	14 50	14 55	15†20			15 55			16 38½
Needham		4											
Stowmarket	arr	5				15 10½	15†40			16 08½			
	dep	6				15 11½				16 10½	16 19		
HAUGHLEY	arr	7									16 23		
	dep	8		14 58½		15 15				16 14½	16 23½		
Finningham		9									16a31		
Mellis		10								[2½]	16 38		
Diss	arr	11								16 28	16 43		
	dep	12								16 30	16 44½		
Burston		13									16 49		
TIVETSHALL	arr	14									16 54		
	dep	15		15 13						16 37	16 54½		
Forncett		16									17 00		
Flordon		17		[2]							17 04½		
Trowse		18								[3]	[1]		
NORWICH THORPE	arr	19		15 30						16 55	17‡18		
	dep	20											
Elmswell (UP)		21											
Thurston (UP)		22				15 25							
BURY (UP)	arr	23				15 33							
(UP)	dep	24				15 35						16 39	
Saxham and Risby (UP)		25				15 41							
Higham (UP)		26				15 46½							
Kennett (UP)		27				15 51½							
Chippenham Jn. (UP)		28				15 55½						16 55	
Warren Hill Jn. (UP)		29				15 57		16 44				16 56½	
Newmarket Yd. Jn. (UP)		30				15 59½		16 46½				16X59	
NEWMARKET (UP)	arr	31				16 01		16 48				17 00½	
(DOWN)	dep	32				16 02						17 02	
Newmarket (Down) (DOWN)		33											
Newmarket Yd. Jn. (DOWN)		34											
Warren Hill Jn. (DOWN)		35											
Snailwell Jn. (DOWN)		36											
Fordham (DOWN)		37											
Soham (DOWN)	arr	38											
(DOWN)	dep	39											
Barway Siding (DOWN)		40											
Ely Dock Jn. (DOWN)		41											
ELY (DOWN)	arr	42											
(DOWN)	dep	43											
Dullingham (UP)		44				16 08						17 08	
Six Mile Bottom (UP)		45				16 12½						17 12½	
Fulbourne (UP)		46				16 18						17 18	
CAMBRIDGE (UP)	arr	47				16 30						17 30	
Westerfield		48	14 44		14 55½								16 45½
Woodbridge		49	14 53		15 06								16 54½
Wickham Market		50			15 14								
SAXMUNDHAM	arr	51			15 22								17 11½
	dep	52	15 09		15 23								17 12½
Darsham		53			15 30½								
Halesworth	arr	54	15 23		15 38								
	dep	55	15 24		15 39				16 54½				17 26½
Brampton		56			15 46				17 01½				
BECCLES	arr	57			15 53½				17 09				17 39½
	dep	58	15 37		15 55½				17 10				17 40½
Oulton Broad South	arr	59	15 50		16 04½				17 19				17 51½
	dep	60	15‡51½		16 05				17 19½				17 52½
LOWESTOFT CEN.	arr	61	15 57		16‡09½				17 24½				17 58
	dep	62	16 02		16 15				17 32				18 03
Lowestoft North		63			16 19½				17 36½				
Corton		64			16 23				17 40				
Hopton-on-Sea		65			16 27½				17 44½				
Gorleston Links Halt		66			16 30½				17 47½				
Gorleston-on-Sea	arr	67	16 15		16 32½				17 49½				18 16
	dep	68	16 17		16 33½				17 50½				18 18
YARMOUTH S.T.	arr	69	16 23		16 40				17 57				18 26
Notes			Not after 5th September; [3] Beccles to Oulton Broad South (‡ 15.48)		[1] Gorleston to Yarmouth S.T.	[2] Thurston to Bury; [3] Fulbourne to Cambridge	To work 16.19 to Norwich		[1] Oulton Broad South to Lowestoft; [1] Gorleston to Yarmouth S.T.		(‡ 17.21)	[3] Fulbourne to Cambridge	Until 5th September inclusive; [2] Gorleston to Yarmouth S.T.

DOWN			1-55	2-73	2-28	2-28	2-71	2-72	1S11	1-59	1S11	1S11	3-79	1-53	1-52	2-72	1-55
			To Yarmouth Vauxhall	To Norwich T.					17.15 Colchester to Glasgow (Qn. St.) SX Edinburgh (W) SO or Peterboro' N'th. (SO)	To Yarmouth Vauxhall	17.15 Colchester to Glasgow (Qn. St.)	17.15 Colchester to Edinburgh (Waverley) §	ECS				To Yarmouth Vauxhall
					DRB	DU	DU	DU								DU	
			♠ HC							♠ HC	SX	SO	SO	♠ HC	SO ♠ HC		♠ HC
LIVERPOOL ST.(Z)	dep	1	15 30							16 30	←	←		16 50	16 50		17 30
IPSWICH	arr	2	16 42						17 45	17 50	17 45	17 45		18 08	18 08		18 42
	dep	3	16 44	16 50		17 00	17 28	17 30	18 00	17 55	18 00	18 00	18†06	18 10	18 10		18 44
Needham		4				17 12	17 40		→								
Stowmarket	arr	5				17 17	17 45			18 08½	18 16	18 16					
	dep	6				17 19	17 45½			18 10½	18 20	18 20					
HAUGHLEY	arr	7				17 23	17 49½										
	dep	8	16 58½			17 23½	17 50			18 14½	18 26	18 26	18 36				18 58½
Finningham		9					17 57½			[2½]							
Mellis		10					18 04½										
Diss	arr	11					18 09½			18 28							
	dep	12					18 10			18 30							
Burston		13					18 14½										
TIVETSHALL	arr	14					18 19½										
	dep	15	17 13				18 20			18 37							19 13
Forncett		16					18 25½										
Flordon		17					18 30			[3]							[2]
Trowse		18	[2]				[2½]										
NORWICH THORPE	arr	19	17 30				18‡45			18 55							19 30
	dep	20	17 36							19 06							19 36
Elmswell (UP)		21				17 30											
Thurston (UP)		22				17 36½					18 36	18 36	18 50				
BURY (UP)	arr	23				17 42½					18 42	18 42					
(UP)	dep	24				17 50					18 52	18 52	19 00				
Saxham and Risby (UP)		25				17 56											
Higham (UP)		26				18 01½											
Kennett (UP)		27				18 06½											
Chippenham Jn. (UP)		28				18 10½					19 09	19 09	19 19				
Warren Hill Jn. (UP)		29				18X12											
Newmarket Yd. Jn. (UP)		30				18X14½											
NEWMARKET (UP)	arr	31				18 16											
(DOWN)	dep	32			17 53	18 17											
Newmarket (Down) (DOWN)		33															
Newmarket Yd. Jn. (DOWN)		34															
Warren Hill Jn. (DOWN)		35															
Snailwell Jn. (DOWN)		36									19 11	19 11	19 21				
Fordham (DOWN)		37															
Soham (DOWN)	arr	38															
(DOWN)	dep	39									19 19	19 19	19 31				
Barway Siding (DOWN)		40									19 23	19 23	19 35				
Ely Dock Jn. (DOWN)		41									19 28	19 28	19 42				
ELY (DOWN)	arr	42									19 30	19 30	19†44				
(DOWN)	dep	43									19 40	19 40					
Dullingham (UP)		44			17 59	18 23											
Six Mile Bottom (UP)		45			18 03½	18 27½											
Fulbourne (UP)		46			18 09	18 33											
CAMBRIDGE (UP)	arr	47			18 18	18 42											
Westerfield		48		16 57				17 35½						18 17	18 17		
Woodbridge		49		17a08				17 46						18a28	18a28		
Wickham Market		50		17 18½				17 54									
SAXMUNDHAM	arr	51		17 29½				18 02						18 46	18 46		
	dep	52		17 30½				18 03						18 49	18 49		
Darsham		53		17 39				18 10½									
Halesworth	arr	54		17 48				18 18						19 04	19 04		
	dep	55		17 49				18 19						19 05	19 05		
Brampton		56		17 57				18 26									
BECCLES	arr	57		18 06½				18 33½						19 19	19 19		
	dep	58		18 08½				18 34½						19 20	19 20		
Oulton Broad South	arr	59		18 19½				18 43½						19 31	19 31		
	dep	60		18‡23½				18 44½						19‡33½	19‡33½		
LOWESTOFT CEN.	arr	61		18 29				18 49						19 39	19 39		
	dep	62		18 49				18 52						19 44		19 58	
Lowestoft North		63						18 56½								20 02½	
Corton		64						19 00								20 06	
Hopton-on-Sea		65						19 04½								20 10½	
Gorleston Links Halt		66						19 07½								20 13½	
Gorleston-on-Sea	arr	67						19 09½						19 57		20 15½	
	dep	68						19 10½						19 58		20 16½	
YARMOUTH S.T.	arr	69						19 17						20 05		20 23	
Notes				(‡ 18.20)			(‡ 18.47)	[1] Gorleston to Yarmouth S.T.			Not to convey extra vehicles from Colchester and Manningtree for stations short of Edinburgh; ♠ beyond March	♠ Beyond March. NOT to convey extra Vehicles from Colchester and Manningtree for stations short of Edinburgh (until 5th September); §Commencing 12th September terminates at Peterborough North Code 1C12	After working 12.33 from Rugby (Midland); Until 5th September inclusive	(‡ 19.32); SX until 4th September Daily from 7th September	(‡ 19.32); Not after 5th September; [1] Gorleston to Yarmouth S.T.	Until 5th September inclusive; [1] Gorleston to Yarmouth S.T.	

F78 WEEKDAYS IPSWICH TO NORWICH, LOWESTOFT AND YARMOUTH S.T.—IPSWICH TO ELY AND CAMBRIDGE

DOWN		2-72	2-28	2-28		2-00	2-71	2-00	1-55	2-73	2-28	1-59		2-73		
						19.51 from Ely			To Yarmouth Vauxhall			To Yarmouth Vauxhall				
		DU		DU		DU	DU	DU		DU	DU			DU		
				SO					HC			HC				
LIVERPOOL ST.(Z) .. dep	1								18 30			19 30				
IPSWICH .. .. .. arr	2								19 50			20 42				
dep	3	18 50	18 55	18 55			19 00		19 55	19 57	20 00	20 44				
Needham	4		19 07	19 07			[1] 19 13									
Stowmarket .. .. .. arr	5		19 12	19 12			19 18		20 08½		20 15½					
dep	6		19 13	19 13			19 19		20 10½		20 16½					
HAUGHLEY .. .. arr	7		19 17	19 17			19 23									
dep	8		19 17½	19 17½			19 23½		20 14½		20 20	20 58½				
Finningham	9						19a31		[2½]							
Mellis	10						19 38									
Diss .. .. arr	11						19 43		20 28							
dep	12						19 44½		20 30							
Burston	13						19 49									
TIVETSHALL .. arr	14						19 54									
dep	15						19 54½		20 37			21 13				
Forncett	16						20 00									
Flordon	17						20 04½		[3]			[2]				
Trowse	18						[1]									
NORWICH THORPE arr	19						20 18		20 55			21 30				
dep	20								21 06			21 56				
UP: Elmswell	21		19 24	19 24												
Thurston	22		19 30½	19 30½							20 30					
BURY .. .. .. arr	23		19 38	19 38							20 36					
dep	24		19 41	19 41				27th July to 5th September inclusive			20 37					
Saxham and Risby	25		19 47	19 47												
Higham	26		19 52½	19 52½												
Kennett	27		19 57½	19 57½												
Chippenham Jn.	28		20 01½	20 01½							20 53½					
Warren Hill Jn.	29		20 03	20 03		20 13					20 55					
Newmarket Yd. Jn.	30		20 05½	20 05½		20 15½					20 57½					
NEWMARKET .. arr	31		20 07	20 07		20 17					20 59					
dep	32	[1½] Oulton Broad South to Lowestoft	20 11½	20 11½						Commences 7th September [1½] Oulton Broad South to Lowestoft	20 59½					
DOWN: Newmarket (Down)	33		[1½] Thurston to Bury	[1½] Thurston to Bury		27th July to 5th September inclusive		20 45								
Newmarket Yd. Jn.	34							20 46½								
Warren Hill Jn.	35							20 49								
Snailwell Jn.	36							20 50½								
Fordham	37							20a56								
Soham .. arr	38							21 01								
dep	39							21‡04								
Barway Siding	40							21 08								
Ely Dock Jn.	41							21 12								
ELY .. arr	42							21 14								
dep	43															
UP: Dullingham	44		20 17	20 17				(‡ 21.02)						Commences 7th September		
Six Mile Bottom	45		20 21½	20 21½												
Fulbourne	46		20 27	20 27												
CAMBRIDGE .. arr	47		20 36	20 36							21 20					
Westerfield	48	18 55½								20 02½						
Woodbridge	49	19 06								20 13						
Wickham Market	50	19 14								20 21						
SAXMUNDHAM .. arr	51	19 22								20 29						
dep	52	19 23	Daily until 5th September SX from 7th September	From 12th September						20 30				[1] Oulton Broad South to Lowestoft		
Darsham	53	19 30½								20 37½						
Halesworth .. arr	54	19 38								20 45						
dep	55	19 39								20 46						
Brampton	56	19 46								20 53						
BECCLES .. .. arr	57	19 53½								21 00½						
dep	58	19 55½								21 01½				21 30		
Oulton Broad South .. arr	59	20 04½								21 10½				21 39		
dep	60	20 05								21 11				21 39½		
LOWESTOFT CEN. arr	61	20 10								21 16				21 45		
dep	62	20 13														
Lowestoft North	63	20 17½														
Corton	64	20 21														
Hopton-on-Sea	65	20 25½														
Gorleston Links Halt	66	20 28½														
Gorleston-on-Sea .. arr	67	20 30½														
dep	68	20 31½														
YARMOUTH S.T. .. arr	69	20 37														

IPSWICH TO NORWICH, LOWESTOFT AND YARMOUTH S.T.—IPSWICH TO ELY AND CAMBRIDGE WEEKDAYS F79

			2-73	2-72	2-71	2-75				1-51	1-51	3-56			2-75		3-56		3-73
												19.38 Parcels Brentwood to Whitemoor					19.38 Parcels Brentwood to Whitemoor		ECS
			DU	DU	DU	DU									DU				DU
			FSO							SX HC	SO HC	SX					SX		SO
1										20 30	20 30						←		
2										21 54	21 54	22 08					22 08		
3			20 50	20 50	21 00	21 07				21 59	21 59	22 50 →			22 10		22 50		
4						21 19									22 22				
5					21 15½	21 24				22 12½	22 12½				22 27		23 09		
6					21 16½	21 25				22 14½	22 14½				22 28		23 14		
7					21 20½	21 29									22 32				
8					21 21	21 29½				22 18½	22 18½				22 32½		23 20		
9			Commences 11th September	Until 5th September inclusive	21 27½					[1½]	22a24								
10											22a32								
11					21 38					22 30	22 37½								
12					21 39					22 32	22 38½								
13						[1½] Thurston to Bury									[1½] Thurston to Bury				
14					21 47														
15					21 48					22 39	22 45½								
16																			
17										[1]	[3½]								
18					[3]														
19					22 11					22 55	23 04								
20																			
21						21 36									22 39				
22						21 42½									22 46½		23 32		
23						21 49									22 54		23 38		
24				[1] Gorleston to Yarmouth S.T.													23 42		
25																			
26																			
27																			
28																	0 02		
29																			
30																			
31																			
32				[1½] Oulton Broad South to Lowestoft															
33																			
34																			
35																			
36																	0 04		
37																	[3]		
38																			
39																	0X15		
40																	0 19		
41																	0 23		
42																			
43																	0 24		
44																			
45																			
46																			
47																			
48			20 55½	20 55½															
49			21 06	21 06															
50			21 14	21 14															
51			21 22	21 22															
52				21 23															Not after 5th September
53				21 30½															
54				21 38															
55				21 39															
56				21 46															
57				21 53½															
58				21 55½															23†32
59				22 04½															
60				22 05															
61				22 10															23†47
62				22 15													Same as page 70		After working 22.45 from Yarmouth S.T.
63				22 19½															
64				22 23															
65				22 27½															
66				22 30½															
67				22 32½															
68				22 33½															
69				22 40															

F134 WEEKDAYS SAXMUNDHAM TO ALDEBURGH — ALL DU

Mileage M	C	DOWN		2–01 § 6.00 from Ipswich (§ Code 3-01 from Ipswich to Saxmundham)	2–01	2–01 9.58 from Ipswich (Until 5th September inclusive)	2–01	2–01 13.58 from Ipswich	2–01	2–01		2–01		2–01 (Until 5th September inclusive)		
0	0	**SAXMUNDHAM**	arr	6 31	......	10 31½	......	14 27½	......	......	......	......	......	......	......	......
			dep	6 37	7 51	10 32½	11 51	14 28	15 51	17 37	..	18 53	..	20 10	..	..
0	34	Saxmundham Jn.		6 38	7 52	10 33½	11 52	14 29	15 52	17 38	......	18 54	......	20 11	......	......
3	75	Leiston		6a46	8a00	10a41½	12a00	14a37	16a00	17a46	..	19a02	..	20a19	..	..
6	22	Thorpeness Halt		6 54½	8 08½	10 50	12 08½	14 45½	16 08½	17 54½	......	19 10½	......	20 27½	......	......
					1	1	1	½	1½	1½		1½		½		
8	26	**ALDEBURGH**	arr	6 59½	8 14½	10 56	12 14½	14 51	16 15	18 01	..	19 16	..	20 33	..	..

WEEKDAYS ALDEBURGH TO SAXMUNDHAM — ALL DU

Mileage M	C	UP		2–01		2–01 To Ipswich	2–01 (Until 5th September inclusive)	2–01 To Ipswich	2–01	2–01		2–01	2 01 (‡ 19.20) (Until 5th September inclusive)	2–01 To Colchester SX Ipswich SO (‡ 19.20) (Commences 7th September)	2–01 To Ipswich (‡ 20.36) (Until 5th September inclusive)	
0	0	**ALDEBURGH**	dep	7 04½	......	8 19½	11 18	12 19½	14 56	17 06	......	18 16	19‡22	19‡22	20‡38	......
2	4	Thorpeness Halt		7a09	..	8a24	11a22½	12a24	15a00½	17a10½	..	18a20½	19a26½	19a26½	20a42½	..
4	31	Leiston		7a18	......	8a33	11a31½	12a33	15a09½	17a19½	......	18a29½	19a35½	19a35½	20a51½	......
7	72	Saxmundham Jn.		7 25	..	8 40	11 38½	12 40	15 16½	17 26½	..	18 36½	19 42½	19 42½	20 58½	..
8	26	**SAXMUNDHAM**	arr	7 26	......	8 41	11 39½	12 41	15 17½	17 27½	......	18 37½	19 43½	19 43½	20 59½	......
			dep	..	..	8 42	..	12 42	..	..	..	..	..	19 44	21 00	..

Pages 240-244 and above:
ER ER passenger WTT 15 June 1964 to 12 June 65, showing the main line service and the Aldeburgh branch.

one. It proposed to modernise working practices, and was effectively a review of the 1955 Modernisation Plan which was clearly floundering. It also proposed some new initiatives to gain new business, notably the introduction of 'Liner Trains' for bulk freight, together with greatly improved handling and transfer facilities, although this went largely unremarked and was little implemented. The popular focus was very much on the closures.

The Eastern Region of British Railways had been in the forefront of the drive to eliminate unprofitable lines. Almost the entire M&GN system had been closed to passengers in 1959, and the East Suffolk's main line had partly followed the same year. The Framlingham and Snape branches had been pruned, likewise the Mid-Suffolk and Waveney Valley, and even the stations on the main line between Ipswich and Norwich were steadily being eliminated. Nevertheless the sweeping cuts proposed by the Reshaping Report caused great consternation. In justification, the report showed the density of freight traffic to be less than 5,000 tons per week on all parts of the East Suffolk, with the only lines in East Anglia over this being the main lines to Norwich via both Ipswich and Cambridge, plus Haughley to Ely, and Cambridge via Newmarket, the Harwich branch and the lines to King's Lynn from both March and Ely. As regards passenger traffic, nothing north of Ipswich–Saxmundham on the East Suffolk showed more than 50,000 passengers per week. Beyond there, to Lowestoft and Yarmouth, the lines came in the 5,000 to 10,000 per week, with the Aldeburgh branch as 0 to 5,000. Under the heading of passenger train receipts both of the Yarmouth stations, Lowestoft Central, Beccles and Saxmundham generated more than £25,000 per annum, whilst Oulton Broad South, Halesworth, Leiston and Woodbridge came in the £5,000 to £25,000 band. The remainder were under this figure. South Town, Lowestoft and Beccles still generated over 25,000 tons of freight traffic each year, with most others in the 5,000 to 25,000-ton category. Nevertheless, Dr Beeching proposed to withdraw all remaining passenger services from the East Suffolk, plus the Lowestoft to Yarmouth direct line. Although the report did not target specific stations and lines for the withdrawal of goods traffic, the report stated that there would be a 'reduction of uneconomic freight traffic passing through small stations by closing them progressively . . .' although it proposed to preserve potentially good railway traffic. More siding-to-siding traffic would be attracted which could be operated as block trains, rather than the expensive wagonload system.

Gerard Fiennes, then General Manager of the Eastern Region, was scathing about the principles applied to rural railways in the report. In his book *I Tried To Run A Railway* he wrote that the Marples/Beeching axis had laid down that rural railways did not and could never pay, and hence decreed their elimination. Gerry Fiennes thought otherwise, and felt that new techniques such as diesel traction, automated level crossings, mechanised track maintenance, tokenless block signalling and bus-stop operation could more than halve costs. The closure procedure was well under way when he took charge of the Eastern Region, but East Suffolk was not going to lose its railway without a fight, and battle was joined along the line. Local MPs — most of whom had voted for the Beeching Report — the local press, local councils and most of the local people, and the railway workers had combined to present an unanswerable case.

British Railways' management retreated before the onslaught, and on 2 March 1964 introduced a revised timetable for the line. This showed a service calling at all stations except Westerfield from Yarmouth to Ipswich roughly every two hours, and taking 1hr 50min overall, or about 80min from Lowestoft. It would be supplemented with other trains between Yarmouth and Lowestoft or Beccles, and also with some of the Aldeburgh branch trains extended to Ipswich. There were to be two through trains to London from Lowestoft, leaving at 7.12am and 6.55pm, both with connections from Yarmouth. The last up trains were the 7.25pm Yarmouth to Ipswich, and 8.42pm to Beccles. In the other direction the service was similar in pattern, with the first down service being the 6.16am from Lowestoft Central to Yarmouth, then the 6.28am from Halesworth, which was actually the newspaper train from Ipswich. The 5.30pm from Liverpool Street was a through train to Lowestoft, as was the 5.30pm from Ipswich on Saturdays in May. The last departure from London was on the 6.30pm, connecting with the 7.57pm to Lowestoft, except on Fridays and Saturdays, when the 7.30pm had a connection as far as Saxmundham. The Aldeburgh branch had seven trains each way, with three working to and from Ipswich.

Passenger counts had shown heavy usage of the line, and detailed analysis on passenger numbers was done in November 1964. On Tuesday 3 November passengers included 93 going from Lowestoft to Liverpool Street or beyond, with 44 from Beccles, 53 from Saxmundham and 61 from Woodbridge. Twelve travelled from Aldeburgh, and there were in all 351 passengers travelling from the East Suffolk to London on one day. A total of 2,222 passengers used the line that day, with 2,683 on the following Saturday when fewer went to London but more to Ipswich, Yarmouth and Lowestoft. Counts were also done on Sunday 4 October, when four up East Suffolk trains carried 87, 164, 198 and 192 passengers into Ipswich, with 97, 60, 71 and 92 joining there on the down services. The numbers of passengers which went forward to Yarmouth from Lowestoft were 43, 23, 41 and 35. Even so, British Railways proposed to introduce conductor-guard working and destaff Wickham Market, Darsham, Brampton, Corton, Hopton and Yarmouth South Town stations in order to cut costs.

The proposed replacement bus services had come in for a great deal of criticism. On the timetables produced in 1964 the journey was scheduled to take 2hr 10min between Lowestoft Central and Ipswich station, or 50min longer than by rail and without the ability take heavy luggage, prams, bikes or the like. The timetable was based on existing Grey-Green express bus services; it turned out that at least 10min extra would be needed for the proposed rail replacement. Donald Newby, then Liberal Parliamentary candidate for the Eye constituency, hired three buses to follow the routes of the proposed replacement services and demonstrated that it was simply impracticable to expect a bus to replace the train service. With two Suffolk mayors and other civic leaders on board, they arrived at Ipswich 23min after the London train had left.

The Halesworth & District Action Committee had the backing of the local Urban District Council, its chairman being councillor J. S. P. Denny. It met at the Town Hall on 20 November 1964 and heard a great many representations. On 4 April 1963 the National Council on Inland Transport had published a highly critical commentary on the Beeching Report, pointing out that it was proposed to save about £18 million per annum by closing 5,000 miles of railway. On the same day the British Road Federation called for a cut in fuel tax and the spending of £1,300 million on new roads. British Railways had had many letters from town and borough opposing closure as well as from the Branch Line Re-Invigoration Society (BLRIS). Proposals had already been put forward to destaff certain places — 'withdrawal of attendance' in the rather quaint official parlance — and level crossings such as Wissett were duly downgraded. The BLRIS had prepared a progress report and felt that the case for closure was marginal. The reported loss on the East Suffolk for 1961 was only £90,800, and a less convenient service would cause a loss of passengers.

The official body appointed to look after passengers' interests, the East Anglian Transport Users' Consultative Committee (TUCC), seemed to be astonishingly indifferent at first, and dismissed claims of hardship that came before it at its official hearings. It held a two-day public enquiry at Saxmundham on 28 and 29 September 1965. There were 1,916 written objections to consider, 75 local authorities and other organisations wishing to be heard and a further 150 individual objectors. Many were not heard because of the large numbers, and the chairman Mr L. A. Carey indicated that a further hearing could be held if necessary. He believed that the TUCC had sufficient evidence on which to base its recommendations to the Minister of Transport, having been forced by the sheer weight and strength of the opposition to conclude that closure should be opposed. The main grounds were the longer journey time, the inability of replacement buses to carry heavy luggage, the absence of toilet facilities, the fact that buses would be less comfortable and cold in winter, and that buses were more prone to disruption in bad weather. Severe hardship would be caused if the main line were to close, but not if the Aldeburgh branch were to go. The prolonged and sometimes bitter struggle to save the line led to the formation of one of the earliest of the rail users' groups, the East Suffolk Travellers' Association (ESTA), which continues to campaign for local passengers today.

There were very large numbers of lines awaiting decisions over their future status: the Beeching axe hung over thousands of stations. It was not until mid-1966 that Barbara Castle, now Minister of Transport, announced her decision to reprieve the East Suffolk and the Lowestoft to Yarmouth lines, but to permit withdrawal of passenger services from the Aldeburgh branch. The closure was to take effect on and from Monday 12 September, but as there were no Sunday services, the last train ran on Saturday 10 September. Services were not strengthened and the usual branch train, a two-car Metro-Cammell unit, was crowded as it left Aldeburgh with the final working, which was the 19.22 to Colchester. Large numbers of people stood on the platform to see the train leave, and away from Leiston as well. Saxmundham Junction signalbox closed soon after, to be replaced by a ground frame and a simplified track layout. Aldeburgh closed completely on that day, its goods service having been withdrawn over six years earlier on 30 November 1959. Sizewell siding became the limit of the line, since although it had closed for general traffic on 7 March 1966 it was retained to serve the nearby nuclear power station. Leiston remained open for goods traffic, but the East Suffolk had not yet reached its lowest ebb. Whilst it was essential to reduce costs to keep the line open, there were more cuts in infrastructure yet to come.

Gerard Fiennes, on his return to the Eastern Region, had proposed *inter alia* to automate the level crossings and single the track as cost-cutting measures on the way to his 'basic railway'. For whatever reason, neither happened. Costs of £250,000 per year had been ascribed to the East Suffolk at the TUCC hearings, with a revenue of about £120,000. Later they were revised to £154,000 earnings and direct costs of £178,000. Fiennes reckoned that the costs could be brought down to £84,000, and that although fares simplification might cost up to £30,000, these measures would bring the line back into balance. The measures that were brought in amounted to no more than a simplification of the signalling and destaffing the stations, as well as withdrawal from goods traffic. The

Above:
The down 'London', 16.50 from Liverpool Street, heads for Lowestoft on 6 September 1966 behind Class 47 No D1758 near Ufford.
G. R. Mortimer

Paytrain concept was to be introduced, whereby conductors on the trains would issue a limited range of tickets to destinations on the line itself, with passengers wanting to travel further afield having to rebook when changing trains at Ipswich or Lowestoft. Intermediate stations on the line were scheduled to become unstaffed on 7 November 1966 with the introduction of Paytrains, but this was postponed to 2 January 1967 as talks with the trades unions failed to reach a conclusion, and was not finally implemented until Monday 10 March 1967, the final tickets having been issued from booking offices on Sunday evening. This allowed the withdrawal of 130 staff from intermediate stations on a number of lines including the East Suffolk, although local guards had agreed that they would not collect fares on the Norwich to Yarmouth, Lowestoft and Cambridge lines.

Goods facilities were withdrawn at different times. Wickham Market, Brampton and Oulton Broad South went on 13 July 1964; Barnby and Aldeby on 28 December 1964 at the end of the sugar beet season; Halesworth closed from 19 April 1965; Bealings, Saxmundham, Darsham, and Woodbridge on 18 April 1966; and finally Beccles on 13 January 1968. Melton was the great survivor, lasting until 1984 for coal traffic. The only other piece of modernisation that had been mooted was at the level crossings, and whilst many were destaffed and reduced to user-operated gates or closed completely, only Darsham was modernised, receiving automatic half-barriers monitored from Saxmundham on 6 March 1967. Beccles bypass also received such a crossing when it opened in the early 1980s, but this was a new installation where none had previously existed.

Demolition of the branch between Aldeburgh and Sizewell siding took place during mid-1968. The siding remained open for traffic although it had officially closed for general goods from 7 March 1966. Leiston remained open for goods traffic, with Garrett's works still operational and the sidings being shunted by their yellow battery-electric locomotive which had replaced *Sirapite*. Meanwhile, the service to Yarmouth South Town had been operated entirely via Gorleston, and the station had become a shadow of its former self. Having been extensively modernised and enlarged in the mid-1950s with new canopies and platform extensions, it was rapidly run down and reduced to unstaffed halt status. General goods facilities had been withdrawn from 6 November 1967, and all the track was lifted apart from that into the former arrival bay, Platform 4, and the line from Lowestoft Central reduced to a long siding. The service was withdrawn on and from Monday 4 May 1970, so that the last trains ran on Saturday 2 May. For its outward journey from Lowestoft Central the usual two-car DMU had an extra four cars added to accommodate the 300 passengers; about 1,500 tickets had been issued on the day. Around 1,000 of them were by Lowestoft guard Norman Riches, who had served almost 50 years on the railway and who retired when the last train finished its journey. The final working was the 21.10 from South Town to Lowestoft Central driven by William George of Beccles, which had a headboard affixed by enthusiasts reading '13th July 1903 — 2nd May 1970. The Last Train. Yarmouth South Town to Lowestoft Central'. The station was taken over as a depot by a company involved in the North Sea oil and gas industry, but was demolished early in 1978.

Today there is little left of the line from Beccles, and probably less of that from Lowestoft. The trackbed north of the Beccles bypass, from roughly where Lowestoft Junction once stood, is mostly used as a farm track and can be walked as far as the swing bridge, where the piers remain intact on both sides of the river. The trackbed is largely intact as far as the first level crossing, but is in private ownership. The

K52 WEEKDAYS — NORWICH TO YARMOUTH VAUXHALL AND LOWESTOFT

DOWN

M C	M C	M C	Station	No.	8–13	4–12	4–12	5–43	5–43
						Not during Sugar Beet Season	D Beet Season only	3.45 from Whitemoor	5.00 from Whitemoor
								MX	MO
0 0	0 0	0 0	NORWICH THORPE dep	1					
0 54	0 54	0 54	Wensum Junction Sdgs. arr	2				5*35	
			dep	3	4 20	4 55	4 55	5*41	6 51
1 66	1 66	1 66	Whitlingham Jn.	4	4 26	5 00	5 00	5 47	6 55
5 63	5 63	5 63	BRUNDALL arr	5					
			dep	6	4 35	5 06	5 06	5 53	7 01
7 79			Lingwood	7					
10 35			ACLE arr	8					[3]
			dep	9			5 15		
	8 2	8 2	Buckenham	10					
	10 2	10 2	Cantley	11					
	12 15	12 15	REEDHAM arr	12					
			dep	13	4 50	5 15	[2]	6 02	7 13
17 15	19 35		Breydon Junction	14		5 26	26		
18 28	20 48		YARMOUTH VAUX. arr	15		5 30	30		[2]
	0 0	16 18	Haddiscoe L.L.	16					
	0 61		Fleet Junction	17					
	2 44		Aldeby	18					
		18 3	Somerleyton	19					
		22 8	Oulton Broad North	20					
		23 43	LOWESTOFT CEN. arr	21	5 21			6 23	7 36

WEEKDAYS — LOWESTOFT AND YARMOUTH VAUXHALL TO NORWICH

UP

M C	M C	M C	Station	No.	8–13	4–47	8–11
						To Whitemoor	
					SX Q		
		0 0	LOWESTOFT CEN. dep	1			
		1 35	Oulton Broad North	2			
	0 0		Aldeby	3	10 50		
	1 72		Fleet Junction	4	10 58		
	2 53	7 25	HADDISCOE L.L. arr	5	11 01		
			dep	6			
0 0	0 0		YARMOUTH VAUX.	7		13 50	14 10
1 13	1 13		Breydon Junction	8		13 54	14X16
	8 33	11 28	REEDHAM arr	9			
			dep	10		14X05	
	10 46	13 41	Cantley	11			
7 73			Acle arr	12			14 34
			dep	13			14X53
10 29			Lingwood	14			
12 45	14 65	17 60	Brundall arr	15			
			dep	16		14 14	15 10
16 42	16 62	21 57	Whitlingham Junction	17		14 19	15 21
17 54	19 74	22 69	Wensum Junction Sdgs. arr	18		[2]	15 27
			dep	19		14 23	15 52
			Trowse arr	20			
			dep	21		14 26	
18 28	20 48	23 43	NORWICH THORPE arr	22			16 00

WEEKDAYS — NORWICH TO YARMOUTH VAUXHALL AND LOWESTOFT — SUNDAYS — K53

No.	8–13	8–13	8–11	4–47	8–13	7*43	8–12	4–13
		Haddiscoe arr. 10.05	Lingwood arr. 11.08	9.15 from Whitemoor	Cantley arr. 12.57	14.00 from Whitemoor		Conveys traffic for 19.15 Lowestoft to Temple Mills
	SX Q				SX	SX	SX	SX
1								19 56
2								20 02
3		9 20	10 37	11 11	12 30	16 37	19 47	
4		9 26	10 43	11*17	12 36	16 41	19 53	
5			R	11*24		[3]		
6		9 35	11 00	11*33	12 45	16 52	20 02	
7			11 20					
8			11 32					
9			12X39	11 42				
10								
11					13 16	R		
12					13*26			
13		9*53			13*44	17 04	20 17	
14			12 58	11 51			20 34	
15			13 04	11 55			20 40	
16	10 27	11 11						
17	10 30							
18	10 38							
19								
20					14 12			
21		11 35			14 21	17 29		

WEEKDAYS — LOWESTOFT AND YARMOUTH VAUXHALL TO NORWICH — SUNDAYS

No.	8–13	4–12	4–43	4–53	8–43	7*43	8–12
			To Whitemoor	To Temple Mills (via Ipswich)		To Whitemoor	
	SO	SX	SX	SX	SX	SX	SX
1	14 48		18 38	19 15	20 35	22 36	
2							
3							
4							
5							
6							
7		18 22					23 10
8		18 26					23X16
9							
10	15 22	18 37	19 00	19 37	21 09	23 02	23 33
11		[5]	[4]				
12							
13							
14							
15							
16	15 37	18 51	19 13	19 46	21 24	23 14	23 48
17	15 46	18 56	19 18	19 51	21 33	23 22	23 57
18	15 52	18 59	19 21	19 54	21 39		0 03
19		19 20	19 32	20 25	21 53	23 25	0 18
20					22 01		0 26
21			19 37	20 30		23 28	
22		19 26					

Above:
A two-car Cravens Class 105 forms the 17.00 Ipswich to Lowestoft service near East Suffolk Junction on 12 May 1980. *Les Bertram*

crossing cottages remain to show where the railway went, and Aldeby station remains in private use; the road bridge is still extant. At Haddiscoe, the abutments of the bridge carrying the East Suffolk over the Lowestoft line still exist on the north side but are in poor condition. The High Level platforms and signalbox still exist, but are again in private hands, and the piers of St Olaves swing bridge are still clearly visible. There is no trace of St Olaves station, although the sign which greeted passengers at the entrance is fixed to the wall of the nearby garage. Some of the trackbed can be traced in nearby Waveney Forest, which has replaced Fritton Warren since the line closed. Belton & Burgh station has been obliterated and a road built on some of the trackbed to the north. There is no trace at all of Yarmouth South Town station.

On the remainder of the line little happened after staff were withdrawn from the stations. Bealings signalbox ceased to be a block post and was downgraded to a gate box. Woodbridge box was closed in 1971 and demolished on 17 February 1974, with Westerfield and Melton marking the ends of the section. Wickham Market box had closed on 19 July 1965, but the junction box survived until March 1971. Snape Junction box closed soon after the branch in March 1960, but Saxmundham survived. The down platform, once bisected by the Chantry Road level crossing, was closed and a new one opposite the up platform, north of the Albion Street crossing, was built. This was made possible by the lifting of the sidings serving the goods yard and shed, although the long siding on the up side running back towards the junction was retained and survives today. Saxmundham Junction box closed soon after the Aldeburgh branch lost its passenger service in 1966, and was replaced by a ground frame released from the station box. The track layout was altered so that instead of a double junction there was a single connection into the up main line. Darsham box had been closed when the AHB (Automatic Half-Barrier) crossing was introduced in 1967, although the crossing remained staffed for some time afterwards. Halesworth signalbox remained open with only the section signals and a crossover to control, closing on the introduction of RETB, while Brampton also survived both as a block post and to control the station level crossing. Beccles South was the last of the many boxes there to survive, Beccles Bank having burnt down in the late 1960s, and Beccles North going about 1970. Beccles South closed when RETB was introduced and was demolished on 12 September 1986. Barnby became redundant once the siding closed in late 1964, as did Oulton Broad South Junction when the South Side branch finally closed in 1967. Oulton Broad swing bridge remained as a block post and to control the bridge, and survives today as a ground frame for the latter purpose, released from Oulton Broad North station box. Coke Ovens ceased to be a junction when the line from Yarmouth closed in 1970, although a stub of it was retained into the 1980s as a coal yard. Lowestoft Yard box remains open to control the station area.

The basic East Suffolk train service continued for several years more or less unchanged. The 1972-3 timetable shows that the first service in the down direction was the 06.25 Halesworth to Lowestoft, actually the newspaper train which was allowed to carry passengers for the last part of its journey.

Left:
BR ER freight WTT, 7 September 1964 to 13 June 1965.
This was the timetable in operation when Aldeby finally closed.

Trains then left Ipswich at roughly two-hourly intervals from 06.52 to 16.48, with a 16.22 thrown in for good measure. There then followed the 17.48 and the 18.09, the latter being the through train from London which left Liverpool Street at 16.50. The 20.03 was the last down train of the day, although there was a 19.38 from Halesworth to Lowestoft, the return working of the 19.01. In the up direction the service started with the 05.29, 06.33 and 07.18 from Lowestoft, the first extended to Colchester, and the third the through train to London. Trains then ran at two-hourly intervals from 08.55 to 14.55, with a 16.15 and 17.55, and a last up service at 20.16. On summer Saturdays there was a through train from Liverpool Street at either 09.46 or 11.10 which did not call at Ipswich or any East Suffolk station except Lowestoft, although the return working at 10.45 or 12.15 did call at Ipswich. The Sunday service showed two trains each way in the morning and three in the afternoon and evening; the morning trains did not run in the winter. In January 1981 Sir Peter Parker held out new hope for rural lines such as the East Suffolk in a speech to the Chartered Institute of Transport. The line now had direct annual costs of £1,200,000 and revenue of £400,000, although BR Divisional management at Norwich had estimated that if all possible cost-saving measures were taken, direct expenses could be cut to match the income. Part of the plan was to try out the experimental lightweight Leyland railbus LEV1, which ran on the line for a period in 1980–1, and although P. W. B. Semmens, writing in the *Railway Magazine*, found that it gave a better ride than conventional DMUs elsewhere, its lack of luggage space and seating made it unpopular with passengers and its stay was relatively short. Replacement of formal signalling by radio despatching, plus the long-mooted automation of level crossings, were also proposed, together with life extension of existing track by the use of lightweight two-part concrete sleepers then under development.

Rumours of closure were fuelled by the Serpell report of 1983, which gave a number of options for the railways, among them being closure of everything in the area except the main line to Norwich. Later the same year Sir Peter Parker's vision was given substance, a package being proposed for the East Suffolk which would give it investment of £1.6 million to pay for the automation of 22 level crossings and installation of the electric token system in train cabs, with Saxmundham becoming the control centre for the line. The line would be singled between Woodbridge and Darsham, and Halesworth and Oulton Broad South. Redundant signalling equipment would be removed, and the scheme was expected to be finished by the end of 1985.

The service continued to be substantially unchanged in the 1983-4 timetable by comparison with the early 1970s, except that the newspaper train had been withdrawn and the early evening Lowestoft to Halesworth and return had gone, but more trains now called at Westerfield. Signs of imminent change and cost-cutting appeared in the following timetable when the through trains to and from London were withdrawn from the start of the 1984 summer timetable. Initially running as a six-car diesel multiple-unit (DMU) as far as Colchester, the replacement was soon cut to a single three-car set, and with the loss of capacity and convenience passengers started to be lost to the line. The summer Saturday through trains were also withdrawn. The first spark of revival came in September of that year, when proposals to reopen Melton came to fruition. The scheme was a joint venture between British Rail, Suffolk Coastal District Council and Suffolk County Council, and was made more affordable by the fact that the line had now been singled through the station, so

Below:
There are many passengers at Darsham on 3 September 1984 for the 10.45 Lowestoft to Ipswich train, which has to stop well short of the level crossing under the new system. It is a long time since trains actually did whistle before proceeding . . . *Mike Macdonald*

that only the former down platform needed to be refurbished. Trains called from the start of service on Monday 3 September, with an official opening on the following Wednesday. The 10.53 train from Ipswich broke a ribbon as it entered the station, which was crowded with local schoolchildren, and the County Council chairman gave the 'right-away' to the 11.14 to Lowestoft.

The single track at this time extended from the crossover opposite Melton signalbox to Saxmundham, where only the up platform could be used because of the position of the crossover. Bealings level crossing had been converted to an AOCL-type (Automatic Open Crossing Locally-monitored) on 31 March 1984. The four at Woodbridge were not done for another 18 months, with Lime Kiln and Sun Wharf on 24 November 1985, and Ferry Lane and Haywards on 8 December. Melton itself had been done on 20 June, Ufford on 25 May, and Blaxhall and Beversham on 3 April. Both crossings at Saxmundham received full barriers worked from the signalbox, Albion Street on 6 October 1984 and Chantry Road a week later. When Melton box was finally abolished the single track section was extended back towards Woodbridge, starting between Haywards and Lime Kiln crossings.

Plans to single the line between Saxmundham and Darsham had been quietly dropped, and in the end the single-line section finished a few yards on the Ipswich side of Chantry Road crossing. This was presented as a major concession to local users lobbying for retention of more double track. Further on, North Green and Middleton crossings were converted to AOCLs on 6 April and 3 March 1985 respectively. Willow Marsh had been the first crossing to be converted to AOCL on 21 August 1983, with Bramfield and Wenhaston not following until early March 1985. Westhall, Brampton and Weston were converted on 22 June of that year

Above:
The level crossing at Darsham takes a heavy pounding from road traffic and needs frequent maintenance. On 26 November 1992 green-liveried No 37216 is involved in delivering rail for renewal work at the site. This locomotive was one of the few fitted with RETB apparatus for working engineers' and freight trains on the East Suffolk. *David Pearce*

and became operational as AOCLs from 17 July. Of the Beccles crossings Cromwell Road and London Road were converted in August 1985, and Grove Road and Ingate the following month, whilst the bypass had been converted in May. Dawdy's, Victoria Road and Gravel Pit were done in September, October and November respectively. In the meantime the line had been singled, using the former up line, from Halesworth, the points being installed on 12 May 1985, and working as far as Beccles South. The section onwards to Oulton Broad North Junction was singled, again using the up line, from 7 September, with lifting of the redundant down road starting a week later. In due course the single line was diverted into the down platform at Beccles, after which the building on the island platform was demolished.

The infrastructure was now in place for the conversion to Radio Electronic Token Block (RETB) signalling, which took place at 08.00 on 16 February 1986. The signalbox at Saxmundham was retained as the control centre for the line, with Oulton Broad North station and Westerfield being able to monitor the progress of trains. The three-car Class 101 Metro-Cammell units working on the East Suffolk became dedicated to the line, although locomotives working the Sizewell freights used portable sets, as could engineers when taking possession of a section. Radio masts sprouted at various points on the line, and the token exchange points

Above:
The present day at Beccles. Single-car No 153306 calls with a working to Lowestoft on 24 November 2002. Only the former down main line remains through the platforms. The footbridge to the Common remains, and is here undergoing heavy maintenance including grit blasting. There is only a bus shelter on this platform, although a real-time information screen has been provided. Plans to refurbish the station have so far come to nothing.
John Brodribb

became Westerfield and Oulton Broad South stations, where trains entered and left the system, and Woodbridge, Saxmundham and Halesworth. Telephones were provided for the occasions when the system failed and drivers had to phone up and get a token. The system was later upgraded to make it more reliable. Sizewell branch trains had their own token, as did those using the siding at Saxmundham. The remaining signalboxes at Melton, Brampton and Beccles South were abolished and quickly demolished, whilst Halesworth was sold into preservation, and Oulton Broad Swing Bridge was downgraded to control the bridge only. Westerfield was subsequently closed on 22 March 1999 and quickly demolished, becoming redundant when the Felixstowe branch was resignalled. The level crossing had received automatic half-barriers on 28 April 1990.

A fatal accident at an open crossing at Lockington, Humberside, in 1986 led to the setting up of an enquiry into level crossing safety chaired by Professor Stott, and as a result of the subsequent report the rules about open level crossings were changed, which greatly affected the East Suffolk. At the busier sites barriers had to be fitted, although they remained locally monitored (in other words, by the train driver rather than remotely by a signaller), and as a result the new ABC-L (Automatic Barrier Crossing Locally-monitored) type started to be installed. Beccles bypass was the very first, on 13 November 1988, and was followed by many others along the line. Bramfield crossing, south of Halesworth on the A144 road, was awaiting conversion when a fatal accident occurred on 11 December 1990, and was one of the very, very few where the railway was at fault rather than the road user.

To the great relief of passengers the experiment with the lightweight railbuses was not pursued, and for a while from the start of the summer 1992 timetable the East Suffolk was operated by two-car Class 156 'Sprinter' units, soon replaced by a mixture of two-car Class 150s and single-car Class 153s. The timetable had settled down after the upheavals caused by the modernisation and singling, although end-to-end times were slowed considerably by the speed limits imposed by the automatic crossings. The new 'Sprinter' units could only partly compensate for this. As with almost all other parts of the national network, the East Suffolk passed back into private hands following passage of the 1993 Railways Act, with Railtrack now owning the fixed assets, and Anglia Railways holding the franchise to operate train services over the line. The concept of the Passenger Service Requirement (PSR) meant that franchisees had to operate a particular minimum level of service over their lines, which on the East Suffolk included a connection out of the 20.30 Liverpool Street to Norwich, as well as year-round Sunday morning services. British Rail had experimented with both, but their future was never felt to be very secure. Anglia Railways, with the smallest route mileage of any of the line's operators since the East Suffolk Railway itself, set about marketing its local services with a will, and on Sunday 26 September 1999 the first timetabled through train to London left Lowestoft at 10.05, formed by one of Anglia's new Class 170 units. The weekday service left at 06.56, arriving at Liverpool Street at 09.31, and returning at 19.00 Mondays to Fridays. Another

Above:
On 9 January 1993 a Class 156 'Sprinter' heads across Oulton Broad swing bridge with the 12.56 to Ipswich. The line has been singled here. The signalbox can be seen on the far left of the picture.
David Pearce

Right:
The up platform at Woodbridge has been transformed by a partnership scheme between Railtrack, Anglia Railways and the local councils. The old buildings, which had become derelict, were swept away and the canopies rebuilt, creating a light and welcoming area for passengers. A café, tourist information centre and taxi office now occupy the buildings on the down side.
John Brodribb

through service was soon provided, at 16.27, and because of the limited capacity of the Class 170s the 19.00 was quickly replaced by a full-length main-line set running to Norwich. Through Sunday services were withdrawn from the start of the summer 2000 timetable.

Britain's railways continue to be in a state of flux at the start of the 21st century. As with many other lines and all of those in East Anglia, passenger numbers are increasing steadily. The work of partnerships which include Anglia Railways has delivered some tangible benefits such as the complete refurbishment of Halesworth station's remaining buildings so that they are once again occupied, with the railway back in the heart of the community. Woodbridge station up side has been rebuilt. Beccles presents a sorry aspect, and is one of the places still to see any benefit from the upturn in the East Suffolk's fortunes. The railway will continue to need a great deal of work and support from its community, but there is no reason why the East Suffolk should not continue to serve the district for very many years to come.

Index

Addison, Col G. W. 100, 133, 188-9
Albion Wharf, Ipswich 45
Alde, river 25, 26, 67, 145, 239
Aldeburgh 8, 9, *17*, 19, 30, 32, 35-6, 149, 158, 164-169, *166*, *167*, *168*, 168M, *169*, *170*, 193, 195-6, 200, 205, 216-9, 222-3, 227-8, 232, 245-7, 249
Aldeby 9, 11, 14, 15, 28, 32, 33, 35, *112*, *113*, 113M, 113-4, 193, 195, 205, 210-1, 226, 239, 247, 249
Anderson, Samuel 14
Anglia Railways 7, 252-3
Ash Abbey 59
Ayres, Edmund 20, 23, 30, 31

Baker, H. 230
Balls, C. 230
Banham, R. 230
Barnby 93, *171*, 171M, 171-3, 188, 211, 216-7, 247, 249
Barnett, George (driver) 169
Baskett, Monty 231
Baugham, J. 230
Bealings 33, 35, 36, 47-51, *47*, *48*, *49*, 49M, 50, 193, 205, 216, 222, 232, 247, 249
Beccles 8-9, *9*, 14-6, *15*, 22, 24, 27, 29, 32-3, 35-7, *37*, *95*, 94-106-7, 96M, *97*, *98*, *99*, *100*, *101*, *102*, *103*, *104*, *105*, *106*, 119, 171, 173, 177, 188, 193, 195-6, 200, 205, 211, 216-8, 220, 223, 226, 239, 245-7, 249, 251-3, *252*
Beccles bank 93, 94M, 94, 249
Beckett, George (signalman) 172
Beeching, Dr Richard 8, 239, 245-6
Belton (and Burgh) 9, 33, 35, 124, 125, *125*, 126M, 193, 205, 216-7, 226, 228, 239, 249
Berkley, George 19, 21, 23, 26
Beversham 26
Bidder, George 19, 20, 22, 28
Bignold, Sir Samuel 19
Billingsgate 192
Birkett, Thomas 19
Birkley (ESR engineer) 17
Bishopsgate 211
Blaxhall 26, 67
Blundeston 11
Blyth, river 19, 23, 25, 79, 80, *82*, 88
Boulton & Paul 192
Bradwell 125
Bramfield .19, 23, 25, 79
Bramford 232
Brampton 14-5, *17*, 32-3, 35-6, 91M, *91*, 91-93, *92*, *93*, 195, 205, 211, 216, 231, 246-7, 249, 252
Branch Line Reinvigoration Society 246
Brandon 11
Brassey, Thomas 20, 23, 24, 30, 31
Breydon bridge .134, 227
Breydon Water .107, 226
British Railways 80, 94, 192, 200, 232, 238-9, 245, 250, 252
Bromeswell 25
Bruce, Henry 14, 20
Bruff, Peter 19, 20, 21, 22, 23, 26, 27, 28, 31
Bruisyard 139
Bungay 16, 27, 36, 103, 107
Burgh St Peter 113
Burleigh (ESR director) 23
Bury St Edmunds .19, 39

Call-boy 218
Cambridge 11, 19, 22, 23, 29, 30
Campsey Ash 19, 25, 30, 59, 61,
Campsey Heath 25
Cantley 93, 223, 231
Carey, L. A. (TUCC chair) 246
Carlton Colville . .17, 28, 29, 35, 68, 171, 173-6, 174M, 188-9, 193, 195-6, 211, 216
Castle, Barbara 246
Cayley (MP) 19
Chelmsford 11, 36, 193
Chittock, Alan (fireman) 238
Clacton 86, 195
Cleaners 218-9
Cliff Quay, Ipswich 45
Cobbold, John Chevallier . .14, 19, 21, 22, 23, 27, 28, 36
Cobbold, R. K. 27, 28
Coke Ovens . . .174, 175M, *176*, 176-7, 189, 249
Colchester 11, 22, 39, 193, 195, 246, 250
Colchester & Pitsea Railway 17, 22, 23, 24
Coleman (chief goods clerk) 229
Coleman, C 230
Common Quay, Ipswich 45
Co-op (Lowestoft) 191-2, *192*, 217
Corton 246
Council, Suffolk Coastal 250
Council, Suffolk County 250

Daines (Woodbridge family) 56
Darsham 25, 30, 33, 35-6, 58, *77*, 77-9, *78*, 79M, *80*, *81*, *82*, 193, 195, 211, 216-7, 230-1, 246-7, 249-51, *250*, *251*
Day, George Game 30
Day, William 19, 32
Deben, river . .25-6, 35, 47, 51, 59, 67, 72, 226-7
Debenham 47, 59
Denny, J. S. P. 246
Derby Road 228
Durham 20
Diss 15
Donop, Col von 133, 159, 189
Double, Harold (driver) 238
Drury, H. G. 133
Dunwich 28

Earsham 196
East Anglian Railway 14, 19, 20, 36
East Suffolk Junction . . .31, 38M, 39-40, 41, *41*, 45, 226-7
East Suffolk Railway . .11, 13, 14, 17, 19, 20, 21, 22, 23, 24, 26, 27, 28, 29, 30, 31, 35, 36, 58
East Suffolk Travellers' Association (ESTA) 7, 246
Easterling, The 200, 210, 220, 238
Eastern Coach Works 187
Eastern Counties Farmers 56, 227
Eastern Counties Railway 11, 13, 14, 15, 16, 17, 19, 20, 21, 22, 23, 24, 26, 27, 28, 29, 30, 31, 32, 35, 36, 39
Eastern Union Railway 13, 14, 16, 17, 19, 20, 21, 22, 23, 26, 27, 28, 29, 30, 31, 36, 39
Evans, J. 230
Eye 27

Farr, Frederick William 11
Felixstowe 39, 45
Felixstowe Dock & Harbour Company 17

Felixstowe Railway Co 45
Ferry Quay 56
Fiennes, Gerard 200, 245-6
Finlays, tobacconist 56
Firemen 219
Fleet Junction *114*, 114-5, 115M, 119, 216-7, 239
Flixton 11
Flooding 226-7, 239
Flunder, A. H. (stn master) 230
Framlingham 9, 13, 17, 19, 23, 25, 26, 27, 28, 30, 32, 33, 35, *35*, 36, 61, 67, 135, 139, 141-2, 141M, *142*, *143*, *144*, 145, 146, 193, 195-6, 200, 205, 211, 216-9, 222-3, 225, 228, 232, 238-9, 245
Freeman (driver) 219
Freezing 227
Freightliner 41
Fritton .60,119, 125, 249
Fynn, river 47, 51

Galton, Capt. 32
Garrett, Newson 26, 36, 141
Garrett, Richard 19, 23, 25, 33, 35, 149
Garrett's works (Leiston) 149-158, 150M, *153*, *154*, 216, 247
Garrod, Russell 231
General Strike 227
George, William (driver) 247
German Ocean 11, 59
Gipping, river 45
Gladwell, Edgar 238
Glemham 139
Goodard, Stanley 219
Goodmayes 211, 216-7, 223
Goodson, James 37
Gorleston . .11, 126, 134, 134M, 195-6, 205, 247
Great Eastern Railway 14, 36-7, 39, 45-6, 51, 56, 58, 83, 94, 100, 107, 133, 135, 139, 142, 164, 166, 171-2, 176, 188, 195-6, 226-8, 230
Great Northern Railway 13, 20
Great Western Railway 39
Griffin Wharf branch .39

Hacheston *139*, 139M, 139, 205, 238
Haddiscoe 11, 13-7, 19, 21-2, 24-5, 27-9, *29*, 31, 113-5, *116*, 117M, *118*, 195-6, 205, 216-7, 223, 226, 239, 249
Haddiscoe Junction 114, 115, *116*,
Halesworth 8, 11, 13-7, 19, 20, 21-31, *32*, 33, 35, 37, 68, 80-90, *83*, 84M, *85*, *86*, *87*, *90*, 103, 105, 193, 195-6, *201*, 211, 216-7, *219*, *220*, *221*, *225*, 225-6, 228, 230-1, 239, 245-7, 249-53
Halesworth & Woodbridge Railway 16
Halesworth, Beccles & Haddiscoe Railway 11, 13, 14, 15, 16, 17, 19, 24, 32, 37, 83, 91, 93, 103, 107, 114, 118, 171
Halifax Junction 26, 39
Hall, James (guard) .172
Hammond, R. (Y&H Rly) 24
Hardy, R. H. N. (Dick) 218
Hardy, W. A. (Bill) 218
Harleston 16, 26, 103, 196
Harrison, Thomas 21
Harvey, D. W. (Bill) .218
Harwich 230, 245

Haughley 47, 245
Haven Bridge, Yarmouth 31, 126
Havers, H. 230
Hembling, J. (motor driver) 229
Herringfleet 26, 115, 119
Holland (Halesworth family) 90, 229
Hopton 11, 246
Howard's Common 125
Howes, Jack (signalman) 188
Hutchinson, Maj Gen 68, 91, 172, 176, 188

Ipswich *2*, 11, 13-4 *13*, 17, 19, 22-3, 25-6, 28-9, 31-3, 35-6, 39, *39*, 41, 45, 90, 93, 169, 193, 195-6, 200, *201*, 211, 216-20, 222, 225, 227-8, 230-2, 238-9, 245-7, 250-1
Ipswich & Bury Railway 13, 39
Ipswich Dock branch 45
Ipswich Goods Junction 41, 45
Ipswich Lower Yard 211
Ipswich Upper Yard 45

Jarvis, Walter Scott 29
Jessup's Wharf (Woodbridge) 25, 28
Johnston, Andrew 11, 19, 23
Joint committee 14, 15, 19, 20, 28, 29, 36, 141
Josselyn (EUR Woodbridge committee) 19, 28

Kelsale 23
Kesgrave 47
Kessingland 192
Kidby, Jas (signalman) 229
King's Lynn 245
Kirkley 17, 171, 173, 178M, 189, 192, *192*

Lacon, Sir E. H. K. 24, 25, 26
Laxfield 88, 238
Leathes, Edward 11, 14, 19, 23, 24, 26, 28, 36
Leiston 17, 19, 23, 25, 26, 27, 28, 32, 33, 35, 36, *149*, 149-159, 150M, *155*, *156*, *157*, *158*, *159*, *161*, *162*, 216, 228, 245-7
Leverick, George 218
Lime Kiln Quay 56
Link system 219-20
Liverpool Street 39, 41, 77, 141, 164, 193, 195-6, 200, 205, 211, 217, 220, 222, 246, 250, 252
LNER 139, 166, 192, 200, 218, 225, 227-8, 232, 238
London 8, 11, 13, 15, 19, 22, 23, 24, 30, 35, 36, 193, 196, 205, 225, 246, 250, 252
Lothing, Lake 17, 27, 176
Loudham 25
Lound 11
Love, Horatio 20, 23, 27, 28, 30, 36
Lowestoft 8, 14, 16, 17, 19, 20, *21*, 22, 23, 24, 27, 28, 29, 30, 31, 32, 33, 35, 36, 37, 88, 93, 98, 100, 133, 171, 176-7, 178-9M, 188, 192-3, 195-6, 200, 205, 211, 216-20, *222*, 223, *224*, 225-8, 231-2, 238-9, 245-7, 249-52
Lowestoft & Beccles Rly 17, 20, 21, 22, 23, 24, 25, 26, 28, 30
Lowestoft Central 22, 171, 176, 177, 178M, *180*, *181*, *182*, *183*, *184*, *185*, *186*, *187*, 191, 196, 217, 245-7
Lowestoft Harbour *176*, 179M, 192, 226-7
Lowestoft Junction 98, 171, 188, 247
Lowestoft North 176, 230
Lowestoft Railway 11, 15, 21, 26
Lowestoft South Side 173, 178M, 191-2, 217, 232
Lucas Bros 176

M&GN 20, 91, 134, 245
Manby (Woodbridge) 28
Manningtree 36, 193, 230
Mark's Tey 36, 195
Marlesford 67, 68, *135*, 135-137, *136*, 136M, *137*, *138*, 145, 205, 217, 239
Marples, Ernest 239, 245
Marsh Junction 114, 115, 196, 216
Martlesham 24, 47
Mells 80
Melton 13, 19, 25, 30, 33, 36, 45, 51, *56*, *57*, 57M, 57-59, *58*, 195, 205, 216-7, 220, 223, 226-7, 232, 238, 247, 249, 250-2
Melton Constable 134, 192
Melton Dock 56
Mid Suffolk Light Railway 47, 80, 232, 238, 245
Modernisation Plan 238, 245
Moore, Pony (fireman) 238
Morton's Cannery 191-2, 238
Moseley (ECR manager) 22, 25
Moutel (driver) 169
Moy, Thomas 46
Mutford 22, 23, 24, 27, 28, 29, 30

National Union of Railwaymen 227
Neptune Quay, Ipswich 45
New Cut 11, 115
Newby, Donald 246
Newmarket 19, 245
Newmarket Railway 14
Nicklin, John (driver) 171-2
Norfolk & Suffolk Joint 126, 133, 134, 181, 189, 195-6, 205
Norfolk Railway 11, 13, 14, 15, 19, 20, 21, 22, 23, 24, 26, 28, 29, 30, 31
North Cove 172
North Quay, Lowestoft 191
North Sea 59
Northern & Eastern Railway 36
Norton, Edward 14, 23
Norwich 13, 14, 27, 35, 36, 41, 191, 193, 196, 200, 216-8, 220, 223, 226, 230, 238, 245, 247

Ogilvie, Alexander 20, 27, 28, 31
Old Man's Gang/Link 219, 225
Ore, river 67, 135, 137, 139,
Orfordness 28
Ormesby, Great 91
Orwell Quay, Ipswich 45
Orwell, river 39
Oulton 11, 195
Oulton Broad 226-7
Oulton Broad North 79, 174M, 176-7, 189, *190*, *191*, 217, 232, 249, 251
Oulton Broad South *172*, *173*, *175*, 189, 191-2, 216-7, 223, 245, 247, 249-50
Owen, J B 20, 30

Packe, James 14
Parham 28, 68, 139, *140*, 141M, 142, 145, 205, 217, 238-9
Parker, Sir Peter 250
Paytrains 247
Peto & Betts (contractors) 13, 15
Peto, James 19, 23
Peto, Samuel Morton 11, 13, 14, 19, 20, 21, 22, 23, 25, 26, 28, 29, 30, 31, 32, 33, 35, 36
Pettistree 25
Plantin, Edward 33
Playford 28, 31, 47
Post Office 15
Pratt, A. D. 230
Pulham St Mary 230
Punchard family 228-31, *229*, *230*, *231*

Rabett, Rev Reginald 25
Railtrack 231, 252-3
Railway Clearing House 24
Reedham 15, 21, 24, 36, 115, 176
RETB 46, 51, 55, 74, 90, 98, 173, 184, 232, 249, 251-2
Riches, Norman (guard) 247
Runnacles, Bill (driver) 169
Rushmere 28, 31

Sandlings, the 59-60, 163
Sandpit farm 59
Saxmundham 13, 14, 19, 23, 25, 26, 30, 32, 33, *33*, 35, 36, 67, 69M, 68-72, *70*, *71*, *72*, *73*, *74*, 103, 149, 166, 193, 195-6, 209, 211, 216-7, 219, 222-3, 225-6, 228-32, 245-7, 250-2
Saxmundham Junction 72, *75*, *76*, 149, 159, 222, 231, 246, 249
Screw bridge 67
Serpell report 250
Shadingfield 11
Shenfield & Pitsea Railway 23, 24
Silcocks 69
Simpson, Lightly 14
Sinclair, Robert 16, 25, 28, 29, 30, 36, 37
Sizewell 159-164, 161M, *161*, *162*, 231-2, 246-7, 251-2
Slaughden Quay 149
Smith, W. H. 36, 56, 62, 69, 83, 100, 103, 105, 168, *186*
Smyth (Joint cttee member) 28
Snape 9, 17, 19, 23, 25, 26, 27, 28, 32, 33, 51, 60, 145-146, *145*, *146*, 146M, *147*, 166, 193, 211, *211*, 216, 222-3, 227, 232, 239, 245
Snape bonus train 51, 146
Snape Junction 26, 30, 35, 67M, 67, *68*, 72, 145, *209*, 216, 219-20, *239*, 249
Somerleyton 115, 119, 196
South Quay, Lowestoft 189
Southtown (Yarmouth) 11, 17, 21, 31, 126, 127,
Southwold 19, 25, 27, 35, 88, 195, 216, 226
Southwold Railway 80, 83, 86, 88, 195, 200, 216, 228, 230
Spencer, Bob (S&T insp) 231
Spitalfields 192, 211, 216-7, 219, 223
St Olaves 33, 35, 67, 107, 117M, 119-125, *122*, *123*, 193, 196, 216-7, 239, 249
St Olaves Exchange station 115
St Olaves Junction 33, 35, 117M, 119, 193, 195
St Olaves Swing Bridge Jct 114, 196, 216
St Peter's Quay, Ipswich 45
Stephenson, Robert 14, 15, 19,
Stevenson, Thomas 172
Stott, Professor 252
Stowmarket 39
Stradbroke, Earl of 13, 14, 19, 20, 22, 23, 25, 26, 27, 28, 29, 33, 36
Stratford 193, 219
Strikes 227-8
Sudbury 22
Suffolk Show 211
Sun Wharf 56

Teed, Thomas 19
Temple Mills 211, 216
Thornton, Henry 196
Thorpe 162M 164,
Thorpe-le-Soken 230
Thorpeness *163*, 164, *165*, 205, 216
Thurkettle (driver) 169
Tidemill Quay 56
Till, Richard 11, 14, 19, 20, 23
Tivetshall 16, 17, 103, 200
TUC 227
TUCC 239, 246
Tunstall 61, 145
Turner, Jack (driver) 238
Tyler, Capt 30, 31, 32

Ufford 25, 226, *227*, *247*

Waddington, David 14, 20
Wagstaffe (ESR solicitor) 30
Walpole 79
Walters, Ralph 22, 23
Wangford 60, 88
Waveney Valley 16, 17, 36, 37, 93, 84, 98, 100, 103, 107, 114, 193, 195, 200, 217, 223, 230, 232, 245
Waveney, river 11, 16, 19, 21, 25, 95, 119, 125, 171
Welnetham 230
Welton, Cornelius .26, 28
Wenhaston 23, 25
Wensum Junction 216
Westerfield 17, *22*, 33, 35, *42*, 42M, 43, *43*, *44*, *45*, *46*, 45-7, 51, 193, 195-6, 205, 211, 216-7, 228, 238, 245, 249, 250-2
Westerfield bank 45
Westhall 11, 13, 14, 19, 91
Weston 11
Wet Dock, Ipswich 45
Wheatacre 113
Wickham Market 13, 25, 26, 30, 33, 36, 59, 61-67, 60M, *61*, *62*, *63*, *64*, *65*, *66*, 68, 135, 137, 193, 195, 196, 211, 216-7, 219-20, 226, 232, 239, 246-7, 249
Wickham Market Junction *1*, 61, *64*, 66M, 135, 137, *217*, 249
Wilford Bridge 25
Wisbech 20
Wissett 25
Witham 36
Wood, Sancton 39
Woodbridge 8, 13, 14, 17, 19, 21, 22, 24, *24*, 25, 26, 27, 28, 30, 31, 33, 35, 45, 47, *51*, 51-56, 52M, *52*, *53*, *54*, *55*, 58, 193, 195, 211, 219, 226-7, 245, 247, 249-50, 252-3, *253*
Wright (EUR Woodbridge committee) 19
Wynne, Lt Col Geo 20

Yare, river .21, 107, 126
Yarmouth 8, 9, 14, 16, 19, 20, 21, 22, 23, 24, 27, 28, 29, 30, 31, 32, 33, 35, 36, 39, 41, 45, 83, 125, 126, 171, 188-9, 193, 195-6, 200, 205, 211, 216-20, 222-3, 225-7, 238-9, 243-7
Yarmouth & Haddiscoe Railway 17, 20, 21, 22, 23, 24, 25, 26, 28, 30, 115, 239
Yarmouth & Lowestoft Rly 11
Yarmouth & Norwich Rly 11
Yarmouth Beach 133, 196, 227, 238
Yarmouth South Town 9, 32, 33, 35, 41, 98, 114, 115, 126, 127M, 126-134, 128, 129, 130, 131, 132, 133, 134, 193, 195-6, 200, 205, 211, 216, 218-20, 222, *223*, 227-8, 232, 238, 246-7, 249
Yarmouth tramways .219
Yarmouth Vauxhall 21, 24, 36, 133, 200, 218-9, 226, 238
Yolland, Maj 14
Yoxford 13, 19, 23, 25, 30, 35, 36, 77

Level crossings
Albion Street 26, 68, 72, 249, 251
Barnby Gate 171
Bealings 51, 232, *232*, 251
Beccles bypass 247, 251-2
Belton *124*, 125, *125*, 126M
Benhall 67
Beversham 67, 251
Black Dam 171
Blackstock 67, 135
Blaxhall (Hall) 67, 251
Blindman's Gate 171-2
Bramfield 79, 225, 251-2
Brampton 91, 252
Brick Kiln 68
Bricklane 141
Broadwater 141
Chantry Row (Road) 68, 225, 249, 251
Clayhills 149
Colville Road 189
Common Lane 96M, 98, 171, 188
Cromwell(s) Lane (Road) 93, 94, 251
Crown Lands 164
Dawdys 173, 251
Durban Road 189, 191, *192*
East Green 72, 77
Ferry Lane 51, 53, 55, 251
Gravel Pit 176, 251
Grove Road 11
Halesworth 83, 88, 88, 89, 225, 231
Harbour Road .176, 189
Haywards 51, 53, 56, 251
Hillings Road 173
Ingate (Street) 93, 94, 251
Ingate Road (Grove Road) 93, *95*,
Jetty Lane 51, 56, 94
Kirkley Run 189
Knodishall 149, *160*,
Lime Kiln 51, 251
London Road 93, 251
Marsh Lane 171
Melton 251
Middleton 77, 230, 251
Mill Lane (Saxmundham) 68
Millpost 90
North Cove 171-2, 226
North Green 77, 228, *229*, 251
Northgate 94
Pound Lane 223
Rendham Road 26, 94, 228
Saxmundham Road .149
Sheepwash 164, 164M
Sizewell 159, 161M, *161*
Spratts Water 173
Staith Road 125
Sun Wharf 51, 251
Thorpe(ness) 164, 164M
Toft Monks 113
Ufford 59, 251
Victoria Road 176, 189, 251
Water Mill 94
Wenhaston .79, 230, 251
Westhall 91, 251
Westhouse 149
Weston 93, 251
Wickham Market station 61, 67
Willow Marsh (Darsham) 79, 251
Wissett 88, 225, 246

Locomotives, steam
B1 . . . . .137, 219
B12 . . . .*9*, *201*, 219, 220, 222
B17 . . . .*42*, 219, *223*, 223
Britannia 41, 200, *201*, 220
C12 . . . .*100*, *111*
D16/Claud Hamilton *106*, *129*, 222
E4 239
F5 . . . .*9*
F6 . . . .*128*, *138*, *209*, 222
J17 219
J20 . . . .*100*
J39 219
K3 . . . .*106*, *175*, 219, 223
L1 93
O1 . . . .*86*, *201*
Sentinel 219, 222, *222*
Sirapite *148*, 151, 152, *153*, *154*, 247
Y14/J15 . . . .*56*, *68*, 145, *146*, *151*, *152*, *175*, *192*, *211*, 222, 239

Locomotives, diesel
Class 03 . . . .*185*
Class 101 . . . .*55*, *130*, *184*, 251
Class 105 . . . .*40*, *183*, *184*, *249*
Class 150 252
Class 153 . . . . .252, *252*
Class 156 . . . . .252, *253*
Class 170 252
Class 31 . . . .*209*
Class 37 . . . .*41*, *43*, *54*, *55*, *183*, *187*, *251*
Class 40 . . . .*66*
Class 47 . . . .*191*, *247*
Deltic *185*
ECW Railbus 187
EE 350HP 222
LEV1 250
Paxman 800HP 222

Coal merchants
Blake, Chas (Woodbridge) 56
Coop (Beccles) 103
Cox, Harry D. (Woodbridge) 56
Craskes (Beccles) 103
Fowlers (Beccles) 103
Jones (Brampton) 93
Manby & Co (Framlingham) 141
Parry, James (Halesworth) 88
Sage, William (Halesworth) 88
Strickson, R. B. (Woodbridge) 56
Sun Wharf Ltd 56

Sidings
Carr's tramway (Leiston) 149, 150M, 158
Clarke, Edwin G. (Framlingham) 141
Coller, R. (Woodbridge) 56
Eastern Counties Farmers (Woodbridge) 56
Gooderham & Heyward (Marlesford) . . .136, 137
Hayward, A (Woodbridge) 56
Ipswich Malting Co (Woodbridge) 56
Leiston Gas Co 158, 159
Lister, T. L. & Sons (Woodbridge) 56
Melton Corn & Coal Company (Melton) 58
Robertson, A. V. (Woodbridge) 56
S Swonnell & Son (Snape) 145
Welton (Marlesford) 135

Swing Bridges
Beccles 9, 11, 14, 107, *107*, 108M, *108*, *109*, *110*, *111*, 109-113, 188, *238*, 239
Carlton Colville 107, 174M, 176, 188, 189
Oulton Broad 26, *188*, *189*, 249, 252, *253*
Reedham 107
Somerleyton 107
St Olaves 17, 26, *27*, 28, 107, 109-113, 115, 117M, *119*, *120*, *121*, 239, 249
Trowse 107, 189

Please note:
M indicates map, eg 96M
Italicised references are to photographs eg *253*